T0223990

Communications
in Computer and Information Science   **923**

Commenced Publication in 2007
Founding and Former Series Editors:
Phoebe Chen, Alfredo Cuzzocrea, Xiaoyong Du, Orhun Kara, Ting Liu,
Dominik Ślęzak, and Xiaokang Yang

More information about this series at http://www.springer.com/series/7899

Shilong Wang · Mark Price
Ming K. Lim · Yan Jin
Yuanxin Luo · Rui Chen (Eds.)

Recent Advances in Intelligent Manufacturing

First International Conference on Intelligent Manufacturing
and Internet of Things and 5th International Conference on Computing
for Sustainable Energy and Environment, IMIOT and ICSEE 2018
Chongqing, China, September 21–23, 2018
Proceedings, Part I

 Springer

Editors

Shilong Wang
Chongqing University
Chongqing
China

Yan Jin
Queen's University Belfast
Belfast
UK

Mark Price
Queen's University Belfast
Belfast
UK

Yuanxin Luo
Chongqing University
Chongqing
China

Ming K. Lim
Chongqing University
Chongqing
China

Rui Chen
Chongqing University
Chongqing
China

ISSN 1865-0929   ISSN 1865-0937   (electronic)
Communications in Computer and Information Science
ISBN 978-981-13-2395-9   ISBN 978-981-13-2396-6   (eBook)
https://doi.org/10.1007/978-981-13-2396-6

Library of Congress Control Number: 2018953022

This Springer imprint is published by the registered company Springer Nature Singapore Pte Ltd.
The registered company address is: 152 Beach Road, #21-01/04 Gateway East, Singapore 189721, Singapore

Preface

This book constitutes the proceedings of the 2018 International Conference on Intelligent Manufacturing and Internet of Things (IMIOT 2018) and International Conference on Intelligent Computing for Sustainable Energy and Environment (ICSEE 2018), which were held during September 21–23, in Chongqing, China. These two international conference series aim to bring together international researchers and practitioners in the fields of advanced methods for intelligent manufacturing and Internet of Things as well as advanced theory and methodologies of intelligent computing and their engineering applications in sustainable energy and environment. The new conference series IMIOT is jointly organized with the well-established ICSEE conference series, under the auspices of the newly formed UK-China University Consortium in Engineering Education and Research, with an initial focus on intelligent manufacturing and sustainable energy.

At IMIOT 2018 and ICSEE 2018, technical exchanges within the research community took the form of keynote speeches, panel discussions, as well as oral and poster presentations. In particular, two workshops series, namely the Workshop on Smart Energy Systems and Electric Vehicles and the Workshop on Communication and Control for Distributed Networked Systems, were held again in parallel with IMIOT 2018 and ICSEE 2018, focusing on the two recent hot topics of the integration of electric vehicles with the smart grid, and distributed networked systems for the Internet of Things.

The IMIOT 2018 and ICSEE 2018 conferences received 386 submissions from over 50 different universities, research institutions, and companies from both China and UK. All papers went through a rigorous peer review procedure and each paper received at least three review reports. Based on the review reports, the Program Committee finally selected 135 high-quality papers for presentation at the IMIOT 2018 and ICSEE 2018. These papers cover 22 topics and are included in three volumes of the CCIS series, published by Springer. This volume of CCIS includes 53 papers covering 8 relevant topics.

Located at the upstream Yangtze basin, Chongqing constitutes the most important metropolitan area in the southwest of China. It has a glorious history and culture and serves as a major manufacturing center and transportation hub. Chongqing is also well-known for its spicy food and hotpot, attracting tourists and gourmets from around the world. In addition to academic exchanges, participants were treated to a series of social events, including receptions and networking sessions, which served to build new connections, foster friendships, and forge collaborations. The organizers of IMIOT 2018 and ICSEE 2018 would like to acknowledge the enormous contribution of the Advisory Committee, who provided guidance and advice, the Program Committee and the numerous referees for their efforts in reviewing and soliciting the papers, and the Publication Committee for their editorial work. We would also like to thank the editorial team from Springer for their support and guidance. Particular thanks are of course due to all the authors, as without their high-quality submissions and presentations the conferences would not have been successful.

Finally, we would like to express our gratitude to our sponsors and organizers, listed on the following pages.

September 2018

Fusheng Pan
Shilong Wang
Mark Price
Ming Kim Lim
Kang Li
Yuanxin Luo
Yan Jin

Organization

Honorary Chairs

Fusheng Pan   Chongqing Science and Technology Society/Chongqing
University, China
Shilong Wang   Chongqing University, China
Mark Price   Queen's University Belfast, UK

General Chairs

Ming Kim Lim   Chongqing University, China
Kang Li   Queen's University Belfast, UK

Advisory Committee Members

Erwei Bai   University of Iowa Informatics Initiative, USA
Zhiqian Bo   China Xuji Group Corporation, China
Tianyou Chai   Northeastern University, China
Phil Coates   Bradford University, UK
Jaafar Elmirghani   University of Leeds, UK
Qinglong Han   Swinburne University of Technology, Australia
Deshuang Huang   Tongji University, China
Biao Huang   University of Alberta, Canada
Guangbin Huang   Nanyang University of Technology, Singapore
Minrui Fei   Shanghai University, China
Sam Ge   National University of Singapore, Singapore
Shaoyuan Li   Shanghai Jiaotong University, China
Andy Long   University of Nottingham, China
Dong Yue   Nanjing University of Posts and Communication, China
Peter Taylor   University of Leeds, UK
Chengshan Wang   Tianjin University, China
Jihong Wang   University of Warwick, UK
Xiaohua Xia   Petoria University, South Africa
Yulong Ding   University of Birmingham, UK
Yugeng Xi   Shanghai Jiaotong University, China
Sarah Supergeon   University College London, UK
Derong Liu   University of Illinois, USA
Joe Qin   The Chinese University of Hong Kong, Hong Kong, China
Savvas Tassou   Brunel University London, UK
Qinghua Wu   South China University of Technology, China
Yusheng Xue   China State Grid Electric Power Research Institute, China
Jiansheng Dai   King's College London, UK

I-Ming Chen	Nangyang Technological University, Singapore
Guilin Yang	Institute of Advanced Manufacturing Technology, Ningbo, China
Zhuming Bi	Indiana University Purdue University Fort Wayne, USA
Zhenyuan Jia	Dalian University of Technology, China
Tian Huang	Tianjin University, China
James Gao	University of Greenwich, UK
Weidong Li	Coventry University, UK
Stan Scott	Queen's University Belfast, UK
Dan Sun	Queen's University Belfast, UK

International Program Committee

Chairs

| Yuanxin Luo | Chongqing University, China |
| Yan Jin | Queen's University Belfast, UK |

Local Chairs

Xuda Qin	Tianjin University, China
Fuji Wang	Dalian University of Technology, China
Yingguang Li	Nanjing University of Aeronautics and Astronautics, China
Adam Clare	University of Nottingham, UK
Weidong Chen	Shanghai Jiaotong University, China
Rui Xiao	Southeast University, China
Furong Li	Bath University, UK
Min-Sen Chiu	National University of Singapore, Singapore
Petros Aristidou	University of Leeds, UK
Jinliang Ding	Northeastern University, China
Bing Liu	University of Birmingham, UK
Shan Gao	Southeast University, China
Mingcong Deng	Tokyo University of Agriculture and Technology, Japan
Zhengtao Ding	The University of Manchester, UK
Shiji Song	Tsinghua University, China
Donglian Qi	Zhejiang University, China
Wanquan Liu	Curtin University, Australia
Patrick Luk	Cranfield University, UK
Guido Maione	Technical University of Bari, Italy
Chen Peng	Shanghai University, China
Tong Sun	City University London, UK
Yuchu Tian	Queensland University of Technology, Australia
Xiaojun Zeng	The University of Manchester, UK
Huaguang Zhang	Northeastern University, China
Shumei Cui	Harbin Institute of Technology, China
Hongjie Jia	Tianjin University, China
Youmin Zhang	Concordia University, USA

Xiaoping Zhang	University of Birmingham, UK
Peng Shi	University of Adelaide, Australia
Kay Chen Tan	National University of Singapore, Singapore
Yaochu Jin	University of Surrey, UK
Yuchun Xu	Aston University, UK
Yanling Tian	University of Warwick, UK

Organization Committee

Chairs

Congbo Li	Chongqing University, China
Minyou Chen	Chongqing University, China
Adrian Murphy	Queen's University Belfast, UK
Sean McLoone	Queen's University Belfast, UK

Special Session Chairs

Qian Tang	Chongqing University, China
Xin Dai	Chongqing University, China
Johannes Schiffer	University of Leeds, UK
Wenlong Ming	Cardiff University, UK

Publication Chairs

Zhile Yang	Chinese Academy of Sciences, China
Jianhua Zhang	North China Electric Power University, China
Hongjian Sun	Durham University, UK
Trevor Robinson	Queen's University Belfast, UK

Publicity Chairs

Qingxuan Gao	Chongqing University, China
Junjie Chen	Southeast University, China
Brian Falzon	Queen's University Belfast, UK
Ben Chong	University of Leeds, UK

Secretary-General

Yan Ran	Chongqing University, China
Dajun Du	Shanghai University, China
Rao Fu	Queen's University Belfast, UK
Yanxia Wang	Queen's University Belfast, UK

Registration Chairs

| Guijian Xiao | Chongqing University, China |
| Shaojun Gan | Queen's University Belfast, UK |

Program Committee Members

Stefan Andreasson	Queen's University Belfast, UK
Andy Adamatzky	University of the West of England, UK
Petros Aristidou	University of Leeds, UK
Vijay S. Asirvadam	Universiti Teknologi Petronas, Malaysia
Hasan Baig	University of Exeter, UK
Lucy Baker	University of Sussex, UK
John Barry	Queen's University Belfast, UK
Xiongzhu Bu	Nanjing University of Science and Technology, China
Jun Cao	University of Cambridge, UK
Yi Cao	Cranfield University, UK
Xiaoming Chang	Taiyuan University of Technology, China
Jing Chen	Anhui University of Science and Technology, China
Ling Chen	Shanghai University, China
Qigong Chen	Anhui Polytechnic University, China
Rongbao Chen	HeFei University of Technology, China
Weidong Chen	Shanghai Jiaotong University, China
Wenhua Chen	Loughborough University, UK
Long Cheng	Chinese Academy of Science, China
Min-Sen Chiu	National University of Singapore, Singapore
Adam Clare	University of Nottingham, UK
Matthew Cotton	University of York, UK
Xin Dai	Chongqing University, China
Xuewu Dai	Northeastern University, China
Li Deng	Shanghai University, China
Mingcong Deng	Tokyo University of Agriculture and Technology, Japan
Shuai Deng	Tianjin University, China
Song Deng	Nanjing University of Posts and Telecommunications, China
Weihua Deng	Shanghai University of Electric Power, China
Jinliang Ding	Northeastern University, China
Yate Ding	University of Nottingham, UK
Yulong Ding	University of Birmingham, UK
Zhengtao Ding	University of Manchester, UK
Zhigang Ding	Shanghai Academy of Science and Technology, China
Dajun Du	Shanghai University, China
Xiangyang Du	Shanghai University of Engineering Science, China
Geraint Ellis	Queen's University Belfast, UK
Fang Fang	North China Electric Power University, China
Minrui Fei	Shanghai University, China
Dongqing Feng	Zhengzhou University, China
Zhiguo Feng	Guizhou University, China
Aoife Foley	Queen's University Belfast, UK
Jingqi Fu	Shanghai University, China
Shaojun Gan	Queen's University Belfast, China
Shan Gao	Southeast University, China

Xiaozhi Gao	Lappeenranta University of Technology, Finland
Dongbin Gu	University of Essex, UK
Juping Gu	Nantong University, China
Zhou Gu	Nanjing Forestry University, China
Lingzhong Guo	Sheffield University, UK
Yuanjun Guo	Chinese Academy of Sciences, China
Bo Han	Xi'an Jiaotong University, China
Xuezheng Han	Zaozhuang University, China
Xia Hong	University of Reading, UK
Guolian Huo	North China Electric Power University, China
Weiyan Hou	Zhengzhou University, China
Liangjian Hu	Donghua University, China
Qingxi Hu	Shanghai University, China
Sideng Hu	Zhejiang University, China
Xiaosong Hu	Chongqing University, China
Chongzhi Huang	North China Electric Power University, China
Sunan Huang	National University of Singapore, Singapore
Wenjun Huang	Zhejiang University, China
Tan Teng Hwang	University College Sedaya International University, Malaysia
Tianyao Ji	South China University of Technology, China
Yan Jin	Queen's University Belfast, UK
Dongyao Jia	University of Leeds, UK
Jongjie Jia	Tianjin University, China
Lin Jiang	University of Liverpool, UK
Ming Jiang	Anhui Polytechnic University, China
Youngwook Kuo	Queen's University Belfast, UK
Chuanfeng Li	Luoyang Institute of Science and Technology, China
Chuanjiang Li	Harbin Institute of Technology, China
Chuanjiang Li	Shanghai Normal University, China
Dewei Li	Shanghai Jiao Tong University, China
Donghai Li	Tsinghua University, China
Guofeng Li	Dalian University of Technology, China
Guozheng Li	China Academy of Chinese Medical Science, China
Jingzhao Li	Anhui University of Science and Technology, China
Ning Li	Shanghai Jiao Tong University, China
Tongtao Li	Henan University of Technology, China
Weixing Li	Harbin Institute of Technology, China
Xiaoli Li	Beijing University of Technology, China
Xin Li	Shanghai University, China
Xinghua Li	Tianjin University, China
Yunze Li	Beihang University, China
Zhengping Li	Anhui University, China
Jun Liang	Cardiff University, UK
Zhihao Lin	East China University of Science and Technology, China
Paolo Lino	University of Bari, Italy
Bin Liu	University of Birmingham, UK

Chao Liu	Centre national de la recherche scientifique, France
Fei Liu	Jiangnan University, China
Guoqiang Liu	Chinese Academy of Sciences, China
Mandan Liu	East China University of Science and Technology, China
Shirong Liu	Hangzhou Dianzi University, China
Shujun Liu	Sichuan University, China
Tingzhang Liu	Shanghai University, China
Wanquan Liu	Curtin University, Australia
Xianzhong Liu	East China Normal University, China
Yang Liu	Harbin Institute of Technology, China
Yunhuai Liu	The Third Research Institute of Ministry of Public Security, China
Patrick Luk	Cranfield University, UK
Jianfei Luo	Chinese Academy of Sciences, China
Yuanxin Luo	Chongqing University, China
Guangfu Ma	Harbin Institute of Technology, China
Hongjun Ma	Northeastern University, China
Guido Maione	Technical University of Bari, Italy
Marion McAfee	Institute of Technology Sligo, Ireland
Sean McLoone	Queen's University Belfast, UK
Gary Menary	Queen's University Belfast, UK
Gillian Menzies	Heriot-Watt University, UK
Wenlong Ming	Cardiff University, UK
Wasif Naeem	Queen's University Belfast, UK
Qun Niu	Shanghai University, China
Yuguang Niu	North China Electric Power University, China
Bao Kha Nyugen	Queen's University Belfast, UK
Ying Pan	Shanghai University of Engineering Science, China
Chen Peng	Shanghai University, China
Anh Phan	Newcastle University, UK
Meysam Qadrdan	Imperial College London, UK
Donglian Qi	Zhejiang University, China
Hua Qian	Shanghai University of Engineering Science, China
Feng Qiao	Shenyang Jianzhu University, China
Xuda Qin	Tianjin University, China
Yanbin Qu	Harbin Institute of Technology at Weihai, China
Slawomir Raszewski	King's College London, UK
Wei Ren	Shaanxi Normal University, China
Pedro Rivotti	Imperial College London, UK
Johannes Schiffer	University of Leeds, UK
Chenxi Shao	University of Science and Technology of China, China
Yuntao Shi	North China University of Technology, China
Beatrice Smyth	Queen's University Belfast, UK
Shiji Song	Tsinghua University, China
Yang Song	Shanghai University, China
Hongye Su	Zhejiang University, China

Guangming Sun	Beijing University of Technology, China
Tong Sun	City University of London, UK
Xin Sun	Shanghai University, China
Zhiqiang Sun	East China University of Science and Technology, China
Wenhu Tang	South China University of Technology, China
Xiaoqing Tang	The University of Manchester, UK
Fei Teng	Imperial College London, UK
Yuchu Tian	Queensland University of Technology, Australia
Xiaowei Tu	Shanghai University, China
Gang Wang	Northeastern University, China
Jianzhong Wang	Hangzhou Dianzi University, China
Jingcheng Wang	Shanghai Jiaotong University, China
Jihong Wang	University of Warwick, UK
Ling Wang	Shanghai University, China
Liangyong Wang	Northeastern University, China
Mingshun Wang	Northeastern University, China
Shuangxin Wang	Beijing Jiaotong University, China
Songyan Wang	Harbin Institute of Technology, China
Yaonan Wang	Hunan University, China
Kaixia Wei	NanJing XiaoZhuang University, China
Lisheng Wei	Anhui Polytechnic University, China
Mingshan Wei	Beijing Institute of Technology, China
Guihua Wen	South China University of Technology, China
Yiwu Weng	Shanghai Jiaotong University, China
Jianzhong Wu	Cardiff University, UK
Lingyun Wu	Chinese Academy of Sciences, China
Zhongcheng Wu	Chinese Academy of Sciences, China
Hui Xie	Tianjin University, China
Wei Xu	Zaozhuang University, China
Xiandong Xu	Cardiff University, UK
Juan Yan	University of Manchester, UK
Huaicheng Yan	East China University of Science and Technology, China
Aolei Yang	Shanghai University, China
Dongsheng Yang	Northeastern University, China
Shuanghua Yang	Loughborough University, UK
Wankou Yang	Southeast University, China
Wenqiang Yang	Henan Normal University, China
Zhile Yang	Chinese Academy of Sciences, China
Zhixin Yang	University of Macau, Macau, China
Dan Ye	Northeastern University, China
Keyou You	Tsinghua University, China
Dingli Yu	Liverpool John Moores University, UK
Hongnian Yu	Bournemouth University, UK
Kunjie Yu	Zhengzhou University, China
Xin Yu	Ningbo Institute of Technology, Zhejiang University, China
Jin Yuan	Shandong Agricultural University, China

Jingqi Yuan	Shanghai Jiao Tong University, China
Hong Yue	University of Strathclyde, UK
Dong Yue	Nanjing University of Posts and Communications, China
Xiaojun Zeng	The University of Manchester, UK
Dengfeng Zhang	University of Shanghai for Science and Technology, China
Huifeng Zhang	Nanjing University of Posts and Communications, China
Hongguang Zhang	Beijing University of Technology, China
Jian Zhang	State Nuclear Power Automation System Engineering Company, China
Jingjing Zhang	Cardiff University, UK
Lidong Zhang	Northeast Electric Power University, China
Long Zhang	The University of Manchester, UK
Qianfan Zhang	Harbin Institute of Technology, China
Xiaolei Zhang	Queen's University Belfast, UK
Xiaoping Zhang	University of Birmingham, UK
Youmin Zhang	Concordia University, USA
Yunong Zhang	Sun Yat-sen University, China
Dongya Zhao	China University of Petroleum, China
Guangbo Zhao	Harbin Institute of Technology, China
Jun Zhao	Tianjin University, China
Wanqing Zhao	Cardiff University, UK
Xingang Zhao	Shenyang Institute of Automation Chinese Academy of Sciences, China
Min Zheng	Shanghai University, China
Bowen Zhou	Northeastern University, China
Huiyu Zhou	Queen's University Belfast, UK
Wenju Zhou	Ludong University, China
Yimin Zhou	Chinese Academy of Sciences, China
Yu Zhou	Shanghai Tang Electronics Co., Ltd., China
Yunpu Zhu	Nanjing University of Science and Technology, China
Yi Zong	Technical University of Denmark, Demark
Kaizhong Zuo	Anhui Normal University, China

Sponsors

Chongqing Association for Science and Technology, China
Shanghai University, China

Organizers

Chongqing University, China
Queen's University Belfast, UK

Co-organizers

Southeast University, Beijing Institute of Technology, Dalian University of Technology, Harbin Institute of Technology, Northwestern Polytechnical University, South China University of Technology, Tianjin University, Tongji University, Shanghai University, University of Birmingham, Cardiff University, University College London, University of Nottingham, University of Warwick, University of Leeds.

Contents – Part I

Manufacturing Material

Manufacturing Optimization

Manufacturing Process

Mechanical Transmission System

Contents – Part II

Fault Diagnosis and Maintenance

Intelligent Computing in Robotics

Intelligent Control and Automation

IoT Systems

Neural Networks and Deep Learning

Precision Measurement and Instrumentation

Image Processing

Contents – Part III

Energy Saving

Energy Storages

Power System Analysis

Digital Manufacturing

Defining Production and Financial Data Streams Required for a Factory Digital Twin to Optimise the Deployment of Labour

C. Taylor[1], A. Murphy[1(✉)], J. Butterfield[1], Y. Jan[1], P. Higgins[2],
R. Collins[2], and C. Higgins[2]

[1] School of Mechanical and Aerospace Engineering, Queen's University Belfast,
Ashby Building, Belfast BT9 5AH, Northern Ireland, UK
a.murphy@qub.ac.uk
[2] N.I. Technology Centre, Queen's University Belfast,
Belfast BT9 5HN, Northern Ireland, UK

Abstract. With the emergence of capable and low cost sensing hardware simulations may be driven from real time production data. Such simulation could be used to predict future system performance. However for effective decision making knowledge of system level behaviour beyond production e.g. financial metrics would also be required. The generation of standard accounting data from simulation models has received little attention in the literature. Herein a modelling approach is demonstrated to generate production and accounting data streams from a Discrete Event Simulation for an idealised production business. The paper demonstrates an approach to assess the influence of production variables (labour arrangement) on system cash flow.

Keywords: Discrete Event Simulation · Factory Digital Twin
Financial metrics · Production demand · Labour resource planning

1 Introduction

A significant volume of research has demonstrated the value of simulation to design and improve production systems. Much work has demonstrated the use of simulation to quantify system behaviour with new or changed system hardware, layout or control. Methods such as Discrete Event Simulation (DES) enable complex process chains to be examined. A key weakness of the current state-of-the-art in this area is the lack of non-engineering metrics typically modelled [1, 2]. For decision makers the critical metrics are often both production and financial. However automatically generating financial data from simulation output is a non-trivial task [2] with financial and production metrics typically dissimilar in fidelity and interval [1]. Thus this paper investigates a modelling approach representing both production and financial variables, in order to define data streams appropriate for monitoring and control interventions. This is achieved through the examination of a simple production problem (using the DES software QUEST) and the representation of the finances of a small production business (using Excel and typical accounting practice).

© Springer Nature Singapore Pte Ltd. 2018
S. Wang et al. (Eds.): ICSEE 2018/IMIOT 2018, CCIS 923, pp. 3–12, 2018.
https://doi.org/10.1007/978-981-13-2396-6_1

2   Literature Review

A number of comprehensive, broad scope and focused review papers have been published which examine the use of DES in understanding and improving manufacturing systems [3–12]. These works have considered simulation software selection and evaluation [3, 4]; manufacturing system design and operation [5, 6]; scheduling and control [7–9]; system optimisation [10]; system maintenance [11]; and real-world applications considering manufacturing and business metrics [12]. Together these works provide an effective summary of progress in manufacturing modelling with DES over the last four decades. Predominantly what–if scenarios are considered, enabling the understanding of the effect of production variable changes on production output metrics; financial impact is frequently considered only indirectly through production metric such as throughput, cycle time, WIP etc. To date there are no procedures or guidelines proposed on how DES may be used to routinely assess the influence of operational level production variables on accounting metrics.

3   Case Study and Methodology

A modified production problem from the literature is modelled [13] to provide a platform for method development. The system creates two outputs and in its standard form includes part manufacture and assembly processes. Typically, the model assumes the processes as machining techniques that require little labour input. In the literature a single operator is required to conduct each process and each operator works on only one process. As labour has been less frequently studied in the literature herein all processes (A, B, C, D) are assumed as tasks with high labour content, Fig. 1. Individual task setup times are incorporated into the process time and are assumed to be used for jig loading and fastener placement.

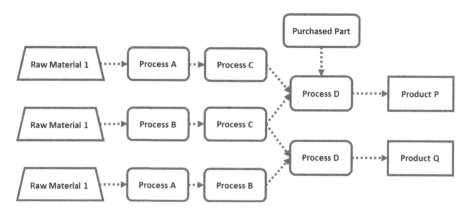

Fig. 1. Case study production arrangement (based on the P&Q problem).

The system produces two products (P's and Q's) to satisfy a demand with variability. One unit each of materials 1 and 2 combined with one purchased part constitutes the chain for product P. One unit each of materials 2 and 3 constitutes the chain for product Q. There are four processes in the system: A, B, C and D. Material 1 is processed by A, C and D, material 2 is processed by B, C and D and material 3 is processed by A, B and D. During process D product Q is made or the purchased part is added to create product P. In the defined problem process B is a constraint. Output from the first two processes are stored in the Manufacturing Component Stores (MCS) until either process D is free, the other product specific component reaches the MCS or the purchased part store is replenished. The product is then assembled and stored in the Final Goods Stores (FGS) before being shipped. The simulation model, Fig. 2, represents each process with its own workstation within three distinct production lines: Processes A and C within Production Line 1 (PL1), Processes B and C within PL2, processes A and B within PL3, and process D as the Final Assembly workstation (FA). To govern the production system in the simulation a Material Requirements Planning (MRP) approach is employed. A weekly sales demand is employed to generate the backward schedule for the MRP. The system demand is calculated weekly based on an individual mean and standard deviation for both P's and Q's. This introduces a controlled level of demand variability into the model. Each simulation is run for an extended period of 24 months such that system behaviour can be considered as stabilised [2].

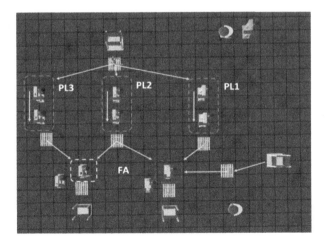

Fig. 2. Simulation model general layout.

In order to model the financial behaviour associated with the production process all activities resulting in financial transactions must be available from the simulation. Herein a prediction of an income statement which records the changes in financial position of a business over a defined period of time is of interest. The three main elements of an income statement are: Revenue – Income earned from trading; Gross profit – Revenue from trading less cost of goods sold (COGS); Net profit – Profit after all other income and expenses have been considered. From the production model the

COGS can be calculated (including materials used to create goods sold and direct labour costs generated from the production of goods). With regards labour cost absorption costing is used which assigns the costs accumulated during the production process to individual products. This approach also enables indirect costs such as variable overheads and fixed overhead to be added to the direct material costs and assigned to the individual products. Moreover from the simulation WIP, MCS and FGS values are also available, describing not only the total system input and output with time but also the state of conversion at discrete time intervals.

The model variables are listed in Table 1. The variables of the model are grouped into several families. The cycle time inputs allow for the manipulation of the cycle time for each part at each process and the cycle time for the assembly of both products. The model represents stochastic failures in the form of a time delay of 15 min occurring every 150 parts for each of the machines. There is a set 5% rework value set within the overhead costing of the model. A stock cap is placed on the MCS for parts 1, 2 and 3 at a maximum capacity of 10 components. Labour is modelled as 3 or 4 operators with training for individual lines or all workstations. The noteworthy model simplifications and assumptions are: the model does not account for travel time between MCS and final assembly, and from final assembly to FGS.

Table 1. Simulation variables grouped into families.

Labour	Financial	Cycle time	Variation
Number of operators	Standard cost of each raw material and purchased part.	Individual process cycle times.	Machine failure percentage.
Operator training (for individual lines or all workstations)	Amount of each raw material purchased per week.	Stock cap on stores (MCS, FGS)	Setup times for each part on each machine.
Operator breaks (UK legal worker breaks are modelled)	P and Q selling prices.		Scrap rate for each part on each machine.
	Wages and salaries.		
	Depreciation.		
	Rent and rates per week.		

4   Results

A series of three simulations are examined with different labour provisions in order to demonstrate the simulation output and identify the key system characteristics. Each simulation has the same initial condition and the same demand profile for 24 months (P's: $\mu = 151$, $\sigma = 6$, Q's: $\mu = 74$, $\sigma = 6$). Each simulation has equal company financial arrangements (fixed costs (rent, rates, consumables, depreciation), variable costs (raw material, purchased part), payment schedules (debtor, creditor)), and equivalent individual process cycle times and process variability.

Dedicated operators on each work-station: Fig. 3 presents the simulation output: part (a) illustrates work-station utilisation. In this case operator and work-station utilisation is the same thus PL1, PL2, PL3 and FA average utilisation is 61%, 30%, 89% and 26% respectively; (b) documents the units produced along with the units demanded; (c) plots the resulting system finances including the cash flow. Examining Fig. 3(a) the average utilisation in PL2 is 89% representing the upper bound achievable with the modelled operator breaks. FA operator utilisation is only 26% and this represents the difference in maximum capacity of PL2 and this downstream process. Average utilisation in PL1 and PL3 is 61% and 30% respectively; with these utilisation levels a result of the FA constrained capacity and the presence of a buffer limit at the end of these lines (MCS buffer limit set to a maximum of 10 units). Thus as in the literature process B on PL2 is the system bottleneck. Examining Fig. 3(b) the average produced and demanded units are the same, however closer inspection reveals a number of weekly instances of over and under production. Across the 24 months, there were 13 weeks with unsatisfied demand for product P and 5 for product Q. The financial predictions are plotted in Fig. 3(c). In general, the cash flow has a negative trend with a final value of £ (71,279) at week 104. This reflects a high level of Labour and Overhead under recovery due to the low utilisation of both the workstations and operators in PL1, PL3 and FA, but also the reduced sales income resulting from the unsatisfied demand for both products.

Shared operator on PL1 and PL3 (three dedicated operators): As in the first simulation case PL2 and FA have dedicated operators but in this simulation case PL1 and PL3 have a single shared operator. Figure 4 presents the simulation output. In this case operator average utilisation for FA, PL1&PL3 and PL2 is 23%, 88%, and 89% respectively. Examining Fig. 4(a) the average utilisation of PL2 and its operator remains high (on average 78%). Average utilisation of work-stations PL 1 and PL3 remain low (55% and 27% respectively) with their combined operator utilisation now 89% representing the upper bound achievable with the modelled operator breaks. Thus the shared operator on PL1 and PL3 appears to be a new system bottleneck. This is further evidenced by the reduction in system output. Across the period weekly output for Ps and Qs are 11% and 10% lower than the demand rate (Fig. 4(b)). Demand of product P is unsatisfied for all 104 weeks and for 73 weeks for product Q. However the financial performance in Fig. 4(c) presents a positive trending cash flow across the period with a final cash flow statement at week 104 of £98,915. Examining in detail the individual finance elements the impact of a lower level of Labour and Overhead under recovery, due to the higher utilisation of the operators, offsets the reduction in the number of goods sold.

Three floating operators: In the first two simulations the operators are assigned to individual production zones or work-stations. In this simulation three floating operators are modelled who can work on any production zone or work-station. The fixed and variable costs associated with labour were also modified to account for higher salary and training requirements. Figure 5 presents the simulation output. In this case operator average utilisation is 87%, 75% and 46%. Line and work-station utilisations have increased by between 3 and 6% over the preceding case with 3 operators with the same rank order of average utilisation with PL2 with the highest level and FA with the lowest. With respect to output, Fig. 5(b), output again fall short of demand with

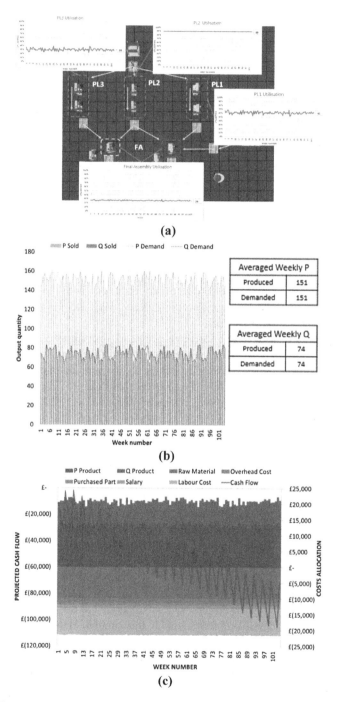

Fig. 3. Dedicated operators on each work-station: (a) illustrates work-station and operator utilisation; (b) documents the units produced along with the units demanded; (c) plots the resulting system finances including the cash flow.

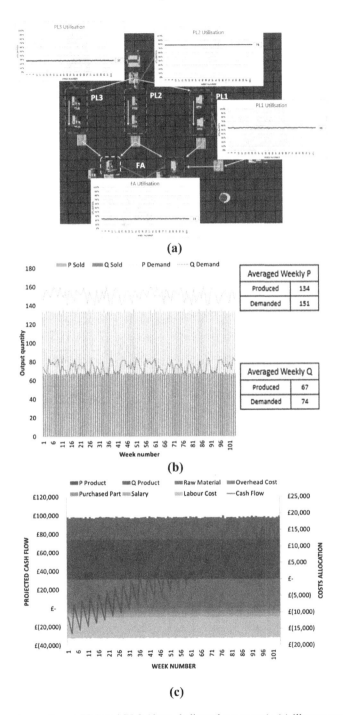

Fig. 4. Shared operator on PL1 and PL3 (three dedicated operators): (a) illustrates work-station and operator utilisation; (b) documents the units produced along with the units demanded; (c) plots the resulting system finances including the cash flow.

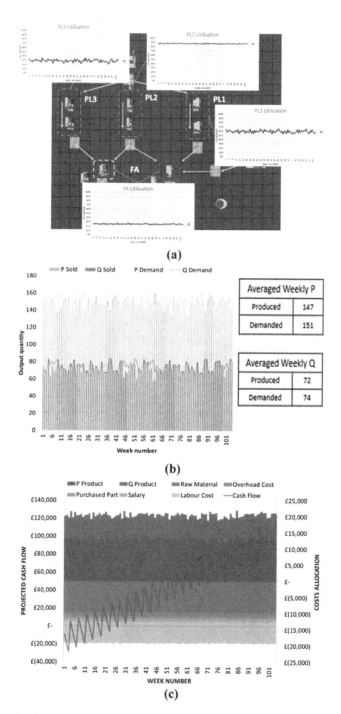

Fig. 5. Three floating operators: (a) illustrates work-station and operator utilisation; (b) documents the units produced along with the units demanded; (c) plots the resulting system finances including the cash flow.

Table 2. Simulation result summary.

	Average P output	Average Q output	Cash flow @wk. 104	% diff from P demand (151)	% diff from Q demand (74)	Total number of weeks in which P demand was unsatisfied	Total number of weeks in which Q demand was unsatisfied
4 dedicated operators	151	74	£(71,279)	0%	0%	13	5
3 dedicated operators	134	67	£98,915	−12%	−10%	104	73
3 floating operators	147	72	£121,948	−3%	−3%	48	26
4 floating operators	165	83	£(233,496)	10%	13%	0	0

unsatisfied demand in a total of 48 and 26 weeks for products P and Q respectively. Examining the financial performance, Fig. 5(c), a positive trending cash flow is predicted with a final cash flow statement at week 104 of £ 121,948. Again the improved Labour and Overhead under recovery with higher utilisation and the greater volume of sales results in the positive cash flow and its final value.

5   Discussion and Conclusions

Table 2 summarises the key simulation results. Four dedicated operators is the approach which best satisfies the demand rate but produces a generally negative cash flow. The next closest to the demand is three floating operators which achieved 3% less output for both products than the required demand rate but yielded the highest cash flow value at the end of the runtime due to the higher operator utilisation and product output. None of the operator arrangements modelled completely satisfies the specified demand thus a final simulation is undertaken with four floating operators. This arrangement of labour satisfies the specified demand with no unsatisfied demand weeks. However this arrangement consistently overproduces Ps and Qs each week and ultimately results in the largest negative final cash flow statement at week 104 of £ (233,496), Table 2. Although the system is arranged for one piece flow and production buffers set to minimise the opportunity for WIP to build up uncontrolled in the system there is no buffer limit on the FGS. Figure 8 presents FGS inventory costs and the clear overproduction for the system throughout the simulation period. Thus the challenge is to resource the production system to match the demand without overproduction. Doing this with the minimum number of operators will minimise the Labour and Overhead under recovery and thus maximise the final cash flow position.

Limited research exists on the use of simulations for the generation of coupled production and non-production data streams. Thus herein a simulation approach is proposed and demonstrated for coupled production and financial data generation for an idealised production system using DSE. The proposed approach enables the prediction of both operational production behaviour and higher level financial metrics (in the case study focusing on system labour arrangement and cash flow). The paper demonstrates how such modelling can enable assessment of specific production strategies which aim to influence both production and financial metrics. The modelling approach also represents the basic capability for simulation based control where real time production and financial data can be used as base conditions for future state prediction, again in both the production and finance domains.

References

1. Acheson, C., et al.: Integrating financial metrics with production simulation models. In: Paper presented at 15th International Conference on Manufacturing Research, London, United Kingdom (2017)
2. Acheson, C., et al.: Using design of experiments to define factory simulations for manufacturing investment decisions. In: Paper presented at 34th International Manufacturing Conference, Sligo, Ireland (2017)
3. Nikoukaran, J., Paul, R.J.: Software selection for simulation in manufacturing: a review. Simul. Pract. Theor. **7**, 1–14 (1999)
4. Alomair, Y., Ahmad, I., Alghamdi, A.: A review of evaluation methods and techniques for simulation packages. Procedia Comput. Sci. **62**, 249–256 (2015). ISSN 1877-0509 http://dx. doi.org/10.1016/j.procs.2015.08.447
5. Negahban, A., Smith, J.S.: Simulation for manufacturing system design and operation: literature review and analysis. J. Manuf. Syst. **33**(2), 241–261 (2014). https://doi.org/10. 1016/j.jmsy.2013.12.007
6. Smith, J.S.: Survey on the use of simulation for manufacturing system design and operation. J. Manuf. Syst. **22**(2), 157–171 (2003)
7. Chan, F.T.S., Chan, H.K., Lau, H.C.W.: The state of the art in simulation study on FMS scheduling: a comprehensive survey. Int. J. Adv. Manuf. Technol. **19**(11), 830–849 (2002)
8. Chan, F.T.S., Chan, H.K.: A comprehensive survey and future trend of simulation study on FMS scheduling. J. Intell. Manuf. **15**(1), 87–102 (2004)
9. Shukla, C.S., Chen, F.F.: The state of the art in intelligent real time FMS control: a comprehensive survey. J. Intell. Manuf. **7**(6), 441–455 (1996)
10. Prajapat, N., Tiwari, A.: A review of assembly optimisation applications using discrete event simulation. Int. J. Comput. Integr. Manuf. **30**(2–3), 215–228 (2017). https://doi.org/10.1080/ 0951192x.2016.1145812
11. Alrabghi, A., Tiwari, A.: State of the art in simulation-based optimisation for maintenance systems. Comput. Ind. Eng. **82**, 167–182 (2015). https://doi.org/10.1016/j.cie.2014.12.022
12. Jahangirian, M., Eldabi, T., Naseer, A., Stergioulas, L.K., Young, T.: Simulation in manufacturing and business: a review. Eur. J. Oper. Res. **203**(1), 1–13 (2010). https://doi. org/10.1016/j.ejor.2009.06.004
13. Youngman, D.K.J.: A Guide to Implementing the Theory of Constraints (TOC). http://www. dbrmfg.co.nz/Overview Introduction.htm

Data Driven Die Casting Smart Factory Solution

Yuanfang Zhao, Feng Qian[✉], and Yuan Gao

School of Mechanical Engineering,
Dalian University of Technology, Dalian 116024, China
qianfeng@dlut.edu.cn

Abstract. Smart factory is the foundation of intelligent manufacturing. Intelligent devices are applied to monitor and adjust factory production process and optimize production performance. Aiming at the problem that traditional decision system in die casting factory ignores the value of manufacturing data, the data driven die casting smart factory solution is developed. The key technology of intelligent factory is reviewed, and a new "Data + Prediction + Decision Support" mode of operation analysis and decision system based on data driven is put forward. Combined with the key technology of die casting and the application of data driven new mode, the "Physics + Information + Decision" three layers of cyber-physical system is designed. This solution digs the value of manufacturing data, and promote the efficient production of die casting smart factory.

Keywords: Smart factory · Intelligent manufacturing · Die casting
Data driven

1 Introduction

With the rapid development of artificial intelligence and network technology, the concept of intelligent manufacturing has been put forward. In 2013, Germany launched "The Industrial 4.0 strategy" [1], and in 2015, China launched the "made in China 2025" plan [2]. Both of them pay attention to Intelligent Manufacturing, which relays on the smart factory. Smart factory is the realization of intelligent manufacturing system in manufacturing factory's level, which is the extension and development of digital factory, connected factory and automated factory [3]. By the intelligent means (e.g. cloud computing, Internet of Things and big data), managers get real-time feedback from factory information system and decision support system, and make decisions based on expert experience. Many researchers studied on key technology in smart factory. Robert et al. [4] described the smart factory as a cyber-physical system, which monitors the factory's production process, builds factory virtual simulation system and

Supported by the project of 2016 Ministry of Industry and Information in the Intelligent Manufacturing: Application of new model of high silicon aluminum alloy engine cylinder block without cylinder 3000 tons high vacuum die casting intelligent workshop.

makes discrete decision. Zhong et al. [5] realized an Internet of Things system in a smart factory based on the radio frequency identification (RFID) technology. Wang et al. [6] proposed a multilayer framework composed of robot, cloud and client, assisted the inter-layer interaction and inter-robot negotiation by the cloud technology. These studies focus on specific technology, and don't propose a framework of whole factory's operational analysis and decision system. Then some researchers began their studies on smart factory's analysis and decision system. Lv et al. [7] proposed a smart factory technology framework based on big data, which combining the emerging technology at home and aboard. Zhang et al. [8] put forward a new mode of factory operational analyzing and decision making, which is "correlation + prediction + regulation". These studies provided method systems for the operational analysis and decision of smart factory, has reference value for realizing data driven smart factory.

Die casting fills the die casting mold cavity with high speed and high pressure, and it's better than traditional casting in casting performance and productivity. Compared with developed countries, die casting technology started late in China, and the development of die casting industry is fast. Therefore, it has great significance for the development of die casting industry in China that put forward the die casting smart factory solution, which combining die casting technology and intelligent manufacturing. Sun [9] designed a hierarchical structure of die casting smart factory manufacturing system after analyzing the production process of die casting factory. Taking a die casting workshop as an example, Xu [10] studied the architecture design, development and implementation of intelligent manufacturing system software. These studies focus on the production process of die casting factory, driving the die casting factory by the causal relationship. The causal relationship will be more complex when factory products are more diverse and technology is more complex. Then driving the die casting factory by the causal relationship will be difficult, so it's necessary to design a new solution.

In this paper, a data driven intelligent factory operation analysis and decision method system is used, and study the key technology of intelligent manufacturing, then a data driven die casting smart factory solution is proposed.

2 Data Driven Smart Factory

2.1 Data Driven Smart Factory Operation System

Intelligent equipment e.g. CNC machine tools, sensors, data acquisition devices are widely used in smart factory with the rapid development of automation and information, and the manufacturing data in factory are more and more scale (Volume), high speed (Velocity) and diversity (Variety) [11]. In general, factory is driven by the causal relationship, and improves production efficiency, product quality and other workshop performance by using factory simulation modeling and algorithm [8]. Take the decision-making process of logistics distribution as an example, to get a good distribution plan, we analyze the causal relationship between distribution parameters and distribution goals, and establish an accurate mathematical model to describe the delivery problem. Then we design an algorithm to solve it. It's possible to get accurate solution when it's a small scale problem. When the problem scale gets big, it's necessary to design excellent optimization method to get a better solution. The "Causality + modeling + algorithm" decision mode ignores the value in manufacturing data, and difficult to cope with the diverse needs of products and complex processes in intelligent factories.

When data is enough, the data guarantees the effectiveness of data analysis. Even if we don't know the causal relationship completely, we can get close to the conclusion of the fact. Combining the value of data and the causality driven analysis and decision system, we propose a "Data + Prediction + Decision Support" mode, showed in Fig. 1. It collects manufacturing data in the smart factory, carries out the pre-processing of cleaning, classification and integration, excavates the law of the influence between data, predicts the performance index of the factory, and provides decision support for the factory regulation and control by combining the prediction results with the traditional decision-making model.

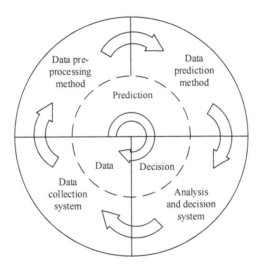

Fig. 1. "Data + Prediction + Decision Support" mode

2.2 Data Driven Smart Factory Organization Structure

Under the "Data + Prediction + Decision Support" mode, smart factory operation analysis and decision system is driven by manufacturing data, which is a cyber-physical system consisted by "Physical-Information-Decision" three-layer structure.

In the smart factory, on the basis of acquiring manufacturing data from the physical layer, the data quality of the workshop is improved by manufacturing data pre-processing method. The prediction is realized by the method of data mining such as artificial neural network. The smart factory control is realized through the smart factory analysis and decision system, and the control signal is passed through the information layer to the physical layer. The physical and information fusion of the smart factory is realized.

Physical layer, consisted by intelligent devices (e.g. AGV) acquires manufacturing data of the production process in the smart factory and transfers it to the information layer, which is consisted by data processing software (e.g. Data Warehouse). Prediction is made based on the data which is collated and pre-processed in the information layer, being the preparation of the decision layer. In the decision layer, managers make decision by expert experience model or the "Causality + modeling + algorithm" model, with the aim to optimize the factory performance by adjusting factory production process. The decision layer is composed of factory management and control software (e.g. ERP).

3   Die Casting Smart Factory Solution

The main operation process in die casting smart factory is shown as Fig. 2. After receiving the order, the die casting enterprises finish the process design according to the order requirements, make the master production plan and purchase raw materials and spare parts. The main production processes include melting aluminum liquid, transporting aluminum liquid, die casting (high temperature injection, hold & cooling), cutting edge and polishing etc. Then the products are packed and delivered in storage.

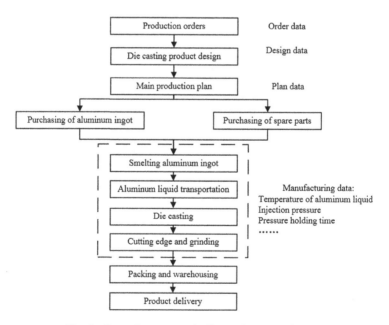

Fig. 2.   Operation process in die casting smart factory

3.1 Solution of Physical Layer in Die Casting Smart Factory

The die casting smart factory physical layer includes intelligent integrated die casting equipment, intelligent aluminum liquid transportation system, intelligent complete logistics equipment and other intelligent devices.

Intelligent integrated die casting equipment is the core of die casting smart factory, which is composed of furnace, aluminum liquid hoisting and dumping device, soup sending machine, die-casting machine, unloading robot and on-line monitoring device etc. The data bus technology is used to control the linkage of all intelligent devices, and complete all the process operations needed to produce die casting blanks. Collects production process data e.g. casting pressure, pressing velocity, temperature of aluminum liquid.

Intelligent aluminum liquid transportation system monitors and alerts of the amount of molten aluminum in the furnace by liquid amount monitoring device, and sets up wireless communication equipment, realize intelligent automatic calling function. Meantime, it connected with intelligent equipment of molten aluminum smelting workshop, collecting data of raw material e.g. composition of aluminum liquid.

Intelligent complete logistics equipment uses AGV and conveyor belts to deliver the semi-finished products of the intelligent integrated die casting equipment to the grinding zone, and uses the auxiliary intelligent equipment e.g. the tray, the RFID chip on the finished product box and the corresponding reading and writing equipment to prevent the error.

Other intelligent devices are interconnected through sensors, RFID and other technologies, and connect with the information layer software, and upload data to the information layer by the mass, multi-source and heterogeneous manufacturing data of the smart factory.

3.2 Solution of Information Layer in Die Casting Smart Factory

The information layer of the smart factory collects and stores the mass multi-source heterogeneous manufacturing data from the data sources of the physical layer. In order to form effective decision support, pre-processes the manufacturing data and uses the data mining technology to predict the key performance of the die casting intelligent factory (Table 1).

Table 1. Null values (-), error values (*) and repeat values (#) in die casting factory physical layer.

Product number	x_1	x_2	x_3	...	x_n	Y
1	102.05	2	0.4		0	2.945079
$2^{\#}$	102.05	2	0.4		0	2.945079
3	98.56	-1.23^{*}	0.398		1	2.741264
4	-	2	0.4		0	2.799336
...						
500	100.25	3	0.4		0	2.625853

There may be many problems in physical layer data collection, such as data errors, data missing, data duplication, etc. Null values and an error values in the time of the product's entry may arises if scavenging gun breakdown when finished products access storage, and repeat values arises if repeated scans. These data quality problems increase the difficulty of mining data's internal value. So it's necessary to define the method to identify and deal with null values, error values and repeat values in information layer. Null values are easy to identify. Error values can be identified by the value meaning e.g. aluminum liquid temperature must be lower than boiling point, and also can be identified by statistical method. Repeat values can be identified by Hamming distance, it will by identified as a repeat value if a value's Hamming distance with another value is smaller than the threshold. To ensure the integrity of the data, interpolation method is used to deal with null values, and correcting method is used to deal with error values and repeat values (Fig. 3).

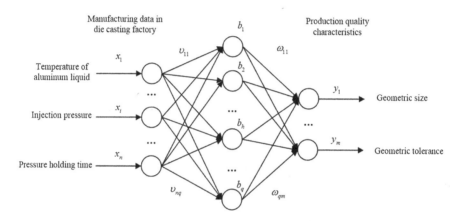

Fig. 3. Die casting production quality prediction model based on neural network

In the data drive mode, the analysis's effectiveness is guaranteed by data scale. Predicting the performance index by the manufacturing data is corresponding classification and regression task in data mining, which can be used to extract models describing important data classes or predict future trends. Commonly used classification and regression methods include support vector machine (SVM), artificial neural network (ANN). Taking the quality prediction of die casting as an example, we take die-casting pressure, aluminum liquid components etc. as the prediction basis, and take geometrical dimensions as the goal of quality prediction. Using BP neural network to train on the historical data in die casting smart factory, we get the die casting quality prediction model (Fig. 4).

Taking an automobile engine cylinder die-casting factory as an example, the 27 parameters, which affect the quality of the die-casting of the cylinder body, are selected as the input of the improved BP neural network, and the 19 dimensions of the three coordinates of the cylinder body are selected as the output. The error back propagation algorithm is used to update the network parameters, and the genetic algorithm is used to

Fig. 4. Cylinder block of automobile engine

optimize the network learning rate and the number of neurons in the hidden layer. Using the continuous production of 51 cylinder data training networks and adopting 90% off cross validation, an improved BP neural network which can predict the quality of the cylinder block is obtained. The mean square error is much smaller than the size parameter, which indicates that the prediction is of high accuracy (Table 2).

Table 2. Related parameters in improved BP neural network.

Input dimension	Output dimension	Learning Rate	Numbers of hidden layer	Mean square error
27	19	0.0003	7940	0.022

Using the improved BP neural network, the die casting intelligent factory can predict the quality of the product in real time, and upload the data to the decision layer of the intelligent factory to provide reference for the intelligent decision making of the die casting factory.

3.3 Solution of Decision Layer in Die Casting Smart Factory

In decision layer in die casting smart factory, basing on the performance prediction offered in the information layer, the managers select expert experience model or causality driven model to regulate and control the die casting process. It aims at improving the operation performance of the smart factory e.g. making main production plan base on the prediction of product quality, production quality and mold life (Fig. 5).

The regulating and control decisions, which are made in the decision layer, are fed back to the information layer and transformed to the adjustment instructions. The instructions are executed in the physical layer to adjust the operating state of the die casting smart factory. After adjusting, manufacturing data is uploaded to the

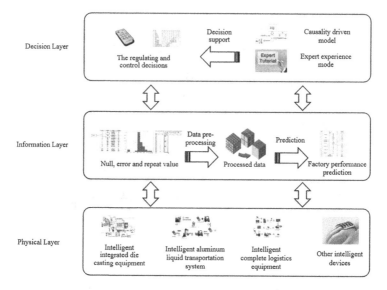

Fig. 5. Die casting smart factory "physical-information-decision" solution

information layer, then to the decision layer. A closed-loop die casting smart factory operation analysis and decision system is formed.

4   Conclusion

This paper has studied some intelligent methods and operation analysis and decision system in smart factory, and put forward a "Data + Prediction + Decision Support" mode smart factory operation analysis and decision system, which is combining the traditional "Causality + Modeling + Algorithm" mode and the value in manufacturing data. Applying the new mode, a die casting smart factory solution is designed as a cyber-physical system, made up by the physical layer, information layer and decision layer, which is a closed-loop die casting smart factory operation analysis and decision system. This solution is useful for the construction of intelligent factory in die casting industry. Future research will focus on the realization and the performance of each layer in this system.

References

1. Zuehlke, D.: Smart factory—towards a factory-of-things. J. Ann. Rev. Control **34**(1), 129–138 (2010)
2. Sun: Commentary of the development trend for intelligent equipment manufacturing industry in the future. J. Process Autom. Instrum. **34**(1), 1–5 (2013)
3. Zhu, H., Li, Y., Liu, K.: Smart factory architecture standard for middle and low-voltage switchgear assembly industry. J. Comput. Integr. Manufact. Syst. **23**(6), 1216–1223 (2017)

4. Harrison, R., Vera, D., Ahmad, B.: Engineering the smart factory. J. Chin. J. Mech. Eng. **29**(6), 1046–1051 (2016)
5. Zhong, R.Y., Xu, X., Wang, L.: IoT-enabled smart factory visibility and traceability using laser-scanners. J. Procedia Manufact. **10**, 1–14 (2017)
6. Wang, S., Zhang, C., Liu, C., et al.: Cloud-assisted interaction and negotiation of industrial robots for the smart factory. J. Comput. Electr. Eng. **63**, 66–78 (2017)
7. Lv, Zhang: Big-data-based technical framework of smart factory. J. Comput. Integr. Manufact. Syst. **22**(11), 2691–2697 (2016)
8. Zhang, J., Gao, L., Qin, W.: Big-data-driven operational analysis and decision-making methodology in intelligent factory. J. Comput. Integr. Manufact. Syst. **22**(5), 1220–1228 (2016)
9. Sun: Research on the key technology of the intelligent manufacturing system in die-casting workshop and system development. D. Zhejiang University (2017)
10. Xu: Research and development and architecture design of die-casting plant manufacturing system software. D. Zhejiang University (2017)
11. Laney, D.: 3D data management: controlling data volume, velocity and variety [EB/OL], 6 February 2001. https://blogs.gartner.com/doug-laney/files/2012/01/ad949-3D-Data-Manage ment-Controlling-Data-Volume-Velocity-and-Variety.pdf. Accessed 15 Jun 2015

The Parametric Casting Process Modeling Method Based on the Topological Entities Naming

Xiaojun Liu[1,2(✉)], Zhonghua Ni[1,2], Xiaoli Qiu[1,2], and Xiang Li[1,2]

[1] School of Mechanical Engineering, Southeast University,
Nanjing 210096, People's Republic of China
liuxiaojun@seu.edu.cn
[2] Jiangsu Key Laboratory for Design and Manufacture of Micro-Nano
Biomedical Instruments, Southeast University,
Nanjing 210096, People's Republic of China

Abstract. In order to maintain the topological relations for the elements of casting process model and rebuild the casting process correctly when process parameters is changed, the topological entities naming method is used in this paper. Firstly, topological entities naming method, including naming rule for entity ID, Geometry_Name, and Process_Name, is proposed, and the mapping strategy between topological entity name and process information is established. Then, the geometry modeling method for casting process is studied in three steps: (1) process parameter setting method for gating and riser system; (2) parametric modeling procedure for gating and riser system; (3) the 3D process dimension design procedure for gating and riser system. Thirdly, the reconstruction method for parametric casting process model based on topological entity identification is given. A prototype of 3D casting process planning system is developed, and the reconstruction method is tested by an example part.

Keywords: Casting process planning · Parametric design
Topological entities naming · Gating system · Riser system

1 Introduction

The 3D casting process planning is mainly to realize the design and modeling of casting part, gating system, riser system and chilling system in 3D modeling environment. And, the casting part modeling procedure includes removing no casting features, adding matching allowance and drafting angle. These functions are generally completed by two key steps. The first step is process parameters selection and calculation, such as size selection for no casting features and machining allowance, dimension calculation and position selection for gating and riser system. And the second step is modeling for the process elements, such as creating of 3D models, marking of the process dimensions and annotation.

For large parts with complex structure, it is difficult to choose the most suitable process parameters at once, so it is necessary to modify the casting process during the process planning. The casting process parameters are always firstly recalculated and

S. Wang et al. (Eds.): ICSEE 2018/IMIOT 2018, CCIS 923, pp. 22–39, 2018.
https://doi.org/10.1007/978-981-13-2396-6_3

reselected when the casting process needs to be changed, then the parameters are transferred to the 3D model, and the 3D model and process dimensions are modified and rebuilt.

The essence of parametric design is to reflect the designer's design intent by adding lots of constraint relations in the parametric model, update the model by changing variable parameters and automatically maintain all invariant parameters and constraints. But it is lack of explicit definition for the descriptions of the features during parametric modeling, so the designer's design intention is difficult to be expressed and maintained accurately in the procedure of parametric reconstruction. The updation of a parametric model may cause boundary geometry entity be added, split, or deleted, the referenced topological entities (point, line, surface) cannot be accurately found in the rebuilt model, and leads to model size updating errors. Therefore, all the referenced topological entities need to be recorded properly during the casting process modeling for the constraint relation analysis and correctly recognition of topological entities. This article will use the topological entities naming method to record the topological entities and process information.

2   State of the Art

Naming and identification of topological entities is one of the key problems in parametric feature modeling system, Bidarra [1] considers it as one of the six problems to be solved in the feature modeling system.

Ever since Kripac [2] proposed a topological naming system first in 1994, the research on persistently naming of topological entities has been extended to the present. This global matching approach involves expensive graph isomorphism procedures in each model re-evaluation [3].

The influence of the feature editing to the design result and the relationship between topological entities naming method and topological entities is analyzed in detailed by Capoyleas [4]. And the topological entities can be named by the local topological relations of topological entities, the local orientation of the edges and vertexes and the direction information of features. The mapping of topological entities is achieved by the comparison of topological names in the old and new model.

The method proposed by Capoyleas and Kripac is based on the similarity to identify topological entities, and the method is not necessarily able to correctly identify the topology entities which fit the user's design intent.

A topological naming method based on faces is given by Wu [5]. The topological face is associated with an original name, and when the face is splitted, the name of previous face is given to the splitted face. Liu [6] integrate the local topology information and geometry characteristics of topological entities on the basis of Wu's work in order to deal with the change of topology structure effectively. However, the reconstruction of the model is still not able to satisfy the design intent when the topology entities disappear. Gao [7] proposes a new mechanism of naming topological entities based on face features and a method of coding topological entities, sub-entities and virtual entities, in which, three mechanisms including inheritance of topological entities, split of topological entities and obliteration of topological entities in semantic feature operations are given. Zhang [8] proposed a persistent naming and identification method based on faces and the method uses dynamic naming and variable long string coding based on the evolution of face topology. A topological entities persistent naming and identification mechanism based on the connection between faces is proposed by Zhu [9]. The system can realize the function of common features creation, history management, constraint management and the access of feature model and geometry model.

The topological naming methods proposed above are all used in CAD system, and all used to realize model reconstruction to satisfy the design intent. As parametric casting process model is multi-state model and more process information related to casting model needs to be handled, so a topological entities naming method for parametric casting process planning needs to be studied.

3   Topological Entities Naming for Casting Process Planning

The topological entities naming method tries to record all the geometry entities of the 3D model persistently, and the entities includes face, edge and vertex.

As the 3D modeling procedure for casting process element involve no complicated edge and face operations, a topological naming method for the parametric design of casting process is put forward. Topological naming mainly includes two steps: naming of original geometry entity and naming of process entity features.

3.1   The Naming Rule for ID

Due to the different design habits, when the parts model is imported to the process planning system, there are usually some problem as follow:

(1) The model of the casting part is composed of many feature components, which are disordered and haven't been arranged and combined.
(2) There are inessential information during design procedure in the exported part model, such as auxiliary surfaces, center lines and positioning points.
(3) The model center may not be set as the coordinate origin, then the imported design model may not be located in the view field.

In order to ensure that the process modeling is executed smoothly, the design model need to be preprocessed.

(1) According the definition of geometry topology in ACIS, a complete entity has at least one block and no wire frame information. Therefore, all the design part model entity should be traversed firstly, and all the geometry entities which fit the requirement should be applied boolean sum operation, the only casting part model will be obtained.
(2) After removing the casting part model, the design model still includes auxiliary information, sketch information, coordinate system, and redundant model entities such as array features, turning features and stretching features. Therefore auxiliary information still needs to be stored, so all of the plane, line and point information

(which may contain entity information) should be copied and stored in auxiliary information container.

(3) Get the internal parameters of coordinate system, and set the center of the part model after boolean sum operation as the origin for the new world coordinate, then redefine world coordinate of the system maintaining the XYZ axis direction of the design model.

The ID is the unique mark of a geometry feature entity, which can be used for the recording and searching of the geometry entities conveniently in the procedure of naming. The geometry entities are classified into faces, edge and vertex, and IDs are given to all geometry entities as their unique mark. Then the geometry entities can be identified and obtained by their IDs which are taken as the first retrieval basis. Meanwhile, the 3D dimension information, process information and process geometry model are associated with each other by the IDs.

The ID is made up of the entity mark and the common mark. The entity mark represents the type of geometry entity, and the common mark represents the number of geometry entity in the entity set. The detailed definition is as shown in Table 1.

Table 1. Geometry classification mark

Geometry entity type	Entity mark	Common mark	ID
body	0	000001	0_000001
face	1	000001 ~ 999999	1_000001 ~ 1_999999
edge	2	000001 ~ 999999	2_000001 ~ 2_999999
vertex	3	000001 ~ 999999	3_000001 ~ 3_999999

3.2 The Naming Rule for Geometry_Name

The naming method of the original geometry entity is to construct the name according to the type of entity and the IDs of their sub entities, and all entities will have unique marks in the initial state. The Geometry_Name is the name of the original geometry entity, defined as:

$$Geometry\_Name = \ <Feature\_Type, Feature\_Entities>$$

where, Feature_Type is the type of feature, and Feature_Entities is the entity list of the feature. Regardless the type of feature is face, edge and vertex, the Feature_Entities is formed by ID list of the key vertexes.

The topological naming examples for edge are shown in Fig. 1. If the type of an edge is a straight line, as shown in Fig. 1a, this edge is named as edge_line_0_1, and the ID list is composed of the two vertexes. If the type of the edge is curve or arc, as shown in Fig. 1b, the edge is named as edge_arc_0, and ID list is composed of the center of the arc. If there are concentric circles, the sequence number should be added to the end of the name such as line_arc_0_(0 ~ 10). If the curve is other irregular curves, as shown in Fig. 1c, this edge is named as line_curve_0_1, and ID list is composed of the two vertexes of the edge.

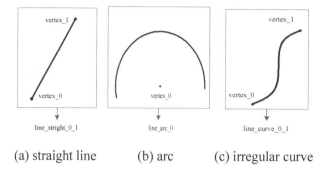

(a) straight line   (b) arc   (c) irregular curve

Fig. 1. Topological naming of edge

The topological naming examples for face are shown in Fig. 2. If the type of face is plane as shown in Fig. 2a, the face is named as face_plane_0_1_2_3, and the ID list is composed of all vertices. If the type of face is curved surface and the curved face is a sphere as shown in Fig. 2b, this face is named as face_sphere_0, and the ID list is composed of the center point of the sphere. If the curved face is a truncated cone, as shown in Fig. 2c, this face is named as face_cone_0_1, and the ID list is composed of the center points of the top face and bottom face. If the curved face is a irregular curved face, as shown in Fig. 2d, this face is named as face_surface_0_1_2_3, and the ID list is composed of all vertexes of the face.

3.3   The Naming Rule for Process_Name

Process_Name is name of topological entities associated with cast process, defined as:

$$Process\_Name = <Process\_Reference, Process\_Num, Process\_Type>$$

where, Process_Reference is the reference name of a process element which is associated with the topological entities, Process_Num is the number of a process step which is associated with the topological entities, and Process_Type is the type of process. The Process_Type may be N, C, E, and D, and N stands for no process, C stands for creating process, E stands for modifying process, D stands for deleting process. If the Process_Num is 0 and the Process_Reference is null, the topological entity is the original geometry entity.

The naming rule of Process_Name has to ensure the association between the process information and the involved topological entities during the parametric modeling procedure, such as the information of creation, modification and deletion, by adding the intention of the process personnel to the topological entities name associated with process. The specific procedure is as follows:

STEP 1: Initialize the names of all the original geometry entities of the design part, including vertexes, lines and faces. Then traverse all the vertexes, lines and faces and add the suffix NULL_0_N to the name of original geometry entity to get the

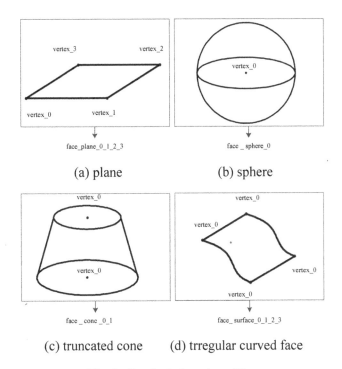

Fig. 2. Topological naming of face

process associated name, and the suffix means that there is no process information associated to the geometry entities.

STEP 2: Enter the waiting state until the relevant procedure events are triggered, if there is no relevant procedure operation. Start the procedure associated naming procedure, if the relevant procedure operation is carried out.

STEP 3: Obtain all the relevant vertexes which are involved in the change of the process model according to the type of procedure event. Obtain all line and face features which include these point by querying the ID of the vertexes.

STEP 4: According to the geometry feature modification type, three kinds of situation are as following: if the event is creating process features, the name of new-created geometry entity feature is composed of original geometry entity name and the procedure type mark "C"; if the event is editing the process features, the procedure type mark is "E"; if the event is deleting process features, the procedure type mark is "D" and the original geometry entity name is kept in order to backtrack.

The creating of casting process feature "machining allowance" and "drafting angle" is set as an example to describe the naming procedure of process associated name. As shown in Fig. 3, machining allowance 1 and drafting angle 2 are created in order.

After creating the process, the topological name of the geometry entities is shown in Table 2, including original geometry entity name and process association name, and

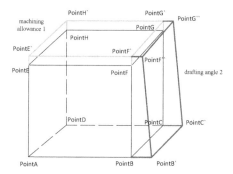

Fig. 3. Schematic diagram of process creating

Table 2. Topological name of point

Geometry entity	Original elelment feature	Process associated name	topological name
pointA	vertex_0	NULL_0_N	vertex_0_NULL_0_N
pointB′	vertex_1	Taper_2_C	vertex_1_Taper_2_C
pointC′	vertex_2	Taper_2_C	vertex_2_Taper _2_C
pointD	vertex_3	NULL_0_N	vertex_3_NULL_0_N
pointE′	vertex_4	Allowance_1_C	vertex_4_Allowance_1_C
pointF″	vertex_5	Allowance_1_C _Taper _2_C	vertex_5_Allowance_1_C _Taper _2_C
pointG″	vertex_6	Allowance_1_C _Taper _2_C	vertex_6_Allowance_1_C _Taper _2_C
pointH′	vertex_7	Allowance_1_C	vertex_7_Allowance_1_C

these two parts are connected by "_". And Tapper represents the process name of drafting angle, Allowance represents the process name of machining allowance.

3.4 Mapping Strategy Between Topological Entity Name and Process Information

The 3D casting process model based on MBD includes process geometry model, 3D process dimensional information, and process information. The topological entity names include the mapping relationship between process geometry model and process information, the data information and the relationship of casting process model, which are shown in Fig. 4.

Take the inner runner process planning as an example: First, the feature model of the inner runner is created and the entity feature name and process association name of the inner runner are created according to the feature model of the inner runner. Then the design history information of the inner runner feature model, such as the profile, the sweep path and the information of API function, is stored corresponding to the process tree nodes. Finally, the corresponding 3D process dimension information of inner

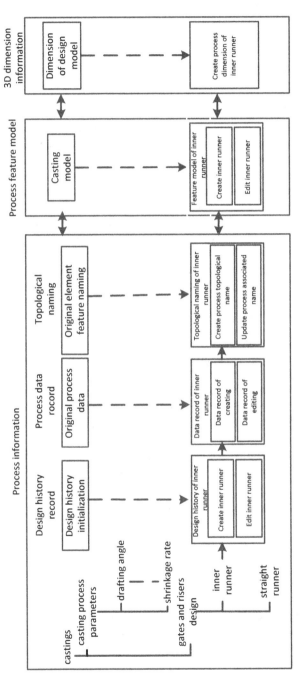

Fig. 4. Mapping of topology name and process planning information

runner model is created according to the user's setting. When the inner runner feature model is modified, the process associated name of the inner runner feature model is updated according to the modified geometry entities, the record of process data and design history need to be kept at the same time.

4 Geometry Modeling Method of Casting Process

4.1 Process Parameter Setting of Gating and Riser System

Gating system of low pressure casting usually plays the role of feeding, so the minimum cross-sectional area of the runners in the low pressure casting system cannot be determined by the usual calculation formula. The metal material of low pressure casting is usually aluminum, magnesium and other materials which can be oxidized easily. Therefore, the open gating system is generally used, and the sum of the cross-sectional area is $\sum F_{inner} > \sum F_{horziontal} > \sum F_{vertical}$, and the specific number can be $2 \sim 2.3{:}1.5 \sim 1.7{:}1$. Taking into account the structural integrity of the casting during the pressure relieving procedure, in order to achieve a bottom-up order filling shrink, the system can also be designed as semi-open gating system.

In the design procedure of gating system, the section area of inner runner is calculated firstly and then the cross sectional area of horizontal runner and vertical runner is determined according to the ratio of each section. The sectional area design of the common casting system is based on the formula:

$$t = h/v_s$$
$$A_g = G_c/(\rho v t)$$

where, t is the filling time(*s*), *h* is the cavity height (*cm*), v_s is the rising velocity of liquid level in cavity, *Ag* is the cross sectional area of inner runner (*cm²*), *Gc* is the weight of casting (*g*), *v* is the linear velocity of inner runner exit (*cm/s*), and ρ is the density of alloy liquid (*g/cm³*).

When determining the cross sectional area of inner runner according to the formula, the cavity filling is taken into account, but the feeding of inner runner is ignored.

4.2 Parametric Modeling of Gating and Riser System

4.2.1 Modeling of Gating System

(1) The establishment of the runner feature model

The runner model is mainly modeled by sweep function. The area of runner is firstly calculated; select the appropriate section shape and size of gating runner, then determine the position and attitude and create the guide line; runner model is completed by sweep the cross section along the guide. In the procedure of modeling, the 3D process model of the gating system is independent of the casting model. When modifying the position and attitude of the gating system, it only needs to translate or rotate the internal coordinate system of the runner and the casting model does not need to be changed.

The inner runner is the last channel when liquid metal enters into the mold cavity, which controls the speed and direction of the metal fluid. For low pressure casting gating system, there are several kinds of the cross section, as shown in Fig. 5(a–d).

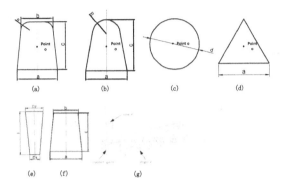

Fig. 5. Cross section of runners

Taking inner runner as an example, the creation procedure of the runner is introduced. Only the type of cross section and necessary gating parameters are needed to be selected, the 3D process runner model can be build. The procedure for creating a runner with trapezoidal cross section is introduced, the workflow is as follows:

STEP 1: Get the information of inner runner, such as size of cross section, position and attitude of the runner. The inner runner location is denoted as O and the section normal vector of inner runner is denoted as n.

STEP 2: Take point O as the origin to create 2D sketch plane, the horizontal axis is denoted as x and vertical axis is y, as shown in Fig. 6.

STEP 3: Calculate coordinates of point 1, point 2, point 3, point 4 in the sketch plane through the values a, b, c.

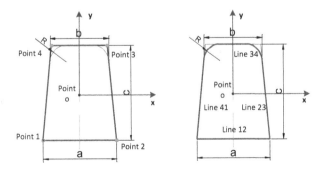

Fig. 6. Draft of inner runner

STEP 4: Create line 12, line 23, line 34, line 41 in the sketch plane using Point 1, point 2, point 3, point 4 and create chamfer feature, and the four line segments are recorded as the inner runner profile.

STEP 5: The normal vector in sketch plane is (0, 0, 1) and the actual of section normal vector is n. Seek the angle between two vectors, denoted as θ.

STEP 6: Position the sketch contour to the actual position, and the normal direction of runner section has been determined. Input the cross section rotation direction, and the default rotation angle is 0.

STEP 7: Sweep and create the 3D feature model of inner runner according to the design parameter set by designer.

Horizontal runner is the channel which connects the end of straight runner and the front of inner gate. Generally, the cross section area of the runner should be uniformly or gradually reduced from the straight runner to the inner runner. Trapezoidal runner, whose height is greater than the width, is usually used in production, as shown in Fig. 5 (e, f). So the reducing proportion of the first section in the sweeping of section should be determined. To complete modeling work, the initial sweeping contour, final contour and guide line need to be defined. The modeling procedure of transverse runner is similar to inner runner.

The casting liquid enters the transverse runner and the inner runner through the straight runner. Straight runner is mostly conical, as shown in Fig. 5(g). The design procedure is similar to procedure of the inner runner.

At present, for cabin type casting parts widely used in the field of aerospace, vertical slot gating systems are mainly used. Slot gating system improves the process performance of top pouring and bottom pouring system.

The vertical slot gating system is conducive to the floating of slag, and can also make up the shrinkage of casting. The vertical tube has the function of heat preservation [17]. The slot gating systems is composed of the vertical tube and the gap, and the structure is shown in Fig. 7.

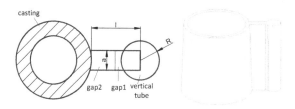

Fig. 7. Cross section and structure of gap runner

The slot gating systems is suitable for cylinder castings. When creating a slot gating, the appropriate gap runner parameters and the joint surface between cylinder castings and slot runner are needed be selected, then the model of slot gating can created by the computer automatically. The procedure of rapid parametric modeling algorithm is as follow:

STEP 1: calculate the parametric size of slot gating and selected the joint surface.
STEP 2: Judge whether the joint surface feature is truncated cone (Cone and cylinder feature belongs to special cone). If it is, go to STEP 3; otherwise, remind that the selected joint surface is wrong and reselect.
STEP 3: Obtain central axis feature of truncated cone surface, and the center of upper ring is denoted as O_1 and radius is denoted as R_1, and the center of under ring is denoted as O_2 and radius is denoted as R_2.
STEP 4: Set the axis direction vector of point O_2 and O_1 as n. Create local coordinate system by taking n as the Z axis and O_2 as the origin of coordinates. The XY axis direction can be set by the system, because the vertical tube is distributed in a circular array on the joint surface.
STEP 5: Create a vertical cylinder cross section with a radius of R, and sweep the vertical cylinder model. Establish the right slot 1 with the width of b/2 + R and the length of a.
STEP 6: Create a sketch profile for left slot 2, and sweep the model. The extruding termination constraint is the joint surface.
STEP 7: Execute boolean sum of the three sweeping parts, and it is the slot gating system.

4.2.2 Modeling of Riser System

Riser system is used for feeding the casting liquid volume shrinkage during solidification, in order to reduce the defects of shrinkage cavity and shrinkage porosity so as to obtain the dense microstructure casting.

For the low pressure casting, feeding capacity of inner runner and slot runner is usually considered, so the design procedure of riser system can be simplified. Mold filling and solidification under pressure of castings improves the feeding distance of riser.

If the riser size needs to be chosen manually, the designer can refer to dimension design standard for cylindrical open riser. The riser modeling procedure is almost the same with the modeling procedure of gating system, positioning by reference point and normal vector of cross section. After modeling, the 3D process model is established according to the process data. Specific procedures are as follows:

STEP 1: Create a reference segmentation plane to split casting
STEP 2: The system automatically calculates the modulus of component based on the geometric information of splitting component.
STEP 3: Set the number of riser pre-design, and get the process attribute of the 3D process model, calculate equivalent diameter riser according to casting material information, the modulus of components and the number of risers.
STEP 4: Retrieve process database for riser, get the riser type and size information from design handbook in accordance with the calculation results.
STEP 5: Select suitable riser type and size, and design the position and attitude of riser.

STEP 6: According to the riser size and location information, complete the establishment of riser feature model in casting model.

Four kinds of commonly used standard cylindrical open riser are shown in Fig. 8.

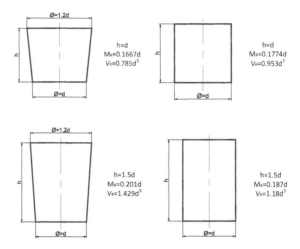

Fig. 8. Size and parameters of standard cylindrical riser

4.3   3D Process Dimension Design of Gating and Riser System

After the establishment of the feature model of the runner and riser, there are two methods for adding 3D process dimensions: one kind is that the designers add dimension manually, the dimension type and dimension entity is selected firstly, and then the display information and value for process dimension are added. The other kind is completing the establishment of dimension automatically according the runner size parameters when the runner feature model is build.

As shown in Fig. 9, the dimensions need to be added for the inner runner model are dimension a, b, c and L. The dimensions of a, b and c are in the cross section of the inner runner, and the dimensions L is in the direction of section normal vector. The data structure of 3D dimension model is defined as:

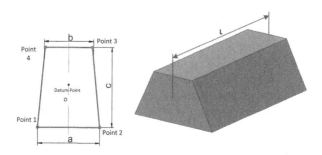

Fig. 9. 3D annotation of inner runner

PMI = <Dimension_Type, PMI_Value, Association, Orientation, Annotation>
and, Orientation = <Line_Start1, Line_Start2, Arrow_1, Arrow_2, Text_Display, n, l>

Take the dimension a as an example, the procedure is as follows:

STEP 1: Obtain the all the edge information of cross section.
STEP 2: Get the endpoints of associated body: point 1 and point 2. Denote them as Line_Start1 and Line_Start2.
STEP 3: Get the midpoint of point 1 and point 2, denote it as point O`. The unit directional vector of OO` is denoted as L1, the unit vector of point 1 and point 2 is denoted as L2.
STEP 4: set Arrow_1 = Line_Start1 + L1 * c/5, Arrow_2 = Line_Start2 + L1 * c/5, Text_Display = $O' + L1 * c/5$ (c/5 indicates the distance between the mark extraction point and the mark arrow points, the c/5 has a better display effect after the test).
STEP 5: The cross section normal vector is defined as N, and the vector L2 is defined as l, the procedure is end.

For dimension L, the procedure is as follows:

STEP 1: Analyze all face information from the runner model, and get the two faces that are parallel and equal in size, then define the two faces as the associated entities of dimension L.
STEP 2: Get the center of the two faces, marked as point 1 and point 2, and record them as Line_Start1 and Line_Start2.
STEP 3: Use vector L1 which is obtained from the calculation of dimension a. Set Arrow_1 = Line_Start1 − L1 * (c/2 + c/5),   Arrow_2 = Line_Start2 + L1 * (c/2 + c/5), Text_Display is the midpoint of Arrow_1 and Arrow_2.
STEP 4: Defined the cross section normal vector as l, define L2 vector, which is obtained from calculation of solving dimension a, as n, and L is defined as the annotation value.

5   Reconstruction of Parametric Casting Model

The gating model is independent with the casting, and the topological naming of the first runner in the gating system is same to the naming of the casting when importing the design model. The topological name of the casting part and gating system is stored separately in order to ensure that the topological name of the gating system and casting don't have the reference relationship. Tables 3 and 4 are the topological entities naming of the casting part and the inner runner for the part in Fig. 10. The NJD stands for the inner runner process name.

    We only need to call the corresponding API function according to the modified process data to update the feature model, when modifying the runner model.

Table 3. Topological entities naming of castings

Geometry entity	Original entity feature	Process association name	Topological name
point1	vertex_0	NULL_0_N	vertex_0_NULL_0_N
point2	vertex_1	NULL_0_N	vertex_1_NULL_0_N
edge1	line_arc_0_0	NULL_0_N	line_arc_0_0_NULL_0_N
edge2	line_arc_0_1	NULL_0_N	line_arc_0_1_NULL_0_N
edge3	line_arc_1_0	NULL_0_N	line_arc_1_0_NULL_0_N
edge4	line_arc_1_1	NULL_0_N	line_arc_1_1_NULL_0_N
face1	face_circle_0_0_1	NULL_0_N	face_circle_0_0_1_NULL_0_N
face2	face_circle_1_0_1	NULL_0_N	face_circle_1_0_1_NULL_0_N

Table 4. Topological entities naming of inner runner

Geometry entity	Original entity feature	Process association name	Topological name
point1	vertex_0	NJD_1_C	vertex_0_NJD_1_C
point2	vertex_1	NJD_1_C	vertex_1_NJD_1_C
point3	vertex_2	NJD_1_C	vertex_2_NJD_1_C
point4	vertex_3	NJD_1_C	vertex_3_NJD_1_C
edge12	edge_line_0_1	NJD_1_C	edge_line_0_1_NJD_1_C
edge13	edge_line_0_2	NJD_1_C	edge_line_0_2_NJD_1_C
edge24	edge_line_1_3	NJD_1_C	edge_line_1_3_NJD_1_C
edge34	edge_line_2_3	NJD_1_C	edge_line_2_3_NJD_1_C
face1234	face_plane_0_1_2_3	NJD_1_C	face_plane_0_1_2_3_NJD_1_C

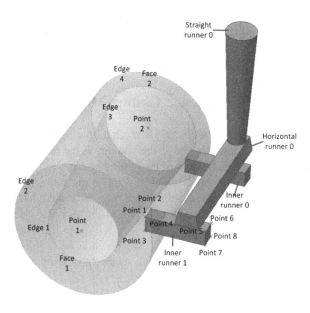

Fig. 10. Topological name of the gating system

STEP 1: Modify the casting process name according to the demand, and find the node refer to the modified procedure in the process tree by traversing the process tree.

STEP 2: Search the database information according to the process name. The process data of the process model which is stored in the database is shown at the dialog for the designer's modification.

STEP 3: Judge whether the process feature model involves the change of geometry entities, if only process data and information is added, goto STEP 5; otherwise, goto STEP 4.

STEP 4: Regenerate the feature model by calling the API function of operating the geometry feature model in design history according to the modification of process data in dialog box.

STEP 5: Retrieve the topology name of points, lines, surfaces according to process name. The process type Process_Type is modified as E, which indicates that the process type in the topology name is editing, update all names that are referenced by the topology entity of the feature model.

STEP 6: Add the modified process model bulletin board in the process planning history,, and the modified operation is recorded.

STEP 7: Store the new process data in the corresponding process database after digitization.

STEP 8: Reconstruct geometry entity location based on the feature model, and recalculat 3D annotation display unit.

6 Prototype System Development

Based on the geometry modeling kernel ACIS and 3D display kernel HOOPS, this paper develops a prototype system for 3D parametric casting process design. Here is an example of casting process design of a part model. As shown in Fig. 11(a), the design model is the cylinder, and the design of gap runner, inner runner, horizontal runner and risers need to be finished. Open the gap runner design panel, modify the value of gap, parameters of vertical tube and number of gap runner according to the system rec-ommendation, then click the gap fitting surface and the gap runner model will be constructed automatically by the system. When gap runner is established, the inner runner whicn is connected with the gap runner can be positioned by selecting datum point and runner direction. Then select the cross section of inner runner according to the system recommendation and the inner runner will be modelled automatically. And select the datum point to position the horizontal runner, the system can calculate and recommend the parameters of runner for designer to choose. After deciding the parameters, the horizontal runner will be modelled. The risers can also be positioned by selecting datum point, and the size of risers can be calculated by filling the number of risers in the design panel. After choosing the type of risers, the riser will be constructed by system, as shown in Fig. 11(b).

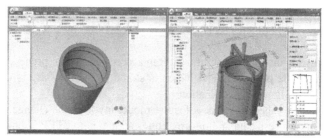

(a) The imported casting part (b) The gating system and
riser system

Fig. 11. A prototype system for 3D parametric casting process design

The parameters of runners can be edited, the feature model and dimensions will be reconstructed automaticly according to the modification. In Fig. 11(b), the first length of the inner runner is 200 and the width is 90, and after modifying the process parameters to 300 and 100 through the panel, the model and process dimension of inner runner are driven to be refreshed automatically, as shown in Fig. 12(a). The parameters of horizontal runner and gap runner can also be modified through panel, as shown in Fig. 12(b).

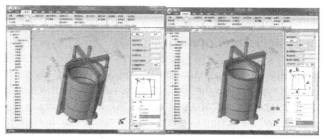

(a) The upated inner runner (b) The updated horizontal
runner

Fig. 12. Parametric design of inner runner and horizontal runner

7 Conclusions

In this paper, topological entities naming method for casting process planning is proposed, and a 3D casting process planning system is developed. The case study shows that the topological entities naming mechanism and the 3D geometry modeling method can support the casting process model reconstruction.

Acknowledgment. The authors acknowledge the financial support from the National Natural Science Foundation of China (Grant No. 51405081), the Fundamental Research Funds for the Central Universities, the six talent peaks project in Jiangsu Province, and sponsored by Qing Lan Project.

References

1. Bidarra, R., Nyirenda, P.J., Bronsvoort, W.F.: A feature-based solution to the persistent naming problem. Comput. Aid. Des. Appl. **2**(1), 517–526 (2005)
2. Kripac, J.: A mechanism for persistently naming topological entities in history-based parametric solid models. Comput. Aid. Des. **29**(2), 113–122 (1997)
3. Wang, Y., Nnaji, B.O.: Geometry-based semantic ID for persistent and interoperable reference in feature-based parametric modeling. Comput. Aid. Des. **37**(10), 1081–1093 (2005)
4. Capoyleas, V., Chen, X., Hoffmann, C.M.: Generic naming in generative, constraint-based design. Comput. Aid. Des. **28**(1), 17–26 (1996)
5. Wu, J., Zhang, T., Zhang, X., et al.: A face based mechanism for naming, recording and retrieving topological entities. Comput. Aid. Des. **33**(10), 687–698 (2001)
6. Liu, J., Chen, Z., Gao, S., Wang, Z.: Design intent maintenance and topological entities naming in design process. J. Comput. Aid. Des. Comput. Graph. **08**, 1106–1117 (2009)
7. Gao, X.Y., Zhang, C.X., Ren, M.Y., et al.: A new mechanism of naming topological entities for semantic feature operations. J. Softw. **7**(3), 705–711 (2012)
8. Zhang, Y., Luo, X.: Wang Huiqi.A face-based approach to persistently naming and identifying topological entities. J. Dalian Univ. Technol. **50**(4), 508–514 (2010)
9. Zhu, Y., Liu, J., He, K., Chen, Z.: Design and implementation of feature modeling system based on ACIS/HOOPS. Comput. Appl. Softw. **30**(2), 71–73 (2013)
10. Tao, W.: CAD system of low pressure castiong process for cylindric magnesium alloy casting. China Academy of Machinery Science & Technology (2000)

Accuracy Analysis of Incrementally Formed Tunnel Shaped Parts

Amar Kumar Behera[1][(⊠)], Daniel Afonso[2], Adrian Murphy[1], Yan Jin[1], and Ricardo Alves de Sousa[2]

[1] School of Mechanical and Aerospace Engineering, Queen's University Belfast, Stranmillis Road, Belfast BT9 5AH, UK
{a.behera,a.murphy,y.jin}@qub.ac.uk
[2] Department of Mechanical Engineering, University of Aveiro, Campus de Santiago, 3810-183 Aveiro, Portugal
{dan,rsousa}@ua.pt

Abstract. Tunnel shaped parts with truncated pyramidal shapes were formed using Single Point Incremental Forming (SPIF) on a Stewart platform. The accuracy behavior of these parts was characterized by an error prediction response surface generated using Multivariate Adaptive Regression Splines (MARS). This response surface predicted over forming for low wall angle parts and under forming for higher wall angle parts. It is based on geometrical parameters associated with features on the part geometry and was used to compensate for inaccuracies in the part geometry. Feature detection was found to work well for tunnel shaped parts using similar thresholds as container shaped parts, while the maximum deviations were found to be lower at a wall angle of 60° compared to a part with wall angle 40°.

Keywords: Tunnel shaped parts · Single Point Incremental Forming (SPIF)
MARS · Accuracy · Sheet metal

1 Introduction

Single Point Incremental Forming (SPIF) is a flexible sheet metal forming process that enables dieless manufacture of 3D shapes. A cylindrical tool with a hemispherical ball end is usually used to deform a flat sheet in incremental steps, conforming to the part geometry. The process has been studied in great detail over the last 15 years, leading to detailed understanding of the deformation mechanics and process outcomes such as sheet thickness variations, formability and achievable accuracy [1]. Several process variants have been developed that include the use of laser support [2], electrical heating [3], two tools [4], part die [5], full die [5] etc.

Most studies in SPIF have focused on the use of fully constrained sheets, clamped on four sides, resulting in parts that have the configuration of a container. The disadvantage in such a configuration is the waste of material when forming parts that are eventually not meant to be containers and limitation in part dimensions. To overcome these limitations, the forming of tunnel shaped parts, as shown in Fig. 1 has been recently proposed by Afonso et al. [6]. This involves the use of semi-constrained sheets

© Springer Nature Singapore Pte Ltd. 2018
S. Wang et al. (Eds.): ICSEE 2018/IMIOT 2018, CCIS 923, pp. 40–49, 2018.
https://doi.org/10.1007/978-981-13-2396-6_4

where only two sides are clamped. The result of this is a reduction in the formability, leading to a lower critical wall angle at failure. Furthermore, the deformation characteristics change leading to inaccuracies with different magnitudes and shape as compared to fully constrained blanks.

Fig. 1. Tunnel shaped parts formed using Single Point Incremental Forming (SPIF)

The objective of the current study was to investigate the effect of semi-constraining on the achievable part accuracy. Pyramidal shapes with three different wall angles were formed and their accuracy behavior studied. The formed surfaces were compared to their nominal CAD models and the resulting data sets were used to train a regression model using Multivariate Adaptive Regression Splines (MARS) for individual planar features on the parts. This model was then used to compensate for the part accuracy, resulting in compensated STL files, which can be used for optimized toolpath generation for tunnel shaped parts.

2 Methodology

The experimental and analysis campaign is described below. First, the experimental setup is discussed. Next, the toolpath generation procedure for forming the parts in these experiments is described. A feature based part geometry compensator that works on part geometries in stereolithographic (STL) file format was used within this research, which is covered next. Finally, the methodology for accuracy prediction using the data from the experiments and linking to the part geometry compensator is discussed.

2.1   Experimental Setup

Experimental tests were performed on the SPIF-A setup at Aveiro [7]. This setup possesses 6 degrees-of-freedom for the tool and uses a parallel kinematics scheme on a Stewart platform as its backbone architecture. Parts were made from aluminium sheets, AA 1050-H111, with a sheet thickness of 2 mm. A 10 mm spherical tip punch was used, with a 0.5 mm constant step down in the z-axis (corresponding to the spindle axis), with a feed rate of 1500 mm/min, free spinning tool and using 10W40 oil as a lubricant. Truncated tunnel shaped pyramids with wall angles 20°, 40° and 60° were formed and analysed for their accuracy behavior.

2.2   Toolpath Generation for Tunnel Shaped Parts

The toolpath strategy uses alternating directions in each forming step, with the travel from one wall of the tunnel to the opposite made outside the part edge, as shown in Fig. 2. The toolpath programming was done using Powermill. The CAD model surface was extended by 5 mm on each edge (to allow a side changing position outside the true part edge) and a constant Z strategy was applied. The direction of the even steps were then changed. The toolpath was then post-processed to a numeric G-code to be run on the SPIF-A machine.

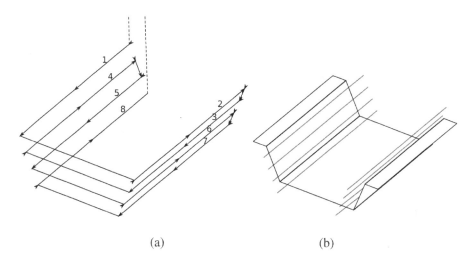

(a)   (b)

Fig. 2. Toolpath strategy for tunnel shaped parts illustrating (a) movements of tool between passes 1–8 (b) length of tool movements on the part geometry

2.3   Feature Detection on STL Files

Past work on accuracy in SPIF has illustrated the strong correlation between geometrical features and the nature and magnitude of deviations in formed parts [8–10]. A taxonomy of 33 features based on geometry, curvature, orientation, location and process related attributes was defined by Behera et al. [11, 12]. These features can be detected within a Visual C# program, developed at KU Leuven, that takes in stereo-lithographic (STL) files as inputs, where the geometry of a part is described using triangles.

The feature detection process involves calculation of the principal curvatures and normal at each individual vertex in the STL model. This is done by following the steps outlined by Lefebvre et al. [13] The curvature tensor at a vertex v is calculated as:

$$\Lambda(v) = \frac{1}{|A|}\sum_{edges} \beta(e)\left\|e \cap A\right\|\frac{ee^T}{e^2} \tag{1}$$

where, $|A|$ is the surface area of the spherical zone of influence of the tensor and $\beta(e)$ is the signed angle between the normal vectors of the STL facets connected by the edge e. $\beta(e)$ is positive for a concave surface and negative for a convex surface. The factor $e \cap A$ gives the weight for the contribution by an individual edge. The normal at each vertex is estimated as the eigenvector of $\wedge(v)$ calculated by the eigenvalue of minimum magnitude. The remaining eigenvalues, k^{min} and k^{max} represent the minimum and maximum curvatures at the vertex v. Using these principal curvatures, four types of features can be classified as defined below:

Planar feature: $k^{min} = 0 \pm \varepsilon_p$ and $k^{max} = 0 \pm \varepsilon_p$, where ε_p is a small number that can be tuned for identifying planar features.

Ruled feature: $k^{min} = 0 \pm \varepsilon_r$ and $k^{max} = X$, where X is a positive non-zero variable. Another possible case is where $k^{min} = X$ and $k^{max} = 0 \pm \varepsilon_r$, where X is a negative non-zero variable. ε_r is a small number that can be tuned for identifying ruled features.

Freeform feature: $k^{min} = Y \pm \varepsilon_f$ and $k^{max} = X \pm \varepsilon_f$, where X and Y are non-zero variables such that $X \leq \rho_{max}$ and $Y \geq \rho_{min}$, where ρ_{max} and ρ_{min} are threshold values for distinguishing freeform and rib features. ε_f is a small number that can be tuned for identifying freeform features.

Rib feature: $k^{min} \leq \rho_{min}$ and/or $k^{max} \geq \rho_{max}$

2.4 Accuracy Predictions Using Multivariate Adaptive Regression Splines

In order to make reliable predictions of accuracy of sheet metal parts formed by SPIF, models can be developed using data from experimental parts. A common approach is to scan these parts with a laser scanner or touch probe, which generates a point cloud of high order (data sets of the order of 100, 000 – 500, 000 points). Once this cloud is generated, it can then be meshed to form a STL file and compared with the CAD model corresponding to the design of the part (also commonly referred to as the nominal model), to generate a dataset of deviations for each individual point. This dataset can then be used to model the accuracy for a given feature as a function of key geometrical parameters on the feature. One technique for doing so that has been shown to effective for parts made by SPIF is the use of Multivariate Adaptive Regression Splines (MARS) [14]. MARS is a non-parametric regression technique that sifts through a data set and finds out the best possible relationship between the predictor variables and a response variable. A continuous response surface is generated with continuous first order derivative. Models typically take the form:

$$\hat{f}(x) = \sum_{n=1}^{N} c_n B_n(x) \qquad (2)$$

The response variable is a weighted sum of basis functions $B_n(x)$, and the coefficients c_n are constants. The basis function $B_n(x)$ takes on one of three forms:

(i)   a constant,
(ii) a hinge function of the type max(0, $x - c$) or max(0, $c - x$), where c is a constant and max(p, q) gives the maximum of the two real numbers p and q or
(iii) a product of two or more hinge functions that models interactions between two or more variables.

The hinge functions have knots that are given by constants which are calculated by a forward pass step that initially over-fits the given data, and is followed by a backwards pruning operation which identifies terms that are to be retained in the model. MARS models provided in this paper were fitted in R, a statistical software suite developed as a GNU project, with functions associated with the 'Earth' library of R [15].

3   Results

In this section, detailed accuracy results from the three truncated tunnel shaped pyramid tests are presented first. Results for detection of features on such parts are covered next, followed by the MARS model for error prediction based on the accuracy data from these three tests. Finally, part compensation results are presented.

3.1   Accuracy Analysis

By comparing the measured part geometries to the nominal CAD model in the software GOM Inspect, accuracy plots were obtained for the three truncated pyramids as shown in Fig. 3. The accuracy results were further analyzed by exporting the deviations for individual points and analyzing the same using a MATLAB code to yield a table of deviations, as shown in Table 1. The results indicate that the low wall angle part with a wall angle of 20° shows a significant amount of over forming, as indicated by a minimum deviation of −3.66 mm, while the under forming is highest for the part with the wall angle of 40°, where a maximum deviation of 5.47 mm is observed. The 60° part shows an even distribution of under formed and over formed regions with a maximum deviation of 3.56 mm and a minimum deviation of −2.62 mm.

3.2   Feature Detection Results

Feature detection was carried out on the three STL files with a set of thresholds, as provided in Table 2. These thresholds have been generated after tuning them for tunnel

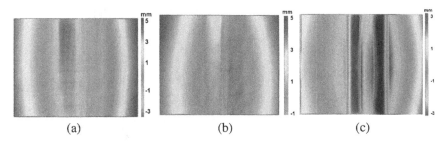

Fig. 3. Accuracy plots for parts with wall angles (a) 20°, (b) 40° and (c) 60°

Table 1. Accuracies of manufactured parts *(All dimensions are in mm)*

Wall angle	Average Positive Deviation	Average Negative Deviation	Maximum Deviation	Minimum Deviation	Average Deviation	Standard Deviation
20°	2.3298	−1.9974	5.2966	−3.6686	0.0541	2.4474
40°	1.8977	−0.3931	5.4758	−1.0077	1.6325	1.4430
60°	1.4554	−1.2095	3.5675	−2.6214	0.1573	1.5693

shaped parts. The detection result for the 20° truncated pyramid is shown in Fig. 4. It was found that for shallow parts with low wall angles, the bottom horizontal plane may get detected as an edge occasionally. This is owing to only a small number of triangles available for feature detection and the presence of an edge when the ordinary non-horizontal planar (ONHP) feature meets the horizontal bottom planar (HBP) feature. It may be noted that the taxonomy adopted is the same as [11, 12].

Table 2. Feature detection thresholds

Threshold	Value
ε_p	$5 * 10^{-4}$
ε_r	10^{-5}
ε_f	10^{-5}
ρ_{min}	−0.01
ρ_{max}	0.01

3.3   Error Correction (Accuracy Prediction) Equation

The accuracy data from the three truncated pyramidal tests were used to train a MARS model. This yielded the following equation:

Fig. 4. Feature detection results on the 20 degree truncated pyramid (Nomenclature follows taxonomy defined in [11]; *HTP: Horizontal Top Planar, NGSVE: Negative General Semi-Vertical Edge, ONHP: Ordinary Non-Horizontal Planar, HBP: Horizontal Bottom Planar*)

$$
\begin{aligned}
e = &-0.58 + 0.57 * \max(0, 0.39 - d_b) + 0.49 * \max(0, d_b - 0.39) + 0.22 \\
&* \max(0, 0.77 - d_o) - 3.4 * \max(0, d_o - 0.77) + 0.0085 * \max(103 - d_h) \\
&+ 0.0028 * \max(0, d_h - 103) - 7.8 * \max(0, 0.7 - \alpha) + 5.5 * \max(0, \alpha - 0.7)
\end{aligned}
\tag{3}
$$

Here, d_b is the normalized distance from the point on the STL file to the edge of the feature in the tool movement direction, d_o is the normalized distance from the point to the bottom of the feature, d_h is the total horizontal length of the feature at the vertex and α is the wall angle at the vertex in radians.

3.4   Part Compensation

Using the model generated in (3), vertices in the STL model of the part were translated normal to the part geometry, following the procedure outlined in [8], using a compensation factor of +1. The result of the compensation for a part with wall angle 40° is illustrated in Fig. 5. This compensated part geometry has been sent to the University of Aveiro for manufacture. It was noted that the model in (3) predicts over forming for low wall angle parts such as the one in the experimental test cases with wall angle of 20°, while it predicts under forming for higher wall angle parts such as the test cases with wall angles 40° and 60°.

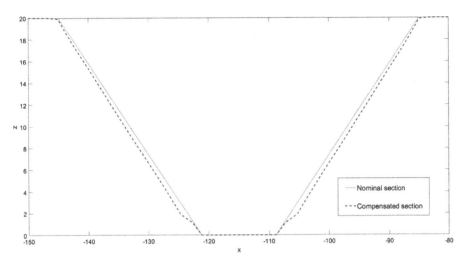

Fig. 5. Sectional view midway through the part at y = 70 mm from the part edge for a part with a length of 140 mm showing nominal and compensated sections

4 Discussion

The accuracy behavior at low wall angles for tunnel shaped pyramidal parts made by SPIF is similar to the behavior observed for fully constrained parts, both showing significant over forming. However, as the wall angle in increased, there appears to be divergence between the accuracy profiles. For fully constrained parts, the under forming at 60° is usually higher than at 40°. For tunnel shaped parts, the opposite behavior was observed in this set of experiments. This suggests that the material flow under deformation could be different for tunnel shaped parts compared to fully constrained parts. However, this will need further validation with additional experimentation such as the use of digital image correlation (DIC). It is also noteworthy that in prior work, Afonso et al. [6] indicated that the accuracy is lower in tunnel shaped parts when tool plunge movements are used in the center of the part, lateral movements of the tunnel bottom while forming due to absence of rigidity and damage at the edge of the parts. These factors influence the accuracy magnitudes that have been reported in this work.

Feature detection for truncated pyramidal parts using an established strategy as shown earlier by Behera et al. [8, 12] worked well here. The detection thresholds also did not change much compared to fully constrained parts. No additional changes to algorithms were necessary. Some cases showed the horizontal bottom being detected as an edge due to the low volume of triangulation for smaller parts and also the transition from a plane to another inducing a positive horizontal edge.

The MARS model shown in Eq. (3) was able to predict and compensate the accuracy behavior of tunnel shaped parts. The efficacy of these predictions in improving the accuracy of parts will need further experiments. The optimized compensation factor for tunnel shaped parts could be different from fully constrained parts, as the results on accuracy at high wall angles indicate that deformation mechanisms seem to be different upon removal of constraints.

5 Conclusions

The analysis of accuracy behavior of truncated pyramids formed as tunnels using SPIF indicates continuation of some patterns observed for fully constrained parts such as over forming at low wall angles and introduction of potentially new phenomena such as higher accuracies at high wall angles compared to moderate wall angles. It is feasible to detect features on STL models of tunnel shaped parts, similar to fully constrained parts, with none or minimal changes to thresholds used for fully constrained parts. Compensation for part accuracy was carried out using a regression model using MARS and generated from the experiments performed in this study. Three distance parameters and the wall angle of the part were found to be the key predictor variables in the MARS model.

Further work shall involve looking into the effect of different compensation factors in improving the accuracy of formed parts. The effect of interaction between features can be studied by forming two slope pyramids and cones, to understand the deformation mechanisms better, make good predictions and form complex parts. The effect of material properties and sheet thickness on accuracy profiles can be studied using digital image correlation leading to better predictions using generic error correction functions.

References

1. Behera, A.K., de Sousa, R.A., Ingarao, G., Oleksik, V.: Single point incremental forming: An assessment of the progress and technology trends from 2005 to 2015. J. Manuf. Process. **27**, 37–62 (2017)
2. Duflou, J.R., Callebaut, B., Verbert, J., De Baerdemaeker, H.: Laser assisted incremental forming: formability and accuracy improvement. Cirp Ann. Technol. **56**, 273–276 (2007)
3. Fan, G.Q., Gao, L., Hussain, G., Wu, Z.L.: Electric hot incremental forming: a novel technique. Int. J. Mach. Tools Manuf **48**, 1688–1692 (2008)
4. Malhotra, R., Cao, J., Ren, F., Kiridena, V., Xia, Z.C., Reddy, N.V.: Improvement of geometric accuracy in incremental forming by using a squeezing toolpath strategy with two forming tools. J. Manuf. Sci. Eng. ASME **133**, 061019 (2011)
5. Jeswiet, J., Micari, F., Hirt, G., Bramley, A., Duflou, J., Allwood, J.: Asymmetric single point incremental forming of sheet metal. Cirp Ann. Technol. **54**, 623–649 (2005)
6. Afonso, D., de Sousa, R.A., Torcato, R.: Incremental forming of tunnel type parts. Procedia Eng. **183**, 137–142 (2017)
7. de Sousa, R.J.A., Ferreira, J.A.F., de Farias, J.B.S., Torrão, J.N.D., Afonso, D.G., Martins, M.: SPIF-A: on the development of a new concept of incremental forming machine. Struct. Eng. Mech. **49**, 645–660 (2014)
8. Behera, A.K., Verbert, J., Lauwers, B., Duflou, J.R.: Tool path compensation strategies for single point incremental sheet forming using multivariate adaptive regression splines. Comput. Des. **45**, 575–590 (2013)

9. Behera, A.K., Lauwers, B., Duflou, J.R.: An integrated approach to accurate part manufacture in single point incremental forming using feature based graph topology. In: Material Forming - Esaform 2012, Pts 1&2, vol. 504–506, pp. 869–876 (2012)
10. Verbert, J., Duflou, J.R., Lauwers, B.: Feature based approach for increasing the accuracy of the SPIF process. Sheet Metal **2007**(344), 527–534 (2007)
11. Behera, A.K., Lauwers, B., Duflou, J.R.: Advanced feature detection algorithms for incrementally formed sheet metal parts. Trans. Nonferrous Metal Soc. China **22**, S315–S322 (2012)
12. Behera, A.K., Duflou, J., Lauwers, B.: Shape feature taxonomy development for toolpath optimisation in incremental sheet forming. Ph.D. thesis. KU Leuven (2013)
13. Lefebvre, P., Lauwers, B.: Multi-axis machining operation evaluation for complex shaped part features. In: Proceedings of the 4th CIRP International Seminar on Intelligent Computation in Manufacturing Engineering, pp. 345–350 (2004)
14. Behera, A.K., Gu, J., Lauwers, B., Duflou, J.R.: Influence of material properties on accuracy response surfaces in single point incremental forming. In: Material Forming - ESAFORM 2012, Pts 1–2, vol. 504–506, pp. 919–924 (2012)
15. Milborrow, S.: earth: Multivariate Adaptive Regression Splines. https://cran.r-project.org/web/packages/earth/index.html. Accessed 16 May 2018

Dynamic Model for Service Composition and Optimal Selection in Cloud Manufacturing Environment

Jawad Ul Hassan[1], Peihan Wen[1(✉)], Pan Wang[1], Qian Zhang[1],
Farrukh Saleem[2], and M. Usman Nisar[2]

[1] School of Mechanical Engineering,
Chongqing University, Chongqing 400044, China
wenph@cqu.edu.cn
[2] The State Key Laboratory of Mechanical Transmission,
School of Mechanical Engineering,
Chongqing University, Chongqing 400044, China

Abstract. A classification model is proposed to allocate, search and match services in cloud environment for Service Composition and Optimal Selection (SCOS). Unlike cloud computing, the services in cloud manufacturing (CMfg) include real time manufacturing resources besides computing services, which makes CMfg environment complicated for allocation of services to the respective tasks. Thus, problem is not having adequate tools for the fast and effective searching and allocation of services for implementation of SCOS. The method described in this paper is to achieve SCOS by organizing the services by an approach named pedigree. For this method to be applied, calculation of semantic cosine distance along with analyzing relationship between different services are required to support the collaboration for managing and matching services in pedigree. Examples are done for service registration along with searching and selecting the services which shows this method to be effective for service composition and optimal selection.

Keywords: Cloud manufacturing · Pedigree · Service model
Cosine similarity · SCOS

1 Introduction

A new manufacturing model developed from the concepts of cloud computing, Internet of Things (IoT), virtualization, service-oriented technologies and advanced computing technologies called Cloud Manufacturing [1]. CMfg has expanded the scope of cloud computing services to include not only Infrastructure as a Service (IaaS), Platform as a Service (PaaS) and Software as a Service (SaaS), but also Manufacturing and Logistics as services [2]. Manufacturing industry is transforming from production to service oriented industry [3]. Considering the user demands and criteria CMfg platform provides secure, reliable, cheap and on-demand manufacturing services from the service providers [4]. The concept of manufacturing here refers to the whole lifecycle of a product and offer services like Argumentation as a Service (AaaS), Design as a Service

© Springer Nature Singapore Pte Ltd. 2018
S. Wang et al. (Eds.): ICSEE 2018/IMIOT 2018, CCIS 923, pp. 50–60, 2018.
https://doi.org/10.1007/978-981-13-2396-6_5

(DaaS), Simulation as a Service (SimaaS), Experiment as a Service (EaaS), Fabrication as a Service (FaaS), Operation as a Service (OaaS), Integration as a Service (IntaaS), Management as a Service (MaaS), Repair as a Service (RaaS). Cloud manufacturing resources are, unlike cloud computing, have dynamic characteristics like geographical distribution of hard resources, physical processes, real time communications and much more [5]. For SCOS multiple services in a certain sequence have to be executed and coordinated for a manufacturing task to be implemented [6] but due to complexities of physical manufacturing processes, service composition has been considered one of the critical challenges of cloud manufacturing [7]. Therefore, Adequate management schemes of SCOS by coordinating huge dispersed services, resources and operations are needed [8].

A dynamic model is presented to increase interoperability by considering common information to define relations between similar and non-similar services. Also, it differentiates services according to their functionalities and made pool of alike services. Thus, creating boundaries between different services to remove the ambiguity and to establish better relationship between alike services for search and selection. Four significant advantages are as follows.

- Improve the coordination of decentralized real resources by converting them into centralized virtual services for effective allocation and optimal selection.
- Narrow down searching spaces and accelerate services scheduling for each SCOS process.
- Dig current services structure and proportion to explore new potential.
- Cover more resources to raise quality of service (QoS) of a CMfg system.

The rest of this paper is organized as follows. Section 2 is about Related work to SCOS whereas Pedigree Model Frame-Work is constructed in Sect. 3, and Applications are discussed in Sect. 4. Finally, conclusions appear in Sect. 5.

2 Related Work

Cloud manufacturing emphases on the collaboration of diverse manufacturing services by considering flexibility and scalability between them. Manufacturing service matching and optimal selection in cloud environment is the serious matter for realizing cloud manufacturing. Researchers have proposed various methods for SCOS such as Ranking Chaos algorithms [9], FC-PACO-RM [10] and others by different intelligent algorithms such as Ant Colony Optimization (ACO), Genetic Algorithms (GAs), Particle Swarm Optimization (PSO) and such other algorithms for dealing with SCOS. In fact, many other similar evaluation and optimization methods also were introduced: QoS with trust function introduced by Tao et al. [12]. According to him trust is an important factor for service scheduling problems. A comprehensive optimization model proposed by Laili et al. [13] for allocation of computing resources in cloud manufacturing environment. Huang et al. [14] proposed a model based on QoS evaluation using optimize chaos control algorithm. Cheng et al. [15] gave a method for energy aware service scheduling by considering different factors such as risk, cost, energy consumptions of utilities. Zheng et al. [16] considered energy consumption during resource allocation a problem and proposed a method using fuzzy similarity degree to select services along with NSGA-II algorithm to had energy aware SCOS. Zhang [17] proposed Flower Pollination Algorithm (FPA) integrated with GA to analyze services correlation along with QoS factors to increase quality of SCOS according to customer demand and many other methods were proposed for various problems of SCOS.

Lacking from the trend, a service platform which is proposed in this paper is to automatically manage services in different classes with unique IDs by using service properties, relations and QoS evaluation for SCOS.

3 Pedigree Model Framework

Service management is becoming difficult with the increasing development of manu-facturing services and increasingly abundant service types. As an essential component of the cloud manufacturing system, creating a logical and realistic classification is vital for different types of manufacturing services for detailed study and description. Cloud manufacturing services are divided into three categories based on the characteristics of manufacturing resources, computing resources and by the perspectives of storage and transportation. Using service classification this model is proposed which starts from level 0 having a root node 'Cloud_Services' as shown in Fig. 1. This classification is not only limited to manufacturing services but also include Computing and Logistics as a service therefore pedigree is a versatile tool and can be used for varieties of services. For the purpose of shortening the scope of effective searching in classification each node on level 1 is classified further to make level 2 and onto level 4. Pedigree is predefined for using as an instance from level 0 to level 2 by considering the common classification accordingly to the product cycle.

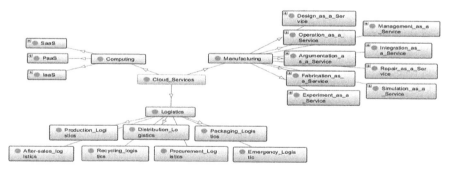

Fig. 1. Pedigree model

This model is not a visible entity but rather a concept in cloud environment using services properties to relate and organize services accordingly. For each service, pedigree classifies it according to four criteria which are common between service descriptions, such criterion is called as level criteria of pedigree. These are defined as follow:

Level 0: Root node
Level 1: Classification according to industry type criteria
Level 2: Classification according to department type criteria
Level 3: Classification according to service type criteria
Level 4: Classification according to service name criteria

Four level classification criteria limits the height of pedigree but allows to expand in width as new and hetrogenous services are added.

3.1 Service Model in Pedigree

Cloud manufacturing has complex, heterogeneous and dynamic environment hence making it difficult to share information and matching services without any ambiguity. Therefore, a service model is required considering the characteristics of a cloud. For the construction of pedigree, a manufacturing service model which was presented in [11] shown in Fig. 2 is reviewed by various market environments and it can support effective cloud service searching, matching and composition for proposed model.

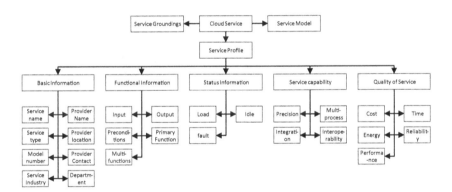

Fig. 2. Cloud service ontology model [11]

Cloud Service consist of three parts: (1) Service Groundings (2) Service Model and (3) Service Profile. Service protocols for communications are defined in **Service groundings** whereas **Service Model** is to give detailed description of service process and **Service Profile** contains all the information of service with respect to provider and user in terms of Name, Quality, capabilities, physical location and etc. The service profile data will store in form of vectors

$$Ser\_Basinfo = R_1 = [Name,\ Type,\ Loc,\ PrvdrN,\ \ldots] \tag{1}$$

$$Ser\_Funcinfo = R_2 = [I,\ O,\ P,\ \ldots] \tag{2}$$

$$Ser\_Statinfo = R_3 = [L, \ Idl, \ Flt, \ \ldots] \tag{3}$$

$$Ser\_Capability = R_4 = [Process, \ Precision, \ \ldots] \tag{4}$$

$$Ser\_QoS = R_5 = [C, \ T, \ E, \ P] \tag{5}$$

3.2   Construction Mechanism

Construction Mechanism is divided into two parts: construction (Offline Period) and utilization (Online Period). As for construction, pedigree classify the services in a smart manner without overlapping and misplacement of services in a model. An automatic mechanism is proposed for the construction of pedigree which uses the semantic cosine distance to find the best path to the suitable location comparing the sibling nodes shown in Fig. 3. Construction of pedigree is explained in following steps:

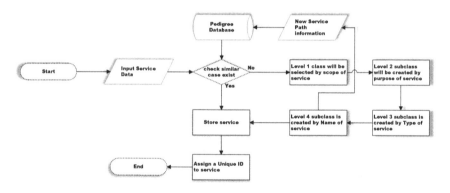

Fig. 3. Pedigree construction flowchart

a. Input service information.
b. Check service similarity with previously stored services.
c. If similar case exists, Add service to predefined path.
d. For a new kind of service, each level is defined by a common factor of services.
e. New subclasses are construct according to level criteria.
f. Services are the leaf nodes of the pedigree.
g. Unique IDs are assigned to services.

Service pool nodes are those nodes which contain the pool of virtual resources. Machine learning is used to understand data from the database and make decisions accordingly to construct the pedigree. When a service is added in the pedigree, it is assigned a unique 'ID' to not only for information transfer but also for keeping track and easy control for providers. When an ID is assigned to a service, it cannot be edited. Pedigree database store the information of relations of current services registered in pedigree and with help of machine learning tools by having some samples of relations pedigree will make decisions more accurate to differentiate service pools from others.

For Utilization, pedigree performs its function of automatically managing services in classes according to defined method and it also meets the requirements of user demands and search optimal services along collecting more information for service classes. The basic purpose of utilization is to have feedback of the model to debug errors and modify pedigree service relations for construction part to make pedigree effective.

3.3   Searching and Matching Mechanism

After the construction of pedigree, next challenge is how to use it. So, this mechanism consists of two parts: searching and matching. This method converts the task and service description into keywords by using POS tagging algorithm to traverse the optimal path for search of the related services using semantic cosine similarity. Cosine distance can be defined as:

$$cosine\ distance = cos\emptyset = \frac{[A][B]}{|A||B|} \tag{6}$$

$$cosine\ similarity = S_c = 1 - cos\emptyset \tag{7}$$

Recalling Eqs. (1) to (5):

$$A = [R_1|R_2|R_3|R_4|R_5];\ B = [T_1|T_2|T_3|T_4|T_5]$$

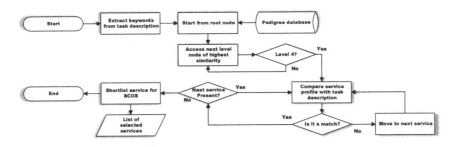

Fig. 4. Flowchart for searching and matching mechanism

Where, A and B are the matrices containing the information of service and task description respectively. So, range of cosine similarity is from 0 to 1 which means that if S_c between two concepts or vectors is 0 indicates dissimilarity. Whereas, 1 will represent both vectors are identical. Service profile contains functional and capability information of services which compared with task description to shortlist services for SCOS as shown in Fig. 4.

After shortlisting services, next challenge is to match service to the task specific requirements from the pool of similar services. So, a service evaluation criterion introduced consisting of QoS parameters described by the service providers are shown in Table 1.

Table 1. QoS evaluation factors

Name	Symbol
Cost	C
Time	T
Reliability	γ
Energy	ε
Performance	ρ

QoS factors selected for optimal selection:

For Service Composition and Optimal Selection (SCOS), QoS functions need to be calculated for the service compositions for optimal selection and to provide best services to the user demand.

4   Application

Proper description of a service is first needed to register the service in a pedigree. The cloud manufacturing service model have a service profile which consists of all the relative information of a service. If a company wants to register a service or services, they have to provide service profile. Along with basic information, functional and other information is also provided to register the service to cloud as shown in Table 2. The required information is then extracted using POS tagging algorithm which also extracts the sense of words for better relationship between words.

Table 2. Service description of a provider

Property name	Property value	Property name	Property value	Property name	Property value
Service ID	MM0268	Contact	+55 280 9500	Primary Func.	Turning
Name	CNC Lathe	Spindle Torque	95.5/70 (N.m)	Turning Dia.	165 mm
Type	Equipment	Spindle RPM	6,000	Turning Length	300 mm
Model	KIT4500	Chuck Size	6″	Available Time	3 months
Scope	Manufacturing	Spindle Output	15/11 kw	Performance	8.0
Department	Fabrication	Tool Size (mm)	20/32	Cost	80 yuan per day

Service ID is a unique number assigned to every service at the end of cloud submission to keep track of services and unambiguous information transfer between cloud and provider. Once a service ID is assigned it cannot be changed unless the service is removed from cloud. Service ID also identifies the location of the node in pedigree. Data from Table 2 converted into vectors respectively and combining these vectors will make service matrix as described in Sect. 3.2. Service name, type, model and primary function will act as keywords to compare with nodes on each level according to the methodology defined in Sect. 3.1. Using C++ platform following are the examples:

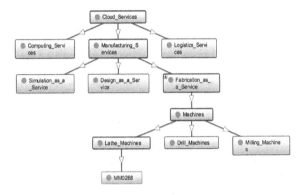

Fig. 5. Addition of a service in Pedigree

4.1 Construction Example

For registering of a service in a cloud there are two cases; either the service being registered has not any similar service in pedigree or it has. Pedigree will construct according to level criteria for a new kind of service as shown in Fig. 5. According to level criteria service addition will be in following steps:

Level 0 Root node.
Level 1 service adds in manufacturing node per industry type criteria.
Level 2 service classifies to fabrication per department type criteria.
Level 3 classifies to machines by evaluating the type of service.
At last, level 4 service registered to lathe class with unique ID.

First level classification is according to evaluation of the type of industry offering service. For instance, three types are shown in Fig. 6: Manufacturing, Computing and Logistics. The differentiation between these types depends upon the infrastructure and process. As second level criteria is from which department the service is being offered and this service provider mentioned the fabrication. Similarly, level 3 and level 4 are constructed for a new type of service. Pedigree samples services for machine learning to learn relationships between similar services for fast and effective classification.

4.2 Searching and Matching Example

Task uploaded or requested to cloud, decomposes into various subtasks to match the services accordingly. While for pedigree concept to take place, task basic information

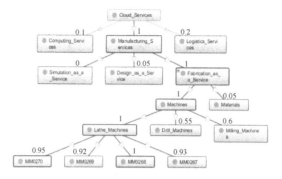

Fig. 6. Searching and matching of services

and relationships between subtasks are required to match service effectively. By assuming the task information as mentioned in Table 2, searching method is defined in following steps:

a. Data extracted from task descriptions using POS Tagging algorithm.
b. Access pedigree data from level 0.
c. Compare data from step 1 with each node of next level to check relations by calculating semantic cosine similarity.
d. Access the node with highest similarity.
e. Repeat step 3 and 4 until level 4. Hence, service pool required according to task description is searched.
f. In the end shortlist or match services according to the specific functional and non-functional requirement from service profile.

For given information and using search mechanism, two services have been searched and matched to the task description. As shown in Fig. 6, search is done from level to level by shortening the search space on proceeding level until the services are matched.

A sample database constructed for the purpose of searching service from pedigree in which data was supposed and assigned to nodes shown in Fig. 6. Then by using cosine similarity, started search for services according to task description as the search completed successfully but out of four services, only two were matched although having high value of similarity because of the functional requirements of task two services didn't meet the requirement to fulfill the task.

Search and match of service to task is important application of pedigree as it reduces the searching space by narrowing down the services based on relationships and functional information used for matching services required to complete the task.

5   Conclusion

Great amount of services data in cloud environment have been a problem for effective and fast SCOS implementation. Therefore, considering different aspect, many researchers have proposed different methods to make efforts to resolve these problems. The contribution of this study is to briefly review of existing methods of arrangement of resources for an automatic pedigree construction along with discussion of service model to extract services data and utilizing that data to classify services to construct pedigree by analyzing relationship between services and using semantic similarity for searching and matching services to tasks.

This model can further cope with new services or data and support automatic service discovery by centralizing services after finding relationships and common information from various service profiles in cloud and then narrowing down the search spaces by tracking services in a certain path using similarity calculation instead of exploring all the services for fast and effective SCOS.

For future work, SCOS functions will be revised and other optimal selection methods will be studied to further improve pedigree effectiveness and efficiency compared to other methods.

Acknowledgement. The research work was granted by the National Natural Science Foundation, China. (No. 71501020).

References

1. Li, B., Hu, B., et al.: Cloud manufacturing: a new service-oriented networked manufacturing model. Comput. Integr. Manuf. Syst. **16**(1), 1–7 (2010)
2. Tao, F., Zhang, L., et al.: Cloud manufacturing: a computing and service-oriented manufacturing model. Proc. Inst. Mech. Eng. Part B J. Eng. Manuf. **225**, 1969–1976 (2011)
3. Li, B., Zhang, L., Ren, L., et al.: Typical characteristics, technologies and applications of cloud manufacturing. Comput.-Integr. Manuf. Syst. CIMS **18**(7), 1345–1356 (2012)
4. Wu, D., Greer, M.J., et al.: Cloud manufacturing: strategic vision and state-of-the-art. J. Manuf. Syst. G Model JMSY-212 **32**(4), 564–579 (2013)
5. Wei, X., Liu, H., et al.: A cloud manufacturing resource allocation model based on ant colony optimization algorithm. Int. J. Grid Distrib. Comput. **8**(1), 55–66 (2015)
6. Tao, F., Zhao, D., Hu, Y., et al.: Correlation-aware resource service allocation and optimal-selection in manufacturing grid. Eur. J. Oper. Res. **201**(1), 129–143 (2010)
7. Zhang, L., Luo, Y., et al.: Cloud manufacturing: a new manufacturing paradigm. Enterp. Inf. Syst. **8**(2), 1–21(2012)
8. Ren, L., Zhang, L., Tao, F., et al.: Cloud manufacturing: from concept to practice. Enterp. Inf. Syst. (2013). https://doi.org/10.1080/17517575.2013.839055
9. Laili, Y., Tao, F., et al.: A Ranking Chaos Algorithm for dual scheduling of cloud service and computing resource in private cloud. Comput. Ind. **64**, 448–463 (2013)
10. Tao, F., LaiLi, Y., Xu, L., et al.: FC-PACO-RM: a parallel method for service allocation optimal-selection in cloud manufacturing system. IEEE Trans. Industr. Inf. **9**(4), 2023–2033 (2013)

11. Minghai, Y., et al.: Manufacturing resource modeling for cloud manufacturing. Int. J. Intell. Syst. **32**, 414–436 (2017)
12. Tao, F., Hu, Y.F., et al.: Application and modeling of resource service trust-QoS evaluation in manufacturing grid system. Int. J. Prod. Res. **47**(6), 1521–1550 (2009)
13. Laili, Y.J., Tao, F., et al.: A study of optimal allocation of computing resources in cloud manufacturing systems. Int. J. Adv. Manuf. Technol. **63**(5–8), 671–690 (2012)
14. Huang, B.Q., Li, C.H., Tao, F.: A chaos control optimal algorithm for QoS-based service composition selection in cloud manufacturing system. Enterp. Inf. Syst. **8**(4), 445–463 (2014)
15. Cheng, Y., Tao, F., Liu, Y.L., et al.: Energy-aware resource service scheduling based on utility evaluation in cloud manufacturing system. Proc. Inst. Mech. Eng. Part B J. Eng. Manuf. **227**(12), 1901–1915 (2013)
16. Zheng, H., Feng, Y., Tan, J.: A hybrid energy-aware resource allocation approach in cloud manufacturing environment. IEEE Access Spec. Section Emerg. Cloud-Based Wirel. Commun. Netw. **5**, 12648–12656 (2017)
17. Zhang, W., et al.: Correlation-aware manufacturing service composition model using an extended flower pollination algorithm. Int. J. Prod. Res. (2017). https://doi.org/10.1080/00207543.2017.1402137

Industrial Product Design

Quality Characteristic Decoupling Method Based on Meta-Action Unit for CNC Machine Tool

Yan Ran[(✉)], Genbao Zhang[(✉)], Zongyi Mu, Hongwei Wang, and Yulong Li

College of Mechanical Engineering and State Key Lab Mech Transmiss, Chongqing University, Chongqing 400044, China
ranyan@cqu.edu.cn, gen.bao.zhang@263.net

Abstract. Since CNC machine tool is a typical complicated electromechanical product with thousands of parts, it is very hard to design and control the whole machine's quality characteristics because of the intricate coupling relationships among them. In this paper, a method of quality characteristic decoupling based on meta-action unit for CNC machine tool was proposed. Besides dozens of meta-action units' own quality, it only needs to control the coupling relationships among different meta-action units' quality characteristics to guarantee the whole machine's quality. Firstly, the definition of "meta-action unit" and "Function—Motion—Action (FMA)" were introduced. Secondly, the coupling constraint models based on meta-action unit were established. Thirdly, the decoupling method using design structure matrix and domain mapping matrix was proposed, while the decoupling models were built and the decoupling planning flow chart was established. Finally, APC rotary motion of CNC machine tool was taken as an example to illustrate the effectiveness.

Keywords: Meta-action unit · Decoupling method · Quality characteristic
CNC machine tool · Coupling constraint model

1 Introduction

As an electromechanical product, CNC machine tool has very complicated structure and dynamic working process. It is very hard to design and control the whole machine's quality characteristics because of the intricate coupling relationships among them [1]. Many scholars home and abroad have been working hard on that. Danilovic and Browning [2] proposed design structure matrices and domain mapping matrices to manage complex product development projects. Guo et al. [3] researched on the decoupling technology and robust design optimization of product's multi-quality characteristics. Zhang et al. [4] and Wei et al. [5] analyzed on the coupling factors of CNC machine tools and established the quality characteristic models. Yang and Duan [6] realized the quantitative modeling and analysis of the correlative relationships among quality characteristics. Fast-Berglund et al. [7] studied on the relationships between complexity, quality and cognitive automation, and quantified complexity by the measure Operator Choice Complexity (OCC). Ouyang et al. [8] combined the

© Springer Nature Singapore Pte Ltd. 2018
S. Wang et al. (Eds.): ICSEE 2018/IMIOT 2018, CCIS 923, pp. 63–72, 2018.
https://doi.org/10.1007/978-981-13-2396-6_6

quality characteristics analysis chart (QCAC), entropy method and technique for order of preference to measure quality characteristics and rank improvements. However, all of the researches before analyzed the coupling relationships from a macroscopic angle, which is very difficult and inaccurate for quality characteristic control.

The working purpose of electromechanical products is to accomplish a specific function [9, 10]. Different function with different physical process, also different mechanical structure and control mode, but there are still some commonness among them: In order to achieve the main function, different action units are needed to cooperate to complete different motions. In general, every action requires a single unit to achieve, and multiple relatively independent action units move synergistically to implement the main function in high quality and efficient. From the perspective of theoretical mechanics, the working process of electromechanical products is a complex synthetic movement, which is composed of several action units through motion [11]. CNC machine tool is also composed of multiple meta-action units (the minimum action units) to achieve one specific function, then the author proposed a new "Function—Motion—Action (FMA)" method, taking the automatic pallet changer (APC) of THM6380 for example (shown in Fig. 1), and analyzed the quality characteristic association of CNC machine tool based on meta-action unit (MU) to guarantee the whole CNC machine tool assembly quality [12].

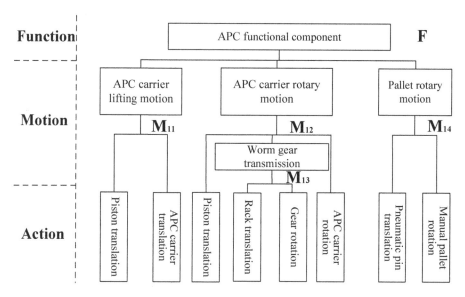

Fig. 1. "FMA" decomposition of APC functional component

In the complex large system of electromechanical product, any one quality characteristic has very close relation with other quality characteristics, and a quality fluctuation usually causes multiple quality characteristics changing, which is called coupling. For example, one unit's precision can affect others', even the whole machine's precision, accuracy life, performance stability and reliability [13].

And decoupling is to minimize the coupling effects among quality characteristics, then control the whole machine's quality characteristics effectively. In this paper, a method of quality characteristic decoupling based on meta-action unit for CNC machine tool was proposed, and the coupling relationships among the whole machine's quality characteristics were simplified as among meta-action units'. The definition of "meta-action unit" and "Function—Motion—Action (FMA)" were introduced firstly. And the coupling constraint models based on meta-action unit were established. Then the decoupling method using design structure matrix and domain mapping matrix was proposed, while the decoupling models were built and the decoupling planning flow chart was established. Finally, APC rotary motion of CNC machine tool was taken as an example.

2 Coupling Constraint Models Based on MU

There are same-layer, different-layer, one-to-one, one-to-many, even many-to-one coupling relationships among quality characteristics of different unit [14]. The whole machine's quality characteristic coupling includes each unit's same-layer coupling and different-layer coupling, shown in Fig. 2. The same-layer coupling mainly embodied in the quality characteristic transfer influence relations among different units in the same level, such as geometric constraints, assembly constraints, and physical (movement) constraints. The different-layer coupling mainly embodied in the quality characteristic decomposing and gathering relations among upper units and lower units, such as function constraints and auxiliary constraints.

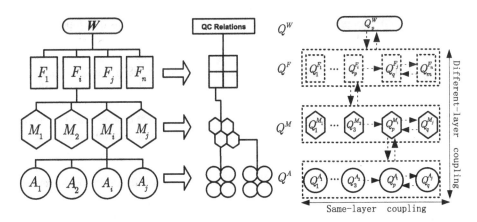

Fig. 2. The quality characteristic coupling relationship diagram of FMA tree

To the quality characteristics of one unit, the coupling relations can be decomposed to the coupling relation between each two quality characteristics of same-layer units and of different-layer units. Quality characteristics of MU layer are taken as an example, of which the upper layer is motion unit, shown in Fig. 3. Then the complex

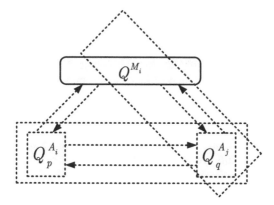

Fig. 3. The simplified model of quality characteristic coupling relationships for MU layer

coupling constraint relations among quality characteristics of whole machine can be simplified to the relation between each two units.

3 Quality Characteristic Decoupling Method Based on MU

3.1 Decoupling Models Using DSM and DMM

Design Structure Matrix (DSM) was first proposed by Steward in 1967, and in 1981 it was introduced to the information flow analysis in product design. It can reduce feedback, ease work, speed up progress and improve quality in the analysis and optimization of design process. Domain Mapping Matrix (DMM) was developed based on DSM in the 1990s. It is widely used in complex systems, such as aircraft, automobiles, etc. DSM is mainly used to analyze information in one domain, while DMM focuses on information among different domains. In this paper, DSM is used to analyze the same-layer coupling, while DMM is proposed to deal with different-layer coupling, shown in Fig. 4. Unlike DSM's square matrix, DMM's matrix is rectangular, which represents the coupling relationships among elements in different domains, and its rows and columns represent different elements belonging to different domains.

To two quality characteristics of same-layer units, if the coupling relationship between them can be considered as their internal constraint (Same-layer matching property), then the coupling relation between upper unit and them can be considered as their external constraint (Different-layer matching property). And to one quality characteristic, it involves in two constraints, one is same-layer matching constraint from other quality characteristics of same-layer unit, which can be analyzed by DSM; the other is different-layer matching constraint from quality characteristics of upper unit, which can settled by DMM. Quality characteristics of MU are taken as an example, shown in Fig. 5.

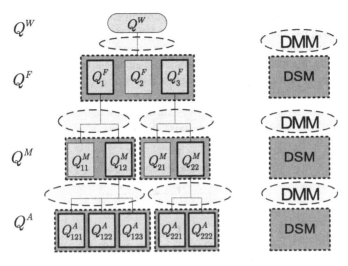

Fig. 4. DSMs and DMMs specifically for FMA

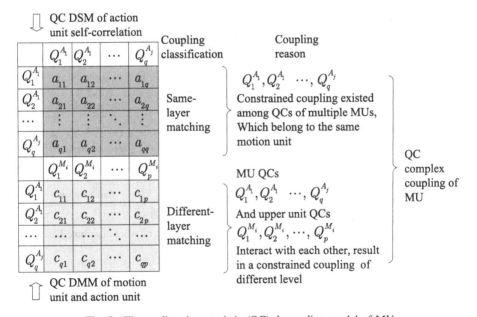

Fig. 5. The quality characteristic (QC) decoupling model of MU

3.2   Decoupling Planning Flow Chart Based on MU

In the quality characteristic decoupling planning of whole machine based on MU, one unit quality characteristic is assumed as one discipline [15]. Firstly, the coupling strengths of different MU quality characteristics should be calculated and brought into DSM, after being fuzzily processed, then the fuzzy DSM based on coupling strength can be obtained. Secondly, the decoupling control method of MDO is adopted to cut apart, aggregate, plan and reconstruct the fuzzy DSM, to reduce the coupling strengths among each unit quality characteristic and to optimize the quality characteristic control sequence. Finally, the result met the requirements can be output. The specific flow chart is shown in Fig. 6, also taking quality characteristics of MU for example.

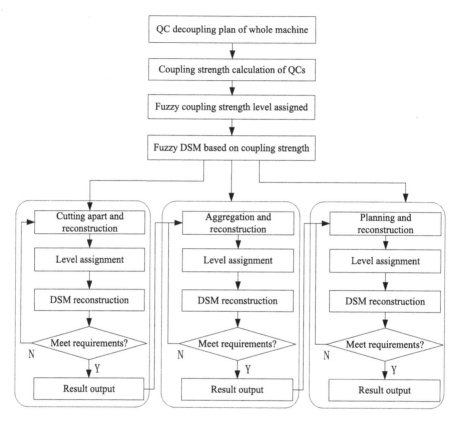

Fig. 6. The quality characteristic decoupling planning flow chart of whole machine based on MU

4 Case Study

In this paper, three meta-action units of piston translation, rack translation and gear rotation in APC rotary motion are taken as an example, the rotation part structure sketch of APC is shown in Fig. 7, and "FMA" decomposition of APC functional component is shown in Fig. 1. Decoupling planning are carried out on their key quality characteristics: precision of piston translation MU ($Q_1^{A_1}$), accuracy life of piston translation MU ($Q_2^{A_1}$), performance stability of piston translation MU ($Q_3^{A_1}$), reliability of piston translation MU ($Q_4^{A_1}$), precision of rack translation MU ($Q_1^{A_2}$), accuracy life of rack translation MU ($Q_2^{A_2}$), performance stability of rack translation MU ($Q_3^{A_2}$), reliability of rack translation MU ($Q_4^{A_2}$), precision of gear rotation MU ($Q_1^{A_3}$), accuracy life of gear rotation MU ($Q_2^{A_3}$),performance stability of gear rotation MU ($Q_3^{A_3}$) and reliability of gear rotation MU ($Q_4^{A_3}$).

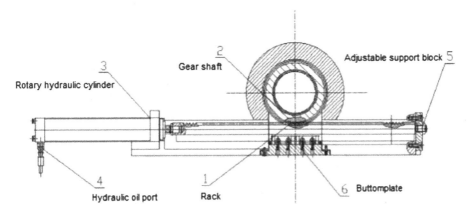

Fig. 7. The rotation part structure sketch of APC

Taking piston translation MU and gear rotation MU (lower meta-action unit layer) in APC rotary motion (upper motion unit layer) as an example, the comprehensive coupling strength between precision of piston translation MU ($Q_1^{A_1}$) and performance stability of gear rotation MU ($Q_3^{A_3}$) is analyzed. The structure of piston translation MU and gear rotation MU can be seen in Fig. 8.

The coupling constraint model of precision of piston translation MU ($Q_1^{A_1}$), performance stability of gear rotation MU ($Q_3^{A_3}$) and APC carrier rotary motion unit is shown in Fig. 9. The relationship between piston translation MU and gear rotation MU is same-layer coupling, both belonging to meta-action unit layer, while the relationship between APC rotary motion unit and gear rotation MU is different-layer coupling. The comprehensive coupling strength of $Q_3^{A_3}$ from $Q_1^{A_1}$ should be calculated by analysing the specific indexes.

Then the coupling strength DSM can be obtained according to the coupling strength calculation of quality characteristics among different meta-action units. According to the quality characteristic decoupling planning flow chart, the reconstructive DSM after programming can be obtained, and the best design and control sequence of quality characteristics based on meta-action can be found, shown in Table 1.

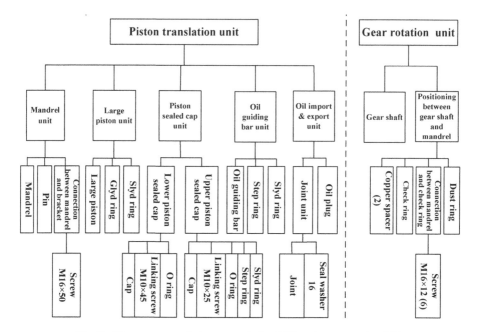

Fig. 8. The structure of piston translation MU and gear rotation MU

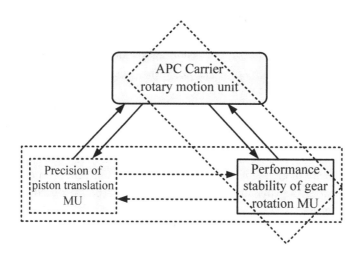

Fig. 9. The coupling constraint model

5 Conclusion

Because of coupling, quality characteristic analysis and control of CNC machine tool is very hard, and quality in the design and manufacturing process can not be guaranteed. Since one whole machine is composed of many MUs to achieve a specific function, and

Table 1. The reconstructive DSM after programming

DSM		1 $Q_2^{A_1}$	2 $Q_3^{A_1}$	3 $Q_2^{A_2}$	4 $Q_3^{A_2}$	5 $Q_4^{A_1}$	6 $Q_1^{A_1}$	7 $Q_1^{A_2}$	8 $Q_3^{A_3}$	9 $Q_1^{A_3}$	10 $Q_4^{A_2}$	11 $Q_4^{A_3}$	12 $Q_2^{A_3}$
1	$Q_2^{A_1}$	1	0	0	×	0	0	0	0	0	0	0	0
2	$Q_3^{A_1}$	0	1	0	×	0	0	0	×	0	0	0	0
3	$Q_2^{A_2}$	0	×	1	0	0	0	0	×	0	0	0	0
4	$Q_3^{A_2}$	0	×	0	1	0	×	0	×	0	0	×	0
5	$Q_4^{A_1}$	0	0	0	×	1	0	0	×	0	0	0	0
6	$Q_1^{A_1}$	0	0	0	×	0	1	×	0	×	0	0	0
7	$Q_1^{A_2}$	×	0	0	0	×	×	1	×	×	0	0	0
8	$Q_3^{A_3}$	0	×	0	×	0	×	×	1	0	0	0	0
9	$Q_1^{A_3}$	×	0	×	×	×	×	×	0	1	0	0	0
10	$Q_4^{A_2}$	0	0	0	0	0	×	0	×	0	1	×	0
11	$Q_4^{A_3}$	0	0	0	0	×	0	×	0	0	×	1	0
12	$Q_2^{A_3}$	0	0	0	0	0	0	×	0	0	×	0	1

there are various combinations among these MUs, besides each MU's quality, it needs to control each MU's same-layer coupling and different-layer coupling to guarantee the whole machine's quality.

In this paper, a new method of quality characteristic decoupling based on MU for CNC machine tool was proposed. Firstly, the definition of "meta-action unit" and "Function—Motion—Action (FMA)" were introduced. Secondly, the coupling constraint models based on MU were built, while MU's same-layer and different-layer coupling were studied. Then the decoupling method using design structure matrix and domain mapping matrix was proposed, while the decoupling models were built and the decoupling planning flow chart was established, which is helpful in the design and manufacturing process. Finally, APC rotary motion of CNC machine tool was taken as an example to illustrate the rightness and effectiveness of this method.

Acknowledgments. This work is supported by the <National Natural Science Foundation of China> under Grant <No. 51705048>; <National Major Scientific and Technological Special Project for 'High-grade CNC and Basic Manufacturing Equipment' of China> under Grant <No. 2016ZX04004-005>; and <Fundamental Research Funds for the Central Universities> under Grant <No. 106112017CDJXY110006> .

References

1. Fortunato, A., Ascari, A.: The virtual design of machining centers for HSM: towards new integrated tools. Mechatronics **23**(3), 264–278 (2013)
2. Danilovic, M., Browning, T.R.: Managing complex product development projects with design structure matrices and domain mapping matrices. Int. J. Proj. Manage. **25**, 300–314 (2007)
3. Guo, H., Ren, P., Zhang, G.: Decoupling of multi-quality characteristics and robust design optimization. Chinese Soc. Agr. Mach. **40**, 203–205 (2009)
4. Zhang, G., Zeng, H., Wang, G.: Decoupling model of quality characteristics for complicated electromechanical products. J. Chongqing Univ. **33**(5), 7–15 (2010). (Chinese)
5. Wei, L., Shen, G., Zhang, Y., et al.: Research on the availability model of NC machine tool. In: 2010 International Conference on Computer, Mechatronics, Control and Electronic Engineering, IEEE Computer Society, vol. 2, pp. 526–529 (2010)
6. Yang, F., Duan, G.: Developing a parameter linkage-based method for searching change propagation paths. Res. Eng. Des. **23**(4), 353–372 (2012)
7. Fast-Berglund, A., Fässberg, T., Hellman, F., et al.: Relations between complexity, quality and cognitive automation in mixed-model assembly. J. Manuf. Syst. **32**, 449–455 (2013)
8. Ouyang, L., Chen, K., Yang, C.: Using a QCAC-Entropy-TOPSIS approach to measure quality characteristics and rank improvement priorities for all substandard quality characteristics. Int. J. Prod. Res. **52**(10), 3110–3124 (2014)
9. Umeda, Y., Tomiyama, T.: Supporting conceptual design based on the function-behavior-state modeler. Artif. Intell. Eng. Des. Anal. Manuf. **10**(4), 275–288 (1996)
10. Hirtz, J., Stone, R., McAdams, D.: A functional basis for engineering design: reconciling and evolving previous efforts. Res. Eng. Des. **13**(2), 65–82 (2002)
11. Wu, J., Yan, S., Zuo, M.J.: Evaluating the reliability of multi-body mechanisms: a method considering the uncertainties of dynamic performance. Reliab. Eng. Syst. Saf. **149**, 96–106 (2016)
12. Ran, Y., Zhang, G., Zhang, L.: Quality characteristic association analysis of computer numerical control machine tool based on meta-action assembly unit. Adv. Mech. Eng. **8**(1), 1–10 (2016)
13. Tang, D., Zhang, G., Dai, S.: Design as integration of axiomatic design and design structure matrix. Rob. Comput. Integr. Manuf. **25**(3), 610–619 (2009)
14. Cao, L.: Coupling learning of complex interactions. Inf. Process. Manage. **51**(2), 167–186 (2015)
15. Yao, W., Chen, X., Luo, W., et al.: Review of uncertainty-based multidisciplinary design optimization methods for aerospace vehicles. Prog. Aerosp. Sci. **47**, 450–479 (2011)

A CAD Based Framework for Optimizing Performance While Ensuring Assembly Fit

Dheeraj Agarwal⬤, Trevor T. Robinson$^{(\boxtimes)}$⬤,
and Cecil G. Armstrong⬤

School of Mechanical and Aerospace Engineering,
The Ashby Building, Queen's University, Belfast BT9 5AH, UK
{d.agarwal, t.robinson, c.armstrong}@qub.ac.uk

Abstract. The optimization of an individual component usually happens in isolation of the components it will interface with or be surrounded by in an assembly. This means that when the optimized components are assembled together fit issues can occur. This paper presents a CAD-based optimization framework, which uses constraints imposed by the adjacent or surrounding components in the CAD model product assembly, to define the limits of the packaging space for the component being optimized. This is important in industrial workflows, where unwanted interference is costly to resolve. The gradient-based optimization framework presented uses the parameters defining the features in a feature-based CAD model as design variables. The two main benefits of this framework are: (1) the optimized geometry is available as a CAD model and can be easily used in the manufacturing stages, and (2) the resulting manufactured object should be able to be assembled with other components during the assembly process. The framework is demonstrated for the optimization of 2D and 3D parametric models created in CATIA V5.

Keywords: Optimization · Industrial product design · CAD systems

1 Introduction

With advances in the field of computers and their progressive use within the industrial design process, the need for costly physical design prototypes has been extensively reduced and replaced with that for digital models which are constructed and analyzed using computers. Nowadays product design typically starts with the construction of a computer-aided design (CAD) geometry of an initial concept, and the goal is to deliver an optimized and validated geometry as a CAD model. If this is achieved the optimized model can then be directly used for downstream applications including manufacturing and process planning.

In recent years, optimization has become an essential part of an industrial design process. However, optimization is usually performed on a component by component basis. Modern CAD systems like CATIA V5, SIEMENS NX, Solidworks etc. uses feature-based modelling strategies to create a parametric CAD model. Also, feature based CAD systems use many parameters when defining the shape. Even simple models can have tens or hundreds of parameters, while complex models can have

© Springer Nature Singapore Pte Ltd. 2018
S. Wang et al. (Eds.): ICSEE 2018/IMIOT 2018, CCIS 923, pp. 73–83, 2018.
https://doi.org/10.1007/978-981-13-2396-6_7

thousands. Therefore, in many processes, the shape of the component is extracted from the CAD systems to be optimized.

However, CAD systems provide significant advantages to companies in the way they capture and unify design information. One good example is how they enable designers to create relationships between parts or assemblies to enforce their design intent on how the products fits together, or in how they can be used to feed manufaturing simulation processes. This means that if the model has been extracted from the CAD system for optimization, it is necessary to bring it back into the CAD system to realise these bigger advantages. This process can be complex for some optimisation processes (e.g. mesh based approaches [1]), and to reassociate an externally optimized geometry with a set of CAD features and parameters is virtually impossible, and if required has to be created from scratch.

In general, mechanical design processes are not only driven by performance but are also subjected to constraints. Often constraints are performance based, e.g. Walther and Siva [2] presented an adjoint-based shape optimization for a multistage turbine design, with the objective to maximize the efficiency while constraining the mass flow rate and the total pressure ratio. Kontoleontos et al. [3] presented a constrained topology optimization approach for ducts with multiple outlets, where the flow constraints are inforced at each outlet defining the volume flow rates, flow direction and/or mean temperature of the outgoing flow. Sometimes constraints can be geometric, for example Shenren et al. [4] presented an approach employing a set of test points to impose the thickness and trailing edge radius constraint for the optimization of a nozzle guide vane. However, one important constraint from a manufacturing perspective is fit within the packaging space defined by the adjacent or surrounding components in an assembly.

Since different components are designed and optimized by different engineers, simultaneously to and in isolation from the components adjacent to them in an assembly, when the components are assembled together, issues such as fit often occur. The consequence is the need for engineering changes late in the product development cycle [5], or rework of the manufactured parts. Either is undesirable, therefore it is important for designers and manufacturers to devise methods to ascertain that the designed component can be assembled within the space available, before the actual component is released for manufacture. Current approaches to achieve this are to specify bounds on parameter ranges acceptable for individual parameters [6], but these bounds can become outdated quickly as all of the components in the assembly are refined.

In modern CAD systems it is possible do the assembly of components, creating a digital mock-up (DMU). Interference checking can be carried out on the DMU within the CAD environment. Some of the early works in the field of interference detection between two solids were found in [7]. Recent developments in this field included the works in [8], which enable interference detection directly using CAD models. Zubairi et al. [9] developed a sensitivity approach to eliminate any interference in a 3D CAD assembly, by identifying which parameters defining the CAD features need to be modified, and by how much, to eliminate interference. The approach is effective in this role (eliminating interferences), but the effect of the resulting shape change on the performance of the individual components was not considered, meaning that the process of eliminating interference could also reduce the performance of a products, or even make it unsuitable for its role.

In this paper, a framework is described which will optimize a component in terms of its performance, but will consider the constraints on packaging space imposed on the system due to adjacent or surrounding components in a CAD system. The developed approach is demonstrated on 2D and 3D parametric CAD models built in CATIA V5 and assembled with other components in CATIA V5 assembly workbench. ABAQUS CAE is used for solving structural mechanics problems, Helyx solver provided by ENGYS [10] is used for flow simulations, and Python 3.5 is used as the programming interface.

2 Background

2.1 Adjoint Methods

The key issue with optimizing models with many parameters is the high computational cost, however this can be mitigated with the use of gradient based optimization. The focus of this work is optimization using adjoint methods, enabling the computation of gradients at a cost which is essentially independent of the number of design parameters. The underlying theory and implementation of adjoint methods is well documented in literature [11, 12]. In Fig. 1 the contours shown are surface sensitivity, ϕ, which represents the change in overall performance which would be caused by a small normal movement of the boundary. For the model in Fig. 1, pulling the model boundary outward in red regions or inward in the blue regions will improve performance. The reverse movements will reduce performance.

Fig. 1. Adjoint sensitivities map: to minimize the objective function the surface should be pulled out at positive values and pushed in at negative values (Color figure online)

Typically, the adjoint is computed as a separate load case after the primal solution, and many adjoint solvers provide ϕ as an output. Once the adjoint sensitivity information is available, the change in performance dJ due to changes in the values of the CAD parameters dP, can be predicted as

$$dJ = \phi \frac{dX_s}{dP}. \tag{1}$$

dX_s is the change in the position of the mesh nodes caused by a change in the parameter values dP.

2.2 Design Velocity

Design velocity, V_n, is the normal component of the movement of the boundary of a model caused by a parametric perturbation. In this work design velocity is computed for the CAD model, and interpolation used to compute the change in position of the surface notes sitting on the boundary. Therefore

$$V_n = \frac{dX_s}{dP} \cdot \hat{n}, \tag{2}$$

where $\hat{n}$ is the outward unit normal of a point on the surface of the model.

Figure 2(a) shows CAD model of a cylinder in solid yellow, where the location of the bottom of the defining sketch is defined to be at the origin. The transparent shape superimposed is the model after the radius defining the cylinder is changed from 25 mm to 26 mm. In Fig. 2(b), the arrows represent the design velocities as the boundary changes from the original to the perturbed model. The convention adopted throughout this work is that a positive design velocity represents an outward movement of the boundary, and negative is inward. The approach used in this work for calculating design velocity is developed by [13], and is applicable to any feature-based CAD modelling package.

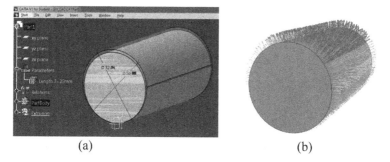

(a)	(b)

Fig. 2. Parametric CAD model, (b) vector representation of design velocity (Color figure online)

2.3 Gradient Computation

For the optimizer to establish a new search direction it is necessary for the gradient to be evaluated with respect to each design variable. In this case, it means evaluating the change in objective function, dJ, and the constraints due to a perturbation of a CAD parameter, dP. This means that for each parameter, i, a sensitivity value S can be computed as

$$S_i = \frac{dJ}{dP_i} = \int \phi V_{ni} dA. \tag{3}$$

where A is the surface area of the model.

3 Interference Detection

Interference occurs when components in an assembly violate each other by attempting to occupy the same physical space. Most CAD systems have interference detection tools, although the name of the function, and the information returned differs from system to system. The interference detection tool in CATIA V5 provides capabilities to obtain the penetration depth between the interfering components, which is described as the minimum distance required to translate a product to avoid interference whereas Solidworks returns the interference volume. In addition, the clearance distance between two components can also be obtained.

Figure 3 displays the part-to-part interference detection interface in CATIA V5 which shows if the selected parts are interfering or are in contact or have a clearance between them. In this work a negative value of interference represents the clearance between components. For this work the main requirements is to automatically compute the amount of interference between the CAD model being optimized and other components in the CAD model assembly. This is obtained using the CAD system API, which is configured to compute the interferences between the component being optimized and the other components in the assembly.

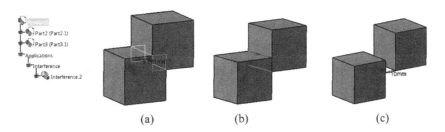

Fig. 3. Interference between two boxes in CATIA (a) Interference, (b) Contact, and (c) Clearance

At each optimization step, the developed CAD system API records the interference values which are used as constraints on the optimization. The other requirement is the computation of gradients of each interference value with respect to the parameters used to define the CAD model. So, to compute the gradients of constraints, each parameter of the CAD model is perturbed by a small amount, and the interference tool is used to obtain the interference values between the component being optimized and the other components. The respective gradients of the constraints are then obtained using a finite difference method.

4 Optimization Framework

In this work a gradient based optimization framework has been developed with the CAD system at its center. The adjoint based optimization process is used to guide the design towards a local optimum over multiple optimization steps.

A general optimization can be defined as:

$$
\begin{aligned}
\textit{Minimize} : &\quad \textit{objective function}, \\
\textit{Subject to} : &\quad \textit{interference} < 0 \\
\textit{Design variables} : &\quad \textit{vector of CAD parameters}
\end{aligned}
$$

In this work, the CAD models are created in CATIA V5 and optimized using Sequential Least Square Programming (SLSQP) method implemented in Scipy. The optimization process (Fig. 4) is implemented using Python 3.5.

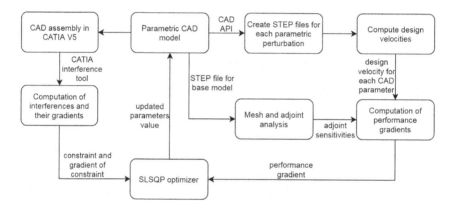

Fig. 4. CAD-based optimization using constraints from assembly components

5 Results

In this work, the use of assembly constraints during optimization is demonstrated for two test cases. One is for a simple cantilever beam, while the other is for the optimization of an automotive ventilation duct.

5.1 Cantilever Beam Optimization

The first test case is a cantilever beam loaded at one end. The optimization is a compliance minimization problem, therefore the objective function for this test case is to minimize the strain energy. This type of problem is self-adjoint, meaning that a special adjoint solver is not required to compute the surface sensitivities. Here the contours of strain energy density on the surface of the model indicate the change in strain energy in the component that can be achieved by moving the boundary.

The beam's geometrical configuration, the loading applied, and boundary conditions are shown in Fig. 5(a). The top edge of the beam is defined by a Bézier curve with four control points, while the bottom, left and right edges are defined using straight lines. The beam is modelled in CATIA V5. In the initial geometrical configuration, the strain energy density (adjoint sensitivity) is higher at the left-hand corners of the beam as shown in Fig. 5(b). This means that when minimizing strain energy, the geometry is expected to move outward in that region. A constant volume constraint was also imposed for the test case to ensure the model did not grow indefinitely (as an objective of minimizing compliance would encourage).

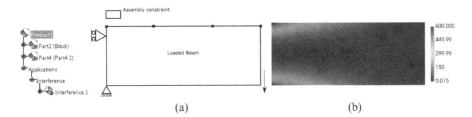

(a)   (b)

Fig. 5. (a) Cantilever beam with boundary conditions, (b) strain energy density plot

The optimization of this component was carried out twice. For the first optimization there was no constraint imposed on the packaging space for the component. For the second optimization a rectangular box was added representing an adjacent component, restricting the amount of outward movement possible by the top edge, Fig. 5(a).

The optimization results are shown in Figs. 6 and 7. The optimization without the constraint on packaging space Fig. 6(a) has resulted in the expected thickening of the left-hand side of the beam, and a subsequent narrowing of the right-hand side to maintain the overall volume of the model. It is obvious that this has caused the boundary to move outwards in the regions of highest strain energy density (remembering that the bottom edge is constrained to be a straight line). In the other optimization, Fig. 6(b), it is apparent that the outward movement of the model is restricted due to the presence of the block component. As a result, the optimizer finds a different solution and as shown in Fig. 7, this results in comparatively lower reduction in the strain energy of the beam. It should be noted that the optimized model in Fig. 6(a) would have interfered with the block component by approximately 8 mm.

5.2 S-Bend Optimization

An automotive ventilation duct is shown in Fig. 8(a). Components such as this are highly constrained in terms of the shape they can adopt due to the number of different vehicle sub-systems they are assembled adjacent to. In this test case a subsection of the duct is optimized. The parametric CAD model of the so-called S-Bend section is created in CATIA V5, with representative assembly components also created in the CATIA V5 assembly workbench as shown in Fig. 8(b). Here, the two cylindrical components are used to represent different components in the assembly that constrain shape optimization of the S-Bend boundary.

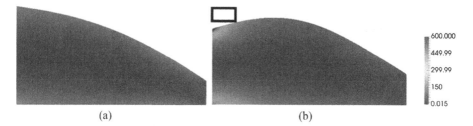

Fig. 6. Optimized cantilever beam with (a) constant volume constraint, (b) assembly constraints

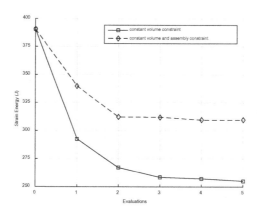

Fig. 7. Optimization history for cantilever beam

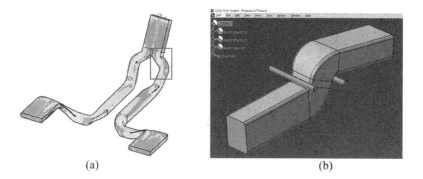

Fig. 8. (a) Automotive airduct [14], (b) S-Bend assembly with other components

The S-Bend was modelled using eight 2D sketches at different positions and orientations along the length of the duct, with multi-section solid features passing through these sketch profiles. The duct is composed of three individual sections i.e. inlet, S-Bend and outlet as shown in Fig. 9(a). As the inlet and outlet ducts will join with other components their shape is fixed, so they are not considered for optimization. Here the

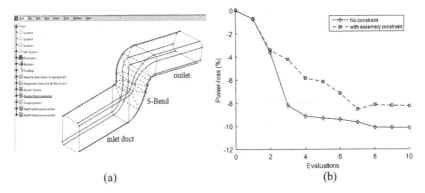

Fig. 9. (a) CAD model of S-Bend duct, (b) Optimization for S-Bend with assembly constraint

optimization variables are the parameters defining the four sketches (shown in broken lines in Fig. 9) describing the interior profile of the S-Bend (48 parameters).

As with the cantilever beam, this optimization was carried out with and without the constraints imposed by adjacent components. Where these constraints were considered, the location of assembly components (shown in Fig. 8(b)) were selected such that they would restrict the shape change in the regions suggested by adjoint sensitivity contours. They are created such that in its initial state the two cylinders are adjacent to the S-Bend with clearance distances of 1.03 mm and 0.53 mm. After optimization a reduction in power-loss of 8.35% was achieved for the S-Bend with the assembly constraints in place, compared to 10.14% achieved when optimized without any constraints imposed by adjacent components. However, the unconstrained optimization result would have interfered with these components by 2.4 mm and 0.38 mm respectively, should assembly have been attempted.

The optimization history for minimizing the objective function is shown in Fig. 9(b). It should be noted that in the optimization subject to the assembly constraint, at iteration-7 of the optimization, the geometry is in interference with one of the parts in the product assembly. To remove the interference the optimizer moves the geometry such that an increase in objective function is observed.

6   Discussion

In this paper, an efficient approach to shape optimization with assembly constraints was demonstrated. It ensures fit between the optimized and adjacent components. The optimization framework was configured to exploit the capabilities of CAD DMU to incorporate assembly constraints imposed by other components in the assembly workbench. However, the framework can also be used for models created in other CAD systems to define these constraints.

The developed framework was first applied to the optimization of a simple beam model (analyzed in ABAQUS) constrained by a 2D block in the assembly. The objective function used was minimization of strain energy of the system which was a self-adjoint problem and thus required only one analysis to provide the surface sensitivities. It is interesting to note that for the unconstrained optimization results in Fig. 6(a), the strain energy density in the entire model is the same color. This indicates that for this model there is no further performance improvement possible (without removing the constraint of constant volume). The optimization process was completed in approximately 11 min.

The objective of the S-Bend duct optimization was to minimize the power-loss in the duct in the presence of two representative cylindrical components restricting the movement of the duct. These constraints are representative of the actual constraints imposed by the steering column and other mechanical equipment. The developed optimization framework successfully optimized the component without introducing interference during the optimization. The optimization process was completed in approximately 4.5 h. It was interesting to note that for both examples, optimizing the models without considering adjacent components, resulted in optimized shapes which would have caused fit issues when assembly would have been attempted.

7   Conclusion

- An efficient shape optimization framework which includes interference information to ensure fit between the optimised components has been demonstrated.
- The constrained optimization employing the prior information from assembly components was successfully demonstrated for minimizing the objective function without violating the space available for storing other components in the assembly.

Acknowledgments. This work has been conducted within the IODA project (http://ioda.sems. qmul.ac.uk), funded by the European Union HORIZON 2020 Framework Programme for Research and Innovation under Grant Agreement No. 642959.

References

1. Helgason, E., Krajnovic, S.: Aerodynamic shape optimization of a pipe using the adjoint method. In: ASME International Mechanical Engineering Congress & Exposition, 9–15 November 2012
2. Walther, B., Nadarajah, S.: Constrained adjoint-based aerodynamic shape optimization of a single-stage transonic compressor. J. Turbomach. **135**, 021017 (2013)
3. Kontoleontos, E., Papoutsis-Kiachagias, E., et al.: Adjoint-based constrained topology optimization for viscous flows, including heat transfer. Eng. Optim. **45**, 941–961 (2013)
4. Xu, S., Radford, D., et al.: CAD-based adjoint shape optimisation of a one-stage turbine with geometric constraints. ASME Turbo Expo GT2015-42237 (2015)
5. Chang, K., Silva, J., et al.: Concurrent design and manufacturing for mechanical systems. Concurrent Eng. **7**, 290–308 (1999)
6. Immonen, E.: 2D shape optimization under proximity constraints by CFD and response surface methodology. Appl. Math. Model. **41**, 508–529 (2017)
7. Ahuja, N., Chien, R.T., et al.: Interference detection and collision avoidance among three dimensional objects. In: AAAI-1980 Proceedings, pp. 44–48 (1980)

8. Pan, C., Smith, S.S., et al.: Determining interference between parts in CAD STEP files for automatic assembly planning. J. Comput. Inf. Sci. Eng. **5**, 56–62 (2005)
9. Zubairi, M.S., Robinson, T.T., et al.: A sensitivity approach for eliminating clashes from computer aided design model assemblies. J. Comput. Inf. Sci. Eng. **14**, 031002 (2014)
10. Karpouzas, G.K., Papoutsis-Kiachagias, E.M., et al.: Adjoint optimization for vehicle external aerodynamics. Int. J. Autom. Eng. **7**, 1–7 (2016)
11. Mader, C.A., Martins, J.R.A., et al.: Adjoint: an approach for the rapid development of discrete adjoint solvers. AIAA J. **46**, 863–873 (2008)
12. Roth, R., Ulbrich, S.: A discrete adjoint approach for the optimization of unsteady turbulent flows. Flow Turbul. Combust. **90**, 763–783 (2013)
13. Agarwal, D., Robinson, T.T., et al.: Parametric design velocity computation for CAD-based design optimization using adjoint methods. Eng. Comput. **34**, 225–239 (2018)
14. Othmer, C.: Adjoint methods for car aerodynamics. J. Math. Ind. **4**, 1–23 (2014)

Design and Optimization Aspects of a Novel Reaction Sphere Actuator

Jie Zhang[1,2(✉)], Li-Ming Yuan[1,2], Si-Lu Chen[1], Chi Zhang[1(✉)], Chin-yin Chen[1], and Jie Zhou[1]

[1] Ningbo Institute of Materials Technology and Engineering, Chinese Academy of Sciences, Ningbo 315201, China
{zhangjie,yuanliming,chensilu,zhangchi,chenchinyin, zhoujie}@nimte.ac.cn
[2] University of Chinese Academy of Sciences, Beijing 100049, China

Abstract. This paper presents the design and optimization aspect of a reaction sphere. Firstly, a novel reaction sphere actuator is proposed, which is composed of 12 curved stators, 6 electromagnets and a spherical rotor. Secondly, the relation between output torque and design parameters are discussed through finite element method (FEM) modeling. Thirdly, due to the difficulty of building a purely analytical model that takes all effects into account as design parameters, a optimization method based on Support Vector Machine (SVM) is studied, where the torque model is built through SVM and the optimized structure parameters are calculated by using genetic algorithm based on the developed SVM torque model. Finally, FEM simulation results validate the effectiveness of the proposed optimization method, showing that the proposed reaction sphere with optimized structure could increase the torque density by 68% as compared to the original prototype.

Keywords: Design optimization · Reaction sphere · Support vector machines Finite element method

1 Introduction

Conventionally, satellite attitude control are realized by 3 or more momentum wheels, which not only increases the mass and volume of the spacecrafts, but also adds much complexity to the attitude control algorithms for eliminating the coupling effects between the torques of different momentum wheels. Reaction sphere is a new type of momentum exchange device, a single reaction sphere that is capable of rotating in any directions can achieve 3-axis attitude control of the spacecrafts, which brings attitude control system the benefits of robustness and redundancy improvement and volume and mass reduction. Due to the compact design, reaction spheres are very suitable in small satellites attitude control.

So far, four kinds of spherical motor have been designed to drive reaction spheres: permanent magnet (PM) spherical motor, spherical induction motor, spherical hysteresis motor and spherical ultrasonic motor. Rossini [1], Emory Stagmer [2], Yan [3] have accomplish a series of research of permanent magnet (PM) spherical motors,

© Springer Nature Singapore Pte Ltd. 2018
S. Wang et al. (Eds.): ICSEE 2018/IMIOT 2018, CCIS 923, pp. 84–93, 2018.
https://doi.org/10.1007/978-981-13-2396-6_8

among whom Rossini [4] have carried out the force and torque analytical models of a PM reaction sphere based on spherical harmonics, which is able to derive linear expressions of forces and torques for all possible orientations of the rotor, Yan [5] have derived an semi-analytic model of a PM spherical motor based on Laplace's equation. The expression that relates the actuator torque and current input to the stator coils are obtained in a matrix form by using Lorentz force law and linear superposition. Doty [6], Iwakura [7], Kim [8], Zhu [9] have proposed different kinds of spherical induction motors to drive reaction spheres, among whom Kim [8] proposed a spherical inductive reaction wheel with concentrated winding, of which the torque model is deduced based uniform magnetic field. Also, Davey [10], Purczyński [11] delivered a general analysis of both the fields and output torque of spherical induction motor, applying magnetic vector potential and scalar magnetic potential independently. FEM simulations were not applied due to the lack of computer resources. Spałek [12] evaluated the electromagnetic field and torque of a spherical induction motor by adopting the separation method for magnetic vector potential. Zhou [13] have tried to apply spherical hysteresis motors to reaction spheres and realize one-axis hysteresis drive with experimental prototype. Paku [14] designed a novel reaction sphere based on spherical ultrasonic motor and conducted experiments with PID controller to confirm the feasibility of proposed reaction sphere in an attitude control system.

2 Structural Design

The proposed reaction sphere is driven by a 3D spherical induction motor, which is composed of a rotor, 12 curved stators, 72 toroidal coils and 6 electromagnets. As shown in Fig. 1(a), the hollow sphere is the rotor of the motor. It is multilayered: the inner layer is made of steel, which is used to form magnetic circuit and so to improve torque performance; the outer layer is made of copper, which is used to induce eddy currents and generate driving torque. A rotating sphere carries angular momentum. The attitude adjustment of the satellite is realized by transferring the angular momentum from the rotating sphere to the satellite body back and forth. Figure 1(b) shows the toroidal coils that go all around the sphere. These 72 coils form 3 circle in total. Each circle can generate a rotating magnetic field when loaded with symmetric alternating currents. Figure 1(c) shows the 12 curved stator that is used to fix coils and form magnetic circuit. The curved stators are assembled by silicon-steel lamination and fixed with the satellite body. Figure 1(d) shows the 6 electromagnets that are used to levitate the sphere. When direct current is applied to the electromagnets, it'll generate static magnetic field. Then the magnetic force will attract the inner layer of the rotor to make it levitated. The 6 electromagnets will keep the sphere stably suspended in 3-dimension space.

Figure 2 shows the assembly model of proposed reaction sphere. Compared to reaction wheels, it obtains the following advantages: Compact design. One reaction sphere can replace 3 or more reaction wheels, so it'll occupy less space and less mass when applied in satellite attitude control systems; More redundancies. Reaction sphere can rotate in any directions while reaction wheel can only rotate in one axis. High reliability. The magnetic levitated rotor eliminates mechanical friction. It can work much longer than reaction wheels.

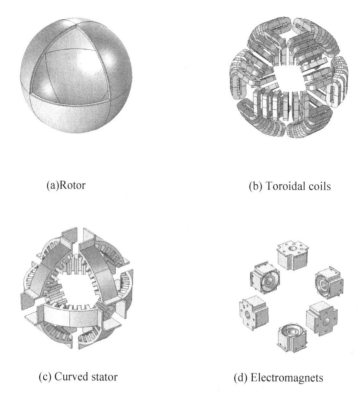

(a)Rotor   (b) Toroidal coils

(c) Curved stator   (d) Electromagnets

Fig. 1. Components of proposed reaction sphere.

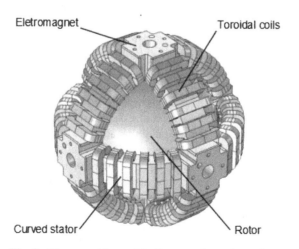

Eletromagnet   Toroidal coils

Curved stator   Rotor

Fig. 2. The assembly model of proposed reaction sphere.

3 Torque Optimization

3.1 Driving Torque Analysis

The exchange of angular momentum between rotating sphere and satellite body can be realized by accelerating and decelerating the rotor, so torque is the key parameter of the reaction sphere, which determines the agility of attitude adjustment.

As show in Fig. 3(a), FEM modeling of 1-dof stator is carried out in COMSOL Multiphysics. Figure 3(b) shows the magnetic flux density of the equatorial cross section, from which we can see that the curved stator steel and the core layer of the rotor obtains a relatively higher magnetic density. Magnetic filed lines and induced eddy currents (that generate driving torque) on the surface are shown in Fig. 3(c). Figure 3(d) shows the main structural parameters that are closely related to the output torque.

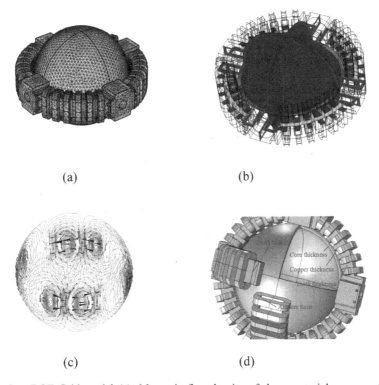

(a)   (b)

(c)   (d)

Fig. 3. One DOF Grid model (a). Magnetic flux density of the equatorial cross section (b). Magnetic field lines and induced eddy currents on the rotor (c). Design parameters (d).

To figure out the relation between design parameters and the output torque, a series of simulations are conducted. Figure 4 shows the influence of five parameters on output torques, from which we can make the following conclusions: There exists a best copper thickness value; The rotor core thickness is not a factor in generating torques if it's not zero; Torque are proportional to ampere turns square; The rotor tooth thickness and tooth width are approximately proportional to output torque of the reaction sphere (it may only works in a certain range).

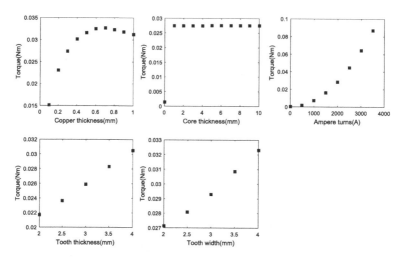

Fig. 4. The relation between output torques and structural parameters.

3.2   Torque Modeling Based on Support Vector Machines

Sample spaces establishment is necessary for SVM modeling. In this case, sample spaces include design parameters (ampere turns, copper thickness, tooth thickness, core thickness, face width) and output torque. Each parameters are set with 5 levels (as shown in Table 1). If we adopt comprehensive test method, then we'll need 3125 samples, which will cost too much time in 3D FEM calculation. Thus, approximately orthogonal design is applied to generate 75 groups representative samples and another 75 local derivation data is designed following uniform random distribution. So there are 150 data in total forming the final sample spaces of the SVM model. The output value are calculated by FEM models. The sample spaces will generate the training and testing data necessary for building SVM models.

Table 1. The parameters table of the sample space.

Element	Level 1	Level 2	Level 3	Level 4	Level 5
δ_{co} (mm)	0.1	0.2	0.3	0.4	0.5
δ_{st} (mm)	1	2	3	4	5
NI (A)	1800	2000	2200	2400	2600
S (mm)	2	2.5	3	3.5	4
B (mm)	20	22.5	25	27.5	30

SVM torque model can be expressed as (1), where torque T is set as the output value, and 5 parameters are set as input values. δ_{co} is copper thickness, δ_{st} is core thickness, NI is ampere turns, S is tooth thickness and B is face width.

$$T = f(\delta_{co}, \delta_{st}, NI, S, B) \tag{1}$$

SVM modeling are performed through Libsvm in Win 10 platform system. The optimization codes are written in Matlab. Gauss kernel function is selected as the kernel function of the SVM model. Cost c, Gauss kernel parameter σ and epsilon p will be optimized by genetic algorithm. The SVM model parameter optimization are carried out by genetic algorithm. The flow chart are depicted in Fig. 5.

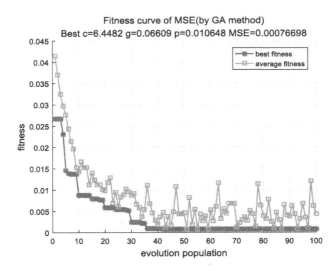

Fig. 5. Flow chart of SVM parameters selection with genetic optimization algorithm.

Data normalization is adopted in sample spaces data processing. As shown in Table 1, the distribution range of each dimension data is very different. To prevent the data with a broad range of values (Ampere turns) from dominating the SVM parameters, data normalization will be carried out in the pre-processing step, making the range 0 to 1. Figure 6 shows the SVM model training and regression performance with data normalization in columns. It promotes the performance in data regression by reducing the Mean Relative Error from 45.03% to 3.22% with the same training and test data (Table 2).

The SVM model parameter optimization are carried out by genetic algorithm. 4/5 of the sample spaces are selected at random for torque model training. The rest are for test regression and so to judge the performance. After 5 rounds of optimization, cost c, gauss kernel parameter σ and epsilon p are determined respectively as 6.45, 0.066 and 0.0106 after taking into account both the mean square error and mean relative error.

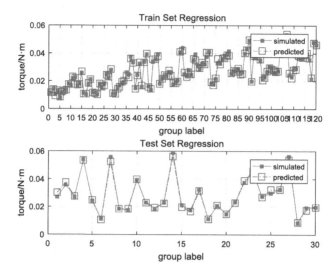

Fig. 6. SVM model regression with data normalization method.

Table 2. Parameter optimization results by ga method.

Iteration	c	σ	p	Mean Square Error	Mean Relative Error
1	74.54	0.037	0.0117	0.0029	4.32%
2	18.49	0.058	0.0187	0.0006	4.00%
3	38.48	0.030	0.0222	0.0006	3.92%
4	6.45	0.066	0.0106	0.0008	3.22%
5	21.96	0.046	0.0103	0.0005	5.04%

3.3   Design Optimization

The problem of reaction sphere optimization can be formulated as a multi-parameter optimization problem with constraints. To ensure the uniform distribution, the copper layer on the surface of the rotor is generated by electrolytic action. Therefore, the tooth thickness are set under 0.5 mm considering time and manufacturing cost. Formula (2) is the moment of inertia expression of spherical shell, where M is the mass of spherical shell, R is the outer radius of the sphere, R_0 is the inner radius of the sphere. From this expression we can see that the outer layer mass are more critical than the inner layer for angular momentum generation. So the core thickness are set under 5 mm.

$$J = \frac{2}{5} M \frac{R^5 - R_0^5}{R^3 - R_0^3} \tag{2}$$

Besides bound constraints, different inputs can affect each other. The number of teeth and the arc length of the stator are fixed, so the ampere turns decrease with increasing tooth thickness. The ampere turns and tooth thickness are limited by tooth pitch. Also, the stator is made up of 3 pairs of orthogonal toroidal coils, so the face wideness cannot be too big otherwise the orthogonal coils will interact with each other. The exact value of the constraints are carried out through prototypes. Based on the analysis above, the mathematical description of the optimization problem of the reaction sphere can be expressed as:

$$\begin{cases} \max T = svmpredict(\delta_{co}, \delta_{st}, NI, S, B) \\ \quad 0.1 \leq \delta_{co} \leq 0.5 \\ \quad 1 \leq \delta_{st} \leq 5 \\ \quad 1800 \leq NI \leq 2600 \\ s.t. \quad 2 \leq S \leq 4 \\ \quad 20 \leq B \leq 30 \\ \quad \frac{NI}{400} + S \leq 9 \\ \quad \frac{NI}{250} + B \leq 37 \end{cases} \tag{3}$$

Genetic algorithm with penalty function method is applied to solve the optimization problem (3). This method is realized through sequential unconstrained minimization, whose principle is to combine objective function with constraints by setting weighting coefficient as a penalty term and so to form a new objective function. The resolution is obtained by calculating the new objective function. The optimized results are listed in Table 3.

Table 3. Optimization results by genetic algorithm.

Labels	Copper thickness (mm)	Core thickness (mm)	Ampere turns (NA)	Tooth thickness (mm)	Face width (mm)	Torque (mNm)
Original	0.3	3	2073.6	3.16	20	26.13
Optimized	0.494	4.371	2391.1	3.01	27.3	43.97

As show in Table 3, the output torque of the reaction sphere with optimized structural parameters has increased over 68% than with the original ones. Figure 7 shows the tangential electromagnetic force distribution at different latitudes, from which we can see that at low latitudes, the distribution of the original reaction sphere is closed to the optimized one. However, with the increasing of latitude, it decreases rapidly compared with the optimized one. The larger driving force distribution ensures that the optimized reaction sphere gains the larger driving force and to some extent improves the stability of the rotating motion.

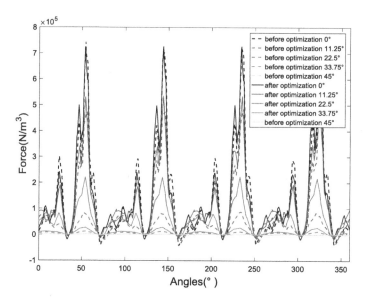

Fig. 7. Tangential components of electromagnetic force of 0°, 11.25°, 22.5°, 33.75° and 45° in latitude on the surface of optimized rotor (solid line) and original rotor (dotted line).

4   Conclusion

This paper designs a novel reaction sphere for satellite attitude control based on a spherical induction motor. The relations between design parameters and the output torque are discussed. Then a torque optimization method based on SVM and FEM is proposed. Simulation results show that the optimized parameters can increase the torque over 68% without increasing the outer radius of the stator. Heat dissipation and efficiency are another two key performance indicators when reaction spheres are applied in space, which will be taken into consideration in the future research. This method can be also applied in other electrical devices when it is not practical to derive an analytical model.

Acknowledgement. The authors acknowledge the support from zhejiang provincial public welfare research program (Grant no. LGG18E070007), NSFC-Zhejiang Joint Fund for the Integration of Industrialization and Informatization (Grant no. U1609206), the Science and Technology Service Network Initiative (STS) Project of the Chinese Academy of Sciences (Grant no. STS-ZJ-2016ZX01).

References

1. Rossini, L.: Electromagnetic Modeling and Control Aspects of a Reaction Sphere for Satellite Attitude Control. EPFL (2014)
2. Stagmer, E.: Reaction Sphere for Stabilization and Control in Three Axes. US, US 20140209751 A1 (2014)

3. Yan, L.: Modeling and design of a three-degree-of-freedom permanent magnet spherical actuator. Nanyang Technological University (2007)
4. Rossini, L., et al.: Force and torque analytical models of a reaction sphere actuator based on spherical harmonic rotation and decomposition. IEEE/ASME Trans. Mechatron. **18**(3), 1006–1018 (2013)
5. Yan, L., Chen, I.M., Yang, G., et al.: Analytical and experimental investigation on the magnetic field and torque of a permanent magnet spherical actuator. IEEE/ASME Trans. Mechatron. **11**(4), 409–419 (2006)
6. John, D.: Reaction Sphere for Spacecraft Attitude Control. WO, WO/2010/117819 (2010)
7. Iwakura, A., Tsuda, S., Tsuda, Y.: Feasibility study on three dimensional reaction wheel. Proc. Sch. Eng. Tokai Univ. Ser. E **33**, 51–57 (2008)
8. Kim, D.-K., et al.: Development of a spherical reaction wheel actuator using electromagnetic induction. Aerosp. Sci. Technol. **39**, 86–94 (2014)
9. Zhu, L., Guo, J., Gill, E.: Reaction Sphere for Microsatellite Attitude Control (2016)
10. Davey, K., Vachtsevanos, G., Powers, R.: The analysis of fields and torques in spherical induction motors. IEEE Trans. Magn. **23**(1), 273–282 (1987)
11. Purczyński, J., Kaszycki, L.: Calculation of power losses and driving torque in spherical symmetry induction motor. Archiv Für Elektrotechnik **69**(1), 69–76 (1986)
12. Spałek, D.: Spherical induction motor with anisotropic rotor-analytical solutions for electromagnetic field distribution, electromagnetic torques and power losses. International Compumag Society. Testing Electromagnetic Analysis Methods (2009)
13. Zhou, L., Nejad, M.I., Trumper, D.L.: One-axis hysteresis motor driven magnetically suspended reaction sphere. Mechatronics **42**, 69–80 (2017)
14. Paku, H., Uchiyama, K.: Satellite attitude control system using a spherical reaction wheel. Appl. Mech. Mater. **798**, 256–260 (2015)

Logistics, Production and Operation Management

Analysis of International Logistics Top Talent Training Based on "One Belt One Road"—Taking the Western China as an Example

Lei Deng[1,2], Zexin Li[1(✉)], Fang Yuan[1], Xu Wang[1,2],
and Yunhuai Zhang[3]

[1] School of Mechanical Engineering,
Chongqing University, Chongqing 400044, China
568185819@qq.com
[2] Chongqing Key Laboratory of Logistics,
Chongqing University, Chongqing 400044, China
[3] School of Graduate, Chongqing University, Chongqing 400044, China

Abstract. Thanks to the "one belt one road" initiative, the international logistics of Western China has made a huge development. However, the shortage of top international logistics talents prevents its further progress. This paper induces the demand types of talents and analyzes it by using the gray forecast model respectively from the qualitative and quantitative aspect. Aiming at the demand, a double-three-spiral talent training model is built, which include school-government optimizing schooling resources; joint practice platforms of school-enterprise; government-enterprise perfecting the mechanism. With perfecting three-year graduate education system, internalizing knowledge, externalizing capability, and improving themselves, the quality of talents training is finally improved.

Keywords: "One Belt One Road" · Gray prediction Double triple helix
International logistics top talents training

1 Background of International Logistics Development in the Western China

With the "One Belt One Road", China-Singapore cooperation and other major national cooperation projects landing one after another, the international Logistics in Western China is facing a golden opportunity [1]. Smooth and high-efficient international logistics channel accelerate the expansion of domestic logistics business to the world. A substantial growth in international logistics and the further expanding scope of services are bound to put forward higher requirements for the logistics talents training [2].

The overall level of international logistics industry of Western China, restricted by the level of economic development and logistics industry itself, is relatively low. And its scattered and diversified pattern make it difficult to achieve the scale management and economies of scale of enterprise. In addition, enterprise's management methods are

S. Wang et al. (Eds.): ICSEE 2018/IMIOT 2018, CCIS 923, pp. 97–107, 2018.
https://doi.org/10.1007/978-981-13-2396-6_9

relatively laggard. The format of the whole logistics service industry is traditional [3], because of lacking international logistics awareness and systematic problem-solving ability, personalized international logistics solutions cannot be provided [4]. The shortage of top talents in international logistics has become the main bottleneck restricting the development of western international logistics. In order to promote the development of western international logistics, and support the implementation of " One Belt One Road", deepening the reform of education and cultivating international logistics top talents required by the society have become important missions of the western colleges [5].

2 Demand Analysis of International Logistics Top Talents in the West

The talents training in western universities, both in quantity and quality, can't meet the needs of the market owing to laggard education in western region [6]. This paper will make a demand analysis of international logistics top talents from two aspects of the quality and quantity.

2.1 Quality Requirements

In the promotion of "One Belt One Road "project, the international logistics development needs a large number of top international logistics talents. The specific talents types are as follows:

1. High end logistics talents with international view

With the globalization of logistics activities in-depth development, talents need to deal with affairs from an international perspective. In international logistics activities, the different countries' economic development, institutional regulations, religious beliefs, cultures, ethics and values have different characteristics. Therefore, the talents who are familiar with the international trade are poorly in need of promoting international logistics trade in an unpredictable international environment [7].

2. Logistics system operation and decision-making talents

Talents who can systematically grasp the overall development of logistics and the future development trend are in urgent need as international logistics supply chain develops rapidly. Meanwhile, in the system operation, macro management and decision-making talents are extremely needed to integrate logistics resources effectively, promote the construction of logistics standardization, achieve the integration of logistics operations, and finally improve logistics efficiency.

3. Professionals in logistics segmentation

After "One Belt One Road" landing, a large number of talents who are good at international trade, warehousing freight and related fields are accordingly needed with the expansion of international cooperation and development of international logistics.

4. Cross-border logistics talents

Many industries and even the capital pay more attention to the logistics industry in recent years, which not only strengthen cross-border competition, but also promote industrial integration, and a new trend of cross-border logistics industry comes into being. Therefore, a corresponding new-type talents of logistics -management, logistics-finance, logistics-information and logistics-electricity business and other new cross-border talents are needed [8].

5. Innovative and entrepreneurial talents

Along with the rapid development trend of international logistics, new interdisciplinary businesses will emerge continually, so top logistics talents who have innovative entrepreneurial awareness are required to further promote the development of logistics and grasp the new format of logistics.

2.2 Quantity Demand

In this paper, the number of practitioners who have a graduate degree or above in logistics industry (transportation, warehousing and postal services, as well as the wholesale and retail) of western China from the end of 2010 to 2015 is taken as actual demand of top talents [9] (Table 1).

Table 1. Postgraduates engaging in western logistics industry

Year	2010	2011	2012	2013	2014	2015
Number of postgraduates engaged in logistics industry	11662	28633	41379	55165	55393	63939
Proportions		0.144169	0.157997	0.165285	0.181603	0.192419	0.210215
Number of postgraduates engaged in western logistics industry	1681	4524	6839	10018	10659	13441

(Source: China Labor Statistical Yearbook. The proportion is the ratio of employments in the western region to the total nation).

Corresponding to the demand of top logistics talents, the number of postgraduate after graduating from the western colleges, employed in the logistics-related industries, are showed in Table 2.

Gray forecast model is used to forecast the demand of top logistics talents in western region in 2016 and 2017. First of all, the paper does test processing for the demand–raw data group, and finds the ratio according to the original time data column. However, most of the ratios don't fall within the interval– $(e^{-\frac{2}{n+1}}, e^{\frac{2}{n+1}}) = (0.7165, 1.3956)$. To make processing datum fall into the intervals, the original datum should be smoothed [11], (Table 3).

Table 2. The number of postgraduates engaging in logistics industry in Western Universities after graduation

Year	2014	2015	2016	2017
Number	7362	8640	8532	8772

(Source: The university employment website. Colleges and universities released employment data from 2014).

Table 3. Data processing of postgraduates engaged in the western logistics industry

Year	2010	2011	2012	2013	2014	2015
Raw data	0.1681	0.4524	0.6839	1.0018	1.0659	1.1583
Stepwise ratio		0.3716	0.6615	0.6827	0.9400	0.9202
Data after processing	1.679	1.3529	1.2071	1.0996	1.0859	0.8480
Stepwise ratio after processing		1.2410	1.1208	1.0978	1.0127	1.0350

According to the gray prediction method, the forecasting model based on the processed datum is constructed:

$$\hat{x}^{(1)}(k+1) = \left(\hat{x}^{(0)}(1) - \frac{b}{a}\right)e^{-ak} + \frac{b}{a}, k = 1, 2, \ldots, n \tag{1}$$

where a is the developing coefficient and u is the grey input. Both of these are parameters to be determined [12].

Use MATLAB software run the data, getting the values of a and b are: a = 0.0782, b = 1.5121. The gray forecast model is:

$$\hat{x}^{(1)}(k+1) = \left(\hat{x}^{(0)}(1) - \frac{b}{a}\right)e^{-ak} + \frac{b}{a} = \left(0.1681 - \frac{1.5121}{0.0782}\right)e^{-0.0782t} + \frac{1.5121}{0.0782} \tag{2}$$

At the same time draw the forecast fitting results of top logistics talents from the end of 2011 to 2015 (Table 4).

Table 4. The forecast fitting results of top logistics talents

Year	2011	2012	2013	2014	2015
Observed data	4524	6839	10018	10659	13441
GM (1,1) Result	4839	6415	8668	10971	12005

To test the forecast result [13], $\bar{\Delta} = 0.018$, $\varepsilon = 0.71$, C = 0.3, P = 1 are obtained. It is clear that the prediction accuracy is qualified (based on the availability of data, the prediction results are only instructive) by referring to the prediction accuracy classification table (Table 5). Then, the model can be used to predict the demand of top

Table 5. Prediction accuracy classification table [10]

Average relative error $\bar{\Delta}$	Correlation degree ε	Small error frequency P	Posteriori difference ratio C	Accuracy level
≤ 0.01	≥ 0.9	>0.95	<0.35	Good
≤ 0.05	≥ 0.8	>0.80	<0.5	Qualified
≤ 0.10	≥ 0.7	>0.70	<0.65	Barely qualified
≤ 0.20	≥ 0.6	≤ 0.70	≥ 0.65	Disqualified

logistics talents in the western region in 2016 and 2017, which are 14541, 16372 people respectively. After comparing talents supply and demand, it is found that the direct gap expands yearly after yearly to even nearly eight thousand people. At present, the gap is mainly compensated by the mid-level talents who have received effective training in the enterprises [14], but supplemented less by the return of talents from the Eastern and Central China [15]. The result is most of the top employees in the western region lacking systematic and professional training [14]. So it is urgent to cultivate international logistics top talents for filling the gap.

3 Top Talents Training System in International Logistics

Owing to the scarcity of logistics talents, many colleges start to set up logistics professionals and expand the scale of enrollment. But their rough talents training system is far from the industry demand. How to cultivate top talents is an subject, which needs to research and explore urgently [4]. This paper designed a training mode of top talents in international logistics based on double-triple-helix model [16] (Fig. 1).

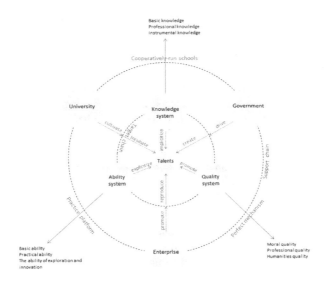

Fig. 1. Talents training model

The training mode consists of two helical chains, including inside and outside. The outer triple helix chains, which aim for the inter triple helix chains, support the whole personnel training process: through the good environment created by the government and the practice platforms built by school-enterprise, the international logistics graduate students incubated by colleges acquire knowledge and improve ability and quality, namely the inter triple helix chain. Ultimately knowledge is constantly internalized to the ability, which is continuously explicit for literacy [17]. And literacy continuously promotes the enrichment of knowledge. Cycling and spiraling by this way. Students will be transformed into top talents.

3.1   Formation of Inner Triple Helix

In this paper, three-year postgraduate training system is further improved by the training mode [18] (Fig. 2).

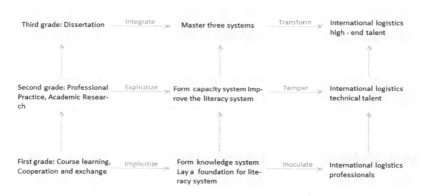

Fig. 2.   Three-year postgraduate training system

The graduate students in the 1st grade systematically learn basic, professional and instrumental knowledge curriculum to form knowledge system, and understand international logistics expertise deeply to improve the knowledge system further, through the international talents exchange platforms Table 6, linking up with international logistics better. At the same time in the good social atmosphere created by government, students could strengthen their own moral cultivation. In process of studying quality education curriculum system, understand the corporate culture, for the purpose of developing their own professional and humanistic qualities [19], and laying the foundation for the formation of literacy system. After one-year courses study, students become an international logistics professional with a perfect knowledge system and an international view.

The graduate students in the 2nd grade, through participating in research and professional practice, improve ability to research and use professional knowledge to solve practical problems; they also need to understand the real technical level of the logistics field and the operation management mode of the enterprises, for the purpose of

Table 6. Knowledge system

Basic knowledge	Knowledge of basic subject and even social sciences
Professional knowledge	Knowledge of international trade and customs clearance
	logistics and supply chain expertise
	Knowledge of risk control
	Laws and regulations, policies,
	Related knowledge: familiar with the cross section's knowledge of logistics and finance, information, electricity suppliers, service industry
Instrumental knowledge	Proficiency in English, computer, software and even data

training the ability to discover and solve the technical and management problems in engineering application, and enhancing the practice and innovation ability [19]. Ability system is Table 7 perfectly formed in the end. In the diverse and complex business scenarios created by enterprises, professionals improve the literacy system imperceptibly Table 8 after the cycle of learning practice. After tempering of practice become an international logistics technical talent with the ability of logistics system operation and decision-making talents and professionals in logistics segmentation.

Table 7. Ability system

Basic ability	Ability to acquire knowledge: Ability to search, read, analyze and understand kinds of books, papers and materials
	Ability to apply knowledge: Ability to analyze and solve engineering problems and management problems in the field
Practical ability	Teamwork and communication ability
	Organization and management ability
	System thinking ability
	Emergency job processing ability
	Continuous improvement of logistics quality ability
The ability of exploration and innovation	Can analyze the logistics of the world system without the thinking mode of domestic logistics, can think about logistics with the perspective of global allocation of resources

The third-year dissertations are the comprehensive reflections of graduate students' ability of scientific research, practicing and innovation, as well as mastery and application of knowledge, which reflect the solid and profound multi-disciplinary knowledge, and are also important index to measure their cultivation quality [20]. Graduate students who have the ability of an innovative and entrepreneurial talents and cross-border logistics talents will transform into an omniscient international logistics top talent after mastering three systems in this year.

Table 8. Literacy system

Moral cultivation	Establish correct moral concept, and strive to strengthen social responsibility; clear their own social responsibility, and strive to cultivate and strengthen their sense of historical mission
Professional accomplishment	In international trade activities, comply with the moral standards and norms; correct the cultural consciousness; respect each other and pay attention to communication and understand characteristics and value of different cultural
Humanities accomplishment	Cultivate and improve physical and mental quality and environmental adaptability with Conscious, purposeful and planned; improve the ability to deal with the relationship between human and society, human and nature

3.2   Support of Outer Triple Helix

(1) College chain - Incubate

As the first step in personnel training, colleges should improve the curriculum and teaching method radically. First and foremost, teacher staff with high-quality must define the ability and literacy of diversified international logistics top talents and then optimize theory curriculum system in accordance to the principle of " foundation, heavy cross, direction and modularity" [20]; besides, linked up with enterprises, the colleges' teaching content should emphasize on the organic combination of theory and practice, such as case study combined with practical manipulate in enterprises and teaching students in accordance with their aptitude using inspiration, discussion and so on [21]. Consequently, a ladder-like practice teaching curriculum system, composed of basic knowledge, professional skills, and innovative research, can be established gradually; last but not least, with the promotion of government, colleges in alliance with the international academic organizations establish a learning pattern, including multi-agent coordination, cross-disciplinary education and master-doctor continuous study. In addition, cross-cultural courses and other special courses should be supplemented in this pattern.

(2) Enterprise chain - reproduce

In the process of talents growth, enterprises should abandon the past behavior of enjoying unilaterally the results of college training and offer feedback of the talents using information timely and effectively [22], to maintain the health relationship with colleges and promote talents training in colleges. Through increasing human, financial and material resources, providing resources for colleges, in the curriculum, teacher building and practical training, and sharing government expenditure on education, enterprises participate gradually in all domains of personnel training [23]: enterprises set up international logistics training platforms, which will be conductive to promote the university to break restrictions of disciplines and majors, set modular, complex practice course system and implement research teaching methods based on problems, projects and cases; implement dual-mentoring system [20], which will combine college teachers with technical staff to guide students in theory and practice. Enterprises carry out interdisciplinary and independent design-style experiment, to enrich students' cross-domain knowledge in constant practice, change the dogmatic way of thinking and solve the practical problems of logistics innovatively.

(3) Government chain-create

As a third party of personnel training, the government make full use of their advantages to service personnel breeding and growth. Strengthen the system construction, and create a good atmosphere of logistics industry [24], to ensure the cooperation among school, government and enterprise in a healthy and sustainable development. Benefit from "One Belt One Road", government should guide colleges to cooperate with other countries along the road and establish international talents training bases in strategy, as well as support colleges and enterprises to set up engineering practice education center in policy. It is crucial to create a good environment, in where care, love talents, and effectively provide quality services for personnel training.

The double-three-spiral model unifies the talents, enterprises and government in personnel training. In the sound environment created by the government, talents are incubated by the university, reproduced by the enterprise. The integrated system, which consisted of knowledge, ability and quality, makes sure the talents master the capacity of developing international logistics and participate in western international logistics actively, so that they could make a great contribution to the development of Western China.

4 Summary

The construction of "One Belt One Road" project has provided a golden opportunity for the development of western international logistics. However, the shortage of top talents in international logistics has become a major short-board in the process of international logistics development in Western China. It is an urgent problem to speed up the training of top talents who could meet the needs of western international logistics market [4].

Through exploring the talent training mode which is suitable for the development of western international logistics, double-three -spiral talent training model is established. In the sound mechanisms established by government, colleges run schools with foreign universities, establish practice bases widely with enterprises and continually promote knowledge internalization, ability externalization, self-improvement. Finally postgraduates are transformed into international logistics top talents, which can alleviate the western talent gap effectively and promote the western economic development.

Acknowledgement. The authors would like to appreciate anonymous referees for their remarkable comments and enormous support by the following projects: analysis of the Master Training Program Major in Logistics Engineering, the "EU-China Tuning Study Project", Ministry of Education of the People's Republic of China, the Specialized Research Fund for the Doctoral Program of Higher Education, China (No. 20130191110045),the National Nature Science Foundation of China (71301177), The National Key Support Program, China (No. 2015BAH46F01,

2015BAF05B03), the Chongqing Science and Technology Research Program, China (No. cstc2014yykfA40096, 2014yykfA40006, 2015yykf-C60002, cstc2015yykfAC0007), and the Fundamental Research Funds for the Central Universities, China (No. CDJZR14110001, 13110048, 106112015CDJSK02JD05).

References

1. Zhao, T., Sun, C., Zhang, F.: Opportunities and Challenges of Regional Economic Development under the Background of "One Belt and One Road". Econ. Probl. **12**, 19–23 (2015)
2. Liangwei, Z.: Synergy analysis of international trade and international logistics under "One Belt, One Road" strategy: case study from Guangdong Province. Finan. Econ. **7**, 81–88 (2015)
3. Chen, H., Wei, X., Wei, X.: The power source and factors driving the development of China in logistics industry—based on the perspective of labor input. J. Bus. Econ. **11**, 13–26 (2015)
4. Ji, X., Luo, Y., Wu, J., Shui, W., Shen, Y.: Analysis on the regional international logistics personnel training mode which oriented bridgehead strategy. Res. High. Educ. Eng. **4**, 121–124 (2014)
5. Chen, J.: deepen the reform of education and teaching comprehensively and promote the quality of personnel training vigorously. Tsinghua J. Educ. **35**(6), 1–5 (2014)
6. Yang, Y.: Aspirations and countermeasures of enhancing the education quality in western local colleges-based on the investigation into some Western Local Colleges. J. Natl. Acad. Educ. Admin. **8**, 30–34 (2013)
7. Wen, J., Jiang, X.: Innovative training path of university international talents using systematic thinking with "Belt and Road Initiative". Int. Bus. **5**, 153–160 (2015)
8. Sun, X., Yao, W.: The talents supporting and educational solutions to the "Belt and Road Initiative". Educ. Res. **10**, 4–9 (2015)
9. Yang, L., He, Z., Han, F.: Forcast on talent demand of strategic emerging industries and relative countermeasures—taking Hunan Province as an example. Forum Sci. Technol. China **1**(11), 85–91 (2013)
10. Zhu, N.: A research on forecasting the value - added of marine economy based on gray model. Math. Pract. Theory **1**, 102–109 (2016)
11. He, B., Meng, Q.: Study on generalization for grey forecasting model. Syst. Eng. Theory Pract. **22**(9), 137–140 (2002)
12. Li, C., Qin, J., Li, J., Hou, Q.: The accident early warning system for iron and steel enterprises based on combination weighting and grey prediction model gm (1, 1). Saf. Sci. **89**, 19–27 (2016)
13. Gao, Y., Bian, Z.: Research on "Double Quantity" demand of scientific and technological foreign language talent in Blue Economic Zone of Shandong Peninsula. Shandong Soc. Sci. **12**, 105–108 (2011)
14. Wang, J., Chen, G.: Simulation-based training model for high-level logistics talent. Mod. Educ. Technol. **21**(6), 145–148 (2011)
15. Li, Y., Zhao, X.: The capability difference, capability need and regional self-development ability in counterpart aid between the Eastern and Western Areas—a case study of Five Frontier Provinces in the Western Areas. Acad. Explor. **9**, 93–99 (2016)
16. Sun, X., Yao, W.: Double Triple Helix Model theory and innovation mode of the talent cultivation. Soc. Sci. Nanjing **12**, 124–130 (2012)

17. Chen, F., Wu, M.: Exploration and practice of high-quality applied talents cultivating system in accordance with the development of the times - an analysis framework of SECI Model based on knowledge innovation. China High. Educ. Res. **8**, 63–65 (2011)
18. Xu, Z.: Double Helix Model of cultivating talents with entrepreneurial skills in higher education. Res. Educ. Dev. **5**, 30–34 (2015)
19. Li, Y., Yu, B., Qin, Z., Xia, Q., Luo, X.: Research on innovation cultivation mode for logistics management application of innovation and talents. Sci. Technol. Manage. Res. **32**(12), 134–136 (2012)
20. Yao, W., Lu, F.: Research on the cultivation mode of full - time engineering Master's Degree based on cooperative education. Acad. Degrees Graduate Educ. **10**, 12–16 (2011)
21. Yao, L.: Constructing the postgraduates cultivation mode with the main line of research and innovation. Jiangsu High. Educ. **2**, 42–44 (2010)
22. Ju, C., Fu, X.: The exploration of hierarchical logistics education system for dynamic social needs—the case of Zhejiang Province. China High. Educ. Res. **6**, 98–101 (2014)
23. Wei, K.: School-enterprise cooperation of higher vocational and technical education under the "Triple Helix" theory. High. Educ. Explor. **1**, 115–119 (2010)
24. Tong, L., Meng, W.: Building regional talent sharing mode based on Triple Helix Theory. Sci. Technol. Manage. Res. **34**(2), 93–95 (2014)

Simulating the Impact of Fuel Prices on Transportation Performance in Aerospace Supply Chains

David Allen[1(✉)], Adrian Murphy[1], Joseph Butterfield[1],
Stephen Drummond[2], Stephen Robb[2], Peter Higgins[3],
and John Barden[3]

[1] Queen's University Belfast, Belfast, Northern Ireland, UK
dallen15@qub.ac.uk
[2] Bombardier Aerospace, Belfast, Northern Ireland, UK
[3] Northern Ireland Technology Centre, Belfast, Northern Ireland, UK

Abstract. Due to the vast distances between aerospace supply chain (SC) members, the logistical implications of outsourcing decisions must be considered, including the uncertainty in transportation costs (TC) caused by fluctuating fuel prices. Analytical models often model the impact of fuel prices without capturing the dynamic behavior of SC networks. Discrete event simulation (DES) can capture such behavior and correlate it with financial performance to support decision making. This paper uses DES to model the impact of fuel prices on TC and inventory holding costs (IHC) in a three-tier SC scenario where suppliers deliver products via land/sea- or air freight. The results show the transportation decisions can be used to mitigate the influence of fuel prices on the TC. The value, weight and size of products transported throughout the SC also influence in whether TCs or IHCs drive total SC costs. Future work could apply the methodology to larger and more complex SCs.

Keywords: Aerospace · Supply chains · Fuel prices · Logistics
DES

1 Introduction

Through the use of advanced communication techniques and the effects of globalization, aerospace SCs have spread over large distances to exploit the competitive advantages available around the world. However, these vast distances make the organization of efficient transportation between SC members a challenge due to operating in a complex and uncertain environment [1]. Transporting goods across such distances also influence SC costs; it was estimated in 2008 that TCs averaged 20% of the total production costs in manufacturing firms [2]. Since the cost of delivering aerospace-grade products are high (due to their value, size and weight), third party logistics (3PL) providers often manage their delivery in aerospace SCs to reduce costs [3, 4]. When bidding for the contracts to manage these logistical operations, 3PL providers quote a 'door-to-door' transit time and price [3]. These contracts are renewed every few years to allow competitors to bid, thus encouraging continual improvement

© Springer Nature Singapore Pte Ltd. 2018
S. Wang et al. (Eds.): ICSEE 2018/IMIOT 2018, CCIS 923, pp. 108–120, 2018.
https://doi.org/10.1007/978-981-13-2396-6_10

in their logistical functions by maintaining an atmosphere of competition between 3PL providers.

An important component of the price quoted by 3PL providers is the fuel surcharge applied to compensate for the uncertainty that fuel prices introduce. This is partly due to fuel prices continuing to outpace inflation caused by concerns over depleting oil supplies [5]. Policies to reduce emissions, or further governmental agendas have also caused fuel prices to fluctuate [6]. Despite the development of more efficient technologies, fuel prices are driving TCs higher; some authors even claim rising fuel prices may potentially reverse the globalization of outsourcing activities [5]. Due to these developments, it is apparent the logistical implications of outsourcing decisions should be considered carefully [7].

1.1 Supply Chain Transportation Modeling

The two main approaches applied to analyze transportation problems are analytical- and simulation modeling. The former aims to represent the behavior of a system as a series of mathematical equations and are typically static in nature (i.e. they don't capture the dynamic behavior of the system over time). In an industrially relevant example, Zeng and Rossetti [7] created an aerospace transportation costing spreadsheet tool, although variable fuel prices are not considered. Gurtu et al. [5] used an analytical model to examine the impact of fuel prices on inventory management policies by modifying the economic order quantity to optimize lot sizes and shipping quantities. The inclusion of fuel prices in inventory management problems is relatively new since the majority of related efforts don't consider variable fuel prices [5, 8]. Fuel prices are also considered in developing delivery strategies; in the example by Wangsa and Wee [8] a vendor decides to send their products to a 3PL provider or use their pick-up policy depending on the price of fuel and subsidies available.

In contrast to analytical models, simulation captures the dynamic behavior of systems by tracking the flow of parts and material through it over time [1, 9]. This capability makes simulation valuable in supporting the integration of production and transport scheduling to improve production and logistical flow efficiency [1, 9]. Simulation is commonly applied to identify cost savings by using different lot sizes based on constraints including transport capacities and costs. Typical applications of simulation include managing logistics to improve inventory levels, transportation scheduling and routing [10]. Despite these strengths, analytical models are generally applied to resolve transportation problems, although some studies are supported with simulation [2, 11]. This is partly due to the time and effort required to use simulation, making it best reserved for problems that analytical models cannot handle. In addition, few research efforts have explicitly incorporated fuel prices into simulation models.

The most relevant literature found is the agent based simulation model developed by Cooper and Jarre [12, 13] to understand the impact of fuel prices, exchange rates and catch uncertainty on the performance of South African fishing companies. They conclude that increasing fuel prices caused smaller companies to merge in order to reduce their vulnerability to fuel price fluctuations. Another study by Gross et al. [14] used simulation to optimize logistics network structure configurations for a range of oil prices. They conclude that while centralized networks make less use of their trucks, thus increasing TCs, they benefit from reduced inventories by leveraging economies of scale. What is of note in the literature is the use of simulation to understand how fuel prices affect SCs and mitigate their impact, suggesting a novel opportunity to apply simulation to the optimization of transport strategies while considering their influence. This paper therefore contributes to the existing literature by simulating the impact of fuel prices on SC transportation performance. Section 2 describes the methodology and simulation model used to analyze the impact of fuel prices on the SC's TC and IHC. Section 3 demonstrates the capability with experimental results and Sect. 4 summarizes the main findings of this paper.

2   Methodology

2.1   Methodology Overview

This paper employs a combined analytical and simulation modeling approach to model the influence of fuel prices on transportation performance (Fig. 1). The simulation model calculates product dispatch dates in the SC. These dates are then correlated with fuel price trends in the analytical model to allocate the appropriate fuel surcharge when calculating the TC. Supplier inventory levels are exported from the simulation to calculate the IHC incurred. By correlating the timing of physical events in the simulation model to independent financial inputs in the analytical model (e.g. fuel prices), it is possible to analyze the impact of multiple factors using the same set of simulation data. Reusing the same simulation data reduces the number of instances required, increasing modeling efficiency. This addresses the common drawback noted for simulation based analysis regarding model building and execution, albeit factors which alter the physical timing of events (e.g. transit times) would require new simulation instances.

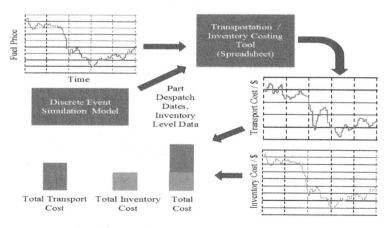

Fig. 1. Overview of the combined modeling methodology

This paper uses Delmia QUEST, a commercial DES software package. DES models dynamic systems by representing them as a series of interconnected activities, resources and queues through which entities flow (e.g. orders progressing through a SC) [15, 16]. The dynamic behavior of the system is captured by updating the system's status every time an "event" occurs (a discrete point in time where the system changes in some fashion (e.g. dispatching an order) [15, 16]. Since the time between events can vary, the system's status therefore "jumps" at discrete points in time and remains constant during the intervals [15, 16]. By tracking the status of every entity, resource and queue in the model, DES is able to model a system in high fidelity, making it a highly flexible technique. A description of DES and its underlying mechanics can be found in [15, 16].

2.2 Supply Chain Simulation Model

The scenario modeled consists of an aircraft OEM, a Tier 1 supplier for an aircraft structure and a Tier 2 supplier providing the structure's machined parts (Fig. 2). Both suppliers could use either land/sea freight or air freight to deliver products to their customer. The different modes of transport were represented through their standard price (SP) rate, fuel surcharge trend and transit time applied (Table 1).

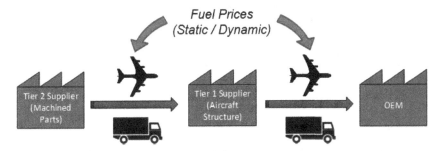

Fig. 2. The three-tier supply chain scenario

Table 1. Modes of transport available of the Tier 1 and Tier 2 supplier

Mode of transport	Transit time (Working days)	Standard price rate (Normalized)	Fuel surcharge trend applied
Land/sea freight	5	100	Diesel fuel
Air freight	1	333	Jet fuel

The raw material inventory store, manufacturing processes, finished goods store and transportation for each SC member were modeled in the simulation and connected as illustrated in Fig. 3. The Tier 2 supplier was a machine house while the Tier 1 supplier included composite fabrication lines and a final assembly line. Due to the many part types and processes involved in the SC (38 part types and 56 processes), tracking the status of each part in the SC would have been too complex to model each supplier as a single element. Each supplier's process flows were therefore modelled to capture their inventory levels over time. The Tier 2 supplier performed machining processes, surface treatments and quality inspections. The Tier 1 supplier performed composite fabrication and final assembly processes. The composite skins and stiffeners were fabricated in parallel before final assembly. The skins also had a structural core located onto them during the ply layup process.

The following assumptions were applied in the simulation model:

1. Parts from suppliers not modeled arrived on time and in perfect quality.
2. There were no losses due to scrapped parts or materials.
3. Both suppliers had enough capacity to meet a demand of 1 aircraft structure/week.
4. Both suppliers had the same interest rate when calculating their IHC.
5. Manufacturing and dispatch schedules were created following the material requirements planning (MRP) technique described in [17].
6. The raw material and finished goods stores applied a one week safety lead-time.

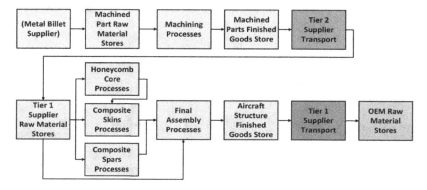

Fig. 3. Process flow diagram of the three-tier supply chain. The orange, green and blue sections are located at the Tier 2 supplier, Tier 1 supplier and OEM respectively. (Color figure online)

2.3   Transportation Cost Modeling

The price quoted by 3PL providers to deliver a product contains fixed and variable components. The fixed component of the price is defined as the SP and acts as a base price from which additional surcharges are applied. The SP is influenced by factors including accessibility to the destination and whether special means of transport are required. The SP is a function of the product's weight and volume and is calculated by multiplying its weight by the SP rate quoted by the 3PL provider (1).

$$\text{Standard Price} = \text{Weight} \times \text{Standard Price Rate} (\text{Cost per Unit Weight}). \quad (1)$$

If the product is lightweight but large, a "volumetric weight" may be applied instead, representing the amount of space it requires to be transported as an equivalent weight (2). When calculating the SP, the larger value is applied to account for the constraints of transporting large and heavy products (3).

$$\text{Volumetric Weight of Product} = (\text{Height} \times \text{Width} \times \text{Depth}) \times \text{Conversion Factor}. \quad (2)$$

$$\text{Weight Applied in Transportation Pricing} = \text{Max}(\text{Weight}, \text{Volumetric Weight}). \quad (3)$$

The volume and weight of products and the conversion factor applied were obtained from logistics managers. The variable components of the price account for the dynamic and uncertain nature of external factors including fuel prices and delivering to high risk areas. The 3PL provider will apply a surcharge known as the Fuel Adjustment Factor (FAF) as an additional percentage of the SP (4, 5). The FAF is a function of the price of jet fuel and diesel for air freight and land/sea freight respectively. The FAF function was generated by plotting a best line of fit from FAF data published by 3PL providers (Fig. 4).

$$\text{Fuel Adjustment Factor} = (1 + n) \times \text{Standard Price}. \quad (4)$$

$$n = f(\text{fuel price}). \quad (5)$$

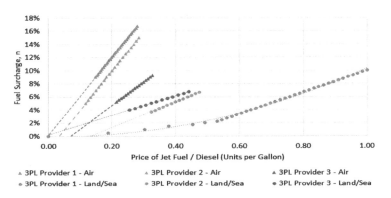

Fig. 4. Fuel surcharge trends for three international 3PL providers

In the aerospace industry, a 3PL provider may be responsible for delivering packages for multiple aircraft programs, meaning they could deliver hundreds of packages each month. To simplify the tracking of payments made by a firm to their 3PL provider, it is common practice to consolidate the invoices generated each month. In addition, contractual agreements with 3PL providers also include payment terms stating how long a firm has to pay their 3PL provider after an invoice is issued. In the simulation model a 30 calendar day payment period was applied to the Tier 1 and Tier 2 suppliers.

2.4   Inventory Cost Modeling

IHCs represent the physical cost to maintain facilities for holding inventory and the opportunity cost due to having cash "tied up" in inventory that could otherwise have been invested elsewhere [18]. This paper used the traditional approach to modeling the IHC as a percentage of the average value of the inventory held (6). It should be noted the interest rate applied varies between firms and can be difficult to estimate accurately, illustrated with textbooks stating estimates ranging between 20–50% [18].

$$\text{Cost of Inventory} = \text{Average Value of Inventory} \times \text{Interest Rate.} \qquad (6)$$

The value of inventory in each supplier was measured by summing the value of each part's raw material and manufacturing cost. The raw material cost is the price a firm paid to acquire it while the manufacturing cost represents the value-added work performed on it to transform it into products to sell. Both types of cost were allocated as a part attribute. Each part's manufacturing cost attribute was increased every time a process was completed on it. The cost to complete a process was the product of its hourly cost rate and its cycle time (7). The process cost was then added to the part's manufacturing cost attribute (8).

$$\text{Process Cost} = \text{Hourly Cost Rate} \times \text{Cycle Time} \qquad (7)$$

$$\text{Part Manufacturing Cost (after)} = \text{Part Manufacturing Cost(before)} + \text{Process Cost} \quad (8)$$

3   Results

3.1   Tier 1 Supplier's Transportation and Inventory Holding Cost

To demonstrate the developed capability, historical fuel price trends covering a five year period were imported into the analytical model. Figure 5 illustrates how the TC for

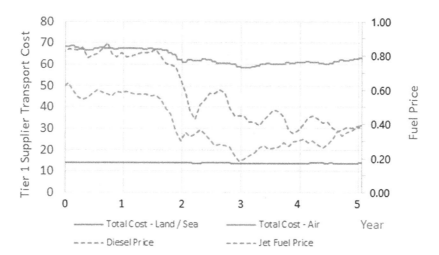

Fig. 5.   Tier 1 supplier's TC using land/sea freight and air freight over time due to the influence of fuel prices. Note data points are non-dimensionalised and normalized.

an aerospace structure supplied by the Tier 1 supplier, either by land/sea or air freight, varied over time in response to the changing fuel price.

The TC's sensitivity to the fuel price depended on the mode of transport used. The cost to deliver products by land/sea was nearly constant despite the price of diesel dropping by nearly 50% while the cost to deliver the same products by air fluctuated within the 55–70 range. Since the fuel surcharge was applied as a percentage of the SP rate, greater SP rates caused the TCs to become more sensitive to the price of fuel. One conclusion that can be drawn from using this result is the importance of using accurate SP rates when modeling the impact of fuel prices on TCs.

While using air freight may be more expensive, being able to transport goods to the customer faster may offer reductions in IHCs. The total IHC and TC were therefore combined to assess the effect of using either mode of transport on the total cost (Table 2). In this example, using air freight caused a net increase of 87% in the total cost, showing the additional TC incurred by using air freight outweighed the IHC savings.

Table 2. The total transportation, inventory and overall costs induced by the Tier 1 supplier. Note data points are non-dimensionalised and normalized.

Mode of transport	TC	IHC	Total cost
Land/sea freight	14	39	53
Air freight	69	31	100

3.2 Design of Experiment

With the modeling methodology and outputs metrics demonstrated, the methodology was applied to the SC scenario in Fig. 2. Whether the price of fuel was considered when using a mode of transport was modeled by assuming it was constant throughout the simulated period or dynamic (i.e. correlating the simulation data to the entire fuel price trend) when calculating the TC. Combined with both suppliers having the option of using either mode of transport (Table 1), this gave four independent factors with two levels each (Table 3). To identify interactions between the factors, a half-fractional factorial design was used to reduce the number of experimental runs. A resolution IV experimental array was used to prevent the main effects being aliased with two-way interactions (three-way interactions were not expected to have any significant effect). The effect of the three-way interaction "ABC" was aliased with the main effect of factor D, resulting in the experimental design array in Table 4.

Table 3. Factor level descriptions

	Mode of transport (Factor A)	Mode of transport (Factor B)	Price (Factor C)	Price (Factor D)
Lower	Land/sea	Land/sea	Static	Static
Upper	Air	Air	Dynamic	Dynamic

Table 4. Partial factorial experimental array (defining relation, I = ABCD)

Experiment	Factor A	Factor B	Factor C	Factor D
1	Land/sea	Air	Static	Dynamic
2	Air	Air	Static	Static
3	Air	Land/sea	Dynamic	Static
4	Land/sea	Air	Dynamic	Static
5	Land/sea	Land/sea	Static	Static
6	Air	Land/sea	Static	Dynamic
7	Air	Air	Dynamic	Dynamic
8	Land/sea	Land/sea	Dynamic	Dynamic

3.3 Tier 1 Supplier Costs

The influence of fuel prices and transport modes were plotted on Pareto- and main effects charts. All of the effects are normalized against the highest total cost measured from all of the experiments (e.g. an effect of 50 units has a magnitude equal to 50% of the highest total cost measured). The Pareto chart (Fig. 6) shows the main effects and interactions between factors. The main effects chart (Fig. 7) shows the direction the main effects, represented by the gradient of the lines. A positive gradient indicates setting a factor to its upper level increases the cost and vice versa (factors with a gradient of zero have no effect). A 5% confidence interval was used to determine if effects were statistically significant (SS), represented by the red dotted line on the Pareto chart; any effects or interactions that crossed the line were SS. In Fig. 6, it can be seen that the Tier 1 supplier's mode of transport dominates their TC while the price of jet fuel and the interaction between these factors are the only other factors that bear any influence. Figure 7 shows that using air freight rather than land/sea freight increases the Tier 1 supplier's TC by an average of 48.18 units. Interestingly, using the dynamic jet fuel price trend decreased the Tier 1 supplier's TC. This was due to using the historical trend (Fig. 5) where a sharp decline in the price of jet fuel occurred within the first two years of the simulated period.

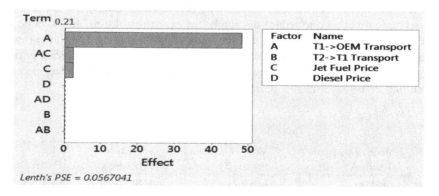

Fig. 6. Tier 1 supplier's TC Pareto Effect Chart (α = 0.05). Threshold value for SS = 0.21 (Color figure online)

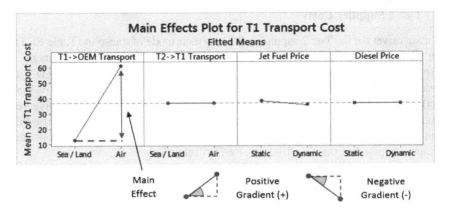

Fig. 7. Tier 1 supplier's TC main effect chart.

Table 5 shows the Pareto- and main effect data for the TCs, IHCs and their combined total (the brackets hold the threshold value for determining SS). The factors that influenced the Tier 1 supplier's IHCs were their mode of transport and interestingly, that of the Tier 2 supplier. Using the faster freight option meant products spent less time as finished goods inventory, thus lowering IHCs. The reason for the Tier 2 supplier's use of air freight increasing the Tier 1 supplier's IHC was due to recording the inventory level at a specific points in time; the cost of holding inventory may vary suddenly depending on the timing of measurements. While the result may be SS, its physical magnitude is 0.56 units and thus is of little practical importance.

The driving factor on the Tier 1 supplier's total cost was their mode of transportation. In this scenario, the cost of air freight outweighed the IHC saving, causing an average increase of 40.41 units in the total cost. The main effect of the jet fuel price and interaction between it and the Tier 1 supplier's mode of transport each caused an average decrease of 2.51 units in the total cost each; an outcome caused by the impact of fuel prices being dependent on the SP and the fuel price data used.

Table 5. Main effects and interactions on the Tier 1 supplier's costs

Factor (+Aliases)	Transport cost			Inventory cost			Total cost		
	Effect	Gradient	ss? (0.21)	Effect	Gradient	SS? (0.01)	Effect	Gradient	SS? (0.43)
A+BCD	48.18	+	Yes	−7.77	−	Yes	40.41	+	Yes
B+ACD	0.00	0	No	0.56	+	Yes	0.56	+	Yes
C+ABD	−2.51	−	Yes	0.00	0	Yes	−2.51	−	Yes
D+ABC	0.08	+	No	0.00	0	Yes	0.08	+	No
AB+CD	0.00	0	No	0.00	0	Yes	0.00	0	No
AC+BD	−2.51	+	Yes	0.00	0	Yes	−2.51	−	Yes
AD+BC	0.08	+	No	0.00	0	Yes	0.08	+	No

3.4   Tier 2 Supplier Costs

The main driver for the Tier 2 supplier's TC was their mode of transport (Table 6). The price of jet fuel and the interaction between it and the Tier 2 supplier's mode of transport decreased their TCs (while the interaction "BC" is aliased with "AD", the interaction "AD" is unlikely to have any effect since factors "A" and "D" had no main effect). Although their effects are SS, with a magnitude of 0.06 units over a five year period, their practical significance are negligible. The price of jet fuel also caused the TC to decrease when the dynamic fuel price trend was applied, providing a consistent outcome compared to the Tier 1 supplier's TC (Table 5).

Only the mode of transport used influenced the Tier 2 supplier's IHC. The magnitude of the transport mode's effect was smaller compared to the Tier 1 supplier's IHC however (−3.69 units compared to −7.77 units (Table 5)). This was due to the nature of both suppliers; the type and volume of materials they bought and their manufacturing processes influenced the average value of their inventory.

The mode of transport used by the Tier 2 supplier had the greatest influence on their total cost (the price of jet fuel and the interaction between these factors also had a minor effect). In contrast to the Tier 1 supplier, using air freight to deliver the machined parts caused a reduction in the total cost. This was due to the IHC savings outweighing the increased TC for using air freight; since the machined parts were smaller, the increase in TC was not as significant compared to that observed in the Tier 1 supplier (Table 5).

Table 6. Main effects and interactions on the Tier 2 supplier's costs

Factor (+Aliases)	Transport cost			Inventory cost			Total cost		
	Effect	Gradient	ss? (0.01)	Effect	Gradient	ss? (0.00)	Effect	Gradient	ss? (0.01)
A+BCD	0.00	0	No	0.00	0	Yes	0.00	0	No
B+ACD	0.88	+	Yes	−3.69	−	Yes	−2.81	−	Yes
C+ABD	−0.06	−	Yes	0.00	0	Yes	−0.06	−	Yes
D+ABC	0.00	0	No	0.00	0	Yes	0.00	0	No
AB+CD	0.00	0	No	0.00	0	Yes	0.00	0	No
AC+BD	0.00	0	No	0.00	0	Yes	0.00	0	No
AD+BC	−0.06	−	Yes	0.00	0	Yes	−0.06	−	Yes

4   Discussion and Conclusions

The logistical implications of outsourcing decisions must be carefully considered in order to fully benefit from the advantages of selecting suppliers in strategic locations, including the impact of fuel prices on TC. Analytical models are often used for this purpose despite the strengths of simulation to model the dynamic behavior of SCs, partly due to the time and effort required to apply it. This paper therefore simulates the impact of fuel prices on the TCs and IHCs of a three-tier aerospace SC problem using a hybrid analytical-simulation approach. Each supplier could either deliver their products via land/sea- or air freight. The simulation captured the dynamic behavior of the SC by exporting order dispatch dates to the analytical model to correlate them to historical fuel price trends and apply the appropriate fuel surcharge when calculating the TC. The average value of inventory in each supplier was also exported to the analytical model to calculate IHCs. A powerful feature of the developed methodology is the ability to reuse simulation data for multiple fuel price trends, transportation price rates and inventory interest rates, thus reducing the number of simulation instances required.

The results show the mode of transport used by the Tier 1- and Tier 2 supplier drove their TC and IHC. The impact of fuel prices was limited due to being modeled as a percentage surcharge of the standard price quoted by the 3PL providers to deliver the products. More expensive modes of freight became more sensitive to fuel price fluctuations. There was no relationship between the price of fuel and IHCs. Instead, the IHC was driven by the value of materials, the time they spent in transit and the nature of the processes performed on them. This suggests suppliers can mitigate the impact of fuel prices via their transportation strategies. However, selecting cheaper modes of transport to do so doesn't necessarily lead to reduced total costs, as illustrated in the Tier 2 supplier's IHC savings outweighing the additional TC from using air freight. A holistic perspective to SC costs is therefore needed when making transportation decisions.

Opportunities for future research include leveraging the strengths of the developed methodology to investigate the impact of variable SP rates while accounting for uncertainty in fuel price and interest rate projections on each supplier's TC and IHC. Other external factors could be included such as disruptions due to extreme weather or man-made disasters. Finally, the methodology could be applied to larger and more complex SCs by including more suppliers along each tier and connections between them.

References

1. Avci, M., Selim, H.: A multi-objective, simulation-based optimization framework for supply chains with premium freights. Expert Syst. Appl. **67**(1), 95–106 (2017)
2. Meixell, M., Norbis, M.: A review of the transportation mode choice and carrier selection literature. Int. J. Logist. Manag. **19**(2), 183–211 (2008)
3. Bayazit, O., Karpak, B.: Selection of a third party logistics service provider for an aerospace company: an analytical decision aiding approach. Int. J. Logist. Syst. Manag. **15**(4), 382–404 (2013)
4. Alfalla-Luque, R., Medina-Lopez, C., Schrage, H.: A study of supply chain integration in the aeronautics sector. Prod. Plan. Control **24**(8–9), 769–784 (2013)
5. Gurtu, A., Jaber, M., Searcy, C.: Impact of fuel price and emissions on inventory policies. Appl. Math. Model. **39**(1), 1202–1216 (2015)
6. Rogat, J.: The politics of fuel pricing in Latin America and their implications for the environment. Energy Environ. **18**(1), 1–12 (2007)
7. Zeng, A., Rossetti, C.: Developing a framework for evaluating the logistics costs in global sourcing processes. Int. J. Phys. Distrib. Logist. Manag. **33**(9), 785–803 (2003)

8. Wangsa, I., Wee, H.: Impact of lead time reduction and fuel consumption on a two-echelon supply chain inventory with a subsidised price and pick-up policy. Int. J. Integr. Supply Manag. **11**(2–3), 264–289 (2017)
9. Mönch, L., Lendermann, P., McGinnis, L., Schirrmann, A.: A survey of challenges in modelling and decision-making for discrete-event logistics systems. Comput. Ind. **62**(1), 557–567 (2011)
10. Galović, P., Čišić, D., Ogrizović, D.: The application of simulation in logistics. In: MIPRO 2011 - 34th International Convention on Information and Communication Technology, Electronics and Microelectronics, Opatija, Croatia, pp. 1402–1407. IEEE (2011)
11. Frazzon, E., Albrecht, A., Pires, M., Israel, E., Kück, M., Freitag, M.: Hybrid approach for the integrated scheduling of production and transport processes along supply chains. Int. J. Prod. Res. **4**(5), 2019–2035 (2018)
12. Cooper, R., Jarre, A.: An agent-based model of the south african offshore hake trawl industry: part II drivers and trade-offs in profit and risk. Ecol. Econ. **142**(1), 257–267 (2017)
13. Cooper, R., Jarre, A.: An agent-based model of the South African offshore hake trawl industry: part I model description and validation. Ecol. Econ. **142**(1), 268–281 (2017)
14. Gross, W., Hayden, C., Butz, C.: About the impact of rising oil price on logistics networks and transportation greenhouse gas emission. Logist. Res. **4**(3–4), 147–156 (2012)
15. Law, A.: Simulation Modeling and Analysis, 5th edn. McGraw-Hill Education, New York (2015)
16. Robinson, S.: Discrete-event simulation: a primer. In: Discrete-Event Simulation and System Dynamics for Management Decision Making, 1st edn., pp. 10–25. Wiley, Chichester (2014)
17. Hopp, W., Spearman, L.: Factory Physics International Edition, 3rd edn. McGraw-Hill Education, New York (2008)
18. Azzi, A., Battini, D., Faccio, M., Persona, A., Sgarbossa, F.: Inventory holding costs measurement: a multi-case study. Int. J. Logist. Manag. **25**(1), 109–132 (2014)

Research on the Process Layout Evaluation of Rail Vehicle Assembly Workshop in the Lean Intelligent Manufacturing Environment

Xiaoying Tong[(⊠)], Li Sun, and Tianming Guan

School of Mechanical Engineering, Dalian Jiaotong University, Dalian, China
txy@djtu.edu.cn

Abstract. In the Lean Intelligent Manufacturing Environment, Improving the level of workshop process layout is the foundation and key for rail transportation equipment manufacturing to improve efficiency and reduce costs. So, it is very important to establish a scientific and reasonable process layout evaluation system. Combining with the process layout features of rail vehicle assembly workshop, an evaluation indicator system including 4 first-level indicators, 13 second-level indicators and 26 third-level indicators is constructed. Group AHP and entropy weight method are used to calculate weights. Grey relational analysis is used to calculate gray correlation between the current state and the ideal level of each indicator, so as to achieve a quantitative evaluation. Three typical urban rail vehicle assembly workshops of CRRC are evaluated, and the evaluation results are consistent with the actual situation.

Keywords: Group AHP · Entropy weight · Grey relational analysis
Rail vehicle assembly · Process layout evaluation

1 Introduction

The process layout is the basis of the overall design of production lines and the basis for decision making of scheduling and operation control, and also the key technology to determine production rhythm, process and product quality [1]. Lean production and intelligent manufacturing can play a better role by improving the level of process layout. Therefore, rail vehicle manufacturing companies need to establish a systematic and scientific process layout evaluation system to evaluate process layout, so as to better grasp their own level, identify problems timely, and constantly optimize the process layout.

As an important part of facility planning process, the layout evaluation has attracted the attention and research of domestic and foreign scholars. Yang and Kuo evaluated the layout of workshop facilities by using AHP and data envelopment [2] Li introduced the average of fuzzy weights in fuzzy evaluation and applied the algorithm model to facility layout evaluation [3]. L Yang and J Deuse evaluated workshop layout from the perspective of energy saving by using rough set-AHP and TOPSIS [4]. Na Zhang established an evaluation index system for the layout characteristics of multi-variety and small-batch production workshops, and evaluated the layout plan based on

© Springer Nature Singapore Pte Ltd. 2018
S. Wang et al. (Eds.): ICSEE 2018/IMIOT 2018, CCIS 923, pp. 121–130, 2018.
https://doi.org/10.1007/978-981-13-2396-6_11

G-TOPSIS [5]. H Charkhand et al. considered environmental, safety, and business indicators, using simulation and random DEA analysis to evaluate the layout plan [6]. Considering cost, adjacency, and distance requirements,N Bozorgi et al. used tabu search algorithm to get dynamic layout optimization [7].

It can be seen that scholars at home and abroad have focused on the evaluation methods, such as simulation software verification, AHP, fuzzy evaluation, and data envelopment. There are few in-depth studies on evaluation indicators and evaluation weights. Evaluation indicators and evaluation weights are related to product manufacturing characteristics and model. Rail vehicle assembly accounts for about 50% of the production cycle, and the level of process layout directly affects the production efficiency. Therefore, this paper proposes the study on the process layout evaluation of rail vehicle assembly workshop in the lean intelligent manufacturing environment.

2 The Process Layout Evaluation Indicators of Rail Vehicle Assembly Workshop

2.1 The Analysis of Process Layout Characteristics of Rail Vehicle Assembly Workshop

Rail vehicles develop rapidly with diversified and individualized demands, require lean production and intelligent manufacturing. Combining with the characteristics of rail vehicle assembly, the workshop process layout must have the following main features:

(1) Meeting the production capacity requirements, and at the same time having the ability to meet the change of variety and quantity of products.
(2) Meeting the requirements of process flow, and making the material handling convenient.
(3) Making full use of equipment and space.
(4) Production is as balanced as possible, otherwise production and logistics are difficult to control.
(5) Improving the automation and intelligence of equipment.
(6) Fully considering the safety of workers and making the operation convenient and comfortable.

2.2 The Process Layout Evaluation Indicators

Combining with the opinions of experts, this paper has established 4 first-level indicators, namely: layout efficiency, layout economy, layout advancement and humanization. Then combining with the process layout features of rail vehicle assembly, an evaluation indicator system including 13 second-level indicators and 26 third-level indicators has established, as shown in Table 1.

Evaluation indicators are divided into 11 qualitative indicators and 15 quantitative indicators. Smoothness of logistics route, frequency of material handling, automation and intelligence of equipment, product flexibility, yield flexibility, promotion effect, safety, human-machine relationship and working environment are qualitative indicators. Others are quantitative indicators.

Table 1. The process layout evaluation indicators of rail vehicle assembly workshop

Layout efficiency	Logistics efficiency	Approach rate of close units
		Cross and return rate
		Carrying rate of long-distance
		Smoothness of logistics route
		Frequency of material handling
	Assembly efficiency	Assembly cycle
		Production capacity
Layout economy	Equipment utilization	Assembly equipment utilization
		Handling equipment utilization
		Storage equipment utilization
	Space utilization	Space utilization
	Balance	Production balance rate
	Equipment universality	Assembly equipment universality
		Handling equipment universality
		Storage equipment universality
	Adjust cost	Adjust cost
Layout advancement	Automation and intelligence	Automation and intelligence of assembly equipment
		Automation and intelligence of handling equipment
		Automation and intelligence of storage equipment
	Assembly flexibility	Product flexibility
		Yield flexibility
	Layout appearance	Setting rate
		Promotion effect
Layout humanization	Safety	Safety
	Human-machine relationship	Human-machine relationship
	Working environment	Sanitation, noise, lighting, etc.

3 The Weight Calculation Method of Process Layout Evaluation Indicators

3.1 Using Group AHP to Calculate First and Second-Level Indicator Weights

The procedure by which group AHP calculates weights is as follows:

Step1: establishing expert judgment matrix.

l Experts separately compare the n indicators one by one and build a judgment matrix $A_k(k = 1, 2, \ldots l)$, $A_k = \left(a_{ij}^k\right)_{n \times n}$, a_{ij}^k takes 1–9 and its countdown [8], $a_{ji}^k = 1/a_{ij}^k$, $a_{ii}^k = 1$, $i = 1, 2, \ldots n, j = 1, 2, \ldots n$.

Step2: Calculating indicator weights of each expert.

① Calculating the geometric mean of elements in each line in expert judgment matrix.

$$\omega_i^{(k)} = \sqrt[n]{\prod_{j=1}^{n} a_{ij}^k} \tag{1}$$

② Normalizing $\omega_i^{(k)}$:

$$w_i^{(k)} = \frac{\omega_i^{(k)}}{\sum_{i=1}^{n} \omega_i^{(k)}} \tag{2}$$

Here, $w_i^{(k)}$ is the weight of i indicator in judgment matrix A_k.

Step3: verifying and modifying the judgment matrix consistency.

Each expert's judgment matrix must be verified. The formula for consistency verification is as follows:

$$A_k W_k = \lambda_{\max} W_k \tag{3}$$

$$C.I. = \frac{\lambda_{\max} - n}{n - 1} \tag{4}$$

$$C.R. = \frac{C.I.}{R.I.} \tag{5}$$

Here, W_k is the weight vector corresponding to A_k, $\lambda_{\max}$ is the maximum eigenvalue of A_k. $C.I.$ is the consistency value. $R.I.$ is the average random consistency value, it can be found in related literature [9]. When $C.R.$ is less than 0.1, the judgment matrix is considered to be consistent, otherwise, it needs to be adjusted, and then be verified again.

Step4: Calculating expert weights λ_k^*.

Using $C.R.$ to calculate expert weights [10]. The method has a simple idea, a small amount of calculation, and has a strong practicality.

$$\lambda_k = \frac{1}{1 + \alpha C.R._K} \alpha > 0, k = 1, 2, \ldots, m \tag{6}$$

Normalizing λ_k to λ_k^*. α plays the role of a regulator. In practical applications, it is generally taken a = 10.

Step5: Calculating indicator weights w_i.

$$w_i = \sum_{k=1}^{m} w_i^{(k)} \lambda_k^* \tag{7}$$

So, $W_F = (w_1, w_2 \ldots w_n)$. Here, W_F is weight vector.

3.2 Using Group AHP and Entropy Weight Method to Calculate Three-Level Indicator Weights

The procedure for calculating objective weights using entropy weight method is as follows:

Step1: Constructing the original evaluation matrix X.

$X = (x_{ij})_{nm}(i = 1, 2, \ldots n, j = 1, 2, \ldots m)$. x_{ij} represents the value of indicator i of workshop. j.

Step2: Data standardization.

Standardizing $X = (x_{ij})_{nm}$ to $R = (r_{ij})_{nm}$, $r_{ij} \in [0, 1]$. The standardization method is shown in formula (8) and (9).

When the indicator is a positive indicator, the standardization formula is:

$$r_{ij} = \frac{x_{ij} - \min x_{ij}}{\max x_{ij} - \min x_{ij}} \tag{8}$$

When the indicator is the inverse indicator, the standardization formula is:

$$r_{ij} = \frac{\max x_{ij} - x_{ij}}{\max x_{ij} - \min x_{ij}} \tag{9}$$

Step3: Calculating entropy value H_i of indicators.

$$H_i = -\frac{1}{\ln n} \sum_{j=1}^{m} f_{ij} \ln f_{ij} \tag{10}$$

$f_{ij} = r_{ij} / \sum_{j=1}^{m} r_{ij}$, when $f_{ij} = 0$, $f_{ij} \ln f_{ij} = 0$.

Step4: Calculating entropy weight w_i of indicators.

$$w_i = \frac{1 - H_i}{n - \sum_{i=1}^{n} H_i} \tag{11}$$

So, $W_E = (w_1, w_2 \ldots w_i)$. Here, W_E is Entropy weight vector.

For the third-level indicators, considering W_F and W_E comprehensively. The formula for calculating the comprehensive weights of the third-level indicators is as follows:

$$W = tW_F + (1 - t)W_E \tag{12}$$

4 Workshop Process Layout Evaluation Based on Grey Relational Analysis

Step1: calculating comparison sequence and reference sequence.

There are m workshops to be evaluated, and there are n evaluation indicators. The comparison sequence is $X_{ij} = \{x_{ij} | i = 1, 2, \ldots n; j = 1, 2, \ldots, m\}$, The reference sequence is $X^* = [x_1^*, x_2^* \ldots x_n^*]^T$. x_i^* is the optimal value of indicator i, it is also the ideal value. Constructing the original evaluation matrix D.

$$D = \begin{bmatrix} x_1^* & x_{11} & x_{12} & \cdots & x_{1m} \\ x_2^* & x_{21} & x_{22} & \cdots & x_{2m} \\ \vdots & \vdots & \vdots & & \vdots \\ x_n^* & x_{n1} & x_{n2} & \cdots & x_{nm} \end{bmatrix} \tag{13}$$

Step2: Non-dimensional treatment for indicators.

The method of Non-dimensional treatment for indicators is initialization transformation. After Non-dimensional treatment, matrix D becomes matrix S.

$$S = \begin{bmatrix} 1 & S_{11} & S_{12} & \cdots & S_{1m} \\ 1 & S_{21} & S_{22} & \cdots & S_{2m} \\ \vdots & \vdots & \vdots & & \vdots \\ 1 & S_{n1} & S_{n2} & \cdots & S_{nm} \end{bmatrix} \tag{14}$$

Step3: Calculating grey correlation coefficient.

$$\xi_i^j = \frac{\min\limits_{i} \min\limits_{j} |1 - s_{ij}| + \rho \max\limits_{i} \max\limits_{j} |1 - s_{ij}|}{|1 - s_{ij}| + \rho \max\limits_{i} \max\limits_{j} |1 - s_{ij}|} \tag{15}$$

ρ is the distinguish coefficient, $\rho \in [0, 1]$, here $\rho = 0.5$.
Step4: Calculating grey correlation.

$$P_j = \sum_{i=1}^{n} W_i \xi_i^j \tag{16}$$

Table 2. Workshop process layout evaluation criteria and description

Gray correlation	Process layout level	Description
0.3–0.5	Level IV	Low level, it need to be renovated
0.5–0.7	Level III	Medium level, it need to be improved
0.7–0.9	Level II	High level, it can be improved
0.9–1	Level I	Higher level, it should be kept

Here, W_i is the three-level indicator weight determined by group AHP and entropy weight method.

Step5: Evaluation result analysis.

Dividing workshop process layout into four levels: low, medium, high, and higher. Evaluation criteria and description are shown in Table 2.

5 The Evaluation Case

In order to illustrate the scientificity of the evaluation indicator system and the practicality of the evaluation method, three typical urban rail vehicle assembly workshops of CRRC are evaluated, they are E_1, E_2 and E_3. The evaluation procedure is as follows:

Step1: Using group AHP to calculate weights of all indicators.

Using four first-level indicators as an example to illustrate the procedure of weight calculation. Selecting three experts from three evaluated workshops to make group decision. The three experts' judgment matrixes are:

$$A_1 = \begin{bmatrix} 1 & 2 & 3 & 4 \\ \frac{1}{2} & 1 & 3 & 3 \\ \frac{1}{3} & \frac{1}{3} & 1 & 3 \\ \frac{1}{4} & \frac{1}{3} & \frac{1}{3} & 1 \end{bmatrix} A_2 = \begin{bmatrix} 1 & 1 & 3 & 5 \\ 1 & 1 & 2 & 2 \\ \frac{1}{3} & \frac{1}{2} & 1 & 4 \\ \frac{1}{5} & \frac{1}{2} & \frac{1}{4} & 1 \end{bmatrix} A_3 = \begin{bmatrix} 1 & 3 & 4 & 5 \\ \frac{1}{3} & 1 & 4 & 5 \\ \frac{1}{4} & \frac{1}{4} & 1 & 2 \\ \frac{1}{5} & \frac{1}{5} & \frac{1}{2} & 1 \end{bmatrix}$$

According to formula (1) and (2), the weights of experts on the first-level indicators are calculated as: $w_i^1 = (0.4580, 0.3014, 0.1565, 0.0841)$, $w_i^2 = (0.4204, 0.3021, 0.1925, 0.085)$, $w_i^3 = (0.5196, 0.2992, 0.111, 0.0702)$.

According to formula (3), (4) and (5), $C.R.1 = 0.0564$, $C.R.2 = 0.0876$ and $C.R.3 = 0.067$. They are all less than 0.1, so A_1, A_2 and A_3 have satisfactory consistency.

According to formula (6), $\lambda_1 = 0.6394$, $\lambda_2 = 0.533$, $\lambda_3 = 0.5988$. Normalizing λ_k to λ_k^*, $\lambda_1^* = 0.361$, $\lambda_2^* = 0.301$, $\lambda_3^* = 0.338$. According to formula (7), the weights of the first-level indicators are: $(w_1, w_2, w_3, w_4) = (0.468, 0.3, 0.152, 0.08)$.

The weight of logistics efficiency is 0.452, the weight of assembly efficiency is 0.548. Limited by space, this article lists the third-level indicator weights under the layout efficiency, as shown in Table 3.

Table 3. The weights of partial evaluation indicators

Third-level indicators	Weights (AHP)	Weights (Entropy)	Comprehensive weights
Approach rate of close units	0.232	0.373	0.303
Cross and return rate	0.339	0.150	0.245
Carrying rate of long-distance	0.162	0.176	0.169
Smoothness of logistics route	0.157	0.145	0.151
Frequency of material handling	0.110	0.156	0.133
Assembly cycle	0.5	0.474	0.487
Production capacity	0.5	0.526	0.513

Step2: Using entropy weight method to calculate weights of three-level indicators.

The calculation of the entropy weight is illustrated by five three-level indicators of logistics efficiency. The calculation methods of other three-level indicators are similar.

The original evaluation matrix for the five indicators is: $\begin{bmatrix} 90\% & 80\% & 80\% \\ 20\% & 25\% & 32\% \\ 15\% & 22\% & 26\% \\ 95 & 90 & 80 \\ 90 & 85 & 80 \end{bmatrix}$.

The original evaluation matrix is standardized according to formula (8) and (9). The matrix after standardization is: $R = \begin{bmatrix} 1 & 0 & 0 \\ 1 & 0.583 & 0 \\ 1 & 0.364 & 0 \\ 1 & 0.667 & 0 \\ 1 & 0.5 & 0 \end{bmatrix}$.

Calculating entropy weights according to formula (10) and (11). The calculation results are shown in Table 3.

Step3: Calculating comprehensive weights of three-level indicators.

Calculating comprehensive weights of three-level indicators according to formula (12), t = 0.5. The calculation results for the five indicators are shown in Table 3.

Step4: Calculating grey correlation of indicators.

Taking the calculation of grey correlation of logistics efficiency as an example to illustrate the calculation procedure. The original evaluation matrix consisting of comparison and reference sequences is: $D = \begin{bmatrix} 90\% & 90\% & 80\% & 80\% \\ 15\% & 20\% & 25\% & 32\% \\ 10\% & 15\% & 22\% & 26\% \\ 95 & 95 & 90 & 80 \\ 95 & 90 & 85 & 80 \end{bmatrix}$.

According to formula (14) and (15), the grey correlation coefficient for the five indicators of the three workshops is: $\xi =$

$$\begin{bmatrix} 1 & 0.7347 & 0.7347 \\ 0.5517 & 0.4348 & 0.3668 \\ 0.48 & 0.3606 & 0.3333 \\ 1 & 0.854 & 0.6609 \\ 0.854 & 0.745 & 0.6609 \end{bmatrix}.$$

Using the comprehensive weights of Table 3, the grey correlation of the three workshops' logistics efficiency is calculated according to formula (16). $P = (0.7839, 0.6181, 0.5565)$.

According to the weights and the grey correlation of first-level indicators, the grey correlation degree of the layout level of the three workshops are calculated: $P_j =$

$$[0.468 \quad 0.3 \quad 0.152 \quad 0.08] \times \begin{bmatrix} 0.8417 & 0.5973 & 0.5084 \\ 0.8622 & 0.7327 & 0.7096 \\ 0.8471 & 0.5712 & 0.6451 \\ 1.0000 & 0.6137 & 0.8638 \end{bmatrix} =$$

$[0.8613 \quad 0.6353 \quad 0.618]$. The grey correlation of E_1 is 0.86136, E_2 is 0.6353, E_3 is 0.618.

Step5: Analysis of evaluation results.

According to the evaluation criteria of Table 2 and the gray correlation of the three workshops, the sequence of workshop process layout is obtained, as shown in Table 4.

Table 4. The evaluation results of workshop layout of the three workshops

Workshops	Gray correlation	Grade	Sequence
E_1	0.8613	level II	1
E_2	0.6353	level III	2
E_3	0.618	level III	3

According to the evaluation results, we can see: E_1 has the highest level of process layout and is at level II, but it can be further improved. E_2 and E_3 are at level III, so they need to be further improved.

The process layout level of E_2 is slightly better than E_3, but comparing with E_1, E_2 and E_3 are significantly lower. The evaluation results are consistent with the actual situation of the enterprises, indicating that the evaluation indicator system and the evaluation method proposed in this paper are reasonable and reliable, and can be used to guide enterprises to implement lean production and intelligent manufacturing.

6 Conclusion

A good workshop process layout is the basis and key to the successful implementation of lean production and intelligent manufacturing in rail transportation equipment manufacturing. A scientific and reasonable workshop layout evaluation system can help enterprises better grasp the level of their own process layout, identify problems timely, and thus make targeted improvements.

The characteristics of the process layout of rail vehicle assembly workshop are analyzed, based on which, the evaluation indicator system for the process layout of rail vehicle assembly workshop is established. The weight calculation method is more scientific by using group AHP and entropy weight method. The level of workshop process layout can be evaluated scientifically by grey relational analysis method which calculates gray correlation between the current state and ideal state of each indicator. The evaluation case shows that the evaluation method is reasonable and reliable.

Acknowledgments. This work was supported by the Guidance Program for Natural Science Foundation of Liaoning (No. 20170540138).

References

1. Wang, W.L., Kang, Y.F.: Importance of process technology in smart machining line design and running controlling. Aeronaut. Manuf. Technol. **511**, 48–51 (2016)
2. Yang, T., Kuo, C.: A hierarchical AHP/DEA methodology for the facilities layout design problem. Eur. J. Oper. Res. **147**, 128–136 (2003)
3. Li, C.L., Li, C.G., Mok, A.C.K.: Automatic layout design of plastic injection mould cooling system. Comput. Aided Des. **37**, 645–662 (2005)
4. Yang, L., Deuse, J.: Multiple-attribute decision making for an energy efficient facility layout design. Procedia CIRP **66**, 795–807 (2013)
5. Zhang, N.: Research of the Evaluation of Workshop Facilities Layout Plans Based on Grey TOPSIS for Multi-variety and Small-batch Production. Chongqing University, Chongqing (2014)
6. Azadeh, A., Nazari, T., Charkhand, H.: Optimisation of facility layout design problem with safety and environmental factors by stochastic DEA and simulation approach. Int. J. Prod. Res. **53**, 3370–3389 (2015)
7. Bozorgi, N., Abedzadeh, M., Zeinali, M.: Tabu search heuristic for efficiency of dynamic facility layout problem. Int. J. Adv. Manuf. Technol. **77**, 689–703 (2015)
8. Wang, Y.L.: System Engineering. Version 5. Machinery Industry Press, Beijing (2015)
9. Mi, T.F., Tian, J.P., Yang, H.L.: Research on machine equipment selection based on fuzzy comprehensive evaluation. In: Combined Machine Tool and Auto-machining Technology, pp. 109–112 (2012)
10. Jiang, W.N.: The ideas and methods of determining experts' weight in group decision. In: Statistics and Decision, pp. 18–24 (2013)

Network Sharing Based Two-Tier Vehicle Routing Optimization of Urban Joint Distribution Under Online Shopping

Longxiao Li[1], Xu Wang[1,2(✉)], Yun Lin[1,2], Kaipeng Liu[3],
and Yingjia Tang[1]

[1] Chongqing University, Shapingba District, Chongqing 400044, China
LongxiaoLi@cqu.edu.cn, wx921@163.com
[2] State Key Laboratory of Mechanical Transmission,
Shapingba District, Chongqing 400044, China
[3] Changan Minsheng APLL Logistics Co., Ltd.,
Yubei District, Chongqing 401122, China

Abstract. The rapid development of online shopping offers new opportunities to the express delivery industry, but also brings enormous challenges due to its characteristics of multi-frequency and small-batch distribution. And the lack of cooperation among express companies in the urban distribution has resulted in uneconomical distribution. In the context of the sharing economy, this paper attempts to solve this problem by implementing joint distribution strategy with sharing the network resources. Based on the customer's time window of receipt, a two-tier vehicle routing optimization model of urban joint distribution considering transfer stations' sharing is established, and a hybrid heuristic algorithm has been designed accordingly. The results of a case study show significant optimization effect by comparing the independent distribution and joint distribution as well as robustness of the designed algorithm.

Keywords: Network sharing · Two-tier vehicle routing optimization
Urban joint distribution · Hybrid heuristic algorithm

1 Introduction

The rapid development of E-commerce has boomed the prosperity of online shopping, plenty of opportunities have been created for the express delivery industry [1]. While enormous challenges have also been brought due to multi-frequency and small-batch distribution of online shopping distribution. Express companies try to optimize their own distribution network to achieve internal optimization under the mode of independent distribution. However, from the point of view of the entire urban distribution, the system is not optimal. With the rapid increase of less-efficient and small-package flows in the urban distribution originating from online shopping, some negative externalities issues are also becoming prominent such as traffic congestion, logistic resource waste and environmental pollution [2]. And more higher standards service as well as sustainability management have been required by the end-customers [3].

© Springer Nature Singapore Pte Ltd. 2018
S. Wang et al. (Eds.): ICSEE 2018/IMIOT 2018, CCIS 923, pp. 131–145, 2018.
https://doi.org/10.1007/978-981-13-2396-6_12

Under this circumstance, establishing a joint distribution alliance by integrating idle resources owned by different express companies is essential for the entire logistics services market. A joint operational plan will enable the companies to achieve a larger profit and become more environmentally friendly [4]. And cooperation between different logistics service providers has risen an effective way to reduce cost and improve service quality [5]. In the context of the sharing economy, this paper attempts to solve problems faced by express companies by implementing joint distribution strategy considering the transfer stations' sharing. While how to optimize the two-tier vehicle routing under the framework of urban joint distribution is an important issue. According to the classification of vehicle types, number of distribution centers, distribution tasks, time windows, there exist extensive research on vehicle routing problems. Aghezzaf et al. formulated the single-vehicle cyclic inventory routing problem as a mixed-integer program with a nonlinear objective function and proposed the corresponding algorithm for its solution. Kovacs et al. set several objective functions including driver consistency improvement, arrival time consistency and routing cost minimization to extend the generalized consistent vehicle routing problem to balance routing cost and service consistency [6]. Spliet et al. viewed the discrete time window assignment vehicle routing problem as a two-stage stochastic optimization problem and develop an exact branch-price-and-cut algorithm to solve it and achieve the objective of minimum expected total transportation cost [7]. Xiao et al. studied a green vehicle routing and scheduling problem by taking general time-dependent traffic conditions and weighted tardiness into consideration. Zhao et al. focused on optimization of two-echelon capacitated location-routing problem for joint distribution in urban logistics to reasonably set the intermediate depots and minimize the total costs [8]. Therefore, vehicle routing problem (VRP) is a multi-objective and multi constraint combinatorial optimization problem, which makes it NP-hard. And, the solution methods can be divided into exact algorithm and heuristic algorithm. Defryn et al. solve the clustered vehicle routing problem by proposing an improved two-level variable neighborhood search algorithm in which customers are grouped into pre-defined clusters, and all customers in the cluster must be continuously served by the same vehicle [9]. Yu et al. sought the solution of hybrid vehicle routing problem by developing a simulated annealing heuristic algorithm with a restart strategy [10]. And, Kalayci et al. designed an ant colony system empowered variable neighborhood search algorithm to find the solution of vehicle routing problem considering simultaneous pickup and delivery [11].

According to the previous research, some beneficial references and research directions can be provided for us to seek the solution of the VRP of urban joint distribution. While it can be seen from above that the background of online shopping is less involved in the existing studies. And they are mainly focused on the VRP optimization of urban joint distribution arising in the "last mile". Moreover, most of the research are concentrated on the VRP optimization of joint distribution under the premise of co-constructing distribution centers. Therefore, vehicle routing optimization of urban joint distribution under online shopping remains to be further studied. Moreover, the existing networks will be mainly considered and consider its sharing among the express companies. The remainder of this paper is organized as follows. Section 2 displays problem description, notations and quantitative model. Section 3 proposed the hybrid heuristic algorithm and its operation for two-tier vehicle routing problem of urban joint distribution. A case study is conducted to validate the proposed model and designed algorithm in Sect. 4. Conclusions are put forward in Sect. 5.

2   Problem Formulation

2.1   Problem Description

Given the location of distribution center and transfer station of each express company, the location and demand of end-customers, and the vehicle parameters of each distribution center and transfer station, the two-tier VRP considering transfer station sharing can be described as shown in Fig. 1.

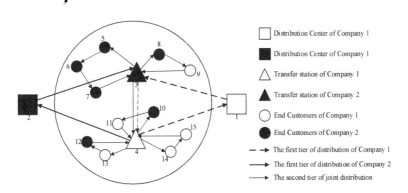

Fig. 1. The second tier of joint distribution considering transfer station sharing

Combined with the actual situation, this paper makes the following assumptions:

- The vehicle capacity of various networks at all tiers can meet the demand for distribution.
- The types of goods delivered by different companies are roughly the same and can be mixed. And the types of vehicles required at the same tier are roughly the same and can be regarded as the same type.
- The time of entire distribution process is limited to half a day.
- The dynamic changes and emergencies of road conditions are not taken into account.

Based on the assumptions, several constraints including vehicle constraint, network facility constraint and time window constraint need to be considered in the practical operation.

This paper explores the VRP optimization model based on the fixed distribution network, and the goal is to complete the distribution task with the minimum cost. As a result, this paper only considers the costs associated with the VRP as the optimization goal, covering fixed cost of vehicle, variable cost of vehicle and penalty cost.

2.2   Notations

The notations and description are listed in the following Table 1.

Based on the problem formulation and parameter notation, the corresponding mathematical model is established.

$$\min F = \sum_{d \in N_D} \sum_{j \in N_S} \sum_{k \in K_d} f_1 x_{djk} + \sum_{s \in N_S} \sum_{j \in N_C} \sum_{k \in K_s} f_2 y_{sjk} + \sum_{i \in N_1} \sum_{j \in N_1} \sum_{k \in K_d} \sum_{d \in N_D} c_1 d_{ij} x_{ijk}$$
$$+ \sum_{i \in N_2} \sum_{j \in N_2} \sum_{k \in K_s} \sum_{s \in N_S} c_2 d_{ij} y_{ijk} + c_e \sum_{i \in N_C} \{\max(a_i - t_i, 0)\} + c_l \sum_{i \in N_C} \{\max(t_i - b_i, 0)\} \quad (1)$$
$$+ M \sum_{i \in N_C} \{\max(e_i - t_i, 0)\} + M \sum_{i \in N_C} \{\max(t_i - l_i, 0)\}$$

$$\sum_{i \in N_1} \sum_{k \in K_d} x_{ijk} \le 1, \forall j \in N_S, d \in N_D \tag{2}$$

$$\sum_{j \in N_1} \sum_{k \in K_d} x_{ijk} \le 1, \forall i \in N_S, d \in N_D \tag{3}$$

$$\sum_{i \in N_1} \sum_{k \in K_d} x_{ijk} = \sum_{i \in N_1} \sum_{k \in K_d} x_{jik}, \forall j \in N_1, d \in N_D \tag{4}$$

$$\sum_{d \in N_D} \sum_{i \in N_1} \sum_{k \in K_d} x_{ijk} \ge 1, \forall j \in N_S \tag{5}$$

$$\sum_{i \in N_S} x_{dik} = \sum_{i \in N_S} x_{idk} \le 1, \forall k \in K_d, d \in N_D \tag{6}$$

$$u_{djk} = \sum_{s \in N_S} p_s z_{sk} \le Q_1, \forall d \in N_D, j \in N_S, k \in K_d \tag{7}$$

$$\sum_{d \in N_D} \sum_{k \in K_d} u_{jsk} - \sum_{d \in N_D} \sum_{k \in K_d} u_{sjk} = P_s, \forall j \in N_1, s \in N_S \tag{8}$$

$$t_d = u_d = 0, \forall d \in N_D \tag{9}$$

$$t_j = (t_i + u_i + d_{ij}/v_1) x_{ijk}, \forall i \in N_1, j \in N_S, d \in N_D, k \in K_d \tag{10}$$

$$0 < t_i \le T_1, \forall i \in N_S \tag{11}$$

$$P_s = \sum_{i \in N_C} p_i h_{is} \le C_s, \forall s \in N_S \tag{12}$$

$$\sum_{s \in N_S} \sum_{i \in N_2} \sum_{k \in K_s} y_{ijk} = 1, \forall j \in N_C \tag{13}$$

Table 1. Notations and description

Sets	Description
N_D	Set of the distribution center, $N_D = \{1, 2, \cdots m\}$
N_S	Set of the transfer station, $N_S = \{m+1, m+2, \cdots, m+r\}$
N_C	Set of the transfer station, $N_C = \{m+r+1, m+r+2, \cdots, m+r+n\}$
N	Sets of distribution network nodes, $N = N_D \cup N_S \cup N_C$
N_1	Sets of distribution nodes in the first tier, $N_1 = N_D \cup N_S$
N_2	Sets of distribution nodes in the second tier, $N_2 = N_S \cup N_C$
k_d	Sets of vehicle where distribution center $d \in N_D$, $K_d = \{1, 2 \cdots, k_d\}$
k_s	Sets of vehicle where transfer station $s \in N_S$, $K_s = \{1, 2, \cdots, k_s\}$
Parameters	**Description**
d_{ij}	Distance between node $i \in N$ and node $j \in N$
c_1	Distribution cost of unit distance in the first tier
c_2	Distribution cost of unit distance in the second tier
c_e	Penalty cost of unit waiting time
c_l	Penalty cost of unit delay time
M	Infinite positive integer
f_1	The fixed departure cost of the vehicle in the first tier
f_2	The fixed departure cost of the vehicle in the second tier
Q_1	The maximum capacity of the vehicle in the first tier
Q_2	The maximum capacity of the vehicle in the second tier
v_1	The average speed of the vehicle in the first tier
v_2	The average speed of the vehicle in the second tier
C_s	Capacity of the transfer station $s \in N_S$
p_s	Demand of the transfer station $s \in N_S$
p_i	Demand of the end-customer $i \in N_C$
t_i	The time the vehicle arrives at node $i \in N$
u_i	The time the vehicle stays at node $i \in N$
u_o^i	Delivery processing time of the vehicle at the node $i \in N$
t_{ij}	Vehicle travel time from node $i \in N$ to node $j \in N$
w_i	The waiting time of vehicle at end-customer $i \in N_C$
T_1	Deadline for delivery of the shipment to the transfer station
H	Average sorting time of delivery at transfer station
T_2	Deadline for completion of second-tiered delivery
$[a_i, b_i]$	Time window of end-customer $i \in N_C$
$[e_i, l_i]$	Tolerable delivery time range of end-customer $i \in N_C$
Intermediate variables	**Description**
u_{ijk}	Loading of the vehicle $k \in K_d \cup K_s$ between node $i \in N$ and node $j \in N$

(continued)

Table 1. (*continued*)

Sets	Description
Decision variables	Description
x_{ijk}	When the vehicle $k \in K_d$ reaches the node $j \in N_1$ from node $i \in N_1$, it is equal to 1, otherwise it is 0
y_{ijk}	When the vehicle $k \in K_s$ reaches the node $j \in N_2$ from node $i \in N_2$, it is equal to 1, otherwise it is 0
h_{is}	When the transfer station $s \in N_S$ serves the end-customer $i \in N_C$, it is equal to 1, otherwise it is 0
z_{sk}	When the vehicle $k \in K_d$ serves the transfer station $s \in N_S$, it is equal to 1, otherwise it is 0
z_{ik}	When the vehicle $k \in K_s$ serves the end-customer $i \in N_C$, it is equal to 1, otherwise it is 0

$$\sum_{s \in N_S} \sum_{j \in N_2} \sum_{k \in K_s} y_{ijk} = 1, \forall i \in N_C \tag{14}$$

$$\sum_{s \in N_S} h_{is} = 1, \forall i \in N_C \tag{15}$$

$$\sum_{i \in N_2} \sum_{k \in K_s} y_{ijk} = \sum_{i \in N_2} \sum_{k \in K_s} y_{jik}, \forall s \in N_S, j \in N_2 \tag{16}$$

$$\sum_{i \in N_C} y_{sik} = \sum_{i \in N_C} y_{isk} \leq 1, \forall s \in N_S, k \in K_s \tag{17}$$

$$u_{sjk} = \sum_{i \in N_C} p_i z_{ik} h_{is} \leq Q_2, \forall j \in N_C, s \in N_S, k \in K_s \tag{18}$$

$$u_{ijk} - u_{jik} = p_j, \forall j \in N_C, i \in N_2, k \in K_s \tag{19}$$

$$t_s = T_1 + H, \forall s \in N_S \tag{20}$$

$$t_j = (t_i + u_i + w_i + d_{ij}/v_2)y_{ijk}, \forall i \in N_2, j \in N_C, k \in K_s \tag{21}$$

$$u_i = u_o^i p_i, \forall i \in N_S \cup N_C \tag{22}$$

$$w_i = \max\{0, a_i - t_i\}, \forall i \in N_C \tag{23}$$

$$T_1 + H < t_i < T_2, \forall i \in N_C \tag{24}$$

$$x_{ijk} = \{0, 1\}, \forall i \in N_1, j \in N_1, k \in K_d \tag{25}$$

$$y_{ijk} = \{0, 1\}, \forall i \in N_2, j \in N_2, k \in K_s \tag{26}$$

$$h_{is} = \{0, 1\}, \forall i \in N_C, s \in N_S \tag{27}$$

$$z_{sk} = \{0, 1\}, \forall s \in N_S, k \in K_d \tag{28}$$

$$z_{ik} = \{0, 1\}, \forall i \in N_C, k \in K_s \tag{29}$$

The objective (1) aims to minimize the total cost, consisting of the fixed cost of departure in both tiers, variable cost of vehicle in both tiers, penalty cost of the end-customer's time window, penalty cost arising from exceeding the maximum acceptable delivery time. Constraints (2)–(11) are related to the distribution of vehicle in the first tier. Among them, constraints (2) and (3) make sure that vehicles from any distribution center can visit the transfer station at most once. Constraint (4) indicates the flow balance of vehicles at any node in the first tier. Constraint (5) represents that any transfer station needs to be visited by the vehicles. Constraint (6) shows that each vehicle at any distribution center performs the distribution task at most once. Constraint (7) guarantees that the total capacity of distribution of any vehicle at the transfer station cannot exceed its maximum load. Constraint (8) is flow constraint for demand of the transfer station. Constraint (9) the requirement for the vehicle's departure time and residence time. Constraint (10) implies the time relation between vehicles reaching two adjacent nodes. Constraint (11) is the time constraint of vehicles arriving at any transfer station. Constraint (12) is the flow balance constraint between two-tiered routings. Constraints (13)–(23) are related to the distribution of vehicle in the second tier. Constraints (13) and (14) restrain that any end-customer can be served by only one vehicle. Constraint (15) means that any end-customer can only be served by one transfer station. Constraint (16) is the flow constraint. Constraint (17) specifies that each vehicle at any transfer station performs the distribution task at most once. Constraint (18) ensures that the total capacity of end-customer's demand cannot exceed the maximum load of the vehicle. Constraint (19) indicates that the difference of the load capacity is equal to the end-customer's demand. Constraint (20) is the departure time of the vehicle from the transfer station. Constraint (21) implies the time relation between vehicles reaching two adjacent end-customers. Constraint (22) shows the relation between the residence time of the vehicle at the node and the delivery capacity. Constraint (23) sets the waiting time of the vehicle at the end-customer. Constraint (24) represents the time vehicle reaching the end-customer. Constraints (25)–(29) are 0–1 constraints.

3 Hybrid Heuristic Algorithm for Two-Tier Vehicle Routing Problem

VRP with time-window constraint (VRPTW) has proven to be an NP hard problem. Adding a two-tier constraint into VRPTW makes it still NP-hard. To solve this problem, heuristic algorithm has been utilized widely such as genetic algorithm and particle swarm algorithm. Based on this, this paper adopts the C-W saving algorithm proposed by Clarke and Wright in 1964 [12]. The C-W algorithm has poor searching ability, and it is computationally intensive when solving large-scale problems. However, the saving algorithm will produce a feasible solution at the end of each iteration. Genetic algorithm has strong search capability, but tend to be "premature". Therefore, combining the advantages of the above two algorithms, a hybrid heuristic algorithm is designed in this paper. And the main steps of the algorithm are as follows:

Step1. Parameter settings: Initial population size M_0, Maximum generation I_{MAX}, Crossover probability p_c, Mutation probability p_m.

Step2. Preliminary allocation of end-customers.

Step3. Generate initial feasible routes with the number of $M_0 * p_f$ (p_f denotes the proportion of feasible initial solutions in the population) through the saving algorithm, and randomly generate initial routes with the number of $M_0 * (1 - p_f)$.

Step4. Generate initial routes with the number of M_0 according to the coding rules and generate the initial population p_0.

Step5. Fitness evaluation;

Step6. Select individuals for cross-operation with probability p_f.

Step7. Select the individuals for mutation operation with probability p_m.

Step8. Individual evaluation of the new population.

Step9. If it meets the termination condition, go to step 10, otherwise go to *step 5*.

Step10. Decode and output the optimal solution.

3.1   Initial Route Generation

The saving algorithm aims to solve the VRP with a single distribution center, and it is necessary to address the issue of end-customer allocation first, so that the multi-distribution center VRP can be transformed into a single distribution center VRP.

- End-customer allocation

In order to minimize the total distribution distance of the vehicle, this paper is based on the principle of distance to the nearest when assigning the transfer station to which the end-customer belongs. The specific allocation steps are as follows:

Step1. Calculate the distance from the end-customer to the transfer station.

Step2. Let M_n be the set of distances from the end-customer's nearest transfer station, for $i \in N_C$, $M_n = \{d_{in} | d_{in} = \min(d_{i1}, d_{i2}, \cdots, d_{is})\}$. If the transfer station $n \in N_S$ satisfies the capacity constraint, all corresponding end-customers i in M_n are assigned to the transfer station n; if not, select the end-customers corresponding to M_n in sequence from the nearest end-customers of other transfer stations and assign it to the nearest transfer station until the constraints is satisfied.

Step3. Other transfer stations perform end-customer assignment according to the principle of step 2 until all end-customers are assigned.

- Initial routing generation

The basic saving algorithm considers the constraint and the saving value to be relatively simple, combined with the actual situation, this paper try to improve the basic saving algorithm. The improved algorithm steps are as follows:

Step1. Calculate the savings $s(i,j)$ between end-customers where $s(i,j) = c_2(d_{0i} + d_{0j} - d_{ij}) + f_2 + pc_i + pc_j - pc_{ij} > 0$, let $G = \{s(i,j)|s(i,j) > 0\}$, and sort the elements in G in descending order.

Step2. Select the first element in G to determine whether i and j can meet one of the following conditions: (1) i and j are in the initial route; (2) i and j are in the initial route, one of which is in the non-initial route and are directly connected to the distribution center; (3) i and j are both in the non-initial route and both are directly connected to the distribution center. If any of the condition is satisfied, turn to *step 3*, otherwise, turn to *step 6*.

Step3. Determine whether the vehicle capacity constraint and the longest delivery time constraint are satisfied after connecting i and j. If it is satisfied, turn to *step 4*, otherwise turn to *step 6*.

Step4. Connect i and j, calculate the amount of time change Δt_j caused by the connection: (1) $\Delta t_j = 0$; (2) $\Delta t_j < 0, |\Delta t_j| \leq \Delta t_{j-}$; (3) $\Delta t_j > 0, |\Delta t_j| \leq \Delta t_{j+}$. If any of the condition is satisfied, turn to *step 5*, otherwise, turn to *step 6*.

Step5. Connect i and j, and calculate the time when the vehicle arrives at each end-customer on the route, and output the route.

Step6. Eliminate of the elements $s(i,j)$ in the set G. Besides, i and j can no longer be used as the starting and ending point of the vehicle, so $s(i,p)$ and $s(p,j)$ will be eliminated at the same time, and then turn to *step 2* for a new round of calculation until the number of initial feasible routes $M_0 * p_f$ is reached.

3.2   Searching the Optimal Solution with Genetic Operations

- Encoding rules

  On the basis of the characteristics of the problem, a two-tiered vector mapping real number coding method is adopted. The chromosome consists of two parts, which correspond to the first vehicle route and the second route respectively. For example, the encoding scheme corresponding to Fig. 1 is shown in Fig. 2 which indicates the first tier vehicle route is: 1-3-4-1, 2-3-4-2; the second tier vehicle route is: 3-5-6-7-3, 3-8-9-3, 4-10-11-4, 4-13-12-4, 4-14-15-4.

The first tier	1	3	4	2	3	4	2									
The second tier	3	5	6	7	0	8	9	4	10	11	0	13	12	0	14	15	4

Fig. 2. Chromosome coding scheme

- Population initialization

  The initial route is used to generate individuals with the number of M_0 according to coding rules, and the initial population p_0 is formed.

- Fitness evaluation

  Since the objective function is the minimization of the total cost, the fitness function is specified as $f'(i) = 1/f(i) + \delta$ where $f(i)$ is the objective function value. δ is a positive real number in the open interval (0,1) in case the denominator is zero and the randomness of the genetic algorithm is increased.

- Selection

  In this paper, the method of fitness proportion selection is adopted. The higher the individual fitness value is, the higher the probability of being selected. Let the population size is M_0 and the fitness value of individual i is $f'(i)$, then the probability that the individual is selected is $p_i = f'(i) / \sum_{i=1}^{M_0} f'(i)$

- Crossover operation

  There exist fewer vehicle route nodes in the first tier and they can be performed through mutation operation. As to the second tier, two-point crossover operation is performed on the chromosomal vector. Moreover, the partial mapping method has been adopted to eliminate the conflict situation where different gene loci values are generated in the crossover process. The cross-schematic diagram is shown in Fig. 3.

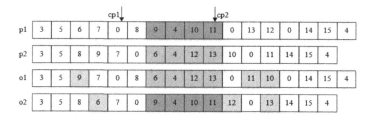

Fig. 3. Two-point crossover operation

- Mutation operation

  According to the characteristics of the two-tiered route, the mutation operation in the first tier is selecting a route randomly, selecting two non-distribution centers and non-virtual zero gene loci in the route, and exchanging the values of them. With respect to the second tier, select two non-transfer stations and non-virtual zero gene loci randomly and exchange the values.

- Individual evaluation

  The pros and cons of new individuals are evaluated by the objective function value.

- Optimal solution output

  The genetic operation stops when the maximum generation is reached. According to the evaluation of the current individual population, the optimal individual is selected as the optimal solution and output.

4   Case Study

A case study based on a real-world distribution network in Chongqing city is conducted to validate the hybrid heuristic algorithm in vehicle routing optimization.

4.1   Data Collection

In the real-world case, two express companies A and B in Nan'an District are selected, and they totally have 2 distribution centers, 6 transfer stations and 75 end-customers (including 51 terminal networks and 24 end-customer groups). According to the data provided by the companies, the information of the distribution center and the transfer station as well as the vehicles at each tier are shown in Tables 2 and 3.

Table 2. The information of distribution center and transfer station

Parameters	D1	D2	S1	S2	S3	S4	S5	S6
k_d/k_s	5	5	5	4	5	4	5	4
C_s	/	/	500	700	800	500	600	600

Table 3. The information of vehicle

Parameters	c_1	c_2	f_1	f_2	Q_1	Q_2	v_1	v_2
Distribution in the first tier	1.35	/	100	/	600	/	35	/
Distribution in the second tier	/	0.8	/	60	/	200	/	25

Given the above information, this paper sets the total distribution time to half a day, that is, 7:00 a.m. to 12:00 a.m. (0–300 min). The start time in the first tier of distribution is 7:00 a.m. (0 min), and the deadline is 9:10 a.m. (130 min), i.e. $T_1 = 130$ min, the average sorting time of express is 20 min, i.e. $H = 20$ minutes, the average speed of the vehicle is 35 km/h. The starting time in the second tier of distribution is $T_1 + H = 150$ min and the deadline is 12:00 a.m., i.e. $T_2 = 300$ min and the average speed is 25 km/h. In addition, the distribution time at the transfer station, terminal network and end-customer is 0.1 min, 0.3 min, and 1 min respectively. The penalty cost of unit waiting time is 30 Yuan/h, and of unit delay time is 40 Yuan/h. The acceptable distribution time range is 20 min in advance or 10 min delayed on the basis of the time window, i.e. $[e_i, l_i] = [a_i - 20, b_i + 10]$.

4.2   Solution Presentation

The algorithm proposed in Sect. 3 is compiled on the MATLAB R2011 and runs on a computer with Intel Core Dual CPU at 2.3 GHz and 4 GB RAM under Windows 7 OS. And the initial population size M_0 is set to 50, the initial feasible solution ratio p_f is 0.5, the maximum evolutionary generation I_{MAX} equals 100, the crossover probability p_c is 0.5, and the mutation probability p_m is 0.1.

According to the results obtained, the first-tier distribution route and the second-tier distribution route for express company A and B are shown in the following Figs. 4 and 5.

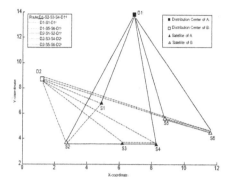

Fig. 4. The first-tier distribution route

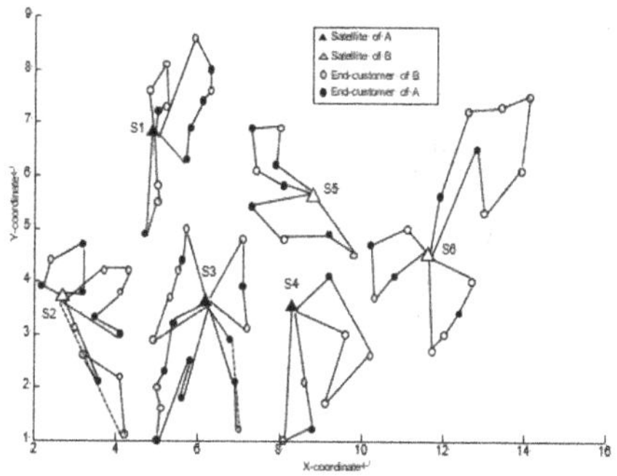

Fig. 5. The second-tier distribution route

4.3 Comparative Analysis

- Comparison of the optimization results

In order to illustrate the effect of optimization, the cost of the independent distribution has been compared with the optimized result as shown in the following Table 4.

Table 4. The comparison of two distribution modes

Comparison of items	Transfer station sharing	Non-transfer station sharing			Amplitude of change
		Comapny A	Comapny B	Total	
TC (Total cost)	2223.8	1499.6	1459	2958.6	−24.8%
$fc1$ (Vehicle cost of the first tier)	236.8	102.6	108	210.6	+12.4%
$fc2$ (Vehicle cost of the second tier)	246	235	186	421	−41.6%
$Fc1$ (Fixed departure cost of the first tier)	600	300	300	600	0%
$Fc2$ (Fixed departure cost of the second tier)	1020	600	600	1200	−15%
$Dt1$ (Travelling distance of the first tier)	175.4	76	80	156	+12.4%
$Dt2$ (Travelling distance of the second tier)	307.6	293.6	233.4	527	−41.6%
ALR (Average loading rate)	77%	71.4%	68.6%	70%	+10%

As can be seen from the above table, the total cost has decreased by 734.8 Yuan with a decrease ratio of 24.8%. Based on the proportional method, Company A can achieve 372.4 Yuan cost saving and Company B can achieve 362.4 Yuan. Among them, the fixed cost of vehicles is reduced by 180 Yuan with a ratio of 10%, the variable cost is reduced by 148.8 Yuan with a ratio of 23.6%, and the travelling distance is reduced by 201 km. More specifically, the sharing of the transfer stations results in an increase in the number of networks in the first tier, and the travelling distance as well as variable costs for the delivery increasing by 12.4%. With the joint distribution in the second tier, the number of vehicles is reduced by 3, the fixed cost is reduced by 15%, and the travelling distance and variable costs are reduced by 41.6%. The overall loading rate has increased by 10%. Moreover, under the independent distribution, there exists no subdivision of end-customer's requirement for delivery time in the second tier, and the distance is too long to meet the customer's timeliness requirements, and often results in secondary delivery. Therefore, the optimization results are obvious through the joint distribution of the two enterprise by sharing the transfer stations.

- Comparison of the algorithm performance

In order to analyze the performance of the proposed algorithm, this paper makes comparison with the standard genetic algorithm (SGA) as are shown in Figs. 6 and 7 respectively. By comparison, it can see that the proposed algorithm can converge faster and the solution quality is much higher.

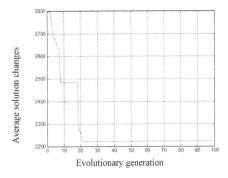

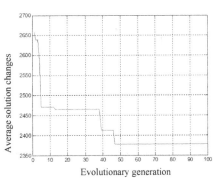

Fig. 6. The evolutionary process of the proposed algorithm

Fig. 7. The evolutionary process of the SGA

To further test the solution performance and stability of the algorithm, this paper run the two algorithms 15 times respectively, and the overall variance of the relevant indicators is estimated by the VAR. S function in excel according to the obtained data, and the average value of the relevant indicators is calculated as well. The statistical results are shown in Table 5.

Table 5. Stability comparison of two algorithms

Comparison of items	Average convergence generation	Variance of the convergence generation	Average optimal solution	Variance of the optimal solution	Solving average time (s)	Variance of the solving time
The proposed algorithm	26	43	2254	288	1.8	0.04
SGA	57	140	2340	1109	7.6	0.26

5 Conclusion

A network sharing based two-tier vehicle routing optimization model for the urban joint distribution under online shopping is constructed in this paper. And a two-stage hybrid heuristic algorithm is designed for approaching the model. To validate the proposed algorithm, a case study has been conducted through the distribution network's sharing of two express companies in Nan'an District, Chongqing City. The optimization results give the evidence that implementing the joint distribution strategy in the urban joint distribution contributes to reducing costs and vehicle usage. Besides, the case study of the two express companies show the effectiveness and robustness of the proposed algorithm. In addition, some implications can be drawn accordingly from the above analysis as well. As to the theoretical implications, it is important to consider the route optimization of the end distribution, that is, to rationally plan the distribution route from the transfer stations to the end customers and fully utilize the resources of the transfer station. For the practical implications, implementing the joint distribution strategy in the urban joint distribution is of great benefit to express companies in the context of sharing economy. The benefits that express companies can obtain are not limited to the economic, as can be seen from the above, the reduction of vehicles and the rational planning of the routes will reduce the carbon emissions in the distribution thus achieving environmental sustainability. Therefore, it is essential for the policy makers to formulate corresponding policies to encourage the development of sharing economy and facilitate the transfer stations' sharing to carry out a wider range of joint distribution among express companies.

We recognize that every study has its limitations, and this paper is no exception. In this paper, end-customers' demand and distribution route of the network are both considered to be static, however, with the randomness of the end-customers' demand and the continuous improvement of the service quality requirements, higher requirements are imposed on the flexibility of urban distribution. Therefore, it is worth considering the dynamic demands of end-customers and the dynamic changes of route network when optimizing the urban distribution route under online shopping.

Acknowledgement. This study was supported by the Fundamental Research Funds for the Central Universities Project (under Grant No. 106112017CDJXSYY001 and 106112015 CDJSK02JD05). We also appreciate the editor and the anonymous reviewers for their manuscript processing and remarkable comments.

References

1. Yu, Y., et al.: E-commerce logistics in supply chain management: practice perspective. Procedia CIRP **52**, 179–185 (2016)
2. Cherrett, T., et al.: Logistics impacts of student online shopping – evaluating delivery consolidation to halls of residence. Transp. Res. Part C Emerg. Technol. **78**, 111–128 (2017)
3. Adenso-Díaz, B., et al.: Assessing partnership savings in horizontal cooperation by planning linked deliveries. Transp. Res. Part A Policy Pract. **66**, 268–279 (2014)
4. Palhazi Cuervo, D., Vanovermeire, C., Sörensen, K.: Determining collaborative profits in coalitions formed by two partners with varying characteristics. Transp. Res. Part C Emerg. Technol. **70**, 171–184 (2016)
5. Vanovermeire, C., et al.: Horizontal logistics collaboration: decreasing costs through flexibility and an adequate cost allocation strategy. Int. J. Logistics Res. Appl. **17**(4), 339–355 (2014)
6. Kovacs, A.A., Parragh, S.N., Hartl, R.F.: The multi-objective generalized consistent vehicle routing problem. Eur. J. Oper. Res. **247**(2), 441–458 (2015)
7. Spliet, R., Desaulniers, G.: The discrete time window assignment vehicle routing problem. Eur. J. Oper. Res. **244**(2), 379–391 (2015)
8. Zhao, Q., Wang, W., De Souza, R.: A heterogeneous fleet two-echelon capacitated location-routing model for joint delivery arising in city logistics. Int. J. Prod. Res. **2**, 1–19 (2017)
9. Defryn, C., Sörensen, K.: A fast two-level variable neighborhood search for the clustered vehicle routing problem. Comput. Oper. Res. **83**, 78–94 (2017)
10. Yu, V.F., et al.: A simulated annealing heuristic for the hybrid vehicle routing problem. Appl. Soft Comput. **53**, 119–132 (2017)
11. Kalayci, C.B., Kaya, C.: An ant colony system empowered variable neighborhood search algorithm for the vehicle routing problem with simultaneous pickup and delivery. Expert Syst. Appl. **66**, 163–175 (2016)
12. Clarke, G., Wright, J.W.: Scheduling of vehicles from a central depot to a number of delivery points. Oper. Res. **12**(4), 568–581 (1964)

The Research of Tripartite Game Between Managers and Executors in Logistics Security Under the Influence of Government

Zhen Guo[1], Yun Lin[1(✉)], Xingjun Huang[1], Jie Li[2], and Wenwen Yang[1]

[1] College of Mechanical Engineering, Chongqing University, Chongqing, China
linyun313@163.com
[2] School of Automotive Engineering, Chongqing University, Chongqing, China

Abstract. Based on logistics security, this paper analysis that people as one of the most important roles affect logistics security, and the games among different hierarchies will lead to different results of logistics security. By constructing a tripartite game model of participating groups, including government, managers and executors, in logistics security, the income matrix of tripartite game can be listed, and then we can find the game equilibrium points through evolutionary game theory. Through using the game model simulation by placing the value which makes the characteristic roots of the Jacobian matrix less than zero, we can get expected game equilibrium point which is {supervising, strengthening, executing}. Meanwhile changing some of the initial values under the government's macro-regulatory effect, such as increasing the cost of punishment and rewards for managers and executors or reducing the input cost and the opportunity cost of doing other inputs appropriately and so on, can promote the three participants to build a stable and safe logistics transportation environment.

Keywords: Logistics security · Tripartite game model
Evolutionary game theory · Stability of game · Numerical simulation

1 Introduction

Nowadays, the global Gross Domestic Product is at a stage of steady growth, at the same time, the logistics industry has also shown rapid development along with the economic development and achieved remarkable results, particularly in

This work was supported in part by the National Social Science Fund of China (Grant No. 18BJY066), Fundamental Research Funds for the Central Universities (Grant No. 106112016CDJXZ338825), Chongqing key industrial generic key technological innovation projects (Grant No. cstc2015zdcy-ztzx60009), Chongqing Science and Technology Research Program (Grant No. cstc2015yykfC60002).

S. Wang et al. (Eds.): ICSEE 2018/IMIOT 2018, CCIS 923, pp. 146–156, 2018.
https://doi.org/10.1007/978-981-13-2396-6_13

China. There still are many problems to be solved in process of logistics. While security issues are particularly prominent in global supply chain logistics. For examples, in 2015, the explosion in Tianjin port international logistics center (8.12 accident) exposed the problems in warehouse, especially chemicals goods. In addition, logistics also has problems with substandard storage facilities, overloading and so on. These problems cause a great threaten to social and country. Therefore, it is imperative to eliminate hidden dangers by means of perfecting laws and regulations, strengthening supervising and innovating management methods to ensure that supply chain logistics develops healthily and steadily.

2   Literature Review

2.1   Connotation of Logistics Security

Jiahong [1] summarized the relationship between logistics and security in practice are inseparable. Zheng [2] believes that information security, transportation security, processing safety and storage safety are the main contents of logistics security.

However, the scholars who study logistics security are from their research fields and points, and haven't formed a unified definition of logistics security. There is also no uniform standard for definition of logistics security issues or term for "logistics security" in logistics terminology. Meanwhile the new concepts which were put forward in recent years such as cycle-logistics, green logistics, reverse logistics and emergency logistics have greatly enriched the connotation of logistics security.

2.2   Research Status of Logistics Security

Due to the adverse impact of logistics on global supply chain, the logistics security field is widely concerned by the academic and the inside. Michelberger [3] conducted research on logistics information security research.

In terms of cargo security, Lu [4] pointed out that terrorist attacks, cargo theft, smuggling and other events in logistics process posed a greater challenge to security of logistics transportation system.

In terms of human, because of the subjective dynamic nature of them, it has become one of the most important factors affecting logistics security. Witkowski [5] pointed out that the most important role in city's logistics is local government. Its main goal is to resolve the conflicts of urban logistics stakeholders and ensure the sustainable development of city. They should be the initiators and coordinators of logistics solutions in city.

Lu [4] has constructed a model of motivational forces over the logistics security life-cycle. The model shows that government as an important factor in logistics security runs through the entire process. And Urciuoli [6] found that three main aspects can improve the security of supply chain logistics, including government, management and implementation showing in Fig. 1.

Fig. 1. The three areas for supply chain security improvement [6]

With the development of the theory of labor division and third-party logistics, more and more companies know the service outsourcing model of freight services and warehousing services, etc. And the proposal of sharing economy makes it more and more common for goods vehicles matching in logistics industry.

The development of these theories and models weakens subordinate relationship between managers and executors. The conflicts of them are further increasing but the relevant requirements of logistics security which can be achieved or not are determined by both of them. Most of existing literature show the importance of logistics security and provides many advice from single viewpoint [6]. While Zhewen [7] applied the game theory to logistics security and analyzed the mutual wrestling situation between government and managers in logistics companies.

When the conflicts between managers and executors become more and more serious, the choices of executors will have influence on the whole situation. The game between two parties will no longer be applicable. Therefore, this paper adopts tripartite game model theory in logistics security. Meanwhile the tripartite game theory has been applied in other fields of academia [8]. Exploring the participation of three parties in interests of different initial conditions, the changes in final selection strategy also provide reference for government, managers and executors to ensure security of the entire supply chain logistics.

3   Problem Description and Model Formulation

3.1   Problem Description

To facilitate the analysis of various stakeholders in the game of logistics security, it is assumed that the main players involved in logistics security are set as government, managers and executors. And the three parties in tripartite game are all rational economic men.

Government in this paper refers to the group of relevant administrative departments that supervise, control and guide logistics security. **Managers** in this article mainly refers to the group of related enterprises in logistics industry supervised by government. **Executor** refers to the group of logistics practitioners (mainly drivers) in this article supervised by government and their companies.

The direct stakeholders of logistics security are government, managers and executives. From the view of government, they can reduce accident rate of logistics security by implementing measures such as supervising and controlling logistics security(as supervising). They may also choose not to supervise to high cost and difficulty (as non-supervising). So, managers can choose strategy of strengthening or as non-strengthening, the same as executors. According to the analysis above, each game participant has two selecting strategies. So the number of combination strategies is eight.

3.2   Model Formulation

Parameter Setting. The game theory is to study the participants' benefits under different strategies and find the best. To research the relationship among costs, benefits and losses of them in logistics security, related parameters are set. The specific meanings of parameters are shown in Table 1 below.

Summarizing existing literatures, we find, in many game model, the balance between cost and benefit will be involved. So in this article, we set parameters

Table 1. Parameters and meanings

Parameters	Meanings
C_1	Supervision cost
C_2	Strengthening cost
C_3	Executing cost
C_G	The impact on society before strengthening
C_G'	The impact on society after strengthening
C_M	The impact on enterprises before strengthening
C_M'	The impact on enterprises after strengthening
C_E	The impact on the executors before strengthening
C_E'	The impact on the executors after strengthening
B_1	The social image of government after supervision
B_2	The benefits after enterprise strengthening
B_2'	The benefits of C_2 for other activities
B_3	Rewards for executors after executing
B_3'	Benefits for executors
F_1	Losses of government for society credibility
F_2	Punishment losses of managers
F_3	Punishment losses of executors
f	The supervision possibility of government.
a	The strengthening possibility of managers.
b	The executing possibility of executors.

C_1, C_2 and C_3 as participants' costs in game, and B_1, B_2, B_2', B_3 and B_3' as interests of participants.

Through the case study of logistics security accidents, the influence of accidents on participants is obviously different before and after they take measures of logistics security. So we set parameters C_G, C_G', C_M, C_M', C_E and C_E' as influence losses of participants respectively for government, managers and executors. Based on the theme of government leading in this article, we set the parameters F_2 and F_3 as punishment of managers and executors under the control of government. Meanwhile, government would face the consequence of declining social credibility because of non-supervising, quantified as loss of government, for F_1.

The Process and Profit Value of Game. Through the hypothesis and setting of relevant parameters of the model above, the tripartite evolutionary game model of government, managers and executors in logistics security is constructed. In this paper, the game tree is used to represent the process of tripartite game, as shown in Fig. 2.

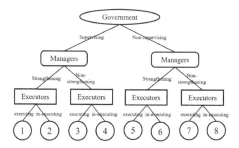

Fig. 2. The game tree of tripartite game

According to the game tree above, the profit value of each participant government, managers, executors in eight different game strategies under the tripartite game model can be analyzed, and the income matrix of tripartite game is listed, as shown in the following Table 2.

Model Construction. We set expected return of government is $\pi_{1(Sup)}$ if government choose the strategy of supervising, while we set expected return of government is $\pi_{1(N-Sup)}$ for choosing the strategy of non-supervising, and the total expected return is set as π_1, then:

$$\pi_{1(Sup)} = ab(B_1 - C_1 - C_G') + a(1-b)(B_1 + F_3 - C_1 - C_G) +$$
$$(1-a)b(B_1 + F_2 - C_1 - C_G) + (1-a)(1-b)(B_1 + F_2 + F_3 - C_1 - C_G)$$

$$\pi_{1(N-Sup)} = ab(-F_1 - C_G') + a(1-b)(-F_1 - C_G) + (1-a)b(-F_1 - C_G) +$$
$$(1-a)(1-b)(-F_1 - C_G)$$

Table 2. The income matrix of tripartite game

Executors		Executing b	In-executing $1-b$
Government	Managers		
Supervising f	Strengthening a	$B_1 - C_1 - C'_G,$ $B_2 - C'_2 - C_M,$ $B_3 - C'_E - C_3$	$B_1 + F_3 - C_1 - C_G$ $-C_2 - C_M, B'_3 - C_E - F_3$
	Non-strengthening $1-a$	$B_1 + F_2 - C_1 - C_G$ $B_2 - F_2 - C_M,$ $-C_E - C_3$	$B_1 + F_2 + F_3 - C_1 - C_G,$ $B'_2 - F_2 - C_M,$ $B_3 - C_E - F_3$
Non-supervising $1-f$	Strengthening a	$-F_1 - C'_G, B_2 - C_2 - C'_M,$ $B_3 - C'_E - C_3$	$-F_1 - C_G, -C_2 - C_M,$ $B'_3 - C_E$
	Non-strengthening $1-a$	$-F_1 - C_G, B'_2 - C_M,$ $-C_E - C_3$	$-F_1 - C_G, B'_2 - C_M,$ $B'_3 - C_E$

After simplifying the formula:

$$\pi_{1(Sup)} = B_1 - C_1 - C_G + \mathrm{ab}(C_G - C'_G) + (1 - a)F_2 + (1 - b)F_3$$
$$\pi_{1(N-Sup)} = \mathrm{ab}(C_G - C'_G) - F_1 - C_G$$

According to the expectation formula, the government's expected return is:

$$\pi_1 = f * \pi_{1(Sup)} + (1 - f) * \pi_{1(N-Sup)}$$

The replicated dynamic equation of government is:

$$F(f) = \frac{df}{dt} = f(\pi_{1(Sup)} - \pi_1) = f(1 - f)(B_1 + F_1 - C_1 + (1 - a)F_2 + (1 - b)F_3) \quad (1)$$

And the same as government, we can get replicated dynamic equation of managers and executors are $F(a)$ and $F(b)$:

$$F(a) = a(1 - a)(b(B_2 + C_M - C'_M) + f * F_2 - C_2 - B'_2) \quad (2)$$
$$F(b) = b(1 - b)(a(B_3 + C_E - C'_E) + f * F_3 - C_3 - B'_3) \quad (3)$$

3.3   The Stable Strategy of Tripartite Game Model

The Evolutionary Stability Strategy of Government. According to the replicated dynamic equation of government, we find the first derivative of $F(f)$

$$F(f)' = \frac{d(F(f))}{df} = (1 - 2f)(B_1 + F_1 - C_1 + (1 - a)F_2 + (1 - b)F_3) \quad (4)$$

(1) When $B_1 + F_1 - C_1 + (1-a)F_2 + (1-b)F_3 = 0$, in this condition, $F(f) = \frac{df}{dt} \equiv 0$, $F(f)' = \frac{d(F(f))}{df} \equiv 0$, this means that f is stable for any value. The ESS's process of government in this state is shown in Fig. 3(a) below.

(2) When $B_1 + F_1 - C_1 + (1-a)F_2 + (1-b)F_3 \neq 0$, in this condition, the two game equilibriums of government are $f = 0$ and $f = 1$, According to the nature of evolutionary stable strategy, When $b < \frac{B_1+F_1+F_2+F_3-C_1-a*F_2}{F_3}$, then $F(f)'_{f=1} < 0$, $F(f)'_{f=0} > 0$, the evolutionary stable state of government is $f = 1$. The ESS's process of government in this state is shown in Fig. 3(b). And when $b > \frac{B_1+F_1+F_2+F_3-C_1-a*F_2}{F_3}$, the evolutionary stable state of government is $f = 0$. The ESS's process of government in this state is shown in Fig. 3(c).

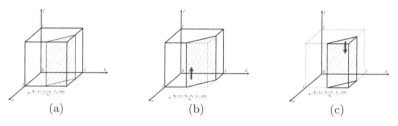

(a)   (b)   (c)

Fig. 3. The ESS's process of government

The Evolutionary Stability Strategy of Managers. According to the replicated dynamic equation of managers, we can find the first derivative of $F(a)$

$$F(a)' = \frac{d(F(a))}{da} = (1-2a)(b(B_2 + C_M - C'_M) + f * F_2 - C_2 - B'_2) \quad (5)$$

(1) When $b(B_2 + C_M - C'_M) + f * F_2 - C_2 - B'_2 = 0$, in this condition, $F(a) = \frac{da}{dt} \equiv 0$, $F(a)' = \frac{d(F(a))}{da} \equiv 0$, the result is shown in Fig. 4(a) below.

(2) When $b(B_2 + C_M - C'_M) + f * F_2 - C_2 - B'_2 \neq 0$, in this condition, the two game equilibriums of managers are $a = 0$ and $a = 1$, when $f > \frac{C_2+B'_2-b(B_2+C_M-C'_M)}{F_2}$, the result is shown in Fig. 4(b). And the result of another situation is shown in Fig. 4(c) below.

The Evolutionary Stability Strategy of Executors. According to the replicated dynamic equation of executors, we can find the first derivative of $F(b)$

$$F(b)' = \frac{d(F(b))}{db} = (1-2b)(a(B_3 + C_E - C'_E) + f * F_3 - C_3 - B'_3) \quad (6)$$

(1) When $a(B_3 + C_E - C'_E) + f * F_3 - C_3 - B'_3 = 0$, in this condition, $F(b) = \frac{db}{dt} \equiv 0$, $F(b)' = \frac{d(F(b))}{db} \equiv 0$, the result is shown in Fig. 5(a) below.

(2) When $a(B_3 + C_E - C'_E) + f * F_3 - C_3 - B'_3 \neq 0$, in this condition, the two game equilibriums of executors are $b = 0$ and $b = 1$, when $f > \frac{C_3+B'_3-a(B_3+C_E-C'_E)}{F_3}$, the result is shown in Fig. 5(b). And the result of another situation is shown in Fig. 5(c) below.

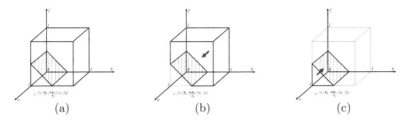

Fig. 4. The ESS's process of managers

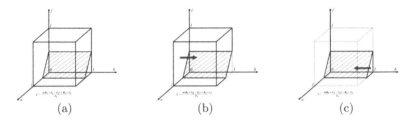

Fig. 5. The ESS's process of executors

3.4 The Evolutionary Stability Points of Tripartite Game

From the process of analysis above, the follow results can be obtained that there are a total of 9 evolutionary stability points in the tripartite game of government, managers and executors. The ninth is $E_9 = \{f^*, a^*, b^*\}$ which value is the solutions of equations in Figs. 3(a), 4(a) and 5(a)

According to the theory of Lyapunov stability, if the point is an ESS, the characteristic roots of the Jacobian matrix must be less than 0. The strategic combination $\mathrm{E} = \{\text{supervising}, \text{strengthening}, \text{executing}\}$ is the best state in game. If we want the strategic combination above become to the ESS, the three characteristic roots $\lambda_1 = -M$, $\lambda_2 = -N$, $\lambda_3 = -P$ of the Jacobian matrix are less than zero which is the same as the results in Figs. 3(b), 4(b) and 5(b)

4 Numerical Simulation

The relationship between Jacobian matrix's characteristic solutions is obtained according to the Lyapunov method. And considering the authenticity of model and simplicity, parameters are assigned as shown in the following Table 3.

Simulating tripartite model by MATLAB, the dynamic phase diagram of participants is obtained as shown in Fig. 6 below. And Figs. 7, 8 and 9 show the trends of each participant's selection strategy during the tripartite evolutionary game. The density of lines in graph indicates the probability of player's choice under the same conditions in tripartite game. The denser the lines, the higher probability of strategy is to be chosen.

In Fig. 10, $b > 0.8$, and in Fig. 11, $a > 0.8$. And $B_2 = 90$ in Fig. 12, $F_2 = 70$ in Fig. 13 while other values remain unchanged.

Table 3. The assignment table of parameters

Parameters	Value	Parameters	Value	Parameters	Value
C_1	30	C_2	40	C_3	15
C_G	35	C_M	25	C_E	10
C_G'	0	C_M'	0	C_E'	0
B_1	35	B_2	45	B_3	20
F_1	25	B_2'	42	B_3'	16
f	$[0,1]$	F_2	35	F_3	20
		a	$[0,1]$	b	$[0,1]$

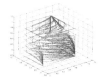

Fig. 6. The dynamic phase diagram of tripartite game   **Fig. 7.** The trends of government's selection strategy   **Fig. 8.** The trends of managers' selection strategy   **Fig. 9.** The trends of executors' selection strategy

  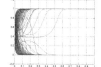

Fig. 10. Managers' strategy ($b > 0.8$)   **Fig. 11.** Executors' strategy ($a > 0.8$)   **Fig. 12.** Managers' strategy ($B_2 = 90$)   **Fig. 13.** Managers' strategy ($F_2 = 70$)

5   Discussion and Conclusion

5.1   Discussion

From the analysis of evolutionary game model above, we can know that in dynamic environment, the initial state and changes of some parameters in tripartite game will lead the convergence of the game evolution system to different equilibrium points.

When the initial state of each participants falls in common area of Figs. 3(b), 4(b) and 5(b), the selection strategy of government, managers and executors will converge on {supervising, strengthening, executing}. And this conclusion is the same as the simulation result of Fig. 6. According to the constraint condition of Fig. 3(b), it is shown the probability of supervising is 1 regardless of the initial state of managers and executors, which is the same as the simulation result of

Fig. 7. Figures 10, 11, 12 and 13 illustrate that different initial states will affect the selection of final strategies by managers and executors in the process of game.

5.2 Conclusion

This article is mainly based on the evolutionary game theory, a tripartite evolutionary game model among government, managers and executors is established and simulated by MATLAB. Through this tripartite evolutionary model, we can get the following conclusions:

(1) According to the inequality $f > \frac{C_2+B_2'-b(B_2+C_M-C_M')}{F_2}$ in the Fig. 4(b), for increasing the probability of choosing 1 in managers group, the value of F_2 and $B_2+C_M-C_M'$ can be increased and the value of C_2+B_2' can be reduced appropriately. So government can increase punishment cost appropriately and award some incentives to enterprises which strengthen logistics security or publicize and praise those enterprises. The effectiveness of these measures is illustrated in simulation results showing Figs. 12 and 13.

(2) According to the inequality $f > \frac{C_3+B_3'-a(B_3+C_E-C_E')}{F_3}$ in Fig. 5(b), for increasing the probability of choosing 1 in executors group, we can reference the methods mentioned above, increasing the value of F_3 and $B_3+C_E-C_E'$ and reducing the value of C_3+B_3' appropriately. Therefore government and managers can increase punishment if executors don't execute regulations but rewards more rewards to executors who fulfill their duties actively.

(3) Comparing Fig. 8 with Fig. 10, and Fig. 9 with Fig. 11, high initial probability of managers and executors will increase probability of final convergence to 1. So government and managers can use technology to reduce the opportunity of executors who don't execute regulations. For example, using logistics security driving aid software including fatigue driving warning system and others.

Government should play a leading role in this tripartite game by using macro-control functions and the convenience brought by modern technology, urge enterprises to strengthen logistics security, encourage executors to implement the relevant regulations and guide society to build a safe and harmonious logistics transport environment.

References

1. Jiahong, Z., Kaili, X.: Logistics and security. Ind. Safety Environ. Prot. **33**(1), 4–6 (2007)
2. Zheng, L.: Research on logistics chain security assurance system. Logist. Sci. Technol. **2810**, 8–10 (2005)
3. Michelberger, P., Lábodi, C.: Development of information security management system at the members of supply chain. Ann. Univ. Petrosani Econ. **IX**(4), 10–10 (2009)

4. Lu, G., Koufteros, X.: Adopting security practices for transport logistics: institutional effects and performance drivers. Soc. Sci. Electron. Publ. **6**(6), 611–631 (2013)
5. Witkowski, J., Kiba-Janiak, M.: The role of local governments in the development of city logistics. Proc. Soc. Behav. Sci. **125**(125), 373–385 (2014)
6. Urciuoli, L.: Supply chain security-mitigation measures and a logistics multi-layered framework. J. Transp. Secur. **3**(1), 1–28 (2010)
7. Yang, L., Zhewen, Z.: Application of nash equilibrium in logistics safety sup in small and medium-sized logistics enterprises. J. Logist. Technol. **27**(8), 115–116 (2008)
8. Jianrong, Y., Binyi, S.: Policy factors and development path of China's real estate market: a game analysis of government, developer and consumer. Res. Financ. Econ. **30**(4), 130–139 (2004)

Quality Improvement Practice Using a VIKOR-DMAIC Approach: Parking Brake Case in a Chinese Domestic Auto-Factory

Fuli Zhou[1], Xu Wang[2,3(✉)], Ming K. Lim[2,3], and Yuqing Liu[2]

[1] School of Economics and Management,
Zhengzhou University of Light Industry, Zhengzhou, People's Republic of China
deepbreath329@outlook.com
[2] School of Mechanical Engineering,
Chongqing University, Chongqing, People's Republic of China
wx921@163.com
[3] State Key Laboratory of Mechanical Transmission, Chongqing University,
Chongqing, People's Republic of China

Abstract. To improve the product quality and customer satisfaction, Chinese domestic automobile industries tend to perform continuous quality improvement procedure (CQIP). In this paper, an integrated VIKOR-DMAIC approach is developed to boom quality improvement practice. Firstly, the critical quality issue is chosen as the pilot program using VIKOR steps. Then, the Six Sigma method including DMAIC operations is performed to scrutinize the cause of quality issue and regulate strategic proposal. A practical case is presented to validate the integrated approach, and the pilot program improvement sets an example for other quality items.

Keywords: Quality improvement practice · Pilot program · VIKOR
DMAIC · Parking brake

1 Introduction

With the development of Chinese domestic automobile industry, China has become the most automobile producing and selling country in recent eight years. Low price has become the competitive advantage compared with joint venture vehicles, and some auto-factories focus much on front processes of the supply chain, overlooking the post-sales business [1]. The warranty policy is regulated that auto-factory should be responsible for their products within 36 months. Furthermore, many firms perform recall business when there occurred serious quality defects [2]. Besides, the supply of vehicles is obviously more than demand owes to the excess expansion of the production line. Increasing fiercer competitive pressures motivate automobile industry to strive for quality improvement, cost reduction and quick responses to customers' complaints. On the other hand, the soaring warranty cost due to un-conformance and quality defectives leads to the increasing attention on product quality. The un-conformity of vehicle's

© Springer Nature Singapore Pte Ltd. 2018
S. Wang et al. (Eds.): ICSEE 2018/IMIOT 2018, CCIS 923, pp. 157–168, 2018.
https://doi.org/10.1007/978-981-13-2396-6_14

experience brings warranty expenditure, as well as quality loss due to customer un-satisfaction. The negative word-of-mouth caused by customer complaint will propagate, which leads to potential consumer loss, loyalty reduction and reputation damage. Therefore, under these situations, Chinese domestic automobile industry tends to conduct continuous improvement (CI) [3].

The strategic continuous quality improvement, as a significant action to improve firm's capability and narrow the gap between Chinese domestic auto-factories and foreign counterparts, has been confirmed over time [4]. Automobile organizations are regarded as a big triumph that can give rapid response and attention to customer feedback and product usage [3]. Auto-factories are striving to improve quality and customer satisfaction by employing competitive strategies. The customer satisfaction improvement for auto-industries not only relies on high quality product, but also service hospitality [5]. And after-sales service is significant to product and brand marketing, and quality information from global quality research system (GQRS) can reflect the vehicle's quality, as well as providing a guide for continuous improvement (CI). Therefore, the quality index system needs to be developed to evaluate the product quality and customer satisfaction. The failure frequency R/1000@3MIS is the most widely used indicator in the industry for quality improvement [6].

Time and again, practitioners and researchers have reported local quality improvement practices by using different kinds of quality techniques, such as 8D, TQM, Six Sigma, and cost of quality method [7]. The 8D procedure, first proposed by the Ford Company, has assisted quality managers to deal with the sudden failure involving multiple related departments. TQM appears to be one of the most management fads, and has proven to be an effective approach and management philosophy encouraging full staff participation. However, it seems that TQM fails to bring about financial improvements for firms and ignores the importance of customer's feedback [8]. Six sigma method, as an efficient approach, is a structural method to help organizations to achieve continuous improvement, and some researchers thought it is a replacement of TQM. In addition, the Six sigma method, as a customer-oriented practice, facilitates to achieve continuous improvement by adopting DMAIC operations. Srinivasan [9] has enhanced the sigma level from 3.31 to 3.67 by using DMAIC phases in furnace nozzle manufacturing. It manifests that even there is not enough investment on belt-based training and infrastructure, the case report of DMACI application is also effective for quality improvement. However, some organizations fail to perform six sigma approach, and there are many publications focusing on the crucial factors of success sigma implementation [10, 11]. Both TQM and Six sigma have not paid much more attention to the economics of quality. Cost of quality, called quality cost as well, aims at the measurement of quality economy, and is an effective method to control financial sector [12]. The lack of leadership concentration and financial consideration leads to the failure and hard dilemma of Six sigma [11, 13]. As for small-and-medium enterprises, the huge investment on infrastructure and belt training may be expensive and thus beyond their burden, the case report or the pilot programme improvement can be implemented instead [9]. Therefore, the cost of quality and Six sigma technique can be integrated to develop a systematic approach to assist automobile industries for continuous improvement. In addition, to expand the availability of the quality practice, especially for small-and-medium firms, the pilot program-based philosophy is adopted. Quality managers can perform strategic improvement on the objective quality item.

In this paper, an integrated VIKOR-DMAIC approach is developed, and the strategic quality management practice driven by pilot improvement is reported. Different with previous practice, the pilot philosophy is adopted, and the warranty cost criterion is taken into account for pilot programme establishment, instead of the single failure frequency consideration.

The reminder of this paper is organized as follows. Section 2 highlights the criteria used in auto-industry and quality improvement practice. In Sect. 3, an integrated VIKOR-DMAIC approach, inducing VIKOR-based quality pilot programme establishment and DMAIC steps, is developed to put quality improvement into practice. Subsequently, a practical case is presented. Section 5 concludes.

2 Continuous Quality Improvement Practice

2.1 Quality Index in Automobile Industry

The most prevailing used quality index in the automobile industry is PP100 (problems per 100 vehicles), and it reflects the frequency of problems occurred. It is employed by many consultant organizations (like J.D. Power and Zhongdiao Co. Ltd) to distinguish the quality performance in different brand for potential consumers. Due to durability characteristics of vehicle product, the product quality and after-sales quality are coupled with consideration during the CQIP implementation. That means, we need to perform quality management practice to improve product quality, as well as promote customer satisfaction at the same time. Therefore, in our study, the quality indexes that reflect product quality and voice of customers are proposed and addressed, providing an improvement objective for quality managers to eliminate problem and negative word-of-mouth. We target failure frequency (R/1000) and customer complaint (Things go wrong, TGW/1000) per thousand cars as key quality indexes, and actually they are applied in Chinese domestic auto-industry recently [1, 6, 14]. The R/1000 criterion reflects failure status occurred within certain period, and the TGW/1000 indicator manifests the degree of customer un-satisfaction when there is even one glitch. We can obtain the quality feedback through the global quality research system (GQRS), tracing the quality deviation and functional problems, and they are denoted as R/1000@xMIS and TGW/1000@xMIS (Month in service, MIS). The symbol x denotes the time (Month in service, MIS) after vehicles' delivery to users. Taken the quick response and validity into consideration, R/1000@3MIS and TGW/1000@3MIS indicators, as critical to quality (CTQ), are proven to be the most appropriate to reflect the quality performance of vehicles in service [14].

2.2 Continuous Quality Improvement Procedure

Continues quality improvement practices are regarded as strategic actions for Chinese domestic auto industry. By tracing the quality defectives and unconformity, the quality managers could correct the existing problems and to make responses. A systematic

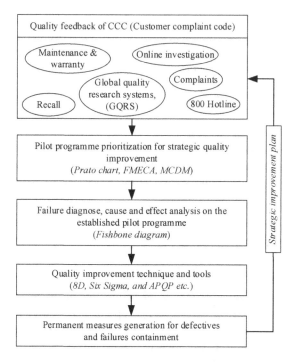

Fig. 1. CQIP in Chinese domestic auto-industry

improvement procedure for automobile industry is find in Fig. 1, which caters to PDCA (Plan-Do-Check-Action) philosophy. Due to the manufacturing characteristics, there are thousands of parts and accessories for vehicle product, as well as multi production processes with multiple involvements. Even one glitch may lead to unconformity and customer complaint for many kinds of factors. Therefore, we start with the quality improvement on a pilot programme, and promote the improvement measures [15].

As we can see from the Fig. 1, the vehicle quality improvement is driven by customers' feedback. We can make concrete actions and perform strategic improvement on pilot programme that may be a single customer complaint code (CCC), a failure part or a system. The 8D method, a qualitative analytic approach introduced by Ford has been widely used in automobile industry in China, India and South Africa, which has dramatically help to deal with high failure rate [7]. Besides, the six sigma technique has proven to be an effective to improve customer satisfaction and reduce quality cost both for manufacturing and service sector [16]. As a strategic plan, the CQIP is adopted by Chinese domestic auto factories and its part manufacturing sector.

3   The Integrated VIKOR-DMAIC Approach

In practice, the critical processes of strategic CQIP are pilot program identification and strategic improvement based on quality techniques. To improve the product quality and customer satisfaction, a two-stage integrated method is developed to perform quality improvement practice, which combines VIKOR, a multi-criteria decision making approach with DMAIC steps, and we can find the strategic improvement process in the following Fig. 2.

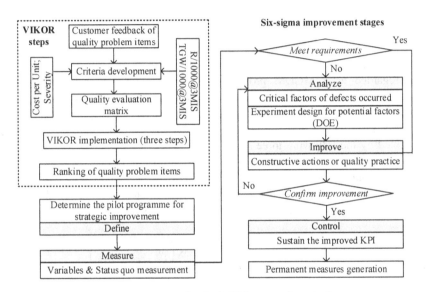

Fig. 2. The VIKOR-DMAIC integrated method

3.1   Criteria Description of Quality Improvement Pilot Programme Identification

The QIP pilot programme as a multi-criteria decision making problem, and therefore, we need to construct the index system that influences the selection. Those characteristics determines quality improvement come from customers' feedback can be introduced to this procedure. Apart from the above-mentioned two quality indexes, the quality improvement efforts or cost also needs to be considered. FMEA analysis and its elements can present a brief overview on certain failure occurred, and is usually employed by quality engineers [17]. Another effective index is cost per unit within the warranty period, which reflects the economics of quality, and the quantification of criteria follows previous publications [1]. The following Table 1 presents the influential criteria for pilot programme selection.

Table 1. Criteria development of pilot programme selection [3]

Item	Criteria	Meaning
C1	R/1000@3MIS	Failure frequency per thousand vehicles within 3 MIS
C2	TGW/1000@3MIS	Customer complaint per thousand vehicles within 3 MIS
C3	Severity (S)	The severity of the failure occurred
C4	Cost per unit (CPU)	Warranty cost per unit calculated based on GQRS

3.2 VIKOR-Based the Establishment of QIP Pilot Programme

To select the objective pilot program from a variety of customer complaint items, the VIKOR, a multi-criteria decision making method, is employed to determine a compromise solution subjecting to multiple conflicting criteria.

The QIP pilot programme establishment is subject to multi conflicting criteria and can be regarded as a MCDM problem. Suppose the influential criteria is $C = (C_1, C_2, \ldots, C_j, \ldots, C_n)$, and the corresponding weight vector is $w = (w_1, w_2, w_3, w_4)$. The existing problem item (CCC, part or sub-system) is $A = (A_1, A_2, \ldots, A_i, \ldots, A_m)$. The quality information from of the problem item is x_{ij}. The VIKOR method is implemented by the following three steps.

Step 1: Generate the decision matrix. The decision matrix $D = (x_{ij})_{m \times n}$ is determined by the quality information of all quality items investigated from GQRS.

Step 2: Calculate the S and R value [1]. The maximum group utility value S_i and minimum individual regret value R_i are determined by the following Eq. (1).

$$S_i = \sum_{j=1}^{n} w_j \cdot \frac{(f_j^* - x_{ij})}{(f_j^* - f_j^-)}, \quad R_i = \max_j \left(w_j \cdot \frac{(f_j^* - x_{ij})}{(f_j^* - f_j^-)} \right) \tag{1}$$

Where $f_j^* = \min(x_{ij}), f_j^- = \max(x_{ij})$.

Step 3: Derive the Q value [1]. The comprehensive group utility value S_i and minimum individual regret value R_i are determined by the following Eq. (2).

$$Q_i = v \frac{S_i - S^*}{S^- - S^*} + (1 - v) \frac{R_i - R^*}{R^- - R^*} \tag{2}$$

Where $S^* = \min_i S_i, S^- = \min_i S_i; R^* = \min_i R_i, R^- = \min_i R_i$.

After the requirement of two conditions (acceptance advantage and stability), the final ranking of alternatives is obtained by the ascending Q value [18]. Then the quality problem item with minimum Q value will be selected as a pilot programme.

3.3 DMAIC Stages

The five DMAIC (define, measure, analyze, improve, control) phases are main components of Six sigma approach. The critical problem item selected using VIKOR method is treated as a pilot programme due to the resources limitation at design phase, and the improvement process is find in the Fig. 2.

Define Stage: The objective is determined at this phase, as well as the work team. The critical item, as a pilot programme, derived by VIKOR method is selected, and the detective item is defined. In addition, the quality improvement team member includes quality manager, production manager, operator and engineers etc.

Measure Stage: In this stage, we need to figure out the status quo and current performance of objective item, also covers data collection and performance measurement. The process capability C_{pk}, and current sigma level are also metrics need to be scrutinized. This stage laid foundation for the following analysis and optimization.

Analyze Stage: The potential factors that influence the metrics of process are analyzed and investigated. To scrutinize the source of problem, the design of experiment is performed on each potential factor by statistical tools. In this stage, we need to identify the causes of problem based on the measurement outcome of DOE.

Improve Stage: After the confirmation of causes may existed, some corresponding solutions are proposed and developed to deal with the defects or un-conformity. The specific improvement actions or operations driven by team members are implemented to achieve established goals. In addition, the quality performance and sigma level after improvement is measured and analyzed as well. If there is no improvement, then the specific actions or solutions need to be checked and revised.

Control Stage: The aim of this stage is to sustain the improvement metric achieved by using quality tools. Once we obtain the correct actions or solutions to achieve the objective improvement, efforts are made to maintain the implementation of proposal, as well as in-process performance control.

The DMAIC stages provide a systematic improvement way for quality problem item. After checking the effectiveness of correct solutions, the actions will be regarded as permanent operations for further manufacturing activities.

4 Case Study

The industrial case comes from the recent quality improvement practice in a famous Chinese domestic automobile factory, who is implementing CQIP by using 8D and Six Sigma technique [7]. The proposed integrated method is employed and used to improve key metrics by quality department.

4.1 Quality Improvement Pilot Programme Selection

The quality information comes from the global quality research system (GQRS) and the warranty platform. We can choose the first 17 problem items based on Pareto analysis in advance. The VIKOR method is conducted to rank the alternative quality problem item, and prioritization results are find in Table 2. Due to the robustness of the method proved in previous publications, we suppose $v = 0.5$, and obtain the critical quality item.

Table 2. Prioritization result of different quality items

Quality item	C1	C2	C3	C4	S	R	Q	Rank
A1	0.3	15	7	0.1	.057	.236	.114	4
A2	1.4	3.4	5	0.75	.344	.447	.389	14
…	…							
A17	0.9	21	8	0.56	.479	.245	.276	9

4.2   Six Sigma Implementation

Based on the previous analysis, the parking brake is the most focusing problem with the first priority for quality enhancement, and is regarded as the pilot program in this improvement.

(1) *Define phase*

Many vehicle consumers claim that the parking brake needs much more force to be pulled when braking on the slope. We try to investigate the problem description about parking brake and define the defective. We perform the parking brake experiment and found the maximum operating force is 250 N. The customer requirement is that the operation force should be [196 N, 259 N], when the number of hand brake teeth is less than 80% of the total teeth number. In addition, the quality improvement team member is established, mainly coming from Chassis group of quality department, manufacturing sector, and financial department etc.

The quality performance of parking brake is analyzed through the experiments, and the statistics results are presented in Table 3. As can be seen, the current performance cannot meet the customers' requirement.

Table 3. Status quo investigation by experiments

Vehicle type	Number of teeth when braking			Hand brake force		
	Teeth	Frequency	Percentage	Max	Min	Average
A-type	3	12	11.9	296	220	244
	4	36	34.7	352	205	279
	5	44	44.6	396	283	331
	6	9	8.9	375	336	355

(2) *Measure phase*

As is defined and investigated that the hand brake needs to much force when braking. The potential factors are investigated based on the cause and effect analysis illustrated in Fig. 3. The sub-system/parts (parking cable, rear brake, brake body) and manufacturing process are covered to scrutinize the cause of this problem.

In this stage, there are two components including process capability analysis and measurement systems analysis (MSA). The MSA using force testing equipment is implemented by performing experiments 38 times involving 2 workers, and the pulling

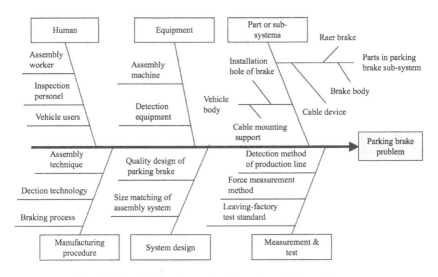

Fig. 3. Potential factors analysis based on fishbone diagram

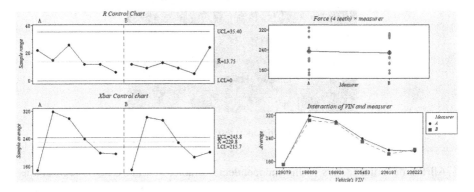

Fig. 4. ANOVA of measurement system

force is measured and recoded at 3, 4, and 5 teeth. For the sake of confidentiality, the experimental data is not exposed in this manuscript, and the ANOVA is implemented in Fig. 4 and the analysis outcome shows that the measurement system can be acceptable (R&R = 15.1%).

(3) *Analyze phase through statistics tools*

This chapter aims at finding the significant factor that influences the existing defective through statistics methods or DOE technique. Through the cause and effect diagram, potential factors are divided into two kinds: controllable and noise factors. To scrutinize the cause of the problem, we need to perform statistics analysis based on experiments. Some potential factors and is the critical to quality (CTQ) is established in Table 4, as well as the current capability.

Table 4. Detail analytic plan of the experiment

Vehicle type	Potential factors	Critical to quality (CTQ)	Standards	Measurement tools	Measurement plan	Current *Ppk*
A-type	Brake body	Screw length	$\mu \pm 1$mm	Vernier caliper	30	1.52
	Vehicle body	Installation hole	± 1.5mm	Three-coordinates	30	1.33
	Cable of the brake	Length	$\mu \pm 2$mm	Special tool	30	1.64
		Cable efficiency	$\geq 70\%$	Special tool	10	~
	....					
	Rear brake	Gap size	$\mu \pm 0.15$mm	Vernier caliper	30	1.13

Fig. 5. Cable efficiency test by simu-platform

All the potential factors as the independent variable, and the CTQ is regarded as dependent variable. Statistics tools like histogram, hypothesis test, regression and process capability analysis are employed to scrutinize the status quo of each potential ingredient. Through the statistical analysis of the experiment data, the brake body, the vehicle body, and rear brake are normal and acceptable, except cable sector.

(4) *Improve phase*

To improve the performance, the further experiment is conducted to trace the original reasons. According to the above-mentioned philosophy in measurement stage, the more detail potential factors (based on assembly processes) are analyzed, of course as well as the experiment is performed (Fig. 5). The low efficiency of braking cable causes the increasing pulling force, which leads to the raising of parking tension. To deal with this matter, there are two actions proposed: ① initial contact area and friction coefficient are improved; ② the design of system tolerance is optimized through quality chain perspective. After the assembly process revision and optimized design, the capability of cable efficiency is dramatically improved, as well as the quality performance.

(5) *Control phase*

After the four stages, we revised the assembly tolerance and improved the cable process. The quality index TGW/1000@3MIS is improved by 30%, and the customer complaint is reduced as well. The process specifications and standards are renewed in the new vehicle manufacturing, and quality control techniques are performed in these special links. Other potential factors and improvement course can abide by the same procedure.

5 Conclusion

This paper presents a quality improvement practice in a Chinese domestic automobile industry. An integrated VIKOR-DMAIC approach is proposed, catering to the CQIP implemented in auto-factories recently. It focuses on the strategic improvement through the pilot program activity, which setting an example for other counterparts. Different with the current practice of local improvement relying on failure frequency indicator, the multi criteria involving in customers' attitude are taken into consideration for pilot programme establishment, also the integrated VIKOR-DMAIC approach provide a systematic improvement strategy for Chinese domestic auto industry.

The VIKOR steps contributes to the pilot issue selection, and DMAIC phases are effective to find the cause of quality items and propose strategic measures. In this paper, the quality performance enhancement driven by the pilot programme improvement is proven to be effective and efficient for auto industries, especially under the TQM atmosphere. However, as the limitation of VIKOR and DMAIC, other systematic implementations and stages are also need to be developed to embrace the strategic quality improvement.

Acknowledgement. The authors would like to thank the anonymous referees and the editor for their valuable comments and suggestions.

References

1. Zhou, F., Wang, X., Lin, Y., He, Y., Zhou, L.: Strategic part prioritization for quality improvement practice using a hybrid MCDM framework: a case application in an auto factory. Sustainability 8(6), 559 (2016)
2. Shah, R., Ball, G.P., Netessine, S.: Plant operations and product recalls in the automotive industry: an empirical investigation. Manage. Sci. 63(8), 2439–2450 (2016)
3. Zhou, F., Wang, X., Samvedi, A.: Quality improvement pilot program selection based on dynamic hybrid MCDM approach. Ind. Manage. Data Syst. 118(1), 144–163 (2018)
4. Lin, L.C., Li, T.S., Kiang, J.P.: A continual improvement framework with integration of CMMI and six-sigma model for auto industry. Qual. Reliab. Eng. Int. 25(5), 551–569 (2010)
5. Guajardo, J.A., Cohen, M.A., Netessine, S.: Service competition and product quality in the U.S. automobile industry. Manage. Sci. 62(7), 1860–1877 (2016)
6. Gaikwad, L.M., Teli, S.N., Majali, V.S., Bhushi, U.M.: An application of Six Sigma to reduce supplier quality cost. J. Inst. Eng. (India) Series C 97(1), 93–107 (2015)

7. Zhou, F., Wang, X., Mpshe, T., Zhang, Y., Yang, Y.: Quality Improvement Procedure (QIP) based on 8D and Six Sigma Pilot Programs in Automotive Industry (2016)
8. Sabet, E., Adams, E., Yazdani, B.: Quality management in heavy duty manufacturing industry: TQM vs. Six Sigma. Total Qual. Manage. Bus. Excellence 27(1–2), 215–225 (2014)
9. Srinivasan, K., Muthu, S., Devadasan, S., Sugumaran, C.: Enhancement of sigma level in the manufacturing of furnace nozzle through DMAIC approach of Six Sigma: a case study. Prod. Plann. Control 27(10), 810–822 (2016)
10. McLean, R.S., Antony, J., Dahlgaard, J.J.: Failure of Continuous Improvement initiatives in manufacturing environments: a systematic review of the evidence. Total Qual. Manage. Bus. Excellence 28(3–4), 219–237 (2017)
11. Montgomery, D.C.: Why do lean Six Sigma projects sometimes fail? Qual. Reliab. Eng. Int. 32(4), 1279 (2016)
12. Lim, C., Sherali, H.D., Glickman, T.S.: Cost-of-quality optimization via zero-one polynomial programming. IIE Trans. 47(3), 258–273 (2014)
13. Laureani, A., Antony, J.: Leadership–a critical success factor for the effective implementation of Lean Six Sigma. Total Qual. Manage. Bus. Excellence 29(5–6), 502–523 (2018)
14. Zhou, F., Wang, X., Chen, S., Ni, L.: COQ math model case study for self-brand automobile industry. In: Proceedings of the 2015 IEEE International Conference on Industrial Engineering and Engineering Management (IEEM), pp. 392–1396 (2015)
15. Chen, Y., Li, B.: Dynamic multi-attribute decision making model based on triangular intuitionistic fuzzy numbers. Scientia Iranica 18(2), 268–274 (2011)
16. Cherrafi, A., Elfezazi, S., Govindan, K., Garza-Reyes, J.A., Benhida, K., Mokhlis, A.: A framework for the integration of Green and Lean Six Sigma for superior sustainability performance. Int. J. Prod. Res. 55(15), 4481–4515 (2017)
17. Kim, K.O., Zuo, M.J.: General model for the risk priority number in failure mode and effects analysis. Reliab. Eng. Syst. Safety 169, 321–329 (2018)
18. Zhou, F., Lin, Y., Wang, X., Zhou, L., He, Y.: ELV recycling service provider selection using the hybrid MCDM method: a case application in China. Sustainability 8(5), 482 (2016)

Delivery Vehicle Scheduling Modeling and Optimization for Automobile Mixed Milk-Run Mode Involved Indirect Suppliers

Tianyu Xiong, Qian Tang$^{(\boxtimes)}$, Tao Huang$^{(\boxtimes)}$, Zhenyu Shen,
Hao Zhou, Henry Y. K. Hu, and Yi Li

State Key Laboratory of Mechanical Transmissions,
Chongqing University, Chongqing 400044, China
{tqcqu, thuang}@cqu.edu.cn

Abstract. On the issues of that the cost of the milk-run logistics mode with multi-level suppliers is hard to reduce, a mixed milk-run logistics mode involved second level suppliers is proposed in this paper. Based on the cost model in the traditional milk-run logistics mode, the transportation cost influenced by second level suppliers is taken into consideration in the new milk-run logistics mode. An improved genetic algorithm is applied to solve the new milk-run optimization problem. The preliminary comparison results indicate that the proposed mixed mode could provide a more practical method to significantly reduce the cost of logistics for the whole supply chain.

Keywords: Logistics · Milk-run · Indirect suppliers · Vehicle routing problem
Genetic algorithm

1 Introduction

1.1 A Subsection Sample

With the vigorous development of the automotive industry and the increasingly intense competition in manufacturing, the prices of cars dropped sharply and the profit margin of automakers continue to shrink. In order to maintain the advantage of market competition and to improve the market share, the problem about how to reduce the total cost of car production to expand profit space is getting more and more attention. Hence, efficient logistics system as 'The third profit source' is focused on. As the cost involved in the logistics of parts and components entering the factory accounts for approximately 70% of the total cost of automotive manufacturing logistics, it becomes the key to reduce the total cost of the logistics system.

Foundation items: This work was supported in part 1. the Key Technology Research and System Integration of Discrete Intelligent Manufacturing Workshop, China (No. cstc2016zdcy-ztzx60001); 2. the National Nature Science Foundation of China under Grant 51805053; 3. the National Nature Science Foundation of China under Grant 51575069; 4. the Fundamental Research Funds for the Central Universities of China under Grant 2018CDXYJX0019.

S. Wang et al. (Eds.): ICSEE 2018/IMIOT 2018, CCIS 923, pp. 169–178, 2018.
https://doi.org/10.1007/978-981-13-2396-6_15

The idea of lean production has increasingly become popular during the past decade. Using the milk-run logistics mode is an efficient strategy to achieve lean production, and the implementation of the logistic strategy is helpful to reduce cost and to improve efficiency. In consequence, the competitiveness of enterprises will be greatly enhanced in this way. The key issues for the implementation of milk-run logistics mode is to handle the supply network control from the suppliers and make it observable. It means the Milk-run Vehicle Routing problem must be solved well in scheduling of vehicles from a central depot to a number of delivery points. The Milk-run Vehicle Routing problem is an extended variation of the Vehicle Routing Problem (VRP). VRP was first discussed by Dantzig and Ramser in 1959 [1]. VRP can be introduced as: There are few vehicles, several delivery centers and customers in a system with a supply-demand relationship. Reasonable arrangement of vehicle routes is required to let the vehicles pass the delivery centers and customers in a certain order under the given constraints and to optimize the objective function. The elementary target of VRP is to minimize the length of the vehicle route. However, there are other goals involved in VRP such as minimizing the time spent, total cost and the number of vehicles needed.

The situation that the vehicle is often required to simultaneously drop off and pick up goods at the same stop was discussed by Min in 1989 [2]. Heuristic algorithms was used to solve the VRP with pickups and deliveries by Nagya [3]. A reactive tabu search metaheuristic that can check feasibility of proposed moves quickly was used to deal with the VRP with pickups and deliveries by Wassan et al. [4]. In previous research, only the direct suppliers were regarded as the customers in the logistics mode. Consequently, just the pickups and deliveries took place in the different direct suppliers so that the indirect suppliers were ignored. This caused some kind of waste.

In consideration of the transportation factors for the multi-level suppliers, this article tries to discuss both the direct suppliers and the indirect suppliers in a milk-run logistics mode. Based on the traditional milk-run logistics mode, a mixed milk-run logistics mode involved second level suppliers is introduced in this article. And improved genetic algorithm is selected to solve the optimization of the mixed milk-run mode. This mixed milk-run mode can not only better organize the automakers entrance logistics, but also balance the material supply of multi-level suppliers. This will greatly shorten the production period of automakers and suppliers, and through the mixed milk-run logistics mode cost afford by the whole supply chain, it can also reduce the logistics cost and improve the efficiency of the time, so as to realize the optimization of the whole supply chain.

2   Mathematical Model

In this section, the mixed milk-run modeling is dealt with. As it's already explained, the proposed mode of this article is a special case of milk-run which is purposely designed and customized for the supply chain with several multi-level suppliers.

This mixed mode can be described as finding the minimum cost of the combined routes of a number of vehicles K that must service a number of customers $(n_1 + n_2)$. Mathematically, this system can be imagined as a weighed graph $G = (V, A, d)$ where $V = \{v_0, v_1, \ldots, v_n\}$ represent the vertices, and the arcs are represented by

$A = \{(v_i, v_j), i \neq j\}$. A central depot where each vehicle starts its milk-run is located at v_0 and n customers are represented by each of the other vehicles. The distances associated with each arc are represented by the variable d_{ij} measured by Euclidean computations. Each vehicle is given a capacity constraint Q_m and a travel length constraint L_m. There is a non-negative demand qi assigned for each customer. The problem is solved under the following constraints [5].

a. Each customer is visited only once by a single vehicle.
b. Each vehicle must start and end its route at the depot, v_0.
c. Total demand serviced by each vehicle cannot exceed Q_m.
   Total route length for each vehicle cannot exceed L_m.
   The constraints above are the common constraints of the typical VRP. Additionally, another constraint must be included in the mixed mode.
d. The direct suppliers and related second level suppliers must be served by a single vehicle.
e. The second level suppliers must be served before related direct suppliers.

2.1   Decision Variables and Parameters

k: The number of vehicles available
k':   The number of vehicles actually used
n_{1i}:   The number of direct suppliers
n_{2j}:   The number of second level suppliers
n_p: The number of suppliers $(p = i + j)$
d_{pq}:   The distance moving from supplier $1i$ to supplier $2j$, $(d_{pq} = d_{qp})$
$d_{n_1 n_2j}$: The distance moving from supplier $1i$ to related supplier $2j$, $(d_{n_{1i}n_{2j}} = d_{n_{2j}n_{1i}})$
$R_{k(p)}$:   The transportation route set of vehicle k, whose subset is $r_{k(p)}$, and $k(p)$ means the sequence number of supplier p in the route
D_{p0}:   The demand of suppliers
Q_m: The maximum capacity for a single vehicle
L_m: The maximum travel length for a single vehicle
R_{kp}:   The transportation route of vehicle k,
C_k: The fixed cost for using a single vehicle
C_{l1}:   The negotiated transportation cost per unit distance between the direct suppliers and the delivery center
C_{l2}:   The negotiated transportation cost per unit distance between the direct suppliers and the second level suppliers

$$X_{pqk} = \begin{cases} 1 \text{ if truck } k \text{ transports from supplier } p \text{ to supplier } q \\ 0 \text{ if not} \end{cases}$$

$$Y_{pk} = \begin{cases} 1 \text{ if truck } k \text{ pick up materials at supplier } p \\ 0 \text{ if not} \end{cases}$$

2.2 The Mathematical Model

Since the main goal of implementation of the mixed milk-run system is to decrease the transportation cost, the following objective function is considered,

$$\min Z = \left(\sum_k \sum_p \sum_q X_{pqk} d_{pq} C_{l1} - \sum_k \sum_i \sum_j X_{n_{1i} n_{2j} k} d_{n_{1i} n_{2j}} C_{l1} \right) - \sum_k \sum_i \sum_j X_{n_{1i} n_{2j} k} d_{n_{1i} n_{2j}} C_{l2} + k' C_k$$

The first part of the objective function explains the total cost which the vehicles start from the direct suppliers to the delivery center.

It's considered that the transportation cost between the direct suppliers and the second level suppliers shouldn't be afforded by the automakers. The second part is considered as a kind of payback through helping transport materials from the second level suppliers to the related direct suppliers.

The third part is the fixed cost for actually used vehicles.

The first three constraints are associated with 'constraints a' listed in the preceding paragraph.

$$\sum_k Y_{pk} = 1 \tag{1}$$

This constraint states that every supplier is only allowed to be served by a single truck.

$$\sum_p X_{pqk} = Y_{qk} \tag{2}$$

$$\sum_q X_{pqk} = Y_{pk} \tag{3}$$

This two constraints state that every supplier is only allowed to be served only once.

$$\sum_p X_{1qk} = \sum_q X_{p1k} \le 1 \tag{4}$$

This constraints states that every vehicle starts its route from the delivery center and ends its route to the delivery center.

$$\sum_p D_{p0} Y_{pk} \le Q_m \tag{5}$$

This constraint investigates that the amount of materials collected from the suppliers for transportation to the delivery center would not exceed the upper limit of transporting vehicles.

$$\sum_k \sum_p \sum_q X_{pqk} d_{pq} \leq L_m \tag{6}$$

This constraint investigates that the route length of each vehicle would not exceed the upper limit of transporting vehicles.

$$r_{k(1i)}, r_{k(2j)} \in R_{k(p)} \forall i = j \tag{7}$$

This constraint states that the direct suppliers and related second level suppliers must be served by a single vehicle in the same route.

$$k(1i) > k(2j) \forall i = j \tag{8}$$

This constraint states that the direct suppliers must be served after related second level suppliers.

3 Improved Genetic Algorithm Design

Genetic algorithm (GA) is a directed random search technique that has been widely applied in optimization problems [6]. It's especially helpful to figure out the optimal solution globally over a domain [7]. In this paper, the standard GA is modified and new operators are introduced to improve its performance.

3.1 Initial Population

The symbolic coding method which is simple and easy to use is applied in the model. The solution to the problem (path set) should be encoded as a natural array of length N. The first set of population is generated randomly.

3.2 Fitness Function

Since the main goal of implementation of the model is to decrease the transportation cost, the formula $f = 1/(Z + M \times P_W)$ is applies as an individual fitness indicator.

Z: Objective function value
M: The number of unfeasible path
P_W: Punishing weight of unfeasible path

The better solution to the problem will return higher values in this process.

3.3 Selection Strategy

Roulette selection strategy is applied. Higher individual fitness, more opportunities or probabilities to be selected. The selected individual will undergo genetic operations for reproduction.

3.4   Genetic Operations

Since the mixed milk-run logistics mode is similar to Traveling Salesman Problem (TSP) in some ways and ordered crossover (OX) has been proved to be one of the best crossover operators for TSP [8] and the milk-run is similar to TSP, OX is applied in this article. Through this crossover operation, the offspring will be generated effectively.

Inversion mutation is applied. If the current optimal solution hold steady for a number of generation, the mutation rate P_m turns ten times until the optimal solution changes. The features of the offspring inherited from their parents can be changed in this way. Hence, the current search field can be expanded.

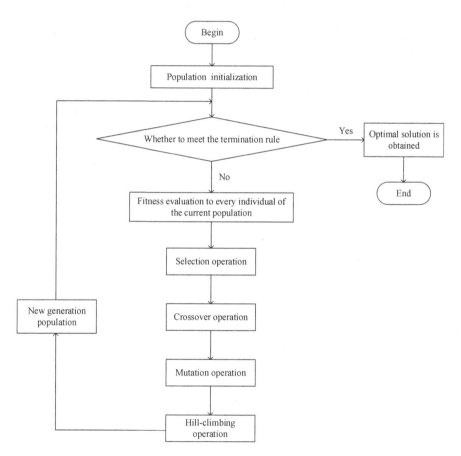

Fig. 1. Algorithm flow chart

3.5   Hill-Climbing Operation

Hill-climbing operation is implemented on the best individual of every generation. The exchange method of gene is used for field selection and new individual will born in this way. Better individual will be generated from the current best individual.

Computing Termination Rule

When the evolutionary generation is up to assigned generation, the evolution come to an end.

Algorithm flow chart is shown in Fig. 1.

4   Simulation Examples

This simulation is based on an automaker (numbered 0) with 20 direct suppliers (numbered 1, 2, …, 20) and 3 second level suppliers (numbered 21, 22, 23). The supplier 21 is the related supplier to the supplier 1. Similarly, the supplier 22 is the related supplier to the supplier 2 and the supplier 23 is the related supplier to the supplier 3. There are 4 same trucks, whose maximum loading capacity are 8t and maximum travel length are 50 km, served in this system.

The position coordinates of the automaker and suppliers are shown in Table 1. The amount of picking up goods demand from every supplier is also listed in Table 1.

Table 1. Parameters of suppliers.

	0	1	2	3	4	5	6	7
X Position/km	14.5	12.8	18.4	15.4	18.9	15.5	3.9	10.6
Y Position/km	13.0	8.5	3.4	16.6	15.2	11.6	10.6	7.6
Demand/t	0	0.1	0.4	1.2	1.5	0.8	1.3	1.7
	8	9	10	11	12	13	14	15
X Position/km	8.6	12.5	13.8	6.7	14.8	1.8	17.1	7.4
Y Position/m	8.4	2.1	5.2	16.9	2.6	8.7	11.0	1.0
Demand/t	0.6	1.2	0.4	0.9	1.3	1.3	1.9	1.7
	16	17	18	19	20	21	22	23
X Position/km	0.2	11.9	13.2	6.4	9.6	15.3	14.2	14.1
Y Position/km	2.8	19.8	15.1	5.6	14.8	5.4	0.2	19.8
Demand/t	1.1	1.5	1.6	1.7	1.5	0.8	1.7	1.9

The negotiated transportation cost per unit distance between the direct suppliers and the delivery center $C_{l1} = 1.78$ yuan/km.

The negotiated transportation cost per unit distance between the direct suppliers and the second level suppliers $C_{l2} = 5$ yuan/km.

The number of vehicles available $k = 4$.

The maximum capacity for a single vehicle $Q_m = 8$t.

The maximum travel length for a single vehicle $L_m = 50$ km.

Model and algorithm are programed by Matlab.

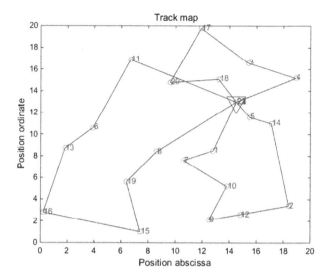

Fig. 2. The traditional optimal route

4.1 Traditional Milk-Run Simulation Example

In this simulation, 3 second level suppliers are not considered. It means there are only 20 direct suppliers in the milk-run simulation example. The example has been run 50 times. The optimal route can be seen in Fig. 2.

The optimal route: Route I: 0—18—20—17—3—4—0; Route II: 0—1—7—10—9—12—2—14—5—0; Route III: 0—8—19—15—16—13—6—11—0. Only 3 vehicles are actually occupied.

The minimum cost is 705.9718 yuan.

4.2 Mixed Milk-Run Simulation Example

In this simulation, 3 second level suppliers are considered. The example has been run 50 times. The optimal route can be seen in Fig. 3.

The optimal route: Route I: 0—5—14—1—7—10—21—2—12—22—9—0; Route II: 0—8—19—15—16—13—6—0; Route III: 0—18—4—3—23—17—11—20—0. Only 3 vehicles are actually occupied.

The minimum cost is 531.3116 yuan.

4.3 Simulation Results Comparison

After simulations of these two mode examples, optimal cost result has been selected from 50 simulations for each example. As the new mixed model lacks an optimal solution as a reference, It cannot be determined that the solution obtained by using the improved genetic algorithm is the global optimal solution. However, it's certain that they are globally satisfactory solutions.

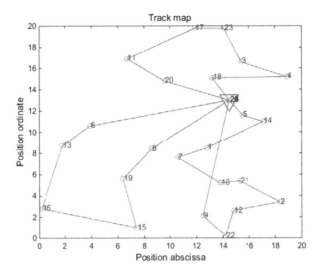

Fig. 3. The new optimal route

From the comparison of the minimum cost of each mode, nearly 180 yuan costs can be saved to per milk-run by the mixed milk-run logistics mode. It's shown that the mixed milk-run logistics mode is more helpful in saving cost than the typical mode under given constraints mentioned before from this simulation results.

5 Conclusion

In this paper, a mixed milk-run logistics mode with second level suppliers is proposed for the logistics of parts and components entering the automobile factory. By scheduling the sequence of vehicles visiting reasonably, this mode can balance the material supply of multi-level suppliers, reduce the inventory level of both automaker and its direct suppliers. Consequently, the total cost of automakers will be reduced and the competitiveness of enterprises will be greatly promoted. In addition, this is beneficial to reduce the vehicles and employees used for material transportation from second level suppliers to related direct suppliers. The result calculated by these examples can be serve as an important reference for the automakers who want to improve their logistics strategies so as to reduce their total cost.

References

1. Dantzig, G.B., Ramser, J.H.: The truck dispatching problem. Manag. Sci. **6**(1), 80–91 (1959)
2. Min, H.: The multiple vehicle routing problem with simultaneous delivery and pick-up points. Transp. Res. Part A General **23**(5), 377–386 (1989)
3. Nagya, G.: Heuristic algorithms for single and multiple depot vehicle routing problems with pickups and deliveries. Eur. J. Oper. Res. **162**(1), 126–141 (2005)

4. Wassan, N.A., Wassan, A.H., Nagy, G.: A reactive tabu search algorithm for the vehicle routing problem with simultaneous pickups and deliveries. J. Comb. Optim. **15**(4), 368–386 (2008)
5. Bell, J.E., Mcmullen, P.R.: Ant colony optimization techniques for the vehicle routing problem. Adv. Eng. Inform. **18**(1), 41–48 (2004)
6. Holland, J.H.: Adaptation in natural and artificial systems. Q. Rev. Biol. **6**(2), 126–137 (1975)
7. Rigelsford, J.: Intelligent optimisation techniques: genetic algorithms, tabu search, simulated annealing and neural networks. Ind. Robot **27**(5) (2000)
8. Abdoun, O., Abouchabaka, J.: A comparative study of adaptive crossover operators for genetic algorithms to resolve the traveling salesman problem. Comput. Sci. **31**(11), 49–57 (2011)

An Optimization Model of Vehicle Routing Problem for Logistics Based on Sustainable Development Theory

Yan Li, Ming K. Lim$^{(\boxtimes)}$, and Weiqing Xiong

Chongqing University, Chongqing City 400044, China
ming.lim@cqu.edu.cn

Abstract. This paper proposes a logistics vehicle routing problem model based on the sustainable development theory, and develops a multi-objective planning model that includes social indicators, economic indicators and environmental indicators. Minimum total cost as a goal,that includes social costs, fixed costs, fuel costs, delay costs, CO_2 emission costs and PM emissions costs. The particle swarm optimization was proposed to solve the case. The impact of different carbon dioxide prices on economic costs and environmental costs were discussed. The results show that increasing carbon dioxide prices can reduce pollutant emissions and lower operating costs. Finally the limitations and future research directions of this study are discussed.

Keywords: Logistics · Vehicle routing problem · Sustainable development
Particle swarm optimization

1 Introduction

In recent years, the increase of greenhouse gas emissions leads to global warming and it has attracted the attention of the international community [1]. The transportation industry accounts for more than 20% of the energy consumption and greenhouse gas emissions. In the transportation industry, CO_2 emissions of the transportation and distribution links accounts for 93%, only 7% for warehousing and other links [2]. So how to develop sustainable distribution has become an important research direction in the logistics [3].

The concept of sustainable development can be traced back to the 1960s, Rachel's "Lonely Spring" made people begin to pay attention to the protection of the environment [4]. Nowadays, sustainable development has increasingly attracted the attention of governments and enterprises [5]. However, there is no unified concept for sustainable development currently. It can be concluded that it contains three major themes: economic development, environmental quality and social equity by analyzing different scholars' descriptions of sustainable development [6, 7].

Optimizing the vehicle routing will reduce carbon emission achieving logistics sustainable development [8]. However, the current research on sustainable vehicle routing focuses on environmental and economic factors. Tiwari proposed a vehicle routing problem(VRP)model with the goal of minimizing pollution and analyzed the

© Springer Nature Singapore Pte Ltd. 2018
S. Wang et al. (Eds.): ICSEE 2018/IMIOT 2018, CCIS 923, pp. 179–190, 2018.
https://doi.org/10.1007/978-981-13-2396-6_16

relationship between carbon emissions and costs [9]. Tavares developed a VRP model of garbage collection with minimizing the fuel consumption [10]. Economic factors and environmental factors were considered when they built the model, and the environmental factors only contain carbon emissions. However, vehicles also produce pollutants such as particulate matter (PM) in the process of transportation [10]. This study fully considers social factors, economic factors and environmental factors aiming at the defects of the existing research, and proposes a vehicle routing problem model based on the sustainable development theory (SDVRP). Nalepa proposed a VRP model with the goal of shortest distance [11]. Kuo established a model consider fuel consumption [12]. However, researchers began to change from single-objective to multi-objective. This study proposed a multi-objective SDVRP model aims at minimizing the total cost, that includes social cost, fixed costs, fuel costs, delay costs, CO_2 emission costs, and PM emission costs.

The method to solve VRP is a hot research direction. Golden classified VRP into two categories from algorithmic perspective: exact algorithms and heuristic algorithms [13]. Exact algorithm and traditional heuristic algorithm were used to solve the VRP in early stages of research, but these two methods will not find the optimal solution as the model complexity increases [14]. The modern heuristic algorithms such as genetic algorithm, ant colony algorithm, and particle swarm optimization has a good ability to solve complex problems [15]. Costa used genetic algorithm to solve the VRP [16]. Goel proposed that the ant colony algorithm was used to solve the VRP [17]. Particle swarm optimization (PSO) was proposed to solve the problem by Norouzi, and the results showed that PSO was faster compared with other algorithms [18]. Therefore, PSO was used in this paper.

In summary, the advantage of the SDVRP model is that it considers social, environmental and economic factors to achieve optimal overall benefits, and propose a particle swarm algorithm to improve the speed of the solution. This article is divided into six sections. This section presents a literature review of vehicle routing problem based on sustainable development theory. Section 2 established a SDVRP model that considers social factors, economic factors, and environmental factors. The particle swarm optimization was introduced in Sect. 3. Section 4 introduces the relevant information of the case. Section 5 discusses the impact of different CO_2 prices on total cost and pollutant emissions. The last section summarizes the conclusions, contributions, limitations, and future work of this article.

2   Formulation of the Optimization Model

2.1   Problem Hypothesis

In the process of turning into a mathematical model, this study makes some assumptions:

(1) This article deals with the problem of a single distribution center delivering to multiple customers.
(2) Vehicles for distribution are the same type and travel at uniform speed.

(3) The weight of the goods carried by the vehicle cannot exceed its maximum carrying capacity.

(4) All vehicles must be return to the distribution center after distribution.

2.2   Objective Function

This study proposes a SDVRP model with multi-objective. The objective function includes social costs, economic costs and environmental costs.

2.2.1   Social Costs

The social cost contain three indicators, the employee's education investment, the employee's welfare protection and the penalty for violating the law (this article refers to whether there is overload or speeding). The expression of social costs is shown in Eq. (1).

$$C_1 = \sum_{n=1}^{N} (T_1 + T_2 + W_n \cdot T_3) \tag{1}$$

In the equation, T_1—employee education investment (yuan/person, day), T_2—employee welfare protection(yuan/person, day), T_3—illegal penalties (yuan/number), W_n— 0,1 variable, when the vehicles violates the laws, $W_n = 1$, otherwise $W_n = 0$. N — vehicles owned by the distribution center.

2.2.2   Economic Costs

Economic costs include the fixed cost of using the vehicle, energy costs, and delay costs due to inappropriate delivery times.

(1)   Fixed costs

The fixed cost of the vehicle refers to the cost in the distribution process, including the loss of the vehicle, the maintenance of the vehicle, the salary of the personnel. The fixed cost is shown in Eq. (2).

$$C_{21} = \sum_{n=1}^{N} T_4 \cdot X_n \tag{2}$$

In the equation, T_4—fixed cost(yuan/vehicle), X_n— 0,1 variable, when the vehicle is used, $X_n = 1$, otherwise $X_n = 0$.

(2)   Energy costs

Energy cost refers to the cost of using fuel in the distribution process, which is related to fuel consumption. The energy costs are shown in Eq. (3), fuel consumption is shown in Eq. (4).

$$C_{22} = \sum_{n=1}^{N}\sum_{i=0}^{M}\sum_{j=0}^{M} Z_{ij}^{n} \cdot T_5 \left[d_{ij} \cdot R(Q_i) \right] \tag{3}$$

$$R(Q_i) = R_0 + \frac{(R_1 - R_0)}{Q} \cdot Q_i \tag{4}$$

In the equation, T_5—fuel cost (yuan/L), d_{ij}—the distance between customer i and j, $R(Q_i)$—the fuel consumption, Z_{ij}^{n}—0,1 variable, when the vehicle passes customer i to customer j, $Z_{ij}^{n} = 1$, otherwise $Z_{ij}^{n} = 0$. Q—the maximum load (t), Q_i—weight of goods on vehicle(t), R_0—fuel consumption when empty(L/km), R_1—fuel consumption at full load(L/km), M—total number of customers.

(3) Delay costs

Delay costs refers to the cost due to the delivery time not meeting the customer requirements. The delay cost is shown in Eq. (5).

$$C_{23} = \sum_{n=1}^{N}\sum_{i=0}^{M} \left(T_6 \cdot max(D_1 - t_i^n, 0) + T_7 \cdot max(t_i^n - D_2) \right) \tag{5}$$

In the equation, T_6—Early penalty cost (yuan/h), T_7—Late delay cost (yuan/h), t_i^n— the operation time from customer i to j, D_1—the earliest delivery time, D_2—the latest delivery time.

Therefore, the total economic cost is shown in Eq. (6).

$$C_2 = C_{21} + C_{22} + C_{23} = \sum_{y=1}^{Y} T_4 \cdot X_n + \sum_{n=1}^{N}\sum_{i=0}^{M}\sum_{j=0}^{M} Z_{ij}^{n} \cdot T_5 \left[d_{ij} \cdot R(Q_i) \right] + $$
$$\sum_{n=1}^{N}\sum_{i=0}^{M} \left(T_6 \cdot max(D_1 - t_i^n, 0) + T_7 \cdot max(t_i^n - D_2) \right) \tag{6}$$

2.2.3   Environmental Costs

Environmental costs contains the carbon dioxide emissions cost and PM emissions costs, and PM emission costs including $PM_{2.5}$ cost and PM_{10} cost.

(1) Carbon dioxide emission cost

According to the '*Accounting Method for Greenhouse Gas Emissions of Land Transport Enterprises by the Chinese Government*' [19], the equation for carbon dioxide emissions is shown in (7).

$$E_{CO_2} = \sum NVC \times FC \times CC \times OF \times \frac{12}{44} \tag{7}$$

In the equation, *NVC*—the average low calorific value of the fuel, *FC*—the fuel consumption, *CC*—the carbon content per unit calorific value of the fuel, *OF*—the carbon oxidation rate of the fossil fuel. For the diesel fuel, $NVC = 43.33$, $CC = 0.0202$, $OF = 0.98$ T8—CO_2 cost (yuan/kg). The cost of carbon dioxide emissions is shown in (8),

$$C_{31} = T_8 \sum_{n=1}^{N} \sum_{i=0}^{m} \sum_{j=0}^{m} Z_{ij}^n \left(NVC \times \left(\left[\sum d_{ij} \times R(Q_i) \right] \right) \times CC \times OF \times \frac{12}{44} \right) \quad (8)$$

(2) PM emission costs

PM emissions measured according to the '*Guidelines for the Preparation of Air Pollutant Emission Inventory for Road Vehicles promulgated by the Chinese government*' [20], that includes $PM_{2.5}$ and PM_{10} as shown in Eqs. (9) and (10).

$$EF_{PM_{2.5}} = BEF_{PM_{2.5}} \times \varphi_{Temp-PM_{2.5}} \times \varphi_{RH-PM_{2.5}} \times \varphi_{Height-PM_{2.5}} \times \gamma_{j-PM_{2.5}} \times \lambda_i$$
$$\times \theta_{i-PM_{2.5}} \quad (9)$$

$$EF_{PM_{10}} = BEF_{PM_{2.5}} \times \varphi_{Temp-PM_{10}} \times \varphi_{RH-PM_{10}} \times \varphi_{Height-PM_{10}} \times \gamma_{j-PM_{10}} \times \lambda_i \times \theta_{i-PM_{10}} \quad (10)$$

In the equations, *BEF*—the comprehensive emission factor coefficient. φ_{Temp}—the temperature correction factor, φ_{RH}—the humidity correction factor, φ_{Height}—the altitude correction factor, γ_j—the speed correction factor, λ_i—the deterioration correction factor, and θ_i other use condition correction factors, $BEF_{PM2.5} = 0.044, BEF_{PM10} = 0.049$, $\varphi_{Temp-PM2.5/PM10} = 1$, $\varphi_{RH-PM2.5/PM10} = 1$, no elevation correction, $\lambda_i = 1.43$, $\theta_{i-PM2.5/PM10} = 0.82$, T9—PM cost (yuan/g). PM emission costs are shown as Eq. (11),

$$C_{32} = T_9 \sum_{n=1}^{N} \sum_{i=0}^{m} \sum_{j=0}^{m} Z_{ij}^n \left(\sum d_{ij} \times 10^{-6} \right.$$
$$\times \left(\begin{matrix} BEF_{PM_{2.5}} \times \varphi_{Temp-PM_{2.5}} \times \varphi_{RH-PM_{2.5}} \times \varphi_{Height-PM_{2.5}} \times \gamma_{j-PM_{2.5}} \times \lambda_i \times \theta_{i-PM_{2.5}} + \\ BEF_{PM_{2.5}} \times \varphi_{Temp-PM_{10}} \times \varphi_{RH-PM_{10}} \times \varphi_{Height-PM_{10}} \times \gamma_{j-PM_{10}} \times \lambda_i \times \theta_{i-PM_{10}} \end{matrix} \right) \left. \right) \quad (11)$$

The total environmental costs is shown in Eq. (12).

$$C_3 = C_{31} + C_{32} = T_8 \sum_{n=1}^{N} \sum_{i=0}^{m} \sum_{j=0}^{m} Z_{ij}^n \left(NVC \times \left(\left[\sum d_{ij} \times \rho(X) \right] \right) \times CC \times OF \times \tfrac{12}{44} \right) +$$
$$T_9 \sum_{n=1}^{N} \sum_{i=0}^{m} \sum_{j=0}^{m} Z_{ij}^n \left(\sum d_{ij} \times 10^{-6} \times \left(\begin{matrix} BEF_{PM_{2.5}} \times \varphi_{Temp-PM_{2.5}} \times \varphi_{RH-PM_{2.5}} \times \varphi_{Height-PM_{2.5}} \times \gamma_{j-PM_{2.5}} \times \lambda_i \times \theta_{i-PM_{2.5}} + \\ BEF_{PM_{2.5}} \times \varphi_{Temp-PM_{10}} \times \varphi_{RH-PM_{10}} \times \varphi_{Height-PM_{10}} \times \gamma_{j-PM_{10}} \times \lambda_i \times \theta_{i-PM_{10}} \end{matrix} \right) \right) \quad (12)$$

2.3 Optimization Model

The optimization goal of this model is to minimize the total cost, contains social costs, economic costs and environmental costs, as shown in Eq. (13).

$$
Zmin = \left(
\begin{array}{l}
\sum\limits_{n=1}^{N}(T_1 + T_2 + W_n \cdot T_3) + \sum\limits_{y=1}^{Y} T_4 \cdot X_n + \sum\limits_{n=1}^{N}\sum\limits_{i=0}^{M}\sum\limits_{j=0}^{M} Z_{ij}^n \cdot T_5 [d_{ij} \cdot R(Q_i)] + \\
\sum\limits_{n=1}^{N}\sum\limits_{i=0}^{M}(T_6 \cdot max(D_1 - t_i^n, 0) + T_7 \cdot max(t_i^n - D_2)) + T_8 \sum\limits_{n=1}^{N}\sum\limits_{i=0}^{m}\sum\limits_{j=0}^{m} Z_{ij}^n (NVC \times ([\sum d_{ij} \times R(Q_i)]) \times CC \times OF \times \tfrac{12}{44}) + \\
T_9 \sum\limits_{n=1}^{N}\sum\limits_{i=0}^{m}\sum\limits_{j=0}^{m} Z_{ij}^n \left(\sum d_{ij} \times 10^{-6} \times \left(\begin{array}{l} BEF_{PM_{2.5}} \times \varphi_{Temp-PM_{2.5}} \times \varphi_{RH-PM_{2.5}} \times \varphi_{Height-PM_{2.5}} \times \gamma_{j-PM_{2.5}} \times \lambda_i \times \theta_{i-PM_{2.5}} + \\ BEF_{PM_{10}} \times \varphi_{Temp-PM_{10}} \times \varphi_{RH-PM_{10}} \times \varphi_{Height-PM_{10}} \times \gamma_{j-PM_{10}} \times \lambda_i \times \theta_{i-PM_{10}} \end{array}\right)\right)
\end{array}
\right) \quad (13)
$$

Constraints:

$$
\sum_{j=1}^{m}\sum_{n=1}^{N} Z_{ij}^n = Y, \quad i = 0 \tag{14}
$$

$$
\sum_{n=1}^{N} Y_i^n = 1, \quad i = 1, 2, \cdots, M \tag{15}
$$

$$
\sum_{j=1}^{m} Z_{ij}^n = \sum_{j=1}^{m} Z_{ij}^n \leq 1, \quad i = 0, \ n = 1, 2, \cdots N \tag{16}
$$

Equation (14) represents having Y deliver paths and it is equal to the number of vehicles.

Equation (15) represents a customer only be served by one vehicle.

Equation (16) represents the vehicle leaves from the distribution center and finally back to distribution center.

3 Algorithm Design

This study uses the particle swarm optimization (PSO) to solve the case in Sect. 4. The POS solves the vehicle routing problem in two stages. The first stage is to initialize the particle population and form the initial solution. The second stage is to find the optimal solution. The specific steps are as follows:

(1) Phase 1 - Initialization of Particle Swarms

Step1: Randomly generated particle swarms containing a total of N particles;

Step2: In each particle position vector, xa is an integer between $(1 - N)$, and xb is an integer between $(1 - M)$.

Step3: In each particle velocity vector, va is an integer between $-(N - 1) \sim (N - 1)$ and vb is an integer between $-(M - 1) \sim (M - 1)$.

Step4: Evaluation of fitness for each particle based on fitness function.

Step5: Take the initial fitness as the individual historical best solution pi, and find the optimal solution within the population pg.

(2) Phase 2 - Finding the Optimal Solution

Step1: Update the speed and position of each particle.

Step2: Evaluation of fitness based on fitness function.

Step3: If a particle's current fitness is better than its historical optimal fitness, the current position is updated to the particle's historical optimal position *pi*.

Step4: Finding the best solution within the population, if it is better than the historical best solute-on update *pg*.

The solution process is shown in Fig. 1.

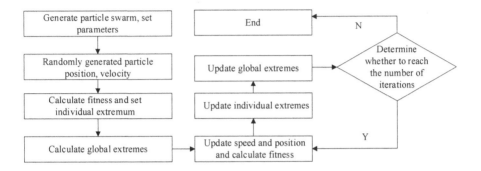

Fig. 1. Particle swarm optimization process

4 Experimental Design

The particle swarm optimization (PSO) proposed in this paper uses Matlab2016b to conduct simulation experiments. This section mainly introduces the information needed for simulation experiments, including customer data and parameter settings.

4.1 Case Description

This research studies the logistics route planning of a distribution company in Chongqing. The coordinates of the distribution center is (622.298, 3281.896). The geographic coordinates, time requirements and demand of the 16 customer sites are shown in Table 1.

4.2 Parameter Settings

Parameter includes the parameter in the model and the parameter in the algorithm.

4.2.1 Parameter in the Model

In the morning, the vehicle departs from the distribution center at 4:30 and the vehicle travels at 30 km/h. The specific parameter setting of the model is shown in Table 2.

Table 1. Customer Information

Customer number	X	Y	Demand (t)	Earliest time	Latest time	Service hours (h)
1	652.962	3272.595	0.4	5:00	7:00	0.52
2	641.474	3269.611	0.2	5:00	7:00	0.26
3	651.208	3268.814	0.1	5:30	7:00	0.13
4	655.236	3271.702	0.35	5:00	6:30	0.46
5	644.652	3275.904	0.2	5:00	6:00	0.26
6	640.402	3277.821	0.4	5:30	7:00	0.52
7	647.522	3270.582	0.25	6:00	7:00	0.33
8	644.408	3263.427	0.35	6:00	6:30	0.46
9	646.248	3275.309	0.15	5:00	6:00	0.20
10	642.683	3272.029	0.45	5:00	7:00	0.59
11	647.325	3267.129	0.2	6:00	7:00	0.26
12	648.584	3279.836	0.3	5:30	7:30	0.39
13	645.184	3270.182	0.25	6:00	7:00	0.33
14	647.937	3275.885	0.15	5:00	6:00	0.20
15	651.609	3275.103	0.2	5:30	7:00	0.26
16	654.799	3276.07	0.1	6:00	7:00	0.13

Table 2. Parameter settings in the model

Parameter	Unit	Parameter value
N——total number of vehicles	number	3
T_1——employee education investment	yuan/person,day	12
T_2——employee welfare protection	yuan/person,day	12
T_3——illegal penalties	yuan/number	1000
T_4——fixed cost	yuan/vehicle	150
T_5——fuel cost	yuan/L	6.68
T_6——early penalty cost	yuan/h	40
T_7——late delay cost	yuan/h	60
T_8——CO_2 cost	yuan/kg	variable
T_9——PM cost	yuan/g	0.1
Q ——the maximum load	t	2
R_0——fuel consumption when empty	L/km	0.165
R_1——fuel consumption at full load	L/km	0.377

4.2.2 Parameter in the Algorithm

The maximum number of iterations of the algorithm is 300, inertia factor is 0.7, learning factor C_1 is 2, learning factor C_2 is 2 and the number of population is 20.

5 Analysis of Case

The effect of changing in carbon dioxide prices on economic indicators and environmental indicators is discussed. The unit price of carbon dioxide is set to 2, 2.5, 3, 3.5, 4, 4.5 yuan/kg. The path planning is shown in Fig. 2. The simplified result obtained are shown in Table 3.

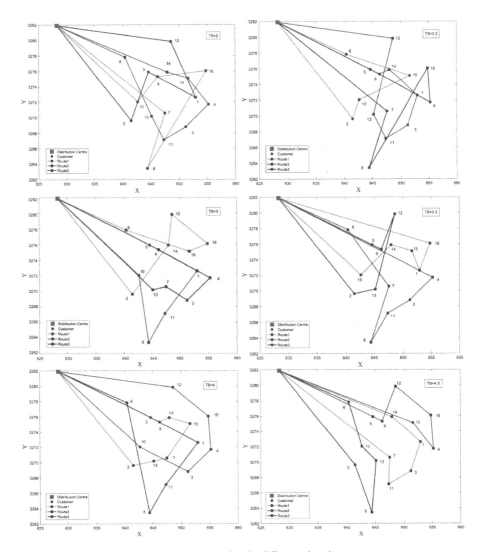

Fig. 2. Path planning in different situations

From Fig. 2, we can draw the vehicle path is constantly changing as the price of carbon dioxide increases, so the price of carbon dioxide will affect the optimal path and

Table 3. Simplified result in different carbon price.

Carbon price (yuan/kg)	Social cost (yuan)	Economic costs (yuan)	Environment cost (yuan)	Total cost (yuan)	CO_2 emission (kg)	PM emission (g)
2	24	742.86	23.85	790.71	8	78.71
2.5	24	730.87	27.59	782.46	7.89	78.59
3	24	718.03	30.04	772.06	7.62	72.13
3.3	24	713.92	33.79	771.71	7.51	71.97
4	24	709.48	36.11	769.59	7.25	71.18
4.5	24	704.84	38.8	767.64	7.03	70.59

thus affect costs. This study continue to explore the impact of carbon prices on total costs, economic costs, and environmental costs.

5.1   Changes in Carbon Dioxide Prices and Economic Costs

This section discusses the impact of changes in carbon dioxide prices on economic costs and total costs. The data of carbon price and economic costs in Table 3 is plotted as a line graph Fig. 3.

The cost of social responsibility is only related to the number of employees joining the distribution. The number of employees is fixed at three under different situations, so the social cost is fixed. The conclusion can be obtained through Fig. 5-1: As the price of carbon dioxide continues rising, both the total costs and the economic costs continue to decline, while the environmental costs gradually increase.

5.2   Changes in Carbon Dioxide Prices and Environmental Costs

This section discusses the impact of changes in carbon dioxide prices on environmental costs. The data of carbon price and environmental costs in Table 3 is plotted as a line graph Fig. 4.

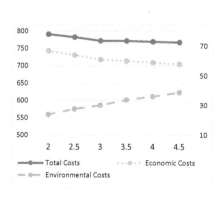

Fig. 3. Effect of CO_2 price on costs

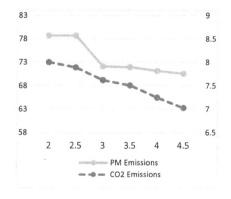

Fig. 4. Effect of carbon dioxide price on emissions.

The conclusion can be obtained through Fig. 5-3: As the price of carbon dioxide continues rising, both the CO_2 emissions and PM emissions continue to decline.

6   Conclusion and Future

This study proposed a vehicle routing problem model of logistics based on the sustainable development theory (SDVRP). It aims at minimizing the total cost, which is divided into three categories: social costs, economic costs and environmental costs. There are seven detailed costs, including social costs, fixed costs, fuel costs, delay costs, CO_2 emission costs, and PM emission costs. Further using particle swarm optimization (PSO) to solve the case and the results discussed the impact of different carbon dioxide prices on economic costs and environmental costs.

This study draws the following conclusion: As the price of CO_2 rises within the range selected in this paper, social costs remain unchanged, total costs and economic costs gradually decrease, environmental costs gradually increase. And CO_2 and PM emissions gradually decrease. These show that raising the price of carbon dioxide within a certain range can reduce operating costs and environmental pollution. This study mainly has the following contributions. In theory, this paper proposes a model based on the theory of sustainable development. Existing research in environmental factors has focused on carbon dioxide emissions, this study adds the PM_{10} and $PM_{2.5}$ factors in addition to carbon dioxide. In practice, this study provides a method for enterprises to implement sustainable path planning and provides a decision-making basis for the country to formulate policies.

This article has some limitations in some aspects. Only one type vehicle was selected in this study, various vehicles should be studied in the future. The fuel consumption only considers the distance and the load, other conditions such as the vehicle speed, weather, and road congestion were not taken into consideration. Research on fuel consumption is a direction worth studying.

References

1. Wang, X.: Changes in CO_2 emissions induced by agricultural inputs in China over 1991–2014. Sustainability **8**(5), 414 (2016)
2. Decker, I.J.: Sustainability and green logistics. In: Proceedings of the Joint German-Singaporean Symposium on Green Logistics, August Singapore City [s.n.] (2011)
3. Gross, W.F., Butz, C.: About the impact of rising oil price on logistics networks and transportation greenhouse gas emission. Logistics Res. **4**(3–4), 147–156 (2012)
4. Carson, R.: Silent Spring. China Youth Press, Beijing (2015)
5. Summers, K., Mccullough, M., Smith, E., Gwinn, M., Kremer, F., Sjogren, M., et al.: The sustainable and healthy communities research program: the environmental protection agency's research approach to assisting community decision-making. Sustainability **6**(1), 306–318 (2014)
6. Zhao, X., Zhang, Y., Liang, J., Li, Y., Jia, R., Wang, L.: The sustainable development of the economic-energy-environment (3e) system under the carbon trading (ct) mechanism: a Chinese case. Sustainability **10**(1), 98 (2018)

7. Sun, Q., Zhang, X., Zhang, H., Niu, H.: Coordinated development of a coupled social economy and resource environment system: a case study in Henan province. China. Environ. Dev. Sustain. **1**, 1–20 (2017)

8. Bektaş, T., Laporte, G.: The pollution-routing problem. Transp. Res. Part B Methodological **45**(8), 1232–1250 (2011)

9. Tiwari, A., Chang, P.C.: A block recombination approach to solve green vehicle routing problem. Int. J. Prod. Econ. **164**, 379–387 (2015)

10. Tavares, G., Zsigraiova, Z., Semiao, V., Carvalho, M.G.: Optimisation of MSW collection routes for minimum fuel consumption using 3D GIS modelling. Waste Manage. **29**(3), 1176–1185 (2009)

11. Nalepa, J., Blocho, M.: Adaptive memetic algorithm for minimizing distance in the vehicle routing problem with time windows. Soft. Comput. **20**(6), 1–19 (2015)

12. Kuo, Y.: Using simulated annealing to minimize fuel consumption for the time-dependent vehicle routing problem. Comput. Ind. Eng. **59**(1), 157–165 (2010)

13. Golden, B.L., Assad, A.A.: Perspectives on vehicle routing: exciting new developments. Oper. Res. **34**(5), 803–810 (1986)

14. Bettemir, Ö.H., Birgönül, M.T.: Network analysis algorithm for the solution of discrete time-cost trade-off problem. KSCE J. Civil Eng. **21**(4), 1–12 (2017)

15. Guo, P., Wang, K., Xue, M.: Research status and prospects of computational intelligence in big data analysis. J. Softw. **26**(11), 3010–3025 (2015)

16. Costa, P.R.D.O.D., Mauceri, S., Carroll, P., Pallonetto, F.: A genetic algorithm for a green vehicle routing problem. Electron. Notes Discrete Math. **64**, 65–74 (2018)

17. Goel, R., Maini, R.: A hybrid of ant colony and firefly algorithms (HAFA) for solving vehicle routing problems. J. Comput. Sci. **25**, 28–37 (2018)

18. Gong, M., Cai, Q., Chen, X., Ma, L.: Complex network clustering by multi-objective discrete particle swarm optimization based on decomposition. IEEE Trans. Evol. Comput. **18**(1), 82–97 (2014)

19. The Central People's Government of the People's Republic of China, 2015. National Development and Reform Commission, People's Republic of China (2015). http://www.ndrc.gov.cn/zcfb/zcfbtz/201511/t20151111_758275.html

20. The Central People's Government of the People's Republic of China, 2014. Ministry of Ecology and Environment, People's Republic of China (2014). http://www.zhb.gov.cn/gkml/hbb/bgg/201501/t20150107_293955.htm

The Prediction of Perishable Products' Sale Volume and Profit in Chongqing Based on Grey Model

Yingjia Tang[1], Xu Wang[1,2(✉)], and LongXiao Li[1]

[1] Chongqing University, Shapingba District, Chongqing 400044, China
422760871@qq.com, wx921@163.com
[2] State Key Laboratory of Mechanical Transmission, Shapingba District, Chongqing 400044, China

Abstract. The cold chain logistics has become an important part of national economy as the plans which the government announced these year, such like 《Development plan of cold chain logistics of agricultural products》. But also the city, Chongqing, paid more attention on its improvement that issued some files like 《The implementation of Municipal People's government to speed up the development of agricultural Cold Chain in Chongqing, and 《Development plan of cold chain logistics in Chongqing》. This paper aimed to help fresh enterprise predicting the sales volume and profit by using Grey Model, which can grasp the trend of the market and developing direction. This paper set an example as TY Co., Ltd in Chongqing to show the operation process then get the answers. The figures of outcome past the consistency test that can prove this method's accuracy and reliability.

Keywords: Perishable goods · Grey model

1 Introduction

The 《Food hygiene law》 published in China have improved the cold chain logistics development in some extent in 1982. Early twenty-first century, some food processing industries become the leader to established the cold chain system self-centered. Most of Chinese enterprises adapt self-management model for their cold chain logistics operation, which can draw up by different condition these companies have. This model not only can keep and control the high quality of goods, but also decrease the potential risk and damage, the most commonly used patterns under such an incomplete social system. In 2006, the average level of dairy consumption in cities is 25.59 kg per person, included fresh dairy 18.29 kg, powdered milk 0.50 kg, yogurt 3.79 kg. The cost of logistics account for 25% among the total expense, 355.6 billion Yuan. Wang et al. had introduced the procedure and the related formula of gray model [1]. Hu et al. did research on the improved gray model which aim at the shortcoming of the traditional Verhulst model and proved the scheme is efficient and applicable [4]. It is important to forecast the sales volume to make right strategies to keep the quality of the dairy products, as the Bio Nano Laboratory and other two institutions' research mentioned

© Springer Nature Singapore Pte Ltd. 2018
S. Wang et al. (Eds.): ICSEE 2018/IMIOT 2018, CCIS 923, pp. 191–197, 2018.
https://doi.org/10.1007/978-981-13-2396-6_17

that there are many kinds of viruses and bacteria can have negative impacts on the dairy goods [2]. To ensure the quality of goods sent to the customer, there are more and more high-tech used in this field, such like the cold plasma science and technology is increasingly used for translation to a plethora of issues in agriculture and dairy food, which can help to keep the right temperature in the room [3] studied by Bourke et al. In Shaikh et al.'s study [5], they utilized the gray model to forecasting Chinese natural gas demand by two optimized nonlinear grey models, and get the conclusion that there will be a significant increase in its demand in the future. Before this paper, Shaikh et al. also analyzed the logistic modelling of natural gas by use LMA in 2016, then this method was placed by gray model in 2017 as the former [6]. Yang et al. had mentioned [8] that the modeling and prediction process is more complicated than the one with real numbers that based on the interval grey parameter numbers, and they found that the grey prediction model for interval grey number by the fractional-order accumulation calculus more freedom with better performance for modeling and prediction. The Grey model not only can used to predict the volume, but also can forecasting system for return flow of end-of life vehicles. Ene et al. used a small amount of the most recent data to create the forecasting models [9].

With the demand of dairy product increased dramatically, it is more and more important to insure the way can be right to transfer and store the large amount of these goods. Because the gray model has a simple but accurate process, accurate data can also be obtained with less continuous data. So this paper choose to use grey model to predict the sales volume.

2 Analysis on the Present Situation of Dairy Products

The dairy industry started late in China, but its has enormous room for developing. Looking from our agricultural structure, the dairy industry only account for 3%, which is far behind some developed countries. Considered the dairy animals' capacity comprehensively, it's forecast to reach 6000 million tons of production in 2020, average 42 kg Per person, which the China and India's demand for dairy will take 1/3 among the worldwide, and this figure in Asia will exceed the other areas again. With the increasing trend of our living standard and the consciousness of healthy life style, people will have higher and higher requirement of dairy's security and quality, which means that the people will prefer to some nutritious dairy. From August 2016 to July 2017, domestic quantity is went up steady and kept over 250 million tons, which illustrate the dairy production has tended to be stable (Figs. 1 and 2).

In our country's dairy industry, few third party took part in it development that make there few third party can offer the technology to control the temperature at the appropriate level during the whole cold chain. Because the most logistics supplier are developed from traditional logistics transporter that can't meet the needs of comprehensive, complete, and integrated logistics services. Moreover, as the specialty the dairy transportation needs, Chinese dairy cold chain development are restricted by shortage of manager. Based on complexity and specialty, the cold chain has higher level of requirement of manager than other industries.

Fig. 1. The data of dairy production quantity in 2016–2017.

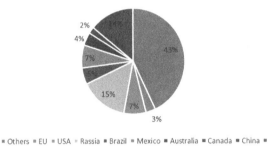

Fig. 2. Proportion of dairy import in different areas.

3 Prediction of Sales Volume and Profits in TY Co., Ltd Based on GM

Dairy production belongs to fast consumables that has high requirement of freshness and security. So the sales volume and profit become important that can make enterprises avoid over-capacity and adjust plans to adapt new situation when there are some changes in market.

Grey Model is used to predicting the changes happened in developed process constantly. In this model, we have to consider impacts of the uncertainty and randomness of the thing itself has, some external factors and environment. So Grey Model can be attributed to one of fuzzy mathematics. However, the advantage the Grey Model has are, it don't need too many samples, and these samples needn't to showed regular distribution. TY Co., Ltd' s situation meet this method requirement– over three samples. Grey Model can do predict work with high accuracy in Short, medium and long term.

There are four types of Grey Model: Sequence prediction, catastrophic prediction, system prediction, topological prediction. Among many kinds of model, we chose GM (1,1) to make the prediction. Additionally, it will be helpful to collect the figures as much as we can to reduce the variability and randomness of sequence. Accumulating data generating series of original data: $x^{(0)} = (x^{(1)}(1), x^{(1)}(2), \ldots, x^{(1)}(n))$.

Then the first linear differential equation is established, in which a is the development coefficient, and the U is the endogenous control grey number:

$$\frac{dx^{(1)}}{dt} + ax^{(1)} = u, a(1, 1)$$

The equation can be obtained by using the least square method to calculate the grey parameters:

$$\hat{a} = \begin{pmatrix} a \\ u \end{pmatrix} = (B^T B)^{-1} B^T Y_n$$

$\hat{a}$ will be brought into the linear differential equation $x^{(1)}(t)$, and the formula can be calculated:

$$\hat{x}^{(1)}(t+1) = (x^{(0)}(1) - \frac{u}{a})e^{-at} + \frac{u}{a}$$

4 Case Study

4.1 Model Formulation

Using the method of sequence prediction, we can get the sales volume and profits of TY Co., Ltd dairy in 2005–2013 during practice (Table 1).

Table 1. The sales volume and profits of TY Co., Ltd during 2005–2013.

	Volume (MT)	Profit (BY)
2005	9.3	3.85
2006	10.05	4.24
2007	11.39	5.5
2008	12.06	7.29
2009	15.63	9.6
2010	18.45	12.22
2011	19.59	15.25
2012	21.2	17.75
2013	23.2	23

The sales volume is taken as an example. First, the sales information is arranged. According to the information of data, the original data sequence can be obtained:

$$X_{(0)} = [9.3, 10.05, 11.39, 12.06, 15.63, 18.45, 19.59, 21.2, 23.2]$$

The cumulative generation sequence is as follows:

$$X_{(1)} = [9.3,\ 19.35,\ 30.74,\ 42.8,\ 58.43,\ 76.88,\ 96.47,\ 117.67,\ 140.87]$$

Make, $Y_n = [X^{(0)}(2), X^{(0)}(3) \ldots, X^{(0)}(n)]$ And construct accumulative matrix B:

$$B = \begin{bmatrix} -\dfrac{1}{2}\left(X^{(1)}(1) + X^{(1)}(2)\right) & 1 \\ -\dfrac{1}{2}\left(X^{(1)}(2) + X^{(1)}(3)\right) & 1 \\ \cdots & \cdots \\ -\dfrac{1}{2}\left(X^{(1)}(n-1) + X^{(1)}(n)\right) & 1 \end{bmatrix} \Rightarrow B = \begin{bmatrix} -14.325 & 1 \\ -25.045 & 1 \\ -36.77 & 1 \\ -50.165 & 1 \\ -67.655 & 1 \\ -86.675 & 1 \\ -107.07 & 1 \\ -129.27 & 1 \end{bmatrix}$$

Therefore, the model can be expressed as:

$$Y_n = B\hat{\alpha}$$

It can be obtained by the least square method:

$$\hat{a} = \binom{a}{u} = (B^T B)^{-1} B^T Y_n$$

$$B^T B = \begin{bmatrix} 44965.48 & -516.975 \\ -516.975 & 8 \end{bmatrix}$$

$$(B^T B)^{-1} = \begin{bmatrix} 0.0000225 & 0.0055908 \\ 0.0014540 & 0.4862878 \end{bmatrix}$$

$$B^T Y_n = \begin{bmatrix} -49924.01 \\ 583.21 \end{bmatrix}$$

$$\hat{a} = \binom{a}{u} = \begin{bmatrix} 0.0000225 & 0.0055908 \\ 0.0014540 & 0.4862878 \end{bmatrix}\begin{bmatrix} -49924.01 \\ 583.21 \end{bmatrix} = \begin{bmatrix} 2.1372 \\ 211.0784 \end{bmatrix}$$

Therefore, the Gm (1, 1) model is as follows:

$$x^{(0)}(t) + 2.1372x^{(1)}(t) = 211.0784$$

4.2 Model Test

$$\varepsilon = \frac{1}{n}\sum_{k}^{n} |\varepsilon(k)| = \frac{1}{9}\sum_{k}^{10} |\varepsilon(k)| = 0.026$$

Therefore, through the residual error test, the method has high accuracy. This method can also predict the sales of TY dairy products from 2014 to 2021 (Tables 2 and 3).

4.3 Outcome of Prediction

By constructing the GM (1, 1) model, the forecast results of the sales volume and profits of TY Co., Ltd milk industry from 2014 to 2021 can be obtained (Table 4).

Table 2. The comparison between the figures of prediction and actual in volume and profits

	Volume (MT)	Outcome	Profit (BY)	Outcome
2005	9.3	9.3	3.85	3.85
2006	10.05	10.48	4.24	4.75
2007	11.39	11.8	5.5	5.95
2008	12.06	12.29	7.29	7.46
2009	15.63	14.97	9.6	9.36
2010	18.45	18.85	12.22	11.73
2011	19.59	18.98	15.25	14.7
2012	21.2	21.37	17.75	18.43
2013	23.2	24.05	23	23.1

Table 3. The average relative error of the residual

Numb	Year	Actual value	Predicted value	Residual	Relative error
1	2005	9.3	9.3	0	0
2	2006	10.05	10.48	0.43	0.042
3	2007	11.39	11.8	0.41	0.035
4	2008	12.06	12.29	0.23	0.019
5	2009	15.63	14.97	0.66	0.042
6	2010	18.45	18.85	0.4	0.022
7	2011	19.59	18.98	0.61	0.031
8	2012	21.2	21.37	0.17	0.008
9	2013	23.2	24.05	0.85	0.036

Table 4. TY Co., Ltd sales volume and profits during 2014–2021

	Volume (MT)	Profits (BY)
2014	27.08	28.96
2015	30.5	36.29
2016	34.33	45.49
2017	38.66	57.01
2018	43.53	71.46
2019	49.01	89.57
2020	55.18	112.26
2021	62.13	140.71

5   Conclusion

Cold chain logistics is an indispensable project to meet the needs of the society which is also developing rapidly. In order to achieve the development goal of Chongqing cold chain logistics in 2020, we need to combine theory with practice, innovate and foundation, promote the perfection of cold chain logistics market, and promote the development of the whole cold chain logistics industry. This paper mainly studies the method of forecasting the sales volume and sales profits of cold chain logistics in dairy products. Taking Chongqing TY Co., Ltd dairy industry as an example, using the Grey Prediction Model to combine the method with practice to provide enterprises with more reliable and credible methods for market prediction as to formulate business development plan and marketing strategy, and set the right sales target and expected value. The residual test is a good response to the accuracy of the whole prediction process and the correctness of the data in time. The application of theory and mathematical methods to practice can give full play to its greatest value. The research [7] use Grey model (1,1) combined with Ant Lion Optimizer as a new intelligence algorithm which can significantly improve annual power load forecasting accuracy.

References

1. Qianru, W., Li, L., Shu, W., Jianzhou, W., Ming, L.: Predicting Beijing's tertiary industry with an improved grey model. Appl. Soft Comput. **57**, 482–494 (2017)
2. Neethirajan, S., Vasanth Ragavan, K., Weng, X.: Agro-defense: biosensors for food from healthy crops and animals. Trends Food Sci. Technol. **73**, 25–44 (2018). BioNano Laboratory, School of Engineering, University of Guelph, Guelph, ON N1G 2W1 Canada
3. Paula, B., Dana, Z., Daniela, B., Patrick, J.C., Kevin, K.: The potential of cold plasma for safe and sustainable food production. Trends Biotechnol. **11**, 1 (2017)
4. Wei, H., Jianhua, L., Xiuzhen, C., Xinghao, J.: Network security situation prediction based on improved adaptive Grey Verhulst Model
5. Faheemullah, S., Qiang, J., Pervez, H.S., Nayyar, H.M., Uqaili, M.A.: Forecasting China's natural gas demand based on optimised nonlinear grey models. Energy **12**, 941–951 (2017)
6. Faheemullah, S., Qiang, J.: Forecasting natural gas demand in China: Logistic modelling analysis. Electr. Power Energy Syst. **77**, 25–32 (2016)
7. Zhao, H., Guo, S.: An optimized grey model for annual power load forecasting. Energy **107**, 272–286 (2016). School of Economics and Management, North China Electric Power University, Beijing 102206, China; School of Natural Resources and Environment, University of Michigan, Ann Arbor, MI 48109-1041, USA
8. Yang Y., Dingyu, X.: An actual load forecasting methodology by interval grey modeling based on the fractional calculus, ISA Trans. (2017)
9. Seval, E., Nursel, Ö.: Grey modelling based forecasting system for return flow of end-of-life vehicles. Technol. Forecasting Soc. Change **115**, 155–166 (2017)

The Establishment of Cloud Supply Chain System Model and Technology System

Weiqing Xiong and Ming K. Lim[(⊠)]

College of Mechanical Engineering,
Chongqing University, Chongqing 400044, China
ming.lim@cqu.edu.cn

Abstract. Cloud manufacturing integrates supply chain resources across the country or even around the world, then virtualizes and services them to cloud platform. This allows users to access and use the services which are safe, reliable, high-quality and low-cost through the Internet at any time. The supply chain in cloud manufacturing (hereinafter referred to as the "cloud supply chain") has a mess of resources and complex transaction status, so it will be disorderly and ill-organized without the support of system management and holistic technology. Therefore, this paper analyzes the characteristics of cloud supply chain, proposes the business model and system hierarchical structure of cloud supply chain, establishes the technical system of cloud supply chain implementation. This lays the theoretical foundation for the further development and implementation of the cloud supply chain.

Keywords: Cloud manufacturing · Supply chain · Hierarchical structure
Technology system

1 Introduction

Traditional supply chain is a system that transform raw materials and components into a finished product or deliver service from supplier to customer [1]. The development of the manufacturing supply chain in the 21st century is based on the requirements of downstream customers. Upstream suppliers design and modify products according to the requirements, and sometimes sub-tier suppliers are required to assist. Although both upstream and downstream perform their production tasks well with traditional relationship, this routine stops them from gaining opportunities to increase production experience [2]. When the traditional supply and demand relationship are proved to be unsuitable, it is difficult and expensive to terminate this relationship. The business relationship within the industrial clusters in China is loose, the manufacturing capacity is duplicative and imbalance. As a result, resource bottlenecks and resource idleness phenomenon exist at the same time, and resource utilization is low [3]. To ensure the overall benefits of the supply chain, it is necessary to integrate various manufacturing resources in the supply chain, share information and strengthen cooperation among the intra-chain organizations.

In this new era of rapid development of information technology, the emergence of cloud manufacturing has brought a key change "Cloudification" to the supply chain. It

© Springer Nature Singapore Pte Ltd. 2018
S. Wang et al. (Eds.): ICSEE 2018/IMIOT 2018, CCIS 923, pp. 198–208, 2018.
https://doi.org/10.1007/978-981-13-2396-6_18

changes the supply chain from a simple, independent hierarchical structure to a complex, resource-sharing hierarchical structure [4]. The concept of cloud manufacturing was first proposed by Bohu Li and his team in 2010 [5], they analyzed the differences among cloud manufacturing and ASP, manufacturing grids, etc., then they presented the architecture of the cloud manufacturing service system. In 2012, they thoroughly studied the various aspects of cloud manufacturing expansion under cloud computing, proposed a complete cloud manufacturing service system and cloud manufacturing technology system [6], which provided theoretical support for further research on management and business operation models.

In the cloud manufacturing environment, the supply chain relationship of the manufacturing industry will become customer-centered and meet the demand of customers, improve efficiency, reduce costs, increase flexibility and improve production capacity for manufacturers [7]. These advantages stem from the establishment of a flexible manufacturing sequence, which allows different manufacturing resource providers get together in a resource pool to solve special service requirements of users [8]. Users are given the right to assign specific tasks in the cloud manufacturing platform. They can set key requirements such as product cost, delivery time, quality and other requirements.

At present, there are few studies on the application of cloud manufacturing to the supply chain. Lin puts forward the definition of logistics cloud service and discusses the key technologies of implement logistics cloud services, he solves many bottlenecks in the promotion and application of current logistics service methods [9]. Tang analyzes closed-loop supply chain information flow, then promotes full life cycle manufacturing and management service through resource integration, demand docking and service integration, and builds a closed-loop supply chain cloud manufacturing service platform for remanufacturing [10]. Li and Qi proposes a collaborative cloud manufacturing system for automotive supply chain, establishes a cloud manufacturing service hierarchy structure and operational flow for the automotive supply chain [11]. Based on the new characteristics of supply chain in cloud manufacturing, Gu analyzes the supply chain structure and management model briefly in cloud manufacturing, looking forward to a series of changes that caused by supply chain management in the cloud manufacturing environment [12]. The above study of the supply chain in cloud manufacturing only by one-side. It lacks a comprehensive analysis. This article analyzes the characteristics of cloud supply chain from three aspects: resource, operating mode and participating members. A platform model, a hierarchical structure model and a complete technical system for implementing cloud supply chain are proposed from the perspective of the system. It provides a theoretical basis for the further development and implementation of the supply chain in the cloud manufacturing environment.

The rest of this paper are organized as follows. Section 2 analysis the characteristics of the supply chain in a cloud manufacturing environment. Section 3 puts forward the platform model and hierarchical structure model of cloud supply chain. Establishes the complete technical system of cloud supply chain in Sect. 4. The last section summarizes the whole paper and points out the future work.

2 Analysis of Supply Chain Characteristics Under Cloud Manufacturing

The cloud supply chain is a network link based on the cloud manufacturing technology system. It is supported by advanced information technologies such as cloud computing, the IoT, big data and human-computer interaction systems, it's a more agile, flexible, open and independent supply chain [12]. Features are analyzed in this paper from the perspective of resources, organization model and participants to achieve a deeper understanding of supply chain in cloud manufacturing, as follows:

2.1 Resources

(1) More Flexible Resources

Traditionally, flexibility of the supply chain is mainly measured by the residual capacity of the resources, the flexibility increases as the residual capacity of the resources increase [13]. In cloud manufacturing, the resource/capacity required by supply chain companies are stored in the cloud service platform. Supply chain companies scattered in different links and locations can flexibly invoke or rent required resources. The centralized resource/capacity service enhances the flexibility of supply chain. Cloud manufacturing can provide a good negotiation mechanism and improve the information exchange for the supply chain, so it makes the supply chain resources more flexible.

(2) Wider Varieties and Wider Range

The cloud supply chain breaks the limit of geographical space locations with advanced Internet technologies, to distribute unite autonomous and heterogeneous manufacturing resource. Decentralized resources include a variety of soft, hard resources and capacities of the supply chain. Companies in the supply chain no longer rely solely on their own resources. Instead, they can have a variety of options. With the help of a networked cloud platform, they can quickly find the resources needed to achieve a rapid combination of supply chain and achieve the overall optimization of the supply chain.

(3) Higher Utilization and Energy Saving

The strong companies have spare resources and capabilities, these are what weak companies in the supply chain lack. Through cloud platform, resources and capabilities are complementary and benefit mutually. With cloud services, companies could use other cloud service to have what they lack and companies could focus on their core competitiveness and make use of own advantages, to achieve a more professional service cloud. At the same time, extra resources and capabilities of the company will also be leased out through the cloud platform to avoid duplicate resource. It a green supply chain which costs less energy.

2.2 Operating Mode

(1) Initiative Innovation
Supply chain companies will virtualize their resources, capabilities into the cloud platform to form different types of cloud services. Companies continuously improve their processes with mutual operations, adopt new operating methods to reduce costs and make improvement. The resources and capabilities contributed by each company are continuously learned and improved through intelligent technologies, and active innovation based on community wisdom is implemented in the supply chain.
(2) Virtualization
In the cloud manufacturing, all supply chain resources and capabilities are accessible through the cloud terminal technology and the IoT technology. Resources are virtualized, packaged, released and then stored as services in the cloud platform. These resources are provided to customers as virtualized services. Thus,the configuration and invocation of supply chain resources become more flexible and efficient.
(3) Fault Tolerance
With various fault-tolerance technologies in the cloud supply chain platform, when failure on single physical point of fault occurs, manufacturing still operating without affecting other tasks. The upstream and downstream nodes of the supply chain will not be affected. Therefore, the supply chain is more available than other supply chains.

2.3 Participating Members

(1) Higher Participation
Participants communicate in a public environment directly and conveniently as the cloud platform is open to all end-customers in the supply chain. The customer's perception and understanding of the product is no longer limited to the final product, they have an intuitive understanding of the entire manufacturing and transfer process. It is possible for them to participate in the development and design of cloud services and provide their ideas as services through the human-computer interaction platform.
(2) Higher Trust
Supply chain members monitor and track the entire product lifecycle with transparent and visualized manufacturing process. Once any link was wrong, the remedial measures will be adjusted in time. Management leader will be able to adopt a flexible and convenient strategy in response to market changes. As a result, supply chain members will long-term trust this model and benefit from it.

3 Architecture Design

3.1 Cloud Supply Chain Business Model Design

This paper presents a supply chain model for business transactions using cloud platform (as shown in Fig. 1). The supply chain is highly integrated in the cloud manufacturing environment, and its various entities are more closely coordinated and mutually integrated. The resources and capabilities included in the entire supply chain process are integrated into the cloud, the "instructions" are accurately sent among suppliers, manufacturers, retailers and consumers through cloud manufacturing to allocate resources and complete the life cycle activities of products efficiently. It looks like each subject has a "cloud" to realize on-demand distribution of resources and on-demand production of consumption.

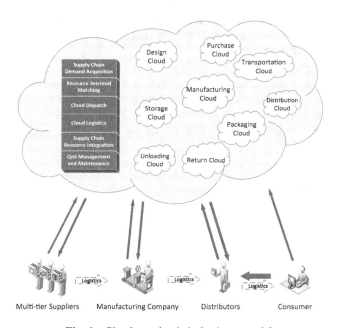

Fig. 1. Cloud supply chain business model

Suppliers, manufacturers, logistics providers and distributors in the supply chain all could serve as resource providers and users in cloud services platforms. After the consumer sent a task to the cloud, the supply chain cloud pool integrate, retrieve, match, and provide logistic cloud scheduling based on customized solution. At the same time, services are managed and monitored by supply chain cloud pool during the whole process. The product design, procurement, manufacturing, transportation, warehousing, packaging, distribution, unloading, returning and other processes could all be achieved as "cloud" in the platform.

3.2 The Establishment of System Hierarchy Model of Cloud Supply Chain

The cloud supply chain emphasizes cooperation, information sharing and intertwined network chain relationships. It is more complicated than traditional supply chain at the structural logic level. This paper combines the existing cloud manufacturing service architecture [6, 13] and supply chain management practices to construct a seven-layer supply chain model in cloud manufacturing (shown in Fig. 2).

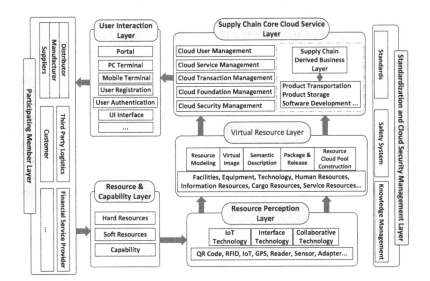

Fig. 2. System hierarchy model of cloud supply chain

(1) Participate Members Layer

The participants in the cloud supply chain include all members of the supply chain, such as suppliers, manufacturers, distributors, third-party logistics, customers, and other members. Members not only use the resources and capabilities from the cloud platform, but also turn their own resources and capabilities to the cloud platform.

(2) Resource/Capability Layer

The resource/capability layer includes all hardware and software resources, capabilities in the supply chain. Hardware resources include computers, machinery equipment, materials, warehouses and transportation tools, etc.; Software resources include database, knowledge base, model library and user information of enterprise supply chain case resources, etc.; Capabilities refer to the special design capabilities, technical capabilities, transportation capabilities, sales networks, staff context and financial strength of the enterprises that they base themselves on the market.

(3) Resource Awareness Layer

The resource awareness layer is a key link for achieving cloud supply chain in technology. Various resources and capabilities need to be perceived, coordinated, accessed to a cloud manufacturing platform to achieve virtualization. This requires the support of IoT technology, interface technology, collaboration technology and other related technologies.

(4) Virtual Resource Layer

The virtual resource layer is mainly to turn distributed supply chain physical resources into virtual resources, and then publish resources to the cloud service platform for consistent access and use. The main functions of this layer include resource modeling, virtual mirroring, semantic description, encapsulation management, release management, and resource cloud pool construction.

(5) Supply Chain Core Cloud Service Layer

This layer is the core part for guaranteeing the service realization and achieving the cloud supply chain. It provides services: cloud user management, cloud service management, cloud- based management, cloud transaction management, cloud security management, cloud derived service management, etc. It is necessary to list the derivative service management separately because it occupies a large proportion of supply chain cloud services, including transportation, storage, software development, financial management, credit guarantee and other services for third-party logistics companies, Internet financial service providers, banks, software service providers.

(6) User Interaction Layer

This layer is the platform portal for communication of system and users. Computers, mobile phones and other equipment can enter the platform and enjoy various services provided with human-computer interaction technology. This layer ensures that users of the supply chain and related industrial chains could communicate with the cloud manufacturing service platform easily and reduce the obstacles caused by the limitations in communication technologies and methods.

(7) Standardization and Cloud Security Management Layer

Cloud manufacturing is an advanced manufacturing model and its supply chain system is huge and complicated. To ensure the safety and reliability of the final products during use, the entire supply chain platform is required to provide standardized interfaces and specifications, efficiently manage of resources and capabilities, and provide cloud security services throughout the entire process to ensure smooth connection at all layers and information security.

4 The Establishment of Key Technology System for Cloud Supply Chain Implementation

The cloud supply chain system model and hierarchical structure only remain in the theoretical framework, it can't live without technology system. The cloud supply chain model is a new model that develop from the existing supply chain management model and integrates supply chain networks, cloud manufacturing, IoT, cloud security and

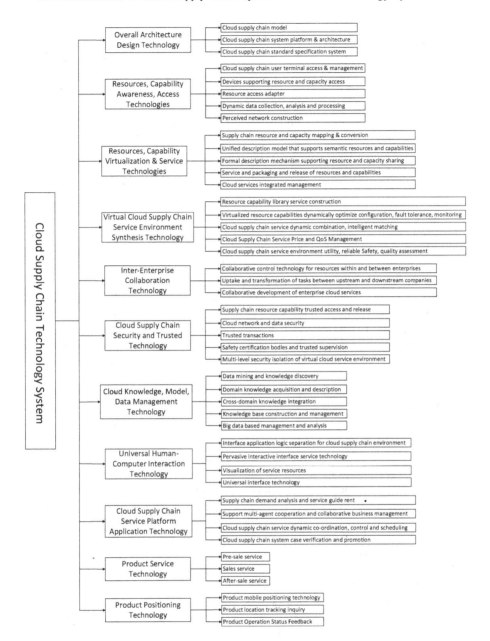

Fig. 3. Cloud supply chain technology system

other technologies. This paper draws on the framework of the technical system implemented by Cloud Manufacturing [13] to put forward a complete key technology system for cloud supply chain, which includes the following 11 aspects and the specific technologies are shown in Fig. 3.

(1) The Overall Architecture Design Technology
The supply chain in cloud manufacturing needs to be reconstructed from the overall system structure. From the perspective of the system, technologies such as the structure, organization, operation modes and the relevant standards for supporting the implementation of the cloud supply chain are studied.

(2) Resources/Capability Awareness and Access Technology
The resources owned by cloud supply chain members and the capabilities of design, technology, transportation, sales, funds owned by the company's members all need to be integrated into the cloud manufacturing platform in order to achieve full sharing, on-demand use and free circulation. Therefore, how to realize the status, performance parameters, IntelliSense, online real-time access of various resources and capabilities is one of the key issues should be solved in the cloud supply chain.

(3) Virtualization Technology of Resources/Capabilities
After integrating various resources and capabilities into the cloud supply chain service platform, it is necessary to virtualize, describe, encapsulate, publish, and invoke these hard resources, soft resources, and capabilities effectively.

(4) Virtual Cloud Supply Chain Service Environment Synthesis Technology
The supply chain cloud pool brings large-scale resources and capabilities together, which need to be configured and deployed to build an autonomous, self-maintaining, dynamically expanding resource library. It needs a comprehensive assessment of the effectiveness, reliability, quality and safety of the cloud supply chain environment to enable the cloud supply chain model to be deployed and applied.

(5) Inter-enterprise Collaboration Technology
It is essential for enterprises to establish a platform for communication and interoperability, and to achieve collaboration among different companies for the implementation of the cloud supply chain.

(6) Cloud Supply Chain Security and Trusted Technology
The cloud platform must provide safe access and prevent resources from malicious access or damage for resource/capabilities providers; The cloud platform must ensure the resources and services accessed are trustworthy, the submitted tasks executed correctly and won't be provided with malicious results for resources/service users; Also, a safe payment and transaction environment must be provided to prevent cloud service data center from being destroyed and attacked for operation platform.

(7) Cloud Supply Chain Knowledge, Model, Data Management Technology
The cloud supply chain is a large system that involves complex knowledge, models and data within companies. Therefore, reasonable and effective management is one of the key technologies in the cloud supply chain.

(8) Cloud Manufacturing Universal Human-computer Interaction Technology
When users of cloud supply chain systems collaborate, trade and interact with the cloud manufacturing service platform, they need a powerful universal human-computer interaction system. Users will extract valuable services from rich resources, enterprises will perform service retrieval and assembly easily through efficient universal human-computer interaction technology.

(9) Cloud Supply Chain Service Platform Application Technology

The cloud supply chain service platform provides a unified transaction interaction environment and regulate, manage, supervise the entire life cycle of the transaction. With the unified management, members could set up a safe and trustable third-party to protect transactions and profits. At the time, some illegal trades will be avoided.

(10) Product Service Technology

The cloud supply chain provides not only service from product manufacturing to sale, but also other kinds of services regarding product entire life circle. And these services will be smarter, more active, more convenient, more reliable, and more economical than traditional services with the strong support of cloud platforms. Generally, services are divided into pre-sales, in-sales, and after-sales.

(11) Product Positioning Technology

The fluidity of resources in cloud supply chain is high, and the products are in various forms. It is necessary to control the task time and process with positioning technology.

5 Conclusion

Cloud manufacturing provides conditions and support for in-depth supply chain coordination and management optimization. The product design, production, transportation, sales and service processes of entire supply chain are cloudified. The resources and capabilities involved in the entire process are virtualized and storage as services in the supply chain cloud pool, users use the resources on the chain to achieve individual needs. The cloud supply chain will be more agile, open, flexible, innovative and manage method will be more integrated, free and transparent. This paper analyzes the business transaction model and hierarchical structure based on the background and new characteristics of supply chain in cloud manufacturing, then proposes a detailed technical system of cloud supply chain. The cloud supply chain system management technology has a bright application prospect and promotion value. The work of this paper deepens the understanding of cloud manufacturing technology and has certain practical significance for the further development and implementation of the supply chain in cloud manufacturing. However, this paper only makes a systematic analysis from the theoretical perspective. The realization of the cloud supply chain needs to be implemented in a great deal of practices driven by the application of demand traction and related technologies. Therefore, the follow work will be applied in cooperation with companies and enterprises to apply the theoretical framework to practice.

References

1. Bhaskaran, S.: Simulation analysis of a manufacturing supply chain. J. Decis. Sci. **29**(3), 633–657 (2010)
2. Wu, D.Z., Greerj, M., Rosen, D.W.: Cloud manufacturing: strategic vision and state-of-the-art. J. Manuf. Syst. **32**(4), 564–579 (2013)

3. Li, F., Qiu, J.: Study on collaborative management of cluster supply chain in small and medium-sized enterprises. J. Ind. Technol. Econ. **30**(4), 84–89 (2011)
4. Xu, X.: From cloud computing to cloud manufacturing. J. Robot. Comput. Integr. Manuf. Syst. **28**(1), 75–86 (2012)
5. Li, B., Zhang, L., Wang, S.: Cloud manufacturing: a new service-oriented manufacturing model. J. Comput. Integr. Manuf. Syst. **16**(1), 1–7 (2010)
6. Li, B., Zhang, L., Ren, L.: Discussion on cloud manufacturing. J. Comput. Integr. Manuf. Syst. **17**(3), 449–457 (2011)
7. Li, B., Zhang, L., Ren, L.: Cloud manufacturing typical features, key technologies and applications. J. Comput. Integr. Manuf. Syst. **18**(7), 1345–1356 (2012)
8. Yang, H.: Cloud manufacturing is a manufacturing service. J. China Manuf. Inf. Technol. **39**(3), 22–23 (2010)
9. Lin, Y., Tian, S.: Logistics cloud services - new model of supply chain-oriented logistics services. J. Comput. Appl. Res. **29**(1), 224–228 (2012)
10. Yan, T., Li, J., Zhang, J.: Remanufacturing closed-loop supply chain cloud manufacturing service platform design. J. Comput. Integr. Manuf. Syst. **18**(7), 1554–1562 (2012)
11. Tianbo, L.I., Ershi, Q.I.: Study on cloud manufacturing model of automobile supply chain collaboration. J. Mach. Des. Manuf. Eng. **46**(04), 11–15 (2017)
12. Gu, C., Zhang, H., An, Y.: Research on supply chain management system in cloud manufacturing environment. J. China Sci. Technol. Forum. **1**(2), 122–127 (2013)
13. Li, B., Zhang, L., et al.: Cloud Manufacturing. Tsinghua University Press, Beijing (2015)

Two Stage Heuristic Algorithm for Logistics Network Optimization of Integrated Location-Routing-Inventory

Hao Wang$^{(\boxtimes)}$ and Ming K. Lim

College of Mechanical Engineering, ChongQing University,
No. 174 Shazhengjie, Shapingba, Chongqing 400044, China
20160713224@cqu.edu.cn

Abstract. To reduce the cost of logistics, optimize logistics warehousing layout and logistics distribution efficiency, logistics network of the integrated location-routing-inventory was studied. In this paper, we present a model of integrated Location-Routing and Inventory problem (ILRIP) that considers the selection of warehouses location, the inventory of products, and vehicle routing. Aiming at the characteristics of proposed model, a two-stage optimization problem is designed, and two main objective functions are established to minimize the expected total cost of inventory and location selection and distribution costs with time windows. Considering multiple constraints, the multi-objective optimization problems is designed. We solve the developed mathematical model by genetic algorithm (GA), then we code in MATLAB, a case study is proposed to prove industrial practicality of the model.

Keywords: Location-inventory-routing problem
Logistics integration optimization · Genetic algorithm

1 Introduction

With the rapid development of economic globalization, logistic plays a more important role in the world economy, known as the third profit source. Particularly as market competition intensifies, the critical challenge to logistic enterprises is to become flexible, cost less and quickly meet customer needs under complex environment. Logistics network optimization has an important meaning to effectively reduce logistics costs, respond quickly to customer needs and reduce carbon emissions. Enterprises need to integrated optimization location-routing and inventory to reduce the cost of total logistics and improve logistics efficiency.

Location-allocation problem [1], vehicle routing problem [2], and inventory management [3] are three key issues in the optimization of logistics networks, many studies in the past have conducted research on them as independent issue or cross combination problems. In fact, inventory-location-routing problem is closely related to each other [4], anyone change will affect the decisions of the other two parties. Previous studies generally assume that the location of the storage is fixed after establishing it in a location, and the impact of warehouse location changes on logistics optimization is lack

© Springer Nature Singapore Pte Ltd. 2018
S. Wang et al. (Eds.): ICSEE 2018/IMIOT 2018, CCIS 923, pp. 209–217, 2018.
https://doi.org/10.1007/978-981-13-2396-6_19

of consideration. Therefore, integrated optimization of logistics network at different stages is one of the most important research fields in the research of logistics optimization.

In this paper we study an integrated inventory-location-routing problem with time window, considering the multi-stage overall optimization. Generally, it is a multi-objective problem of logistics network integration optimization, which includes location-allocation problem, inventory-location problem and vehicle routing problem. However, some optimization decisions may conflict (e.g. storage location and transport). As the problem examined in this paper is of multi-objective type, the vehicle routing problem with time windows is a constrained NP-hard problem in multi-objective. Genetic algorithm can solve effectively the NP-hard problem of combinatorial optimization, GA has become one of the best methods for searching satisfactory solution, in this paper, genetic algorithm (GA) is used to solve multi-objective problems.

The paper proceeds as follows. Section 2 reviews previous studies conducted on logistics integrated optimization (location- routing problem, inventory–routing problem, location–inventory problem). In Sect. 3, the mathematical model of the problem is provided and the equations are described. Section 4 presents a solution approach, and a real case application is described. In Sect. 5, conclusions and future researches are discussed.

2 Literature Review

For the past few years, many scholars have studied and investigated on vehicle-routing problem, facility location problem and inventory control. The study of logistics activity integration optimization mainly includes the following aspects: inventory routing problem, location routing problem, location inventory problem and integrated location inventory routing problem.

Location Routing Problem (LRP) is one of the earliest integrated optimization problems in logistics management. Previous studies have shown that the location of distribution centres (DC) and tracing of distribution routes has an important impact on the complete supply chain. (Bramel and Simchi-Levi 1997) [5], Laporte et al. (1992) [2] and Char et al. (2001) [6] make a thorough research on the location routing problem, Prodhon and Prins (2014) makes an overview of location routing problem by previous studies [7]. For inventory routing problem, it was surveyed by Vidovic et al. (2014) [8] and Soysal et al. (2015) [9], Andersson et al. (2010) [10] reviewed a number of literatures about inventory-routing problem. Finally, about inventory location problem (ILP), Tanonkou (2005) [11] and Miranda (2004) [12] studied stochastic Inventory-Location problem. Diabat (2015) [13] studies the inventory routing problem under uncertain demands. Reviewing previous studies conducted on logistics activity integration optimization, the studies deal with two groups of optimal decisions on logistics activities.

Recently, many scholars have studied the inventory location-routing problem, Liu and Lee (2003) [14] established an integrated optimization model of location inventory routing problem, using a two-phase heuristic method to find solutions for this problem.

Ahmadi-Javid (2012) studies an integration problem that incorporates location, inventory and routing decisions in designing a multisource distribution network [15], other reviews have been made in this direction recently by Rafie-Majd and Pasandideh (2018) [16]. According to the analysis above, we can note that many scholars have respectively made important contributions to the research of the ILRP. However, previous studies on the integrated location-routing and inventory problem do not investigate the existence of multiple distribution centers and the requirements of customers for the product's demand time. In this paper, we study the integrated location-routing and inventory problem with the existence of multiple distribution centers and consider the time of delivery of the product.

3   Model Formulation

3.1   Problem Description

In this study, based on inventory-location-routing problem, first of all, location-allocation is selected according to the fixed cost of the warehouse and the unit stock cost. Then the distribution center service customers are divided according to the distance from customers to distribution centers. Forecasting the inventory of each distribution center through customer demand in a certain period helps route optimization for distribution based on customer location and demand time.

The goals that will be taking into account in this model are to minimize the total cost, optimal distribution rout and location. The first objective function includes the opening and operating costs of distribution centers and the inventory costs. The second objective function minimizes the delivering cost from distribution centers to customers.

3.1.1   Indexes

i Set of distribution centers $\{i\,|\,i = 1, 2, 3, \cdots, m\}$;
j Set of customers $\{j\,|\,j = 1, 2, \cdots, n\}$;
e Set of vehicles $\{e\,|\,e = 1, 2, \ldots, l\}$;
E_i Set of vehicle of the distribution center i;
M_i Set of customers accepting services from the distribution center i;

3.1.2   Parameters

W_i The fixed investment and management costs of the distribution center i;
I_i Inventory holding cost per unit of product per year at distribution center i;
L_i Average inventory level of distribution center i;
Q_j Demand of customer j; Mean of weekly demand at customer j;
q_i The maximum capacity of the distribution center i;
P_{ij} The distance from the distribution i to the customer j;
F Unit cost per kilometer;
g_j The earliest time that customer j allowed the vehicle to arrive;
h_j The latest time that customer j allows the vehicle to arrive;
s_{ij} Customer i service time in distribution center j;

Y_e Capacity of vehicle e;
c_{ab} Customer a to customer b driving distance;
t_{ab} Customer a to customer b driving time;
H_E Unit time opportunity cost arising from arriving at customer location ahead of time;
H_L Unit-time penalties for late arrivals at customer locations;
T_{Ej} The earliest time for the customer j to allow the vehicle to arrive;
T_{Lj} The latest time the customer j allows the vehicle to arrive;
T_{ej} Time when vehicle e arrives at customer j;
C_E Unit time opportunity cost arising from reaching customer location before T_{Ej};
C_L The unit time penalty cost arising from reaching the customer position after T_{Lj};

3.1.3   Decision Variables

$$x_{ij} = \begin{cases} 1 & \text{if customer } j \text{ is assigned to distribution center } i \\ 0 & \text{else} \end{cases}$$

$$y_i = \begin{cases} 1 & \text{if you choose to open this distribution center} \\ 0 & \text{else} \end{cases}$$

$$z_{ieab} = \begin{cases} 1 & \text{Vehicle } e \text{ in distribution center } i, \text{ from customer } a \text{ to customer } b \\ 0 & \text{else} \end{cases}$$

3.2   The Proposed Mathematical Model

Assume the demand of the customer j follow normal distribution $N(\mu_j, \sigma_j^2)$ in this analysis. So, Customer j order quantity $Q_j = \mu_j$. The average inventory level of distribution center j can be calculated by formula (1).

$$L_i = \frac{1}{2} \sum_{j \in M_i} \mu_j, \ i = 1, 2, \cdots, m \tag{1}$$

$$\min f_1 = \sum I_i L_i + \sum W_i y_i \tag{2}$$

$$s.t. \ 1 \le \sum_{i=1}^{m} y_i \le m \tag{3}$$

$$y_i \in \{0, 1\} \tag{4}$$

$$\min f_2 = \sum_{i=1}^{m} \sum_{j=1}^{n} p_{ij} x_{ij} \tag{5}$$

$$s.t. \sum_{j=1}^{n} Q_j x_{ij} \leq q_i, \ i = 1, 2, \cdots m \tag{6}$$

$$\sum_{i=1}^{m} x_{ij} = 1, \ j = 1, 2, \cdots n \tag{7}$$

$$x_{ij} \in \{0, 1\}, \ \forall i, j \tag{8}$$

$$\min f_3 = F \sum_{i=1}^{m} \sum_{e \in E_i} \sum_{a,b \in M_i} c_{ab} z_{eiab} + C_E \sum_{e \in E_i} \sum_{j \in M_i} \max(T_{Ej} - T_{ej}, 0)$$
$$+ C_L \sum_{e \in E_i} \sum_{j \in M_i} \max(T_{ej} - T_{Lj}, 0) \tag{9}$$

$$s.t. \sum_{e \in E_i} \sum_{a \in M_i} z_{eiab} = 1, \ \forall j, b \in M_i \tag{10}$$

$$\sum_{a,b \in M_i} Q_k z_{eiab} \leq Y_e, \ \forall i, e \in E_i \tag{11}$$

$$\sum_{b \in M_i} z_{eiib} = 1, \ \forall e \in E_i, \forall i \tag{12}$$

$$\sum_{a \in M_i} z_{eiab} = \sum_{b \in M_i} z_{eiab}, \ \forall e \in E_i, \forall i \tag{13}$$

$$\sum_{a \in M_i} z_{eiab} = 1, \ \forall e \in E_i, \forall i \tag{14}$$

3.3   The Description Objective Function and Constraint

Objective function Eq. (2) is the minimized total cost expected, including distribution centers fixed costs and the holding inventory costs. Objective function Eq. (5) is the minimized total distance between the distribution center and the customer. Objective function Eq. (9) minimizes total traveling cost from distribution center to Customer.

Equation (1) predicts the average inventory level of distribution center. The number of distribution centers are controlled by Constraint (3). Constraint sets (4) is the binary requirements on the decision variables. Capacity constraints for the distribution center are given in (6). Constraints (7) ensures that each customer is visited exactly once. Constraint set (8) is the binary requirements on the decision variables. Constraint (10) require that each customer be assigned to a single route. The capacity of vehicles is controlled by constraints (11). Constraint (12), (13) and (14) are to ensure that vehicles departing from the distribution center must return to the original distribution center.

4 Solution Method and Case Study

Because location-routing-inventory problem is a NP-hard problem in combinatorial optimization, it is very difficult to solve with traditional optimization methods. In this paper, a two stage heuristic algorithm is proposed to solve multi-objective optimization problems. The first stage consists of selecting the distribution center, classifying the customers and assigning the customer sets to the distribution centers. The second stage is to forecast distribution center inventory based on the demands of each customer sets, and finally optimize the vehicle routing problem with time windows.

In order to evaluate the model, the case analyzes the product distribution of Chongqing Puyue company. City location information is taken from the map. Assume that the product demand of each customer follows normal distribution $N(\mu_j, \sigma^2)$ of each month. This distribution area has three potential distribution centers and 24 customer groups. The fixed cost, capacity, and inventory cost of the candidate distribution center are listed in Table 1. The information of customers and related parameters is given in Table 2. The assumptions of the genetic algorithm are as follows: population size is 50, iteration is 500, crossover rate is 0.9, and mutation rate is 0.1. Each distribution center has 3 vehicles, the maximum load of vehicle is 30, the longest running distance of the vehicle is 50, the starting cost per vehicle is 20, the cost per unit distance is 2, and the vehicle speed is 2.

Table 1. Distribution center parameters

DC_i	(x,y)	W_i	q_i	Storage cost
DC_1	(10,12)	20000	500	0.5
DC_2	(5,13)	15000	750	0.3
DC_3	(15,6)	18000	800	0.25

Table 2. Customer information

j	(x,y)	Q_j	T_{Ej}	T_{Lj}	T_{ej}	C_E	C_L	$N(\mu_j, \sigma_j^2)$
1	(8,10)	4	6	8	0.4	2	12	$(40,10^2)$
2	(3,9)	10	8	12	0.4	1	20	$(100,18^2)$
3	(12,8)	9	9	12	0.4	1	8	$(75,16^2)$
4	(5,11)	6	7	9	0.4	3	16	$(60,12^2)$
5	(13,5)	5	7	10	0.4	1	12	$(45,10^2)$
6	(8,13)	5	15	17	0.4	2	8	$(45,10^2)$
7	(19,6)	7	6	8	0.4	2	10	$(65,12^2)$
8	(10,14)	6	13	15	0.4	1	10	$(60,12^2)$
9	(16,8)	5	18	20	0.4	1	6	$(50,10^2)$
10	(15,13)	10	10	12	0.4	3	8	$(90,202)$
11	(7,15)	6	10	13	0.4	1	12	$(60,122)$
12	(6,17)	4	11	14	0.4	3	7	$(40,10^2)$

(*continued*)

Table 2. (*continued*)

j	(x,y)	Qj	T_{Ej}	T_{Lj}	T_{ej}	C_E	C_L	$N\,(\mu_j,\sigma_j^2)$
13	(17,12)	6	11	15	0.4	1	12	$(60,12^2)$
14	(17,4)	8	14	16	0.4	3	8	$(70,13^2)$
15	(3,15)	5	16	18	0.4	1	12	$(50,10^2)$
16	(12,10)	5	9	10	0.4	1	20	$(35,9^2)$
17	(6,8)	6	17	19	0.4	1	9	$(55,11^2)$
18	(18,9)	6	16	18	0.4	2	10	$(60,12^2)$
19	(20,7)	4	18	20	0.4	1	12	$(40,10^2)$
20	(2,11)	4	18	20	0.4	1	10	$(40,10^2)$
21	(4,6)	8	8	12	0.4	1	8	$(90,15^2)$
22	(11,4)	4	8	12	0.4	1	15	$(45,10^2)$
23	(9,18)	7	16	20	0.4	1	16	$(70,13^2)$
24	(14,11)	3	12	16	0.4	2	6	$(35,9^2)$

Table 3. Results of distribution center location and average inventory

Selected distribution center	Average inventory	Total cost
DC2	355	18195
DC3	335	20512.5

At the first stage, DC_2 and DC_3 are selected according to the fixed cost and Inventory cost, the inventory and cost of each distribution center are shown in Table 3.

At the second stage, vehicle routing problem with time windows is optimized. Genetic algorithm is used to optimize distribution route and the Figs. 1 and 2 show the results, the corresponding trend diagram of optimal solution is shown in Figs. 2, 3 and 4 (Table 4).

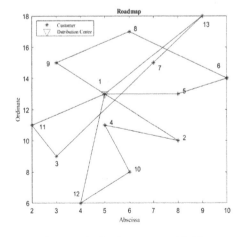

Fig. 1. Distribution routes of DC2

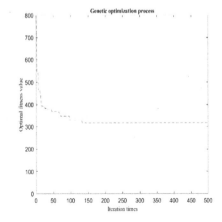

Fig. 2. Iterative graph of optimal solution

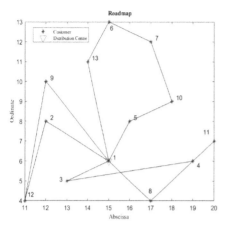
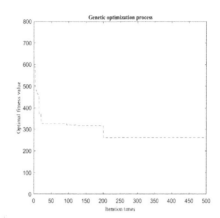

Fig. 3. Distribution routes of DC3   **Fig. 4.** Iterative graph of optimal solution

Table 4. Results of distribution routing

Selected distribution center	Routing	Distance	Total cost
DC$_2$	$1 \to 11 \to 3 \to 7 \to 13 \to 1$ $1 \to 5 \to 6 \to 8 \to 9 \to 1$ $1 \to 2 \to 4 \to 10 \to 12 \to 1$	60.2	355
DC$_3$	$1 \to 9 \to 12 \to 2 \to 1$ $1 \to 5 \to 10 \to 7 \to 6 \to 13 \to 1$ $1 \to 3 \to 4 \to 11 \to 8 \to 1$	60	335

5 Conclusions and Suggestions for Future

In this paper, we presented heuristic solutions to solve logistics network optimization of integrated location-routing-inventory. First, we modeled the problem as multi objective programming which includes minimization of transportation cost, minimization of total inventory cost and location-allocation cost. Then, the location of the distribution center is selected. the customer is assigned to the different distribution centers to minimize the total distance from the customer to the distribution center. According to the set of customers served by multiple distribution centers, genetic algorithm is used to optimize vehicle routing problem with time windows in multiple distribution centers. In the end, to validate the model, some tests data instances have been generated. The results show that the proposed model solves medium instances with a reasonable computational time.

For future research, we consider the following aspects: product inventory and distribution routing optimization under stochastic customer demand; optimization of location inventory routing under shared warehousing.

References

1. Cooper, L.: Location-allocation problems. J. Oper. Res. **11**(3), 331–343 (1963)
2. Laporte, G.: The vehicle routing problem: an overview of exact and approximate algorithms. J. Eur. J. Oper. Res. **59**(2), 231–247 (2007)
3. Dooley, F.J.: Logistics, inventory control, and supply chain management. J. Choices Mag. Food Farm Resour. Issues **20**(4), 287–291 (2005)
4. Ahmadi-Javid, A., Seddighi, A.H.: A location-routing-inventory model for designing multisource distribution networks. J. Eng. Optim. **44**(6), 637–656 (2012)
5. Bramel, J., Simchi-Levi, D.: Integrated logistics models. The Logic of Logistics. Springer Series in Operations Research, pp. 219–235. Springer, New York (1997). https://doi.org/10. 1007/978-1-4684-9309-2_13
6. Chan, Y., Carter, W.B., Burnes, M.D.: A multiple-depot, multiple-vehicle, location-routing problem with stochastically processed demands. J. Comput. Oper. Res. **28**(8), 803–826 (2001)
7. Prodhon, C., Prins, C.: A survey of recent research on location-routing problems. J. Eur. J. Oper. Res. **238**(1), 1–17 (2014)
8. Vidović, M., Popović, D., Ratković, B.: Mixed integer and heuristics model for the inventory routing problem in fuel delivery. J. Int. J. Prod. Econ. **147**(147), 593–604 (2014)
9. Soysal, M., Bloemhof-Ruwaard, J.M., Haijema, R., et al.: Modeling an Inventory Routing Problem for perishable products with environmental considerations and demand uncertainty. J. Int. J. Prod. Econ. **164**, 118–133 (2015)
10. Andersson, H., Hoff, A., Christiansen, M., et al.: Invited Review: Industrial aspects and literature survey: combined inventory management and routing. J. Comput. Oper. Res. **37**(9), 1515–1536 (2010)
11. Tanonkou, G.A., Benyoucef, L., Bisdorff, R., et al.: Solving a stochastic inventory-location problem using Lagrangian relaxation approach. In: IEEE International Conference on Automation Science and Engineering, pp. 279–284. IEEE (2005)
12. Miranda, P.A., Garrido, R.A.: Incorporating inventory control decisions into a strategic distribution network design model with stochastic demand. J. Transp. Res. Part E **40**(3), 183–207 (2004)
13. Diabat, A., Theodorou, E.: A location-inventory supply chain problem: reformulation and piecewise linearization. J. Comput. Ind. Eng. **90**(C), 381–389 (2015)
14. Liu, S.C., Lee, S.B.: A two-phase heuristic method for the multi-depot location routing problem taking inventory control decisions into consideration. J Int. J. Adv. Manufact. Technol. **22**(11–12), 941–950 (2003)
15. Ahmadi-Javid, A., Seddighi, A.H.: A location-routing-inventory model for designing multisource distribution networks. J. Eng. Optim. **44**(6), 637–656 (2012)
16. Rafie-Majd, Z., Pasandideh, S.H.R., Naderi, B.: Modelling and solving the integrated inventory-location-routing problem in a multi-period and multi-perishable product supply chain with uncertainty: lagrangian relaxation algorithm. J. Comput. Chem. Eng. **109**, 9–22 (2018)

Manufacturing Material

Electrical and Dielectric Properties of Multiwall Carbon Nanotube/Polyaniline Composites

Suilin Shi[1(✉)], Honggang Gou[1,3], Guijian Xiao[2],
Jing Li[1], and Daiyun Weng[1]

[1] Chongqing Skyrizon Aero-Engine Co., Ltd.,
Chongqing 401120, People's Republic of China
woyunzhoushi@126.com
[2] The State Key Laboratory of Mechanical Transmissions,
Chongqing University, Chongqing 400044, People's Republic of China
[3] School of Mechanical Engineering, Southwest Jiaotong University,
Chengdu 610031, People's Republic of China

Abstract. In this paper, electrical and dielectric properties of multiwall carbon nanotubes (MWCNTs)/insulating polyaniline (PANI) composites were studied. A mixture of MWCNTs and insulating polyaniline was dispersed in an ethanol solution by ultrasonic process, subsequently dried, and was hot-pressed at 200 °C under 30 MPa. Electrical and dielectric properties of the composites were measured. The experimental results show that the DC conductivities of the composites exhibit a typical percolation behavior with a low percolation threshold of 5.85 wt.% MWCNTs content. The dielectric constant of the composites increases remarkably with the increasing MWCNTs concentration, when the MWCNTs concentration was close to percolation threshold. This may be attributed to the critical behavior of the dielectric constant near the percolation threshold as well as to the polarization effects between the clusters inside the composites.

Keywords: Multiwall carbon nanotubes · Polyaniline · Composite
Electrical conductivity · Dielectric properties

1 Introduction

The unique physical properties of carbon nanotubes (CNTs), which combine high strength and low weight, high electrical and thermal conductivity, have been of great interest for developing new classes of multifunctional composites that incorporate CNTs into polymers [1–5]. Kymakis et al. [2] reported the optoelectronic properties occurring in single-walled carbon nanotubes/poly(3-octylthiophene) composites, and found that the composite represents an alternative class of organic semiconducting material that is promising for organic photovoltaic cells with improved performance. Alexandrou [3] prepared the single-walled carbon nanotubes/poly(3-octylthiophene) composites and showed excellent field emission properties. Hughes [4] found that aligned multi-walled carbon nanotubes/polypyrrole (PPy) composite films offer an

© Springer Nature Singapore Pte Ltd. 2018
S. Wang et al. (Eds.): ICSEE 2018/IMIOT 2018, CCIS 923, pp. 221–227, 2018.
https://doi.org/10.1007/978-981-13-2396-6_20

exciting combination of exceptional charge storage capacities (several times larger than that of either carbon nanotubes or PPy) and have potential applications in supercapacitors and secondary batteries. In particular, carbon nanotubes possess high flexibility, small diameter and large aspect ratio (100–1000), make carbon nanotubes excellent candidates to substitute or complement the conventional nanofillers in the fabrication of multifunctional polymer nanocomposites. For example, as carbon nanotubes is dispersed in an insulating polymer matrix to make a composite, it is expected that the electrical properties of the composite can be greatly improved with a very low percolation threshold. Many experimental studies [6–10] have also verified the CNTs as conductive filler in polymer matrix resulting in very low percolation thresholds from 1×10^{-4} to several percent of CNTs concentration, which are much less than 16 vol% of the theoretical value of percolation threshold derived from the percolation theory [11], and which suggest an advantage of small perturbations of bulk physical properties of polymer matrix, such as strength and lower cost. According to the percolation theory, the dielectric properties of the composites can be enhanced as the conductive CNTs concentration is close to the percolation threshold, which suggest the potential applications for the composites.

It has been known that polyaniline (PANI) can be applied for many practical fields such as chemical sensor, supercapacitor, corrosion protection, battery and energy storage, and antistatic coating. Therefore, the preparation and properties of CNTs/polyaniline composites have also been investigated [12–15], however, the polyaniline in the composites are almost the conducting polyaniline, and the preparation and properties of CNTs/insulating polyaniline composite has few reported. In this work, we prepared MWCNTs/insulating polyaniline (PANI) composites and investigated systematically the behaviors of the DC electrical conductivity and dielectric properties at room-temperature.

2 Experimental Study

The composites were prepared by solution blending and subsequently hot-pressing processes. MWCNTs used in this study were prepared from chemical vapor deposition grown and treated by dilute nitric acid and fluorhydric acid by removing nickel and silica, respectively. It typically consists of eight to fifteen graphite layers wrapped around a hollow 20 nm core, and with typical average diameters 30 nm while lengths are between 0.05 and 1.0 μm. Insulating polyaniline used in this study was obtained from the Zheng Ji Company (Ji Lin, China). The starting materials of MWCNTs and PANI were mixed in different weight fraction of MWCNTs by ball milling, further ultrasonic dispersing and drying simultaneously in ethanol solution. Subsequently, the mixtures were molded by hot pressing at about 200 °C under 30 MPa. Disk-shaped samples (20 mm in diameter, 1 mm in thickness) were prepared for electrical testing. The ac conductivity and dielectric measurements were conducted using an impedance analyzer (Model HP4194A, Hewlett-Packard Corp. Palo Alto, CA) in the frequencies range from 100 Hz to 40 MHz at a bias voltage of 1.0 V. The DC conductivity was measured using the four-point probe method. The microstructure of the composites was observed by scanning electron microscopy (SEM, Jeol-6301F, Japan).

3   Results and Discussion

Figure 1 shows scanning electron microscopy (SEM) micrograph of fracture surface of the composite with 5 wt.% MWCNTs content. The SEM micrograph shows that the excellent dispersing of the MWCNTs in the PANI matrix. Figure 2(a) is the plot of DC conductivity measured at the room temperature of the composites versus mass fraction of MWCNTs. It can be observed that DC conductivity of the composites follows a typical percolative behavior, when the MWCNTs concentration is below 4 wt.%, it is only slightly elevated from the insulating PANI matrix, and with the increasing MWCNTs concentration is between 4 wt.% and 6 wt.%, it displays a dramatic increase. This behavior can be described by the following percolation theory [16–18]:

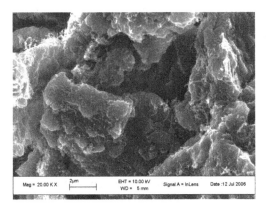

Fig. 1. Scanning electron microscopy (SEM) micrograph of fracture surface of MWCNT/insulating PANI composite with 5 wt.% MWCNT content

$$\sigma_m = \sigma_c (f - f_c)^t, \ for f > f_c \tag{1}$$

where σ_m, σ_c are the effective DC conductivity of the composites and conducting component, respectively, f is the weight fraction of the conducting component, fc is the critical weight fraction of the conducting component or percolation threshold. The t is the critical exponent. By using a least-squares fit, the percolation threshold f_c and exponent t are determined to be $f_c = 0.0585 \pm 0.0003$, $t = 2.20 \pm 0.12$. It should be noted that the value of critical exponent t is much close to the universal 3D lattice value ($t \sim 2$). Long et al. synthesized multi-walled carbon nanotube/polyaniline composite by an in situ chemical oxidative polymerization directed with cationic surfactant cetyltrimethylammonium bromide. They found that the conductivity of the composites increases by two orders of magnitude with increasing carbon nanotube loading from 0 to 24.8 wt.%, however, our results exhibit a lower percolation threshold, which may be attributed to the excellent dispersion of MWCNTs in PANI matrix. Figure 2(b) is the plot of dielectric behavior of the composites measured at the room temperature versus mass fraction of MWCNTs. It can be seen that dielectric constant of the

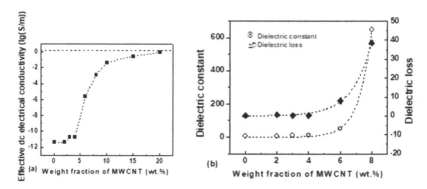

Fig. 2. (a) Effective DC electrical conductivity of MWCNT/insulating PANI composites vs. MWCNT concentration at room temperature and (b) dielectric behaviors of composites at room temperature, vs. MWCNT concentration at a frequency of 100 Hz of electric field

composites is enhanced when the MWCNTs concentration is close to the percolation threshold, according to the percolation theory, the following power law is given [16]:

$$\varepsilon_m = \varepsilon_0 (f_c - f)^{-s}, \; for f < f_c \tag{2}$$

where ε_m, ε_0 are the dielectric constant of the composites and the matrix, respectively. The s is the critical exponent. The data for the composites with $f_c = 0.0585 \pm 0.0003$ (Fig. 1a) yield s = 0.81 ± 0.02. It is noted that the value of s is lower than the universal 3D lattice value (s ~ 1), which can be attributed to effect of the large aspect ratio of MWCNTs fillers. In addition, it is seen that the dielectric constant of the composites remains increase above the percolation threshold but does not decrease as expected from Eq. (2). Such behavior has been reported earlier for polymer composites [19–22], and which was attributed to "micro capacitors" remaining in the sample above the percolation threshold. The "micro capacitors" are assumed to be formed by gaps between multiwall carbon nanotubes. Another possibility for formation of capacitances is parallel strength and free ends of the percolation structure.

According to the percolation theory, the frequency dependence of the dielectric constant and effective conductivity of the random mixture results from two important effects: (a) polarization effects between clusters inside the mixture and (b) anomalous diffusion within each cluster, and as considering only the polarization effects between clusters, many researchers have derived the following relation [23–25]:

$$x = t/(t+s), \; y = s/(t+s) \tag{3}$$

where t, s are the critical exponent in the Eqs. (1) and (2), respectively. The x and y is the critical exponent, and Bergman derived the power law for the effective conductivity $\sigma(2\pi v, f_c)$ and dielectric constant $\varepsilon(2\pi v, f_c)$:

$$\sigma(2\pi v, f_c) \propto (2\pi v)^x, \quad \varepsilon(2\pi v, f_c) \propto (2\pi v)^{-y} \qquad (4)$$

where f_c and v is the percolation threshold and frequency, respectively. Figure 3 shows the frequency dependence of the dielectric constant and ac conductivity of the composites. From Fig. 3a, it can be seen that the composites exhibited a typical dielectric behavior below the percolation threshold, i.e., ac conductivity increased linearly with the frequency. This may be explained by the polarization effects between the clusters, as the MWCNTs concentration is below the percolation threshold, due to a lack of percolating clusters, the polarization between the clusters and the motion of electrons in the finite cluster will determine ac conductivity of the composites, hence, the ac conductivity of the composites increases with the increasing of frequency. In addition, we can experimentally obtain the critical exponent x = 0.76 ± 0.03 from the ac conductivity of the composite with the MWCNTs concentration is just above the percolation threshold and 6 wt.%, which is much close to the universal 3D value (~0.72). From the above determined critical exponent t and s, we can theoretically calculate critical exponent x = 0.74 ± 0.02 from the Eq. (4), which is much close to the experimentally obtain the critical exponent x, and which suggest that polarization effects between clusters inside the mixture play dominant part for the frequency dependence of the dielectric constant and effective ac conductivity of the composites. Subsequently, as the MWCNTs concentration is much above the percolation threshold, the ac conductivity of the composite is manly determined by the many paths of the percolating clusters rather than the small effect of the capacitors, therefore, a finite conductivity led to a plateau at low frequency corresponding to the electrical response of the percolating network.

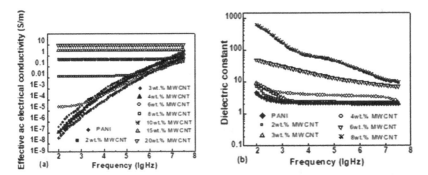

Fig. 3. (a) Effective ac electrical conductivity and (b) dielectric constant of MWCNT/insulating PANI composites vs. frequency of electric field

From Fig. 3(b), it is seen that the dielectric constant of composites are nearly frequency independent as the MWCNTs concentration is less than 4.0 wt.%, which follow the tendency of insulating PANI matrix, which is approximately frequency independent at room temperature. As the MWCNTs concentration is higher than 4.0 wt.%, the dielectric constant decrease with the increasing of frequency, which can be attributed to the MWCNTs become larger clusters, the dielectric relaxation become evident as the frequency of the electric field increases, results in the decrease of the dielectric constant. However, the dielectric constant of the composites is greatly enhanced by addition of MWCNTs toward low frequency, and a maximum value of the dielectric constant is achieved 650 at the frequency of 100 Hz, as the MWCNTs concentration is 4 wt.%, which suggests that it should be promising way for addition of MWCNTs to enhance the dielectric constant of materials.

4 Conclusions

MWCNTs/insulating PANI composites were prepared by solution blending and subsequently hot-pressing process. The electrical and dielectric behaviors of the composites were investigated. A low percolation threshold of 5.85 wt.% MWCNTs concentration in the system was determined by percolation theory. The dielectric constant of the composites can be greatly enhanced when the MWCNTs concentration is close to the percolation threshold, which may be attributed to the critical behavior of the dielectric constant near the percolation threshold as well as the polarization effects between inclusters inside the composites. The electrical and dielectric behaviors of the MWCNTs/insulating PANI composites suggest that it should be attractive for some electrical applications.

Acknowledgements. This work was supported by the National Natural Science Foundation of China (Grant No. 50572122).

References

1. Moniruzzaman, M., Winey, K.I.: Polymer nanocomposites containing carbon nanotubes. Macromolecules **39**, 5194–5205 (2006)
2. Kymakis, E., Amaratunga, G.A.J.: Single-wall carbon nanotube/conjugated polymer photovoltaic devices. Appl. Phys. Lett. **80**, 112 (2002)
3. Alexandrou, I., Kymakis, E., Amaratunga, G.A.J.: Polymer–nanotube composites: burying nanotubes improves their field emission properties. Appl. Phys. Lett. **80**, 1435 (2002)
4. Hughes, M., et al.: Electrochemical capacitance of nanocomposite films formed by coating aligned arrays of carbon nanotubes with polypyrrole. Adv. Mater. **14**, 382–385 (2002)
5. Ago, H., Pertritsch, K., Shaffer, M.S.P., Windle, A.H., Friend, R.H.: Composites of carbon nanotubes and conjugated polymers for photovoltaic devices. Adv. Mater. **11**, 1281–1285 (1999)
6. Kymakis, E., Alexandou, I., Amaratunga, G.A.J.: Single-walled carbon nanotube–polymer composites: electrical optical and structural investigation. Synth. Met. **127**, 59–62 (2002)
7. Sandler, J.K.W., Kirk, J.E., Kinloch, I.A., Shaffer, M.S.P., Windle, A.H.: Ultra-low electrical percolation threshold in carbon-nanotube-epoxy composites. Polymer **44**, 5893–5899 (2003)
8. Seoul, C., Kim, Y.T., Baek, C.K.: Electrospinning of poly(vinylidene fluoride)/dimethyl-formamide solutions with carbon nanotubes. J. Polym. Sci. Part B Polym. Phys. **41**, 1572–1577 (2003)
9. Ramasubramaniam, R., Chen, J., Liu, H.Y.: Homogeneous carbon nanotube/polymer composites for electrical applications. Appl. Phys. Lett. **83**, 2928 (2003)

10. Bryning, M.B., Islam, M.F., Kikkawa, J.M., Yodh, A.G.: Very low conductivity threshold in bulk isotropic single-walled carbon nanotube-epoxy composites. Adv. Mater. **17**, 1186–1191 (2005)

11. Scher, H., Zallen, R.: Critical density in percolation processes. J. Chem. Phys. **53**, 3759–3761 (1970)

12. Zengin, H., et al.: Carbon nanotube doped polyaniline. Adv. Mater. **14**, 1480–1483 (2002)

13. Sainz, R., et al.: A soluble and highly functional polyaniline–carbon nanotube composite. Nanotechnology **16**, S150 (2005)

14. Mottaghitalab, V., Spinks, G.M., Wallace, G.G.: The influence of carbon nanotubes on mechanical and electrical properties of polyaniline fibers. Synth. Met. **152**, 77–80 (2005)

15. Wu, T.M., Lin, Y.W.: Doped polyaniline/multi-walled carbon nanotube composites: preparation, characterization and properties. Polymer **47**, 3576–3582 (2006)

16. Nan, C.W.: Physics of inhomogeneous inorganic materials. Prog. Mater Sci. **37**, 1–116 (1993)

17. Bergman, D.J.: Exactly solvable microscopic geometries and rigorous bounds for the complex dielectric constant of a two-component composite material. Phys. Rev. Lett. **44**, 1285 (1980)

18. Meir, Y.: Percolation-type description of the metal-insulator transition in two dimensions. Phys. Rev. Lett. **83**, 3506 (1999)

19. Tchmutin, I.A., Ponomarenko, A.T., Shevchenko, V.G., Ryvkina, N.G., Klason, C., McQueen, D.H.: Electrical transport in 0–3 epoxy resin-barium titanate–carbon black polymer composites. J. Polym. Sci. B Polym. Phys. **36**, 1847–1856 (1998)

20. Flandin, L., Prasse, T., Schueler, R., Schulte, K., Bauhofer, W., Cavaille, J.Y.: Anomalous percolation transition in carbon-black–epoxy composite materials. Phys. Rev. B **59**, 14349 (1999)

21. McLachlan, D.S., Heaney, M.B.: Complex ac conductivity of a carbon black composite as a function of frequency, composition, and temperature. Phys. Rev. B **60**, 12746 (1999)

22. Pötschke, P., Dudkin, S.M., Alig, I.: Dielectric spectroscopy on melt processed polycarbonate-multiwalled carbon nanotube composites. Polymer **44**, 5023–5030 (2003)

23. Bergman, D.J., Imry, Y.: Critical behavior of the complex dielectric constant near the percolation threshold of a heterogeneous material. Phys. Rev. Lett. **39**, 1222 (1977)

24. Stroud, D., Bergman, D.J.: Frequency dependence of the polarization catastrophe at a metal-insulator transition and related problems. Phys. Rev. B **25**, 2061 (1982)

25. Wilkinson, D., Langer, J.S., Sen, P.N.: Enhancement of the dielectric constant near a percolation threshold. Phys. Rev. B **28**, 1081 (1983)

26. Song, Y., Noh, T.W., Lee, S.-I., Gaines, J.R.: Experimental study of the three-dimensional ac conductivity and dielectric constant of a conductor-insulator composite near the percolation threshold. Phys. Rev. B **33**, 904 (1986)

Experiment and Modelling on Biaxial Deformation of PLLA Materials Under Designed Strain History for Stretch Blow Moulding

Huidong Wei$^{(\boxtimes)}$, Gary Menary, Shiyong Yan, and Fraser Buchanan

Queen's University Belfast, Belfast BT9 7DB, Northern Ireland, UK
hwei02@qub.ac.uk

Abstract. Stretch blow moulding in manufacturing bioresorbable vascular scaffold (BVS) from poly (l-lactic acid) (PLLA) provides a biaxial deformation process of raw materials to enhance the mechanical performance. Current knowledge on the mechanical behaviour of PLLA materials in this deformation process is still lacked and trial-and-error tests are relied to develop a successful operation, causing significant waste of material and cost. Motivated by this circumstance, mechanical properties of PLLA materials were investigated by biaxial stretching test at designed strain history mimicking the stretch blow moulding process. A nonlinear viscoelastic material model, i.e. Glass-rubber model was calibrated based on the experimental data from equal biaxial (EB) and constant-width (CW) stretching tests. Material anisotropy was implemented into the original model by introducing the initial orientation factor from the extrusion process. Biaxial deformation process of PLLA materials under variable strain history was modelled by the calibrated and modified model. Modelling results exhibited good agreement with the experimental data, highlighting the potential application of material modelling in improving the understanding on stretch blow moulding of PLLA materials in the industrial manufacture.

Keywords: Biaxial deformation · Poly (l-lactic acid) · Glass-rubber model
Strain history · Anisotropy

1 Introduction

Bioresorbable vascular scaffolds (BVS) from poly (l-lactic acid) (PLLA) usually have a strut thickness of around one hundred microns. To manufacture this medical product with tiny wall thickness, stretch blow moulding was employed to offer a secondary processing of extruded PLLA tubes [1]. During this operation, a thick walled PLLA tube (~ 500 µm) is placed in a closed mould and heated to temperature above the material glass transition point ($T_g \approx 60$ °C) and below the melting temperature (T_m 150 °C). Axial elongation is applied by stretching one end or both ends of the tube whilst pressure is supplied to inflate the tube inside the cavity of the mould. By stretch blow moulding, the expanded tube has a dimension of $3 \sim 5$ times over the original

© Springer Nature Singapore Pte Ltd. 2018
S. Wang et al. (Eds.): ICSEE 2018/IMIOT 2018, CCIS 923, pp. 228–238, 2018.
https://doi.org/10.1007/978-981-13-2396-6_21

diameter and dramatically reduced thickness (~ 150 μm). Compared with the extruded tubes, stretch blow moulding introduced highly oriented molecular chains along the axial and hoop direction by the biaxial deformation, thus enhancing the mechanical properties of post-stretched products, e.g. strength and fracture toughness [1]. It has been found the strain history experienced in stretch blow moulding dramatically influenced the final mechanical properties of blown PLLA tubes by applying a simultaneous (SIM) and sequential (SEQ) process at 74 °C [2]. In a more wide range of processing temperature from 73 °C to 93 °C [3], it was discovered that there was decreased orientation factor in hoop direction at high temperature conditions with axial strain rate increasing from 0.1 to 2.1 s^{-1}.

Evolving strain rate and unequal in-plane strain history happened in the stretch blow moulding of PET materials revealed by a free stretch blow (FSB) test [4, 5]. After pressurization, there was slow strain rate (<0.3 s^{-1}) at the first stage until the yielding point (~ 0.2 s) was reached. A rapid inflation process followed after 0.2 s with strain rate as high as 50 s^{-1} and then stable stage was attained without further evident increase of strain. The axial strain achieved in this blowing process was approximately 200% whilst the final hoop strain reached 250% (exterior layer) and 300% (middle layer) [5]. To study the correlations between mechanical behaviour and strain history, the uniaxial test of PLLA materials at 75 °C was inspected and different hardening behaviour at strain rates ranging from 0.01 s^{-1} to 0.2 s^{-1} was found [6]. In a biaxial deformation of PLLA sheets at 70 °C and strain rate of 0.025 s^{-1}, the mechanical response of PLLA materials exhibited strong dependence on deformation modes, i.e. equal biaxial (EB), constant width (CW) and sequential (SEQ) deformation [7]. One limit of the previous study was mechanical tests were performed at constant and low strain rates (<1 s^{-1}) monotonically, lack of the reproduction of the strain history in stretch blow moulding with evolving and high strain rate. One potential approach on treating this circumstance is designing a strain history close to actual processing from stretch blow moulding, which was recently proposed and showed sound correspondence with the results directly from blow forming [5].

Viscoelastic behaviour of amorphous polymers above T_g can be simulated by a reliable material model. In stretch blow moulding of PET bottles, a nonlinear viscoelastic model, glass-rubber model (GR) was developed and successfully applied in predicting the biaxial deformation behaviour of PET materials at wide range of temperature and strain rates [8, 9]. PLLA materials displays the similar mechanical response to PET materials [7], enabling an idea to model its deformation behaviour by the glass-rubber model.

In this article, viscoelastic properties of PLLA materials were investigated by biaxial stretching test at 70 °C. Experimental data was used to calibrate the GR constitutive model. Material anisotropy was determined by studying the mechanical response in two stretching portfolios on machine direction (MD) and transverse direction (TD) of extrusion by constant-width deformation. Furthermore, multiple strain history cases were designed at 72 °C to mimic the biaxial deformation experienced in stretch blow moulding. The developed material model incorporating the orientation factors was validated by comparing the modelling results with the experimental data at the designed strain history.

2 Biaxial Stretch Experiment

2.1 Material Preparation

Poly (L-lactic acid) (PLLA) materials with a commercial grade of PURAC LX175 was kindly supplied by Corbion in Netherland. This material is a highly viscous material with a minimum of 96% L-isomer of stereochemical purity. The density of the material is 1.24 g/cm^3 and it has the weight-average molecular weight of 231131 g/mol. The supplied PLLA pellets were dried at 60 °C for 8 h. Then the PLLA pellets were extruded into sheets with a thickness of 1 mm by an extruder. PLLA sheets were cut into a square samples with dimension of 75 × 75 mm to fit the biaxial stretch tests.

2.2 Biaxial Stretch Test at 70 °C

Mechanical tests were conducted by the home-made biaxial stretcher in QUB, which is shown in Fig. 1 (a). A top and bottom heater were used to heat the polymer sheet sample to reach desirable processing temperature as high as 200 °C. The stretch can provide varied stretching speed leading to the strain rate from 1 s^{-1} to 32 s^{-1}. In the operation, the sample was clamped by two groups of grips equally spaced along the edges of the sheet. Homogeneous biaxial deformation was acquired by a scissor like motion mechanism [10]. By measuring the axial forces along two directions and recording the displacement during stretching, mechanical properties of polymer materials during biaxial deformation were obtained. Figure 1 (b) displays a constant width deformation (CW) and equal biaxial (EB) deformation of sheets were provided by controlling the deformation in two orthogonal directions. Biaxial stretching test of PLLA materials at EB and CW deformation were performed at 70 °C at strain rate of 1 s^{-1}, 4 s^{-1} and 16 s^{-1}.

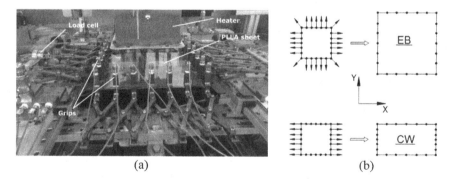

(a)   (b)

Fig. 1. Biaxial stretch test, (a) the biaxial stretcher in QUB, (b) two stretching modes at 70 °C

2.3 Biaxial Stretch Test at 72 °C

Multiple biaxial tests were conducted at 72 °C. In the CW test, PLLA samples were marked machine direction (MD) along extrusion and transverse direction

(TD) perpendicular to extrusion. Mechanical tests along MD and TD were performed separately to examine the material anisotropy. To mimic the strain history in stretch blow moulding, four customized biaxial testing cases in Fig. 2 were designed and performed on the biaxial stretcher. An initial stretch along TD of PLLA sheet was conducted at a low strain rate of 1 s^{-1} to simulate the deformation from prior pressurization in stretch blow moulding of PLLA tubes [2]. Four levels of deformation ratios in the initial stretch were achieved by controlling the stretching time (0.25 s, 0.5 s, 1.0 s, 1.5 s) whilst the MD of sheet was constrained to replicate the absence of axial stretch. At the second stage, the stretch along MD was conducted at a strain rate of 3 s^{-1} to gain an ultimate strain level of 150% to reconstruct the inflation period and the stretch in TD progressed as well to achieve the equivalent strain level in two directions. Four terminating points marked (1) to (4) in Fig. 2 were achieved and the total time for the deformation last approximately 0.75 s, 1.0 s, 1.5 s and 2.0 s respectively.

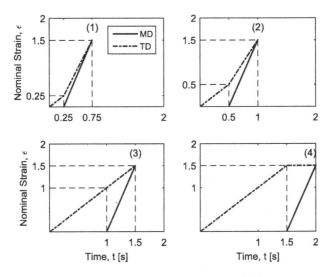

Fig. 2. Designed strain history at 72 °C

2.4 Experimental Results

EB and CW Test at 70 °C. The experimental result of biaxial deformation at varied strain rates from 1 s^{-1} to 16 s^{-1} at 70 °C was shown in Fig. 3. Figure 3 (a) exhibits in EB deformation, no apparent stress deviation at the same strain level was found in MD and TD. Viscoelastic behaviour is addressed by the increased stress with growing strain rate at the identical strain level. Only CW deformation with stretch along MD is shown in Fig. 3 (b). It shows that except the similar tendency of stiffer response at elevated strain rates, bigger stress values were found in EB deformation than CW at equal strain level, e.g. 9.00 MPa in EB and 7.23 MPa in CW at strain level of 50% and strain rate of 4 s^{-1}. In CW deformation, a stable stress response in TD was observed after yielding, independent of the further stretch in MD, revealing no strain introduced conformation change in the constrained direction, which has been proved by relevant studies using X-ray diffraction and polarized light microscopy [7].

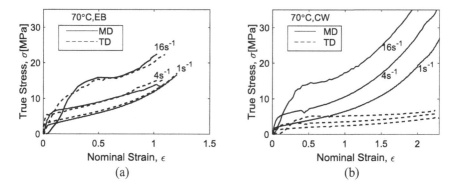

Fig. 3. Mechanical behaviour of PLLA materials at 70 °C, (a) EB deformation, (b) CW deformation (dashed line from bottom: 1 s^{-1}, 4 s^{-1}, 16 s^{-1})

CW Test at 72 °C. CW deformation was further investigated by applying stretch in MD and TD in two separated experiments at the strain rate of 1 s^{-1} and 3 s^{-1} at 72 °C. The stress response of two directions in each case is plotted against the strain in stretching direction in Fig. 4. Figure 4 (a) and (b) displays the stress response at two strain rates coincided at low strain level independent of MD and TD. When strain increased to the regime higher than 100%, elevated stress response was found in the stretching case along MD (top solid line), highlighting the material anisotropy. This initial anisotropy took effects only when apparent strain hardening stage was reached, i.e. the onset of conformational entanglement. No remarkable difference existed in the un-stretched direction (bottom lines) indicating no contribution of material anisotropy at zero strain.

Designed Strain History at 72 °C. Figure 5 displays the stress response of four cases in the designed strain history replicating stretch blow moulding at 72 °C. Figure 5 (a) plots the stress history of four cases. Recalling that Case 4 had the sequential deformation with a primary stretch at 1 s^{-1} and secondary stretch at 3 s^{-1}, the stress history of other three cases need to follow the stress path before the bifurcation point in both MD and TD, which is clearly proved by Fig. 5 (a). The coincident stress response between MD and TD in Case 1 and 2 demonstrated the negligible effect from the small initial stretch and closed strain rate. Difference arises between two directions in Case 3 due to the differed strain rate in TD ($\sim$1 s^{-1}) and MD ($\sim$3 s^{-1}) with large initial stretch. Figure 5 (b) provides the stress response in two directions under the respective deformation strains. Similar trend of stress response along MD under continuous stretch was observed. Higher stress response along TD was found in Case 1 and 2 with similar stress-strain slope with MD due to the high strain rate of its secondary stretch close to MD. Case 3 shows a bigger slope due to a sequential effect from the low strain rate in TD (1 s^{-1}) compared with MD (3 s^{-1}).

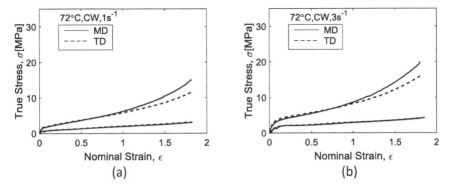

Fig. 4. Mechanical behaviour of PLLA materials at 72 °C in CW deformation (bottom lines: constrained direction; top lines: stretching direction), (a) 1 s^{-1}, (b) 3 s^{-1}

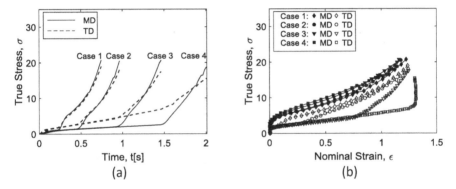

Fig. 5. Mechanical response of PLLA materials in designed strain history, (a) stress evolution, (b) stress-strain curve

3   Constitutive Model

The stress-strain response of PLLA material has three distinct stages as shown in Fig. 6 (a) whilst Fig. 6 (b) displays a simple 1D representation of glass-rubber (GR) model capable of capturing the mechanical characteristics. The total stress (σ) in the model comprises bond-stretching stress (σ^b) in glassy branch and conformational stress (σ^c) in rubbery branch. The initial elastic response in stage a (Fig. 6 (a)) is described by isotropic linear elasticity in glassy part. The stress flow stage b after yielding point is represented by the Erying viscosity. After arrest of stress flow, hyper-elasticity in rubbery part contributes to the strain hardening behaviour in stage c. More details on the GR model can be found in the literatures [12–13]. Traditional GR model disregards the material anisotropy, incapable of catching the anisotropic mechanical response of materials in Fig. 4 under CW deformation. To incorporate this effect, an initial orientation factor along MD (λ_{MD}) from the extrusion process was introduced. To maintain the volumetric balance, the orientation factor matrix (λ^{or}) need to have a

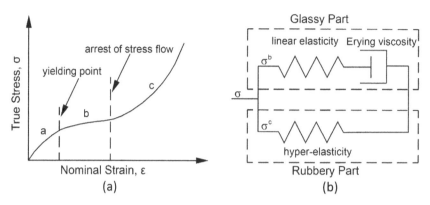

Fig. 6. Mechanical response of PLLA materials, (a) deformation stages, (b) 1D representation of glass-rubber (GR) model

determinant of 1.0. A uniaxial deformation in extrusion process along MD by Eq. (1) is proposed, acting in the conformational part with enhancement along MD and weakening effect along TD and thickness direction.

$$\lambda^{or} = \mathrm{diag}\left[\lambda_{\mathrm{MD}}, \frac{1}{\sqrt{\lambda_{\mathrm{MD}}}}, \frac{1}{\sqrt{\lambda_{\mathrm{MD}}}}\right] \qquad (1)$$

4   Material Modelling

4.1   Modelling EB and CW Deformation

Modelling Result at 70 °C. A calibration process has been developed to obtain the parameters of the GR model for PLLA materials from the biaxial data at 70 °C [14]. The comparison between modelling and experiment is shown in Fig. 7. Figure 7 (a) displays at EB deformation, good agreement is achieved by material modelling, perfectly catching the strain rate dependence. Small deviation happens for the initial elastic response at 16 s^{-1} since constant shear modulus was employed and resulted a constant elastic slope at all strain rates. This discrepancy can be corrected by introducing rate dependent modulus by experiment, such as dynamic mechanical analysis (DMA). It is ignored in the current model as modelling demonstrated consistency with experiment at increased strain level (>0.5). In CW deformation in Fig. 7 (b), significant offset between modelling and experiment exists at 1 s^{-1}. Although the model presents coincident mechanical response at initial elastic stage, the lack of conformational slippage leads to the independence of strain rate at large strain level. The disagreement at 1 s^{-1} in CW deformation reveals the ineligible conformational viscosity.

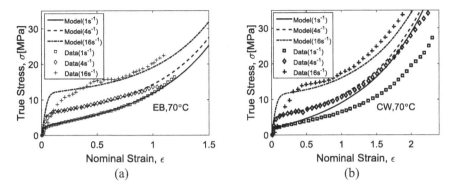

Fig. 7. Comparison of results between experiment and modelling at 70 °C, (a) EB deformation, (b) CW deformation

Modelling Result at 72 °C. Figure 8 shows the modelling result in CW deformation at 72 °C, where the stress response in stretching direction along both MD and TD is plotted to study the material anisotropy. It clearly demonstrates the model with orientation factor ($\lambda_{MD} = 1.15$) presents the distinguished stress response in two CW testing cases at two strain rates. The ignorance of conformational slippage leads to the deviation at 1 s^{-1} in Fig. 8 (a), with reason described in the above part. As the strain rate increases to 3 s^{-1} in Fig. 8 (b), growing contribution from bond-stretching stress weakens the deviating and presents more reasonable results from the material modelling.

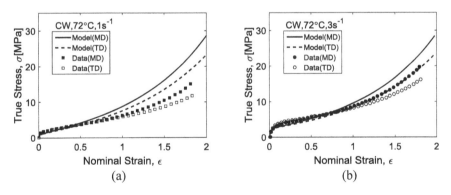

Fig. 8. Comparison of results between experiment and modelling in CW deformation at 72 °C, (a) 1 s^{-1}, (b) 3 s^{-1}

4.2 Modelling Deformation with Designed Strain History

The material model with initial orientation factor was then used to simulate 4 cases in the designed strain history and comparison of modelling results with experiment are shown in Fig. 9. Figure 9 (a) and (b) display in Cases 1 and 2, close to the EB deformation, the introduction of orientation factor enhance the stress response in MD and decease it in TD, with acceptable offsets in two directions. In the sequential deformation in Fig. 9 (d) for Case 4, negligible weakening effect in the first stretch and enhancing result in the second stretch exist along TD, and good agreement is found in the secondary stretch along MD. An intermediate deformation between EB and CW in Case 3 in Fig. 9 (c) discloses the consistence of modelling with experiment. The consistency of modelling result with experiment of the four cases covering the strain history from EB to sequential modes (including CW) proves the good robustness of the material model and its applicability for stretch blow moulding.

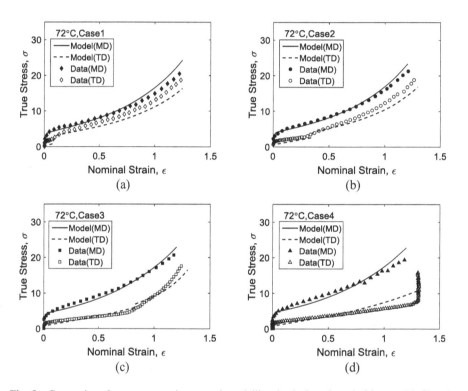

Fig. 9. Comparison between experiment and modelling in designed strain history, (a) Case 1, (b) Case 2, (c) Case 3, (d) Case 4

5   Conclusion

Strong viscoelastic behaviour of poly (l-lactic acid) (PLLA) materials above the glass transition temperature (T_g) was found by the equal biaxial (EB) and constant width (CW) deformation at different strain rates (1 s^{-1}, 4 s^{-1} and 16 s^{-1}) at 70 °C. The established mechanical characteristics of PLLA materials with three distinct stages suggested the applicability of the glass-rubber (GR) model. The calibrated constitutive model showed good consistency with the experimental data at 70 °C for both EB and

CW, except at 1 s^{-1} in CW deformation due to the ignorance of the conformational slippage. Material anisotropy was proved by performing the CW stretch in both machine direction (MD) and transverse direction (TD) respectively at 72 °C at two strain rates (1 s^{-1}, 3 s^{-1}). Multiple biaxial cases with designed strain history covering EB deformation and sequential deformation were developed to mimic the stretch blow moulding and corresponding stress evolution behaviour was found. The material model with implemented orientation factors was validated by the consistent modelling result with the numerous designed strain history cases, thus highlighting its capability in predicting deformation process of processing PLLA materials by stretch blow moulding in the manufacture of bioresorbable vascular scaffold (BVS).

References

1. Oberhauser, P.J., Hossainy, S., Rapoza, R.J.: Design principles and performance of bioresorbable polymeric vascular scaffolds. EuroIntervention **5**, F15–F22 (2009)
2. Løvdal, A., Andreasen, J.W., Mikkelsen, L.P., Agersted, K., Almdal, K.: Characterization of biaxial strain of poly (l-lactide) tubes. Polym. Int. **65**, 133–141 (2016)
3. Løvdal, A.L., Andreasen, J.W., Mikkelsen, L.P., Agersted, K., Almdal, K.: Mechanical properties of biaxially strained poly (l-lactide) tubes: Strain rate and temperature dependence. J. Appl. Polym. Sci. **134**, 45192 (2017)
4. Nixon, J., Menary, G., Yan, S.: Free-stretch-blow investigation of poly (ethylene terephthalate) over a large process window. Int. J. Mater. Form. **10**, 765–778 (2016)
5. Yan, S., Menary, G., Nixon, J.: A novel methodology to characterize the constitutive behaviour of polyethylene terephthalate for the stretch blow moulding process. Mech. Mater. **104**, 93–106 (2017)
6. Zhang, X., Schneider, K., Liu, G., Chen, J., Brüning, K., Wang, D., Stamm, M.: Structure variation of tensile-deformed amorphous poly (l-lactic acid): Effects of deformation rate and strain. Polymer **52**, 4141–4149 (2011)
7. Ou, X., Cakmak, M.: Influence of biaxial stretching mode on the crystalline texture in polylactic acid films. Polymer **49**, 5344–5352 (2008)
8. Menary, G.H., Tan, C.W., Armstrong, C.G., Salomeia, Y., Picard, M., Billon, N., Harkin-Jones, E.M.A.: Validating injection stretch-blow molding simulation through free blow trials. Polym. Eng. Sci. **50**, 1047–1057 (2010)
9. Nixon, J., Menary, G.H., Yan, S.: Finite element simulations of stretch-blow moulding with experimental validation over a broad process window. Int. J. Mater. Form. **10**, 793–809 (2017)
10. Menary, G.H., Tan, C.W., Harkin-Jones, E.M.A., Armstrong, C.G., Martin, P.J.: Biaxial deformation and experimental study of PET at conditions applicable to stretch blow molding. Polym. Eng. Sci. **52**, 671–688 (2012)
11. Adams, A.M., Buckley, C.P., Jones, D.P.: Biaxial hot-drawing of poly (ethylene terephthalate): dependence of yield stress on strain-rate ratio. Polymer **39**, 5761–5763 (1998)
12. Buckley, C.P., Jones, D.C., Jones, D.P.: Hot-drawing of poly (ethylene terephthalate) under biaxial stress: Application of a three-dimensional glass—rubber constitutive model. Polymer **37**, 2403–2414 (1996)

13. Buckley, C.P., Jones, D.C.: Glass-rubber constitutive model for amorphous polymers near the glass transition. Polymer **36**, 3301–3312 (1995)
14. Wei, H., Yan, S., Goel, S., Menary, G.H.: Characterization and modelling the mechanical behaviour of poly (l-lactic acid) for the manufacture of bioresorbable vascular scaffolds by stretch blow moulding (under review)

DEM Modelling of a New 'Sphere Filling' Approach for Optimising Motion Control of Rotational Moulding Processes

Jonathan Adams[1]($^{(\boxtimes)}$), Yan Jin[1], David Barnes[2], and Joe Butterfield[1]

[1] School of Mechanical and Aerospace Engineering,
Queen's University Belfast, Belfast, UK
jadams25@qub.ac.uk
[2] School of Mathematics and Physics, Queen's University Belfast, Belfast, UK

Abstract. Rotational moulding is a polymer forming process used to create hollow, stress-free products using both heat and rotation. The basic principles behind the machines which execute the process of rotational moulding have not changed significantly over the last 60 years. A factor restricting the growth of the rotational moulding industry is the limited wall thickness uniformity that can be achieved using the current machines which have limited motion control. Improved flexibility of motion control over the mould is now available and will be investigated with the aim of providing a more efficient process and higher quality products. Using a mathematical 'sphere filling' curve approach, a rotational path can be designed which allows every area of a spherical mould to spend a more uniform time period in contact with the powder pool (Wall thickness uniformity is affected by the powder-wall contact time). This paper proposes a new approach to mould motion control optimisation and provides validation using Discrete Element Method (DEM) simulations. This method has been found to increase the uniformity of powder-wall contact time by up to 19%.

1 Introduction and Background

Rotational moulding is increasingly competitive with other polymer forming processes, namely injection and blow moulding. However, a comparative limitation of rotational moulding is the uniformity of wall thickness that can be achieved (wall thickness for many product shapes is able to be controlled to within $\pm 20\%$ [1]). This is largely due to the fact that no pressure is used to force the polymer into cavities. Instead, the polymer lays up layer by layer against an internal mould wall under rotation. Wall thickness uniformity is an important factor, as for many applications, the higher the uniformity, the lower the amount of material that is required to achieve a nominal wall thickness of the part. Therefore, material, weight, energy and processing times can be reduced with better wall thickness uniformity.

A number of factors influence the wall thickness uniformity. These include: powder-wall contact time, mould wall 'recharge' time, powder flowability

© Springer Nature Singapore Pte Ltd. 2018
S. Wang et al. (Eds.): ICSEE 2018/IMIOT 2018, CCIS 923, pp. 239–248, 2018.
https://doi.org/10.1007/978-981-13-2396-6_22

(how well powder can travel into tight spaces), mould geometry (powder can be held up at corners or protrusions), heating system (uniformity of heat supply to mould), mould mount (shielding heat transfer to mould wall), mould wall thickness variations (decreasing the mould surface temperature uniformity), warpage effects, and presence of bubbles [2]. The key factor that controls the wall thickness uniformity is the powder-wall contact time where the areas that see the most of the powder bed are expected to be the thickest.

A method of creating a more uniform wall-powder contact time is to rotate the mould in such a manner that every area of the mould will spend an equal time period in and out of the powder pool. Motion control parameters, which are the rotational speeds about two perpendicular axes for bi-axial rotational machinery, are the key factors that affects the uniform distribution of the powder across the mould surface [3]. The mould rotation is currently limited to two degrees of freedom (2-DOF) with both axes having to rotate at constant speeds throughout the cycle. This restriction of mould rotation and speed is a limiting factor in obtaining optimised uniformity of powder-wall contact time. Crawford et al. [4] predicts that in future advances of motion control, the rotational speed and speed ratios will not be fixed to improve uniformity.

While the rotational speed (ranging from 4–30 RPM [5]) is important to provide the optimum powder flow conditions at the bottom of the mould [6–8] and to allow all areas of the mould surface sufficient time to 'recharge', it is the speed ratio between the two perpendicular axes that largely dictates the powder-wall contact time uniformity. The speed ratio determines the number of times a specific area on the mould wall passes through the powder bed and the direction in which it enters and exits the powder bed. As well as wall thickness uniformity, Ramkumar et al. [9–11] found that choosing the correct speed ratio is crucial for the mechanical properties of the finished part such as tensile, impact and flexural strength.

For a given mould geometry, a rotational speed ratio is chosen to obtain a suitable uniform (or non-uniform) wall thickness [7,12]. The thickness of plastic on the mould wall is dependent on how often each point on the mould surface passes through the powder bed and for how long. Due to machinery limitations and a lack of technical understanding, little has been achieved in this area beyond a wasteful trial and error approach to find suitable speed ratios (e.g. 4:1 for a sphere, 8:1 for a horizontally mounted cylinder, and 1:5 for a vertically mounted cylinder) for certain mould geometries using the conventional bi-axial rotational moulding machine.

Conventional bi-axial rotational moulding machines are limited to two degrees of freedom and many can only be used for a constant rotational speed about two perpendicular axes, i.e. they lack the functionality to be controlled to alter rotational speeds effectively throughout a moulding cycle. Robotic technologies have the potential to fundamentally change and significantly improve production practices through the introduction of automated processing and digital control benefits but they need to be proven as being technically and commercially viable for rotational moulding. AMS [13] have developed a robot arm which can hold an electrically heated mould. This lifts the restriction and opens a new potential for improving product quality, namely wall-thickness uniformity.

Discrete Element Method (DEM). RotoSim is the only commercially available simulation package of rotational moulding processes. However, it lacks a powder flow model and is limited to constant speed bi-axial motion control. The discrete element method (DEM) is a means of simulating the flow of powder and granular matter. This is achieved by modeling a number of discrete particles and calculating the contact and non-contact forces acting on each particle over a period of time. For every particle, its position, velocity and acceleration are found using Newton's equations of motion. Nguyen et al. [14] were the first to use DEM for modeling rotational moulding processes. They used DEM to simulate the flow and heat transfer within the powder bed in a uni-axial rotating cylinder during the initial stage of a rotational moulding cycle (up to point of polymer powder starting to adhere to mould wall). The aim is that the discrete element method can be used to replace current trial and error optimisation techniques with predictive methods which optimise conditions and enable Industry 4.0 practices around automated control and data management.

Knowledge Gap. There has been no research to date investigating the possible benefits from utilizing the improved motion control of bi-axial rotation via altering the speed or utilizing increased flexibility of mould rotation beyond 2-DOF. How to utilise this increased flexibility of mould rotation to improve part quality and cycle times is an unknown. Using a mathematical method to utilise the increased flexibility and control of the mould rotation by designing an optimised rotational path is a new and challenging task.

2   Mathematical Foundation and Hypothesis

The lack of rotational flexibility and control within current rotational moulding machines, restricts the uniformity of powder-wall contact time that can be achieved. This hypothesis assumes that improving the uniformity of powder-wall contact time will lead to enhanced product wall thickness uniformity. With the aim to improve powder-wall contact time uniformity, a new rotational path will be defined. This path will bring all areas of the mould surface through the bottom-most point of the mould (assumed to be the core of the powder bed) in regular equal time periods. It is predicted that this approach will improve on the uniformity currently achieved through conventional speed ratios.

Taking a sphere shaped mould as a case study, if its surface is covered with a number of regular equidistributed nodes (Fig. 1), the problem can be clearly visualized, which is how best to rotate the mould as to bring each of the nodes through the powder pool (at the bottom of the mould) to achieve contact time uniformity.

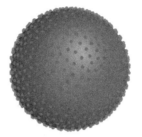

Fig. 1. Sphere mould surface covered by equidistributed nodes

2.1 Sphere Filling Curves

Gerlach and von der Mosel [15] investigated a mathematical approach of how to cover the surface of a sphere with a closed curve and a constant thickness without overlaps or self-intersection. They found that by plotting a series of latitudinal circles on the sphere surface an equal circumferential distance apart (number of circles depending on the desired 'thickness' of the curve), splitting the sphere into a western and eastern hemisphere, and rotating the western hemisphere by a specific angle, that the longest closed curve of a specified minimum thickness is found which covers the mould surface.

Figure 2 shows the curves covering a sphere for a range of circles. The number of circles, n, depends on the minimum thickness of the curve that is desired. The curves are shown in Fig. 2 with the same thin thickness. If the thickness is increased for each curve they would cover the sphere completely before coming into contact with another part of the curve. The number of circles is chosen according to the thickness or width of the powder bed which is expected to provide a uniform covering across the mould surface.

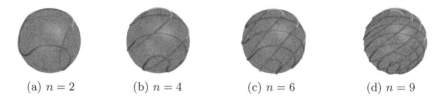

(a) $n = 2$ (b) $n = 4$ (c) $n = 6$ (d) $n = 9$

Fig. 2. Sphere filling curves with varying circles, n

Figure 3 shows the paths that the bottommost point of the sphere mould travels for a range of speed ratios which use constant speeds. Comparing these paths to the sphere filling paths shown in Fig. 2, it can be seen how a more uniform powder-wall coverage can be expected using the sphere filling curve approach.

From analysing these constant speed ratios, it can be expected that it is at the poles of the sphere mould (or rather the areas of the mould surface around

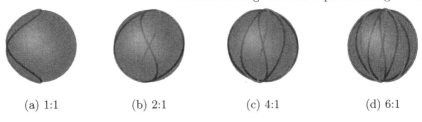

(a) 1:1   (b) 2:1   (c) 4:1   (d) 6:1

Fig. 3. Trace of lowest point on sphere surface during constant speed biaxial rotation for range of speed ratios

the secondary axis of rotation) that see the most traffic as it is here that the path crosses over and intersecs on itself. This pattern of increased traffic at the poles cannot be changed for any constant speed bi-axial rotation, which limits the uniformity that can be achieved using this approach.

3 New Motion Control Method for Spherical Mould Rotation

3.1 Designing the Rotational Path

Gerlach and von der Mosel describe a curve that covers a sphere's surface (given a minimum curve thickness) as a series of semi-circles. In order to turn these series of semi-circles into one continuous path the order and direction in which each semi-circle follows must be defined. To achieve this, Mathematica was used to map the coordinate at the end of each semicircle to a coordinate at the start of another. Using this approach the correct sequence of semi-circles can be found (Fig. 4(a)).

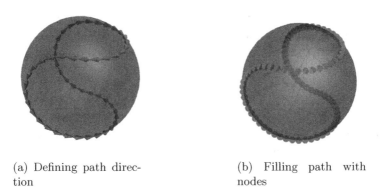

(a) Defining path direction

(b) Filling path with nodes

Fig. 4. Defining path of a sphere filling curve

The next step is to rotate the sphere so that the bottom-most point of the sphere (assumed to be core of the powder bed) traces out the sphere filling curve. To achieve this, a series of nodes were plotted along the sphere filling path (Fig. 4(b)). With knowing the co-ordinates and the sequence of the nodes, a point-to-point approach was used to find the spherical co-ordinates to rotate the next node in the sequence to the bottom point of the sphere($[0, 0, -1]$ for unit sphere). This was repeated until all the nodes have been passed sequentially through point $[0, 0, -1]$ to provide a list of rotations about two perpendicular axes.

3.2   Development of DEM to Model Rotational Moulding Processes

Currently, the only simulation package that provides a powder-wall contact uniformity is with RotoSim. RotoSim can be used to calculate the powder-wall contact time uniformity. However, as previously discussed, RotoSim does not have a powder flow models incorporated within it. Rather, it assumes that the powder fills the mould from the bottom most point up to a horizontal surface.

The use of DEM as a new method of obtaining the powder-wall contact uniformity is proposed in this paper. DEM holds two key advantages. Firstly, varying rotation speeds and speed ratios required to rotate the sphere through the sphere filling path can only be modeled with DEM. Secondly, DEM provides a more accurate representation of the position and flow of the powder.

In order to use DEM to find the powder-wall contact time, a way of determining (for every defined time period) whether or not a mould element is in contact with the mould wall must be found. One method of achieving this is to track the position of each mould wall element during the rotation and if the position of the element is within a certain distance (particle radius) of any particle then it is said to be in contact at that time. However, this approach was found to be too computationally intensive. Another approach is to utilise a function within the DEM package, LIGGGHTS [16], which is to record the pressure being applied to each mould element in the mesh. A non-zero pressure reading on the mesh element represents contact with powder particles. This method was used as it is less computational. The output files from the DEM simulations were then manipulated to find the powder-wall contact time for each element in the mesh over the simulation.

4   Simulation Setup

Discrete Element Method(DEM) was used to investigate and compare the powder-wall contact time uniformity of rotating the sphere by the novel rotational paths proposed in Sect. 2.1 and the conventional bi-axial rotations. The DEM package used for these simulations was LIGGGHTS [16]. This paper will focus on investigating the benefit of using the sphere filling curve approach which uses 2 circles, n (Fig. 2(a)).

4.1   Procedure

The procedure to find the powder-wall contact time is detailed below.

1. **Construct mould geometry.** Model sphere using CAD and create a mesh. Insert mesh into LIGGGHTS environment specifying position and orientation relative to the axes of rotation.
2. **Insert powder particles.** Specify particle insert region within the mould and allow particles to fall to the bottom of mould under gravity (Powder parameters as per Table 1).
3. **Rotate mesh.** Once particles have settled begin the rotation of the mesh. Sphere mould rotated using a 4:1 speed ratio and a sphere filling curve rotation $(2\ n)$.
4. **Record pressure values.** Record values of each mesh elements every 1000 time-steps (every 0.01 s). Non-zero pressure values represents contact with the powder. This information is used to find powder-wall contact time.

4.2   Input Variables

DEM input parameters are shown in Table 1. These parameters were obtained from Nguyen et al. [14] who simulated and analyzed powder flow of HDPE during the initial heating stage of the rotational moulding cycle using DEM. Note that spherical shaped particles were chosen to aid simulation time. In reality, particle shapes are irregular.

For the sphere mould, the literature suggests that a speed ratio of 4:1 is optimum. Therefore, the results from the 'sphere filling' rotations will be compared to the 4:1 speed ratio. A range of powder loads from 5% to 30% will be tested, which is common within rotational moulding.

Table 1. Parameters used in DEM simulations.

	Value	Unit
Radius of mould	0.05	m
Particle density	965	$Kg.m^{-3}$
Particle radius	50–350	μm
Young's modulus	$1.4.10^{6}$	Pa
Poisson ratio	0.45	
Particle-particle friction	0.5	
Particle-mould friction	0.5	
Coefficient of restitution	0.4	
Time-step	1.10^{-5}	s
Particle shape	Spherical	
Powder load	5–30	%

5   Results

Table 2 shows the average element time over the mould for a 4:1 speed ratio rotation and a 2 circle sphere filling curve with a 25% powder fill. At this fill level, the sphere filling approach is found to reduce the standard deviation of contact time when compared to a 4:1 speed ratio. For 4:1 speed ratio, it can be seen how the areas at the poles spend most time in contact with the powder bed compared to the areas around the equator. This was expected and can be correlated to the rotational path of the mould (See Fig. 3), where the path insects itself at the poles. For the sphere filling approach, the opposite trend was observed, where the areas around the poles were seen to spend the least time in contact with the powder bed.

Results (Fig. 5) show that for powder fills between 20–30% using the sphere filling approach increases the uniformity of powder-wall contact between the powder bed and the mould wall (compared to the conventional constant speed 4:1 speed ratio). As the powder fill level drops below 20%, the conventional 4:1

Table 2. Comparison of DEM outputs for sphere filling curve and 4:1 speed ratio rotations

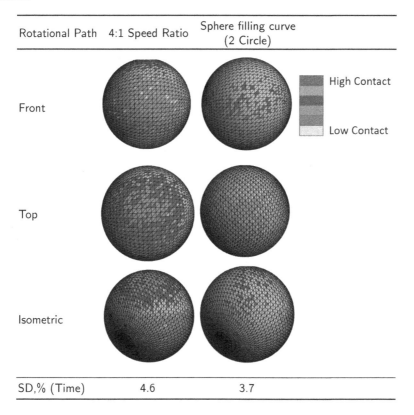

Rotational Path	4:1 Speed Ratio	Sphere filling curve (2 Circle)
Front		
Top		
Isometric		
SD,% (Time)	4.6	3.7

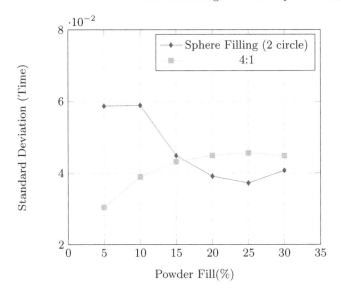

Fig. 5. Contact Time Uniformity from sphere filling and 4:1 speed ratio rotations for range of powder fills.

ratio was found to have better contact time uniformity (Fig. 5). This finding could be due to the width of the powder bed dropping below the minimal width needed to cover the mould surface with 2 circle, n. It is predicted that increasing the circle number with decreasing powder fills will improve uniformity.

6   Conclusions and Future Work

This research is the first to investigate a mathematical 'sphere filling' approach to define a path in which to rotate a mould during the rotational moulding heating cycle. A numerical model of powder flow (DEM) was used to demonstrate the advantages of this mathematical approach by studying the powder-wall contact uniformity, which affects the wall thickness uniformity. It was found that with the 'sphere filling' method (for the case of 2 circles,n), it can increase the powder-wall contact uniformity for a spherical mould by up to 19%, when compared to the conventional 4:1 speed ratio. For powder fill levels below 20%, 4:1 speed ratio was found to be better. It is predicted that increasing the number of circles (Fig. 2) will improve the powder-wall conact uniformity at these powder levels.

These findings open a new avenue of research into altering the rotational speed ratio to achieve a designed rotational path throughout the heating cycle to optimise the uniformity of wall thickness. Future work will investigate increased number of circles in the 'sphere filling' curves and further validate the benefits of the 'sphere filling' method with experimental testing. This space-filling approach will be developed to other mould geometries beyond a sphere.

Acknowledgments. The authors thank the Department of Education and Learning (DEL) for funding provided for this research project.

References

1. Crawford, R.J.: Rotational Moulding of Plastics, 2nd edn. Research Studies Press Ltd., London (1996)
2. Walls, K.: The dimensional control of rotationally moulded products. Ph.D thesis, Queen's University, Belfast (1998)
3. Roa, A., Throne, J.: Principles of rotational molding. Polym. Eng. Sci. **12**(4), 237–264 (2004)
4. Crawford, R.J., Kearns, M.: The future for rotational moulding. In: Practical Guide to Rotational Moulding, chap. 6, pp. 163–169, Smithers Rapra Press (2003)
5. Crawford, R.J., Gibson, S.: Rotational molding: a review. popular plast. Packag. 19–23 (2015)
6. Olinek, J., Anand, C., Bellehumeur, C.T.: Experimental study on the flow and deposition of powder particles in rotational molding. Polym. Eng. Sci. **45**(1), 62–73 (2005)
7. Aissa, A.A., Duchesne, C., Rodrigue, D.: Characterization of polymer powder motion in a spherical mold in biaxial rotation. Polym. Eng. Sci. **52**(5), 953–963 (2012)
8. Ma, L., Wang, C., Yang, W.: Heat transfer during rotational molding of a single axis device. Adv. Powder Technol. **87**, 116–118 (2010)
9. Ramkumar, P.L., Kulkarni, D.M., Chaudhari, V.V.: Parametric and mechanical characterization of linear low density polyethylene (LLDPE) using rotational moulding technology. Sadhana-Acad. Proc. Eng. Sci. **39**(3), 625–635 (2014)
10. Ramkumar, P.L., Ramesh, A., Alvenkar, P.P., Patel, N.: Prediction of heating cycle time in rotational moulding. Mater. Today: Proc. **2**(4–5), 3212–3219 (2015)
11. Ramkumar, P.L., Waigaonkar, S.D., Kulkarni, D.M.: Effect of oven residence time on mechanical properties in rotomoulding of LLDPE. Sadhana-Acad. Proc. Eng. Sci. **41**(5), 571–582 (2016)
12. Pethrick, R.A., Hudson, N.E.: Rotational moulding - a simplified theory. Proc. Inst. Mech. Eng., Part L: J. Mater. Design Appl. **222**(3), 151–158 (2008)
13. Trebing, M.: AMS Robotics - Robomould (2017). https://www.rotomolding.org/pdf/Fully.pdf
14. Nguyen, H.T., Cosson, B., Lacrampe, M.F., Krawczak, P.: Numerical simulation on the flow and heat transfer of polymer powder in rotational molding. Int. J. Mater. Form. **8**(3), 423–438 (2014)
15. Gerlach, H., von der Mosel, H.: On sphere-filling ropes. Am. Math. Monthly **118**(10), 863–876 (2010)
16. Kloss, C., Goniva, C., Hager, A., Amberger, S., Pirker, S.: Models, algorithms and validation for opensource DEM and CFD-DEM. Prog. Comput. Fluid Dyn. **12**(3), 140 (2012)

Review on Structure-Based Errors of Parallel Kinematic Machines in Comparison with Traditional NC Machines

Rao Fu[1], Yan Jin[1(✉)], Lujia Yang[2], Dan Sun[1], Adrian Murphy[1],
and Colm Higgins[3]

[1] School of Mechanical and Aerospace Engineering, Queen's University Belfast,
Stranmillis Road, Belfast BT9 5AG, UK
y.jin@qub.ac.uk
[2] School of Innovation and Entrepreneurship, Dalian University of Technology,
Dalian 116024, People's Republic of China
[3] Northern Ireland Technology Centre, Queen's University Belfast,
Cloreen Park, Malone Road, Belfast BT9 5HN, UK

Abstract. Machining technology is developed with increasing flexibility to adapt to the rapid changes of the market. Parallel kinematic machines (PKMs) have demonstrated great flexibility to suit the demands, but it is still not possible to achieve as high accuracy as the traditional NC machines (TNCMs). This paper presents a general review on the structure-based errors of PKMs in comparison with TNCMs to reveal the root causes of the errors and their relevance to the machining uncertainty. The geometric/kinematic, gravitational, and thermal aspects in both TNCMs and PKMs are identified as structure-based error sources. Errors in each aspect are comparatively analyzed, and inherent differences are found to bring new challenges to the accuracy of PKMs. Finally, perspectives in each aspect are highlighted for accuracy improvement of PKMs.

Keywords: Parallel kinematic machine · Geometric/kinematic
Gravitational · Thermal · Error

1 Introduction

Machining technology is developed with increasing flexibility in order to adapt to the changes (e.g., short lead-time, more variants, low and fluctuating volumes, low price) taking place in the market [1–3]. The effective use of robot machine tools has proved critical towards that direction [2–6]. A parallel kinematic machine (PKM), also known as parallel robot exhibits its superior dynamic performance to achieve quality, reliability, and productivity demands while possessing great flexibility, which will be the key technology in future 'plug and play' machining systems [7]. After first PKM publicly presented on the IMTS fair in 1994, commercialized PKMs have been adopted in industrial application [3, 7]. Up to now, PKMs (e.g., Exechon [8], Tricept [9], Z3 [10] and A3 [11] Sprint Head) have demonstrated great flexibility and relatively improved precision capability for the machining of large parts, such as milling and drilling aero-structures [6, 12, 13].

© Springer Nature Singapore Pte Ltd. 2018
S. Wang et al. (Eds.): ICSEE 2018/IMIOT 2018, CCIS 923, pp. 249–256, 2018.
https://doi.org/10.1007/978-981-13-2396-6_23

However, the development and implementation of parallel theoretical capabilities into the PKMs are rather in infancy compared to the long experience of traditional NC machines (TNCMs), which have an open-loop serial kinematic chain. That highlights the double-edged sword effects of applying parallel structure. Although PKMs theoretically should gain high accuracy due to its closed-loop kinematic chain resulting in few error accumulating effects, it also introduces new problems, such as the coupled errors (e.g., a single axis error will cause sources in all DOF of the end-effector) [14] which still cannot be well controlled. Specific accuracy comparisons between PKMs and TNCMs could be found in reference [7, 14–17] under certain levels, which have proved that there are still great barriers to achieve as high accuracy as TNCMs with PKMs, and deviations of PKMs could be induced by vast of reasons.

As we know, machining, specifically in subtractive one, is the removal of material from a clamped workpiece, by using specific cutting tool and parameters on a certain machine tool, whether a PKM or a TNCM, to obtain the component with desired profiles. Machine tool, cutting tool, processing method and clamping system as shown in Fig. 1 are the basic elements to perform the machining on a raw material to obtain a machined component. However, the machined component is not always in accordance with the requirements on dimensional and geometrical accuracy. It is because that each of the basic elements will induce deviations in the actual cutting positions from the theoretical values, defined as errors. The high accuracy component could only be achieved beyond the error effects of each element in Fig. 1 and that is what high precision machining pursues. Therefore, significant differences of structure, movability, control, etc. between PKMs or TNCMs definitely contribute to distinguishing errors within the four elements.

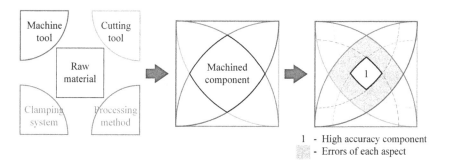

Fig. 1. Subtractive machining process to obtain high accuracy component

To improve the accuracy of PKMs, the first step and key factor are to identify the error sources within the four elements and of the errors and their relevance to the machining uncertainty. PKMs are unique for their structures, and structured-based error source should be one of the most influential factors on their final accuracy. Restricted by the article length, the focus of this review is only to address structured-based errors, and to emphasize their inherent differences in comparison with TNCMs, to provide a perspective view of challenges.

2 Structure-Based Error Sources

Structure-based errors here refer to the static and quasi-static errors induced by specific configurations of assembly structures as well as each moving (e.g., slide) and fixed components (e.g., bed). Tracing the root causes of those errors, they could be classified into geometric/kinematic, gravitational, and thermal aspects. The root causes of the three aspects have been deeply investigated in TNCMs [7, 18–24].

    i. Geometric errors are basically derived from design, manufacturing and assembly of the machine tool and its components, such as the misalignments of axes, slideways degradation or other guide imperfection issues induced by the mechanical imperfections. These errors are stable or changing slowly over time e.g. due to foundation drifts, wear or material aging. Kinematic errors are concerned with the motion errors induced by the components. The boundary to define an error as geometric or kinematic is diffuse.

    ii. Since no object is perfectly rigid, the gravity of the structural components in any machine tool will cause some deflections. The combined deflections of all the components consequently form the finial gravity-induced errors, and they are generally dependent on the real-time pose (i.e., position and orientation) during the actual machining process.

    iii. Causes of thermal errors are more complicated. These include the thermal expansion of guideways heated by the ball screw drives, the expansion of the frame heated or cooled by the machine tool itself or external heat sources (e.g., environment), etc. In addition, most heat sources are time-dependent and at universal/local workspace levels, which lead to non-uniform temperature distributions and rather difficult to control.

3 Structure-Based Errors Comparisons

TNCMs generally consist of bed, column, spindle and various linear and/or rotary axes, and that is no exception for PKMs, which makes these two kinds of machine tools almost share the same error sources as well as their causes. However, the more complex the structure and constraints, the more errors and difficulties to calibrate. PKMs are quite complex in the structure such as the non-orthogonal driven legs and contain far more constraints than TNCMs. Therefore, errors of PKMs exhibit some new features.

3.1 Geometric/Kinematic Errors

When designing machine tools, the geometric error of each component is always a significant factor to be considered [25]. Actually, each component of machine tools has independent geometric errors, and what is critical between PKMs and TNCMs lies on how the errors are accumulated to affect the final position of the tool endpoint and how to calibrate its accuracy. Errors from components or from the assembly (e.g., axis misalignment) will fundamentally affect the accuracy through the kinematic chain transmissions. For TNCMs, abundant studies have revealed that errors could be added step-by-step through the open-loop kinematic chains as illustrated in Fig. 2(a), and consequently, the corresponding calibration and compensation could be implemented to minimize geometric errors [19, 20, 26]. Comparatively, PKMs have a closed-loop kinematic chain always with non-orthogonal legs, see Fig. 2(b), and their kinematic relationships are considerably complex. The final errors induced by geometric errors of components can't be simply added up, and the evaluation of the geometric error effects mainly faces two aspects of difficulties.

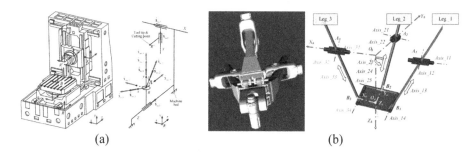

(a)   (b)

Fig. 2. Schematic diagram of machine tools (a) 4-axis TNCM [26], (b) Exechon PKM [30]

i. Typically, the kinematic model of a PKM is established neglecting the geometric errors. However, geometric errors (e.g., parallelism errors of two theoretically parallel legs) sometimes are under high constraints and will even lead to great uncertainty to the normal PKM kinematic model [27], which makes the normal model unsuitable for calibration and control of the PKM precisely in actual motion.

ii. Much more geometric parameters are needed to calibrate PKMs than TNCMs [28] which definitely leads to heavy computational burden if following each step of the closed-loop kinematic chain. More importantly, the accurate identification of calibration required geometrical parameters is the key to accurate positioning capability for PKMs [24], but not all the calibration required data could be obtained exactly.

Up to now, the applications of the simplified reverse kinematic model and limited numbers of calibration poses to averagely complete the whole workspace calibration are popular to reduce PKM geometric/kinematic errors [29]. However, based on the above two facts, to further minimize geometric/kinematic errors, constraint errors should be first checked and measured independently, before determining the reverse simplified kinematic model, so that a better calibration model could be established. Certainly, the more measuring poses are applied, more accuracy the PKMs will be achieved in the whole workspace.

3.2   Gravity-Induced Errors

The gravity-induced errors exhibit more interesting and distinct features between TNCMs and PKMs. TNCMs always have the relatively fixed structure resulting in the approximately constant gravity-induced errors in the whole workspace, which could be easily compensated by current calibration methods [31]. In contrast, the gravity of a PKM will significantly change due to that the slides protrude different lengths for the end-effector reaching within a large range especially like at a singular point, near an edge of the workspace or under a large tilt angle. This leads to the remarkable non-consistent stiffness of a PKM as well as gravitational effects at different poses, and consequently, the gravity-induced errors are highly pose-dependent. Therefore, the stiffness mapping considering gravitational effects [32] and specific gravity-effect modeling [33] have been investigated to effectively reduce gravity-induced errors.

In addition, in the development of future flexibility machining system, reconfig-urable position and orientation concepts are proposed and put into practice in both TNCMs [34, 35] and PKMs [36–38], and the gravity-induced errors are particularly highlighted in PKMs. Due to the great advantages (e.g., high payload-to-weight ratio) of reconfigurable tooling, the PKM has been recognized as a standard module to extend workspace to a more universal space as shown in Figs. 3(a) and (b). The gravity effects on PKMs face flexible change especially in machining large components like the fuselage in Fig. 3(b). Meanwhile, some up-to-date walking PKMs [39, 40] are developed to contribute more flexibility to the machining process, and their operating positions also affect the gravity-induced errors. Therefore, the reconfigurability brings the PKMs great challenge of the complex gravitational effects on the machining accuracy, but the relevant studies are still in infancy. Gravity-induced errors due to reconfigurability, as well as the corresponding compensation strategies, need to be further investigated.

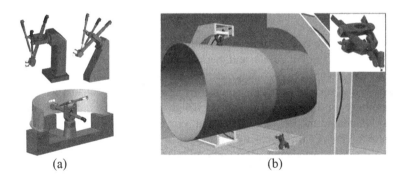

(a)   (b)

Fig. 3. Reconfigurable PKMs (a) TriVariant [41], (b) Exechon [42]

3.3 Thermal Errors

Although the thermal error sources in TNCMs and PKMs are similar, the effects of errors feature differently. Thermal errors in TNCMs are independent on each compo-nent, and their combined effects could also be added up due to the open-loop structure, but the non-uniform temperature distributions make it difficult to predict and com-pensate in Fig. 4(a). For PKMs, the thermal effects of the legs induced by screw drives are the major thermal error source [24], and the parallel structure makes the legs always perform asymmetry movement simultaneously resulting unequal temperature elevations [5]. Meanwhile, the thermal effects such as actual thermal defection of legs and frame are not independent and will be affected by each other within the closed-loop structure in Fig. 4(b). Thus, both of these make the PKM more susceptible to thermal loads, even besides the non-uniform temperature distributions. Although some studies on cooling structure components [19, 35], modeling thermal error [43] and compensating [40] have been conducted to decrease thermal errors of PKMs, it is far beyond the high accuracy expectation even compared with TNCMs. And co-thermal effects within the closed-loop structure could be an attractive aspect in increasing the accuracy.

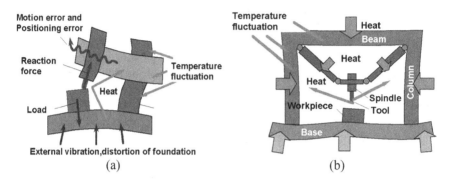

Fig. 4. Thermal expansion machine tools (a) TNCMs [44], (b) PKMs [45]

4   Conclusion

In this paper, structure-based error sources of both TNCMs and PKMs are identified in geometric/kinematic, gravitational, and thermal aspects. These structure-based errors in each aspect are comparatively analyzed between TNCMs and PKMs, and inherent differences show that the structure complexity, the close-loop chains as well as the reconfigurability of PKMs bring new challenges to the final accuracy of PKMs. Modified kinematic model with constraint errors, gravity-induced errors due to reconfigurability, and co-thermal effects within the closed-loop structure are highlighted for further investigations on improving the accuracy of PKMs. Machining errors induced by the other three basic elements i.e., cutting tool, processing method and clamping system in the application of PKMs will be reviewed in the future.

Acknowledgments.   It is supported by EPSRC UK under project EP/P025447/1, EP/P026087/1, and EU H2020 RISE 2016 - ECSASDPE 734272 project.

References

1. Chryssolouris, G.: Manufacturing Systems: Theory and Practice. Springer, New York (2006). https://doi.org/10.1007/0-387-28431-1
2. Gadalla, M., Xue, D.: Recent advances in research on reconfigurable machine tools: a literature review. Int. J. Prod. Res. **55**, 1440–1454 (2017)

3. Neugebauer, R., Harzbecker, C., Drossel, W.G., et al.: Parallel Kinematic Structures in Manufacturing. Dev Methods Appl Exp Parallel Kinematics. Fraunhofer Institute for Machine Tools and Forming Technology IWU, Chemnitz, Germany, pp. 17–47 (2002)

4. Gao, Z., Zhang, D., Member, S.: Performance analysis, mapping, and multiobjective optimization of a hybrid robotic machine tool. IEEE Trans. Ind. Electron. **62**, 423–433 (2015)

5. Boër, C.R., Molinari-Tosatti, L., Smith, K.S.: Parallel Kinematic Machines: Theoretical Aspects and Industrial Requirements. Springer, London (2012). https://doi.org/10.1007/978-1-4471-0885-6

6. Webb, P: Automated aerospace manufacture and assembly. Encycl. Aerosp. Eng. 1–10 (2010)

7. Weck, M., Staimer, D.: Parallel kinematic machine tools - current state and future potentials. CIRP Ann. Manuf. Technol. **51**, 671–683 (2002)

8. Neumann, K.-E.: Parallel Kinematical Machine. US Patent 8783127 (2014)

9. Neumann, K.-E.: Robot. US Patent 4732525 (1988)

10. Hennes, N., Staimer, D.: Application of PKM in aerospace manufacturing-high performance machining centers ECOSPEED, ECOSPEED-F and ECOLINER. In: Proceedings of the 4th Chemnitz Parallel Kinematics Seminar, pp. 557–577 (2004)

11. Ni, Y., Zhang, B., Sun, Y., Zhang, Y.: Accuracy analysis and design of A3 parallel spindle head. Chin. J. Mech. Eng. **29**, 239–249 (2016)

12. Jin, Y., Mctoal, P., Higgins, C., et al.: Parallel kinematic assisted automated aircraft assembly. Int. J. Robot. Mech. **3**, 89–95 (2014)

13. Neumann, K.-E.: Adaptive In-Jig High Load Exechon Machining Technology & Assembly. SAE Technical Papers 2008-01-2308 (2008)

14. Pandilov, Z., Rall, K.: Parallel kinematics machine tools: history, present, future. Mech. Eng. Sci. J. **25**, 1–46 (2006)

15. Tlusty, J., Ziegert, J., Ridgeway, S.: Fundamental comparison of the use of serial and parallel kinematics for machines tools. CIRP Ann. Manuf. Technol. **48**, 351–356 (1999)

16. Geldart, M., Webb, P., Larsson, H., et al.: A direct comparison of the machining performance of a variax 5 axis parallel kinetic machining centre with conventional 3 and 5 axis machine tools. Int. J. Mach. Tools Manuf **43**, 1107–1116 (2003)

17. Jia, Z., Ma, J., Song, D., et al.: A review of contouring-error reduction method in multi-axis CNC machining. Int. J. Mach. Tools Manuf. **125**, 34–54 (2018)

18. De Lacalle, N.L., Mentxaka, A.L.: Machine Tools for High Performance Machining. Springer, London (2008). https://doi.org/10.1007/978-1-84800-380-4

19. Ramesh, R., Mannan, M.A., Poo, A.N.: error compensation in machine tools - a review Part I: geometric, cutting force induced and fixture depend errors. Int. J. Mach. Tools Manuf. **40**, 1235–1256 (2000)

20. Ramesh, R., Mannan, M.A., Poo, A.N.: Error compensation in machine tools - a review Part II: thermal errors. Int. J. Mach. Tools Manuf. **40**, 1257–1284 (2000)

21. Zhang, C., Gao, F., Yan, L.: Thermal error characteristic analysis and modeling for machine tools due to time-varying environmental temperature. Precis. Eng. **47**, 231–238 (2017)

22. Mayr, J., Jedrzejewski, J., Uhlmann, E., et al.: Thermal issues in machine tools. CIRP Ann. Manuf. Technol. **61**, 771–791 (2012)

23. Zhu, S., Ding, G., Qin, S., et al.: Integrated geometric error modeling, identification and compensation of CNC machine tools. Int. J. Mach. Tools Manuf. **52**, 24–29 (2012)

24. Wavering, A.J.: Parallel kinematic machine research at NIST: past, present, and future. In: Boër, C.R., Molinari-Tosatti, L., Smith, K.S. (eds.) Parallel Kinematic Machines, Advanced Manufacturing, pp. 17–31. Springer, London (1999). https://doi.org/10.1007/978-1-4471-0885-6_2

25. Majda, P.: Modeling of geometric errors of linear guideway and their influence on joint kinematic error in machine tools. Precis. Eng. **36**, 369–378 (2012)
26. Tian, W., Gao, W., Zhang, D., Huang, T.: A general approach for error modeling of machine tools. Int. J. Mach. Tools Manuf. **79**, 17–23 (2014)
27. Jin, Y., Chen, I.M.: Effects of constraint errors on parallel manipulators with decoupled motion. Mech. Mach. Theory **41**, 912–928 (2006)
28. Knapp, W.: Metrology for parallel kinematic machine tools (PKM). WIT Trans. Eng. Sci. **44**, 77–87 (2003)
29. Jin, Y., Chanal, H., Paccot, F.: Parallel robot. In: Nee, A. (ed.) Handbook of Manufacturing Engineering and Technology, pp. 1–33. Springer, London (2013). https://doi.org/10.1007/978-1-4471-4976-7_99-1
30. Bi, Z.M., Jin, Y.: Kinematic modeling of exechon parallel kinematic machine. Robot. Comput. Integr. Manuf. **27**, 186–193 (2011)
31. Pandilov, Z.: dominant types of errors at parallel kinematics machine tools. FME Trans. **45**, 491–495 (2017)
32. Lian, B., Sun, T., Song, Y., et al.: Stiffness analysis and experiment of a novel 5-DOF parallel kinematic machine considering gravitational effects. Int. J. Mach. Tools Manuf. **95**, 82–96 (2015)
33. Ibaraki, S., Okuda, T., Kakino, Y., et al.: Compensation of gravity-induced errors on a hexapod-type parallel kinematic machine tool. JSME Int J., Ser. C **47**, 160–167 (2004)
34. Girsang, I.P.: Handbook of Manufacturing Engineering and Technology (2015)
35. Landers, R.G., Min, B., Koren, Y.: Reconfigurable machine tools. CIRP Ann. Manuf. Technol. **50**, 1–6 (2001)
36. http://www.loxin2002.com/fixed-structure-c-frame
37. Li, Z., Katz, R.: A reconfigurable parallel kinematic drilling machine and its motion planning. Int. J. Comput. Integr. Manuf. **18**, 610–614 (2005)
38. Bi, Z.M.: Development and control of a 5-axis reconfigurable machine tool. J. Robot. **2011**, 1–9 (2011)
39. Olarra, A., Axinte, D., Uriarte, L., Bueno, R.: Machining with the WalkingHex: a walking parallel kinematic machine tool for in situ operations. CIRP Ann. Manuf. Technol. **66**, 361–364 (2017)
40. Pan, Y., Gao, F.: A new six-parallel-legged walking robot for drilling holes on the fuselage. Proc. Inst. Mech. Eng. Part C J. Mech. Eng. Sci. **228**, 753–764 (2014)
41. Huang, T., Li, M., Zhao, X.M., et al.: Conceptual design and dimensional synthesis for a 3-DOF module of the trivariant - a novel 5-DOF reconfigurable hybrid robot. IEEE Trans. Robot. **21**, 449–456 (2005)
42. Neumann, K.-E.: Modular Parallel Kinematics Intelligent Assembly Automation. SAE Technical Papers 2011-01-2534 (2011)
43. Soons, J.A.: Error analysis of a hexapod machine tool. WIT Trans. Eng. Sci. **16**, 347–358 (1997)
44. Oiwa, T.: Accuracy improvement of parallel kinematic machine - error compensation system for joints, links and machine frame. In: Proceedings of the 6th International Conference on Mechatronics Technoly, pp. 433–438 (2002)
45. Oiwa, T.: Study on accuracy improvement of parallel kinematic machine (compensation methods for thermal expansion of link and machine frame). In: International Proceedings of Korea-Japan Conference on Positioning Technology (CPT 2002), pp. 1–6 (2002)

Design and Testing of a Novel Vane Type Magnetorheological Damper

Allah Rakhio, Xiaomin Dong$^{(\boxtimes)}$, and Weiqi Liu

State Key Laboratory of Mechanical Transmission, Chongqing University,
Chongqing, China
allahrakhio54@gmail.com, xmdong@cqu.edu.cn,
1228395565@qq.com

Abstract. A vane Magnetorheological (MR) damper for the purpose of suspension system was designed, manufactured and tested. The working methodology of the designed rotary damper was outlined and its theoretical model was also defined in the article. The magnetic field working as well as design was modelled on ANSYS. It is clearly defined in the results that damping ability of the designed damper is more than enough to be used for automotive suspension system. The manufactured damper was tested on MTS 858 table top system and performance of damper was analyzed at different currents and frequencies. Extra ordinary results proved that proposed vane type MR damper has high torque density and compact structure.

Keywords: Vane type MR damper · Magnetic field simulation
Experimental evaluation

1 Introduction

Magnetorheological technology has achieved a lot importance from the last few decades and because of rapid reaction and unique control properties its importance increasing every single day. Meanwhile, MR damping devices have been investigated and successfully applied in several suspension mechanisms. MR damper are categorized in two main types which are linear MR dampers and rotary MR dampers [1]. Linear Magnetorheological dampers are used more practically and there are unlimited research articles available on this type of damper but there are some disadvantages which are important to consider. In dampers it is necessary that the cylinder of damper must needs to be full of fluid so it's costly to use so much amount of MR fluid in a damper [2]. It is important to mention another major disadvantage which the big size of the damper so it's cannot be used where space is comparatively [3]. Rotary Magnetorheological dampers are the damper in which operations are conducted by angular velocity and incorporate one or more MR fluid working modes as the working principle. From the design point of view, rotary MR damper can be separated into continuous angle damper and limited angle rotation damper.

First type mostly of the time used in rotor-based applications like some kind of semi active brakes and clutches. Second type in this category is also known as vane magnetorheological damper and it has ability to generate more damping as compare to

© Springer Nature Singapore Pte Ltd. 2018
S. Wang et al. (Eds.): ICSEE 2018/IMIOT 2018, CCIS 923, pp. 257–266, 2018.
https://doi.org/10.1007/978-981-13-2396-6_24

first type of damper [4], it is fact that vane dampers cannot rotate continuously but still these can produce good amount of damping. It can be simply concluded that vane dampers are better options in applications where high damping torque is required. In terms of device improvement, limited angle damper has not been used for so many experimental purposes. Few written publications were found over the past decades. First publication on limited angle damper using was done by Zhang [5], which based on the principle of basic vane type hydraulic damper used in car suspension, it is called as Lever arm shock absorbers. In Zhang's model, MR fluid was pressurized to move from one part of the damper to other part of chamber by using a vane, a valve named as MR arc valve was used as path of MR fluid, these valves were inserted between the space of moving part and stationary part. In valves there is charged field, where fluid will come under effect of magnetic field while crossing from the valve. In limited angle dampers it's very hard and challenging job to seal the damper body properly. In Zhang's design maintenance is very time consuming task especially in case when problem is related to magnetic coil. Giorgetti's [6] proposed his work on limited angle MR damper, in his work there are some similarities in mechanical design with Zhang's design but valve design is totally different from Zhang's design. In this design, valves were fixed in stationary part of damper and its design was based on flow mode. Different and more detailed research with mathematical modeling and torque calculation at different currents and speeds were provided in Giorgetti's research. Yang [7] proposed another design of vane MR damper which has some similarities to Giorgetti's design and also working mode was also based on flow mode but magnetic field design was totally different. Yang installed the coil in inner radius while in Giorgetti's design coil was located in outer radius of the fluid path. Fitrian's [8] design was state of art and very much unique; he specially worked on an ease and reliability of damper from maintenance point of view as well as on increasing in damping torque. His design was named as bypass rotary MR damper. The valves were located outside of the damper body and that's the main uniqueness of the design which makes it unique from previous designs. This novel design is reliable from leakage point of view as well as from maintenance point of view.

There are four basic working modes on which magnetorheological damper works, these basic types are the flow mode, the shear mode, the squeeze mode and the magnetic gradient pinch mode [9]. Practically, in this novel vane type, MR dampers are operating on a mixed mode of valve mode and shear mode. Most of the limited angle vane damper designed and manufactured are double vane MR dampers and most of them are with elliptical outer body so it is a bit hard to make a leakage free damper with elliptical outer body. Furthermore, most exiting dampers are elliptical because stationary part needs to locked, so ellipse section is used to insert the stationary part in the outer body of damper and mostly it needs a deep groove otherwise MR fluid will leak from corners of stationary part. Here in this research the grove made for the stationary part was not so deep so MR damper outer body didn't need elliptical section to fix the damper because sealing grooves were made on all sides of stationary part in order to prevent the leakage of MR fluid. The objective of this paper is to design and manufacture a single vane MR damper which will provide more angular moment. The designed and manufactured damper is cylindrical which will provide a big advantage to prevent the leakages with ease because that circular O-rings are easily available which can provide better sealing for a cylindrical body. However, there are still disadvantages for cylindrical body that vane MR damper needs more volume because of more diameter as compare to elliptical body so it is hard to fix it exactly under the seat. The most important factor on the design is using bearings for the first time in any vane MR damper. It will result in less friction than the previously tested vane MR dampers.

This article organized in following way, part 2 elaborates a detailed introduction of the design and the working principle. Mathematical modelling of damper is in part 3. Here the part 4 analyzes the feasibility of its magnetic field design and the experimental setup is shown in part 4. Part 5 includes analysis and discussion of the experimental results and part 6 provides the conclusion.

2   Structure of Designed Damper

Designed damper is a rotary damper with certain allowable limits of rotation so its design is one of the most fundamental designs in limited angle MR damper design. Design and structure aspects include lot of engineering disciplines for example structure, determination of weights, available space and economics. Configuring the vane MR damper geometry, load estimation and available space calculation are an important process. Kinematics, structural sizing and required torque are some of the steps to be considered in vane MR damper design. Structure of damper is very simple and is basic vane structure. The maximum outer diameter of the designed vane MR damper is 130 mm, the maximum length of vane including shaft is 160 mm, and width of stationary is 20 mm. Single Vane MR damper absorbers operate entirely on the principle change in viscosity while crossing from the area of magnetic field resistance. MR fluid will be forced from one side of stationary part to another by the movement of vane. The working chamber will be kept full by the MR fluid in the reservoir.

Design consists of an outer body, vane, and the stationary part with valves, covers, and seals as shown in Fig. 1. The outer body has to contain all the parts inside it and the stationary part with valves is also attached to outer body.

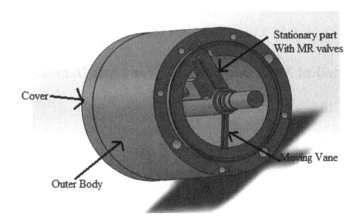

Fig. 1. Single vane MR damper

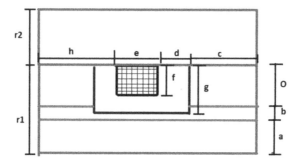

Fig. 2. Magnetic field simulation model

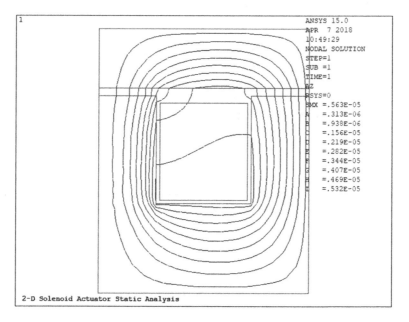

Fig. 3. Flux lines

3　Mathematical Modelling of Single Vane MR Damper

$$T = \int_{0}^{l} \frac{F \cdot D}{2} \sin \theta x dx \tag{1}$$

Where T is damping torque, F is the force, and θ is the angle.

$$F = \Delta P \cdot A \tag{2}$$

Where ΔP is the pressure difference between both sections and A is the cross sectional area.

$$A = \frac{\pi(R^2 - r^2)}{4} \tag{3}$$

In the given are formula R represents the radius of damper, r is the radius of vane shaft.

$$\Delta p = \frac{12\eta LQ}{bh^3} + \frac{3L\tau_Y}{h} \tag{4}$$

Where η the viscosity of MR fluid, Q is is the volume flow rate due to pressure drop, b is the width of the plates and h is the gap between the plates.

$$Q = A \cdot v \tag{5}$$

Where v is the Velocity.

$$\tau_y = (-0.565B^4 + 0.627B^3 + 0.811B^2 + 0.192B - 0.00393)10^5 \tag{6}$$

Where B is the magnetic induction.

$$B = 1.91\phi^{1.133}[1 - e^{(-10.97\mu_0 H)}] + \mu_0 H \tag{7}$$

The value of B is obtained by magnetic field simulation on ANSYS. H is magnetic field strength; μ_0 represents the permeability constant normally taken as $4\pi * 10^{-7} H/m$

According to Ampere's law

$$B = \frac{\mu_0 I}{2\pi r_0} \tag{8}$$

The basic formula for Current Density is [10]

$$J = \frac{NI}{A} \tag{9}$$

Where J is current density, number of turns represented by (N), the current (I), and the coil area is (A).

4 Magnetic Field Simulation

This section will provide all results generated by the finite element model in ANSYS. A model was built with curved corners farthest from the coil, as shown in Fig. 4. In this model, the MR fluid gap is represented by b. The coil is supplied a current of 2.0 Amps. The program required the current to be input in the form of current density (current over area of the electrical coil). The shaded section in the middle is the coil.

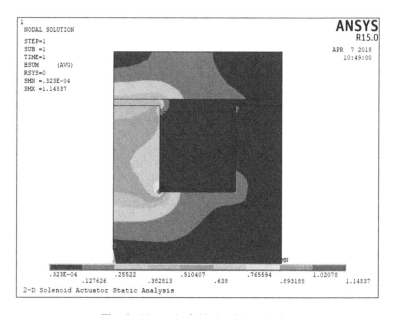

Fig. 4. Magnetic field simulation design

The single vane MR damper has 2 similar coils so just one was analyzed by ANSYS software, analyzed as a 2-D axisymmetric model. The stationary part of damper, MR fluid gap and the pump are the stationary component that form the complete magnetic circuit around the coil i.e., the static magnetic circuit for analysis. Coil is of 150 windings which provides the magnetic flux field that is necessary for energizing the MR fluid. The magnetic field model shown in Fig. 2 has been modeled in ANSYS software. After modeling, meshing is done and then boundary conditions are applied and solutions are done to get the results.

No leakage in the field was assumed during modelling, which means that the flux will be acting parallel to this surface. In Fig. 3 the flux lines are clearly shown, these lines represent the path which will be followed by the field. Meanwhile, the magnetic field in the gap of effective work area reaches 0.7T at a current of 2.0A

5   Test and Discussion

The parts of manufactured damper were shown in the figures given below. Designed damper was manufactured with special focus on leakage problem, which is the biggest issue for most of the vane MR dampers, and grooves were made in order to prevent leakage. For the first time a vane MR dampers is designed and manufactured composed of bearings, and the purpose of using bearings is to decrease the friction between shaft and body of damper, which results in smoother moment of vane inside the damper. Different internal parts of the damper are shown in the figure and the applications of different parts are described below. The vane is the rotary part and its function is to force the MR fluid to cross from one side of stationary part. Since stationary part is the most important part of damper and it needs special focus to seal from all sides, grooves were made in the stationary part to use O-ring sealing in it. Figures 5 and 6 show the parts of design and the stationary parts after assembling all parts together, respectively.

Fig. 5. Vane type MR damper with annular duct valve design parts

As shown in Fig. 6, the proposed design was tested on MTS 858 table top system. In this experiments, a DC power was utilized to generate current to the coils. After selecting stroke control mode, the physical dials on the console were used to specify the set-point, zero the load cell signal, and set limits on the amplitude of oscillation. The loading frequency of the sinusoidal routine was changed from 0.2 Hz to 0.4 Hz, to obtain the frequency-dependent performances. In these tests, MR damper at current levels of 0A, 0.5A, 1A, 1.5A and 2A were tested (Fig. 7).

Figure 8 and 9 show the variable damping results at different currents and frequencies. Results proved the increase in the damping capability at different currents

Fig. 6. Vane type MR damper after assembling all parts together

Fig. 7. Experimental set-up

such as I = 0A, 0.5a, 1A, 1.5A and 2A, respectively. It is seen that the enclosed area of the torque-angle loops increasing with the increase of current and that the peak force shows a saturation trend. This means that increasing current leads to the increase in the equivalent damping of the MR damper. It can be easily observed from Fig. 8 that the change in value current from 0A to 2A leads to the torque increasing from 26 N.m to 59 N.m. It can be clearly analyzed that, just like the other dampers tested in the field of

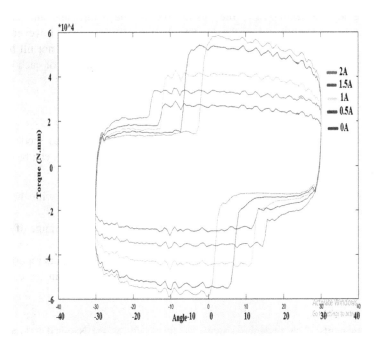

Fig. 8. Torque and angle graphs at 0.2 Hz

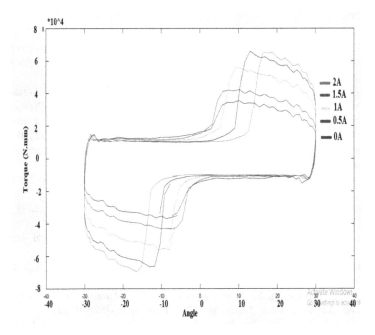

Fig. 9. Torque and angle graphs at 0.4 Hz

magnetorheological technology, the higher the torque value and the equivalent damping increase slightly when the loading frequency increases. However, torque-angle loops are obviously not full. The reason is the MR fluid does not fill the entire chamber, and the residual air causes the force loss at the beginning of each cycle.

6   Conclusion

In this study, a single vane damper was designed, based on a mixed mode of valve mode and shear mode is prototyped and tested. The main conclusions can be drawn as follows.

- This innovative scheme uses an annular gap flow mode valve with the electro-magnetic axis perpendicular to the rotation axis of the damper.
- The results obtained from the tests show a very wide operational range of damping characteristic.
- Compared with the performance of the proposed rotary MR dampers reported in the literature, this novel vane type damper shows the bigger torque in the case of the same volume.

Acknowledgements. This research is supported financially by the National Natural Science Foundation of People's Republic of China (and 51675063), this research is also supported by graduate research and innovation foundation of Chongqing, China (Grant No. CYB17023).

References

1. Dong, X., Liu, W., Wang, X., Yu, J., Chen, P.: Research on variable stiffness and damping magnetorheological actuator for robot Joint. In: 10th International Conference on Intelligent Robotics and Applications, Wuhan, pp. 109–119 (2017)
2. Goncalves, F.D.: A review of the state of the art in magnetorheological fluid technologies - part I: MR fluid and MR fluid models. Shock Vibr. Digest. **38**, 203–219 (2006)
3. Giorgetti, A., Baldanzini, N., Biasiotto, M., Citti, P.: Design and testing of a MRF rotational damper for vehicle applications. Smart Material Structures **19**(6), 065006 (2010)
4. Imaduddin, F., Mazlan, S.A., Zamzuri, H.: A design and modelling review of rotary magnetorheological damper. Mater. Des. **51**(5), 575–591 (2013)
5. Zhang, J.Q., Feng, Z.Z., Jing, Q.: Optimization analysis of a new vane MRF damper. J. Phys. Conf. Series **149**, 012087 (2009)
6. Giorgetti, A., Baldanzini, N., Biasiotto, M., Citti, P.: Design and testing of a MRF rotational damper for vehicle applications. Smart Mater. Struct. **19**(6), 065006 (2010)
7. Yang, L., Chen, S.Z., Zhang, B., Feng, Z.Z.: A rotary magneto rheological damper for a tracked vehicle. Adv. Mater. Res. **328–330**, 1135–1138 (2011)
8. Imaduddin, F., Mazlan, S.A., Zamzuri, H.: Bypass rotary magnetorheological damper for automotive applications. Appl. Mech. Mater. **663**, 685–689 (2014)
9. Zhu, X., Jing, X., Cheng, L.: Magnetorheological fluid dampers: A review on structure design and analysis. J. Intell. Mater. Syst. Struct. **28**, 3839–3873 (2012)
10. Yu, J., Dong, X., Wang, W.: Prototype and test of a novel rotary magnetorheological damper based on helical flow. Smart Mater. Struct. **25**(20), 2500 (2016)

Low-Cycle Fatigue Life Prediction of D5S for Application in Exhaust Manifolds

Farrukh Saleem[1], Ling Ma[1(✉)], Yuanxin Luo[1], Junfeng Xu[1],
Muhammad Arshad Shehzad Hassan[2], Waheed Ur Rehman[1],
Muhammad Usman Nisar[1], Jawad Ul Hassan[1],
and Muhammad Shoaib[1]

[1] The State Key Laboratory of Mechanical Transmission, School of Mechanical
Engineering, Chongqing University, Chongqing 400044, China
ml5923282420@163.com
[2] State Key Laboratory of Power Transmission Equipment & System Security
and New Technology, School of Electrical Engineering, Chongqing University,
Chongqing 400044, China

Abstract. With reference to imminent emissions regulation, the temperature is presumed to elevate in engines exhaust manifolds. To consider the present material in the manifolds, it's necessary to study the performance of the material in the working temperature. In designing part for increase life, important material characteristics to be noted, as like creep, corrosion by oxidation and fatigue resistance. Alloys are considered for improving these material properties in exhaust gases at high temperature. In this present study, analysis of D5S is observed experimentally which is used for evaluating the damage mechanism of exhaust manifolds at variant temperature and strain amplitude. Mechanical properties are examined physically by optimizing the method of uniaxial stress-strain testing and low-cycle fatigue testing with different temperature range from 300 °C to 800 °C. Behavior of the material, experimentally analyze with these cyclic softening and cyclic hardening properties. Concisely, life cycle of material D5S confers during fatigue testing. Ni-resist D5S at high temperature, reduction in fatigue life is observed during transition from elastic part to plastic part under strain dominance. In addition, the results are achieved from low-cycle fatigue experiments lead towards the selection of rank material for these applying conditions.

Keywords: Low-cycle fatigue · Cyclic deformation
Stress-strain hysteresis loops · Exhaust manifold · Mechanical properties

1 Introduction

Automotive industries have been facing major challenges regarding sensitive parts of the engine. The core issue comes with inlet and outlet parts of the engine due to temperature variation. To overcome these issue, alloy materials are used because of their better efficiency. Low-cycle fatigue (LCF) and thermo-mechanical fatigue (TMF) experiments are the efficient way to distinguish the endurance of material versus low cycle fatigue at different degree of the temperatures [1]. The combine effect of

© Springer Nature Singapore Pte Ltd. 2018
S. Wang et al. (Eds.): ICSEE 2018/IMIOT 2018, CCIS 923, pp. 267–276, 2018.
https://doi.org/10.1007/978-981-13-2396-6_25

fatigue and mechanical constraints has been observed via automotive engine parts during LCF experiments. The mechanical behavior of the material has been verified either in-phase or out-phase loadings [2]. The LCF experiment is an easy way to evaluate the fatigue strength of the material subjected to different mechanical loadings. The low-cycle and mechanical behaviors are studied previously to evaluate the damage and fatigue phenomenon of the materials as verified by [3]. However, strain with respect to time and heat diffusivity and conductivity regarding material characteristics at different temperatures have not been considered.

Number of publications have been done on the thermal behavior of the material for different applications with distinct mechanical properties. According to the requirement, most up-to-date methods are used for stress and thermal analysis of materials under different histories of loading [4]. In the previous research, most of the techniques are not efficient as compared to today techniques (LCF and TMF) for different materials analysis while keeping experiment efficiency under consideration. Analysis of automotive exhaust part has strongly link with temperature strain cycles according to above literature in the sense of damage mechanism [5].

Selection of material plays an important role in constitutive model and point out the specific region of test specimen with some define types of materials regarding usage and damage mechanism. The unique actual conditions must apply to testify the specimen but difficulty comes with the prototype and real-life deformation of materials [6].

Some restrictions for environmental effects are limited in the exhaust of heavy automobile engines which responsible for different strain mechanism. Regarding these restrictions, thermal property of exhaust parts has increased to defecate the effect of exhaust gases for efficient working. In the near time, thermal property increases more as 1000 °C which indicates to change the material ferritic ductile cast iron because of its limitation at 750 °C. Material named as Ni-resist D5S with its competent physical behavior by enhancing thermal property of exhaust parts in spark engines leads to better results. Due to its complexity in the shape of exhaust manifolds, mechanical properties such as bearing load, vibrations, thermal low-cycle fatigue (LCF) and oxidation generally leads to cast alloys as with all systematic physical properties for this purpose [7]. With the ignition-in and ignition-out of engine repeated physical behavior changing in thermally expansion and contraction causes deformation. Manufacturing procedure has also considered some generalize rules in designing with its casting and cooling temperature rate factors. Due to cyclic loading strain rate depends on microstructure behavior of material which is considered during casting. For example, strain hardening of different materials effects the crack initiation during deformation due to factors apply in casting [8].

Few effective reasons are discussed to describe the different deformation mechanism like hardness to fatigue limit in case of crack initiation at boundaries and grains effect [10]. The plasticity deformation occurs in ductile irons due to defects interlinked at nodules. The [7, 8] examines the impact of graphite structural plastic behavior of cast iron. Microstructure effect of cast iron on cyclic loading behavior is also explained by [9].

Under the present circumstances, some factors are influenced in the reduction and prediction of fatigue life such as scratches and irregularity on the surface of material. According to [11, 12], the notching effect fatigue badly occurs during experimentation.

On the other hand, inspection of notched specimens is not considered as Low-cycle Fatigue-data, usually frictionless specimen used to estimate the physical properties of exhaust manifolds during loading.

For efficient results outcomes, many test specimens have been tested separately by comparison, choosing few efficient results specimens experiment data for analyses. This paper addresses, Ni-resist D5S experimentation at varying temperature like-wise in exhaust manifold conditions. Different material properties are examined according to their reality-based behavior. As analyses in this paper, LCF test compare the results of experiments by observing the resistance to temperature cycling and hysteresis loops in out-turn of fatigue life cycles at distinct conditions.

2   Materials and Methods

2.1   Material

Alloy is used for exhaust manifold. Ni-resist D5S with the chemical composition of Ni 34–37%, Cr 1.15–2.25%, Si 4.9–5.5%, Cu 0.5 max % and Mn 1.0 max % respectively. Test specimen is designed according to Metallic Materials-Fatigue Testing-Axial-strain-controlled method under ISO 12106:2003, MOD and the requirement of MTS material test system as shown in Fig. 1. Specimens dimension changes because of two ranges of MTS control machine R1 and R2 between the hydraulic wedge grip, furnace and extensometer signals control. This specimen is used as model reference to real application for simulation in software.

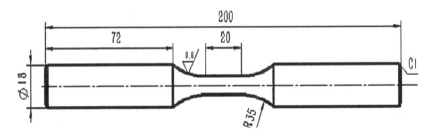

Fig. 1. Sketch of low-cycle fatigue specimen

An improved material for turbocharger housings. Automotive turbocharger housings are complex castings of predominantly thin section requiring a demanding combination of properties. Ni-resist Type D5S, a highly castable austenitic ductile iron containing 36%Ni, 5.3%Si, 2%Cr, provides the required combination of properties and is finding increased application in turbo-charger housing. A series of investigations has been conducted into the influence of melting/casting and compositional variables on microstructure, mechanical and physical properties, and machinability of this iron.

2.2   Low-Cycle Fatigue Testing

Low-cycle fatigue testing is performed on tensile test machine (100 KN) equip with MTS control system FT40, 647 Hydraulic Wedge Grip and model 653 high temperature furnace as shown in Fig. 2(a–c).

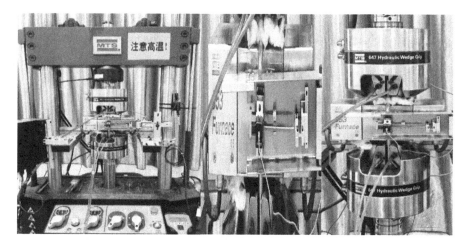

a) MTS control testing machine   b) Furnace   c) Hydraulic wedge grip

Fig. 2. Experimental setup

3   Experimental Observation

In this experimental study, some factors pen down to present physical behavior of the material into two different ways which described below graphically. These parameters are chosen in test section due to application of material in automobile and its standard test conditions for low-cycle fatigue testing.

The basic purpose is to describe the material behavior against cyclic loading and identify the used parameters. Low-cycle fatigue (LCF) components are defined as design calculation parameters for this kind of applications.

3.1   Stress Vs Strain Hysteresis Loops

The experiment discusses a pattern of the material behavior between stress and strain as shown in Fig. 3(a–e). As seen in all the figures, strain-controlled experiment represents data in five parts a, b, c, d and e in the form of hysteresis loops at different temperature range from 300 °C to 800 °C with strain amplitude 0.2% to 0.7%. Strain amplitude increases as well as stress amplitude increases with the increment in cycle. By keeping this fact in view, material additionally shows cyclic stable behavior.

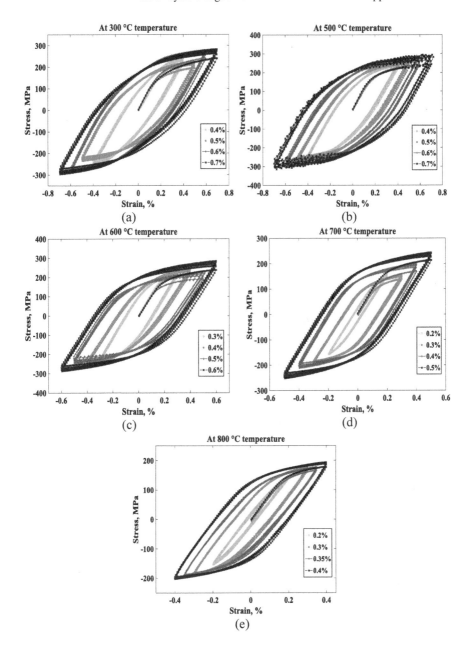

Fig. 3. Hysteresis loops presents graphical data (a, b, c, d and e) at temperature range from 300 °C to 800 °C and strain amplitude range from 0.2% to 0.7%.

The specified deformation response can be described as: (1) Cyclic softening by showing changes comes in hysteresis loops with increasing width range and decreasing peak of loop. (2) Cyclic hardening different effect is examined by the contraction of loop.

3.2   Stress Amplitude Vs Number of Cycles N_f

Strain controlled cycling response are shown in Fig. 4 in the conditions of varying temperature from 300 °C to 800 °C and different strain amplitude. Fatigue life curve and distortion phenomenon have been examined. For the most part; mainly analyses of material D5S expresses deformation mechanism. The LCF life curves in Fig. 4 interpret dual outcome. Effect of strain amplitude with the number of cycles to failure, explain the loading behavior in-phase of material. With increase in strain load and strain amplitude, overlying intrinsic damage mechanism occur certainly presenting material properties. Opposite to this, number of cycles to failure increases with low strain amplitude behave inversely cycle which shows that crack mechanism influences over by ductility of material.

The strain-controlled data presents in the temperature range from 300 °C to 800 °C a consequential result by reduce in number of cycles to failure up-to crack beginning, predominantly at high strain amplitude are observed.

4   Results and Discussions

4.1   Part I: Hysteresis Loops

Differentiate mechanical behavior of material by hysteresis loops are compared. The criterion of cyclic softening and cyclic hardening are described in hysteresis loops with different conditions. For cyclic hardening material by contract an adverse effect has been observed in the case of a similar experiment. In addition, comparison of cyclic softening and cyclic hardening is exposed according to strain amplitude and temperature dependency. During increment in the strain amplitude which is larger than plastic deformation as compared cyclic softening monopolize leads to change hysteresis loops in initial cycles.

As long as deformation proceed, imprecise changing hysteresis loops are examined, when strain amplitude is less than opening plastic mark point-out. This kind of behavior testify on LCF experiment by tension and compression at variant temperature and strain amplitude according to different conditions which are important factors in the design of engine parts.

Although in the Fig. 3, closure of hysteresis loops at different temperature and strain amplitudes shown. With more perfection in closure of hysteresis loops is observed at low strain amplitude. Results shows the effect of temperature changing on the material with different loading.

4.2   Part II: Fatigue Life Cycles

Effect of temperature and strain amplitude on fatigue life of material is expressed in Fig. 4. Comprehensive relations, express results clearly between number of cycles to failure and stress amplitude with changing temperature and strain amplitude.

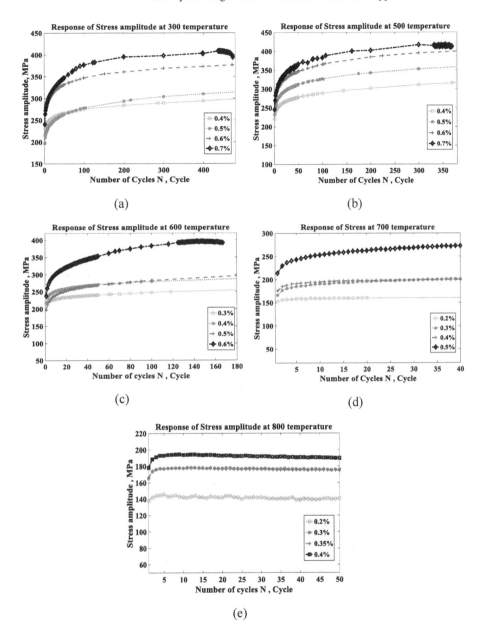

Fig. 4. Response of stress amplitude presents in graphical data (a, b, c, d and e) at temperature range from 300 °C to 800 °C and strain amplitude range from 0.2% to 0.7%

Effectively key-points observed:

(1) Temperature$_{Constant}$, Strain amplitude$_{variable}$
(2) Temperature$_{variable}$, Strain amplitude$_{constant}$

$$T_v \propto \frac{1}{N_{f,v}}$$

$$N_{f,v} \propto \frac{1}{\varepsilon_{ampl.v}}$$

$$\sigma_{ampl.v} \propto \varepsilon_{ampl.v}$$

Equations above explain behavior of material at constant and varying temperature and strain amplitude according to out-comes get from experiment. With increase in strain amplitude, stress increases but a decreasing trend shown in fatigue life cycles of material. At the same time, by increasing in temperature fatigue life cycles decreases depending on strain amplitude.

The figure demonstrates that the model describes several aspects of the material behavior well: (1) the stress level decreases with increasing temperature, (2) strain amplitude sensitivity and stress relaxation become more pronounced with increasing temperature. In contrast, fatigue life curve trend behaving differently with changing conditions. In Fig. 5, break test specimens are shown at different conditions. With macro analysis of break surface, no physical change has been observed.

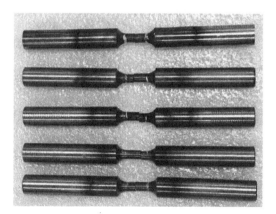

Fig. 5. Tested specimens

Data analyze as given in Table 1; (a) at same temperature with increasing strain amplitude as maximum stress increases which effect fatigue life in decreasing response, (b) at different temperature variation comes in maximum stress and fatigue life with same and increasing strain amplitude. From 300 °C to 800 °C at varying load, unique

Table 1. Data analyzation strain-controlled low-cycle fatigue test parameters and results for D5S material.

Temperature, °C	Strain amplitude, %	Maximum stress, MPa	Minimum stress, MPa	Mean stress, MPa	Fatigue life cycles, N_f
300	±0.4	335	−310	12.5	4852
300	±0.5	336	−340	−2	3478
300	±0.6	384	−377	3.2	1424
300	±0.7	409	−339	35	486
500	±0.4	345	−351	−3.2	3640
500	±0.5	381	−393	−6.2	2516
500	±0.6	405	−426	−10.3	809
500	±0.7	417	−440	−11.7	380
600	±0.3	299	−306	−3.3	2265
600	±0.4	317	−343	−13	1535
600	±0.5	325	−345	−10.5	728
600	±0.6	397	−325	36	174
700	±0.2	160	−159	0.12	6908
700	±0.3	233	−250	−8.2	833
700	±0.4	200	−206	−2.87	544
700	±0.5	289	−300	−5.8	185
800	±0.2	146	−151	−2.4	5110
800	±0.3	179	−185	−3.3	1109
800	±0.35	178	−191	−6.6	478
800	±0.4	194	−203	−4.2	381

fatigue life trend is observed as number of cycles to failure mark in above table. By experimental results, as describe in table material behave differently at high temperature and 0.2% strain amplitude. This table presents, physically behaving property of material during above conditions.

5 Conclusion

LCF life curves establish a way to evaluate number of cycles to failure up-to crack initiation. In this work, material behavior is analyzed with two unique terminologies, relation between stress and strain in hysteresis loops and stress amplitude at peak against number of cycles to failure to calculate fatigue life according to some real condition which occur in exhaust manifold at different temperature and load. In this low-cycle fatigue testing, test specimen used to examine the behavior of material in a realistic condition. Closure of hysteresis loop, plays important role to distinguish the fluctuation of material behaving property under different loading conditions. Alternation in hysteresis loops shows deformation with the variation of strain amplitude and temperature. Material fatigue life cycles depend on stress amplitude which increases directly according to strain amplitude. According to above trend of stress and strain amplitude, at the same conditions fatigue life cycles of material shows decreasing behavior as mentioned in above table. These results show the behavior of material in real condition, changing with same condition like in the exhaust manifold burning gas temperature with the start and shut down of engine at different loads stress. These results distinguish the material behaving properties according to above conditions. Material ranked with loading conditions by testing specimens. Ni-resist D5S alloy, life behavior put into words for use in exhaust manifolds.

Acknowledgement. This work is supported by the National Natural Science Foundation of China (Grant No. 51405044).

References

1. Itoh, T., Sakane, M., Ohsuga, K.: Multiaxial low cycle fatigue life under non-proportional loading. Int. J. Press. Vessels Pip. **110**, 50–56 (2013)
2. Ekström, M., Jonsson, S.: High-temperature mechanical-and fatigue properties of cast alloys intended for use in exhaust manifolds. Mater. Sci. Eng. A **616**, 78–87 (2014)
3. Murakami, Y.: Material defects as the basis of fatigue design. Int. J. Fatigue **41**, 2–10 (2012)
4. Ferro, P., Lazzarin, P., Berto, F.: Fatigue properties of ductile cast iron containing chunky graphite. Mater. Sci. Eng. A **554**, 122–128 (2012)
5. Era, H., Kishitake, K., Nagai, K., Zhang, Z.Z.: Elastic modulus and continuous yielding behaviour of ferritic spheroidal graphite cast iron. Mater. Sci. Technol. **8**(3), 257–262 (1992)
6. Sjögren, T., Svensson, I.L.: Studying elastic deformation behaviour of cast irons by acoustic emission. Int. J. Cast Met. Res. **18**(4), 249–256 (2005)
7. Sjögren, T., Svensson, I.L.: The effect of graphite fraction and morphology on the plastic deformation behavior of cast irons. Metall. Mater. Trans. A **38**(4), 840–847 (2007)
8. Čanžar, P., Tonković, Z., Kodvanj, J.: Microstructure influence on fatigue behaviour of nodular cast iron. Mater. Sci. Eng. A **556**, 88–99 (2012)
9. Sakane, M., Zhang, S., Kim, T.: Notch effect on multiaxial low cycle fatigue. Int. J. Fatigue **33**(8), 959–968 (2011)
10. Berto, F., Lazzarin, P., Gallo, P.: High-temperature fatigue strength of a copper–cobalt–beryllium alloy. J. Strain Anal. Eng. Des. **49**(4), 244–256 (2014)
11. Berto, F., Lazzarin, P.: Recent developments in brittle and quasi-brittle failure assessment of engineering materials by means of local approaches. Mater. Sci. Eng. R Rep. **75**, 1–48 (2014)
12. Berto, F., Lazzarin, P.: A review of the volume-based strain energy density approach applied to V-notches and welded structures. Theor. Appl. Fract. Mech. **52**(3), 183–194 (2009)

Manufacturing Optimization

Task-Driven QoS Prediction Model Based on the Case Library in Cloud Manufacturing

Jian Liu[✉], Youling Chen, Long Wang, Yufei Niu,
Lidan Zuo, and Lei Ling

College of Mechanical Engineering, Chongqing University,
Chongqing 400044, China
liujiancqu@126.com

Abstract. With the great development of cloud manufacturing (CMfg), currently accurate prediction about quality-of-service (QoS) has become a hot issue. However, as task diversity increases, most existing QoS prediction methods mainly focus on the similarity measure between users and services, and thus ignore the impact of task characteristics in CMfg. Therefore, to solve above problem, a task-driven QoS prediction model with the case library is established to predict unknown QoS value. First, we present a similarity measure method in the case library including service similarity and task similarity, to search similar services and corresponding historical tasks. Then, QoS prediction model is established considering task similarity and the time decay function as well as service similarity. According to the experiments, our model outperforms current methods with respect to prediction accuracy, and the key parameters have also been studied.

Keywords: Cloud manufacturing (CMfg) · QoS prediction · Task similarity
Case library

1 Introduction

With the great development of modern emerging technologies (Big Data, Cloud Computing, et al.), manufacturing industries have undergone enormous changes recently [1]. Under this background, cloud manufacturing (CMfg) [2–4] was first proposed by Li et al., as an emerging networked manufacturing paradigm, which is inspired by cloud technology and takes advantage of the previous manufacturing modes [5–7]. However, since there are a huge number of services share similar functionality but different value of QoS in CMfg, it becomes challenging for user to make a better decision [8].

Quality-of-service which is also called QoS, is a critical concept in CMfg, which contains a lot of non-functional attributes of cloud service, like cost, time, reliability, energy consumption, etc. A common assumption was that all QoS values are already known in CMfg. However, in real life, some QoS values are unknown.

Nowadays, collaborative filtering (CF) [9–11] is an effective method, and which has been commonly applied to estimate the unknown QoS value in CMfg. On the basis of historical records of QoS, some similarity measures, like Pearson Correlation

© Springer Nature Singapore Pte Ltd. 2018
S. Wang et al. (Eds.): ICSEE 2018/IMIOT 2018, CCIS 923, pp. 279–289, 2018.
https://doi.org/10.1007/978-981-13-2396-6_26

Coefficient (PCC) [12], which have been utilized to select similar cloud user or service vendor.

Although CF is simple to implement, its prediction accuracy cannot meet dynamic requirements and falls sharply since task diversity increases in CMfg. Task similarity and the time factor involved in the historical QoS records have been ignored, which might makes the prediction results inaccuracy.

Based on the above analysis, QoS prediction is becoming more and more essential in CMfg. Therefore, to effectively tackle with the issue, we first establish a task-driven QoS prediction model with the case library to obtain unknown QoS value.

The rest part of this paper is placed as follows. Section 2 focus on introducing the related studies. Section 3 gives a motivating scenario and briefly describe the case library. Section 4 is about our proposed task-driven QoS prediction model. Section 5 is about the experiments based on our proposed model. Finally, some conclusions and a few future work are drawn in Sect. 6.

2   Related Work

A brief review of QoS prediction methods is given in this section, which have been studied recently. Rehman et al. [13] developed a novel QoS ranking method by utilizing QoS historical records of cloud services over different time periods. To enhance the prediction accuracy, Yu et al. [14] designed a novel CF algorithm, in which time factor have been employed. However, time decay function in the real time has been ignored, and is simply limited for web services. Jayapriya et al. [15] proposed another QoS prediction approach, in which a data smoothing technique is adopted to obtain a better result. Karim et al. [16] established a model for QoS prediction based on user information as well as historical records. To overcome the data sparsity, Feng et al. [17] developed a matrix factorization approach to extract the information of similar neighbors. Also, Wu et al. [18] presented another matrix factorization approach called CSMF to help users access to appropriate services, in which context information are considered.

From the existing approaches in the literature, we can find that current QoS prediction approaches suffer from average performance of QoS. Also, much previous research effort mainly focuses on how to improve the similarity measures in CF algorithms, but seldom takes the task characteristics into consideration.

Therefore, a task-driven model is established to accurately predict unknown QoS value. Firstly, we take task similarity into account, which is extracted in the case library. Then, a QoS prediction model is established considering task similarity and the time decay function as well as service similarity, so as to acquire a more accurate QoS value in CMfg.

3 Motivation and Case Library

3.1 Motivation

Before introducing the above problem, a simple example about task-driven QoS prediction is presented to illustrate the problem that is addressed in this study.

As shown in the Fig. 1, there are two tasks (*Task*1 and *Task*2) submitted by a user in CMfg, and they have been decomposed into several subtasks, for example, $Task1 = \{T_{11}, T_{12}, \cdots, T_{1n}\}$ where n denotes the number of subtasks. $SS(CS) = \{SS_1, SS_2, \cdots, SS_m\}$, where $SS(CS)$ represents similar services of CS and m denotes maximum number of similar services, $T_h(CS) = \{T_h^1, T_h^2, \cdots, T_h^k\}$, where $T_h(CS)$ means the historical tasks of CS and k denotes maximum number of similar historical tasks in the case library. Unfortunately, the QoS of CS which has been both chosen by T_{14} and T_{24} is unknown. However, existing QoS prediction methods assume that same cloud service is likely to have similar QoS values when invoked by same user, and the impact of task characteristics have been totally ignored, which makes it an urgent problem to be solved so far.

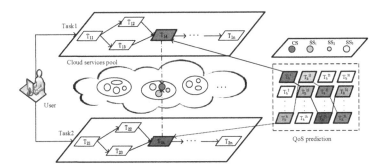

Fig. 1. Example of task-driven QoS prediction.

3.2 The Structure of Case Library

In this section, a brief explanation of case library [19] is given, in which the structure of historical task cases are designed to support the similarity measure mentioned above. The task description model can be expressed as $TaskCase = \{TaskProfile, TaskType, TaskInfor\}$.

Task Profile is the set of task collected in the case library. $TaskType = \{Type^1, Type^2, \cdots, Type^n\}$ denotes the type of task, for instance, design task, manufacture task, assembly task, and logistics task, etc. $TaskInfor = \{Infor^1, Infor^2, \cdots, Infor^n\}$ denotes the different task information requested by users. Furthermore, $Infor^j = \{FuncInfor^j, QoSInfor^j\}$ denotes the detailed task information of j th historical task, including functional request information of task and quality request information of service, in which $FuncInfor^j = \{Fc_1^j, Fc_2^j, \cdots, Fc_N^j\}$ includes N functional requests. In addition, $QoSInfor^j$ stores historical QoS records of j th historical task in the case library. But, the number of historical task has a upper bound *Case_limit*, to ensure high efficiency of similar task search, as well as save the space of historical QoS records database.

4   QoS Prediction Model

4.1   Similarity Computation

Similarity computation is a critical part for QoS prediction, and there are two kinds of similarity involved in this section: service similarity and task similarity. The detail computation process is presented below.

Service Similarity
One important step in the case library is to compute the service similarity and then to select similar services according to Top-K ($K = m$) algorithm. Since Pearson Correlation Coefficient (PCC) [12] is easy to implement, there are a lot of methods for similarity computation based on the PCC in recent years.

The service similarity is computed as follows:

$$Ss\langle CS, SS_i\rangle = \frac{\sum_{t\in T}\left(r_{CS,t} - \bar{r}_{CS}\right)\left(r_{SS_i,t} - \bar{r}_{SS_i}\right)}{\sqrt{\sum_{t\in T}\left(r_{CS,t} - \bar{r}_{CS}\right)^2}\sqrt{\sum_{t\in T}\left(r_{SS_i,t} - \bar{r}_{SS_i}\right)^2}} \tag{1}$$

where $Ss\langle CS, SS_i\rangle$ denotes the service similarity between CS and i th similar service SS_i, $T = T_{CS} \cap T_{SS_i}$ is the set of tasks that are both invoked by CS and SS_i, $r_{CS,t}$ is the QoS value when task t finished by CS, $\bar{r}_{CS}$ is an average value of QoS when CS has finished the co-invoked tasks. Thus, a higher value of Ss computed by Eq. 1 indicated that they are more similar. In addition, assume that there are not m similar services selected ($Ss < \alpha$), then the others are null and α is the threshold of service similarity.

Task Similarity
In order to compute the task similarity as accurately as possible, we take full use of above task semantic description model in the case library. Therefore, the task similarity is computed as follows:

$$Ts\langle T_j, T_h^j\rangle = 1 - \sqrt{\sum_{i=1}^{N} w_i^j D\left(Case(Fc_i^j) - Fc_i^j\right)^2} \tag{2}$$

where Ts represents the task similarity, T_j represents j th subtask of requested task, and T_h^j represents j th historical task in *TaskCase* of candidate service, $Case(Fc_i^j)$ represents functional requests of T_h^j, thus, $Ts\langle T_j, T_h^j\rangle$ denotes task similarity between T_j and T_h^j. And, $W^j = \{w_1^j, w_2^j, \cdots, w_N^j\}$ is the corresponding weight to the different functional requests, in which $\sum_{i=1}^{N} w_i^j = 1$. Also, k denotes the number of similar task ($Ts \geq \beta$), if there are not k similar tasks selected ($Ts < \beta$), then the others are null, and β is the threshold of task similarity.

$D\left(Case(Fc_i^j) - Fc_i^j\right)^2$ is the quantization distance of attributes between $Case(Fc_i^j)$ and Fc_i^j. However, it should be performed according to the task type. For example, if $D\left(Case(Fc_i^j) - Fc_i^j\right)^2 = 1$, then the task similarity is 0. And the formula of $D\left(Case(Fc_i^j) - Fc_i^j\right)$ is calculated as follows:

$$D\left(Case(Fc_i^j) - Fc_i^j\right) = \frac{\left|Case(Fc_i^j) - Fc_i^j\right|}{\left|Fc_{\max} - Fc_{\min}\right|} \tag{3}$$

where $\left|Fc_{\max} - Fc_{\min}\right|$ represents the charge range of the threshold.

Time Decay Function

As mentioned previously, the dynamic characteristic of time is considered when calculating W^T. To be specific, historical performance of QoS occurred to recent time generally have a large proportion on QoS prediction than the performance in older time.

Therefore, according to the dynamic characteristic of time, we aim to obtain an appropriate weight to different historical tasks. And the time decay function [20] is calculated as follows:

$$w_i = \Delta t_i^{-1} / \sum_{i=1}^{k} (\Delta t_i)^{-1} \tag{4}$$

where w_i denotes the corresponding time weight for i th historical task, Δt_i is the time interval from the invoked time of i th historical task.

4.2 QoS Prediction Model

To obtain the missing value of QoS, in this section, a task-driven model for QoS prediction is established. The implementation process and several key steps are depicted as below (Fig. 2):

Step A: In this step, we take task similarity and service similarity into account to achieve appropriate similar services (m) and similar tasks (k). Then, the similarity threshold are set. After that, we would collect some matrices in the case library, for example, $Matrix = \{M_1, M_2, \cdots, M_{m+1}\}$, where $m + 1$ represents the number of candidate service (1) and similar services (m), respectively, and each matrix contains a series of QoS information of historical tasks.

Step B: After Step A, we focus on the two key factors Ss and Ts (Sect. 4.1). Unlike some previous approaches, we comprehensively consider task similarity and the time decay function, as well as service similarity.

Step C: On the basis of Step A and Step B, a novel task-driven model is established to calculate the unknown value of QoS, and the formula is proposed as follows:

$$QôS(r_{S_i}) = \overline{r_{S_i}} + \sum_{j=1}^{k} ((Ts_i^j \cdot w_{ij})(r_{ij} - \overline{r_{S_i}})) / \sum_{j=1}^{k} (Ts_i^j \cdot w_{ij}) \qquad (5)$$

where r_{ij} is the value of j th similar task invoked by S_i, $\overline{r_{S_i}}$ is the average value of S_i, Ts_i^j is the j th task similarity of S_i, w_{ij} is the time weight of j th similar task invoked by S_i, $QôS(r_{S_i})$ denotes the predicting QoS value of S_i.

$$QôS(r_{CS}) = \overline{QôS(r_{S_i})} + \sum_{i=1}^{m+1} \left(Ss_i (QôS(r_{S_i}) - \overline{QôS(r_{S_i})}) \right) / \sum_{i=1}^{m+1} Ss_i \qquad (6)$$

where $\overline{QôS(r_{S_i})}$ denotes the average QoS value, Ss_i is the service similarity of S_i, $QôS(r_{CS})$ is the final predicting QoS value of candidate service.

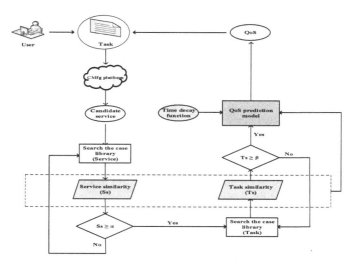

Fig. 2. The process of QoS prediction model based on the case library.

5   Experiment

5.1   Experiment Setup

Since the public dataset of CMfg application platform is unavailable, the experiments are constructed by using real QoS data of cloud services, which is collected form the case library in topology system [19]. In this section, we take the Time (T) and reliability (Rel) as the QoS attribute for performance comparison.

We remove the QoS value of the candidate services, and the value which is removed is considered as the predicted value. Meanwhile, current QoS approaches are also used to estimate the unknown value. And, our task-driven model can also deal with other QoS attributes easily without any modification. The parameters are clearly given in Table 1.

Table 1. Experimental parameters.

Parameters	Value
m: the number of maximum similar services	20
α: the lower threshold of service similarity for service selection	0.6
k: the number of maximum similar historical tasks	10
β: the lower threshold of task similarity for historical task selection	0.6

To make a performance comparison of prediction accuracy, we take both Mean Absolute Error (MAE) and Root Mean Squared Error (RMSE) into account, and they are computed as follows:

$$\begin{cases} MAE = \frac{1}{N}\sum_{i,j} |r(i,j) - \hat{r}(i,j)| \\ RMSE = \sqrt{\frac{\sum_{i,j} |r(i,j) - \hat{r}(i,j)|^2}{N}} \end{cases} \tag{7}$$

where $r(i,j)$ is the value (QoS) of service j invoked by user i, $\hat{r}(i,j)$ is the predicted value of QoS, N is the overall number of values which are predicted.

Without loss of generality, the experiment is repeated for ten times. Then the prediction metrics are accordingly averaged (called AMAE and ARMSE correspondingly).

5.2   Performance Comparison

For QoS prediction, our task-driven QoS prediction model (TQPM) is compared with three other classical approaches: cloud services similarity incorporated tensor factorization model (CSSTF) [16] and neighbourhood enhanced matrix factorization (NEMF) [17], as well as context-sensitive matrix-factorization (CSMF) [18]. The results of our experiments are shown in Tables 2 and 3, respectively.

Table 2. Performance comparison of QoS prediction (T) with other approaches.

Methods	$N = 100$		$N = 200$		$N = 500$	
T(d)	AMAE	ARMSE	AMAE	ARMSE	AMAE	ARMSE
CSSTF	1.4660	2.2453	1.6140	2.6754	2.2780	3.0250
NEMF	1.2170	1.8867	1.3490	2.2275	1.6070	2.4321
CSMF	1.1770	1.8362	1.2710	2.0117	1.5080	2.2919
TQPM	1.1330	1.7417	1.2180	1.8340	1.3660	2.0366

Table 3. Performance comparison of QoS prediction (Re*l*) with other approaches.

Methods	$N = 100$		$N = 200$		$N = 500$	
Re*l*(%)	AMAE	ARMSE	AMAE	ARMSE	AMAE	ARMSE
CSSTF	1.4730	2.2673	1.6380	2.7124	2.3100	3.1670
NEMF	1.2290	1.9037	1.3690	2.2675	1.6280	2.5121
CSMF	1.1860	1.8512	1.2880	2.0837	1.5140	2.3089
TQPM	1.1410	1.7647	1.2170	1.8330	1.3690	2.0382

From Tables 2 and 3, it is obvious that our task-driven model achieves smaller AMAE and ARMSE for both respond time (T) and reliability (Re*l*) with different number of candidate services ($N = 100, 200, 500$), which indicates better prediction accuracy. Compared to other methods, although the AMAE and ARMSE grow gradually as the number N increases, our model always has a better performance with respect to both MAE and RMSE.

To sum up, our proposed task-driven QoS prediction model based on the case library mainly focuses on the task characteristics which has been ignored before, then task similarity and time decay function, as well as service similarity have been taken into account. And, the experiments have proved that our model is feasibility and effectiveness.

5.3   Impact of Parameters

To explore the impact of several parameters (Table 1), we construct experiments by changing a specific parameter while keeping the others unchanged. For simplicity, we only consider the Time (T) in this part, and the detail analysis process is presented below.

Impact of m and k

As a key parameter, m is the number of maximum similar services. We investigate the impact of m in the condition of $N = 100, 200$, in which the value of m is varying from 5 to 50 with a step of 5. At the same time, other key parameters remain unchanged as Table 1.

As shown in Fig. 3, our model has the highest accuracy, especially when $m = 20$ with respect to both MAE and RMSE. Considering the fact that too small of m provide few historical QoS records, while too large of m inevitably introduce some dissimilar services. Thus, we set $m = 20$ in the experiments.

Similarly, k determines the number of maximum similar tasks in the case library. And the impact of k is investigated when $N = 100, 200$, varying the value of k from 2 to 20 with a step of 2 while remaining other settings unchanged.

From Fig. 4, we can observed that our model generate better results when k becomes relative larger. Also, both the MAE and RMSE decrease sharply, particularly when k reaches to 10. After that, the metrics seem to be a stable value. But, a larger k may be ask for more computation time. Therefore, we set $k = 10$ as the default value in the experiments.

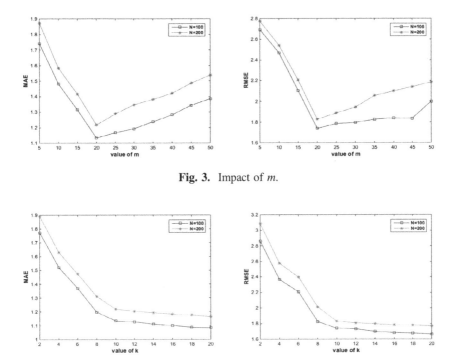

Fig. 3. Impact of *m*.

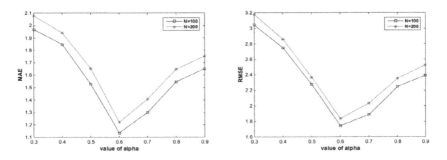

Fig. 4. Impact of *k*.

Impact of α and β

In our model, as key parameters α and β are the threshold of service similarity (*Ss*) and task similarity (*Ts*), respectively. We carry out multiple experiments to research the impact of α and β, in which the values are both varied from 0.3 to 0.9 with a step of 0.1 while keeping other settings unchanged.

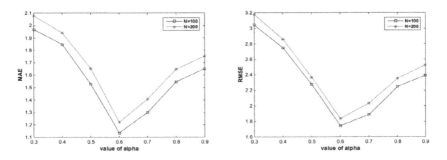

Fig. 5. Impact of α.

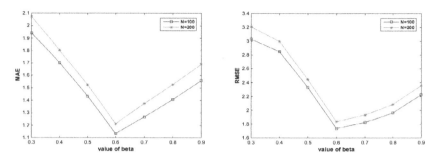

Fig. 6. Impact of β.

Figures 5 and 6 indicate that our model has the highest performance, particularly when $\alpha = 0.6$ and $\beta = 0.6$ with respect to both MAE and RMSE. The reason is that too large of α and β cannot promise enough similar services or tasks for our model, while too small value of α and β will certainly introduce some dissimilar services or tasks into the QoS prediction process, which also inevitably makes the prediction results inaccurate. And this is why we set $\alpha = 0.6$ and $\beta = 0.6$ in the experiments.

6   Conclusion and Future Work

For QoS prediction, a task-driven model based on the case library is established to accurately predict unknown QoS value. The primary contribution is mainly summarized as follows: (1) task characteristic and task similarity are first considered and extracted in the case library; (2) task similarity and the time decay function, as well as service similarity are employed together to establish a model for QoS prediction; (3) experiments are carried out by using real data of QoS to show the efficiency of our proposed model, and the key parameters are also studied.

In future work, we prefer to study the complex relationship among cloud user, task and cloud service in CMfg environment. The robustness of our model is another problem that need to be improved.

Acknowledgments. This project was supported by the National Natural Science Foundation of China under grant No. 71271224. The authors would like to appreciate the constructive and helpful comments from the editors and anonymous reviewers.

References

1. Yao, X., Lin, Y.: Emerging manufacturing paradigm shifts for the incoming industrial revolution. Int. J. Adv. Manuf. Technol. **85**, 1665–1676 (2015)
2. Li, B.H., Zhang, L., Wang, S.L., Tao, F., Cao, J.W., Jiang, X.D., Song, X., Chai, X.D.: Cloud manufacturing: a new service-oriented networked manufacturing model. Comput. Integr. Manuf. Syst. **16**, 1–7 (2010)
3. Xu, X.: From cloud computing to cloud manufacturing. Robot. Comput. Integr. Manuf. **28**, 75–86 (2012)

4. Zhang, L., Luo, Y.L., Tao, F., Li, B.H., Ren, L., Zhang, X.S., Guo, H., Cheng, Y., Hu, A.R., Liu, Y.K.: Cloud manufacturing: a new manufacturing paradigm. Enterp. Inf. Syst. **8**, 167–187 (2014)
5. Sanchez, L.M., Nagi, R.: A review of agile manufacturing systems. Int. J. Prod. Res. **39**, 3561–3600 (2001)
6. Smith, M.A., Kumar, R.L.: A theory of application service provider (ASP) use from a client perspective. Inf. Manag. **41**, 977–1002 (2004)
7. Tao, F., Hu, Y.F., Zhou, Z.D.: Study on manufacturing grid & its resource service optimal-selection system. Int. J. Adv. Manuf. Technol. **37**, 1022–1041 (2008)
8. Wu, Q.W., Zhu, Q.S., Zhou, M.Q.: A correlation-driven optimal service selection approach for virtual enterprise establishment. J. Intell. Manuf. **25**, 1441–1453 (2014)
9. Su, X.Y., Khoshgoftaar, T.M.: A survey of collaborative filtering techniques. Adv. Artif. Intell. **2009**, 4 (2009)
10. Wu, J., Chen, L., Feng, Y., Zheng, Z., Zhou, M., Wu, Z.: Predicting quality of service for selection by neighborhood-based collaborative filtering. IEEE Trans. Syst. Man Cybern. Syst. **43**, 428–439 (2013)
11. Wang, D., Yang, Y., Mi, Z.: A genetic-based approach to web service composition in geo-distributed cloud environment. Comput. Electr. Eng. **43**, 129–141 (2015)
12. Yu, Z.Y., Wang, J.D., Zhang, H.W., Niu, K.: Services recommended trust algorithm based on cloud model attributes weighted clustering. Autom. Control Comput. Sci. **50**, 260–270 (2016)
13. Rehman, Z., Hussain, O.K., Hussain, F.K.: Parallel cloud service selection and ranking based on QoS history. Int. J. Parallel Program. **42**, 820–852 (2014)
14. Yu, C.Y., Huang, L.P.: A Web service QoS prediction approach based on time- and location-aware collaborative filtering. SOCA **10**, 135–149 (2016)
15. Jayapriya, K., Mary, N.A.B., Rajesh, R.S.: Cloud service recommendation based on a correlated QoS ranking prediction. J. Netw. Syst. Manage. **24**, 916–943 (2016)
16. Karim, R., Ding, C., Miri, A., Rahman, M.S.: Incorporating service and user information and latent features to predict QoS for selecting and recommending cloud service compositions. Cluster Comput. **19**, 1227–1242 (2016)
17. Feng, Y., Huang, B.: Cloud manufacturing service QoS prediction based on neighbourhood enhanced matrix factorization. J. Intell. Manuf. (2018). https://doi.org/10.1007/s10845-018-1409-8
18. Wu, H., Yue, K., Li, B., Zhang, B.B., Hsu, C.H.: Collaborative QoS prediction with context-sensitive matrix factorization. Future Gener. Comput. Syst. **82**, 669–678 (2018)
19. Xiang, F., Jiang, G.Z., Xu, L.L., Wang, N.X.: The case-library method for service composition and optimal selection of big manufacturing data in cloud manufacturing system. Int. J. Adv. Manuf. Technol. **84**, 59–70 (2016)
20. Yan, K., Cheng, Y., Tao, F.: A trust evaluation model towards cloud manufacturing. Int. J. Adv. Manuf. Technol. **84**, 133–146 (2016)

Reliability Analysis of Meta-action Unit in Complex Products by GO Method

Hong-Yu Ge$^{(\boxtimes)}$, Yang Gao, and Hong-Wei Fan

College of Mechanical Engineering, Xi'an University of Science and
Technology, Xi'an 710054, China
9203631@qq.com

Abstract. The stability and reliability of meta-action unit is the basis for ensuring the reliability of the whole machine. Based on the analysis of the structure of meta-action units,a fishbone diagram of influencing factors of meta-action unit reliability is established. Then, the GO method is used to analyze the reliability of the meta action unit, and the universal GO diagram model and probabilistic model of the unit action reliability are established. Taking the reliability analysis of spindle rotation element motion as an example, the application of the proposed method is verified.

Keywords: Meta-action unit · Reliability · GO method

1 Introduction

With the rapid development of science and technology, the demand for product diversification has become increasingly strong in the society. Products have been updated faster and faster. The proportion of multi-species, medium and small batch production has increased significantly. With the rapid growth of aviation, automotive and light industrial products, the demand for parts is increasing, and the precision requirements are getting higher and higher. In addition, fierce market competition requires shorter and shorter production cycles for product development. Machining tools must adapt to this versatile, flexible and complex shape of high-efficiency and high-reliability machining requirements. CNC machine tools, as the foundation of manufacturing, are the most important processing tools in the current manufacturing industry, and represent the manufacturing technology and development level [1].

Reliability is one of the key indicators to measure the performance of CNC machine tools. The number of machine tools in China is more than 8 million units, but the overall reliability level is low. Every year, a large number of machine tools face functional or technical elimination, and it is urgent to implement reliability growth technology. CNC machine tools are complex mechanical and electrical products. In order to ensure effective analysis of product reliability, it is necessary to decompose the

Work partially supported by National Natural Science Foundation of China (51705417), Shaanxi Provincial Department of Education Project (17JK0501).

S. Wang et al. (Eds.): ICSEE 2018/IMIOT 2018, CCIS 923, pp. 290–299, 2018.
https://doi.org/10.1007/978-981-13-2396-6_27

reliability of the entire machine. At present, there are many documents dedicated to the reliability of numerically-controlled machine tools, but there are few reference that analyze and research the reliability of the whole machine decomposed. In [2], the fault tree model of Monte Carlo method is used to establish the fault tree model of the mechanical system of CNC machine tools, and the specific process algorithm and simulation results are given. In [3] uses a four-parameter in-homogeneous Poisson process model to quantitative evaluate the early failure period of a machine tool. In [4], using the DIC information criterion, BGR diagnosis principle, Monte Carlo simulation error and interval length of model parameters and reliability index posterior estimation, a comprehensive evaluation method of Bayesian reliability model for NC machine tools is proposed. In [5] divides the machine tool subsystem according to the function principle of the numerically-controlled machine tool, uses the maximum likelihood estimation method and deviation correction to obtain the reliability function of the whole machine and subsystem, and uses the D-test to obtain the reliability function of the whole machine and each subsystem. All meet the requirements. The literature [6] established a series of mathematical models for the distribution of time between failures of numerically controlled machine tools and established the relevant indicators for reliability of numerically controlled machine tools. The literature [7] applied the Bayesian method to analyze the reliability of a few sample fault data CNC machine tools, and presented the two-parameter Weibull model parameters and point and interval estimations of the numerical indicators of the reliability of the CNC machine tools. The Monte Carlo chain Monte Carlo sampling was used. Solved the problem of solving complex posterior integrals in Bayesian reliability analysis.

By analyzing related literature, there are many studies on the reliability of the whole machine, and there is less research on the reliability of the meta-action. However, failure of the whole machine is caused by failure of one meta action function or multiple meta action functions. The reliability of the whole machine is ensured by the reliability of each element action. In the selection of trace ability methods and reliability analysis methods, taking into account the simple structure of the meta-action, fish-bone diagram can describe the reliability of meta-action; According to the GO method-oriented modeling features, the fishbone diagram can be more accurately converted to GO diagram. Therefore, the choice of fishbone diagram and GO method combined with the reliability analysis of the meta-action.

Based on the above analysis, this article begins with the analysis of meta-action units and explores the component factors that complete the meta-action function. Establish the functional block diagram of the meta action unit. Using fish-bone diagram to analyze the influencing factors of meta-action unit. Finally, reliability analysis of the GO method is performed to lay the foundation for the reliability of the entire machine.

2 Meta-action Unit Reliability Analysis Process Framework

2.1 Concept of Meta-action Unit

The working process of CNC machine tools is a complex synthesis movement. The realization of the main function requires multiple different units to complete different actions. Each action requires an independent unit to achieve the function. Meta-action unit structure is independent, able to achieve a certain action goal or achieve a certain purpose. The action unit is controllable for analysis and does not need to (and cannot) subdivide, namely Meta-action [8, 9].

The meta-action is a basic unit in the motion system of CNC machine tools. The reliability of all meta actions determines the reliability of the entire machine function. The meta-action reliability attribute is guaranteed by the correct motion of the meta-action unit. The typical meta-action unit consists of five parts: support frame, power source, connector and actuator. Meta-action structure unit model shown in Fig. 1.

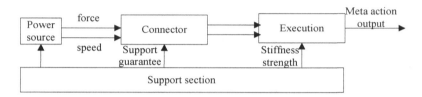

Fig. 1. Function structure diagram of the meta-action unit

2.2   Flow of Reliability Analysis of Meta-action Unit Based on GO Method

The GO method is based on probabilistic analysis and translates system operation schematics, flow charts or engineering drawings into GO diagrams according to certain rules. The GO method analyzes the probability of each step or unit in the system based on the GO diagram [10].

(1) Operators

Operators represent the logical relationship between unit functions and unit input and output signals. According to the composition of a specific system, elements, components, subsystems, or influencing factors in the system may be collectively referred to as units. The attributes of an operator include types, data, and operation rules, and the operator type reflects unit functions and characteristics.

(2) Signal flow

The signal flow represents the association between the input and output of the system unit. The signal flow connection operator constitutes a GO diagram. The attributes of signal flow are state values and state probabilities. The factors affecting the operational reliability of meta-action units mostly belong to a 2-state system. State 1 represents normal, and state 2 represents failure.

(3) GO operation

Starting from the output signal of the input operator of the GO diagram, the operation is performed according to the operation rules of the next operator. The state and probability of the output signal are obtained, and the operations are performed one by one according to the sequence of the signal stream until a set of output signals of the system.

For the concept and characteristics of the reliability of the CNC unit, the GO method can intuitively represent the interaction and correlation between the reliability of the meta-action and the influencing factors. The GO legal analysis can determine the set of meta action motion success events. GO method quantitative analysis can calculate the probability of the successful movement of the meta-action movement and the failure status. To sum up, a method for reliability analysis of meta-action units based on the GO method can be established, as shown in Fig. 2.

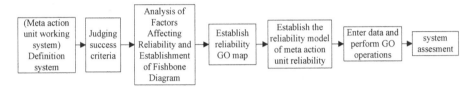

Fig. 2. Meta-action unit reliability GO method analysis flow

The steps of the reliability analysis of the meta-action unit working process are as follows.

(1) Define the working process of the meta-action unit, determine the scope of system reliability analysis, and determine the judging basis and criteria (success criteria) for the reliability of the meta action unit.

(2) Analyze the factors that affect the reliability of the unit of action. Such as whether the power source can guarantee the torque, speed, and motion stability, whether the support can guarantee the rigidity, strength, position accuracy and shape accuracy of the geometric elements, and the transmission parts. Whether it can be fixed firmly, whether the action of the actuator output can guarantee the speed torque, accuracy, precision life and reliability.

(3) Establish the fishbone diagram of the influencing factors of the reliability of the meta-action. Convert the fishbone diagram into a GO diagram model, and introduce the GO operation rules to establish a probabilistic model for reliability analysis of the meta-action.

(4) Evaluate and analyze the reliability of each element of the operation, lock down the key faults, and propose improvement measures.

3   Reliability Analysis of Meta-action Unit by GO Method

3.1   Meta-action Reliability Systematic Analysis and Fishbone Model

The reliability of meta-action unit is ensured by its constituent parts. The main component of the meta-action unit is composed of a support, a power source, a connector, and an actuator.

The support part in the meta-action structural unit is the basic part that supports the meta-action structural unit. It assembles the relevant parts in the meta-action unit into a whole, keeps the parts in the correct mutual position, and drives in a coordinated manner according to a certain transmission relationship. Therefore, the quality of the support directly affects the accuracy, performance, and reliability of the meta-action unit. To ensure the reliability of the meta-action unit, the support must meet the shape accuracy, surface roughness, hole size accuracy, and geometry accuracy of the main plane, the main hole and plane mutual position accuracy, strength, stiffness and other requirements.

The power source is a power device, which can be a DC or AC speed governing motor and a servo motor, and can also be the output of other meta-action units. The torque, speed, and motion stability of the power source are the basis for ensuring the reliable realization of the meta-action.

Both ends of the connector are respectively connected to the supporting portion and the actuator. The requirements for the connectors are fixed and reliable, ensuring correct and stable movement of the actuators.

The executor, the action output of the meta-action unit. Its task is to deliver power to another unit. Since the actuator must complete some form of movement (movement or rotation), the actuator has parameters such as motion accuracy, structural rigidity, and speed adaptability in terms of performance and functionality.

Based on the above analysis, the factors affecting the reliability of the meta-action can be analyzed with fishbone diagrams, as shown in Fig. 3.

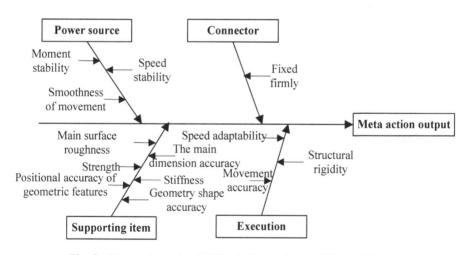

Fig. 3. Meta-action unit reliability influence factors fishbone diagram

3.2   Rules for Converting Fishbone Diagram to GO Diagram

Fishbone diagram is a kind of causality diagram, and it is an event-oriented traceability diagram. GO diagram is a success-oriented system analysis diagram. Both have the same logical relationship analysis points, so follow the following principles in the conversion process:

(1) According to the characteristics of each factor in the fishbone diagram, various factors are converted into corresponding operators;
(2) Connect each element with the corresponding signal flow;
(3) Take the power source, support member, connector, and actuator as input operators;
(4) Concatenate the performance factors of the input operators in the form of two-state operators;
(5) The coupling points of the performance factors of the input operators are logically connected to the gates;
(6) Final output meta-action reliability;
(7) The fishbone diagram is converted to a GO diagram.

3.3   Meta-action Reliability GO Diagram Model

Based on the basic principle of GO diagram creation and the characteristics of reliable implementation of meta-actions, the factors affecting the reliability of meta-actions are represented by operators. The connection between each influencing factor is represented by a signal flow, and a GO diagram of meta-action reliability can be established. The model is shown in Fig. 4.

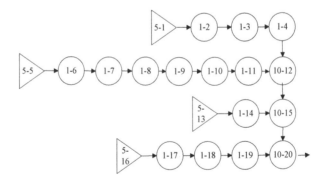

Fig. 4. The reliability of a meta action unit GO diagram

The power source, the support point of the support, the connection point of the connector, and the execution point of the actuator are input terminals (start points) of the system. Each of the above-mentioned inputs generates an output signal and has two states. The type 5 is used input operator $\overset{R}{\underset{5-}{\rhd}\rightarrow}$ representation; Power source output (smoothness, torque stability, smoothness of movement), Support properties (main surface roughness of support, main dimension accuracy, strength, stiffness, position accuracy of geometric elements, geometric element shape accuracy), transmission performance (Fixed firmly), Execution attributes (movement accuracy, structural rigidity, and speed adaptability) have both normal and abnormal states, which are represented by the type 1 two-state $\xrightarrow{S}$⊙$_{1\text{-}}\xrightarrow{R}$ operator; The joints between the parts have the characteristics of multiple input and single output, and are represented by the

type 10 $\quad$
and operator.

3.4 Probability Model of Meta-action Reliability Based on GO Method

From Fig. 4, we can see that there are 17 function operators and 3 logical operators in the meta-action working process. The system is a series system, that is, when the performance of one of the components fails, the reliability of the entire meta-action unit must be affected. It is assumed that the reliability characteristic quantity of each component is: $P_i(1)$, $P_i(2)$, λ_i, represents the normal probability, failure probability, and failure rate of the unit; then the reliability feature quantity of the meta-action unit is: $P_R(1)$, $P_R(2)$, λ_R.

Assuming that the 20 processes are completely independent, the normal probability of the meta-action unit should be the product of the normal probabilities $P_R(1)$ of all components. The formula is as follows:

$$P_R(1) = \prod_{i=1}^{20} P_i(1) \tag{1}$$

The equivalent failure rate of the meta-action unit is the sum of all process failure rates. The formula is as follows:

$$\lambda_R = \sum_{i=1}^{13} \lambda_i \tag{2}$$

The failure probability of the meta-action unit is:

$$P_R(2) = 1 - P_R(1) \tag{3}$$

4 Analysis of Example

The spindle system is an important functional part of the CNC machine tool. The spindle rotation action unit is the main motion transmission unit of the spindle system. Taking the spindle rotation element motion in the THM6380 CNC machine tool as an example, the reliability analysis of the spindle rotation element action unit using the fishbone diagram and GO method proposed in this paper is adopted.

The THM6380 spindle rotation action unit includes a spindle actuator, an arc pulley power source, bearings and connectors, and a chuck. The effect of each element on the output of the meta-action will now be established, as shown in Fig. 5.

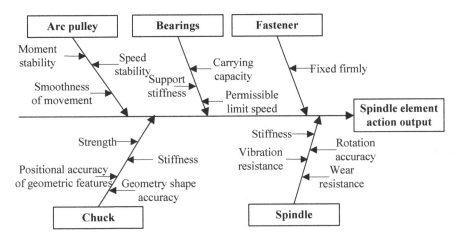

Fig. 5. Spindle Rotary Element Action Influence fishbone Figure

The unit action GO diagram is shown in Fig. 6.

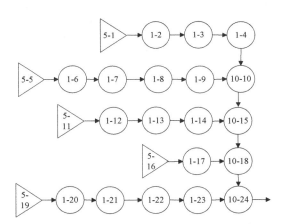

Fig. 6. Spindle rotation unit reliability GO diagram

Spindle rotation unit is mainly composed of pulley, bearing, chuck, connecting piece and spindle. Table 1 describes the normal state data of each main part structure of the spindle rotation unit.

The probabilities of the abnormalities of the main parts in Table 1 were obtained by collecting data and statistics. Investigate 500 spindle units and analyze faults and maintenance data (the cumulative number of abnormal performance factors in each

Table 1. Spindle rotation unit main parts status data

No.	The main parts	Normal state probability	Abnormal state probability
1	Pulley	0.965	0.013
2	Bearings	0.998	0.002
3	Chuck	0.936	0.024
4	Connector	0.995	0.005
5	Spindle	0.943	0.014

year). The ratio of the number of abnormalities of all performance factors of each part to the total number of parts is the probability value of the abnormal state in Table 1, that is, the probability value of the normal state is obtained.

According to the failure rate data of each component in Table 1 and Eq. (1), the normal probability (reliability) of the spindle rotation unit is:

$$P_5(1) = \prod_{i=1}^{5} P_i(1) = 0.8458$$

This result shows that the reliability of the spindle rotation unit operation is not high. After analyzing the performance of the components that make up the spindle rotation unit: The main abnormal mode of the pulley is that the moment is not stable (Traceable pulleys perform abnormalities as upstream element action units of actuators). When the bearing is supporting the shaft and bears radial load appear abnormal state. The chuck has an abnormal position when it is fixed. Spindle running for a long time causes abnormal wear resistance. The above abnormal mode affects the reliability of the meta-action unit.

5   Conclusion

(1) The meta-action unit group constitutes the whole system, and the source reliability problem is started from each element action unit to provide basic data for the reliability growth of the whole machine, which makes the reliability analysis of the whole machine more accurate.

(2) The unit reliability model is a typical tandem mode in the absence of redundant units, and has a "wood barrel" effect, that is, as long as one of the components is abnormal, it will affect the reliability of the meta action unit. Therefore, to improve the reliability of the entire series system by improving the reliability of a certain element, the performance of the element with the lowest reliability in the meta-action unit should be improved. In the example of the paper, in order to improve the reliability of the spindle rotation unit action unit, the accuracy of the chuck position will be focused on, and a more accurate positioning method will be adopted.

(3) Each type of meta-action unit can be composed of a power source, supporting parts, transmission parts, and actuators, but different components are formed, and

the specific factors that affect the reliability of various types of meta-action units are different. Therefore, the trace ability of various factors is a necessary task to improve the reliability of meta-action unit. In the next research process, various types of influencing factors of meta-action unit will be accurately located, and the trace ability mechanism will be analyzed, and the various factors will be aligned. Sensitivity analysis of machine reliability, thus establishing a theoretical basis for improving overall machine reliability.

References

1. Du, Y., Li, C., Liu, S.: Reliability assessment method of remanufacturing process for machine tools based on GO method. J. Mech. Eng. **53**(11), 203–210 (2017)
2. Li, Y., Zhang, W., Huang, Z.: Reliability simulation of NC machine tool based on Monte Carlo method. J. Manufact. Technol. Mach. Tool **1**, 33–37 (2017)
3. Ren, L., Rui, Z., Li, J.: Reliability analysis of numerical control machine tools with bounded and bathtub shaped failure intensity. J. Mech. Eng. **50**(16), 13–20 (2014)
4. Ren, L., Wang, Z., Lei, C.: Comprehensive evaluation approach to Bayesian reliability assessment model of NC machine tools. J. Shanghai Jiaotong Univ. **50**(7), 1023–1029 (2016)
5. Hu, Z., He, X.: Establishing reliability functions of CNC machine tools based on failure information. J. Modular Mach. Tool Autom. Manufact. Techn. **3**, 97–100 (2016)
6. Li, H., Jia, X., Zhang, T.: Reliability analysis of NC machine tools based on Weibull distribution. J. Mach. Tool Hydraul. **42**(19), 191–194 (2014)
7. Wang, Z., Yang, J.: Bayesian reliability analysis for numerical control machine tools with small-sized sample failure data. J. Central South Univ. (Sci. Technol.) **45**(12), 4201–4205 (2014)
8. Ran, Y.: Research on Meta-action Unit Modelling and Key QCs Predictive Control Technology of Electromechanical Products. Chongqing University, Chongqing (2016)
9. Dongying, L.: Research on Quality Modeling and Diagnosis Technology for the Assembly Process of CNC Machine Tool. Chongqing University, Chongqing (2014)
10. Shen, Z., Huang, X.: Principle and Application of GO Methodology. Tsinghua University Press, Beijing(2004)

Batch Scheduling of Remanufacturing Flexible Job Shop for Minimal Electricity- and Time-Cost

Mengyun Li[(✉)], Tao Li, Shitong Peng, and Yanchun Guo

School of Mechanical Engineering, Dalian University of Technology,
Dalian, China
li_mengyun@163.com

Abstract. The sustainable production has received extensive attention. With the aim, reducing the energy consumption in the manufacturing stage is particularly important. This paper presents a new mixed-integer linear programming (MILP) model for the complex production scheduling of remanufacturing job shop. This model is suitable for the job shop that batch processing machines and non-batch processing machines exist at the same time. According to the time-of-use (TOU) electricity pricing, dispatch reasonably to optimize the makespan and the electricity cost. Reach the target of increasing production efficiency and reducing environmental impact, promoting sustainable production.

Keywords: Remanufacturing job shop scheduling · Genetic algorithm
Electricity cost · Makespan

1 Introduction

The rapid development of the global economy requires more energy, but energy shortages are threatening the development of many countries [1]. At the same time, environmental issues are urgently needed. Therefore, it is important to actively promote sustainable production as a way of seeking development. Manufacturing energy consumption accounts for the largest proportion of global resources. Some studies have shown that impeller remanufacturing compared with conventional manufacturing and additive manufacturing has the smallest environmental impact and energy consumption [2]. Therefore, the development of remanufacturing is a powerful method of alleviating energy consumption and environmental issues.

Reducing energy consumption during the manufacturing phase plays a key role in improving sustainable production [3]. The scheduling of remanufacturing workshop, the same as the traditional workshop, is related to energy distribution, labor force distribution, production efficiency, and environmental impact, that is, economic, environmental, and social aspects [4]. The issue of optimizing the makespan, lateness and tardiness in scheduling has been widely focused, and the production scheduling based on energy saving awareness has drawn attention. For example, Che et al. [1] addressed unrelated parallel machines scheduling problem considering the total

© Springer Nature Singapore Pte Ltd. 2018
S. Wang et al. (Eds.): ICSEE 2018/IMIOT 2018, CCIS 923, pp. 300–307, 2018.
https://doi.org/10.1007/978-981-13-2396-6_28

electricity cost under TOU price and investigated a mixed-integer linear programming model. Gong et al. [5] and Shrouf et al. [6] dealt with the job scheduling on a single machine to reduce the energy cost and environmental impact. Because of the variety of energy price during one day, they changed the start-up, idle, and shutdown states of the machine. Zhang et al. [7] analyzed scheduling of a single flow shop, and established a mixed-integer nonlinear model in order to reduce the power cost based on the real-time electricity price.

The above scheduled jobs one by one. There're also a lot of batch scheduling for the workshop. Zhou et al. [8] and Shahidi et al. [9] proposed batch scheduling methods for parallel batch machines, with the aim of reducing the electricity consumption. Zheng et al. [10] chose the flexible flow shop as the research object, and constructed a multi-objective optimization model, including the completion time, electricity consumption and material waste, carrying out batch scheduling.

Nevertheless, the above batching scheduling simply divides all jobs into batches and schedules each batch as a single job. As we all know, batch and non-batch processing machines exist simultaneously in the remanufacturing job shop. For example, in the crankshaft remanufacturing production workshop, the cleaning machine of the crankshaft cleaning station can process 4 parts at one time, but the detection and repair stations will detect and process one by one only. Therefore, this paper proposes a new batch scheduling method that allows parts to be batch processed at the batch processing station while can be processed one-by-one at non-batch processing station, without being affected by batches. Thereby reducing energy Consumption and makespan.

In this paper, we offer a bi-object mixed-integer linear programming model in Sect. 2, which contains batch and non-batch processing machines. Based on the China's electricity price policy, electric power centralized bidding transactions are being implemented. Pricing standards can be priced under the amount of electricity and divided into on-peak, mid-peak and off-peak periods. With this condition, minimize the makespan and total electricity cost. In Sect. 3, apply this model to a remanufacturing job shop to verify the mathematic model. Note the computational conclusion. At last, we present our summary.

2 Mathematical Model

The mathematic model in this paper is based on the flexible job shop. There're G stages at the job shop. And it has m_G unrelated parallel machines at the g stage, as shown in Fig. 1. But at some stages, the operations are various from job to job.

The objectives of scheduling are to minimize the makespan and the electricity cost of all the jobs. In this model, the sequence and the processing time of every job are determined. The average power of each job in any station has been known in advance. The uncertainties of some production process are not taken into account, such as machine breakdown, different processing speeds at the same stage. No preemption between jobs and there is no limit to the buffer capacity between machines. The parameters and variables that will be used in the model are as follows.

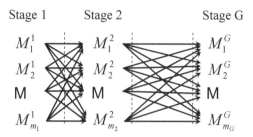

Fig. 1. Flexible job shop layout

Parameters

j, Index of job, $j \in \{1, 2, 3 \cdots, n\}$
g, Index of stage, $g \in \{1, 2, 3, \cdots, G\}$
i, Index of machine, $i \in \{1, 2, 3, \cdots, m\}$
b, Index of batch, $b \in \{1, 2, 3, \cdots, B\}$
Q, Quantity of jobs at every batch
T_{gj}, Due process time of every job j at stage g
P_{gj}, The average power consumption of each job at stage g
$EP(t)$, The electricity price at the t th unit time
C_a, The capacity of the batch processing machines

Variables

S_{ij}^{bg}, the start time of job j belonging to batch b which is processed on machine i at stage g

$X_{ij}^{bg} \in \{0, 1\}$, $X_{ij}^{bg} = 1$ if job j which is assigned to batch b, is processed on machine i at stage c, $X_{ij}^{bg} = 0$ otherwise

$Y_g \in \{0, 1\}$, $Y_g = 1$ denotes stage g is a batch processing station, $Y_g = 0$ otherwise
$C_{\max}$, makespan
TEC, electricity cost of all the jobs

MILP formulation

$$\min C_{\max} \tag{1}$$

$$\min TEC \tag{2}$$

$$\sum_{b=1}^{B} \sum_{i=1}^{m} X_{ij}^{bg} = 1, \forall j, g \tag{3}$$

$$\sum_{i=1}^{m} \sum_{j=1}^{n} X_{ij}^{bg} \le C_a, \forall b, g \tag{4}$$

$$\sum_{i=1}^{m} S_{ij}^{b(g+1)} - \sum_{i=1}^{m} S_{ij}^{bg} \ge T_{gj}, g \in \{1, 2, 3, \cdots, G-1\}, \forall b, i, j \tag{5}$$

$$\sum_{g=1}^{G} \sum_{i=1}^{m} \sum_{j=1}^{n} Y_g X_{ij}^{bg} = \sum_{g=1}^{G} Y_g, \forall b \tag{6}$$

$$\sum_{g=1}^{G} \sum_{i=1}^{m} Y_g S_{ij}^{bg} = \sum_{g=1}^{G} \sum_{i=1}^{m} Y_g S_{ij'}^{bg}, \forall b, j, j' \tag{7}$$

$$S_{ij}^{bg} - S_{i(j-1)}^{bg} \geq T_{gj}, \forall b, g, i, j \tag{8}$$

$$Y_g \sum_{i=1}^{m} S_{ij}^{bg} \geq \max(Y_g \sum_{i=1}^{m} S_{ij}^{b(g-1)} + T_{gj}), \forall b, c, j \tag{9}$$

$$C_{\max} = \max(S_{ij}^{bG} + T_{Gj}), \forall b, i, j \tag{10}$$

$$TEC = \sum_{t=0}^{C_{\max}} (Y_c \frac{EP(t)P_{gj}}{Q} + (Y_g + 1)EP(t)P_{gj}), \forall b, c, i, j \tag{11}$$

It is a bi-objective optimization model. The objective function (1) seeks to minimize the makespan. The objective function (2) seeks the minimum electricity consumption. The constraint (3) ensures that each job can only be assigned to one batch, and processed on one machine at any stage. Constraint (4) limits the number of jobs in one batch cannot exceed the maximum capacity of the batch processing machines. Constraint (5) guarantees that each job must be processed as the defined production order. The constraint (6) requires that a batch of jobs is processed on the same machine at the batch processing stage. Meanwhile, the constraint (7) restricts start processing time is the same, if a batch of jobs is processed on a machine. Constraint (8) guarantees that the processing of each job will not be interrupted. Constraint (9) ensures that before batch processing, all jobs in the batch have completed the previous processes. Constraint (10) calculates the makespan. Constraint (11) calculates the cost of electricity required to process all jobs.

3   Model Assessment

Combined with the case analysis, the genetic algorithm is used to solve the model. Finally it is compared with the global batch schedule to prove the validity and feasibility of the above mathematical model.

In this case, we integrate the multiple objectives into one comprehensive goal, by weighting respectively. There are 100 recovery crankshafts in the remanufacturing job shop that need to be repaired. The workshop is divided into five parts: cleaning, detection, repair, cleaning, and inspection. The batch processing stations are cleaning stations, that is, the first and fourth stations are batch processing stations. Each of batch processing machines can process 4 crankshafts at one time. The number of parallel machines in each stage is 2, and the machine performance is the same, that is, the processing rate, energy consumption, etc. are equal. At last, the jobs will be processed as soon as possible.

Due to the different degree of damage for each crankshaft, the machining of the crankshaft at the repair station is divided into two categories, as shown in Fig. 2.

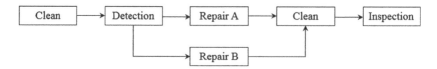

Fig. 2. Crankshaft remanufacturing process flow chart

Type A only requires polishing and silk-hole repair, but type B also demands laser spraying and subsequent processing. The processing times and average power for the various stations of the two kind of crankshaft remanufacturing processes are listed in Table 1.

Table 1. Process time and average power of two type of crankshaft

Type		Clean	Detection	Repair	Clean	Inspection
A	Time/min	8	0.5	18	8	0.5
	Average power/kW	42.76	76	5.6	26.3	76
B	Time/min	10	0.5	87	8	0.5
	Average power/kW	42.76	76	8.36	26.3	76

In this scenario, the electricity price standard selects Beijing's industrial TOU pricing, which consists of on-peak, mid-peak and off-peak period [11]. Its pricing standards are shown in Table 2.

Table 2. Beijing's industrial TOU pricing for a single day

Type	On-peak	Mid-peak	Off-peak
Period	10:00–15:00 18:00–21:00	7:00–10:00 15:00–18:00 21:00–23:00	23:00–7:00
Price (CNY/kW · h)	1.3782	0.8595	0.3658

As for coding, we adopt two genes to stand for decision variables. The first gene is the processing code, and the second is the corresponding machines code. With this special mathematical model, the first job number of the batch represents the batch processing station in the genetic code. Take the first batch as an example to introduce the coding method. Figure 3 is a directed acyclic graph (DAG) of the processing sequence of the first batch of jobs. The first and fourth stations in the figure are batch processing stations, and the number 1 under the clean stations represents the process of job 1, 2, 3, and 4. The rest stations are non-batch processing stations. The number below each station represents the respective process. When the in-degree of a number is 0, the process represented is able to be processed. For example, at the fourth station, only the repair processes of four jobs are finished the cleaning station can be started.

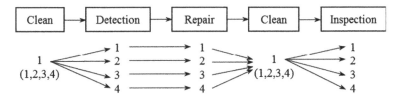

Fig. 3. the DAG of the first batch of jobs

The machine code only needs to correspond to the process code and indicate the processing machine for each job. Cross and mutation of genes can generate a feasible solution.

According to the actual situation of the factory, taking the average of fifty random global batch scheduling results as a reference, the validity of this model is analyzed.

At the result, Fig. 4 is the solution of the objective function of the new mathematical model. The optimal objective function value is 476.95, at the 278th iteration. Figure 5 depicts the optimal schedule of the remanufacturing job shop. In the optimal scheduling result, the makespan is 3736 min, that is, 62.3 h, and the electricity cost is 891.6 CNY, that is, 139.27 USD.

In the Fig. 5, the machines from 1 to 2 means the machines at the first station, the machines from 3 to 4 means the machines at the second station, and so on. Each rectangle in the figure shows the process of a job. The number in the rectangle is the job number.

The average objective function value of fifty random global batch schedules is 517.9, where the average makespan is 72.3 h, and the electricity cost is 963.5 CNY. Obviously, this new model consumes less time and electricity cost, which is 13.8% and 7.5% lower than the global schedule, respectively. Because of at the non-batch processing stations, each job is separated from the batch, saving the waiting time in the line.

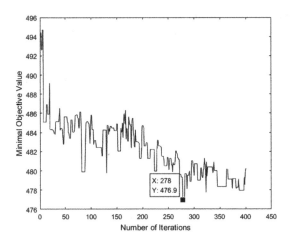

Fig. 4. Minimal objective value of the methods

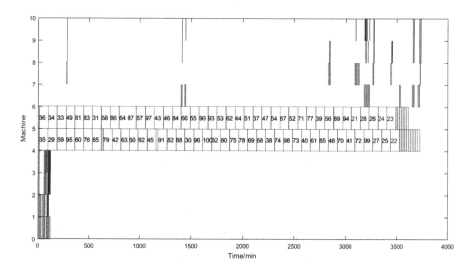

Fig. 5. Optimal production schedule Gantt chart

This proves the feasibility and effectiveness of the mathematical model, which can reduce the maximum completion time and electricity cost.

4   Conclusion

The situation of remanufacturing job shop is complex. This article tackle the flexible job shop with both batch and non-batch processing machines. There are unrelated parallel machines at each stage. As the uncertainty of job select the machine to be machined, optimize the makespan and electricity cost.

In this paper, a mixed-integer linear programming model is established and genetic algorithm is used to solve the model. A new gene coding method is conducted. Finally, the optimal job schedule obtained a reduction under TOU pricing, compared to the global batch schedule.

Eventually, this model enhances the production efficiency of the workshop, reduces the environmental impact, and further achieve sustainable production.

Acknowledgment. The authors are grateful to the support of the National Natural Science Foundation of China under grant number 51775086 and the Fundamental Research Funds for the Central Universities under grant number DUT18JC13.

References

1. Che, A., Zhang, S., Wu, X.: Energy-conscious unrelated parallel machine scheduling under time-of-use electricity tariffs. J. Clean. Produ. **156**, 688–697 (2017)
2. Peng, S., et al.: Toward a sustainable impeller production: environmental impact comparison of different impeller manufacturing methods. J. Ind. Ecol. **21**(S1), S216–S229 (2017)

3. Giret, A., Trentesaux, D., Prabhu, V.: Sustainability in manufacturing operations scheduling: a state of the art review. J. Manuf. Syst. **37**, 126–140 (2015)
4. Pinedo, M.: Scheduling: Theory, Algorithms, and Systems. Tsinghua University Press, Beijing (2005)
5. Gong, X., et al.: An energy-cost-aware scheduling methodology for sustainable manufacturing. Procedia CIRP **29**, 185–190 (2015)
6. Shrouf, F., et al.: Optimizing the production scheduling of a single machine to minimize total energy consumption costs. J. Clean. Prod. **67**, 197–207 (2014)
7. Zhang, H., Zhao, F., Sutherland, J.W.: Scheduling of a single flow shop for minimal energy cost under real-time electricity pricing **139**(1) (2017)
8. Zhou, S., et al.: A multi-objective differential evolution algorithm for parallel batch processing machine scheduling considering electricity consumption cost. Comput. Oper. Res. **96**, 1–44 (2018)
9. Shahidi-Zadeh, B., et al.: Solving a bi-objective unrelated parallel batch processing machines scheduling problem: a comparison study. Comput. Oper. Res. **88**, 71–90 (2017)
10. Zeng, Z., et al.: Multi-object optimization of flexible flow shop scheduling with batch process — consideration total electricity consumption and material wastage. J. Clean. Prod. **183**, 925–939 (2018)
11. State Grid Corporation of China. http://www.95598.cn/static/html//person/sas/es///PM06003001_2016037918467080.shtml

A New Robust Scheduling Model
for Permutation Flow Shop Problem

Wenzhu Liao[(⊠)] and Yanxiang Fu

College of Mechanical Engineering, Chongqing University,
Chongqing 400044, China
liaowz@cqu.edu.cn

Abstract. As traditional flow shop scheduling model is usually designed for
deterministic production environment and under single optimization objective,
this paper considers a permutation flow shop scheduling problem with uncertain
processing time so as to overcome the deficiency. Moreover, a multi-objective
robust scheduling model is constructed to minimize the tardiness and total
completion time under min-max regret criterion. Directed graph is used to
analyze the scenario of the maximum regret value scenario (i.e. the worst-case
scenario). Finally, genetic algorithm is applied to solve this robust scheduling
model. Through the experimental simulation results, the proposed model shows
its efficiency and effectiveness.

Keywords: Permutation flow shop · Uncertain · Robust · Min-max regret
Directed graph

1 Introduction

Flow shop scheduling problem (FSP) has been extensively researched in real manufacturing situation with the scheduling objective to obtain a processing sequence for
minimizing the total flow time. And permutation flow shop scheduling problem (PFSP)
is one kind of more complicated FSP with processing restriction, which has been
proved to be a typical NP-hard problem [1].

Nowadays, heuristic methods and Meta-heuristic methods have been broadly
applied for solving this kind of permutation flow shop scheduling problem, such as
CDS heuristic method [2] and heuristic NEH method [3]. A hybrid genetic local search
algorithm was proposed by Tseng et al. to minimize the total production time of PFSP
[4]. Liu et al. applied an estimation of distribution method to particle swarm optimization algorithm for solving PFSP [5]. Then, Tasgetiren et al. [6] and Liu et al. [7]
used artificial bee colony algorithm to solve PFSP. However, the abovementioned
methods usually assume the parameter are determined whereas there are always
uncertainties in real manufacturing environment. For example, the processing time of a
job is uncertainty but normally belongs to a range, machine breakdown, urgent order,
order cancel and the skill level of workers. Therefore, it is necessary to consider the
uncertainty for PFSP so as to meet more practical situations.

This paper thus proposes a robust scheduling model with the consideration of the
uncertainty about the processing time of jobs. The max-regret value is selected to be the

© Springer Nature Singapore Pte Ltd. 2018
S. Wang et al. (Eds.): ICSEE 2018/IMIOT 2018, CCIS 923, pp. 308–317, 2018.
https://doi.org/10.1007/978-981-13-2396-6_29

robustness indicator, and then the solution with minimum max-regret (i.e. min-max regret) is searched in solution space [8]. Although some researchers have studied on this subject such as Kouvelis et al. [9], Xu et al. [10], Xu et al. [11] and Feng et al. [12], they set the total flowtime as the only objective and ignore the tardiness. As a result, the derived processing sequence can only satisfy the minimum of total flowtime, but job's completion time might exceed customers' acceptance which would further impair customer satisfaction and the reputation of the enterprise. Thus, in order to overcome this kind of shortage, this paper proposes a robust permutation flow shop scheduling model based on min-max regret criterion with the aim of minimizing the total flowtime and tardiness.

2 Problem Statement

2.1 PFSP with the Robustness of Total Flowtime

Considering a flow shop problem with a set $M = \{M1,\ldots, Mi,\ldots, Mm\}$ of m machines and a set $J = \{J1,\ldots, Jj,\ldots, Jn\}$ of n jobs. Jj is composed of m operations being its parts and performed by consecutive machines. Oi,j denotes the operation performed by Mi refers to the part of Jj. The operations for Jj constitute a sequence $(O1,j,\ldots, Om,j)$. And the operation time of Oi,j is pij.

The main difference between a determined PFSP and an uncertain PFSP is that pij is uncertain in an uncertain PFSP and belongs to a known range $\left[\underline{p_{ij}}, \overline{p_{ij}}\right]$. The matrix with all specified values of pij is called a scenario that is the element of the Cartesian product $p = \left[\underline{p_{11}}, \overline{p_{11}}\right] \times \cdots \times \left[\underline{p_{mn}}, \overline{p_{mn}}\right]$, $p \in P$. This paper proposes min-max regret method to solve this PFSP with uncertain processing time. Given a feasible solution π and a scenario p, the regret value can be calculated as below:

$$R(\pi, p) = C_{\max}(\pi, p) - C'_{\max}(p) \tag{1}$$

where $C_{max}(\pi, p)$ denotes the total flowtime of solution π under scenario p, and $C'_{max}(p)$ denotes the optimal total flowtime under scenario p.

For a given solution, there would be a scenario p that can maximize the regret value. Hence, this scenario p^π is called worst-case scenario while the regret value is called max regret value for the given solution π. There is

$$\begin{aligned} Z_1(\pi) &= \max_{p \in P}[C_{\max}(\pi, p) - C'_{\max}(p)] \\ &= C_{\max}(\pi, p^\pi) - C'_{\max}(p^\pi) \end{aligned} \tag{2}$$

Therefore, the purpose of min-max regret method to solve this PFSP is to find a solution $\pi \in \Pi$ that can minimize $Z_1(\pi)$, shown as

$$Z_1(\pi^*) = \min_{\pi \in \Pi} \left(\max_{p \in P} \left(C_{max}(\pi, p) - C'_{max}(p) \right) \right) \tag{3}$$

2.2   PFSP with the Robustness of Total Flowtime and Tardiness

Although the scheduling solution obtained by the min-max regret method considering the robustness of total flowtime has a certain degree of robustness, it does not consider the tardiness. This paper assumes that there is a cap limit ε for the tardiness of each job, called as the maximum tardiness limit. Once one job's tardiness exceed the maximum tardiness limit ε, it is unacceptable. This ensures the total flowtime is robust and maintains good service level. The maximum tardiness under uncertain processing time can be

$$Z_2(\pi) = T_{\max}(\pi, p) = \max_{p \in P} [T(\pi, p)] \tag{4}$$

For a given solution $\pi \in \Pi$ under scenario $p \in P$, the tardiness $T(\pi, p)$ can be calculated as

$$T(\pi, p) = \max(C_{m\pi_n}(\pi, p) - D(\pi), 0) \tag{5}$$

$C_{m\pi_n}(\pi, p)$ denotes the completion time of job n processed on machine m in solution π under scenario p, and $D(\pi)$ denotes the due date given by solution π and the upper and lower bound of job's processing time. There is

$$D(\pi) = C_{m\pi_n}(\pi, p_{mid}) \tag{6}$$

where p_{mid} is the processing time solved by MIH algorithm [13]. $T_{max}(\pi, p)$ denotes the maximum tardiness under different scenario $p \in P$. Hence, the overall objective of this proposed model with the robustness of total flowtime and tardiness is

$$Z(\pi) = Z_1(\pi) + [Z_2(\pi) - \varepsilon] * I \tag{7}$$

Assume ε is $D(\pi)/6$, I could be defined as

$$I = \begin{cases} 0 & Z_2(\pi) - \varepsilon < 0 \\ M & Z_2(\pi) - \varepsilon > 0 \end{cases} \tag{8}$$

$M = 10^4$ is a large number. Therefore, the optimal solution π is the processing sequence that can minimize $Z(\pi)$.

3   Min-Max Regret Method

Worst-case scenario analysis includes the analysis respectively regard to the total flowtime and tardiness. Worst-case scenario analysis of total flowtime is to find a scenario which can maximize $R(\pi, p)$ for a given solution π. Worst-case scenario analysis of the tardiness is to find a scenario which can maximize $T(\pi, p)$ for a given solution.

3.1 Worst-Case Scenario Analysis of Total Flowtime

The problem of maximize $R(\pi, p)$ is to find a worst-case scenario within all possible scenarios for a given π. However, there are countless scenarios, which makes complex computation. This paper applies directed graph $G(V, A)$ to solve this problem. Thus, this problem could be changed to determine the longest path between vertexes $v_{0,0}$ and $v_{m,n}$ in directed graph $G(V, A)$. $C_{max}(\pi, p)$ can be calculated as

$$C_{\max}(\pi, p) = \sum_{(i,j) \in S(\pi, p)} p_{i\pi_j} \tag{9}$$

$S(\pi, p)$ denotes the set of tuple (i, j) that identifies the weight that sum up to the longest path between vertexes $v_{0,0}$ and $v_{m,n}$ for a given π under scenario p. Therefore, the regret value of a given solution π under scenario p can be converted to be

$$\begin{aligned} &C_{\max}(\pi, p) - C'_{\max}(p^{\pi}) \\ &= \sum_{(i,j) \in S(\pi, p)} p_{i\pi_j} - \sum_{(i,j) \in S(\pi', p)} p_{i\pi'_j} \end{aligned} \tag{10}$$

$S(\pi', p)$ denotes the set of tuples (i, j) that identifies the weight that sum up to the longest path between $v_{0,0}$ and $v_{m,n}$ for a given π' under scenario p. There are

$$\forall (i,j) \in S(\pi, p) \backslash S(\pi', p) : p_{i\pi_j} = \overline{p_{i\pi_j}} \tag{11}$$

$$\forall (i,j) \in S(\pi', p) \backslash S(\pi, p) : p_{i\pi_j} = \underline{p_{i\pi_j}} \tag{12}$$

The worst-case scenario can convert to the form below:

$$\forall (i,j) \in S(\widetilde{\pi, p}) : p_{i\pi_j} = \overline{p_{i\pi_j}} \tag{13}$$

$$\forall (i,j) \notin S(\widetilde{\pi, p}) : p_{i\pi_j} = \underline{p_{i\pi_j}} \tag{14}$$

$S(\widetilde{\pi, p})$ denotes all the set of tuples (i, j) that between the path from vertexes $v_{0,0}$ to $v_{m,n}$. The extreme point scenario can be reduced enormously from 2 mn through the method. For example, there are 4096 extreme point scenarios for 3 jobs processed by 4 machines, but there are only 10 possible paths using this method. Hence, it can greatly improve computation efficiency.

3.2 Worst-Case Scenario Analysis of Tardiness

As directed graphs is also adopted for worst-case scenario analysis of tardiness, the maximum tardiness for a given schedule π under scenario p would be

$$T_{\max} = \max_{p \in P}[\max(C_{m\pi_n}(\pi, p) - D(\pi), 0) \tag{15}$$

Since each operation's upper and lower bound of processing time is known, $D(\pi)$ can be obtained. $C_{m\pi_n}(\pi, p)$ is the longest weighted path between vertexes $v_{0,0}$ to $v_{m,n}$. Hence, the problem can be convert like worst-case scenario analysis of total flowtime. There are

$$C_{m\pi_n}(\pi, p) = \sum_{(i,j) \in S(\pi, p)} p_{i\pi_j} \tag{16}$$

$$\begin{aligned} T(\pi, p) &= \max[C_{mn}(\pi, p) - D(\pi), 0] \\ &= \max[(\sum_{(i,j) \in S(\pi, p)} p_{i\pi_j}) - D(\pi), 0] \end{aligned} \tag{17}$$

According to Eq. (17), it could be seen that the worst-case scenario is extreme point scenario and satisfies the following form

$$\forall(i,j) \in S(\widetilde{\pi, p}) : p_{i\pi_j} = \overline{p_{i\pi_j}} \tag{18}$$

where $S(\widetilde{\pi, p})$ denotes the possible path between $v_{0,0}$ and $v_{m,n}$. The corresponding path that maximizes T_{max} is the worst case scenario.

3.3   Solution

As PFSP is proved to be NP-hard problem, genetic algorithm is used to solve this proposed model. The input is the upper and lower bound of processing time, the number of machines and the number of jobs, and the output is the processing sequence. The brief procedure is given as below:

Coding and Initial Solution. This paper chooses real-number coding. A chromosome is constituted of n real numbers. To generate the initial population, 10 random solutions are generated. MIH algorithm is used to solve this proposed model. The obtained solution undergoes 9 random mutations to obtain another 10 solutions. Hence, the initial population composed of 10 random solutions is obtained.

Selection. This paper applies the strategy of elitist preservation. The objective values of solutions are in ascending order. This paper adopts the method proposed by Ćwik [14] using the lower bound of $C'_{max}(p)$. For any machine k, the following inequality holds.

$$\sum_{j=1}^{n} p_{kj} \leq C'_{max}(p) \tag{19}$$

Before the kth machine starts processing, there is at least one job needs to be processed on all machines indexed from 1 to k − 1, unless k = 1. The processing time is $\min_j \sum_{i=1}^{k-1} p_{ij}$. On the other hand, after the ith machine completes the processing, there is at least one job that needs to be processed on all machines indexed from k + 1 to m, unless k = m. The processing time is $\min_j \sum_{i=k+1}^{m} p_{ij}$. Thus, it can be found that for each k, the following inequality holds.

$$\min_j \sum_{i=1}^{k-1} p_{ij} + \sum_{j=1}^{n} p_{kj} + \min_j \sum_{i=k+1}^{m} p_{ij} \le C'_{max}(p) \tag{20}$$

In order to obtain even tighter bound, the job processed before the kth machine must not be the same as the job processed after the kth machine. In addition, as Eq. (20) holds for all machines, the highest value could be obtained. Therefore, the lower bound of the deterministic flow-shop problem is defined as

$$C_{max,LB}(p) = \max_{k=1,m}$$
$$(\min_{j=1,n} (\sum_{i=1}^{k-1} p_{ij}) + \sum_{j=1}^{n} p_{kj} + \min_{\substack{l=1,n \\ l\ne j}} (\sum_{i=k+1}^{m} p_{ij})) \tag{21}$$

Crossover and Mutation. Since the coding scheme is the arrangement of n real numbers. Each number represents a job and the sequence of number represents the sequence of jobs under processing. This paper uses PMX method to ensure the feasibility of solutions. In addition, in order to ensure the richness of offspring individuals, the mutation strategy of swapping two random genes at a certain probability is adopted.

4 Computational Experiments

4.1 Instance Generation

This paper uses two constants K and C to generate instances: K = 100 and C = 50. The lower bound of processing time $p_{i\pi_j}$ denoted as $\underline{p_{i\pi_j}}$ is randomly generated from $[0, K]$ with uniform distribution. The upper bound $\overline{p_{i\pi_j}}$ is then generated from $\left[\underline{p_{i\pi_j}}, \underline{p_{i\pi_j}} + C\right]$ with uniform distribution.

There are three set of experiments and each set of experiments consists of 20 experiments, in which the number of machine is 3 and the number of jobs increases from 6 to 25. Each experiment repeats five times in case of deviation. The first set of experiment take $Z(\pi)$ as the objective which means the model considers both the robustness of total flowtime and tardiness. The second set of experiments take $Z_1(\pi)$ as the objective which means the model only considers the robustness of total flowtime. The third set of experiments uses the solved solution of the second set of experiment to calculate $Z(\pi)$ for the first set of experiment.

4.2 Result Discussion

As shown in Table 1 and Fig. 1, it can be seen that all $Z(\pi)$ in the first set of experiments are lower than 200. This shows that the maximum tardiness $Z_2(\pi)$ of solution π obtained by the model in which taking $Z(\pi)$ as the objective is under, which means the solution π could simultaneously satisfy the robustness of total flowtime and tardiness limitation.

Table 1. the experimental results while taking $Z(\pi)$ as the objective function

n	Experiment 1	Experiment 2	Experiment 3	Experiment 4	Experiment 5
6	104.1997	60.24807	113.2297	113.2297	107.2286
7	100.3967	90.00704	78.7677	78.7677	80.62649
8	36.86021	27.24108	52.63523	52.63523	82.89806
⋮	⋮	⋮	⋮	⋮	⋮
15	20.2855	44.74217	38.91425	38.91425	111.1387
16	65.78526	21.29847	59.16599	59.16599	72.79513
⋮	⋮	⋮	⋮	⋮	⋮
24	93.21831	120.3178	25.84408	25.84408	75.65229
25	91.88376	123.0026	79.76912	79.76912	67.2639

The results of the second and third sets of experiments are demonstrated in Table 2 and Fig. 2. It can be found that $Z_1(\pi)$ in the second set of experiments is always lower than 160. Hence, the solution obtained are acceptable if only considering the robustness of total flowtime. However, Table 2 shows that while calculating $Z(\pi)$ using the solution obtained by the second set of experiments, it might be huge and higher than the maximum tardiness limit. There are respectively 50%, 70%, 45%, 50% and 40% possibility that the tardiness would exceed ε in the five repeated experiments.

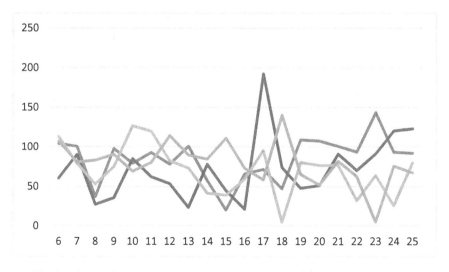

Fig. 1. The trend of experimental results while taking $Z(\pi)$ as objective function

Table 2. The experimental results of the second and third experiment

Experiment 1				Experiment 2			
$Z_1(\pi)$	$Z(\pi)$	Maximum tardiness	ε	$Z_1(\pi)$	$Z(\pi)$	Maximum tardiness	ε
47.45	47.45	37.12	92.44	57.42	1324134.46	197.11	64.70
30.15	441195.14	129.94	85.83	78.77	580046.96	142.31	84.32
77.16	413213.65	129.80	88.49	52.64	52.64	74.44	106.66
⋮	⋮	⋮	⋮	⋮	⋮	⋮	⋮
24.39	24.39	120.85	133.15	58.08	2127826.12	279.51	66.73
39.65	39.65	139.53	151.77	119.66	80456.30	124.84	116.81
⋮	⋮	⋮	⋮	⋮	⋮	⋮	⋮
136.36	136.36	−85.27	342.61	51.20	51.20	−28.72	306.69
17.63	17.63	187.47	302.06	90.35	620952.54	293.68	231.59
Rate of exceed ε 50.00%				Rate of exceed ε 70.00%			
Experiment 3				Experiment 4			
$Z_1(\pi)$	$Z(\pi)$	Maximum tardiness	ε	$Z_1(\pi)$	$Z(\pi)$	Maximum tardiness	ε
107.23	107.23	1.07	122.55	60.25	60.25	56.16	83.46
99.79	715214.21	148.32	76.81	116.93	116.93	73.14	98.28
82.90	82.90	33.45	137.05	27.24	460586.54	143.40	97.34
⋮	⋮	⋮	⋮	⋮	⋮	⋮	⋮
71.92	1154669.90	207.81	92.35	118.00	118.00	34.96	169.62
73.31	73.31	14.60	178.15	62.10	504193.72	200.31	149.90
⋮	⋮	⋮	⋮	⋮	⋮	⋮	⋮
75.65	75.65	117.13	278.68	148.83	1829329.55	389.86	206.94
67.26	1002307.42	375.47	275.25	23.15	4783512.34	713.14	234.79
Rate of exceed ε 45.00%				Rate of exceed ε 50.00%			

Experiment 5			
$Z_1(\pi)$	$Z(\pi)$	Maximum tardiness	ε
11.92	11.92	75.58	87.49
82.49	181835.37	107.08	88.90
53.89	53.89	-28.92	146.49
⋮	⋮	⋮	⋮
50.76	50.76	77.12	174.12
27.43	27.43	69.63	179.98
⋮	⋮	⋮	⋮
79.03	1540359.38	391.03	237.00
21.79	21.79	159.34	321.83
Rate of exceed ε 40.00%			

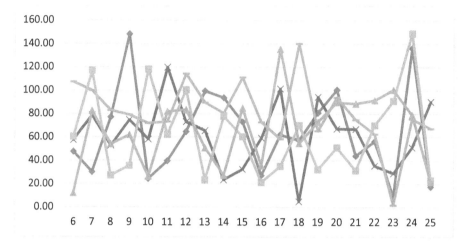

Fig. 2. The trend of experimental results of the second and third experiment

5   Conclusion

Although there are some literatures for solving PFSP with uncertain processing time, they are usually focused on the robustness of total flowtime and ignore the great influence of the tardiness on customer satisfaction. This paper establishes a robust scheduling model for PFSP with the robustness of total flowtime as well as the tardiness. Based on the uncertainty of jobs' processing time, it could meet more real production environment. Then, directed graph is applied to analyze the worst-case scenario and the min-max regret method with the assistant of genetic algorithm is developed to solve this proposed model. Finally, the result obtained through experimental simulation show that the maximum tardiness does not exceed its upper limit while satisfying the robustness of total flowtime, which compensates for the lack of consideration of tardiness in previous PFSP research. Further, it also effectively guarantees customer satisfaction about delivery requirement and maintains a stable and good service level of the enterprise.

References

1. Gonzalez, T., Sahni, S.: Flowshop and jobshop schedules: complexity and approximation. Oper. Res. **26**(26), 36–52 (1978)
2. Campbell, H.G., Dudek, R.A., Smith, M.L., et al.: A heuristic algorithm for the n job, m machine sequencing problem. Manage. Sci. **16**(10), 630 (1970)
3. Nawaz, M., Enscore Jr., E.E., Ham, I.: A heuristic algorithm for the m -machine, n -job flow-shop sequencing problem. Omega **11**(1), 91–95 (1983)
4. Tseng, L.Y., Lin, Y.T.: A hybrid genetic local search algorithm for the permutation flowshop scheduling problem. Eur. J. Oper. Res. **198**(1), 84–92 (2009)

5. Liu, H., Gao, L., Pan, Q.: A hybrid particle swarm optimization with estimation of distribution algorithm for solving permutation flowshop scheduling problem. Expert Syst. Appl. **38**(4), 4348–4360 (2011)
6. Tasgetiren, M.F., Pan, Q.K., Suganthan, P.N., et al.: A discrete artificial bee colony algorithm for the total flowtime minimization in permutation flow shops. Inf. Sci. Int. J. **181** (16), 3459–3475 (2011)
7. Liu, Y.F., Liu, S.Y.: A hybrid discrete artificial bee colony algorithm for permutation flowshop scheduling problem. Appl. Soft Comput. J. **13**(3), 1459–1463 (2013)
8. Aissi, H.: Min–max and min–max regret versions of combinatorial optimization problems: a survey. Eur. J. Oper. Res. **197**(2), 427–438 (2009)
9. Kouvelis, P., Daniels, R.L., Vairaktarakis, G.: Robust scheduling of a two-machine flow shop with uncertain processing times. IIE Trans. **32**(5), 421–432 (2000)
10. Xiaoqing, X., Cui, W., Lin, J., et al.: Robust makespan minimisation in identical parallel machine scheduling problem with interval data. Int. J. Prod. Res. **51**(12), 3532–3548 (2013)
11. Xiaoqian, X., Wentian, C., Jun, L., Yanjun, Q.: Robust identical parallel machines scheduling model based on min-max regret criterion. J. Syst. Eng. **28**(6), 729–737 (2013). (in Chinese)
12. Feng, X., Zheng, F., Xu, Y.: Robust scheduling of a two-stage hybrid flow shop with uncertain interval processing times. Int. J. Prod. Res. **54**(12), 1–12 (2016)
13. Kasperski, A.: A 2-approximation algorithm for interval data minmax regret sequencing problems with the total flow time criterion. Elsevier Science Publishers B.V. (2008)
14. Ćwik, M., Józefczyk, J.: Evolutionary algorithm for minmax regret flow-shop problem. Manage. Prod. Eng. Rev. **6**(3), 3–9 (2015)

Research on Optimal Stencil Cleaning Decision-Making Based on Markov Chain

Jiangyou Yu, Le Cao$^{(\boxtimes)}$, Ji Zhang, Linjun Xie,
Bangjie Zhang, and Shilin Niu

State Key Laboratory of Mechanical Transmission,
Chongqing University, Chongqing, China
lecao@cqu.edu.cn

Abstract. Deteriorated stencil is the main cause of product quality failure for solder paste printing. Frequent stencil cleaning helps to reduce the quality loss, but usually results in an increased cost of downtime. In this paper, an approach for controlling the stencil cleaning is proposed and the optimal decision which balances the quality losses and the downtime losses is obtained based on renewal reward theorem. The degradation of the stencil printing capability is modelled by a Markov chain, and the product quality loss is estimated.

Keywords: Stencil cleaning · Degradation · Renewal reward theorem
Optimal decision making

1 Introduction

The solder paste printing is a key process for SMT (Surface Mount Technology) production lines and substantial researches shows that up to 50% of the defects found in the assembly of printed circuit boards (PCBs) are attributed to stencil printing [1]. There are many factors that affect the quality and efficiency of solder paste printing. A large number of scholars have made efforts to research on this in different aspects.

Amalu [2] studied the rheological properties and printing efficiency of fine-pitch stencil printing and concluded that the type of paste, the opening of the steel mesh, and the interaction between them affected the printing efficiency and quality. Focusing on stencil making materials, Shea [3] obtained the determining factors for manufacturing stencils by changing the laser cutting parameters and coating materials using DOE experimental design methods, which achieved the goal of optimizing the stencil printing performance. Literature [4] reviewed the development and application of lead-free solder paste in the electronic printing industry since the release of the ROSH in 2006. The literature [5] mainly focusing on improving the printing performance of fine-pitch stencils through Taguchi method and Taguchi algorithm based on fuzzy model. Yang [6] proposed a neural network method to solve the quality problem in the solder paste printing process.

In the stencil printing process, however, stencil cleaning will also largely affect the quality and efficiency of solder paste printing. If the stencil cleaning cycle is too short, the cost of downtime caused by cleaning will be greatly increased. If cleaning is not

© Springer Nature Singapore Pte Ltd. 2018
S. Wang et al. (Eds.): ICSEE 2018/IMIOT 2018, CCIS 923, pp. 318–324, 2018.
https://doi.org/10.1007/978-981-13-2396-6_30

performed for a long time, the printing capacity of stencils will be reduced and the number of unqualified products will increase. That is, the cost of quality loss will increase as well. All these information shows that the stencil cleaning control study is very important. However, there are very few studies in this area at home and abroad now. Thus we develop Markov chain model of the stencil printing capability degradation, and take into consideration the loss cost of downtime for stencil cleaning and the cost of product quality loss. The stencil cleaning decision was studied by minimizing the average cost unit time in a cleaning cycle based on the renewal reward theorem.

2 Stencil Printing Capacity Degradation Modeling

As shown in Fig. 1, the discrete-time, discrete-state homogeneous Markov process is used to model the degradation process of stencil printing capability with a single cleaning cycle. The stencil printing capacity includes a total of K states. From state 1 to state K, it represents the process of degradation of printing capacity and the F-state represents the final process of degradation of the stencil printing capability. When the stencil printing capacity reaches the F-state, it indicates that the stencil can no longer be used for printing products, and must be immediately transferred to the M-state and clean it. The parameter p defines the speed of degradation of the stencil printing capability.

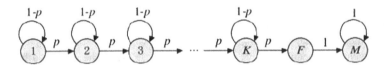

Fig. 1. Markov model of the stencil printing capacity degradation

In addition, we assumed that the cleaning of the stencil is perfect, that is, the stencil printing capability returns to its original state after cleaning. Given a type of printed stencil, we can get the parameters K and p through using the Pascal distribution to fit the empirical distribution of the stencil life.

3 Decision-Making Modeling of Stencil Cleaning

3.1 Stencil Cleaning Quality Loss Cost Estimation

In each printing state, it is assumed that the probability of the qualification of the PCB board printed by stencil printing is constant. And $y(i)$ indicates the probability of the qualified quality of the stencil printing PCB board in the printing state i. Based on the established stencil printing capability degraded Markov chain and the evaluated parameters K and p, a method is proposed to obtain the probability of qualified stencil product quality in each printing state.

Assume that we can detect the quality inspection information of printed PCB boards during the life cycle of N pieces of the same type stencil and the quantities of printed PCB that can be printed before each stencil must be cleaned are $T_1, T_2, \ldots, T_N$, respectively. And then, the quantities of printed PCB of each stencil is divided into K groups and each group contains a same number of printed PCB. The percentage of qualified products in each same group of N pieces same type stencil can be obtained through statistical methods. That is the product quality qualification probability $y(i)$ in each printing state of stencils.

According to the Markov chain model of the stencil printing capability degradation and product quality deteriorating model that have proposed above, we can get the expected quality loss cost $E(Q)$ in a cleaning cycle:

$$E(Q) = C_P \cdot \sum_{n=1}^{T} \sum_{i=1}^{K} (y_n(i) \cdot ((1 - y(i))) \tag{1}$$

The C_P represents the penalty cost due to additional cleaning of the unit's unqualified product. The $y_n(i)$ represents the probability that the stencil printing capability is in i-th printing state at the time step n $(n = 0, 1, 2, 3, \ldots, n)$. The $y(i)$ represents the probability of the qualified quality of the stencil printing PCB board in the printing state i.

3.2 Decision-Making Modeling

We have assumed that the printing state can return to state 1 after each stencil cleaning. So each stencil cleaning is independent of each other. Therefore, stencil cleaning meets the requirements of the renewal process. The renewal reward theorem (RRT) is an important technical means to solve the asymptotic case. Thus the objective function is as following

$$AC = \frac{E(C)}{E(T)} \tag{2}$$

Where AC represents the average cost per unit time during a cleaning cycle, $E(C)$ represents the sum of quality loss cost and stencil cleaning downtime loss cost and $E(T)$ represents the expected cleaning cycle time.

In Sect. 3.1, the expected cost of quality loss during a cleaning cycle has been calculated. According to the Markov chain model of the stencil printing capability degradation, we can get the expected cleaning cycle

$$E(T) = \sum_{n=1}^{T} (1 - y_n(F) - y_n(M)) = \sum_{n=1}^{T} \sum_{i=1}^{K} y_n(i) \tag{3}$$

Let t_Q represents the expected average time spent on stencil cleaning, and C_Q the unit time cost of production line downtime for stencil cleaning. So the total expected cost over a cleaning cycle

$$E(C) = E(Q) + t_Q \cdot C_Q = C_P \cdot \sum_{n=1}^{T} \sum_{i=1}^{K} (y_n(i) \cdot (1 - y(i)) + t_Q \cdot C_Q \quad (4)$$

To optimize the stencil cleaning time T with the goal of minimizing the average cost AC per unit time by Eq. (2), we have the decision model as following

$$AC(T) = \frac{C_P \cdot \sum_{n=1}^{T} \sum_{i=1}^{K} (y_n(i) \cdot (1 - y(i)) + t_Q \cdot C_Q}{\sum_{n=1}^{T} \sum_{i=1}^{K} y_n(i) + t_Q} \quad (5)$$

In order to compute the optimal printing cleaning policy, a numerical iterative search procedure using Eq. (5) is developed and implemented by MATLAB. Assume that k = 6, p = 0.02, $y(i) = 1(i - 1)/K$, $C_P = 15$, $t_Q = 4$, $C_Q = 20$. The average cost per unit time can be calculated by MATLAB software. Figure 2 depicts the average cost per unit time with respect to the printing cleaning time T. As can be seen from the Fig. 2, the average cost per unit time decreases rapidly from a very large value until reaching a minimum value, and then continues to rise, approaching a asymptotic value. So it is apparent that there exists a unique optimal cleaning time T_O which minimizes the average cost per unit time and the value is $AC(T_O)$.

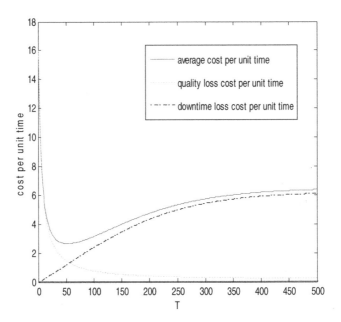

Fig. 2. Cost per unit time respect on cleaning time

4 Numerical Analysis

In this section, the effect of parameter changes on the optimal decision of stencil cleaning will be analyzed through experimental simulation. In the experiment, the degradation of stencil printing capability is divided into two modes that p = 0.02 represents the rapid degradation of stencil printing capability and p = 0.1 represents the slow degradation of stencil printing capability. Besides, assume that there exists three modes of product quality deterioration, as shown in Fig. 3. Where $y_1(i)$ and $y_3(i)$ respectively represent the slowest deteriorating mode and fastest deteriorating mode of the product quality, and then $y_2(i)$ represents the general deteriorating mode of product quality.

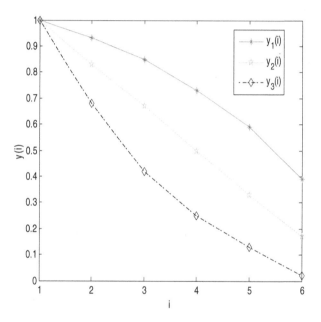

Fig. 3. Different modes of $y(i)$ respect on printing state i

4.1 Effect of Parameter C_P on Optimal Decision of Stencil Cleaning

Table 1 shows the effects of C_P, p and $y(i)$, on the optimal stencil cleaning time T_O and the minimal average cost per unit time slot $AC(T_O)$. The minimal average cost per unit time $AC(T_O)$ increases and the optimal cleaning time T_O decreases as the increase of C_P. In addition, when the stencil printing capability is rapidly degraded and the quality of the product deteriorates rapidly, the effects on the minimal average cost per unit time $AC(T_O)$ and the optimal cleaning time T_O are the same as C_P. This is because in the changing modes of the three parameter, the cost of quality loss will increase, which will cause the average cost per unit time increases while in order to reduce the cost of product quality loss, the decreases of the optimal cleaning time is reasonable.

Table 1. The values T_O and $AC(T_O)$ vs. C_P, p and $y(i)$

C_p	$y_1(i)$				$y_2(i)$				$y_3(i)$			
	P = 0.02		P = 0.1		P = 0.02		P = 0.1		P = 0.02		P = 0.1	
	$AC(T_O)$	T_O	$AC(T_O)$	T_O	$AC(T_O)$	T_O	$AC(T_O)$	T_O	$AC(T_O)$	T_O	$AC(T_O)$	T_O
15	1.86	75	4.09	31	2.66	53	5.48	22	3.51	39	6.92	17
20	2.11	65	4.62	26	3.04	45	6.21	19	4.02	33	7.85	14
25	2.34	58	5.06	23	3.37	40	6.82	16	4.46	29	8.61	12
30	2.54	53	5.45	21	3.66	36	7.36	14	4.84	26	9.26	10
35	2.72	49	5.79	19	3.93	33	7.83	13	5.19	24	9.82	9
40	2.89	46	6.11	18	4.18	31	8.25	12	5.50	22	10.33	8

4.2 Effect of Parameter C_Q on Optimal Decision of Stencil Cleaning

Table 2 shows the effects of C_Q, p and y(i), on the optimal stencil cleaning time T_O and the minimal average cost per unit time slot $AC(T_O)$. The minimal average cost per unit time $AC(T_O)$ increases and the optimal cleaning time T_O increases as the increase of C_Q. This is because the loss cost of downtime for stencil cleaning increases with the increasing of C_Q, which will cause the average cost per unit time increases while in order to reduce loss cost of downtime f5or stencil cleaning, it is wise to decrease the optimal cleaning time. In addition, we can also conclude when the stencil printing capability is rapidly degraded and the quality of the product deteriorates rapidly. We can obtain the same conclusion as the above Sect. 4.1.

Table 2. The values T_O of and $AC(T_O)$ vs. C_Q, p and $y(i)$

C_q	$y_1(i)$				$y_2(i)$				$y_3(i)$			
	P = 0.02		P = 0.1		P = 0.02		P = 0.1		P = 0.02		P = 0.1	
	$AC(T_O)$	T_O	$AC(T_O)$	T_O	$AC(T_O)$	T_O	$AC(T_O)$	T_O	$AC(T_O)$	T_O	$AC(T_O)$	T_O
20	1.86	75	4.09	31	2.66	53	5.48	22	3.51	39	6.92	17
23	2.00	80	4.42	34	2.86	57	5.92	25	3.78	43	7.47	19
26	2.14	85	4.74	37	3.05	61	6.33	27	4.03	46	7.97	21
29	2.28	90	5.03	40	3.23	65	6.71	29	4.26	49	8.44	23
32	2.40	94	5.31	43	3.40	68	7.07	31	4.48	52	8.88	25
35	2.52	98	5.57	46	3.56	72	7.40	33	4.69	55	9.29	26

5 Conclusions

In this paper, we proposed an approach for optimal stencil cleaning control based on renewal reward theorem. The optimal decision which balances the quality losses and the downtime losses is obtained. It shows that the approach is helpful for improving the productivity of solder paste printing and reducing production costs. This research provides a practical method for plant engineers and managers to determine the optimal stencil cleaning time. Finally, the influence law of the change of model parameters and cost parameters on the optimal cleaning decision of stencil cleaning is analyzed and managers can make the best choice based on the actual production situation based on it.

References

1. Amalu, E.H., Lau, W.K., Ekere, N.N.: A study of Sn-Ag-Cu solder paste transfer efficiency and effects of optimal reflow profile on solder deposits. Microelectron. Eng. **88**, 1610–1617 (2011)
2. Amalu, E.H., Ekere, N.N., Mallik, S.: Evaluation of rhological properties of lead-free solder pastes and their relationship with transfer efficiency during stencil printing process. Mater. Des. **32**(6), 3189–3197 (2011)
3. Shea, C., Whittier, R.: Fine-Tuning the Stencil manufacturing Process & other stencil printing experiments. SMT Surface Mount Technology (2014)
4. Cheng, Shunfeng, Huang, Chien-Ming, Pecht, M.: A review of lead-free solders for electronics applications. Microelectron. Reliab. **75**, 77–95 (2017)
5. Tsai, T.-N.: Improving the fine-pitch stencil printing capability using the Taguchi method and Taguchi fuzzy-based model. Robot. Cim-int. Manuf. **27**, 808–817 (2011)
6. Yang, T., Tsai, T.-N., Yeh, J.: A neural network-based prediction model for fine pitch stencil-printing quality in surface mount assembly Engineering. Eng. Appl. Artif. Intel. **18**, 335–341 (2005)

Decision-Making of Stencil Cleaning for Solder Paste Printing Machine Based on Variable Threshold Sequence

Shilin Niu, Zhengjun Bo, Le Cao[(⊠)], Lieqiang Li, Piao Wan, Hao Fu, and Jiangyou Yu

State Key Laboratory of Mechanical Transmission,
Chongqing University, Chongqing, China
lecao@cqu.edu.cn

Abstract. Stencil cleaning is a necessary operation step in solder paste printing process. Frequent cleaning operation usually leads to an excessive waste of cleaning agency and increased standby time. This paper proposes an approach for controlling the cleaning operation through variable stencil cleaning threshold sequences. A downtime ratio model is established to obtain the sequences, and a case study is given to show how to acquire the threshold sequences and makes decisions of stencil cleaning.

Keywords: Solder paste printing · Stencil cleaning · Decision making
Threshold sequences

1 Introduction

Solder paste printing is an important operation for surface mount technology (SMT) lines. Amalu et al. [1] mentioned that 50% of the defects found in the assembly of printed circuit boards (PCBs) are attributed to solder paste printing process.

Solder paste printing has a great influence on the quality of PCBs. A lot of researchers have been conducted to improve the performance of solder paste stencil printing operations. Huang [2] analyzed the influence of process parameters such as printing speed, temperature and printing pressure on solder paste printing. Tsai T N. [3, 4] proposed a Taguchi method based on fuzzy logic to optimize the fine-pitch stencil printing process. However, few researchers studied stencil cleaning to improve the performance of solder paste printing.

Stencil cleaning plays an important role in solder paste printing process. Literature [5] points out that stencil cleaning is an important part of solder paste printing, it ensures the quality of the printing process. However, frequent cleaning operation, usually leads to an excessive waste of cleaning agency, and increased standby time which may greatly decrease the productivity of the solder paste printing machine. In most manufactures, the solder paste printing machines are simply installed with a fixed cleaning cycle without consideration of the real time printing status. In this paper, we develop a dynamic approach for controlling the stencil cleaning operation based on variable threshold sequences.

© Springer Nature Singapore Pte Ltd. 2018
S. Wang et al. (Eds.): ICSEE 2018/IMIOT 2018, CCIS 923, pp. 325–331, 2018.
https://doi.org/10.1007/978-981-13-2396-6_31

2 Stencil Printing Capacity Index and State Index

This chapter evaluates the printing capability and printing state of stencils using real-time production data of solder paste.

2.1 The Calculation of Stencil Printing Capacity Index

Taam [6] proposed a multivariate process capability index, MCpm, to describe the quality of products under multi-parameter conditions. Because the solder paste is printed on the PCBs through the holes of stencil, the printing performance of the stencil is closely related to the parameters of the solder paste. We use the parameters of the solder paste instead of the quality indexes in MCpm to describe the printing capacity of stencils. This is defined as the printing capacity index P_{CI}. Thus we have:

$$P_{CI} = \frac{\frac{\pi(a/2)(b/2)}{|\Sigma|^{1/2}(\pi\lambda(c))^{\nu/2}[\Gamma(d/2)+1]^{-1}}}{[1 + \frac{k}{k-1}(\bar{X} - T)'\Sigma^{-1}(\bar{X} - T)]^{1/2}} \tag{1}$$

Notations:

a, b: The allowable interval for areas and heights of solder paste respectively;
$\bar{X}$: The average vector of solder paste parameters;
$\sum$: Represents the co-variance matrix; $\Sigma = \frac{1}{n-1}\sum_{i=1}^{n}(X_i - \bar{X})(X_i - \bar{X})'$
v: The number of solder paste parameters;
$\lambda(c)$: The value of Chi-square distribution with a lower quantile of 0.9973 and degree of freedom c which is equal v;
k: The number of printed PCB currently, $k \geq 2$;
T: Solder paste target value vector;
$\Gamma(d)$: Gamma function and d = v.

This article uses two parameters of solder paste that are percentage height and area. so the number of variables v equal 2. The working states of stencil can be reflected by P_{CI}. In order to ensure the reliability of the process in this paper, the value of P_{CI} is at least 1.33.

2.2 The Calculation of Stencil State Index C_I

In order to provide the actual operators with a clearer indicator, we propose a state indicator C_I. Equation 2 is a mapping function from the capability index P_{CI} to the state index C_I. The shape of the mapping function can be changed by adjusting the values of f and g, where parameter f controls the position and g controls the inclination of the mapping function graph.

$$C_I = \frac{1 - e^{-(P_{CI}/g)}}{1 + e^{-((P_{CI}-f)/g)}} \times F \tag{2}$$

This article sets (f, g) = (1.09, 0.45), F = 100 which indicates the ideal state of the stencil. Table 1 lists the C_I value corresponding P_{CI} by Eq. 2.

Table 1. Mapping of C_I values in the range (0,4)

P_{CI}	0	1	1.2	1.33	1.5	2	3	4
C_I	0.00	40.14	52.18	59.75	68.78	87.27	98.46	99.83

We divide the stencil into 9 states according to the state index C_I, with states 1–8 and failure status F respectively. From the table below, it can be seen that the status of the stencil from F to 8 is getting better and better. Table 2 shows the relationship between the C_I and state s.

Table 2. Stencil state index and state correspondence table

C_I	<60	60–65	65–70	70–75	75–80	80–85	85–90	90–95	95–100
s	F	1	2	3	4	5	6	7	8

3 Modeling of Variable Threshold Sequences

3.1 Printing Machine Minimization Downtime Ratio Model

Assume that there are only two kinds of downtime during stencil printing: automatic cleaning time and manual cleaning time. Automatic cleaning is preventive maintenance and manual cleaning is corrective maintenance. Generally, the manual cleaning time is longer than the automatic cleaning time and adequate automatic cleaning can reduces total downtime, but this will increase the automatic cleaning downtime. Therefore, a trade-off between automatic and manual cleaning is required to minimize long-term downtime.

It can be seen from Fig. 1. that cleaning has been done before the start of a cycle, which means stencil is in good working condition at the beginning of a cycle. The length of one cycle is equal to the sum of the printing time and the time of the next cleaning. In the following we define the expectations of the downtime ratio. Let α be the downtime ratio, then the function of expected α can be obtained:

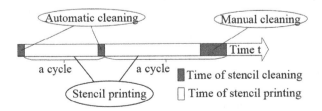

Fig. 1. The cycle length of minimization downtime ratio model for stencil cleaning

$$E(\alpha(m,n)|s) = \frac{Z + A \cdot P_{s,F}^n(m)}{m\Delta + Z + \Delta(n - \sum_{l=0}^{n-1} P_{s,F}^{(l)}(m) + A \cdot P_{s,F}^n(m)} \qquad n \geq 1 \qquad (3)$$

Where:

m: The number of PCBs that have been processed since the last stencil cleaning;

s: The status of the stencil;

n: The number of PCBs that can be processed before the next cleaning under the current m, s;

Z, A: Represent the time of automatic cleaning and manual cleaning respectively;

Δ: Indicates the time for printing one PCB;

$P_{iF}^n(m)$: The element of matrix $M_m^{(n)}$.

3.2   Modeling of Stencil Cleaning Threshold Sequences Based on Downtime Ratio

In order to control stencil cleaning, we need to find appropriate stencil printing state index thresholds. If real-time C_I of stencil is lower than the threshold sequences, stencil need to be cleaned before the next PCB is printed.

Calculated by Eq. 3, there exist n*(s, m) to minimize the expected α. Thus the minimum expected value of α can be expressed as formula 4:

$$E(\alpha(m,n^*)|s) = \min_n E(\alpha(m,n)|s) \qquad (4)$$

Here, we describe the model of stencil cleaning threshold sequences based on the minimum downtime ratio. Since our goal is to minimize the downtime per unit time, the smallest downtime ratio decisions can be described as follows. If the minimum downtime is at n*(s, m)>1, the automatic stencil cleaning schedule at n*(s, m)>1 will minimize the downtime; If α is at minimum when n*(s, m) = 1, the stencil is cleaned immediately. In Sect. 2.2 we divide the stencil into 9 states whose state space is: S = {F, s1, s2, ..., s8}. Each state other than the F state has n* values: n*(s1, m), n* (s2, m), ..., n*(s8, m) and n*(si, m) are non-decreasing function with the increase of A. Here we define the stencil cleaning threshold by the following equation:

$$s^*(m) = \max\{s_i : n^*(s_i, m) = 1\} \qquad (5)$$

Where s*(m) is the stencil cleaning threshold states and represents the best of all the states which satisfy n*(s1, m) = 1 at mΔ. Stencil cleaning threshold is actually the minimum allowable C_I of stencil printing at the moment. Once the stencil C_I is lower than the stencil cleaning threshold, the stencil is automatically cleaned immediately. This rule constitutes the decision making of stencil cleaning in this paper.

At different times, the threshold states of stencil cleaning is different, so we call it a variable threshold sequences. Threshold sequences line also is a alert line for stencil cleaning as shown the red line in Fig. 2.

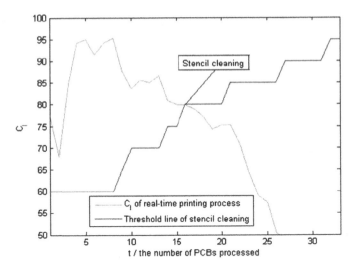

Fig. 2. Stencil cleaning decision threshold sequence and real-time stencil state index (Color figure online)

4 Case Study

We assume that the initial state transition probability matrix M_0 is known and given $Z = 20$ s, $A = 100$ s, the expected downtime ratio α is calculated by Eq. 3 at $t = 15$ and 16, which means 15th, 16th PCBs has been processed. Then a threshold sequence is obtained through the cleaning decision model in one cycle. All the values are shown in Table 3:

The minimum downtime ratio calculated by Eqs. 3 and 4 is indicated by the underline in Table 3. Then it can be observed that when printing 15th PCB and n^* (m) = 1, state 4 is the best state. Therefore, when printing 15th PCB, the threshold state is 4. Similarly, we can get that when $t = 16$, $s^*(m) = 5$. A threshold sequence consisted of all threshold states in one cycle of processing is shown in the red line in Fig. 2. Through formula 1 and we get the real-time printing capacity P_{CI} of the stencil and convert it to the state index C_I by Eq. 2 as shown in the green line in Fig. 2.

When the line of stencil real-time printing states intersects the threshold sequences line, automatic cleaning is triggered. The abscissa, approximately 16, is the cleaning decision time, meaning that cleaning is performed before processing the next board. The cleaning method actually adopted in the factory is periodic, that is, the stencil is cleaned after 7 PCBs processed. The experimental results show that the cleaning cycle is more than twice of the actual one but the printing quality has not changed significantly, which means that the printing efficiency can be improve a lot.

Table 3. Expected downtime ratio (%) and stencil cleaning threshold states

t	n	$s_8 = 8$	$s_7 = 7$	$s_6 = 6$	$s_5 = 5$	$s_4 = 4$	$s_3 = 3$	$s_2 = 2$	$s_1 = 1$	$s^*(m)$
...										...
15	1	7.76	8.04	8.14	8.24	**8.72**	9.20	10.61	12.43	
	2	7.38	7.79	7.97	8.24	9.07	9.90	12.17	14.32	
	3	7.11	7.57	7.82	8.23	9.33	10.38	13.04	15.29	
	4	6.88	7.38	7.68	8.21	9.48	10.65	13.51	15.78	
	5	6.71	7.22	7.55	8.17	9.54	10.79	13.73	15.99	
	6	6.58	7.09	7.44	8.11	9.55	10.82	13.79	16.02	
	Min	**6.58**	**7.09**	**7.44**	**8.11**	**8.72**	**9.20**	**10.61**	**12.43**	4
16	1	7.28	7.55	7.65	**7.74**	8.21	8.68	10.04	11.80	
	2	6.95	7.35	7.53	7.79	8.60	9.41	11.60	13.69	
	3	6.72	7.17	7.42	7.83	8.90	9.92	12.50	14.69	
	4	6.54	7.02	7.32	7.85	9.09	10.24	13.01	15.22	
	5	6.41	6.90	7.23	7.84	9.20	10.41	13.26	15.46	
	6	6.31	6.80	7.15	7.82	9.23	10.48	13.36	15.54	
	Min	**6.31**	**6.80**	**7.15**	**7.74**	**8.21**	**8.68**	**10.04**	**11.80**	5
...										...

5 Summary and Outlook

In this paper, we propose a dynamic cleaning method for stencils of solder paste printing machines using real-time state index and variable threshold sequences. The real-time printing capability index P_{CI} and state index C_I of stencils are calculated from the parameters of solder paste. This paper also present a method for acquiring the variable threshold sequences of stencil cleaning by downtime ratio. Through experiments we found that our method is more effective than just setting a fixed stencil cleaning cycle.

Influence factor analysis of stencil cleaning decision making and comparison with other methods can be studied in the future.

Acknowledgement. The authors gratefully acknowledge the support of Mengxun corporation in providing the experiment environment used for this work. This research is funded by national intelligent manufacturing project.

References

1. Amalu, E.H., Lau, W.K., Ekere, N.N.: A study of SnAgCu solder paste transfer efficiency and effects of optimal reflow profile on solder deposits. Microelectron. Eng. **88**(7), 1610–1617 (2011)
2. Huang, C., Lin, Y., Ying, K.: The solder paste printing process: critical parameters, defect scenarios, specifications, and cost reduction. Solder. Surf. Mt. Tech. **23**(4), 211–223 (2011)

3. Tsai, T.N., Liukkonen, M.: Robust parameter design for the micro-BGA stencil printing process using a fuzzy logic-based Taguchi method. Appl. Soft. Compt. **48**, 124–136 (2016)
4. Tsai, T.N.: Modeling and optimization of stencil printing operations: a comparison study. Comput. Ind. Eng. **54**(3), 374–389 (2008)
5. Cala, F., Reynolds, R.: Stencil cleaning: an area of increasing importance. Solder. Surf. Mt. Tech. **7**(3), 17–19 (1995)
6. Taam, W., Subbaiah, P., Liddy, J.W.: A note on multivariate capability indices. J. Appl. Stat. **20**(3), 339–351 (1993)
7. Chen, A., Wu, G.S.: Real-time health prognosis and dynamic preventive maintenance policy for equipment under aging Markovian deterioration. Int. J. Prod. Res. **45**(15), 3351–3379 (2007)

Consumers' Green Preferences for Remanufactured Products

Yacan Wang[(✉)], Xiaoyu Yin, Qianqian Du, Siqi Jia, Yunhan Xie, and Siyuan He

School of Economics and Management, Beijing Jiaotong University, Shangyuancun 3, Haidian District, Beijing 100044, China
ycwang@bjtu.edu.cn

Abstract. This paper empirically investigates how consumers' preference towards remanufactured products is determined with consideration of their greenness, price and green attributes. A mixed between and within-subject experiment was conducted to test four hypotheses of the correlations between consumers' preferences for remanufactured products and the level of consumer greenness, the level of price discount and green attributes of the products respectively. By analyzing data results of the experiment, the paper reveals how consumers' preferences and utility towards remanufactured products was determined, thus providing remanufacturers with new understanding of consumers' demand and insights into pricing strategy.

Keywords: Remanufactured products · Green consumer · Preference Behavioral experiment

1 Introduction

Remanufacturing is a production strategy where the goal is to recover the residual value of used products via reusing, refurbishing, and/or replacing components such that the end-item is restored to a like-new condition (Debo et al. 2005).

Traditionally, remanufacturing research has focused on operational issues and product acquisition management from a supply point of view, and less attention has been paid to factors affecting consumers' preferences for remanufactured products from the end consumer (Wang and Hazen 2016, Wang et.al 2013). This paper contributes to the remanufacturing and closed-loop supply chain literature by examining the following question: How is consumer preference for remanufactured products determined?

To answer this question, this paper conducts an experimental study to test the hypotheses concerning consumers' preferences for remanufactured products, and through analyzing the data results to reveal the mechanism of consumers' preferences for remanufactured products. The results reveal positive relations between consumer greenness and preference for remanufactured products. Within a certain discount level, preference for remanufactured products becomes stronger as discount level increases, while after a certain discount level, the preference weakens. The result also indicates under different levels of green attributes, there is no significant difference on consumers' preference for remanufactured products.

© Springer Nature Singapore Pte Ltd. 2018
S. Wang et al. (Eds.): ICSEE 2018/IMIOT 2018, CCIS 923, pp. 332–342, 2018.
https://doi.org/10.1007/978-981-13-2396-6_32

2   Literature Review

Psychologically, it is difficult for consumers to equate remanufactured products with new products (Abbey et al. 2015a, b and c; Ge and Huang 2007; Follows and Jobber 2000; Ferrer and Ayres 2000). There are different evaluations (Dang and Ding 2010; Debo et al. 2005).

Existing literature often adopts the method of investigating consumers' willingness to pay for products in dealing with consumer preference or consumer utility. Michaud and Llerena (2011) conduct experimental research on green consumers' behavior. They measured consumers' willingness to pay for new products and remanufactured products respectively and compared experimental results to verify the difference.

In the research of Guide and Li (2010), they conduct an online experiment to study the cannibalization effect that remanufactured products have on new products. To avoid the impact of products' categories on the experiment, the auction adopted two categories of products: consumer products and industrial products. Results indicated consumers' preference for new or remanufactured products differentiates under the two different categories.

Different from Guide and Li's research, Abbey et al. (2015a, b and c) classified the products in three types, i.e., technology products, household products, and personal products. Abbey used attractiveness preference ratings to show consumers' preference.

This paper adopts the same method as Abbey's in revealing the products' attractiveness to consumers by asking consumers to rate their preference for new and remanufactured products. Further, using consumers' ratings as variables is better to control when evaluating.

Compared with existing research, this paper also believes that there is a kind of consumers named green consumers in the market.

In fact, Atasu et al. (2008a, b) have previously suggested that green consumers exist in the market. However, he did not provide any empirical support. While, on this basis, this paper argues that each consumer in the market has a corresponding level of greenness and the level of each consumer's greenness can be obtained by remanufacturers through market research.

In Atasu's research, after dividing consumers into two groups, he thinks that functional consumers' preference for new and remanufactured products are different, represented as v and αv respectively; while green consumers' preference for new and remanufactured products should be the same. However, this paper argues that, regardless of functional consumers and green consumers, their preference towards different products should be different. This paper creatively thinks that consumers' preferences for remanufactured products are related to their greenness levels.

In comparison with the research of Abbey et al. (2015a, b and c), they studied the existence of green consumers through a scale, but the scale used was relatively too simple. On this point, this paper has questioned Abbey's conclusion and assigned consumer greenness as a continuous variable to each consumer.

Another main innovation of this paper is the development of a new consumer greenness scale. The scale is formed based on massive literature research and from the perspective of three dimensions, which are attitude, behavior and value respectively.

This paper uses the corresponding greenness level x as a continuous variable in the experiment to test the hypothesis of consumers' preferences towards remanufactured products with relations to their greenness levels.

3 Experimental Hypothesis

When the manufacturers put a remanufactured product into the market, they generally sets a price discount on it based on the price of the new product (Apple website 2016). Therefore, the following hypothesis is suggested:

H1: Consumers' preference for remanufactured products is positively related to the discount level of remanufactured products.

Some scholars speculated that if green consumers exist, they would be willing to pay more for the remanufactured products due to the environmental attributes (Atasu et al. 2008). Atasu et al. (2008) introduced the green environmental attributes of remanufactured products as a variable into the model to explore the impact of the environmental attributes of remanufactured goods on consumer preferences. Therefore, the following hypothesis is suggested:

H2: The consumer's preference for remanufactured products is positively related to the green attributes of the remanufacturer.

The definition of the consumer greenness is the consumer's perception of and concern for environmental issues (Laroche et al. 2001). For each independent consumer in the market, there is a certain degree of greenness that indicates its level of greenness. In a market where new products and remanufactured goods coexist, the higher the consumer's greenness, the greater the effect that remanufactured goods may have (Atasu 2008a, b) on these consumers. Therefore, the following hypothesis is suggested:

H3a: Consumers' preference for remanufactured products is positively related to the greenness of the consumer, and the stronger the consumer's greenness, the greater his utility on the remanufacturer.

To further verify the existence of consumer greenness, it is necessary to further prove that consumers' preference for new products is not affected by their greenness, that is, the following hypothesis should be verified at the same time:

H3b: Consumers' preference for new products and consumer greenness level have no significant correlation.

To test these two hypotheses, this paper forms a consumer greenness survey scale according to Laroche et al.'s (2001) conceptual framework. The item of each scale was adopted from the existing literature and scale. Specifically, the scale contains 3 dimensions: attitude dimension, behavior dimension and value dimension.

4 Consumer Behavioral Experimentation

The main purpose is to explore the consumer preferences for remanufactured products; and to test the hypotheses.

4.1 Experiment Design

Through a nationwide online questionnaire, 972 people participated in the experiment. The experiment uses consumers' greenness level, prices of remanufactured products and environmental attributes as variables and uses a between and within-subjects mixed model.

The consumer greenness level was researched through a new developed consumer greenness scale, based on massive literature research. The greenness distribution of consumers in the market was figured out and was used in testing hypotheses H3a and H3b, that is, consumers' preferences for remanufactured products with relations to consumers' different greenness levels.

The questionnaire included the experiment itself as well as the survey on demographic variables of the subjects. Thus, after finishing the two surveys, and before starting the options of the behavioral experiment, the consumer is provided with information on "remanufactured productions".

In order to avoid the stochastic error, exclude the situation that consumers have specific disgust or preference on some products, the experiment chose 4 corresponding products in each product category. In addition, the price discount is used as one of the experimental variables to reduce the impact of the overall price level of the experimental products may have on consumers. In addition, this study only focuses on the effect of prices and other factors on consumers' preferences. Therefore, in order to eliminate consumers' consideration on the quality of products, the experiment only retains the relevant experimental variables.

The experimental new products and the corresponding remanufactured products are shown in Table 1.

The demographic variables segment focused on the gender, age, education level and monthly consumption level of the subjects (Abbey 2015a, b and c; Laroche et al. 2001) (Table 2).

4.2 Experimental Manipulated Variables

This paper uses discount levels instead of prices of remanufactured products. The experimental manipulation for discounting randomly assigned respondents to a between-subject single discount level, relative to the price of an identical new product, of 20%, 40%, 60%, 80%, or 95% to study the effect of different price discounts on consumers' preferences for remanufactured products and to verify the hypothesis 2:

This paper takes the greenness of remanufactured products as a possible influencing factor into the experiment, and indicate the different levels of greenness of remanufactured products by two statements:

Table 1. Experimental items and price

Item categories	Item names	New product price (yuan)
Technology products	Color printer	800
	Laptop	5500
	Digital camera	2000
	MP3	300
Household products	Air purifier	3000
	Electric Iron	600
	Drinking fountain	400
	Juicer	300
Personal products	Massage foot tub	400
	Hair dryer	80
	Electric shaver	400
	Electronic sphygmomanometer	250

Table 2. Participant descriptive statistics

	Frequency	Percentage
Gender		
Male	421	43.3%
Female	551	56.7%
Age		
<18	39	4.0%
18–25	309	31.8%
26–35	263	27.1%
36–45	194	20.0%
46–55	117	12.0%
56–65	46	4.7%
>65	4	0.4%
Education Background		
Junior high or below	25	2.6%
Senior high	55	5.7%
Bachelor's degree	558	57.4%
Master's degree	315	32.4%
Doctor's degree or higher	19	2.0%
Individual Monthly Expenses		
¥ 1000 or below	252	25.9%
¥ 1001–2000	405	41.7%
¥ 2001–3000	161	16.6%
¥ 3001–4000	75	7.7%
¥ 4001–5000	25	2.6%
¥ 5001 or higher	54	5.6%

Low Green attribute refers to remanufactured products that can save materials and energy by 15%; While high Green attribute refers to remanufactured products that can save materials and energy by 65%

In the experiment, each consumer will face one of the above green level with equal chance. This is to study consumers' preference for remanufactured products under different greenness level and to verify hypothesis 2 in this article.

4.3 Between-Subjects Experiment Design

This experiment sets $5 \times 2 = 10$ scenarios, considering discount levels of remanufactured products and green attribute levels. Each consumer will be randomly assigned a scenario with 10% probability and answer the corresponding question (Table 3).

Table 3. Between-subjects experiment design

Between-subjects experiment design	20% discount	40% discount	60% discount	80% discount	95% discount
Green Attributes-High	Group1	Group4	Group5	Group8	Group9
Green Attributes-Low	Group2	Group3	Group6	Group7	Group10

Consumers are divided into 10 groups under 10 scenarios as above. Among them, Group 1,2; Group 3,4; Group 5,6; Group 7,8; Group 9,10 correspond to different price discount level respectively. Thus, we can see consumer's different preferences (Table 4).

Table 4. Within-subjects experiment design

Within-subjects experiment design	Technology products	Household products	Personal products
New products	√	√	√
Remanufactured products	√	√	√

4.4 Within-Subjects Experiment Design

When we study consumers preference for remanufactured products, it is also necessary to investigate consumers' preference for new products to form a control. Meanwhile, to avoid the uncertain effect of types of products on consumer preferences, the experiment chose 3 types, 12 in total of the corresponding new and remanufactured products and let consumers rate their attractiveness, thus forming the within-subjects experiment.

4.5 Experiment Results

To achieve the above objectives, the experiment will conduct a survey of consumer greenness scale and an experiment of consumer behavior.

4.5.1 Testing Experimental Hypotheses

Testing Hypothesis 1: Price of Remanufactured Products and Preference

H1: Consumers' preference for remanufactured products is positively related to the discount level of remanufactured products.

In order to test hypothesis 1, we still consider the three types of products to study the consumption of the corresponding remanufactured products in the discount level of 20%, 40%, 60%, 80%, 95%. For each product type, the corresponding consumers' preference data (average of nearly 200 data) are averaged at each price level, yielding results as follow (Fig. 1):

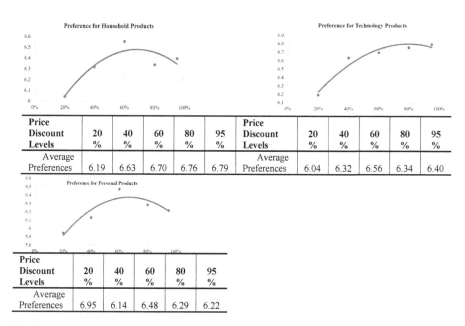

Price Discount Levels	20 %	40 %	60 %	80 %	95 %
Average Preferences	6.19	6.63	6.70	6.76	6.79

Price Discount Levels	20 %	40 %	60 %	80 %	95 %
Average Preferences	6.04	6.32	6.56	6.34	6.40

Price Discount Levels	20 %	40 %	60 %	80 %	95 %
Average Preferences	6.95	6.14	6.48	6.29	6.22

Fig. 1. Preference for technology, household and personal products at discount levels (Color figure online)

Based on experimental result, we come to the conclusion that:

First, within a certain discount level, the consumer's preference for remanufactured products gets stronger when the price discount level increases. Hypothesis 2 is supported.

Second, after a certain level of price discounts, the consumer's preference for remanufactured products has weakened (Ovchinnikov 2011).

Testing Hypothesis 2: Green Attributes of Remanufactured Products and Preference

H2: The consumer's preference for remanufactured products is positively related to the green attributes of the remanufacturer.

The environmental attributes of the different remanufactured products in the experiment are expressed as "15% of energy and materials saving" and "65% of energy and materials saving" respectively (Fig. 2).

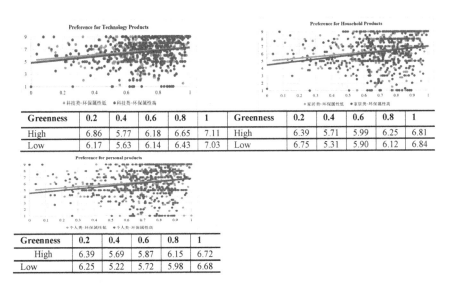

Greenness	0.2	0.4	0.6	0.8	1	Greenness	0.2	0.4	0.6	0.8	1
High	6.86	5.77	6.18	6.65	7.11	High	6.39	5.71	5.99	6.25	6.81
Low	6.17	5.63	6.14	6.43	7.03	Low	6.75	5.31	5.90	6.12	6.84

Greenness	0.2	0.4	0.6	0.8	1
High	6.39	5.69	5.87	6.15	6.72
Low	6.25	5.22	5.72	5.98	6.68

Fig. 2. Preference for technology, household and personal products of green attributes (Color figure online)

Red dot represents low level of green attributes, while blue dots high.

If hypothesis 2 is supported, it indicates that consumers' preference for remanufactured products is distinctly stronger when the green attributes are higher. However, the experimental result shows that under different levels of green attributes, there is no significant difference on consumers' preference for remanufactured products. It's surprising that it happens when the consumer's greenness and the green attributes of the product are both low, however, the preference is relatively higher. Thus, we think there is no significant correlation between the consumer's preference for remanufactured products and the green attributes of the remanufacturer. And we refuse hypothesis 2.

Testing Hypothesis 3: Consumer Greenness and Preference

H3a: Consumers' preference for remanufactured products is positively related to the greenness of the consumer, and the stronger the consumer's greenness, the greater his utility on the remanufacturer.

H3b: Consumers' preference for new products and consumer greenness level have no significant correlation.

Hypothesis 3 includes the relationship between consumers' preference for new and remanufactured products and their greenness. Thus, according to the experimental control scheme, after obtaining the consumer preference data, we conduct a regression verification on the preference and consumption of the three types of products to study the relationship between consumers' preference for new and remanufactured products and their own greenness. And it is found that consumers' preference for new and remanufactured products of the three types are similar to each other (Figs. 3, 4 and 5).

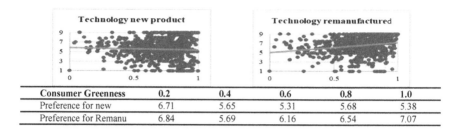

Consumer Greenness	0.2	0.4	0.6	0.8	1.0
Preference for new	6.71	5.65	5.31	5.68	5.38
Preference for Remanu	6.84	5.69	6.16	6.54	7.07

Fig. 3. Preference for technology products (Color figure online)

There is no significant correlation between consumers' preference for new products and their greenness level while consumers' preference for remanufactured products and greenness level is positively correlated. Hypothesis H3a and H3b are verified.

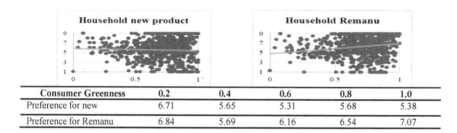

Consumer Greenness	0.2	0.4	0.6	0.8	1.0
Preference for new	6.71	5.65	5.31	5.68	5.38
Preference for Remanu	6.84	5.69	6.16	6.54	7.07

Fig. 4. Preference for household products (Color figure online)

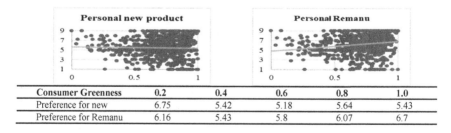

Consumer Greenness	0.2	0.4	0.6	0.8	1.0
Preference for new	6.75	5.42	5.18	5.64	5.43
Preference for Remanu	6.16	5.43	5.8	6.07	6.7

Fig. 5. Preference for personal products (Color figure online)

5 Conclusion

According to the results, consumers' preference for remanufactured products is positively related to consumers' greenness. With higher level of greenness, consumers intend to perform stronger preference for remanufactured products.

With regard to price discount, within a certain discount level, the consumer's preference for remanufactured products gets stronger when the price discount level increases. While beyond a certain level of price discount, the consumer's preference for remanufactured products has weakened, perhaps because the price discount level is too high which leads to consumers' doubts on product quality and some other factors.

In conclusion, this paper has verified a positive relation between consumers' greenness and their preference for remanufactured products.

Through a mixed between and within-subject behavioral experiment, this paper has tested another two hypotheses which verified the relations between consumers' preferences for remanufactured products and price discount levels and green attributes of the products in three categories, namely technology, household and personal products. By analyzing data results of the experiment, the paper reveals how consumers' preferences and utility towards remanufactured products was determined. Referring to these results, a utility function can be built to inform remanufacturers how to set price discounts that generate the maximum utility for remanufactured products and how consumers' greenness level can affect their preferences for the remanufactured goods. Hence a deeper insight into the demand of consumers can be gained, which helps remanufacturers to form an effective pricing strategy to maximize their profits.

References

Abbey, J.D., Blackburn, J.D., Guide Jr., V.D.R.: Optimal pricing for new and remanufactured products. J. Oper. Manage. **36**, 130–146 (2015a)

Abbey, J.D., Meloy, M.G., Guide, V.D.R., Atalay, S.: Remanufactured products in closed-loop supply chains for consumer goods. Prod. Oper. Manage. **24**(3), 488–503 (2015b)

Abbey, J.D., Meloy, M.G., Blackburn, J., Guide Jr., V.D.R.: Consumer markets for remanufactured and refurbished products. Calif. Manage. Rev. **57**(4), 26–42 (2015c)

Atasu, A., Sarvary, M., Van Wassenhove, L.N.: Remanufacturing as a marketing strategy. Manage. Sci. **54**(10), 1731–1746 (2008a)

Atasu, A., Guide, V.D.R., Wassenhove, L.N.: Product reuse economics in closed-loop supply chain research. Prod. Oper. Manage. **17**(5), 483–496 (2008b)

Guide Jr., V.D.R., Li, J.: The potential for cannibalization of new products sales by remanufactured products. Decis. Sci. **41**(3), 547–572 (2010)

Ferrer, G., Ayres, R.U.: The impact of remanufacturing in the economy. Ecol. Econ. **32**(3), 413–429 (2000)

Debo, L.G., Toktay, L.B., Van Wassenhove, L.N.: Market segmentation and product technology selection for remanufacturable products. Manage. Sci. **51**(8), 1193–1205 (2005)

Ovchinnikov, A.: Revenue and cost management for remanufactured products. Prod. Oper. Manage. **20**(6), 824–840 (2011)

Laroche, M., Bergeron, J., Barbaro-Forleo, G.: Targeting consumers who are willing to pay more for environmentally friendly products. J. Consum. Mark. **18**(6), 503–520 (2001)

Follows, S.B., Jobber, D.: Environmentally responsible purchase behaviour: a test of a consumer model. Eur. J. Mark. **34**(5/6), 723–746 (2000)

Binshi, X., Shishen, L., Peijing, S., Zhong, X., Jianjun, X.: Analysis of benefits of automobile engine remanufacturing and contribution to circular economy. China Surf. Eng. **18**(1), 1–7 (2005)

Bin, D., Xuefeng, D.: Optimal pricing of remanufactured goods and analysis of market cannibalization and market growth. Syst. Eng. Theory Pract. **30**(8), 1371–1379 (2010)

Wang, Y., Hazen, B.T.: Consumer product knowledge and intention to purchase remanufactured products. Int. J. Prod. Econ. **181**, 460–469 (2016)

Ge, J.Y., Huang, P.Q., Li, J.: Social environmental consciousness and price decision analysis for closed-loop supply chains—based on vertical differentiation model. Ind. Eng. Manage. **4**, 6–10 (2007)

Michaud, C., Llerena, D.: Green consumer behaviour: an experimental analysis of willingness to pay for remanufactured products. Bus. Strategy Environ. **20**(6), 408–420 (2011)

Atasu, A., Sarvary, M., Van Wassenhove, L.N.: Remanufacturing as a marketing strategy. Manage. Sci. **54**(10), 1731–1746 (2008)

Wang, Y., Wiegerinck, V., Krikke, H., Zhang, H.: Understanding the purchase intention towards remanufactured product in closed-loop supply chains: an empirical study in China. Int. J. Phys. Distrib. Logistics Manage. **43**(10), 866–888 (2013)

Methodology – A Review of Intelligent Manufacturing: Scope, Strategy and Simulation

Peiliang Sun$^{(\boxtimes)}$ and Kang Li

School of Electronic and Electrical Engineering,
University of Leeds, Leeds LS2 9JT, UK
PeiliangSUNelpsu@leeds.ac.uk

Abstract. This paper presents a critical review of some existing modelling, control and optimization techniques for energy saving, carbon emission reduction in manufacturing processes. The study on various production issues reveals different levels of intelligent manufacturing approaches. Then methods and strategies to tackle the sustainability issues in manufacturing are summarized. Modelling tools such as discrete (dynamic) event system (DES/DEDS) and agent-based modelling/simulation (ABS) approaches are reviewed from the production planning and control prospective. These approaches will provide some guidelines for the development of advanced factory modelling, resource flow analysis and assisting the identification of improvement potentials, in order to achieve more sustainable manufacturing.

Keywords: Intelligent manufacturing · Production planning · Scheduling
Agent-based modelling · Discrete event system

1 Introduction

The manufacturing sector in industry, has a nonnegligible environmental impact coupled with the production process. In the manufacturing factory, materials and significant amounts of energy are consumed and only a part of them are renewable which impose considerable stress upon the earth. Some manufacturing activities release hazards solid, liquid and gaseous waste streams that leads to detrimental impact on to the environment.

There are increasing causes for the current manufacturing system [1]: environmental concerns, diminishing non-renewable resources, stricter legislations and inflated energy costs, and increasing consumer preference for environmentally friendly products, etc. The concept "sustainability" is gradually received more attentions from innovative industry. Efforts to develop a manufacturing system meeting the sustainable criteria have to make considerations of multi-level from product, process and of the whole factory system. Isolated approach cannot succeed in the sustainable upgradation.

The three pillars of sustainable development include environmental, economic and social aspects [2]. Efforts along the tree pillars should be synthesized for a more energy efficient and environment benign manufacturing. To meet the more stringent standards,

© Springer Nature Singapore Pte Ltd. 2018
S. Wang et al. (Eds.): ICSEE 2018/IMIOT 2018, CCIS 923, pp. 343–359, 2018.
https://doi.org/10.1007/978-981-13-2396-6_33

proactive green behaviour such as conservation of energy, water, materials, reduction and recycle of the wasted energy and material treatment are extensively developed in recent years.

There are opportunities widely existing for efficient energy usage and improved material utilization in the manufacturing sectors to a resource efficient production. We can use efficiency and effectiveness to evaluate the energy and materials resource used in manufacturing cycle [3]. The definition of efficiency is about the amount of resources used to produce a required amount of product in which the efficiency index should be minimized as much as possible. We would like to use less resource to finish certain amount of output. However, the word "effectiveness" is defined by whether the resources are effectively used. In [4] the author name efficiency as "doing the things right", and describe effectiveness as "doing the right things".

Previous researchers have posed extensive works on makespan optimization and the minimization of makespan has been widely studied as the main objectives to improve production efficiency. In terms of green or energy-aware manufacturing, more attention should be paid in the sector to consideration of non-renewable resource consumption in the product life-cycle. In the [2], the authors focus on "sustainable manufacturing operations scheduling" approach and make summary on key challenges and research trends in the proposed area. These emerging challenges are high energy intensity machining, unsustainability and only partial consideration in control of the industrial operation.

The increasing complexity of the manufacturing environment makes it difficult to find easy solutions to modern energy/environment-oriented upgrading. Operations in widespread industrial manufacturing systems can be viewed as a discrete set [5] which provides the opportunity to implement complex scheduling and control method on the system. Successful simulation of the process modules, evaluation and visualization is one of the keys for enhancing the of strategic and operational management of the production planning and control. This survey discusses a broad manufacturing issues and challenges associated with energy and resources conservation techniques.

The remainder of the paper is organized as follows.

- Section 2 discusses the scope for energy/material managing improvement inside a single factory where solutions, possible techniques and strategies are reviewed for facilitating a more energy and resource efficient manufacturing. Structured approaches are used to distinguish the difference between different system levels.
- Section 3 focuses on manufacturing operation scheduling problems concerning typical objectives can be concerned in manufacturing operations and multi-objective optimization-based scheduling for production lines.
- Section 4 reviews two important modelling techniques for the support of production simulation. The discrete event system and agent-based modelling, and their capabilities for operation planning, process resource modelling and flexible system-based simulation.

2   The Scope of Intelligent Manufacturing Systems

Manufacturing activities are complex that can be discomposed into multiple scopes of production levels [3]. The lower level starts from single machine where unit processes is conducted within a small region, and then to a wider scope contains multiple devices forming a process chain. When comprising all the production line within the factory to deliver the final products, all of the activities can be considered in a holistic view through which production planning and control regarding all of the sustainable potentials can be achieved. In the context of this section we only distinguish three levels of activities: one single machine/unit process, multi-machine/process chain system, and the whole factory level. Manufacturing types can be broadly separated into process and discrete where process manufactures using batch or continuous operation; discrete manufactures parts and assembling products in sequential steps. The difference in the production type leads to different scheduling problems. Nevertheless, both types will be examined below in term of green manufacturing.

2.1   Unit Process/Machine Level

Each single machine in a process can be treated as a subsystem in a process. Successful auditing and identification, determination of energy and material consumption at each unit is one of the key to facilitate a detailed in-depth and more complete understanding in ways to improve sustainability in manufacturing.

Operations adopted on a single machine such as machining tools allocation in the discrete manufacturing and production planning to unit machine for better duty control are part of the approaches. Other solutions include all machines and the whole production are allocated near the nominal capacity level, the parameter settings are set at the optimum, and the machines and processes are optimally controlled, and thus the energy consumption is minimized.

2.1.1   Energy and Material Flow Auditing

At this level, to identify how a single process unit consumes energy and material is the first step towards transparency. This energy/material auditing on each machine provides a fundamental reference for researchers and practitioners to identify any critical problem in the system.

Not only the consumption of energy and resources, but also the waste/emission generation during the production process should be identified to each process unit. Inspired by Abele et al. [6], the energy consumption can be separated into essential energy requirement of the normal production process, the extra energy demands of processing and peripheral demand in product development. Auditing one or series of production units requires to calculate the cost of energy, losses of materials and to identify improvable process variable. [7] Proposed a more instructive approach about different aspects can be analysed in the input/output details. The time, power consumption, consumable and emission studies are analysed thoroughly. After acquiring detailed description of each process to a data inventory, statistical study of these industrial measurements results will assist understanding behaviours in the process for better management.

2.1.2   Strategies for Minimizing Energy and Resource Consumption

At this level, strategies for minimizing energy/resource consumption need to be considered firstly to reduce environmental impact. Fundamentally, most production device can be improved from a better efficiency design, while for a machine at a fixed production line, to optimize the process parameters, and its working duty can be considered as energy/resource demand reduction methods.

Re-design and Structural Improvement of Process Unit

Once the most energy intensive machines or processes are identified and audited, significant improvement of efficiency can be achieved by using more efficient components, and re-designing towards more energy efficient tools [8]. Instead of redesigning of current machine and process, the new technologies transplant on existing production line can guarantee improvement. For instance, it is reported that updating the conventional laser source with new technology in the forming industry can lead to 18% increase of efficiency [9].

Energy and resource efficiency of a single process can be improved by recovery of energy (heat, kinetic) and materials within a machine. [10] developed a method to recycled the powder materials in a polymer laser sintering process. [11] investigated kinetic energy recovery system to improve energy efficiency of high-speed cutting process up to 25%. This kind of strategies can be implemented at different levels which will be discussed in the following subsections. Peripherals like compressed air, heated air, cooling air and lubrication etc. are consumables supplied locally or centrally to each machine. The energy of compressed air can be paid back and recovered at the machine level [12].

Process Control and Optimization Methods

The aforementioned methods in fact change the inherent structure of the process unit though effective, may not be cost effective or may need significant investment. New control methods are however relatively easy to implement on the existing production line. Machine duty can be flexible controlled and the process parameters can be relatively easily optimized.

Controlling the load condition of machines is a straightforward approach to reduce the energy cost where the most convenient way is to shut down machines that are not used. Machines usually have several operating such as heavy duty, nominal duty, light duty, idle and stand-by mode when turned on. Therefore, to minimize the overload and idle time during a manufacturing process will save energy. In [13] the author used a self-learning solution to control the process of a production line system to have a reduced time and efforts. For the process with fixed power level, the energy waste is significant at a non-loaded mode. There is a need for the optimal production plan which uses the nominal capacity of each equipment.

For the process units, the setting parameters are always related to resource consumption. [14] examined the parameter settings for cutting conditions and acceleration control to achieve a reduced power consumption in machine tool operation. Process control, in some cases, can maintain or even improve the quality with less energy cost. For instance, [15] optimized the process parameters of a paper machine's dryer section to reduce the steam consumption in the multi-cylinder dryer and to decrease the loads of centrifugal blowers.

In most industrial processes the process units are interconnected and system level optimization with multi-objective control methods. [16] analysed the historical process data in a paper mill and proposed a multi-objective energy optimization method. They were able to reduce the thermal energy consumption by changing vacuum pressure at an upstream subsystem and optimized the stream usage.

2.2   Production Line/Multi-machine Level

2.2.1   Resource Recycle and Reuse

The optimization of a single machine has limited effect on the reduction of energy and resource consumption, and practical industrial processes are often complex with multiple process units. Production plan or control wide control exhibit specific energy consumption characteristics. When multi-machine or even a process chain in the factory is involved, problems of interactions and synergies between different machines often arises. According to different process structure, the network of connected machines in a plant can be organized in parallel or sequence topology, and in these machine networks the output of one machine might be treated as input for another. Therefore, it is important to get enough knowledge on the trace of resource flow in these multi-machine production chain systems. In iron and steel plants, it is possible to reuse scrap to reduce material cost. During the steel production, the by-product and semi-finished product contain much of the thermal energy which can be harvested to reduce energy consumption [17]. Establishment of cogeneration systems exist in these environments where the valuable steam and fuels can be partially recovery to be utilized to generate electricity in combined cycles.

Energy flow such as steam can be perceived as an energy-cascade system. The concepts, exergy and entropy describe the quality and quantity of energy inside multi-machine ecosystem. These set up analytic foundation to acquire, describe and analyse energetic flow through connected machines. The exergy concept clarifies the different interactions like in- and outputs, work and heat in a system; and helps determine the extent to which the system destroys exergy [18]. By accounting the exergy in a multi-machine system, it is easier to pinpoint the exergy distribution. Then using exergy cascading analysis method, energy and material recycle ability can be estimated. To minimize exergy losses is to minimize energy consumption of the processes. In [19], Wang et al. applied the flowrate-exergy diagram for thermodynamic analysis and energy integration and achieved 37.5% decrease on natural gas consumption through acetylene and power polygeneration.

Waste heat exists in many industries like melting furnace in steel company where excessive heat can be reused for a heat treatment process. For instance, the flue gases which flow in the opposite direction against material flow can make the flue gas reused. Rankine cycle is another way to generate electricity from waste heat besides recycle the heat flow directly and organic Rankine cycle (ORC) has been a hot research topic in recent years. [20] reported that ORC can be used in aluminium, steel, food and battery manufacturing. Analysing the system energetically and exergetically assist efficiency boosting, in [21] used water-steam Rankin cycle and an organic Rankine cycle to recover heat in cement industry.

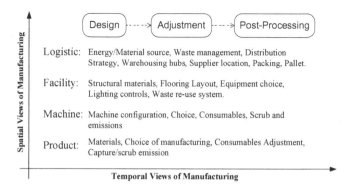

Fig. 1. Manufacturing design level with decision on each stage in respect of temporal view and spatial view.

Similarly, the material flow at multi-machine level can also be optimized to reduce the waste. Resources flow can be described between different machines in a factory. [22] investigated the aluminium recycling economic efficiency by examining the in-plant transportation between different units as material input or output and optimized the model with linear optimization method. [22] revealed that environmental and economic objectives are not always contradictory and their approach was able to lower the emissions up to 10%.

2.2.2   Process Chain Control and Scheduling

In a multi-machine scope, each unit has its load profile and they are accumulated in a production line to exhibit specific energy and resource consumption behaviour. [23] reviewed the potential of production efficiency improvement by the production control. The interlinkage of process units and production features such as batch size and scheduling orders/speed can all influence the efficiency.

Electricity is widely used by many kinds of machines. Appropriate selection of machine, optimal duty control setting and minimizing idling state of each machine can reduce electrical work. In many systems, if some machines in a production line can be switched on and off during the process, the operation control of multi-machine switching considering their transients performance may achieve high energy efficiency [24] where a the serial production line has a number of Bernoulli machines with finite capacity buffers and switching capability has been studied.

Another aspect of cost reduction method is to avoid consumption peak. By optimization methods in production simulation, improved planning solution can be found to minimize peak power and to some extent reduce total energy cost. The peak power in some places causes cost extra charges in the electric bill and similarly, it is possible to shift electricity consumption from day to night when the price is less expensive.

In the process chain, depending on the complex interaction within multiple machines with different states, energy and material consumption behavior is not static but dynamic. To handle those dynamics changes, simulation is a promising approach [23]. This means an energy-oriented manufacturing system simulation is needed to provide the information for decision support. Figure 1 describes a conceptual structure of a systematic approaches of a highly flexible simulation environment with relevant energy flow of the subsystems in the factory [25].

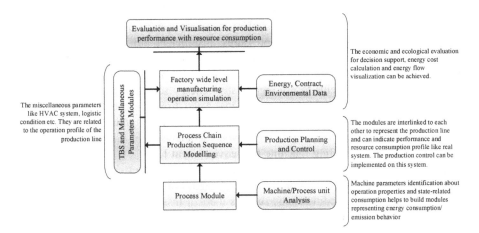

Fig. 2. Conceptual structure of energy-oriented manufacturing system simulation.

2.3 Factory Level

At the factory or whole plant level, there is a greater scope to adopt higher level simulation tools covering whole system configuration, production flow and management to improve efficiency. [3] the author elaborated two orthogonal frameworks: spatial and temporal consideration at factory level. The spatial framework is concerns with the spatial views of product feature, machine, line and supply chain. These spatial levels define the material choice, geometric design, machine-facility configuration, energy-source-waste chain and logistics issues. [26] summarizes the temporal framework characterizes the control of the whole environmental impact and the influence of facility consumptions. It covers the considerations through product design to manufacturing live-cycle assessment such as product/facility design, process/logistics design, process adjustment and pros-processing etc. As the decision-making moves along the temporal axis, the flexibility decreases which means less control over the planning.

Factory wide planning and scheduling methodologies are critically needed. The method should have the ability to accommodate complex interactions. Monitoring and data communication strategies are able to track the facility performance over spatial and temporal dimensions views. Production planning can be optimized at a facility level which is wider than the multi-machine scope in order to limit the total energy consumption.

Load management can also be conducted at the factory level where the peak load surcharge can be minimized; different workloads can be predicted and controlled. However, the monitoring and control at the whole factory level require significant amount of information about the machine/process status and more complex interdependencies between systems.

There are a number of building services that account for energy consumption in support of production, and in [23] Hermann and Thiede incorporated the energy efficiency improvement with production and technical building service (TBS). In support of production and demand for higher productivity, the TBS must consider facility management energy optimization. Technical measures can be used to locate unnecessary demands in temperature and pressures, insufficient utilization. And efficient process control (e.g. continuous runs, processing at favourite working points) to avoid unnecessary cost. Using techniques like combined heat and power cycles, and heat recovery with linked systems to use regenerative energy source and to reduce system losses (e.g. leakages and lacking of insulation). Apart from the energy consumed by machines, it is also found that the energy cost in HVAC and lighting of the working hall were found to be significant (40–65%) when he analysed the energy consumption and CO_2 emission for milling machine tool environment [27].

The concept of "green factory" is important for the process design where the energy and resources waste can be minimized and recovered. For the existing factories which cannot be re-designed, modifications, such as thermal insulation of facades, improvement on fenestration and control of gates or material ports, and illumination control can lead to energy saving (Fig. 2).

2.4   Section Summary

In this section, we have summarized different methods for three levels scope of more energy awareness and resource conservation at three levels, namely the unit process, multi-machine system and the whole factory (plant). The methods are further summarized in Table 1.

3   Scheduling for Sustainability

All relevant aspects must be taken into account to develop manufacturing systems, and with a systematic approach including product, process and system. To understand the linkage among these levels are crucial to achieve of sustainability. In Sect. 2, the most fundamental work needed includes the resource monitoring, analysis and reporting.

To make the whole manufacturing process truly intelligent with energy-ware capability. Scheduling is a prominent methodology in operation to determine the quality, quantity, and cost of production. Besides, scheduling can influence resource consumption efficiency and waste output. In the early stage, waste reducing with process efficiency improvement realized by process sequence scheduling was introduced in chemical industry [28]. More recent interests focus on wider industrial activities concerning operation scheduling for sustainable production has increased.

3.1   Operation Scheduling

The author in [29] reviewed several issues related to the sustainability in current manufacturing system including diverse nature of different conflicting objectives handled by the scheduling system, large numbers of objectives with complex relation

Table 1. Stratergies for promoting efficient and effectiveness manufacturing within a factory.

Methods	Scope	Objectives
Monitoring of energy or resource consumptions	I II III	Build profile for each unit/process Understanding energy/material flow Identify the saving/reuse potentials
Re-design and improvement of process unit	I	More energy efficient tool design
Process control, parameter optimization	I II	Working duty control to balance consumption and to improve energy efficiency and machine life-cycle Improve quality/cost ratio
Energy/Exergy cascade description	I II	Clarify the energy/exergy cascade pattern Re-use of waste heat, steam, water, scratch etc.
Production planning and scheduling	II III	Switch control of machines to energy efficiency Avoid consumption peak Take advantage of electricity price shift Enable energy-oriented manufacturing decision support
Spatial and temporal consideration	III	To have an integrated view of manufacturing design concerning energy consumption and environmental impact
Green building	III	To save the energy cost in the technical building services

I, II, III represent the scope level discussed in Sects. 2.1, 2.2 and 2.3 respectively.

with classical ones, increasing volatility of resources and mechanisms in processes, difficulty in designing accurate model for decision making and evaluation, and the oversized range of elements needed to be considered.

Giret et al. [29] analysed the common procedures for finding a satisfying sustainable operation scheduling solution. These procedures are described in Table 2, where four main steps are explained in the table. Firstly, a model representing operation system be developed with several objectives to optimize, and secondly, the scheduling model needed to be solved where multi-criteria must be handled. Depending on the objective models, the energy consumption, gas emission and waste generation etc. can all be modelled in relationship to the production operation state and control. However, due to the conflicting nature of many objectives, the scheduling problem may not have optimum solution and the problem is usually solved using a Pareto front and a satisfactory solution within multi-constrains can be achieved instead.

For example [30] proposed a pareto-based estimation of distribution algorithm to solve the multi-objective multi-mode resource-constrained project scheduling model with makespan and carbon emissions criteria in metal forming industry. The authors adopt an activity-mode list to encode and a modified serial schedule generation scheme to decode. A hybrid probability model to predict and track the probability distribution of the makespan and carbon emission scheduling solution space. The non-dominated solutions explored in search process and newly found updated solutions are stored in

Table 2. Steps to solve sustainable manufacturing operations scheduling problems.

Step	Task	Approaches
1	Build Optimization Model	Consider Sustainability Features (Consumption, emission) such as: Energy Consumption Model, CO2 Emission Model, Pollution Model, Waste Model
2	Formulize Scheduling Model	Multi-criteria (a) Optimize sustainability features subject to maintaining quality (e.g. effectiveness) of the scheduling (b) Optimize scheduling quality subject to maintaining a minimal level of sustainability (c) Optimize Jointly sustainability level and scheduling quality
3	Solve the Scheduling Problem	Scheduling method to use to solve the problem: (a) Find the Pareto front, using the selected scheduling method (b) Find the solution in the Pareto front that satisfies the constraints
4	Evaluate the solution	To judge whether the solution is feasible To judge whether relaxation or modification are needed

two Pareto archives. The newly updated individuals stored in archive are sampled in probability model.

3.2   Multi-objective Approaches for Solving Production Scheduling Problems

The production system inputs include energy, material, inventory, machine, etc. and the output are products, waste/pollution and scrap etc. A low-carbon production process might take more than one objectives, e.g. to minimize cost, to improve efficiency or to lower the pollution. In the multi-objective scheme, optimisation is to get an estimation of the Pareto optimal front, where the non-dominated solutions to the problem are presented.

3.2.1   Objective Considerations

It is a common practice to consider several performance indicators as the objectives in scheduling problems, e.g. processing time, the cost and quality of production. With the advent of green manufacturing, most of researchers prioritize energy as the key objective. Some researchers further consider green-house-gas (GHG) emissions, pollutions, or waste materials. The indicators relating to energy input and waste output can also be combined into a multi-objective operation problem, forming a mixed target with different priorities.

3.2.2   Case Examples of Manufacturing Operation Scheduling

Single Machine Systems

Considerable changes on energy consumption (mainly electricity) and the associated cost can be achieved when both dynamic pricing and peak energy reduction are combined as scheduling and control objectives [29]. [31] used a greedy randomised adaptive search procedure to solve the scheduling problem, in order to minimising the total energy consumption and total tardiness on a single machine with unequal release dates. [32] Considered the continuous changes in energy prices, the study shows that reduced energy consumption during peak times can be reduced and the proposed heuristic approach can provide optimal solutions in most cases.

In [33], the operational decision-making problem incorporating both economic and environmental performance on single machine system was studied. Focusing on deterministic product arrival time and processing rule, an optimization model with multi-objectives was developed to minimize the total completion time and at the same time reduce total carbon dioxide emission. A non-dominated sorting genetic algorithm II was shown to be superior to a previous proposed multi-objective genetic algorithm [34].

Job Shop Scheduling
[35] developed a genetic algorithm which excels for many classical job-shop scheduling problems where each operation has to be executed by one machine and that machine can work at different speeds, and the proposed method is better than commercial tools which are not able to solve large scale problem in a reasonable time. In [35] energy consumption was coded in a genetic algorithm to guide effective search for the optimized solution.

Energy and Makespan Consideration
[36] introduced a hybrid honey-bee mating optimization and simulated annealing to optimize multi-criteria including energy consumption, makespan, and machine utilization balancing. Similarly, [37] explored a multi-objective energy efficient scheduling problem with two objectives: makespan and energy consumption using mathematical model based on an energy-efficient mechanism in flexible flow shop scheduling problem. In order to generate Pareto-efficient solutions the weighted additive utility function technique was used, together with an improved genetic simulated annealing algorithm inspired from a hormone modulation mechanism.

[38] investigated a hybrid flexible system scheduling problem considering the energy efficiency aspect. The electricity price at different time of use was incorporated into a multi-objective optimization problem concerning production and energy efficiency. An ant colony optimization (MOACO) metaheuristic was developed to optimize both makespan and electric power consumption cost. They further compared MOACO with two popular multi-objective evolutionary algorithms: NSGA-II and SPEA2 and it was shown that though MOACO was slower but had generated better solutions.

In [39] the energy consumption for each operation was modelled and parameterized as a function of the operation execution time, and the energy-optimal schedule was derived by solving a mixed-integer nonlinear programming problem. Further, different objectives including the cycle time, energy consumption and sequences were considered.

Waste Management and Low-Carbon Manufacturing
Scheduling plays an important role in optimal allocation of plant resources. [40] used a non-dominant sorting genetic and local search algorithm to search for the minimal makespan, and minimal cleaning cost, and optimal solutions for composed objectives in paint industry batch production.

Focused on scheduling problem for a single machine, [41] used a mixed integer programming scheduling model to minimize the total carbon emissions during the whole planning horizon.

[42] developed a ε-archived genetic algorithm (ε-AGA) multi-objective genetic algorithm to obtain a wide range of near-Pareto-optimal solutions for two bi-criteria batch scheduling problems where the CO_2 emissions and due date-based objective are minimized. The proposed ε-AGA outperformed NSGA-II in the solutions by the former converge near the true Pareto-optimal set.

4 Modelling and Simulation Techniques

A feature of the intelligent manufacturing is transparency which means the details of manufacturing activities can be gained by manufactures. Then managers can use production control methods to control different aspects to fulfil various objectives, such as producing low cost products without compromising quality or even improving quality, and yet maintain the ability to prepare for production demand change with enough flexibility. When the optimization scope contains multiple machine interactions in production chain, advanced modelling techniques are extremely useful to cope with the complex individual cooperation and resource prediction.

The manufacturing system may experience structural changes during their operational life span resulting from adding new system components, replacing or retiring old equipment to react to the changes in products, technology or markets [43]. Because of the complexity and dynamic nature in the manufacturing systems the spreadsheet and flowcharts are almost impossible to capture the complicated process configuration and its complex constraints. [44] used Energy Blocks methodology for accurate energy consumption prediction, based on the segmentation of the production process into unit operations.

Simulation method provides practical and plausible way to investigate and evaluate manufacturing system issues. Using this tool, system information details and material flow can be clearly simulated and managed. And the simulation realizes the validation of production plan, control policy and reactions to operational problems. The discrete event system (DES) and agent-based simulation are two popular modelling tools for operation scheduling and control in manufacturing.

4.1 Discrete Event System Technique

The discrete event system is suitable for visually modelling dynamic nature of a complex discrete system. For example, problems like queue set up, visualization of each process status and process resource behaviours. Examples include: system simulation during the design stage, evaluating system performance such as utilization of machines, system design, and comparing operation strategies [43]. Discrete event system/ Discrete event dynamic system (DES/DEDS) can be defined as an interacting set of entities that evolve through different states as internal or external events occur [45]. In the discrete event system modelling, simulated system changes only at discrete time when the event is triggered to change.

4.1.1   Planning and Queues, Delivering

In manufacturing, the supply is not constant and the production schedule of resources varies frequently. [46] investigated the procedures used for the planning of a material delivery system in a manufacturing line of an electronic company. [47] used discrete event simulation model to allow dynamic interaction with the scheduler of the planning support system. A virtual steel yard model is built to manage the steel-plate piling plan efficiently.

4.1.2   Behaviour of Process Resources

In [32] the authors used discrete system modelling to identify three states of a machine: processing' (i.e., productive), 'idle' (i.e., working but non-productive), and 'shut down'. Two transition times and their energy costs are incorporated in this model, including the elapsed time when switching from shut down to processing (i.e., turning on) and vice versa (i.e., turning off).

In electronics assembly line where many decisions are based on workers experience, [48] introduced the DES to provide better understanding of the production environment showing the bottlenecks and the impact of each production parameters. [49] investigation on the capacity planning of a mobile phone remanufacturing industry is discussed by Franke et al. The discrete event system was applied to represent quick changing product, process and market constraints. A flexible discrete event system model for identifying production resource usage and line capacity planning with cost analysis in a manufacturing system was proposed in [50].

4.2   Agent-Based Modelling

The agent-based system is often built using the bottom up approach. It starts with individual agents, define their characteristics and behaviours, and let them interact in the agent's environment [51]. Each agent can be defined as a computational system which means that the knowledge of discrete event system techniques can be used to represent the dynamics of the agent. In the dynamics of the environment where an agent may have an environment that includes other agents, community of interacting agents as a whole operates as a multi-agent system [52]. A typical agent can contain attributes, goals, rules, behaviour and memories, then each agent can interact with other agents, the agents can also interact with environment.

4.2.1   Multi-agent Modelling Simulation

A multi-agent system (MAS) can be formed by a network of computational agents that interact and typically communicate with each other as the big family of distributed information system [53]. Each agent has the ability to represent a production resource, not only the machines can be modelled, but the production itself can be represented. Therefore, the production order and logistical scheduling can be modelled using MAS. The MAS needs advanced algorithms in distributed control where each agent representing machine/product can generate decisions for manufacturing control. The distributed control solution takes the advantage of resource allocation possibility and coordination result from automated negotiation among agents.

Yeung proposed a formal approach to address the potential behavioural problems of multi-agent systems for manufacturing control applications, and verified the [54].

Li et al. applied a pheromone based approach using the multi-agent system for a scheduling problem in a cellular manufacturing system to establish flexible route for machine performing in multiple jobs [55]. And the colony optimization technique was used for negotiation among agents.

In [56], a system-based simulation methodology was proposed to solve a backward on-line job change scheduling problem. The system performed with a state transition defined as a combination of the job and machine states. It has been widely believed that the future work of agent-based manufacturing should focus on the integration of agent-abased planning and scheduling with existing systems used in the manufacturing enterprises. The most important integration is with real time data collection systems, including SCADA systems and RFID systems as well as ERP and MRP systems.

5 Conclusion

Currently most of the research of intelligent scheduling are for discrete manufacturing system, and less effort in continuous batch processing. Practical case study on factory level wide planning and scheduling methodologies considering multiple interactions are required to solve complex interdependent and synergistic problems. Some prospects about future research can be drawn from the literatures. Proactive and reactive response to scheduling under uncertainty need further investigation.

In this paper, the resource efficient intelligent manufacturing is reviewed at three different levels, namely the unit process, production line and factory wide where strategies of energy saving, resource recycling and process control are discussed. Various methodologies to describe the energy/material flow and process states are reviewed, which can support decision-making for and identification of the bottlenecks of further improvements. Resource recycle scheme and process chain control play a key role in production line energy-aware optimization. The load and capacity control can be conducted through each level and performs well in energy cost reduction. At the factory level, considerations other than direct manufacturing subsystem like building service cannot be neglected. The energy awareness and resource flow need to be taken into account throughout the design, processing, post-processing stages.

Approaches to the multiple objective scheduling problems approaches are also surveyed in Sect. 3. The diverse nature of different conflicting objectives in production scheduling constitutes complex operation control problem. The problem is usually solved through a pareto front based on which a desirable solution is selected. Simulation is the required to investigate and evaluate manufacturing issues. Various simulation models also help manage material and information flows in the system. The discrete event system is able to build up a queue system and include information about the process resources, while assist to visualize internal aspects for supervision. Agent-based modelling technique which is more flexible than the DES method, allows adaptability, scalability and modularity which are essential for modelling a plant-wide complex system.

References

1. Mařík, V., Schirrmann, A., Trentesaux, D., Vrba, P. (eds.): HoloMAS 2015. LNCS (LNAI), vol. 9266. Springer, Cham (2015). https://doi.org/10.1007/978-3-319-22867-9
2. Trentesaux, D., Prabhu, V.: Sustainability in manufacturing operations scheduling: stakes, approaches and trends. In: Grabot, B., Vallespir, B., Gomes, S., Bouras, A., Kiritsis, D. (eds.) APMS 2014. IAICT, vol. 439, pp. 106–113. Springer, Heidelberg (2014). https://doi.org/10.1007/978-3-662-44736-9_13
3. Duflou, J.R., et al.: Towards energy and resource efficient manufacturing: a processes and systems approach. CIRP Ann. **61**, 587–609 (2012)
4. Roghanian, P., Rasli, A., Gheysari, H.: Productivity through effectiveness and efficiency in the banking industry. Procedia Soc. Behav. Sci. **40**, 550–556 (2012)
5. Brandimarte, P., Villa, A.: Modeling Manufacturing Systems: From Aggregate Planning to Real-Time Control. Springer, Heidelberg (2013). https://doi.org/10.1007/978-3-662-03853-6
6. Abele, E., Anderl, R., Birkhofer, H.: Environmentally-Friendly Product Development. Springer, London (2005). https://doi.org/10.1007/b138604
7. Kellens, K., Dewulf, W., Overcash, M., Hauschild, M.Z., Duflou, J.R.: Methodology for systematic analysis and improvement of manufacturing unit process life-cycle inventory (UPLCI)—CO$_2$PE! initiative (cooperative effort on process emissions in manufacturing). Part 1: Methodology description. Int. J. Life Cycle Assess. **17**, 69–78 (2012)
8. Zein, A.: Transition Towards Energy Efficient Machine Tools. Springer, Heidelberg (2012). https://doi.org/10.1007/978-3-642-32247-1
9. Duflou, J.R., Kellens, K., Dewulf, W.: Environmental performance of sheet metal working processes. In: Key Engineering Materials, pp. 21–26. Trans Tech Publ. (2011)
10. Dotchev, K., Yusoff, W.: Recycling of polyamide 12 based powders in the laser sintering process. Rapid Prototyp. J. **15**, 192–203 (2009)
11. Diaz, N., Helu, M., Jarvis, A., Tonissen, S., Dornfeld, D., Schlosser, R.: Strategies for minimum energy operation for precision machining (2009)
12. Saidur, R., Rahim, N.A., Hasanuzzaman, M.: A review on compressed-air energy use and energy savings. Renew. Sustain. Energy Rev. **14**, 1135–1153 (2010)
13. Bittencourt, J.L., Bonefeld, R., Scholze, S., Stokic, D., Uddin, M.K., Lastra, J.L.M.: Energy efficiency improvement through context sensitive self-learning of machine availability. In: 2011 9th IEEE International Conference on Industrial Informatics, pp. 93–98 (2011)
14. Mori, M., Fujishima, M., Inamasu, Y., Oda, Y.: A study on energy efficiency improvement for machine tools. CIRP Ann. **60**, 145–148 (2011)
15. Li, Y., Liu, H., Li, J., Tao, J.: Process parameters optimization for energy saving in paper machine dryer section. Dry. Technol. **29**, 910–917 (2011)
16. Afshar, P., Brown, M., Maciejowski, J., Wang, H.: Data-based robust multiobjective optimization of interconnected processes: energy efficiency case study in papermaking. IEEE Trans. Neural Netw. **22**, 2324–2338 (2011)
17. Zhang, L., Wu, L., Zhang, X., Ju, G.: Comparison and optimization of mid-low temperature cogeneration systems for flue gas in iron and steel plants. J. Iron. Steel Res. Int. **20**, 33–40 (2013)
18. Bejan, A.: Fundamentals of exergy analysis, entropy generation minimization, and the generation of flow architecture. Int. J. Energy Res. **26**, 1–43 (2002)
19. Wang, Z., Zheng, D., Jin, H.: Energy integration of acetylene and power polygeneration by flowrate-exergy diagram. Appl. Energy **86**, 372–379 (2009)

20. Thekdi, A., Nimbalkar, S.U.: Industrial Waste Heat Recovery - Potential Applications, Available Technologies and Crosscutting R&D Opportunities. Oak Ridge National Laboratory (ORNL), Oak Ridge, TN, USA (2015)

21. Karellas, S., Leontaritis, A.-D., Panousis, G., Bellos, E., Kakaras, E.: Energetic and exergetic analysis of waste heat recovery systems in the cement industry. Energy **58**, 147–156 (2013)

22. Logožar, K., Radonjič, G., Bastič, M.: Incorporation of reverse logistics model into in-plant recycling process: a case of aluminium industry. Resour. Conserv. Recycl. **49**, 49–67 (2006)

23. Herrmann, C., Thiede, S.: Process chain simulation to foster energy efficiency in manufacturing. CIRP J. Manuf. Sci. Technol. **1**, 221–229 (2009)

24. Jia, Z., Zhang, L., Arinez, J., Xiao, G.: Performance analysis for serial production lines with Bernoulli Machines and Real-time WIP-based Machine switch-on/off control. Int. J. Prod. Res. **54**, 6285–6301 (2016)

25. Herrmann, C., Thiede, S., Kara, S., Hesselbach, J.: Energy oriented simulation of manufacturing systems – concept and application. CIRP Ann. **60**, 45–48 (2011)

26. Reich-Weiser, C., Vijayaraghavan, A., Dornfeld, D.: Appropriate use of green manufacturing frameworks (2010)

27. Diaz, N., Helu, M., Jayanathan, S., Chen, Y., Horvath, A., Dornfeld, D.: Environmental analysis of milling machine tool use in various manufacturing environments. In: Proceedings of the 2010 IEEE International Symposium on Sustainable Systems and Technology, pp. 1–6 (2010)

28. Grau, R., Espuña, A., Puigjaner, L.: Environmental considerations in batch production scheduling (1995)

29. Giret, A., Trentesaux, D., Prabhu, V.: Sustainability in manufacturing operations scheduling: a state of the art review. J. Manuf. Syst. **37**, 126–140 (2015)

30. Zheng, H., Wang, L.: Reduction of carbon emissions and project makespan by a Pareto-based estimation of distribution algorithm. Int. J. Prod. Econ. **164**, 421–432 (2015)

31. Mouzon, G., Yildirim, M.B.: A framework to minimise total energy consumption and total tardiness on a single machine. Int. J. Sustain. Eng. **1**, 105–116 (2008)

32. Shrouf, F., Ordieres-Meré, J., García-Sánchez, A., Ortega-Mier, M.: Optimizing the production scheduling of a single machine to minimize total energy consumption costs. J. Clean. Prod. **67**, 197–207 (2014)

33. Liu, C., Yang, J., Lian, J., Li, W., Evans, S., Yin, Y.: Sustainable performance oriented operational decision-making of single machine systems with deterministic product arrival time. J. Clean. Prod. **85**, 318–330 (2014)

34. Yildirim, M.B., Mouzon, G.: Single-machine sustainable production planning to minimize total energy consumption and total completion time using a multiple objective genetic algorithm. IEEE Trans. Eng. Manag. **59**, 585–597 (2012)

35. Escamilla, J., Salido, M.A., Giret, A., Barber, F.: A metaheuristic technique for energy-efficiency in job-shop scheduling. Knowl. Eng. Rev. **31**, 475–485 (2016)

36. Li, X., Li, W., Cai, X., He, F.: A honey-bee mating optimization approach of collaborative process planning and scheduling for sustainable manufacturing. In: Proceedings of the 2013 IEEE 17th International Conference on Computer Supported Cooperative Work in Design (CSCWD), pp. 465–470 (2013)

37. Dai, M., Tang, D., Giret, A., Salido, M.A., Li, W.D.: Energy-efficient scheduling for a flexible flow shop using an improved genetic-simulated annealing algorithm. Robot. Comput.-Integr. Manuf. **29**, 418–429 (2013)

38. Luo, H., Du, B., Huang, G.Q., Chen, H., Li, X.: Hybrid flow shop scheduling considering machine electricity consumption cost. Int. J. Prod. Econ. **146**, 423–439 (2013)

39. Vergnano, A., et al.: Embedding detailed robot energy optimization into high-level scheduling. In: 2010 IEEE International Conference on Automation Science and Engineering, pp. 386–392 (2010)

40. Adonyi, R., Biros, G., Holczinger, T., Friedler, F.: Effective scheduling of a large-scale paint production system. J. Clean. Prod. **16**, 225–232 (2008)

41. Wang, X., Ding, H., Qiu, M., Dong, J.: A low-carbon production scheduling system considering renewable energy. In: Proceedings of 2011 IEEE International Conference on Service Operations, Logistics and Informatics, pp. 101–106 (2011)

42. Liu, C.-H.: Approximate trade-off between minimisation of total weighted tardiness and minimisation of carbon dioxide (CO_2) emissions in bi-criteria batch scheduling problem. Int. J. Comput. Integr. Manuf. **27**, 759–771 (2014)

43. Seleim, Azab, A., AlGeddawy, T.: Simulation methods for changeable manufacturing. Procedia CIRP **3**, 179–184 (2012)

44. Weinert, N., Chiotellis, S., Seliger, G.: Methodology for planning and operating energy-efficient production systems. CIRP Ann. **60**, 41–44 (2011)

45. Robinson, S.: Simulation: The Practice of Model Development and Use. Wiley, Chichester, Hoboken (2004)

46. Costa, B., Dias, L.S., Oliveira, J.A., Pereira, G.: Simulation as a tool for planning a material delivery system to manufacturing lines. In: 2008 IEEE International Engineering Management Conference, pp. 1–5 (2008)

47. Lee, S., et al.: Steel-yard planning support system: Optimizing the steel-yard planning and performance evaluation with simulation. In: 2012 12th International Conference on Control, Automation and Systems, pp. 605–609 (2012)

48. Gebus, S., Soulas, A., Juuso, E.: Short term scheduling in electronics manufacturing using discrete-event simulation. Proc. SIMS–Scand. Simul. Soc. 2013, 1–7 (2013)

49. Franke, C., Basdere, B., Ciupek, M., Seliger, S.: Remanufacturing of mobile phones—capacity, program and facility adaptation planning. Omega **34**, 562–570 (2006)

50. Gregg, M.L., Van Andel, S.M., Saylor, S.E.: Lean+ manufacturing process analysis simulation (LPAS+). In: Proceedings of the Winter Simulation Conference. Winter Simulation Conference, Phoenix, Arizona, pp. 2171–2180 (2011)

51. Van Dyke Parunak, H., Savit, R., Riolo, Rick L.: Agent-Based Modeling vs. Equation-Based Modeling: A Case Study and Users' Guide. In: Sichman, J.S., Conte, R., Gilbert, N. (eds.) MABS 1998. LNCS (LNAI), vol. 1534, pp. 10–25. Springer, Heidelberg (1998). https://doi.org/10.1007/10692956_2

52. Jeon, S.M., Kim, G.: A survey of simulation modeling techniques in production planning and control (PPC). Prod. Plan. Control. **27**, 360–377 (2016)

53. Monostori, L., Váncza, J., Kumara, S.R.T.: Agent-based systems for manufacturing. CIRP Ann. **55**, 697–720 (2006)

54. Yeung, W.L.: Behavioral modeling and verification of multi-agent systems for manufacturing control. Expert Syst. Appl. **38**, 13555–13562 (2011)

55. Li, D., Wang, Y., Xiao, G., Tang, J.: Dynamic parts scheduling in multiple job shop cells considering intercell moves and flexible routes. Comput. Oper. Res. **40**, 1207–1223 (2013)

56. Kim, T., Choi, B.K.: Production system-based simulation for backward on-line job change scheduling. Simul. Model. Pract. Theory **40**, 12–27 (2014)

Manufacturing Process

Experimental Research on Synchronous Manufacturing Technology for Blisk Using Different Polishing Method

Guijian Xiao[(⊠)], Yun Huang, Lai Zou, Ying Liu, Wentao Dai,
Quan Li, Shui He, Geshan Luo, and Suolang Jiahua

The State Key Laboratory of Mechanical Transmissions,
Chongqing University, Chongqing 400044, China
xiaoguijian@cqu.edu.cn

Abstract. Blisk is one of the most important parts in advanced aero-engine, its surface processing quality directly affects the performance of aero-engine. However, it is difficult to polish the blisk at once, because of deep and narrow space, free-form surfaces, easy deformation and interference, poor reach ability, difficult-to-cut materials, and so on, so, it is difficult to guarantee the surface quality for compliance with strict industrial standards to blisk. For this aims, two different polishing methods, called six-axis linkage belt polishing and robot wire-wheel polishing, are used in this paper. The experimental results show that the surface quality meets the manufacturing requirements when different methods are used for different areas of the blisk. It is proved that this method could be integrated to enable automated polishing of blisk full-area surfaces.

Keywords: Blisk · Belt polishing · Wire-wheel polishing · Six-axis linkage
Robot

1 Introduction

As a key part of an aero-engine, the profile accuracy and surface qualityof blisk influence the engine usability. At present, the main manufacturing technology for blisk is precision forging-precision milling. However, the characteristics of the blisk machining process, including the elastic contact, shape change from weak-rigidity and non-uniform margin distribution, make it difficult to ensure high surface precision and quality [1]. The abrasive belt polishing technology is considered to be an ideal processing method for titanium alloy parts because of the characteristics of high efficiency, high precision, flexibility and cold grinding [2]. At present, the precision machining of the blisk surface is achieved by manual grinding mostly, for improving the efficiency and quality of machining processing, the belt polishing technology is combined with multi-axis CNC machine tools and robot grinding [3].

There have mainy researches on using the method of belt polishing as a final machining operation for components, including blade, blisk and so on, has also been investigated. The effects of different grinding methods, bob polishing or belt polishing, on the surface quality and integrity of workpiece for the the GH4169 nickel-based

© Springer Nature Singapore Pte Ltd. 2018
S. Wang et al. (Eds.): ICSEE 2018/IMIOT 2018, CCIS 923, pp. 363–370, 2018.
https://doi.org/10.1007/978-981-13-2396-6_34

superalloy have also been reported [4]. Huang et al. [5] presented the method of new belt polishing to forming micro-stiffener on the workpiece surface to improving the fatigue life with, and then the formation rule of residual stress, surface and sub-surface, with different belt polishing parameters is studied. Xiao et al. [6] introduced a method to obtained longitudinal micromarks along the root-fillet of blisk, and the interference avoidance and path planning are also studied to realize the belt polishing for the root-fillet of blisk. Klaus er al. [7] proposed a simulation method to predict the regenerative vibration of workpiece during milling in order to solve the problems of flutter in the milling of thin wall structural parts of five-axis machine tools, this method carries out real-time simulation analysis of the dynamic characteristics of workpieces in the process of machining by means of finite element method, and verified the feasibility of the simulation method through experiments.

An effective process based on robotic belt polishing for material removal from geometrically complex workpieces has been examined for optimal selection of the grinding parameters [8]. Zhang et al. [9] proposed a new structure of a robotic grinding system, including active frame and passive tool frame, and the dexterity of the system is affected by the position of the contact wheel relative to the robot. Zhang et al. proposed a new model, support vector regression technique, to calculate the force distribution, and then the errors of less than 5% were achieved [10]. Sun et al. [11] studiedthe system calibration and force control to improving the grinding performance, and the position error is reduced from 100 μm to 50 μm. Xiao et al. [12] using the integrated method with CNC belt polishing and robot bob polishing for blade, and the surface roughness and the profile precision are meeting the requrements. Ren et al. [13] calculateed the acting force by incorporating the local geometry information, which is changed from the cutting depth parameter with only one certain value, and the simulation accuracy can be improved to below 5%. The new concepts of the dexterity grinding point and the dexterity grinding space have been proposed to improving the surface quality of robotic belt polishing systems for complex surface shapes [14].

From the above analysis, the methods of belt polishing and wire-wheel polishing both have their own advantages; both methods would be able to perform surface polishing of titanium alloy materials, and the overall surface roughness would also be improved. Therefore, if these methods could be integrated, by combining the six-axis linkage with automated robot technology, the blisk full-area surface would be polished using a single machine.

2   Experiment and Methodology

2.1   Experimental Equipment and Aim

The experimental equipment for the blisk machining was carried out by using a self-developed multi-station integrated numerical control equipment, which integrated with two six-axis linkage machine and a automatic robot. The experimental equipment is comprised with new belt polishing head, bed, column and guide, as shown in Fig. 1. The blisk full-area surface, including disc flowing surface (DFS), blade root (BR), leading edge (LE), training edge (TE), blade concave (CC) and blade convex (CV), are all shown in Fig. 1. The TE, LE, CC and CV surfaces are polished based on a complex surface reconstruction process with a allowance using the six-axis linkage and the method of force precision control.

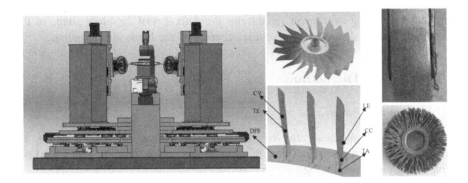

Fig. 1. Experimental equipment

The robot wire-wheel polishing machine, which included the robot, with the flexible shaft and the clamping system, is used to polish the TA and RP of blisk, as shown in Fig. 1. The TA and RP are polished based on a free-form surface reconstruction process with a removal allowance via auto-control of the robot. And the wire-wheel is also commonly used in coated abrasive tools, which are known as super beautician tools, as shown in Fig. 1. These wheels are highly efficient, economical and widely used grinding and polishing tools, and provide good grinding and polishing performances. In addition to being economical, the wheels are flexible and adaptable, and are commonly used for grinding the flat, circular, cylindrical, and deep holes, even many kinds of specially-shaped surface.

2.2 Experimental Methodology

The blisk was installed on a high-precision turntable, the rotary motion of the work-table is realized by connecting the blisk and worktable. The blisk sample from an aircraft engine was used. The blisk was made from precision-milled, Ti-6-4 heat-resistant alloy. The parameters that were used in this experiment were rotation speed of 15 m/s, feeding speed of 0.5 m/min, and grinding pressureof 6 N. The belt and wire-wheel is shown in Firue1, and other important parameters were as follows:

(a) The belt polishing process used a backward feed direction and 3 M nylon belts (5 mm width) with the following grades: (i) randomly distributed grains; and (ii) grains formed into pyramids.
(b) The wire-wheel polishing process used a backward feed direction and off-the shelf and custom 10 mm diameter tools made from the following 3 M abrasive materials/grades: SiC Scotch-Brite 2 Fine; and polycrystalline diamond (PCD74 —mesh 250).

The blisk full-area test planning is as follows:A1 and A6 are the testing points for the surface roughness and topography, A2 and A4 are the CC testing points, and A3 and A5 are the V testing points. L1–L6 represents the profile precision testing line. In this experiment, roughness instrument TR200 manufactured by Beijing Times Group was used to determine the roughness parameter Ra. The Hexagon-made three-coordinate measuring instrument suitable for the detection of the blade shape of the entire blade was used to detect the profile accuracy of the blade after grinding.

3   Results and Discussions

3.1   Surface Roughness

The blisk surface roughness after belt polishing are shown in Fig. 2. 5 points are measured on each sections, and then, the max-roughness, the min-roughness and the average-roughness, are obtained.

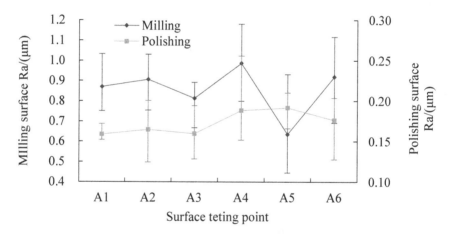

Fig. 2. Surface roughness

The surface roughness Ra after precision-milling is from 0.45 μm to 1.18 μm, as shown in Fig. 2. However, the surface roughness Ra of the blisk blade is from 0.138 μm to 0.242 μm after belt polishing. And the average surface roughness Ra of A1, A2 and A3 are from 0.131 μm to 0.212 μm, at the same time, the average surface roughness Ra of A4, A5 and A6 are from 0.108 μm to 0.281 μm.

According to the analysis of the surface roughness, after belt polishing, the blisk full-area surface Ra values would be all less than 0.30 μm, which meeting the requirements of the blisk surface roughness ($\leq$ 0.4 μm), irrespective of the method used in this experiment.

3.2 Surface Topography

The microscopic analysis after belt polishing for the compressor blade surface is shown in Fig. 3. The surface topography is measured by the fe-SEM (JSM-7800F), the electronic resolution is 2 nm. The surface topographies at A1, A2 and A3 are better than those at A4, A5 and A6. The surface is scratched by the cracked grain. This mainly because of the charateristics of belt polishing process, including the flexible and cold characteristics, and so on. So, the method of belt polishing plays a inportant role in improving the surface quality, the surface texture, and the microscopic surface structure.

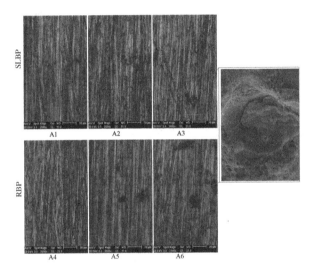

Fig. 3. Surface topography

3.3 Profile Precision

The surface profile precision errors of the CC and CV surfaces are shown in Fig. 4, and the the average values of surface profile precision errors are obtained by testing each line three times. The CC surface profile precision errors range from 0.019 mm to 0.049 mm, and the CV surface profile precision errors range from 0.03 mm to 0.05 mm.

The above analysis shows that the CV profile precision is better than the CC profile precision. This is mainly because of contact area between the belt and the CV surface is small, so the profile precisiona is improved.

The test results for edge profile shape are shown in Table 1, where the edge shape represents the TE and LE requirements for each test line, and the errors for the TE and LE are shown in Fig. 5. Figure 5 shows the profile precision of the LE and TE of the edge shape, where the errors range from −0.045 mm to 0.05 mm.

The TA profile shape test results are shown in Table 2, where the TA requirement is 5 mm, and the error is ±1 mm for each test line, and the TA errors are as shown in

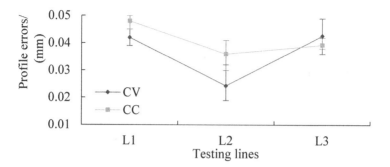

Fig. 4. The profile precision errors for the CC and CV surface

Table 1. TE and LE testing results

Data		Type					
		Leading edge			Trailing edge		
Line 1	Real-R	0.34	0.3	0.32	0.19	0.21	0.23
	Testing		0.27			0.26	
Line 2	Real-R	0.21	0.26	0.22	0.45	0.42	0.39
	Testing		0.24			0.38	
Line 3	Real-R	0.31	0.28	0.29	0.49	0.47	0.5
	Testing		0.25			0.51	

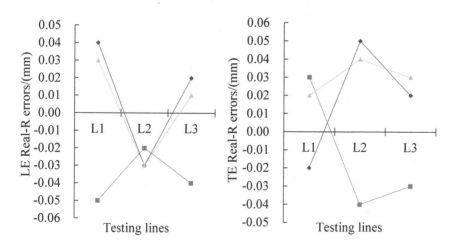

Fig. 5. The Profile precision of LE and TE real-R: (a) LE profile (b) TE profile

Fig. 5. As shown in Table 2, the TA test results range from 4.24 mm to 5.8 mm, which are all under the manufacturing requirement. Figure 6 shows the TA profile precision, where the errors range from −0.86 mm to +0.70 mm.

Table 2. TA testing results

Data	Type					
	CV			CC		
L4	4.5	4.7	4.6	5.5	4.7	4.2
L5	5.8	5.3	5.7	5.6	4.9	5.1
L6	5.2	5.4	04.8	4.4	5.2	5.0

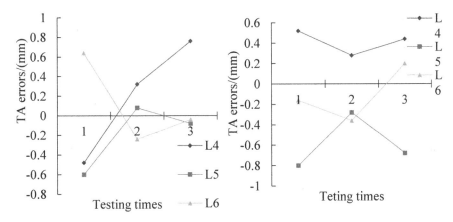

Fig. 6. The Profile precision of TA: (a) TA profile for CV surface (b) TA profile for CC surface

The profile precision errors for the TE, LE, CC and CV surfaces are all ±0.05 mm, and the TA errors are ±1 mm. According to the analysis indicates that the method used in this paper is verified.

4 Summary

The polishing planning of blisk full-area surfaces are introduced with six-axis linkage belt polishing and robot wire-wheel polishing. The results are summarized as follows:

1. After CNC belt polishing and robot wire-wheel polishing, the surface texture is smooth and shows good consistency, the surface defects and the transition region are completely eliminated, and the surface texture is fine.
2. The blisk full-area surface Ra would be less than 0.30 μm throughout, which meeting the surface roughness requirements (≤ 0.4 μm), irrespective of the methods used in the experiments.
3. The profile precision errors for the TE, LE, CC and CV are ±0.05 mm, and the TA errors are ±1 mm. They are all under the requirements of blisk profile precision.

The overall results suggest that the integrated methods could be used to automated polishing of blisk full-area surfaces.

Acknowledgments. This work was supported by National Natural Science Foundation of China (Grant No. 51705047) and the fundamental research funds for the central universities (Grant no. 2018CDQYCD0038, 106112017CDJXY110005, 106112017CDJRC000011, 106112017CDJPT 280003).

References

1. Huang, Y., Xiao, G.J., Zou, L.: Current situation and development trend of polishing technology for blisk. Acta Aeronautica et Astronautica Sinica **37**(7), 2045–2064 (2016)
2. Volkov, D.I., Koryazhkin, A.A.: Adaptive belt grinding of gas turbine blades. Russ. Eng. Res. **34**(1), 37–40 (2014)
3. Xu, W.X., Shi, Y.Y.: Automatic polishing technology of blisk robot. J. Mach. Des. **27**(7), 47–50 (2010)
4. Axinte, D.A., Kwong, J., Kong, M.C.: Workpiece surface integr ity of Ti-6-4 heat-resistant alloy when employing different polishing methods. J. Mater. Process. Technol. **209**, 1843–1852 (2009)
5. Huang, Y., Xiao, G.J., Zhao, H.Q., Zou, L., Zhao, L., Liu, Y., Dai, W.T.: Residual stress of micro-stiffener surface with belt polishing for the titanium alloys. Procedia CIRP **71**, 11–15 (2018)
6. Xiao, G.J., Huang, Y., Wang, J.: Path planning method for the longitudinal micro-marks on the root-fillet of blisk with belt grinding. Int. J. Adv. Manuf. Technol. **95**(1–4), 797–810 (2018)
7. Kersting, P., Biermann, D.: Simulation concept for predicting workpiece vibrations in five-axis milling. Mach. Sci. Technol. **13**(2), 196–209 (2009)
8. Ren, X.Y., Kuhlenkötter, B.: Real-time simulation and visualization of robotic belt grinding processes. Int. J. Adv. Manuf. Technol. **35**(11–12), 1090–1099 (2008)
9. Zhang, D., Yun, C., Song, D.Z.: Dexterous space optimization for robotic belt grinding. Procedia Eng. **15**, 2762–2766 (2011)
10. Zhang, X., Kuhlenkotter, B., Kneupner, K.: An efficient method for solving the Signorini problem in the simulation of free-form surfaces produced by belt grinding. Int. J. Mach. Tools Manuf. **45**, 641–648 (2005)
11. Sun, Y.Q., Giblin, D.J., Kazerounian, K.: Accurate robotic belt grinding of workpieces with complex geometries using relative calibration techniques. Robot. Comput. Integr. Manuf. **25**, 204–210 (2009)
12. Xiao, G.J., Huang, Y., Yin, J.C.: An integrated polishing method for compressor blade surfaces. Int. J. Adv. Manuf. Technol. **88**(5–8), 1723–1733 (2017)
13. Ren, X., Cabaravdic, M., Zhang, X., Kuhlenkotter, B.: A local process model for simulation of robotic belt grinding. Int. J. Mach. Tools Manuf **47**, 962–970 (2007)
14. Gao, Z.H., Lan, X.D., Bian, Y.S.: Structural dimension optimization of robotic belt grinding system for grinding workpieces with complex shaped surfaces based on dexterity grinding space. Chin. J. Aeronaut. **24**, 346–354 (2011)

Research on Early Failure Elimination Technology of NC Machine Tools

Yulong Li[✉], Genbao Zhang, Yongqin Wang,
Xiaogang Zhang, and Yan Ran

State Key Laboratory of Mechanical Transmission,
Chongqing University, Chongqing 400044, China
1004762383@qq.com

Abstract. The frequent occurrence of early failure has long been restricting the corrective of the reliability of domestic numerical control (NC) machine tools. At present, there is a lack of a systematic and effective method to eliminate the early failure of machine tools. The difficulty in eliminating the early failure of the machine tools lies in how to calculate its early failure period accurately and design the failure closed-loop elimination program properly. So, a 4-parameter non-homogeneous Poisson process (NHPP) modeling method and a closed-loop elimination system for the early failure of the machine tools were proposed to solve those problems in this paper. The method proposed in this paper is applied to the enterprise, and its feasibility is verified. The research of this paper lays a foundation for the elimination of the early failure and the improvement of the reliability level of the domestic NC machine tools.

Keywords: Early failure · NC machine tools · Closed-loop elimination Reliability

1 Introduction

Generally speaking, NC machine tools will experience three stages: early failure period, accidental failure period and wearing failure period, and the causes and manifestations of the failures in each stage are different [1]. The early failure occurs in the early operation stage of the machine tools, which greatly reduces the reliability of the machine tools and increases the company's maintenance costs and damages the company's market image. At the same time, it also makes the reliability level of domestic machine tools far lower than that of the European and American countries [2]. Therefore, it has a great significance to study the early failure elimination technology of the machine tools.

At present, the difficulty in the early failure elimination technology of machine tools lies in the rational design and implementation of the failure closed-loop elimination system. Failure Report, Analysis and Corrective Action System (FRACAS) is a relatively mature and effective closed-loop management system, which utilizes the principle of "information feedback and closed-loop control" to promptly report product failures and analyze failures causes and formulate and implement effective corrective actions to prevent similar failures from recurring [3, 4]. The purpose of improving the

S. Wang et al. (Eds.): ICSEE 2018/IMIOT 2018, CCIS 923, pp. 371–381, 2018.
https://doi.org/10.1007/978-981-13-2396-6_35

reliability of the machine tools can finally be achieved by FRACAS. At present, there are few literatures about NC machine tools FRACAS system, and these researches are mostly about machine tools parts, such as literature [3], and lack of exploration for establishing the closed-loop elimination system of the whole machine tools. The pre-condition of the design of the early failure closed-loop elimination system of the machine tools is to calculate the early failure period, and the early failure period cannot be calculated accurately without the reasonable failure model. The existing failure models of NC machine tools are built all most on the basis of the assumption that the maintenance is a "repair as new" process, such as literature [5, 6]. However, for the maintainable complex mechanical and electrical products such as NC machine tools, it is more reasonable to regard the repair process as "repairing as old" [7]. At the same time, the failures of NC machine tools occur randomly in its operation, and the failure intensity is not a constant [8]. So, it is more practical to use the NHPP model based on random point process to describe the failure of machine tools.

Based on the idea of "information feedback and closed-loop control", an early failure closed-loop elimination system for NC machine tools is established in this paper. A 4-parameter NHPP modeling method is also put forward and the early failure period of machine tools is obtained. The research is applied to a machine tools manufacturing enterprise, and has achieved good results. The results also verify the feasibility of this method.

2 Early Failure Model

2.1 Early Failure Definition

Numerous studies and practices have shown that the relationship between the failure characteristics of machine tools and time is in the form of a "bathtub" under the prescribed operation environment, use and maintenance conditions, which is commonly called the bathtub curve [9], and its shape is shown in Fig. 1 [10].

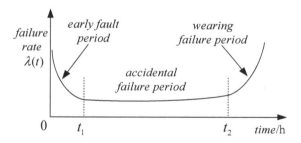

Fig. 1. Bathtub curve

In the Fig. 1, t_1 is the transition point between the early failure period and accidental failure period of the machine tools, namely early failure time inflection point, and the time from 0 to t_1 is called the early failure period of the machine tools. It can be seen that the failure rate of machine tools is higher in this period and decreases with the increase of operation time. During the early failure period, the failures of machine tools are mainly caused by unreasonable product design, quality defects of parts processing, quality defects of purchased parts and unreasonable assembly process. Therefore, the failure caused by defects in the process of design, manufacture and assembly in the early failure period is defined as the early failure of the machine tools.

2.2   Early Failure Modeling

The failure rate of NC machine tools is generally presented as the shape of the bathtub curve, and the failure rate curve does not have a monotonous trend. Therefore, the NHPP process needs to be improved. It is well known that the superposition of a number of independent non-homogeneous Poisson processes is still a non-homogeneous Poisson process [11], so the failure intensity function of NC machine tools can be expressed as follows:

$$\lambda(t) = \lambda_1(t) + \lambda_2(t) \tag{1}$$

For the bathtub curve, its early failure period can be described by the power law process (PLP) model [12], but the failure intensity function of the model will have a large mutation in the vicinity of $t = 0$, which is quite different from the actual situation. Therefore, the log-linear process (LLP) model is used to describe the early failure period of the machine tools [13], and its failure intensity function can be expressed as follows:

$$\lambda_1(t) = exp(a_0 + bt) = ae^{-bt} \quad a, b > 0 \quad t \geq 0 \tag{2}$$

The failure intensity function of the machine tools' accidental failure period can be directly given by the literature [7] as follows:

$$\lambda_2(t) = \frac{c}{d}(\frac{t}{d})^{c-1} \quad c > 1 \quad d > 0 \quad t \geq 0 \tag{3}$$

The formula (2) and (3) are substituted into the formula (1), and the failure intensity function of the NC machine tools can be obtained as follows:

$$\lambda(t) = ae^{-bt} + \frac{c}{d}(\frac{t}{d})^{c-1} \quad a, b, d > 0 \quad c > 1 \quad t \geq 0 \tag{4}$$

Then, the average failure number of the NC machine tools in the (0, t] can be expressed as follows:

$$E[N(t)] = \omega(t) = \int_0^t \lambda(t)d_t = \frac{a}{b}(1 - e^{-bt}) + (\frac{t}{d})^c \tag{5}$$

The time truncation failure data of the m machine tools occurred at the test site is counted, and assuming that the truncated time of the i-th ($0 < i < m$) machine tools is T_i, and a total of n_i failure data are collected during $(0, T_i]$. Then the moment when the i-th machine tools fails at time j can be expressed as t_{ij}, and the total number of failures occurring within the truncated time is $N = \sum\limits_{i=1}^{m} n_i$.

The joint probability density likelihood function of the failure time of the m machine tools is as follows:

$$L = \prod_{i=1}^{m} \{\prod_{j=1}^{n_i} [ae^{-bt_{ij}} + \frac{c}{d}(\frac{t_{ij}}{d})^{c-1}] \times \exp[-\frac{a}{b}(1 - e^{-bT_i}) - (\frac{T_i}{d})^c] \tag{6}$$

The following formula can be obtained by the logarithmic transformation of the formula (6):

$$l = \ln L = \sum_{i=1}^{m} \{\sum_{j=1}^{n_i} \ln[ae^{-bt_{ij}} + \frac{c}{d}(\frac{t_{ij}}{d})^{c-1}] - [\frac{a}{b}(1 - e^{-bT_i}) + (\frac{T_i}{d})^c]\} \tag{7}$$

From the formula (5), it can be seen that the number of failures of the i-th machine tools during the $(0, T_i]$ can be expressed as:

$$n_i = \frac{a}{b}(1 - e^{-bT_i}) + (\frac{T_i}{d})^c \tag{8}$$

Substituting formula (8) to formula (7), and the formula (7) can be expressed as:

$$l = \ln L = \sum_{i=1}^{m} \sum_{j=1}^{n_i} \ln[ae^{-bt_{ij}} + \frac{c}{d}(\frac{t_{ij}}{d})^{c-1}] - N \tag{9}$$

Calculate partial derivatives of parameters a, b, c, and d in formula (9) separately, and make them equal to 0. Then the result can be expressed as follows:

$$\begin{cases} \dfrac{\partial l}{\partial a} = \sum\limits_{i=1}^{m} \sum\limits_{j=1}^{n_i} \dfrac{e^{-bt_{ij}}}{ae^{-bt_{ij}} + \frac{c}{d}(\frac{t_{ij}}{d})^{c-1}} = 0 \\[3mm] \dfrac{\partial l}{\partial b} = \sum\limits_{i=1}^{m} \sum\limits_{j=1}^{n_i} \dfrac{-at_{ij}e^{-bt_{ij}}}{ae^{-bt_{ij}} + \frac{c}{d}(\frac{t_{ij}}{d})^{c-1}} = 0 \\[3mm] \dfrac{\partial l}{\partial c} = \sum\limits_{i=1}^{m} \sum\limits_{j=1}^{n_i} \dfrac{(1 + c\ln(\frac{t_{ij}}{d}))(\frac{t_{ij}}{d})^{c-1}/d}{ae^{-bt_{ij}} + \frac{c}{d}(\frac{t_{ij}}{d})^{c-1}} = 0 \\[3mm] \dfrac{\partial l}{\partial d} = \sum\limits_{i=1}^{m} \sum\limits_{j=1}^{n_i} \dfrac{-(\frac{c}{d})^2(\frac{t_{ij}}{d})^{c-1}}{ae^{-bt_{ij}} + \frac{c}{d}(\frac{t_{ij}}{d})^{c-1}} = 0 \end{cases} \tag{10}$$

Calculate the maximum likelihood estimation of each parameter in formula (10) and substitute them into formula (4). Finally, the early failure period of the machine tools can be obtained.

3 Closed-Loop Elimination System for Early Failure

3.1 Analysis the Causes of Early Failure

The early failures of NC machine tools are mainly caused by defects occurred in the process of product design, manufacturing and assembly, as shown in Table 1.

Table 1. Causes of the early failure of the machine tools at each stage

Failure phase	Failure causes
Design	Defective structure design, inappropriate material selection, unreasonable selection of purchased parts, the lack of reliability expectations and allocation, the missing of parts and complete machine reliability design, and the lack of analysis of dynamic and static characteristics, etc.
Manufacture	Unreasonable processing technic, defective heat treatment, erroneous clamping, incomplete residual stress elimination, the arbitrariness of the worker's operation, poor control of quality inspection process and so on
Assembling	Defective assembly process, poor assembly consistency, unreasonable electrical parameters setting, the arbitrariness of the worker's operation and so on
Test	The design of the experimental scheme is unreasonable, and the link of reliability evaluation is lacking, etc.
Debugging	Incorrect operation of machine tools debuggers when they are not familiar with the machine manual
Use	Improper operation, poor cleanliness of liquid, gas and oil and improper maintenance, overload operation of machine tools, etc.

In addition, the cause of early failure of machine tools is also related to the transportation process of products.

3.2 Design of Closed-Loop Elimination System for Early Failure

According to the causes of early failure of machine tools, the elimination methods can be roughly divided into two categories, that is, early failure active elimination technology and passive elimination technology. The early failure active elimination technology is mainly implemented within the machine tools manufacturing enterprise. It usually uses FMEA technology and experimental to discover and actively eliminate early failures that may occur in the design and manufacture process of machine tools. The early failure passive elimination technology mainly analyzes the reliability of these failures which collected from users at the initial stage of machine tools operation.

FRACAS is developed from the management and control technology of US weapon equipment failure information in the middle of the last century [3]. The related research on this technology is relatively late in China. After years of development, FRACAS technology has been more mature in China, but it is not widely used in manufacturing [15]. FRACAS can accurately report product failures that have already occurred through a set of standardized procedures. By analyzing the causes of failures, we can promptly formulate and implement effective corrective measures to reduce or prevent the recurrence of the same or similar failures so as to improve the reliability of the products. In this paper, a closed-loop elimination system for the early failure of NC machine tools is established based on the principle of FRACAS, and its running process is shown in Fig. 2.

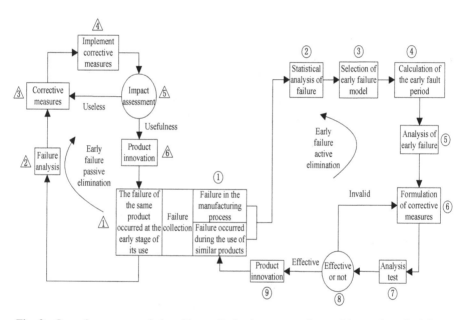

Fig. 2. Operation process of closed-loop elimination system for machine tools early failure

From the Fig. 2, we can see that the specific implementation process of the machine tools early failure closed-loop active elimination technology can be divided into four steps. Firstly, collect machine tools failure data. These failure data mainly come from the after-sales statistics of similar products in recent years and the inspection and test records in the process of product manufacturing. Secondly, calculate the early failure period of machine tools. This part mainly includes the statistical analysis of failure data, the selection of failure model and the solution of early failure time inflection point. Thirdly, analyze the early failure. Analyze the failures occurred in the early failure period to find out the early failure location, mode and cause of the machine tools. Finally, formulate corrective measures. In view of the causes of the early failure of the machine tools, the corresponding corrective measures are made and the relevant reliability test is designed to verify the effectiveness of the corrective measures. If the corrective measures are effective, they will be applied to the production process of the new product. Otherwise, the corrective measures will be reformulated until the failure is completely eliminated. The specific implementation process of the machine tools early failure closed-loop passive elimination technology can be divided into three steps. Firstly, collect machine tools failure data. The data mainly come from failures collected by users in the early operation stage of the machine tools. Secondly, analyze failure. The failures occurred in the early stage of the machine tools are analyzed and the mechanism of these failures is also studied. Finally, formulate corrective measures. According to the mechanism of the early failure, the corresponding corrective measures are made. After reliability evaluation, effective corrective measures are applied to the production process of the new products. On the contrary, the corrective methods will be reformulated until they work well.

4   Application

4.1   Early Failure Period Calculation

Four NC machine tools manufactured by a domestic enterprise are selected for the study. The data collected is calculated according to formula (1) to (10), and the estimated values of the model parameters can be obtained as shown in Table 2, and the failure intensity function is shown in Fig. 3.

Table 2. The estimated values of the model parameters of the machine tools

Parameters	a	b	c	d
Estimated value	2.31×10^{-2}	3.45×10^{-3}	2.27	2585.41

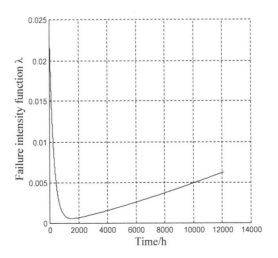

Fig. 3. Failure intensity function of machine tools

According to literature [16], the value of fitting goodness of machine tools failure model can be calculated as $r = 0.925$, which shows that the model used in this paper fits better to the failure data of the selected machine tools. From the Fig. 3, it is can be seen that the failure intensity function of machine tools is a single valley function, and there is a unique minimum value during its operation. The inflection point t_1 of the early failure time of the machine tools is the moment when the slope value of the failure intensity function is zero. The formula (7) is solved by MATLAB, and the result shows that the inflection point $t_1 = 1552.7$ h. Therefore, the failures occurred before 1552.7 h can be considered as early failures of the machine tools.

4.2   Early Failure Analysis

The dressing frame of the machine tools is selected as an example for early failure analysis. It is found that its early failures are mainly caused by diamond roller failures and dressing process failures. The diamond wheel failures are mainly caused by diamond wheel bearing wear, diamond roller nut loosening, core shaft breakage, and dressing motor tripping, etc. Diamond wheel bearing wear and diamond roller nut loosening are the most frequent failures and need to be analyzed emphatically. Diamond wheel bearing wear is caused by poor sealing, and it must be controlled at the design and assembly stages. The looseness of the nut is caused by the poor design of the nut against loosening, and it must be controlled during the design process. The failure of the dressing process is mainly caused by the knife collision and pause during dressing. Unstandardized operation of users and poor engagement state of the end face clutch are the main reasons for the phenomenon of knife collision during dressing. The problem of hydraulic system and the bad lubrication state of the three-π screw are the main reasons for the knife pause during dressing.

4.3   Early Failure Corrective Measures

In view of the reasons for the early failure of machine tools dressing frame, the enterprise technical department made the following corrective measures after discussion.

4.4   Experiment

An experiment is designed to evaluate the feasibility of the corrective measures proposed in this paper, and the experiment process is roughly as shown in Fig. 4.

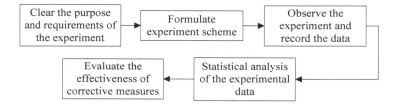

Fig. 4. The procedure of evaluation experiment

The corrective measures given in the Table 3 are applied to the dressing frame, then a 72 h simulation accelerated cutting experiment is carried out according to the Fig. 4. The experiment methods and steps are as follows. Firstly, the dressing frame of the machine tools is debugged to ensure that it meets the requirements of simulation accelerated cutting experiment. Secondly, check the geometric accuracy and positioning accuracy of the dressing frame and adjust it to the value required for normal operation. Thirdly, load the dressing frame and set the running speed to 120% of the operating speed. Fourthly, input simulation accelerated cutting experiment program and debug it. Finally, run the experiment and record the failures that occurred in the experiment. The results of the experiment are shown in Table 4.

Table 3. Measures for the early failure elimination of the dressing frame

Failure	Cause	Corrective measures	Specific implementation
Diamond wheel failure	Diamond wheel bearing wear	Improvement of sealing of diamond roller	Redesign the seal structure of the motor to prevent coolant and impurity from entering the bearing
		Control the assembly process of diamond roller bearings	Refine the installation process of bearings, formulate inspection methods and equipment for key processes
	Nut loosening	Control the loosening of the nut	Quantify tightening torque of the nut and design anti-loose structure of the nut
	Core shaft breakage	Control the machining quality of core shaft	Refine the processing technology, and determine the key quality control points and the corresponding inspection items. Optimize the material of the core shaft. Check the geometric accuracy of the core shaft in the processing, operation, and assembly process
		Strengthen the maintenance awareness of the users	Strengthen training for users on machine tool operation
	Tripping frequently	Prevent the damage and short circuit of the cable of the diamond roller	Control the quality of the cable. Refine the assembly process and optimize the layout of the circuit. Add protective devices at the cable joints to avoid coolant and abrasive entering the cable
Dressing process failure	Knife collision	Normalize the dressing operation of the users	Remind the users to re-adjust the U-axis to zero when replacing a new wheel for dressing

Table 4. Results of the experiment

Number	Failure time/h	Failure phenomenon	Treatment method
1	25	Abnormal sound	Adjust the gap of the dresser
2	69	Diamond wheel run-out	Replacement bearing of the dresser

The results of the experiment show that the failure rate of the modified dressing frame is reduced and its reliability is improved.

5   Conclusion

Based on the idea of "information feedback and closed-loop control", a closed-loop elimination system for early failure of NC machine tools, including active elimination and passive elimination, is proposed in this paper, and the causes and elimination mechanisms of the early failure of the machine tools are also analyzed. A 4-parameter NHPP modeling method is proposed, and the early failure period of the machine tools is obtained. The research is applied to a machine tools manufacturing enterprise, and has achieved good results. The results verify the feasibility of this research. This research is also applicable to the early failure elimination analysis of other repairable systems with the feature of "repairing as old", which lays a foundation for eliminating early failures within the enterprise and improving the reliability and market competitiveness of the products.

Acknowledgments. This work was supported by the National Nature Science Foundation of China (No. 51705048), the National Major Scientific and Technological Special Project for "High-grade CNC Basic Manufacturing Equipment" of China (No. 2016ZX04004-005), and the Fundamental Research Funds for the Central Universities of China (No. 106112017CDJ XY110006).

References

1. Wang, Y., Jia, Y., Jiang, W.: Early failure analysis of maching centers: a case study. Reliab. Eng. Syst. Saf. **72**, 91–97 (2001)
2. Jia, Z., Shen, G., Hu, Z., et al.: Lifetime distribution model and control for CNC lathes based on life cycle. Mach. Tool Hydraul. **36**, 164–167 (2008)
3. Zhang, P.: Reliability Analysis of CNC Machine Tool Main Drive System Based on Functional Hazard Analysis. Lanzhou University, Lanzhou (2010)
4. GJB841-1990: Failure Reporting, Analysis and Corrective Action Systems (1990)
5. Liao, X.: Quantitative Modeling & Application Study of Failure Rate Bathtub Curve of Machine Tool. Chongqing University, Chongqing (2010)
6. Chen, D., Wang, T.M., Wei, H.X.: Sectional model involving two Weibull distributions for CNC lathe failure probability. J. Beijing Univ. Aeronaut. Astronaut. **31**(7), 766–769 (2005)
7. Xu, B., Yang, Z.J., Chen, F., et al.: Reliability model of CNC machine tools based on non-homogenous Poisson process. J. Jilin Univ. (Eng. Technol. Edition) **41**(2), 210–214 (2011)

8. Wei, L.: Coupling Modeling and Influence Analysis for Availability of Numerical Control Machine Tools. Jilin University, Jilin (2011)
9. Huang, X.: Reliability Engineering. Tsinghua University Press, Beijing (1990)
10. Zhang, Z.: Reliability-Centric Quality Design, Analysis and Control. Publishing House of Electronics Industry, Beijing (2010)
11. Ren, L., Rui, Z., Li, J.: Reliability Analysis of numerical control machine tools with bounded and bathtub shaped failure intensity. Chin. J. Mech. Eng. **50**(16), 13–20 (2014)
12. Guida, M., Pulcini, G.: Reliability analysis of mechanical systems with bounded and bathtub shaped intensity function. IEEE Trans. Reliab. **58**(3), 432–443 (2009)
13. Zhang, G., Zhang, K., Wang, Y., et al.: Research on intensity function bathtub curve model for multiple CNC machine tools. Mech. Sci. Technol. Aerosp. Eng. **35**(1), 104–108 (2016)
14. Xu, Z.: Research on Reliability Technology of Machining Center and Its Functional Units. Chongqing University, Chongqing (2011)
15. Wang, H.: Design and Implementation of KN Failure Reporting, Analysis and Corrective Action System. University of Electronic Science and Technology of China, Chengdu (2014)
16. Shu, J., Guo, B., Zhang, J., et al.: Research on probability distribution of parameters of rock and soil based on fitting optimization index. J. Min. Saf. Eng. **2**(25), 197–201 (2008)

Analysis of the Soft Starting of Adjustable Speed Asynchronous Magnetic Coupling Used in Belt Conveyor

Lei Wang[1,2]([✉]), Zhenyuan Jia[1], Li Zhang[2], and Hao Liu[2]

[1] School of Mechanical Engineering,
Dalian University of Technology, Dalian 116023, China
960262968@qq.com
[2] CCTEG Shenyang Research Institute, Fushun 113122, China

Abstract. Aiming at the speed regulation problems of the constant torque load such as adjustable speed asynchronous magnetic coupling (ASAMC) matching belt conveyors, based on the analysis of the magnetic field characteristics of the coupling, its slip speed-air gap-torque equation is obtained, which matches the load start characteristics. The variation of the acceleration under the matching condition of the air gap at the start of the belt conveyor is quantified. On this basis, a soft start control strategy for the matching of ASAMC and the belt conveyor is established. A 125 kW ASAMC experimental platform was set up and experiments were conducted. The experimental results and field applications verified the reliability of the algorithm.

Keywords: Adjustable speed asynchronous magnetic coupling
Belt conveyor · Soft start · 3D-FEM

1 Introduction

Since its extensive application in underground coal mines, belt conveyor is developing towards the direction of large volume, long distance and high speed. As most belt conveyors are driven by asynchronous machines, direct starting of motors may cause rollers to slip and wear, which makes it difficult to start belts; in addition, direct starting will exert relatively strong and continuous impact on the power gird, which will affect the stable operation of the other equipment. Therefore, during the practical application, soft starting should be applied in belt conveyors.

Adjustable speed asynchronous magnetic coupling (ASAMC) is a type of non-contact transmission equipment with magnetic field as the medium. It generates eddy current through the magnetic field produced during the copper plate's cutting the permanent magnet plate. And then the eddy current will generate electromagnetic force, which will then transmit torque. Since ASAMC, which is a non-contact device, enjoys dominant advantages in terms of shock insulation, energy conservation, etc., it has been widely used in power plants as well as chemical plants [1, 2]. What's more, this feature can better satisfy the requirements of belt conveyors.

© Springer Nature Singapore Pte Ltd. 2018
S. Wang et al. (Eds.): ICSEE 2018/IMIOT 2018, CCIS 923, pp. 382–393, 2018.
https://doi.org/10.1007/978-981-13-2396-6_36

2 Soft Start of Current Common Equipment

In the present market, it is equipment like fluid coupling, CST, variable-frequency drive and so on that is used in belt conveyors for soft start [3, 4].

Fluid coupling: fluid coupling is the most widely used equipment for soft start at the present. Through adjusting the internal liquid volume, fluid coupling is able to transmit different output torques when started with constant torque load, which helps increase load speed slowly. However, the overall efficiency of fluid coupling is not quite high, and it needs frequent maintenance;

CST: CST is a product designed especially for the smooth start of great inertia load. During the starting process of belt conveyor, its belt speed can be promoted slowly in the shape of S-curve via control. Thanks to its characteristics of controllable starting time and apparent energy-saving effect, CST is widely used in the field of coal mine. Nevertheless, installation and trial run as well as maintenance of CST should all be guided by professional personnel on spot. Moreover, it has higher demands for the quality of lubricating oil;

Variable-frequency drive: with the development of power electronic components, the application of variable-frequency drive is becoming more and more widespread. By adjusting the frequency of variable-frequency drive's output voltage, the rotating speed of motor can be increased slowly, so as to achieve the purpose of soft start. However, variable-frequency drive has high order harmonic. In coal mine underground, harmonic interference may lead to malfunctions of sensor devices. In addition, environment in coal mine underground affects the life span of variable-frequency drive, which will bring about damages of key components, influencing production in the end.

3 Characteristics of ASAMC

Since ASAMC depends on copper plate's cutting of magnetic field to transmit torque, it is necessary that there must be certain rotating-speed difference between copper plate's rotating speed and the permanent magnet plate. As for ASAMC, by adjusting the size of the air gap between copper plate and permanent magnet plate, transmission torque can be adjusted and then rotating speed of the load end can be changed.

Based on the physical characteristics of ASAMC and aiming at the magnetic field characteristics of ASAMC, the following model is established in software (Fig. 1).

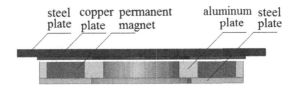

steel   copper permanent   aluminum steel
plate   plate   magnet   plate   plate

Fig. 1. Simulation model of ASAMC

In the above figure, steel plate and copper plate, which act as input end components, are connected with the motor; magnetic steel, which is placed in the aluminum plate and acts as output end component, is connected with load. When there is relative displacement between the input end and the output end, it seems that the copper plate is cutting the magnetic field. According to Faraday's law of electromagnetic induction, there will be eddy current on the copper plate. And then under the effect of magnetic field, eddy current will produce force. In this way, the transmission process of power from motor to load through ASAMC is realized [5, 6].

Scholars at home and abroad have conducted studies on ASAMC, yet there has been no mathematical model which can relatively well indicate the relationship between ASAMC torque and air gap as well as slip speed [7, 8]. The current agreed conclusion is that the changing trend of the ASAMC's transmission torque is only related to the slip speed of ASAMC during its operation, and amplitude of transmission torque has something to do with the air gap during ASAMC's operation.

The relationship between ASAMC transmission torque and slip speed is shown in Fig. 2, among which, s refers to the slip ratio of ASAMC, s_N is the nominal slip ratio of ASAMC, s_m stands for the maximal slip ratio of ASAMC and T_n refers to the nominal torque of ASAMC, T_{max} is the maximal transmission torque of ASAMC.

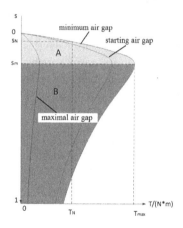

Fig. 2. Diagram of ASAMC's transmission torque

Since the relationship among T, n and g is relatively complex, ASAMC's curve is divided into two parts at the point of its transmission torque peak, as shown in Fig. 2. In area A, ASAMC's transmission torque reduces with the decrease of slip ratio, which represents that ASAMC can work stably in this area when the load is certain; on the contrary, in area B, with the reduction of slip ratio, ASAMC's transmission torque increases. That is to say, when the load is certain, ASAMC will work faster in area B. Therefore, area B is the starting area of ASAMC. During the starting process of belt conveyor, its stable starting is achieved mainly through ASAMC's working points in area B.

Since the transmission characteristics of ASAMC show a continuous curve surface of monotonic change in area B, mathematical equation of ASAMC's transmission torque in this area is set as:

$$T = f(n, g) \tag{1}$$

among which, T refers to the torque which can be transmitted by ASAMC, n is the rotating speed of ASAMC's output end and g stands for the size of air gap of ASAMC.

4 ASAMC's Simulation Analysis

For a set of ASAMC which has been designed well, its transmission torque only has a connection with the size of air gap and slip speed. By solving the coupling of different air gaps and slip speeds, transmission torques of ASAMC under different operating conditions can be acquired. Then fit the acquired values, characteristic curve surface of ASAMC of corresponding type can be obtained [9–11].

Step 1. Rotating speed of ASAMC's copper plate is n_1 and stays the same;

Step 2. The distance between the copper plate and aluminum plate of ASAMC changes according to vector quantity $\vec{g} = [g_1, g_2, \cdots g_n]$;

Step 3. The rotating speed of ASAMC's output end changes according to vector quantity $\vec{n} = [n_1, n_2, \cdots n_m]$.

Transmission torque T_{mn} of ASAMC at different rotating speeds and with variations of air gaps can be obtained through software simulation. By processing the data, characteristics of ASAMC's transmission torque at different rotating speeds and with variations of air gaps are shown in the following Fig. 3:

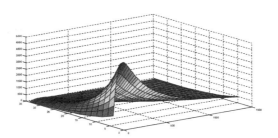

Fig. 3. 3D diagram of ASAMC's transmission torque

Fitting the data obtained via equations, we can get the transmission torque of ASAMC at any rotating speed-air gap:

$$T_{ij} = \vec{N_i} * [C_{m \times p}] * \vec{G_j} \tag{2}$$

Among which:

$$\vec{N_i} = [1, n_i, n_i^2, n_i^3, \ldots, n_i^m] \quad m \in N \tag{3}$$

$$\vec{G_j} = [1, g_j, g_j^2, g_j^3, \ldots, g_j^p]^T \quad p \in N \tag{4}$$

Different coefficient matrix can be acquired based on the values of m and p. Entering the matrix into the controller, the transmission torque of ASAMC can be calculated in real time. Usually: selecting relatively big values for m and p, the accuracy of the fitting equation can be guaranteed. However, because of the limited calculating ability of the controller, m and p should not be too big. In the fitting equation of the present thesis, $m = 5$ and $p = 3$. In this way, the curve surface of ASAMC under such a state equation is shown in Fig. 4:

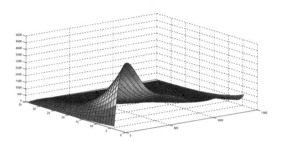

Fig. 4. Fitting diagram of ASAMC's transmission torque

5   Soft Start of ASAMC

After the starting of belt conveyor, ASAMC's air gap is adjusted with the use of electric actuator. With the increase of ASAMC's air gap, its transmission torque T will rise, too. Till load begins to function, the control device will record the size of ASAMC's air gap at this time. The value of load torque of this starting process, T_l, can be acquired through characteristic equation. According to Newton's Second Law of Rotary Motion System:

$$T - T_1 = J \frac{d\omega}{dt} = \frac{\pi J}{30} \frac{dn}{dt} = C_p \alpha \tag{5}$$

J refers to the rotational inertia of belt conveyor's roller;
α is accelerated speed of ASAMC's output rotating speed.
C_p stands for constants related to belt conveyor.

Taking the mathematical model of ASAMC into the equation above, we can get:

$$f(n, g) - f(0_+, g_0) = C_p \alpha \qquad (6)$$

Among which, g_0 is the air gap of ASAMC when belt conveyor starts to act. At this time, ASAMC's transmission torque is the belt conveyor's load torque at this starting. Taking the derivative of the equation above with respect to t, we can get:

$$C_p \frac{d\alpha}{dt} = \frac{\partial f(n, g)}{\partial n} \bullet \alpha + \frac{\partial f(n, g)}{\partial g} \bullet \frac{dg}{dt} \qquad (7)$$

If ASAMC's air gap is not adjusted after the action of belt conveyor, namely, $dg/dt = 0$, then the equation above will be changed into:

$$C_p \frac{d\alpha}{dt} = \frac{\partial f(n, g)}{\partial n} \bullet \alpha \qquad (8)$$

$$\alpha = C_1 e^{\int \frac{1}{C_p} \frac{\partial f(n,g)}{\partial n} dt} \qquad (9)$$

In other words, when load starts to act, if ASAMC's air gap stays the same, then the accelerated speed of ASAMC's output rotating speed will increase at an exponential rate. The rapid change of ASAMC's output end rotating speed will impose great impact on belt as well as roller.

This output characteristic of ASAMC restricts its application in permanent torque load. The present thesis, by adjusting ASAMC's air gap during the staring process of load, will make ASAMC's transmission torque fluctuate within a certain range, keeping the accelerated speed of ASAMC stable in a certain interval until the starting process of load is completed, so as to achieve the effect of soft start.

Before the belt conveyor starts, its soft start time t can be set, which will be used to obtain the ideal average accelerated speed of soft start's rotating speed

$$\alpha_1 = \frac{n_1}{t} \qquad (10)$$

Among which: α_1 stands for the ideal average accelerated speed of rotating speed and n_1 is the motor's nominal rotating speed.

The air gap of ASAMC is controlled by angular travel electric actuator. The adjustment of air gap is at a constant speed, namely, $dg/dt = C_g$. Then we can get the following equation:

$$\frac{d\alpha}{dt} = \frac{1}{C_p} \frac{\partial f(n, g)}{\partial n} \alpha + \frac{C_g}{C_p} \frac{\partial f(n, g)}{\partial g} \qquad (11)$$

α, namely, $d\alpha/dt = 0$. In this way, belt conveyor will not be shocked. Since it is hard to start at a constant accelerated speed during the process of soft start, the lower the change rate of accelerated speed $d\alpha/dt$ is, the weaker the shock on belt is. At this time, set $d\alpha/dt$ as a minimal value, namely, $d\alpha/dt = \varepsilon$. When $\varepsilon \to 0$, we can get:

$$\alpha = \frac{C_P\varepsilon - C_g \frac{\partial f(n,g)}{\partial g}}{\frac{\partial f(n,g)}{\partial n}} \approx \frac{-C_g \frac{\partial f(n,g)}{\partial g}}{\frac{\partial f(n,g)}{\partial n}} \tag{12}$$

In the equation, if

$$\frac{\partial f(n, g)}{\partial g} < 0, \frac{\partial f(n, g)}{\partial n} > 0 \tag{13}$$

We can get,

$$\alpha = C_g h(n, g) = H(n, g) \tag{14}$$

among which,

$$h(n,g) = \frac{-\frac{\partial f(n,g)}{\partial g}}{\frac{\partial f(n,g)}{\partial n}} \tag{15}$$

6 Soft Start of Belt Conveyor

According to the starting characteristics of belt conveyor, the following diagram of soft start control system is designed [12, 13].

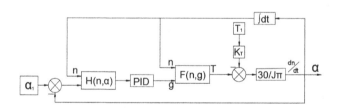

Fig. 5. Diagram of soft start control system

Figure 5 is mainly divided into the following steps (Fig. 6):

1: When starting the motor, ASAMC's air gap will be the biggest and only very small transmission torque can be transmitted. In this way, the motor's no-load starting is realized, the duration time of motor's peak current is reduced and the power grid's pressure drop during the motor's starting process is impaired;

2: When ASAMC is in a big air gap, the transmitted torque cannot take load, and there is a relatively big difference between the accelerated speed of ASAMC's output rotating speed and the preset accelerated speed. After PID controller

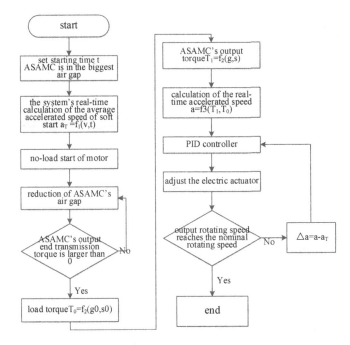

Fig. 6. Flowchart of soft start

Fig. 7. Testing platform of ASAMC

processes signals, the air gap of ASAMC will decrease rapidly until its output end rotating speed is not 0. At this time, the value of torque required for belt conveyor's starting of this time, which is recorded as T_1, can be calculated based on ASAMC's mathematical model;

3: Monitor ASAMC's output end rotating speed and the size of the air gap in real time. Obtain its transmission torque through calculation and compare the result with T_1, after which calculate the accelerated speed of rotating speed. After PID controller, ASAMC's air gap will be further adjusted, keeping its transmission torque T_1 and maintaining the accelerated speed of belt conveyor's rotating speed;

4: When belt conveyor's belt speed reaches the nominal speed, ASAMC will operate under the condition of minimal air gap. During this phase, the controller will compare the duration time of this time's starting with the set time of duration and correct PID control parameter;

5: When belt conveyor stops, the air gap of ASAMC will be adjusted to the maximal value, so as to guarantee that the motor can start with no load in the next time.

Since belt conveyor relies on the fiction between roller and belt to transmit torque, and the maximal static friction force between them is a bit larger than kinetic friction force, after calculating the starting torque of belt conveyor, T_l, through ASAMC's mathematical model, T_l should be corrected. After each time's starting of belt conveyor, control system will record the current starting duration time and count it into starting time matrix $\vec{t} = [t_1, t_2, \ldots t_{10}]$. In addition, a comparison operation will be carried out between starting time matrix and the preset starting duration time, which will work out the correction factor K_T, achieving the effect of self-adaption.

$$\vec{K_T} = g\left(\vec{t}\right)$$

After accessing ASAMC's mathematical model into the controller, ASAMC can work normally, only needing to set starting time on the spot. During the working process, belt conveyor's performance will be adapted automatically, satisfying the requirements of coal mines.

7 Prototype Test and Field Application

ASAMC's testing platform is similar to that of motor. Place ASAMC between two motors and the motors will be tested in the form of using one motor as the motor and the other as the generator. In this way, the transmission torque and transmission power of the prototype tested under different slip speed-air gaps can be obtained.

Through testing, the problem whether the ASAMC designed satisfies the needs of transmission power can be verified. In addition, testing mode can be set according to the field conditions, so as to verify the feasibility and stability of control algorithm.

In order to verify practicability of control algorithm, a 125 kW ASAMC is produced to conduct tests on the testing platform. The motor in the input side employs a common control mode and the rotating speed is set as 1500r/min; and the motor in the output side adopts vector control mode, decoupling load's rotating speed and torque and setting load torque as a fixed value. Simulate the working conditions of permanent torque load and make it similar to filed characteristics as much as possible.

During the tests, several pairs of load torques are set to test control algorithm. According to the results, the algorithm involved in the content above satisfies the soft start of permanent torque load, and also makes it realizable to adjust as well as control starting time (Fig. 8).

As shown in Fig. 7, a set of 125 kW ASAMC has been installed in a coal mine in Shanxi Province. The original coupling used in the field is a set of fluid coupling, which went through 16-h equipment transformation in April, 2015. After field debugging, the

Fig. 8. Field application of ASAMC

starting time of belt conveyor is set as 40 s. After starting the motor, ASAMC will begin to operate normally. Belt conveyor can start smoothly with any load of coal quantity and its starting time is about 40 s. After many start and stop tests, the control system operates smoothly and the starting time just fluctuates slightly, as shown in the Fig. 9 below:

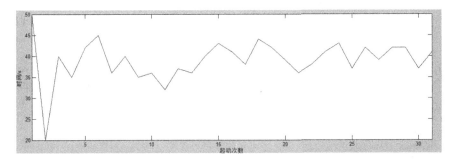

Fig. 9. Starting time curve of ASAMC

During the starting process of belt conveyor, the rotating speeds of ASAMC's input end and output end change as shown in the Fig. 10 below:

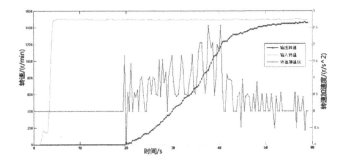

Fig. 10. Starting effect of ASAMC

It can be observed that ASAMC's input end rotating speed reaches the nominal condition rapidly when belt conveyor starts, which reduces the duration time of motor's peak current. After that, ASAMC begins to adjust, and when its input end starts to function, its output end rotating speed increases slowly along the S curve until it reaches the nominal rotating speed. The entire process, from the emergence of rotating speed in ASAMC's output end to its reaching the nominal speed, lasts for 40 s. And the accelerated speed of the output end rotating speed maintains at 1.5 rad/s^2 or so. The accelerated speed of maximal instantaneous rotating speed reaches 2.5 rad/s^2.

This set of ASAMC has been operating smoothly for continuous 15 months before the change of working face, without any malfunctions. What's more, with a reduction in maintenance and also a drop in belt abrasion, its energy-saving effect is remarkable.

8   Conclusion

(1) During the starting process of ASAMC, its transmission torque increases at first and then drops. When the constant torque load is taken, the accelerated speed of load's rotating speed will rise gradually, failing to achieve the effect of soft start.

(2) After load starting, real-time control will be conducted on ASAMC's air gap, which makes it possible for ASAMC's transmission torque to stay within a certain scope until the load rotating speed tends to be stable, so as to achieve the effect of soft start. The maximum acceleration is less than 2.5 rad/s^2 and ASAMC can protect the constant torque loads nicely.

(3) The control system of ASAMC designed can be applied in belt conveyors effectively; self-adaption algorithm can correct mathematical models and enhance the adaptability of control system on the basis of history starting time; testing platforms and field applications have verified the practicability and stability of control system.

References

1. Krasil'nikov, A.Ya.: Cylindrical magnetic coupling having active length of high-coercivity permanent magnet smaller than magnet width. Chem. Pet. Eng. **53**(1–2), 1–3 (2017). https://doi.org/10.1007/s10556-017-0304-z
2. Wang, R.: The application of magnetic coupling in water supply system of thermal power plants. Urban Constr. Theory Res. **12** (2013). 王仁才.磁力耦合器在火电厂供水系统中的应用[J].城市建设理论研究
3. Davydov, S.Y., Zolkin, A.P., Shvarev, V.S., et al.: Determination of the dynamic characteristics of a charge in the bucket of a steeply inclined pivoted bucket belt conveyor. Refract. Ind. Ceram **58**(1), 1–6 (2017). https://doi.org/10.1007/s11148-017-0045-8
4. Qu, J.: The current situation and development trend of belt conveyors used in coal mines. Coal Sci. Techno. **4** (2015)
5. Wan, Y.: Study on performance of adjustable-speed permanent magnet coupling. Shenyang University of Technology (2013). 万援.调速型稀土永磁磁力耦合器的性能研究[D].沈阳工业大学
6. Cai, C., Wang, J., Meilin, H., et al.: Electromagnetic properties of cylinder permanent magnet eddy current coupling. Int. J Appl. Electromagn. Mech. **54**(4), 655–671 (2017)

7. Krasilnikov, A.Y., Krasilnikov, A.A.: Calculation of the reaction force of high-coercively permanent magnets in half-couplings of a magnetic clutch with dismantling of a sealed vertical pump. Chem. Pet. Eng. **48**(3–4), 246–251 (2012). https://doi.org/10.1007/s10556-012-9605-4

8. Dai, X., Liang, Q., Cao, J., et al.: Analytical modeling of axial-flux permanent magnet eddy current couplings with a slotted conductor topology. IEEE Trans. Magn. **52**(2), 1–15 (2016)

9. Ni, C., Hua, L., Wang, X., et al.: Coupling method of magnetic memory and eddy current nondestructive testing for retired crankshafts. J. Mech. Sci. Technol. **30**(7), 3097–3104 (2016). https://doi.org/10.1007/s12206-016-0618-3

10. Yang, J., Liu, F., Tao, X., Wang, X., Cheng, J.: The Application of evolutionary algorithm in b-spline curved surface fitting. In: Lei, J., Wang, F.L., Deng, H., Miao, D. (eds.) AICI 2012. LNCS (LNAI), vol. 7530, pp. 247–254. Springer, Heidelberg (2012). https://doi.org/10.1007/978-3-642-33478-8_31

11. Li, K., Bird, J.Z., Acharya, V.M.: Ideal radial permanent magnet coupling torque density analysis. IEEE Trans. Magn. 1 (2017)

12. Blazej, R., Jurdziak, L., Kawalec, W.: Operational safety of steel-cord conveyor belts under non-stationary loadings. In: Chaari, F., Zimroz, R., Bartelmus, W., Haddar, M. (eds.) Advances in Condition Monitoring of Machinery in Non-Stationary Operations, pp. 473–481. Springer, Cham (2016). https://doi.org/10.1007/978-3-319-20463-5_36

13. Nguyen, H.H., Duong, V.T., Yim, H., Van, C.H., Kim, H.K., Kim, S.B.: A model reference adaptive controller for belt conveyors of induction conveyor line in cross-belt sorting system with input saturation. In: Duy, V.H., Dao, T.T., Kim, S.B., Tien, N.T., Zelinka, I. (eds.) AETA 2016. LNEE, vol. 415, pp. 129–139. Springer, Cham (2017). https://doi.org/10.1007/978-3-319-50904-4_13

Estimating Reliability-Based Costs in the Lifecycle of Intelligent Manufacturing Service

Xianlin Ren[1(✉)], Yi Chen[2], Deshun Li[1], Zezhao Pang[1],
and Zhehan Zhang[1]

[1] School of Mechatronics Engineering, University of Electronic Science
and Technology of China, Chengdu 611731, China
renxianlin0@163.com
[2] School of Engineering and Built Environment,
Glasgow Caledonian University, Glasgow G4 0BA, UK

Abstract. *The reliability of IMSS is an important factor that influences the lifecycle cost of the systems.* However, there is little existing research that investigates relationships between the reliability of systems and their cost in the whole lifecycle. This paper reviews these costs, and proposes a method of estimating business losses due to the failure of an individual component/subsystem. *When compared with the reliability and maintenance of manufacturing systems, IMSS exhibit specific, differing characteristics.* The present paper also compares IMSS with other systems on three factors: operating mode, usage intensity, and preventive maintenance, which have effect on maintenance costs.

Keywords: IMSS · Reliability · Lifecycle cost · Maintenance

1 Introduction

Manufacturing system, is a complex system composed by a set of sub-systems including: mechatronics, security & safety, software & algorithm, information and communication systems, which have been designed to implement the specific functions of the intelligent manufacturing. To meet the end-user's requirements, it is important that a manufacturing system can operate with less interruption or failure events. In other words, it needs to be reliable with cost effectiveness throughout its whole life-cycle (LC), namely, *life-cycle cost* (LCC), which means, a manufacturing system's LCC performance is vital important.

The LCC is the cost summation of systems, products and business projects from conceptual design through to delivery. The basic LCC involve: costs for acquisition, operating, maintenance and disposal or recycling, etc., whose objective is to search for the most cost-effective way among a few solution alternatives and to obtain the minimum long-term owner-ship cost.

The research of LCC has recently been applied to the development and management of IMSS. The acquisition cost is still widely adopted as the one of the most

© Springer Nature Singapore Pte Ltd. 2018
S. Wang et al. (Eds.): ICSEE 2018/IMIOT 2018, CCIS 923, pp. 394–407, 2018.
https://doi.org/10.1007/978-981-13-2396-6_37

principal criteria for equipment selection. This single criterion is simple to use but often results in increased long-term expenditure and poor value for money and seldom addresses the impact upon business effectiveness. The low acquisition cost of some equipment may be easy to afford but may result in high operation, maintenance or disposal costs. In order to obtain a better value solution the LCC should be taken into consideration and carefully analysed at each stage of system life cycle. Depending on the type of system, the owner-ship cost over the LC span varies from ten to one hundred times of the acquisition cost [1].

The definition of reliability the ability of a component to perform its required function under stated conditions for a specified period. It is an essential factor used in assessing the configuration and the life performance of an intelligent manufacturing service system (IMSS). System reliability is one of the most important factors impacting on the LCC of an IMSS. The IMSS with poor reliability has a poor health, security, safety as well as business continuity, in which, the products with higher reliability may involve higher acquisition costs; lower operating costs and lower maintenance costs resulting from longer operation time; and they may also incur lower disposal costs because of possible reuse, recycling or reselling. As shown in Fig. 1, the total costs with various levels of reliability have the different cost trend curves, resulting from maintenance and acquisition costs, for various levels of reliability. Research associated with both reliability and LCC follows two directions: LCC-based reliability analysis, and LCC modelling.

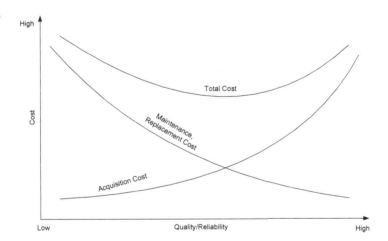

Fig. 1. Costs for various levels of reliability

Basically, the LCC-based reliability analysis usually focuses on two aspects: (1) availability allocation and (2) maintenance policy optimisation. Specifically,

- The optimisation of the availability allocation problem, being applied to either repairable or non-repairable systems, addresses a situation where a system with a given configuration is to be assembled and the individual components which will make up the system may be selected at different levels of cost and reliability/availability. There is a detailed review of availability allocation in Kuo and Prasad [2].

- The optimisation of maintenance policies attempts to provide engineers with optimal system availability and safety performance at lowest possible maintenance costs. After installation and commissioning, the maintenance of intelligent manufacturing services becomes a major concern, which has to be anticipated during the design stage. In the past several decades, a huge number of maintenance policies have been introduced (see [3, 4]).

Recently, within the construction industry, life-cycle costing is gradually finding many applications. For example, it has been applied to the maintenance of bridges [5]; concrete structures in nuclear plants [6]; hydraulic structures [7]; mechanical ventilation systems [8] and HVAC systems [9].

Research on LCC modelling usually concentrates on analysing and estimating elements in the whole life-cycle cost, which is reviewed by Durairaj *et al.* [10] and Woodward [11]. The reader can also refer to Clements-Croome, *et al.* [12] and John *et al.* [13] for the application of LCC to IMSS.

However, both the two research areas – Reliability and LCC – have limitations. In the LCC-based reliability analysis, availability allocation problems are simply concerned with balancing the components' acquisition, maintenance costs with their availability. The development of maintenance policy is commonly to optimise an objective function on the basis of maintenance cost. The two research areas usually consider only one or two costs in LCC instead of all of the costs associated with reliability. Research on LCC modelling ignores detailed information about the systems under study, such as maintenance policies and failure patterns.

The LCC of IMSS includes acquisition costs, business losses due to failures, operation cost (or running costs), maintenance cost and reuse/recycling/salvage costs. However, operation cost might be indirectly impacted by reliability; it will not be studied in this paper. Only costs shown in Eq. (1) are considered as main components making up of the LCC:

$$\Delta C_{LC} = \Delta C_A + \Delta C_B + \Delta C_M \tag{1}$$

ΔC_{LC}: Lifecycle cost
ΔC_A: Acquisition costs
ΔC_B: Business Losses
ΔC_M: Maintenance costs

This paper reviews classical approaches to estimating cost elements influenced by reliability for intelligent manufacturing services system. It investigates special features of IMSS, which differentiate other products. Meanwhile, failure of identical components in a system might cause different business losses; an approach to estimating business losses caused by the failure of an individual component is therefore introduced. This paper also categorises preventive maintenance on the basis of possible failure modes.

The remainder of the paper is organised as follow. Section 2 reviews the relationship between acquisition cost of components and their reliability. Section 3 introduces approaches to estimating business losses caused by the failure of a component in a system. Section 4 discusses factors impacting on maintenance costs, and introduces approaches to developing optimal maintenance policy. Section 5 gives the conclusions and remarks for this paper.

2   Acquisition Costs

Understanding the relationship between a component's reliability and its cost is helpful at the design stage. It may provide designers with useful information on searching for the optimum balancing point between reliability and costs.

There are two main approaches to assessing the relationship between cost and reliability. The first stipulates that cost cannot be formulated as a closed function. Therefore, a discrete function, for example, a table form, of the relationship can be employed. From the real procurement point of view, the discrete function may be more widely used as it may not be able to be provided by product suppliers. The second method is that the relationship between cost and reliability is as described by Eq. (2), which may be helpful when there is no reliability information available during the system design. The basic way is to formulate the cost function from actual cost data and reliability data from field trials and experience.

Generally, the acquisition cost of a given component can be expressed as an increasing function of its reliability, which is assumed as an exponentially increasing, closed-form function relating cost and reliability as be given in Eq. (2).

$$C_A = a_0 e^{-b_0 \lambda} \tag{2}$$

where, C_A is the acquisition cost, a_0 and b_0 are constants, and λ is the component failure rate.

Practically, such functions are often difficult to construct. Moreover, while such an assumption occasionally tends to make the optimisation procedures easier, there is no compelling reason put forward as to why such a relationship is appropriate. As mentioned by Tillman et al. [14] that such a relationship is not always necessarily true.

3   Business Losses

Business losses are an important cost element incurred by failures of IMSS. According to Evans et al. [15], the business losses can be 200 times the acquisition cost. Unfortunately, previous research on LCC has not considered business losses caused by failures of components. People would like to estimate the whole LCCs of these components and hence subsystems when they are selecting components. From a reliability point of view, identical components/components installed in different positions

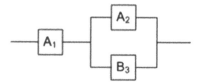

Fig. 2. An example

may cause different business losses. Hence, there is a need to understand the business losses caused by an individual component or subsystem.

For example, for a system shown in Fig. 2, although component A_1 and A_2 may be identical, the probability of a failure component A_1 causing the system failure is larger than component A_2. Hence, business loss caused by the failure of the component A_1 is larger than by A_2.

The business losses caused by failure of components may depend on the number of failures, which in turn depend on the maintenance policy. However, to measure this is difficult. If a repair is allowed on a system, the failure criticality index introduced by Wang *et al.* [16] can be employed. However, to calculate the failure criticality index needs much computing time. The simplest assumption is that 'no repair' is performed on a system; then a well-known importance measure of this type is the one suggested by Barlow and Proschan [17].

Denoting the density of the life distribution of the kth component by f_k, $k = 1,...,$ n, this importance measure is given as in Eq. (3).

Definition *The probability that the kth component causes system failure when the system eventually fails is* [17]:

$$I_{B-P}^{(k)} = \int_0^\infty [\Pr(1_k, X) - \Pr(0_k, X)] f_k(t) dt \tag{3}$$

Where, $\Pr(1_k, X)$ is the system reliability when item k works, and $\Pr(0_k, X)$ is the system reliability when item k fails.

If the business loss due to system failure is C_b, then the business losses due to the failure of component k to the business loss is $C_b I_{B-P}^{(k)}$. An example on estimating the business losses caused by a component is given at Appendix A.

4   Maintenance Cost

Maintenance costs influence LCC. IMSS has their features that need more attention when the maintenance policy is developed. The features include operating modes, usage intensity, failure patterns, and failure causes.

The failure patterns distributions of manufacturing system helps to provide useful information which can be used at the design stages of reliability and maintainability.

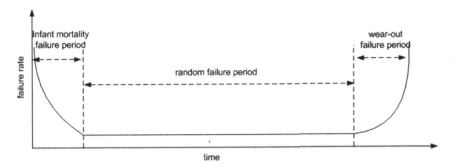

Fig. 3. A traditional bathtub curve

As shown in Fig. 3, a traditional bathtub curve against time has three sections: (1) the infant mortality period, which is usually marked by a rapidly decreasing failure rate; (2) the random failure period, in which the failure rate continues at a steady level; (3) the period of increasing failure rate represents the onset of product wear-out.

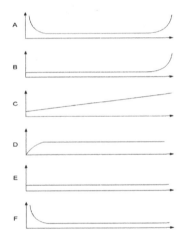

Fig. 4. The six types typical failure patterns of manufacturing system. (see [19])

As given in Fig. 4, a manufacturing system has six types typical failure patterns which demonstrates six most found failure distributions in a manufacturing equipment, associated systems and components [18, 19], in which, each system can be considered individually as 'a component'. The six types typical failure patterns are:

(A) A 'bath-tub curve' with high incidence of failure followed by constant failure rate, then by a wear-out period;
(B) A constant or slowly increasing failure rate, ending in a wear-out period;
(C) A slowly increasing rate, but there is no identifiable wear-out period;

(D) A low failure rate when the component is new or just out of the shop, then a rapid increase to a constant level;
(E) A constant failure rate for the whole life;
(F) A high infant mortality, then drops eventually to a constant or very slowly increasing failure probability.

According to Moubray's research [19], in the Civil Aviation Industry, 4% of components conform to pattern A, 2% to B, 5% to C, 7% to D, 14% to E, and 68% to pattern F. This group of failure patterns has been referred to in research papers on reliability of manufacturing system [20].

4.1   Operating Modes

IMSS is often operated intermittently in a two-successive-states: (A) up state: working state (B) down state: off-work state, which operates in A → B→A → B→.... Specifically, (1) In state A, the system is working but may fail, and the corrective maintenance can help to it's in state A and reduce its failures possibilities. (2) In state B, the system is off-work or not operating, but available for any maintenance.

An active failure occurs in state A, but systems can deteriorate in state B and passively fail. For example, (1) the state A of some systems can be only eight or sixteen hours a day. If a maintenance activity is performed during state A, the costs incurred by system failures combine both business losses and maintenance costs; (2) the systems are then put into the state B for rest of the day. If a maintenance activity is carried out during state B, the costs incurred by system failures include only maintenance costs.

If the system as mentioned above requires the maintenance policies optimisation, the costs for maintenance should be composed of two elements: (1) business losses, and (2) maintenance costs for different time periods. In such scenarios, maintenance time may have two parts: (a) the first one within the state A, and (b) the second one within the state B. When ignoring the maintenance period time, it will lead to the unrealistic results.

In order to formulate preventive maintenance policies for the case mentioned above, one should have failure rate functions and other information including the time intervals between two operating states. Wu and Clements-Croome [20] present the following three models to obtain optimum preventive maintenance policies:

- Model A: it performs the corrective maintenance (CM);
- Model B: it performs the imperfect preventive maintenance (PM) and CM, sequentially
- Model C: it performs PM periodically, and then CM, in which, this PM can restore the system back to the same state as just after the latest CM.

For a detailed discussion on preventive maintenance models, the author is referred to [21].

4.2   Usage Intensity

The life of an intelligent manufacturing services system may include long dormant time periods, in which the system is not used. There are two kinds of dormant periods.

The first occurs when an IMSS, is installed in a building. They are not usually used until the building is commissioned and then completed for use. The time from the installation to the commissioning – a dormant state – may take several years for a large building. It is not a short period compared with the whole life time. In addition to construction, buildings can also be left in a dormant state if the owner cannot find someone to occupy them. Or defects in the building construction delay the availability of the building.

For example, the IMSS for a project is completed and, during the testing and commissioning period, it is established that the building envelope has a defect that is unacceptable. For the duration of the repairs to the building envelope, the IMSS would be available to operate, but they would not be used.

The IMSS products have the features as follow: *in the dormant state, the products may age and deteriorate, and they may, therefore, fail to function when they are put into use at commissioning*, which is different from the other products that are usually put into use after they are purchased. Hence, in order to develop an optimum preventive maintenance policy, the dormant state as mentioned above needs to be taken into account.

The failure rate of an IMSS may be lower in the dormant state than in the operating state. Figure 5 shows a typical failure pattern of a system having only the first dormant state. In this figure, the failure pattern before the commissioning time is lower [22, 23].

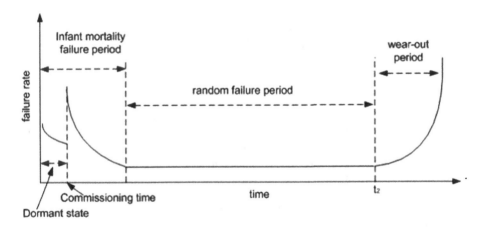

Fig. 5. Failure pattern with the first type dormant

The second kind of dormant period is the time when the system is not in use due to natural events, such as a heating system may not be used in summer, or a cooling system may not be used in winter. Figure 6 shows a typical failure pattern when a

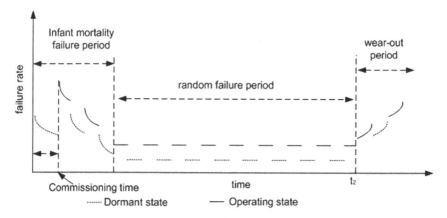

Fig. 6. Failure pattern with the first and the second type dormant

system has both the first dormant state and the second dormant state. In this figure, the failure rate at the dormant state is lower than that at the operating state.

4.3   Reliability-Based and Performance-Based Maintenance

In the research of reliability, *maintenance* is called 'reliability-based maintenance (RbM)' which is expressed as '*any activity intended to retain a functional unit in, or to restore it to, a state in which it can perform its required function*' [24], in which, the *required function* is specified by the products' manufacturer. As such, an **RbM** activity can be carry out on the basis of the consideration of how properly the *required function* is utilised in various scenarios, and how well the CM or PM can be deployed.

Practically, an IMSS may perfectly perform the *required function* as defined by the manufacturer. However, maintenance is still needed in order to meet the end-users' requirements. There are two examples,

(1)   A ventilation system is designed to provide fresh air to the IMSS facility and then remove stale air from the IMSS facility. However, the ventilation system may become contaminated if not properly cleaned and maintained, and as the consequence, it could spread airborne contamination.

(2)   A cooling tower that may also become contaminated, and therefore the whole cooling system may fail to *required function properly*, possibly leading to the development of the organisms that cause Legionnaire's disease. Cleaning, a form of maintenance, is required even if the required function specified by the manufacturer performs perfectly.

We call this sort of maintenance performance-based maintenance (PbM), in which, the maintenance for this kind of failure is not associated with the reliability defined by the manufacturer. As such, the external environmental factors, such as, the degree of cleanliness of the operating environment of a ventilation system, is one of the key factors that may impact on the failure pattern of an IMSS. The real failure rate of an IMSS $r(t)$ can be defined in Eq. (4).

$$r(t) = r_e(t) + r_i(t) \tag{4}$$

where, $r_e(t)$ is the failure rate of the system incurred by the external environmental factors, called *extrinsic failure rate*. $r_i(t)$ is the failure rate of the system due to factors such as the improper design of the manufacturer and incorrect ways to operate the system, called *intrinsic failure rate*.

In the previous literature, PM policies can be defined on the basis of the two factors: (1) failure patterns; (2) costs, such as: business losses and costs on PM. It is assumed that an IMSS can preventively be repaired as good as new, or a PM action can bring the IMSS back to the as new state in terms of the performance; then the optimum PM time can be found by minimising the cost per unit time, C_t, given in Eq. (5).

$$C_t = \frac{C_p R(t) + C_u(1 - R(t))}{\int_0^t R(\tau)d\tau} \tag{5}$$

in which, $R(t)$ is the component reliability at time t; C_p is the cost of planned preventive maintenance; and C_u is the cost of unplanned PM.

However, on developing an optimal PM policy for IMSS, both the failure patterns and costs may be associated with more factors.

A PbM action is employed to rectify the failure state of a system caused by external environmental factors, and an RbM action is responsible for the failure caused by intrinsic factors. The failure patterns need to be considered may include intrinsic failure rate, external environmental factors and dormant states. Instead of only the intrinsic failures, the maintenance policies are to be developed based on a consideration of both the external environmental factors and the intrinsic factors, or failure rate $r(t)$.

As for the costs in Eq. (4), apart from costs such as business losses and cost on preventive maintenance, the following factors should also be considered:

- economic,
- company reputation,
- environmental,
- personnel (i.e., health and safety),
- operational.

4.4   Preventive RbM

The life of components is influenced by myriad factors, some of the more important of which are [25]:

- quality of workmanship on site,
- quality of production,
- quality of maintenance,
- change of use,
- relationships to other materials/components,
- obsolescence,
- exposure to the elements,
- exposure to wear and tear,

- maintenance regime,
- the intelligence of design.

Apart from the above factors, developing maintenance policies for an intelligent manufacturing services system may also be impacted by the following factors:

- business losses,
- manufacturers' recommendations,
- regulations/standards, and
- user's experience.

Preventive RbM is the maintenance carried out at pre-determined intervals or according to prescribed criteria and is intended to reduce the probability of failure or the degradation of a component. One of the most important objectives of preventive RbM is to add value to the business process. In real practice, preventive RbM policy is usually developed based on reliability data, manufacturers' recommendations and relevant regulations and laws. In the absence of good reliability data, it is sensible to rank the possibility of a failure being realised depending on local conditions [26]. It is conducted only if the following two conditions are satisfied:

(a) the component in question has an increasing failure rate;
(b) performing a preventive RbM is cost-effective. As such, the overall cost of the preventive RbM action must be less than the overall cost of the corrective RbM action.

When satisfying the two conditions above, the failure patterns as shown in Fig. 4, the following result can be concluded that it is unnecessary to undertake any preventive RbM on components with failure patterns E and F as patterns, when E and F do not have an increasing failure rate.

Bartlett and Simpson [18] state that in manufacturing system patterns E and F are likely to become more common because intelligent mechanical and electrical manufacturing services components grow more complex. It can therefore be inferred that more components among manufacturing system become unsuitable for preventive RbM. Eventually embedded sensors in components will make it easier to observe failure and wear-out patterns.

4.5   Preventive PbM

Just as the intrinsic failure rate, $r_i(t)$, could vary with systems, the failure rate, $r_e(t)$, may be associated with the external operating environment. For the ventilation system we mentioned above, it can be assumed that $r_i(t) = kt$, where k is a constant number; t is a factor associated with the external operating environment.

If we look into patterns E and F in Fig. 4, although preventive RbM is not needed, preventive PbM could be necessary for improving the system's performance, or cleanness in the ventilation system, or the cooling tower.

5 Conclusions

This paper has reviewed classical approaches to estimating cost elements of intelligent manufacturing service system that are influenced by reliability, and investigated special features which influence the life cycle. The cost elements discussed in this paper include acquisition costs, business losses, maintenance costs, and salvage costs. The following findings and achievements are recorded in the paper:

(1) an approach to estimating business losses caused by the failure of an individual component (or subsystem) was introduced. These can be employed when the whole lifecycle cost of a subsystem or a component is estimated;
(2) IMSS have special operating modes: long time periods at dormant states, and operating intermittently;
(3) there is a need to differentiate between two different sorts of maintenance, performance-based maintenance and reliability-based maintenance, in order to develop an optimal maintenance policy.

The results of the paper are helpful for the designers of IMSS, and researchers in order to develop reliability and maintenance policies.

Acknowledgements. Project supported by NSFC of Guangdong province (2018A030313320);
Project supported by National Natural Science Foundation of China (51305068);Supported by Doctoral Fund of Ministry of Education of China (20130185120034);
Project supported by the Fundamental Research Funds for the Central Universities (ZYGX2012J104);

Appendix A

Business losses caused by failures of a component, for example, component A, can be calculated as follows.

Step 1: compute system reliability when component A works, say $R_1(t)$,
Step 2: compute system reliability when component A fails, say $R_2(t)$,
Step 3: assume component A has density distribution function, $f(t)$,
Step 4: compute importance $I_{B\text{-}P}$ according to Eq. (3), and $C_B I_{B\text{-}P}$.

For example, consider the 3-component system shown in Fig. 2. Suppose components A_1 and A_2 have the same failure rate, $f_a(t) = \lambda_a e^{-\lambda_a t}$, and assume that for component B_3 $f_b(t) = \lambda_b e^{-\lambda_b t}$

Then, for component A_1

$$I_{B-P}^{(1)} = \int_0^\infty [\Pr(1_k, X) - \Pr(0_k, X)]f_k(t)dt$$

$$= \int_0^\infty [system\, reliability\, if\, component\, A_1\, works$$

$$- system\, reliability\, if\, component\, A_1\, fails]f_k(t)dt$$

$$= \lambda_a(\frac{1}{3\lambda_a} + \frac{1}{2\lambda_a + \lambda_b} - \frac{1}{3\lambda_a + \lambda_b})$$

Similarly, for component A_2

$$I_{B-P}^{(2)} = \lambda_a(\frac{1}{3\lambda_a} + \frac{1}{2\lambda_a + \lambda_b} - \frac{2}{3\lambda_a + \lambda_b})$$

If the business loss incurred by a failure of the system is C_b, then, the business losses caused by the failure of component A_1 is $C_b I_{B-P}^{(1)}$, and $C_b I_{B-P}^{(2)}$ by component A_2. Obviously, $C_b I_{B-P}^{(1)} > C_b I_{B-P}^{(2)}$.

For example, let $\lambda_a = 0.001$, $\lambda_b = 0.002$, and $C_b = $ £1000. Then $C_b I_{B-P}^{(1)} = $ £383.3, and $C_b I_{B-P}^{(2)} = $ £183.3, which means the business losses caused by component A_1 is £383.3, and the business losses caused by component A_2 is £183.3.

References

1. Dhillon, B.S.: Life Cycle Costing: Technique, Models and Applications. Gordon and Breach, New York (1989)
2. Kuo, W., Prasad, V.: An annotated overview of system reliability optimization. IEEE Trans. Reliab. **49**, 176–187 (2000)
3. Pham, H., Wang, H.: Imperfect maintenance. Eur. J. Oper. Res. **94**, 425–438 (1996)
4. Wang, K.S., Hsu, F.S., Liu, P.P.: Modelling the bathtub shape hazard rate function in terms of reliability. Reliab. Eng. Syst. Saf. **75**, 397–406 (2002)
5. Frangopol, D.M., Gharaibeh, E.S., Kong, J.S., Miyake, M.: Optimal network-level bridge maintenance planning based on minimum expected cost. Trans. Res. Rec. **2**, 26–33 (2000)
6. Ellingwood, B.R., Mori, Y.: Stability-based service life assessment of concrete structures in nuclear power plants: optimum inspection and repair. Divisions H,J and M, Porto Allegre, Brazil. vol. 4, pp. 529–538 (1995)
7. Van Noortwijk, J.M., Cooke, R.M., Kok, M.: Inspection and Repair Decisions for Hydraulic Structures under Isotropic Deterioration, p. 533. Operations research, Amsterdam (1993)
8. CIBSE.: Improved life cycle cost performance of mechanical ventilation systems. Chartered Institution of Manufacturing services Engineers, London (2003)
9. Schaufelberger, J.E., Jacobson, R.H.: Selecting optimum mechanical systems for office buildings. Cost Eng. **42**, 40–43 (2000)
10. Durairaj, S.K., Ong, S.K., Nee, A.Y., Tan, R.B.: Evaluation of lifecycle analysis methodologies. Corp. Environ. Strategy **9**, 30–39 (2002)

11. Woodward, D.G.: Life cycle costing-theory, information acquisition and application. Int. J. Proj. Manag. **15**, 335–344 (1997)
12. Clements-Croome, D., Jones, K., John, G., Loy, H.: Through life business modeling for sustainable architecture. In: CIBSE Proceedings of Conference on Building Sustainability, Value and Profit, Edinburgh, 24–26 September
13. John, G., Loy, H., Clements-Croome, D., Fairey, V., Neale, K.: Contextual prerequisites for the application of ILS principles to the manufacturing services industry. ECAM J. **40**, 406–428 (2005)
14. Tillman, F.A., Hwang, C.L., Kuo, W.: Optimization of System Reliability. Marcel Dekker (1980)
15. Evans, R., Haryott, H., Haste, N., Jones, A.: The Long-Term Costs Of Owning And Using Buildings. Royal Academy of Engineering, London (1998)
16. Wang,W., Loman, J., Vassiliou, P.: Reliability Importance of Components in a Complex System. In: Proceedings of The Annual Reliability and Maintainability Symposium, pp. 6–11 (2004)
17. Barlow, R.E., Proschan, F.: Importance of system components and fault tree events. Stoch. Process. Appl. **3**, 153–173 (1975)
18. Bartlett, E.V., Simpson, S.: Durability and Reliability, Alternative Approaches to Assessment of Component Performance Over Time, pp. 35–42. World Building Congress, Gavle, Sweden (1998)
19. Moubray, J.: RCM II Reliability Centred Maintenance. Butterworth-Heinemann, Oxford (1996)
20. Wu, S., Clements-Croome, D.: Optimal maintenance policies under different operational schedules. IEEE Trans. Reliab. **54**, 338–346 (2005)
21. Wu, S., Zuo, M.J.: Linear and nonlinear preventive maintenance models. IEEE Trans. Reliab. **59**(1), 242–249 (2010)
22. Wu, S., Xie, M.: Warranty cost analysis for nonrepairable services products. Int. J. Syst. Sci. **39**(3), 279–288 (2008)
23. Wu, S., Li, H.: Warranty cost analysis for products with a dormant state. Eur. J. Oper. Res. **182**(3), 1285–1293 (2007)
24. BS-3811 Glossary of terms used in terotechnology. British Standard, UK (1993)
25. Hurst, R., Williams, B., Lay, M.: Whole-life Economics of Manufacturing Services. International Facilities and Property Information Ltd, Kent (2005)
26. Harris, J., Hastings, P.: Business-Focused Maintenance: Guidance and Sample Schedules. BSRIA (2004)

Weave Bead Welding Based Wire and Arc Additive Manufacturing Technology

Zhihao Li[1], Guocai Ma[1], Gang Zhao[1,2], Min Yang[1], and Wenlei Xiao[1,2(✉)]

[1] School of Mechanical Engineering and Automation, Beihang University, Beijing 100191, China
xiaowenlei@buaa.edu.cn
[2] MIIT Key Laboratory of Aeronautics Intelligent Manufacturing, Beihang University, Beijing 100191, China

Abstract. For wire and arc additive manufacturing (WAAM) technology, the instable formation and the quality of the weld bead is still a problem. In welding technology, the weave bead welding can improve welding efficiency and welding quality. Besides, the weaving arc can reduce the presence of defects in the weld seam. This paper explores the application of weave bead welding in WAAM to improve forming stability and quality of the weld bead. In single-layer experiments, different parameters of weave length and weave amplitude are investigated to analyze their influences to the weld bead geometry. The forming stability of welding beads with weaving and without weaving are compared in multi-layer experiments. A large component is manufactured using the weave bead method, showing that the application of weave bead welding is a good way to improve forming stability in fabricating large scale parts.

Keywords: WAAM · Weave bead welding · Weaving parameters
Forming stability

1 Introduction

Additive manufacturing (AM) has a great potential for reducing material waste, life cycle impact and energy consumption [1]. In recent years, additive manufacturing technologies for metal components arouse great interest. Depending on the energy source used in melting materials, AM of metal components can be mainly classified into three groups: laser-based, electron beam-based and arc welding-based [2]. Among these, arc welding based AM has high energy efficiency and deposition rate [3].

The arc welding-based AM can be divided into the Gas Mental Arc Welding (GMAW) based, the Gas Tungsten Arc Welding (GTAW) based and the Plasma Arc welding (PAW) based technologies. The features of GMAW-based AM are wide applicability, high density and high production efficiency. For the control of the GMAW deposition process, a new modified GMAW, known as Gas Metal Arc Welding-Cold Metal Transfer (GMAW-CMT), offers low initial cost, controllable spatter and low heat input [4]. GMAW-CMT integrates the wire motions with metal transfer condition via a digital process control. The system can detect short circuits.

© Springer Nature Singapore Pte Ltd. 2018
S. Wang et al. (Eds.): ICSEE 2018/IMIOT 2018, CCIS 923, pp. 408–417, 2018.
https://doi.org/10.1007/978-981-13-2396-6_38

The system mechanically controls the retraction of the wire to help separate the droplets when each time a short circuit occurs, which greatly reduces heat input and spatter at the welding [5–7].

In the deposition process, with the number of the weld beads increases, the molten pool easy to flow. The shape of beads cannot be easily controlled, especially located at the boundaries of components [8]. It causes the weld beads of forming to be unstable. When deposit wide weld seams, multi-bead overlapping is prone to generate defects on the surface of the seam. In welding applications, there are many researches on weave bead welding technology which has many advantages. The linear energy of weave bead welding is much lower than that of normal Metal Inert-Gas (MIG) welding, while heat input remains almost unchanged. In addition, the weaving arc accelerates the effusion of impurities and bubbles, which reduces the presence of defects in the weld seam, such as inclusions and porosity [9]. In the study of Zhan et al. [10], compared to multi-pass welding, the weave bead welding increases welding efficiency and reduce the molten pool temperature. Besides, the shape of the weld is good and the welded joint has a high quality.

The weave bead welding is a high efficiency welding technology which can generate weld seam with good quality. However, there are few reports on the application of this technology in WAAM. In this paper, the weave bead for WAAM process is investigated. Experiments are designed to explore the influence of the weaving parameters to the geometry of the seam. The forming stability and quality of the weave bead are tested in multi-layer experiments. And finally a large-scale component is manufactured by using the weave bead welding technology.

2 Experiments

2.1 Experimental Setup

Experiments are conducted under a robotic wire and arc additive manufacturing (WAAM) system as shown in Fig. 1. The system mainly includes a robot and its controller, a welding machine and a working platform. A KUKA KR30 robot is adopted to control the movement of a welding torch to deposit metal materials. As for the welding power supply, a Fronius CMT Advanced4000 welding machine is employed. A three-dimensional welding platform is used to place the substrate. The computer generates the robot programs that are executed by the control center to control the robot motion and welding process.

The wire electrode used in the experiments is ER4043 wire of 1.2 mm diameter and the substrate is 5A06. The chemical compositions of the wire and the substrate are shown in Table 1. Argon (99.998%) is the shielding gas with a flow rate of 15 L/min. The distance between the welding torch and work piece is 15 mm.

2.2 The Weave Bead Welding Method

The diagram of the weave bead welding method is shown in Fig. 2. Weave length and weave amplitude are the main parameters of the weave bead welding method. The

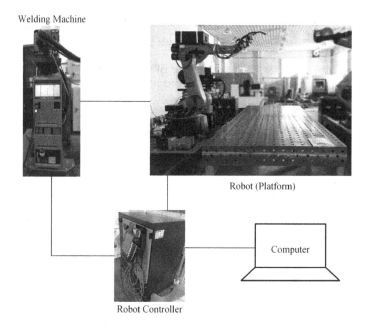

Fig. 1. The robotic wire and arc additive manufacturing system.

Table 1. The chemical composition of ER4043 wire and 5A06 substrate(mass fraction/%)

Material	Si	Mg	Cu	Fe	Mn	Zn	Al
Wire	5	0.10	0.05	0.04	–	–	Bal.
Substrate	0.4	5.8	0.10	0.400	0.5	0.20	Bal.

weave length is the track length from start point to end point of the weave pattern in the X direction, and the weave amplitude is sideways in the Y direction. Appropriate match of weave amplitude and weave length is important for weld bead forming. Otherwise it will cause problems, such as weld bead bending and uneven surface. The influence of weave bead welding parameters on weld geometry is analyzed through experiments in the following section.

2.3   Single-Layer Experiment

2.3.1   Single-Layer Experiment Method
Different parameters of weave length and weave amplitude were used to test the weave forming weld bead. The weave welding bead experimental parameters of single layer are shown in Table 2. A weld bead without weaving is also deposited as a contrast to the weaving welding beads.

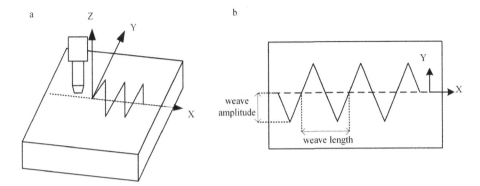

Fig. 2. The weave bead welding method diagram. (*a, the welding torch weaving triangle. b, weaving parameters*)

Table 2. The single-layer experimental.

No.	Wire feed rate (m/min)	Travel speed (m/min)	Weave length (mm)	Weave amplitude (mm)	Weld bead width (mm)
1	7.0	0.3	–	–	10.00
2	7.0	0.3	2	5	14.20
3	7.0	0.3	2	6	15.49
4	7.0	0.3	3	4	14.33
5	7.0	0.3	3	5	15.16
6	7.0	0.3	4	4	12.48
7	7.0	0.5	4	4	11.43
8	6.0	0.5	4	4	9.98

2.3.2   Single-Layer Experiment Result and Discussion

The single-layer experimental samples with different parameters are shown in Fig. 3. The width of weld bead without weaving is 10 mm, while the width of the weld beads with weaving are about 10–15 mm in range that are shown in Table 2. As shown in the Fig. 4, the beads of weave welding show a wider range in width.

The shapes of the welding beads vary with different parameters of weave length and weave amplitude. The weld bead samples of No. 2, No. 3, and No. 5 are bent. It is because that when the weave amplitude is large, the speed of weaving is fast, resulting in uneven distribution of droplets. By comparison, with the same wire feed rate and travel speed, samples of No. 4 and No. 6 have better shapes. It can be seen from Fig. 3 that with the increase of the weave amplitude, the width of the weld bead increases, but the bead bends when the weave amplitude is too large as shown No. 2 and No. 3. With the increase of weave length, the distance between adjacent droplets increases. Therefore, to guarantee the forming of the weld bead, the weave length should not be too large. In addition, wire feed rate and travel speed also affect the geometry of the

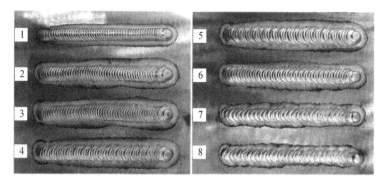

Fig. 3. Single-layer experimental samples. (*The sample number corresponds to the* Table 2)

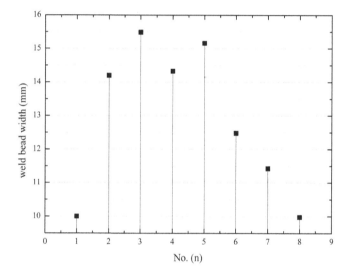

Fig. 4. The width of weld bead.

weld bead. By comparing the samples of No. 6, No. 7 and No. 8, to obtain good weld beads, the weaving parameters should vary with the wire feed rate and travel speed.

2.4   Multi-layer Experiment

2.4.1   Multi-layer Experiment Method

According to the result of the single-layer experiments, multi-layer experiments are carried out by using the optimized parameters.

Firstly, contrasting different deposition formations including that the multi-layer weld bead without weaving and the weld bead overlapping without weaving and the weld bead with weaving which under the same welding parameters were shown in Table 3. Then, the sample were deposited forming that parameters were shown in Table 3. A multi-layer weld bead without weaving was also deposited as a contrast.

The sample deposited with weaving is milled and scanned by a Micro Computed Tomography (Micro-CT) system to observe the internal defects. Finally, a large structure with size of 3000 × 1000 × 1000 mm was manufactured using the weave bead method. The parameters set in the large structure column display in Table 3. In depositing lower layers of the large structure, the inter-layer cooling time is short. Due to the large sample size and the long deposition time of each layer, the temperature can cool down without too much waiting time between two adjacent layers. When depositing the high layers, because the number of welding path was reduced and the deposition time became short for each layer, the inter-layer cooling time was set as about 2 to 3 min.

Table 3. The multi-layer experimental parameters.

Parameters	Single pass			Sample	Large structure
Wire feed rate (m/min)	7.0	7.0	7.0	7.0	7.0
Travel speed (m/min)	0.3	0.3	0.3	5.6	7.0
Weave length (mm)	–	–	4	0.3	0.3
Weave amplitude (mm)	–	–	4	4	4
Other	–	Overlapping	–	4	4

2.4.2 Multi-layer Experiment Result and Discussion

The results of first multi-layer experimental are shown in Fig. 5. No. 1 is the multi-layer weld bead without weaving. No. 2 is the multi-layer weld bead overlapping without weaving and the multi-layer weld bead with weaving is No. 3. According to the single-layer results, the width of the weld bead without weaving is less than that with weaving. In order to get wider welds, the weld bead overlapping should be carried out. As shown in the Fig. 5, there is the uneven surface of the weld with overlapping and defects from the starting and ending positions of the weld. Compared with overlapping, the weaving weld bead is stable and the surface quality is better.

Fig. 5. Contrasting different deposition welds

The weld beads of sample with weaving and without weaving are compared as shown in Fig. 6. The weld bead with weaving has higher forming stability than that without weaving. It is because the weaving arc has a role of stirring to the molten pool and thus there is less fluctuation of the shape of the weld bead. It is easy to meet the requirement of layer flatness. Under the same wire feed rate and travel speed conditions, the weave bead welding method can deposit a wider multi-layer weld bead with a higher stability.

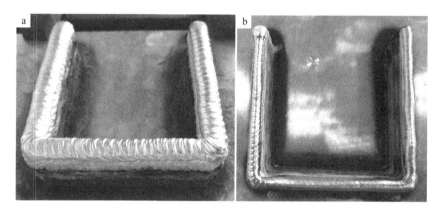

Fig. 6. Comparison of the multi-layer weld beads with weaving and without weaving. (*a, weaving. b, without weaving*)

The final deposited sample is shown in Fig. 7(a) and (b) shows the part after milling. The milled part is scanned by using a Micro Computed Tomography (Micro-CT) system, and the results are shown in Fig. 8. It can be seen that there is only a small number of pores in the part.

A large structure is manufactured as shown in Fig. 9. The design model of the structure is shown in Fig. 9(a) and the dimensional parameters are marked in the

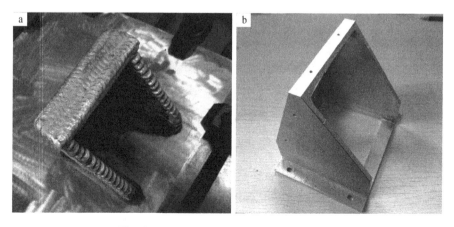

Fig. 7. The multi-layer experimental sample.

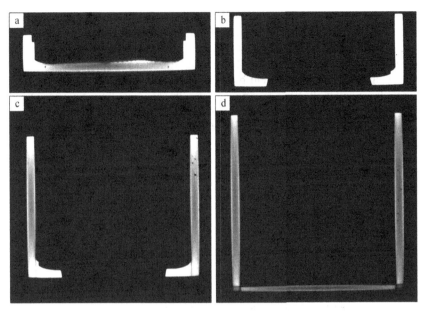

Fig. 8. The scanning result of the milled sample. (*a, b, c, d are sequentially from top to bottom of the milled sample*)

Fig. 9. The large structure.

diagram in detail. Figure 9(b) shows the finally formed structure. Figure 9(c) displays the smooth appearance of the top surface of a thin wall of the structure, and Fig. 9(d) shows the side surface of the thin wall. The structure was deposited continuously and the manufacturing process was stable. The results show that the formation of weld bead with weaving is stable and the weld beads have a good shape.

Single-layer and multi-layer experimental results show that the weave bead welding method can be used in WAAM to improve forming stability and quality of the weld bead. In particular, stable manufacturing of large parts has great significance for the development of WAAM. It is important to further explore the mechanical properties and microstructure of the fabricated parts. Carrying out related researches and extending the applications of the WAAM technology will be the following work.

3   Conclusion

In this paper, the weave bead welding based WAAM technology is investigated. The following conclusions can be drawn.

(1) The weld bead with weaving is more stable forming than without weaving and is easier to flatten and control than with overlapping.
(2) With the increase of the weave amplitude, the width of the weld bead increases, but the bead bends when the weave amplitude is too large. With the increase of weave length, the distance between adjacent droplets increases. So the weave length should not be too large to guarantee the forming of the weld bead.
(3) Multi-layer experiments show that the use of weave bead welding in WAAM can improve the stability of the shapes of the weld beads. The ICT scanning results shows that there is only a small number of pores in the sample deposited with weave bead welding.
(4) A large component is manufactured using the weave bead method. The result shows that the method has wide application prospect in manufacturing large scale parts using WAAM technology.

Acknowledgments.   This research is supported by the Beijing Municipal Science & Technology Commission of China.

References

1. Huang, R., Riddle, M., Graziano, D.: Energy and emissions saving potential of additive manufacturing: the case of lightweight aircraft components. J. Clean. Prod. **135**, 1559–1570 (2016)
2. Ding, D., Pan, Z., Cuiuri, D.: Wire-feed additive manufacturing of metal components: technologies, developments and future interests. Int. J. Adv. Manuf. Technol. **81**, 465–481 (2015)
3. Kazanas, P., Deherkar, P., Almeida, P.: Fabrication of geometrical features using wire and arc additive manufacture. J. Proc. Inst. Mech. Eng. B J. Eng. Manuf. **226**(6), 1042–1051 (2012)

4. Zhang, H.T., Feng, J.C., He, P.: The arc characteristics and metal transfer behaviour of cold metal transfer and its use in joining aluminium to zinc-coated steel. J. Mater. Sci. Eng. A. **499**, 111–113 (2009)

5. Wagiman, A., Bin Wahab, M.S., Mohid, Z.: Effect of GMAW-CMT heat input on weld bead profile geometry for freeform fabrication of aluminium parts. J. Appl. Mech. Mater. **465–466**, 1370–1374 (2013)

6. Pickin, C.G., Young, K.: Evaluation of cold metal transfer (CMT) process for welding aluminium alloy. J. Sci. Technol. Weld. Join. **11**(4), 1–3 (2006)

7. Feng, J., Zhang, H., He, P.: The CMT short-circuiting metal transfer process and its use in thin aluminium sheets welding. J. Mater. Des. **30**(5), 1850–1852 (2009)

8. Xiong, J., Zhang, G., Qiu, Z.: Vision-sensing and bead width control of a single-bead multi-layer part: material and energy savings in GMAW-based rapid manufacturing. J. Clean. Prod. **41**(1), 82–88 (2013)

9. Zhan, X., Liu, X., Wei, Y.: Microstructure and property characteristics of thick Invar alloy plate joints using weave bead welding. J. Mater. Process. Tech. **244**, 97–105 (2017)

10. Zhan, X., Zhang, D., Liu, X.: Comparison between weave bead welding and multi-layer multi-pass welding for thick plate Invar steel. Int. J. Adv. Manuf. Technol. **88**(5–8), 1–15 (2016)

11. Hu, J.F., Yang, J.G., Fang, H.Y.: Numerical simulation on temperature and stress fields of welding with weaving. J. Sci. Technol. Weld. Join. **11**(3), 358–365 (2006)

12. Chen, Y., He, Y., Chen, H.: Effect of weave frequency and amplitude on temperature field in weaving welding process. Int. J. Adv. Manuf. Technol. **75**(5–8), 803–813 (2014)

13. Yang, D., Wang, G., Zhang, G.: Thermal analysis for single-pass multi-layer GMAW based additive manufacturing using infrared thermography. J. Mater. Process. Tech. **244**, 215–224 (2017)

The Effect of Process Parameters on the Machined Surface Quality in Milling of CFRPs

Guangjian Bi, Fuji Wang[✉], Xiaonan Wang, Chen Chen,
Dong Wang, and Zegang Wang

The Key Laboratory for Precision and Nontraditional Machining Technology
of Ministry of Education, Dalian University of Technology,
Dalian 116024, China
727952523@qq.com, 1206318725@qq.com, 271293404@qq.com,
wfjsll@dlut.edu.cn,
{18842660282,S201265044}@mail.dlut.edu.cn

Abstract. Milling is inevitable for CFRP components to remove excess material in manufacturing industries. Multi-flute sawtooth milling tool was widely used because of its cutting stability and high machining quality. However, obvious damage was observed on the machined surface of the CFRPs when fiber orientation is larger than 90°. Therefore, it is important to optimize the process parameters regarding the surface quality in case of multi-flute sawtooth milling tool. To this aim, the experiment of slotting of the CFRPs was conducted by the multi-flute sawtooth milling tool in this paper. The pit depth was proposed as the criterion to quantify the quality of the machined surface. The milling forces for different parameters and the relationship between the forces and the machined surface quality were researched. Based on the experimental results, it can be obtained that low cutting speed and high feed rate are the optimal cutting conditions for the good machined surface quality and high material removal rate when the up milling surface is the mating surface of CFRP components.

Keywords: Milling · Surface quality · Damage · Force · Process parameter

1 Introduction

Carbon Fiber Reinforced Polymers (CFRPs) are widely used in aerospace, automotive, and sports goods due to its high strength-to-weight ratio and good dimensional stability [1, 2]. Although CFRP components are manufactured near-net-shape by layup and curing, drilling and milling must be performed to assure that the CFRP components meet dimensional tolerance, surface quality and other functional requirements [3, 4]. Milling is one of the main processes of machining CFRP due to its flexible machining trajectory and high machining quality [5, 6]. However, CFRP is a typical difficult-to-machine material. CFRP is the mixture of carbon and matrix at micro level, and it is characterized by laminating, heterogeneity and anisotropy at macro level. The cutting damage, such as burring, delamination and cracking, easily occurs because of

© Springer Nature Singapore Pte Ltd. 2018
S. Wang et al. (Eds.): ICSEE 2018/IMIOT 2018, CCIS 923, pp. 418–427, 2018.
https://doi.org/10.1007/978-981-13-2396-6_39

unreasonable process parameters and tool geometries during the machining of the CFRPs [7], which result in the serious reducing of the carrying capacity of the CFRP components.

The machining quality of the CFRPs is closely related to the tool geometry [8]. The general helical milling tool, PCD milling tool, double helix milling tool and multi-flute sawtooth milling tool are used frequently for the milling of the CFRPs. Chatelain [9] and Yang [10] conducted experimental comparisons using general helical milling tool, double helix milling tool and multi-flute sawtooth milling tool. It was found that the milling force conducted by the general helical milling tool is more stable than that of the others, and the machining quality of the double helix milling tool was worse than that of the multi-flute sawtooth milling tool. Lopez De Lacalle [11] compared the PCD milling tool and the multi-flute sawtooth milling tool by the slotting of the CFRPs. It was concluded that the PCD milling tool do not reach enough conditions to be economically feasible with respect to their high price. It was better to improve the machining quality with multi-flute sawtooth milling tool.

Many studies on the effects of the process parameters on the machining of the CFRPs have been done in recent years. Wang [12] found that the feed rate is the main factor influencing the milling force, followed by cutting speed. It was concluded that the low cutting speed, minimum feed rate, and maximum radial depth of cut are preferred to obtain good surface quality and high material removal rate. Colak [13] observed that the milling force is the smallest under the condition of maximum cutting speed and minimum feed rate. The surface roughness increased with the increase of the feed rate and the reduction of the cutting speed. Madjid [8] conducted milling experiments with different tool geometries and process parameters. It was obtained that the surface roughness decrease with the increase of the feed rate when using general helical milling tool. And an opposite phenomenon was observed in the case of the multi-flute sawtooth milling tool. Therefore, it is important to choose the advisable variable process parameters regarding the surface quality in case of multi-flute sawtooth milling tool.

Quantifying the quality of the machined surface based on the average roughness (e.g., Ra, Sa, etc.) is not suitable for composite materials [14]. During the machining of the CFRPs when the fiber cutting angle is $135°$, pits are result on the machined surface generally, which distribute discretely. Meanwhile, the pits and facets alternate on the machined surface as a sawtooth [15]. Considering the damage size is related to the pits depth, and the pit depth is proposed as the criterion to quantify the quality of machined surface in this paper.

The objective of this paper is to research the effect of the process parameters on the cutting force and surface quality. To this aim, the experiment of slotting of the CFRPs was conducted by the multi-flute sawtooth milling tool firstly. Different feed rates and cutting speeds were applied, and the milling force and the surface quality of the machined CFRPs were recorded. In addition, the morphology and the topography of the machined surface were obtained by Scanning Electron Microscope (SEM) and Laser Confocal Microscope (LCM), respectively. Meanwhile, the relationship between milling force and surface quality was studied. Finally, the main factor affecting the surface quality was analyzed according to the required results, which can be as the reference for the CFRP manufacturing.

2 Experiment

Experiments were conducted on the aerospace grade T800 multi-directional CFRP laminates. And the workpiece is manufactured by prepregs in the layout of $[(-45/0/45/90)_2/0]_s$, which is layered with 21 layers by laying and curing. The thickness of the workpiece is 4 mm. The fiber volume of the prepreg is around 60%, and detailed physical properties are listed in Table 1. The multi-flute sawtooth milling tool was conducted to milling of the CFRPs, which made the cutting process stable and reduced the milling force compared to others. The diameter of the tool is 6 mm. Slotting was used to obtain the surface quality of down milling and up milling. Tool geometries and process parameters of milling are listed in Table 2. The cutting edge radius is about 7–9 µm, and the depth of cut influences the chip formation. Moreover, the chip formation affects the machined surface quality and cutting force. Therefore, the feed rate is set to less than cutting edge radius, equal to the cutting edge radius and larger than the cutting edge radius. And the milling tool is shown in Fig. 1.

Table 1. Mechanical properties of the T800 prepreg.

Items	Value
Density/(g/cm^3)	2.7
Longitudinal young's modulus/Gpa	160
Longitudinal shear modulus/GPa	6.21
Transverse poisson's ratio	0.36
Tensile strength/MPa	2843
Compressive strength/MPa	1553

Table 2. Experiment conditions

Tool		Cutting conditions	
Clearance angle γ	10°	Cutting speed V_c	0.5/1/1.5/2/2.5/3 mm/s
Rake angle α	5°	Feed rate f_z	0.005/0.01/0.015/0.025/0.035 mm/z
Number of flutes	12	Axial depth of cut	4 mm
Helix angle β	15°	Coolant	none

Fig. 1. Multi-flute sawtooth milling tool

The experimental setup is shown in Fig. 2. The milling experiment was carried out on MIKRON HSM 500. The CFRP workpiece is clamped on the fixture which is mounted by 4 fastening bolts on the dynamometer. The width of the workpiece is 30 mm. The milling force is measured by Kistler 9257B dynamometer in real time.

The signal of milling force goes through charge amplifier (Charge Amplifier 5080) and AD conversion (Dynoware 5697), then the signal is transmitted to a laptop for data acquisition. Figure 3 shows the schematic of slotting of the CFRPs. Fiber orientation (Φ) of the laminate is calculated by considering the direction of feed and orientation of the fibers in the laminate. The fiber orientation is measured clockwise with reference to the direction of feed (V_f). The fiber cutting angle (θ) is measured clockwise with reference to the instantaneous direction of cutting (V_c). The fiber cutting angle changes as the cutting tool rotates during milling. The φ represents tool rotation angle, which starts at $0°$ and end at $180°$. The component F_X represents milling force in the direction of feed, and the component F_Y represents milling force in the radical direction. The morphology of the machined surface is observed by SEM, and the topography of the machined surface is obtained by LCM.

Fig. 2. Experimental setup   **Fig. 3.** The schematic of slotting of the CFRPs

3   Results and Discussion

3.1   Milling Force

The signal of the milling forces for various feed rates as the cutting speed is 1 m/s in real time is shown in Fig. 4, which increased with the increase of feed rate. The instantaneous depth of cut increased with the increase of feed rate, which resulted in increased milling forces. The component F_X was higher compared to the component F_Y as $f_z = 0.005$ mm/z. However, an opposite phenomenon was observed while the feed rate is 0.035 mm/z. The sawtooth are distributed on the circumference according to certain rules for the multi-flute sawtooth milling tool. The sawtooth of half of the circumference are involved in cutting while slotting of the CFRPs. The sawtooth deemed to be symmetric distribution along the center as shown in Fig. 5. The cutting force F_c and thrust force F_t are decomposed in the direction of feed rate and radical direction by the following Eq., respectively.

$$F_X = (F_{At} + F_{Ct})sin\varphi + F_{Bt} + (F_{Ac} - F_{Cc})cos\varphi$$
$$F_Y = (F_{Ac} + F_{Cc})sin\varphi + F_{Bc} + (-F_{At} + F_{Ct})cos\varphi$$

Where the F_{Ac}, F_{Bc} and F_{Cc} are the cutting forces in the position of A, B and C, respectively; the F_{At}, F_{Bt} and F_{Ct} are the thrust forces in the position of A, B and C, respectively; the φ is the tool rotation angel.

The instantaneous depth of cut was small when the feed rate is 0.005 mm/z. The cutting force F_c was lower than the thrust force F_t at each instantaneous cutting position as $f_z = 0.005$ mm/z. Therefore, the component F_X was higher than the component F_Y as shown in Fig. 4.

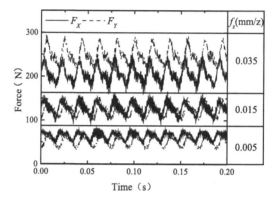

Fig. 4. Signal milling forces for different feed rates ($V_c = 1$ m/s)

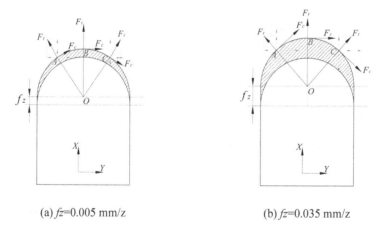

(a) f_z=0.005 mm/z   (b) f_z=0.035 mm/z

Fig. 5. The schematic of distribution of milling forces for different feed rates

The cutting force for large fiber cutting angle increased with the increase of the depth of cut which is related to feed rate, while the thrust force of large fiber cutting angle decreased. The cutting force and thrust force for small fiber cutting angle increased with the increase of the depth of cut [16]. However, the increasing rate of the cutting force for small fiber cutting angle was lower compared to that for large fiber cutting angle. The increasing rate of the component F_X was smaller than that of the component F_Y. It is noted that the component F_Y was higher than the component F_X when the feed rate reached the maximum, as shown in Fig. 4.

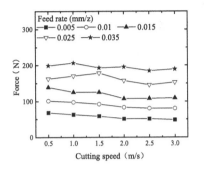
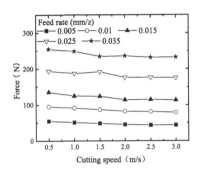

(a) Average milling forces in the direction of feed

(b) Average milling forces in the radical direction

Fig. 6. Average milling forces for different feed rates and cutting speeds

Figure 6 demonstrated the trend of changes in average milling forces with the feed rate and cutting speed. The results showed that the average milling force increased with the increase of feed rate, while reduced slightly with the increase of cutting speed [13]. Compared to feed rate, the cutting speed has no much effect on the milling force. The feed rate was the important factor affecting milling force versus to cutting speed.

3.2   Surface Quality

It occurred unobvious damage in the machined surface for $\Phi = 0°$, $45°$, $90°$ when the feed rate was 0.005 mm/z as shown in Fig. 7. The reason is that the fiber cutting angles are approximate to $0°$, $45°$ and $90°$ for $\Phi = 0°$, $45°$, $90°$ when the cutting edge of milling tool cuts into and cuts out workpiece, respectively. And the chip formation for $\theta = 0°$, $45°$, $90°$ resulted in good machined surface quality under small depth of cut. However, it occurred obvious pit damage on the machined surface for $\Phi = 135°$. The reason is that the fiber cutting angle is approximate to $135°$ for $\Phi = 135°$ when the cutting edge of milling tool cuts into and cuts out workpiece. The fiber first approached with the rake face of the tool near the position of cutting into and cutting out for $\Phi = 135°$. The fiber bent as the tool feeds, which caused cracks of the fiber beneath the machined surface. Then the fiber fractured due to the further feed of tool. Finally, the pit was formed showed in Fig. 7. Comparing Fig. 7(a) and (b) showed that the pit damage in the downing milling surface was severer than that in the up milling surface, which can be clearly observed by the topologies of the machined surface as shown in Fig. 8.

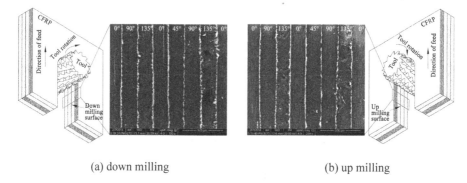

(a) down milling   (b) up milling

Fig. 7. The morphology of the machined surface for down milling and up milling ($f_z = 0.005$ mm/z)

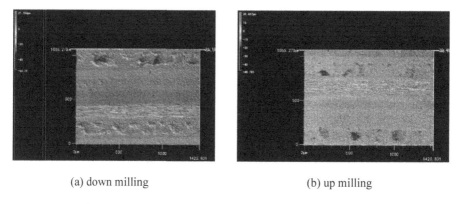

(a) down milling   (b) up milling

Fig. 8. Topography of the machined surface ($f_z = 0.005$ mm/z)

The machined surface of the $\Phi = 135°$ was the roughest, which was focused in the paper. Therefore, only the machined surface profile of $\Phi = 135°$ was extracted by the topographies, as shown in Fig. 9. The pit depth can be obtained by the profile. The profiles of machined surface of down milling and up milling when the feed rate is 0.005 mm/z are shown in Fig. 10. Results showed that the pit depth is in the range of 50 μm to 60 μm for the down milling surface, and the pit depth is in the range of 40 μm to 50 μm for the up milling surface. However, the augment of cutting speed caused increase of pit depth through the comparison for Fig. 10(a) and (b). The effect of cutting speed on the machined surface quality was different from that of cutting speed on the milling force. Compared to Fig. 10, there was a great difference of pits depth between down milling and up milling when $f_z = 0.035$ mm/z as shown in Fig. 11. Comparing Fig. 10(a) and Fig. 11(a) showed that the pits depth are approaching under the condition of up milling. The pit depth increased with the increase of cutting speed, and the maximum pit depth was up to 120 μm.

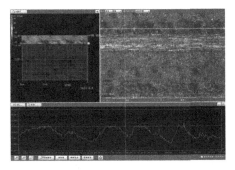

Fig. 9. The schematic of extracting profile

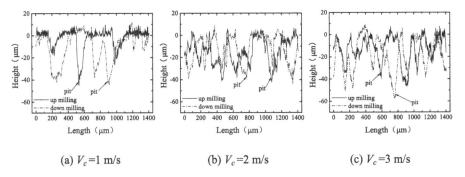

(a) V_c=1 m/s   (b) V_c=2 m/s   (c) V_c=3 m/s

Fig. 10. The profiles for different cutting speeds ($f_z = 0.005$ mm/z)

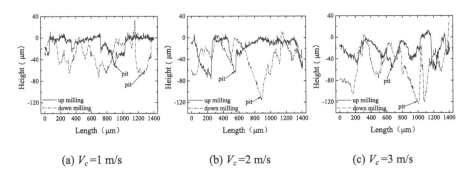

(a) V_c=1 m/s   (b) V_c=2 m/s   (c) V_c=3 m/s

Fig. 11. The profiles for different cutting speeds ($f_z = 0.035$ mm/z)

4   Conclusion

In this paper, an experimental approach is presented to study the milling force and the quality of machined surface under the condition of different process parameters in case of multi-flute sawtooth milling tool by slotting of the CFRPs. The following observation were made:

(1) Presented results confirmed feed rate as a factor with strongest influence on the milling force, in a way that increasing in feed rate resulted in increasing of milling force. The cutting speed has no much effect on the milling force.

(2) Results showed that the down milling and up milling influence the quality of machined surface when the fiber orientation is 135°. The pit depth for up milling was lower compared to that for down milling, especially for the large feed rate.

(3) From the machining results, it can be asserted that low cutting speed and high feed rate are the optimal cutting conditions for the good machined surface quality and high material removal rate when the up milling surface is the mating surface of CFRP components

Acknowledgments. This work is supported by National Natural Science Foundation of China, No. 51575082, National Natural Science Foundation of China-United with Liaoning Province, No. U1508207, National Key Basic Research Program of China (973 Program), No. 2014CB046503, National Innovative Research Group, No. 51621064.

References

1. Soutis, C.: Fiber reinforced composites in aircraft construction. Prog. Aerosp. Sci. **41**(2), 143–151 (2005)
2. Sheikh-ahmad, J.Y.: Machining of Polymer Composite. Springer, New York (2009). https://doi.org/10.1007/978-0-387-68619-6
3. Henerichs, M., Voss, R., Kuster, F., et al.: Machining of carbon fiber reinforced plastics: influence of tool geometry and fiber orientation on the machining forces. CIRP J. Manufact. Sci. Technol. **9**, 136–145 (2015)
4. Ghafarizadeh, S., Chatelain, J.F., Lebrun, G.: Finite element analysis of surface milling of carbon fiber-reinforced com-posites. Int. J. Adv. Manuf. Tech. **87**(1–4), 399–409 (2016)
5. Davim, J.P., Reis, P.: Damage and dimensional precision on milling carbon fiber-reinforced plastics using design exper-iments. J. Mater. Process. Tech. **160**(2), 160–167 (2005)
6. Norlida, J., Ahmad, R.Y.: Electromagnetic actuator for determining frequency response function of dynamic modal testing on milling tool. Measurement **82**, 355–366 (2016)
7. Slamani, M., Gauthier, S., Chatelain, J.F.: Analysis of trajectory deviation during high speed robotic trimming of carbon-fiber reinforced polymers. Robot. CIM-INT. Manuf. **30**, 546–555 (2014)
8. Madjid, H., Redouane, Z., Florent, E., et al.: Study of the surface defects and dust generated during trimming of CFRP: Influence of tool geometry, machining parameters and cut-ting speed range. Compos. Part. A-Appl. S. **66**, 142–154 (2014)

9. Chatelain, J.F., Zaghbani, I.: Effect of tool geometry special features on cutting forces of multilayered CFRP laminates. In: International Conference on Manufacturing Engineering, Quality and Production Systems: proceedings of the 4th International Conference, Barcelona, Spain, pp. 85–90 (2011)
10. Yang, X.F., Li, Y.S., Yan, G.H., et al.: The analysis of tool wear in milling CFRP with different diamond coated tool. Key Eng. Mater. **667**, 231–236 (2016)
11. Lopez De Lacalle, L.N., Lamikiz, A., Campa, F.J., et al.: Design and test of a multitooth tool for CFRP milling. J. Compos. Mater. **43**(26), 3275–3290 (2009)
12. Wang, H.J., Sun, J., Li, J.F., et al.: Evaluation of cutting forces and cutting temperature in milling carbon fiber-reinforced polymer composites. Int. J. Adv. Manuf. Tech. **82**(9–12), 1517–1525 (2016)
13. Colak, O., Sunar, T.: Cutting forces and 3D surface analysis of CFRP milling with PCD cutting tools // Procedia CIRP: Proceedings of the 3rd CIRP Conference on Surface Integrity. Charlotte: North Carolina. **45**, 75–78 (2016)
14. Saleem, M., Toubal, L., Zitoune, R., et al.: Investigating the effect of machining processes on the mechanical behavior of composite plates with circular holes. Compos. Part. A-Appl. S. **55**, 169–177 (2013)
15. Liu, G.J., Chen, H.Y., Huang, Z., et al.: Surface quality of staggered PCD end mill in milling of carbon fiber reinforced plastics. Appl. Sci. **7**, 1–12 (2017)
16. Su, Y.L., Jia, Z.Y., Niu, B., et al.: Size effect of depth of cut on chip formation mechanism in machining of CFRP. Compos. Struct. **164**, 316–327 (2017)

Influence of Dynamic Change of Fiber Cutting Angle on Surface Damage in CFRP Milling

Dong Wang, Fuji Wang[(⊠)], Zegang Wang, Guangjian Bi, and Qi Wang

Dalian University of Technology, Dalian 116024, China
wfjsll@dlut.edu.cn

Abstract. The milling process of carbon fiber reinforced polymer (CFRP) is prone to damages like burr and tear. The fiber cutting angle is generally recognized as an important factor in damage formation. In this study, through up milling and down milling experiments with unidirectional CFRP laminates at four typical orientations, the influence of the dynamic change of fiber cutting angle on surface damage was clarified by burr height, burr morphology and tear degree. The research shows that the dynamic change of fiber cutting angle is the basis of CFRP surface damage formation. Damage accumulates gradually in damage-prone zone, which ultimately determines burr height. When the variation range coincides 90°–135° partially or completely, a significant subsurface tear occurs. If it covers both acute and obtuse areas, the tear degree and burr morphology are determined by the order of the two regions.

Keywords: Carbon Fiber Reinforced Polymer (CFRP) · Milling
Fiber cutting angle · Surface damage

1 Introduction

Carbon fiber reinforced polymer (CFRP) has many advantages such as high specific strength, high specific stiffness, corrosion resistance and designability, which makes it widely used in low- and high-technology engineering applications [1–3]. During the manufacture of components from CFRP, a large number of milling processes are required in order to meet the required tolerances and to manufacture fitting and joining surfaces after curing. However, the heterogeneity and anisotropy of CFRP make its machinability completely different from that of homogeneous metal materials. Lamination, tear and burr are especially easy to occur in the processing. These damages have extremely serious effects on the performance of components and the assembly performance between components, and even result in the rejection of components [4]. If not controlled effectively, it will lead to the decline of production efficiency and serious economic loss. Therefore, it is very important to realize high quality milling of CFRP components.

At present, some researchers are devoted to exploring the influence of cutting quantity and tool geometry parameters on machining quality. Davim et al. [5] and Sheikh-Ahmad et al. [6] conducted a study to determine the effect of typical process parameters on burr length and obtained an empirical formula between the processing

© Springer Nature Singapore Pte Ltd. 2018
S. Wang et al. (Eds.): ICSEE 2018/IMIOT 2018, CCIS 923, pp. 428–439, 2018.
https://doi.org/10.1007/978-981-13-2396-6_40

parameters and the burr length by fitting experimental data. Yin et al. [7] found that the machining quality can be effectively improved by reducing the single cutting thickness and controlling the cutting temperature in the reasonable range. Hintze et al. [8] investigated the influence of tool diameters and helix angles on the maximum burr length. These researchers have explored the influence of cutting quantity or tool geometry parameters on machining quality by experimental methods and used to guide actual production. To a certain extent, it plays a role in improving the machining quality. However, as a link of high-quality machining of CFRP, the optimization of process parameters still needs to cooperate with other links to play its role fully. And revealing the mechanism of damage formation in milling is the basic step to complete the whole optimization process.

Because of the anisotropy of CFRP, fiber cutting angle which is the angle between fiber orientation and cutting speed direction is a key factor influencing the damage formation. In related studies, Koplev et al. [9] used orthogonal cutting experiments to correlate surface quality with fiber orientation and found that the fiber orientation had a significant impact on the form of fiber fracture. Wang et al. [10] analyzed the cutting mechanism of unidirectional and multidirectional CFRP experimentally and adopted orthogonal cutting method to obtain the effect of fiber cutting angle on the quality of machined surface. According to the size of fiber cutting angle and rake angle, Sheikh-Ahmad [11] divided the chip formation modes of CFRP into five categories. Jia et al. [12] established a finite element model of orthogonal cutting that can realize the simulation analysis of continuous dynamic cutting process of unidirectional laminates with arbitrary fiber orientations, and obtained the influence of fiber orientation on the depth of subsurface damage. In addition, numerous other studies [13–16] on the chip formation mechanisms of CFRP have demonstrated the importance of fiber cutting angle for material removal process and damage formation.

Researchers at home and abroad often use orthogonal cutting method to explore the influence of fiber cutting angle on damage formation. However, milling differs from orthogonal cutting in that the removal of material requires multiple actions by the cutting edge. Rotational cutting changes the fiber cutting angle dynamically, resulting in that the damage formation is also a dynamic process. Therefore, the theory of orthogonal cutting alone cannot reveal the influence of the dynamic change of fiber cutting angle on damage formation in milling. Considering the movement characteristics of milling cutters, it is of great significance to deeply explore the mechanism of damage formation affected by the dynamic change of fiber cutting angle, so as to guide the optimization process of CFRP milling.

Based on the edge trimming experiments of unidirectional CFRP laminates under different milling methods which are up milling and down milling respectively, the aim of this study is to explore the influence of the dynamic change of fiber cutting angle on surface damage. The optimal scheme of milling methods in edge trimming is determined to minimize surface damage and to establish a good basic environment for the optimization of later process parameters. The conclusions of this study have certain significance to the damage formation theory of CFRP and the research of damage suppression technology.

2 Preparation Works

2.1 Definition of Fiber Cutting Angle

CFRP has anisotropy and its behavioral characteristics in cutting are largely determined by the angle between fiber orientation and cutting speed direction, which is defined as fiber cutting angle. In milling, the fiber cutting angle can be determined by two factors, fiber orientation angle and cutter engagement angle. It is defined that θ is fiber orientation angle, φ is cutter engagement angle, and β is fiber cutting angle. Taking the up milling as an example, Fig. 1 describes the actual geometric meanings of θ, φ and β.

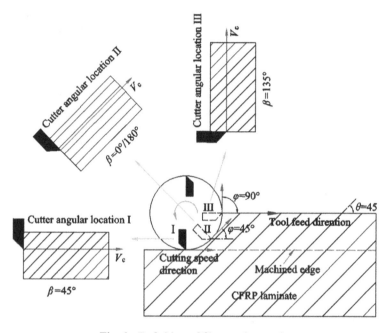

Fig. 1. Definition of fiber cutting angle

The feed direction is taken as the reference line and it is rotated to the side of removed material until it coincides with fiber orientation. The rotated angle is fiber orientation angle. Cutter engagement angle is used to indicate the cutter angular position. The cutter position is defined as the initial measurement position of cutter engagement angle when the cutting speed direction is in the same direction as the feed direction. Define the rotation direction of spindle is positive. β can be deduced from θ and φ. The specific expressions are shown in formula (1) and (2). The fiber cutting angle in down milling are complementary to that of up milling at the same position.

$$\beta = \theta - \varphi(\varphi \le \theta) \tag{1}$$

$$\beta = 180^{\circ} - (\varphi - \theta)(\varphi > \theta) \tag{2}$$

2.2 Experimental Approach

In order to reveal the influence of the dynamic change of fiber cutting angle on surface damage, the edge trimming experiments of unidirectional laminates at four typical orientations are performed using two milling methods which are up milling and down milling respectively. In addition, the slotting experiment of 0° unidirectional laminate is performed to determine the range of fiber cutting angle in which surface damage occurs easily. It can be used as the basis for dynamic analysis in edge trimming. This is mainly due to the particularity of 0°. The fiber cutting angle experienced by each individual fiber does not change with the movement of milling cutter. And the semi-circular machined edge in slotting experiment covers the entire range of fiber cutting angle from 0° to 180°, which is convenient for data acquisition.

The workpiece material used in this study is unidirectional CFRP laminate and individual layer is made of T800 class fiber impregnated with P2352 epoxy resin. The experimental pieces include four typical orientations of 0°, 45°, 90°, and 135° and the dimensions are 32 mm × 32 mm × 3 mm.

In this paper, the surface damages such as burr and tear in milling are mainly studied. Because the interlaminar bonding strength of CFRP is relatively low, spiral end mill may produce large axial force and cause severe delamination. Therefore, the end mill with 0° helix angle is selected as experimental tool. At the same time, large cutting edge radius is selected to obtain a more obvious macroscopic experimental phenomenon. The material of end mill is carbide GK05A. The specific parameters are shown in Table 1.

Table 1. Structural parameters of the end mill with 0° helix angle

Rake angle/°	Relief angle/°	Diameter/mm	Edge length/mm	Cutting edge radius/μm
4	9	8	20	20

The experiment is carried out under dry cutting conditions on a Mikron HSM 500 vertical high-speed CNC machining center. The spindle speed and feed per tooth are 5000 r/min and 0.05 mm/tooth respectively. The radial depth of cut is 4 mm in edge trimming and the slot length is 20 mm in slotting. The morphology and distribution of surface damage are observed by Japanese KEYENCE VHX-600E and the magnification is ×30. The specific experimental setup and VHX-600E are shown in Fig. 2.

(a) Experimental setup   (b) VHX-600E

Fig. 2. Equipment used for the experiment

3 Results and Discussions

Figure 3 illustrates the images of surface damage of CFRP laminates in up milling and down milling, including four typical orientations of 0°, 45°, 90° and 135°. The degree of surface damage in each group is shown in Table 2. It is found that when different milling methods are adopted for the same unidirectional laminate, the degree of surface damage will change significantly. In general, up milling and down milling mainly changes the range and process of fiber cutting angle. Therefore, the dynamic change of fiber cutting angle is the key factor affecting the quality of CFRP edge trimming. Specific analysis is as follows.

3.1 Influence of Dynamic Change of Fiber Cutting Angle on Burr Height

Figure 4 shows the image of surface damage in slotting 0° unidirectional laminate. In AutoCAD, measure the range of cutter engagement angle represented by the AB segment, namely the surface damage area, and obtain the corresponding range of fiber cutting angle according to formula (1) and (2). It is found that obvious burr phenomenon exists in the fiber cutting angle range of 0°–135° and severe tear is also accompanied in the fiber cutting angle range of 90°–135°.

In order to describe the dynamic change of fiber cutting angle more clearly, a single fiber is taken as an example. Figure 5 shows the specific change of fiber cutting angle when unidirectional laminates at four typical orientations are milled in up milling and down milling. The removal of fibers in milling requires multiple actions by the cutting edge. Rotational cutting causes the dynamic change of fiber cutting angle and forms the basis for dynamic damage accumulation. Based on the results of slotting experiment, the range of fiber cutting angle is divided into two parts, 0°–135° and 135°–180°. They are identified in Fig. 5 using different labeling formats.

Because of the particularity of 0°, the fiber cutting angle experienced by each individual fiber does not change with the movement of milling cutter, but depends only on its position. In down milling, the variation range of fiber cutting angle is 0°–90° and it is in the range where surface damage occurs easily. Therefore, attached burrs equivalent to the processing length are formed. The fiber cutting angle in up milling varies from 90° to 180°. Although the upper range of 90°–135°is damage-prone zone, the attached burrs

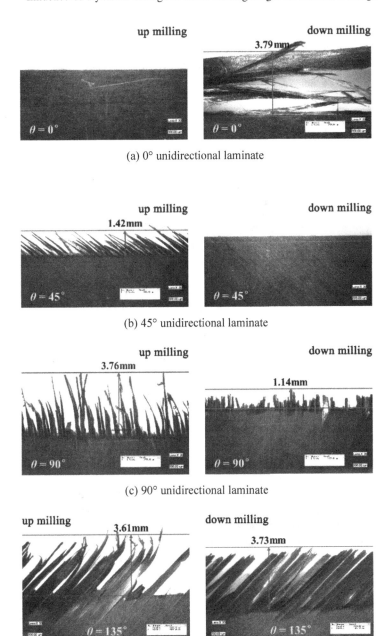

(a) 0° unidirectional laminate

(b) 45° unidirectional laminate

(c) 90° unidirectional laminate

(d) 135° unidirectional laminate

Fig. 3. The images of surface damage of CFRP laminates at four typical orientations

Table 2. The degree of surface damage under different milling methods

Fiber orientation	Radial depth of cut	Up milling		Down milling	
		Burr height	Tear degree	Burr height	Tear degree
0°	4 mm	0 mm	None	3.79 mm	None
45°	4 mm	1.42 mm	Slightly	0 mm	None
90°	4 mm	3.76 mm	Slightly	1.14 mm	Seriously
135°	4 mm	3.61 mm	Seriously	3.73 mm	Seriously

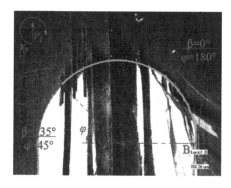

Fig. 4. The morphology and distribution of surface damage in slotting

formed are not retained because the fiber cutting angle range of 135°–180° is closer to the machined edge.

In the 45° unidirectional laminate, there is a tangent position between cutting edge and fiber. Therefore, the fiber can be divided into two parts. In the subsequent processing, both sides of the fiber undergo different changes of fiber cutting angle. The change of fiber cutting angle on the upper side can be ignored because the material on the side is completely removed. The variation process of fiber cutting angle on the lower side is 0°⟶45° and 180°⟶135° respectively in up milling and down milling. Combined with the damage-prone zone in slotting 0° unidirectional laminate, there is no obvious damage to the machined edge in down milling and burrs are formed in up milling. The cumulative range of damage is 0°–45° and the converted burr height is 1.17 mm.

In the 90° unidirectional laminate, the variation process of fiber cutting angle in up milling and down milling are 0°⟶90° and 180°⟶90° respectively. Combined with the damage-prone zone in slotting 0° unidirectional laminate, burrs are formed in up milling. The cumulative range of damage is 0°–90° and the converted burr height is 4 mm. Burrs also occur in down milling, but the cumulative range of damage is 90°–135° and the converted burr height is 1.17 mm.

In the 135° unidirectional laminate, the variation process of fiber cutting angle in up milling and down milling are 45°⟶135° and 135°⟶45° respectively. Both of these variation ranges are within damage-prone zone. Therefore, both generate burrs which are converted to 4 mm in height.

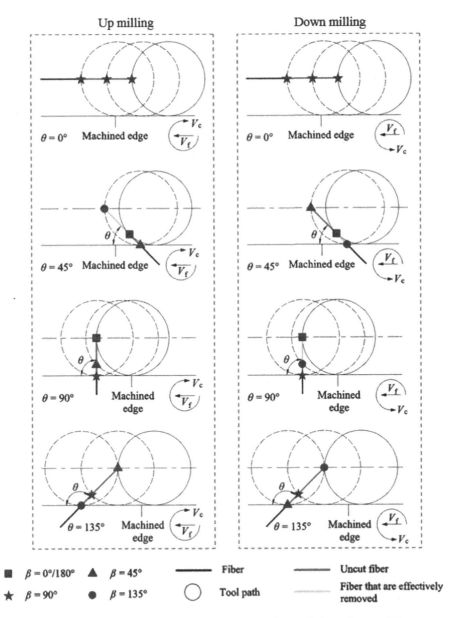

Fig. 5. The specific variation process of fiber cutting angle in up/down milling

Based on the combined analysis of the fiber cutting angle range where surface damage occurs easily in slotting and the dynamic change of fiber cutting angle in edge trimming, theoretical burr height is basically the same as the measured value. It indicates that the formation of burr in milling is related to the dynamic change of fiber cutting angle. The dynamic damage accumulation occurs in the damage-prone zone, which finally determines the burr height.

3.2   Influence of Dynamic Change of Fiber Cutting Angle on Tear Degree

In the analysis of the slotting experimental results, burrs are accompanied by severe tear in the fiber cutting angle range of 90°–135°. It is related to the material removal mode dominated by bending fracture in this range.

In edge trimming, the tear degree is also significantly affected by the dynamic change of fiber cutting angle. Since tear always propagates along the fiber/resin interface, no subsurface tear damage will occur on the 0° unidirectional laminate regardless of up milling or down milling. From the statistical results in Table 2, except the 0° unidirectional laminate, burrs are accompanied by tear at the same time in the others, but the tear degree is significantly different. In the up milling of 45° and 90° unidirectional laminate, since the variation ranges of fiber cutting angle forming damage are both acute angle regions, the tear degree is slight. While, in the down milling of 90° and 135° unidirectional laminate and up milling of 135° unidirectional laminate, the cumulative range of damage includes 90°–135°, so all of them produce visible tear damages. Further, the tear degree is closely related to the variation process of fiber cutting angle. Taking the up and down milling of 135° unidirectional laminate as an example, the variation ranges of fiber cutting angle are the same, both being 45°–135°, but the variation process is exactly opposite. In up milling, the range of 90°–135° is closer to the machined edge, resulting in more severe tear.

In order to further verify the influence of the dynamic change of fiber cutting angle on tear degree, the 135° unidirectional laminate is trimmed in down milling and radial depth of cut is adjusted to 1 mm. The adjustment can limit the range of fiber cutting angle to 45°–90°. Figure 6 shows the comparison of surface damage with radial depths of cut of 1 mm and 4 mm. It is found that tear is significantly inhibited at the depth of 1 mm, indicating that there is a close relationship between the variation process of fiber cutting angle and the tear degree. Therefore, in the down milling of the 135° unidirectional laminate, the range of 90°–135° can be avoided by reducing the radial depth of cut to suppress tear damage.

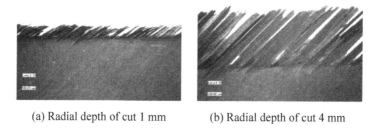

(a) Radial depth of cut 1 mm   (b) Radial depth of cut 4 mm

Fig. 6. Comparison of surface damage under different radial depths of cut

3.3   Influence of Dynamic Change of Fiber Cutting Angle on Burr Morphology

When fiber cutting angle is acute or obtuse, the material removal mode is different. It is represented by the fracture failure under the shearing action and the fracture failure under the bending action respectively. And burr morphology will change accordingly. From Fig. 3, it is clear that the burr morphology can be divided into two types. One is needle-shaped, easy to form in the range of 0°–90°, such as up milling of 45° and 90° unidirectional laminate. The other is sheet that is easily formed in the range of 90°– 135°, such as down milling of 90° unidirectional laminate.

Specially, in the up milling and down milling of 135° unidirectional laminate, the variation range of fiber cutting angle includes 0°–90° and 90°–135° at the same time. Therefore, the two experiments can better reflect the influence of the dynamic change of fiber cutting angle on burr morphology. Figure 7 is the corresponding diagram of fiber cutting angle's variation process and burr morphology in the two experiments. In up milling, the fiber cutting angle first undergoes the process of 45°——→90° and then 90°——→135°. At this time, the burr morphology is a combination of needle and sheet. The distal end is needle-shaped and sheet morphology is near the machined edge. However, the fiber cutting angle changes on the contrary in down milling. At this time, the burr morphology is no longer the combination of them, but uniform sheet morphology. In addition, by observing the burr morphology in Fig. 6(a), it is again in needle-shaped form when the radial depth of cut of 1 mm is adopted. It shows that the first process of 135°——→90° plays a leading role. The interface cracking caused by this process makes fiber in a severely weakly constrained state, so that material removal mode dominated by shear fracture cannot be maintained in the subsequent process of 90°——→45°.

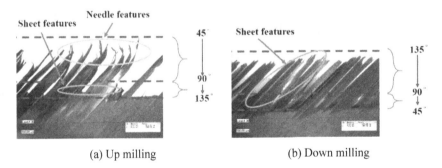

(a) Up milling   (b) Down milling

Fig. 7. Corresponding diagram of fiber cutting angle's variation process and burr morphology

The dynamic change of fiber cutting angle has a significant influence on surface damage in CFRP milling. As the main factors influencing the variation range and process of fiber cutting angle, the up/down milling and radial depth of cut should be given full attention in the actual processing. For CFRP laminates with different orientations, the change of fiber cutting angle should be within an acceptable range by reasonably selecting the up/down milling and appropriately adjusting the radial depth of cut so as to obtain a better machining quality. If there are cases where high-quality trimming cannot be obtained, the scheme with a smaller damage degree should be selected and the damage can be suppressed again by optimizing the subsequent process parameters, such as 90° and 135° unidirectional laminates. With respect to burr, the tear below the machined surface has a more severe effect on the performance of CFRP and should be avoided during actual processing. Therefore, for the unidirectional laminates used in this experiment, up milling for 0°, down milling for 45°, up milling for 90° and down milling for 135° are the optimal schemes. And in the down milling of 135° unidirectional laminate, radial depth of cut should be reduced to suppress tear damage.

4 Conclusions

This study clarified the influence of the dynamic change of fiber cutting angle on the surface damage in CFRP milling process, and determined whether to choose up or down milling, which can effectively inhibit surface damage The results can be summarized as follows:

(1) The fiber cutting angle changes dynamically due to the influence of milling cutter's movement, which causes dynamic damage accumulation in the damage-prone zone, and ultimately determines the burr height.

(2) Except 0° unidirectional laminate, when the variation range coincides 90°–135° partially or completely, severe subsurface tear will occur. The tear degree is determined by specific angle variation process. When down mill at 135°, tear occurs at the distal end and extends below the machined surface. And the tear degree is less than that of up milling.

(3) When the variation process of fiber cutting angle is within 0°–90°, the burr is needle-shaped and when it is within 90°–135°, it is sheet. When these two ranges are partially or completely included, the burr morphology is related to their order. When the acute angle region is first experienced, it is the mixed form of needle-shaped and sheet coexistence, and conversely it is sheet form.

(4) Up/down milling and radial depth of cut have a significant impact on surface damage. Up milling for 0°, down milling for 45°, up milling for 90° and down milling for 135° are the optimal schemes. Specially, when down mill at 135°, the radial depth of cut can be reduced to avoid the range of 90°–135°, thus to suppress tear damage.

Acknowledgments. This work is supported by National Natural Science Foundation of China, No. 51575082, National Natural Science Foundation of China-United with Liaoning Province, No. U1508207, National Key Basic Research Program of China (973 Program), No. 2014CB 046503, National Innovative Research Group, No. 51621064.

References

1. Marsh, G.: Composites in commercial jets. J. Reinf. Plast. **59**(4), 190–193 (2015)
2. Che, D., Saxena, I., Han, P., Guo, P., Ehmann, K.F.: Machining of carbon fiber reinforced plastics/polymers: a literature review. J. Manuf. Sci. Eng. **136**(3), 034001 (2014)
3. Yang, N.B.: Composite structures for new generation large commercial jet. J. Acta Aeronautica et Astronautica Sinica. **29**(3), 596–604 (2008)

4. Tsao, C.C., Hocheng, H.: Computerized tomography and C-scan for measuring delamination in the drilling of composite materials using various drills. J. Int. J. Mach. Tools Manuf. **45**(11), 1282–1287 (2005)
5. Davim, J.P., Reis, P.: Damage and dimensional precision on milling carbon fiber-reinforced plastics using design experiments. J. Mater. Process. Technol. **160**(2), 160–167 (2005)
6. Sheikh-Ahmad, J., Urban, N., Cheraghi, H.: Machining damage in edge trimming of CFRP. J. Mater. Manuf. Process. **27**(7), 802–808 (2012)
7. Wang, F., Yin, J., Jia, Z., Ma, J., Xu, Z., Wang, D.: Measurement and analysis of cutting force, temperature and cutting-induced top-layer damage in edge trimming of CFRPs. J. Mech. Eng. **54**(3), 186–195 (2018). (in Chinese)
8. Hintze, W., Cordes, M., Koerkel, G.: Influence of weave structure on delamination when milling CFRP. J. Mater. Process. Technol. **216**, 199–205 (2015)
9. Koplev, A.A., Lystrup, A., Vorm, T.: The cutting process, chips, and cutting forces in machining CFRP. J. Compos. **14**(4), 371–376 (1983)
10. Wang, D.H., Ramulu, M., Arola, D.: Orthogonal cutting mechanisms of graphite/epoxy composite. part I: unidirectional laminate. Int. J. Mach. Tools Manuf. **35**(12), 1623–1638 (1995)
11. Sheikh-Ahmad, J.Y.: Machining of Polymer Composites. Springer, New York (2009). https://doi.org/10.1007/978-0-387-68619-6
12. Jia, Z., Yin, J., Wang, F., Chen, C., Zhang, B.: FEM simulation analysis of subsurface damage formation based on continuously cutting process of CFRP. J. Mech. Eng. **52**(17), 58–64 (2016)
13. Niu, B., Su, Y., Yang, R., Jia, Z.: Micro-macro-mechanical model and material removal mechanism of machining carbon fiber reinforced polymer. Int. J. Mach. Tools Manuf. **111**, 43–54 (2016)
14. Qi, Z., Zhang, K., Cheng, H., Wang, D., Meng, Q.: Microscopic mechanism based force prediction in orthogonal cutting of unidirectional CFRP. Int. J. Adv. Manuf. Technol. **79**(5–8), 1209–1219 (2015)
15. Xu, W., Zhang, L.: Mechanics of fibre deformation and fracture in vibration-assisted cutting of unidirectional fibre-reinforced polymer composites. Int. J. Mach. Tools Manuf. **103**, 40–52 (2016)
16. Li, H., Qin, X., He, G., Jin, Y., Sun, D., Price, M.: Investigation of chip formation and fracture toughness in orthogonal cutting of UD-CFRP. Int. J. Adv. Manuf. Technol. **82**(5–8), 1079–1088 (2016)

Experimental Study on Tool Wear of Step Drill During Drilling Ti/CFRP Stacks

Qi Wang, Fuji Wang$^{(\boxtimes)}$, Chong Zhang, Chen Chen, and Dong Wang

The Key Laboratory for Precision and Nontraditional Machining Technology
of Ministry of Education,
Dalian University of Technology, Dalian 116024, China
wfjsll@dlut.edu.cn

Abstract. Ti/CFRP stacks are widely used in the aviation field. However, the life of existing Ti/CFRP drilling tool is extremely low. This paper analyzes the wear process of chisel edge and cutting edge of the carbide step drill to reveal the wear mechanism. Based on the microscopic observations and the variation of cutting edge rounding, it is found that tool wear is affected by the carbon fiber/Ti-adhesion interaction. This interaction makes the rake face more susceptible to occur adhesive wear, and slows down the flank wear. It also reveals the secondary sharpening effect of the rake wear and flank wear on cutting edge. In addition, the relationship between thrust force and tool wear is investigated. Results indicate that the variation of thrust force is related to the flank wear width and the degree of Ti-adhesion attached to chisel edge, but not to the cutting edge rounding.

Keywords: Ti/CFRP stacks · Step drill · Wear mechanisms · Flank wear
Thrust force

1 Introduction

Carbon fiber reinforced plastic (CFRP) composites have excellent properties such as high specific strength, high specific rigidity, low density, corrosion resistance, ect. Large scale structural parts based on CFRP have been widely used in aviation [1–3]. However, titanium alloys are still used in some critical load-bearing locations [4, 5]. The connection of different material components is usually bolted or riveted. Therefore, a large number of holes need to be machined on the CFRP/Ti stacks. The quality of the connecting hole will directly affect the safety and reliability of the equipment [6, 7]. But due to the fact that these two kinds of two materials are difficult to machine, and the mechanical and physical properties of materials are different, which leads to the extremely low life of available drilling tools for stacks holes.

The low life, namely severe tool wear in drilling stacks have draw much attention in the industry and research fields. In terms of tool wear evaluation, the rake wear of the CFRP cutting tool starts directly from the cutting edge and it is different from the crater wear of the metal cutting tool [8, 9]. Thus Montoya et al. [10] believe that the flank wear width measured by microscope will be affected by the rake wear, which can not accurately reflect the degree of tool wear. Ali et al. [11] quantify the sharpness of the

© Springer Nature Singapore Pte Ltd. 2018
S. Wang et al. (Eds.): ICSEE 2018/IMIOT 2018, CCIS 923, pp. 440–450, 2018.
https://doi.org/10.1007/978-981-13-2396-6_41

cutting edge and propose cutting edge rounding (CER) to evaluate the wear of the CFRP cutting tool. In terms of tool wear patterns and mechanisms, Ramulu et al. [12] believe that the CFRP/Ti stacks drilling process can be divided into multiple sections depending on the position of the tool relative to the workpiece, and the high cutting temperature when drilling titanium alloy is the cause of tool wear. Park et al. [13] have found that the wear of the CFRP/Ti stacks cutting tool includes flank wear and edge wear by alternating drilling of CFRP and CFRP/Ti stacks, and believe that the edge wear is the result of abrasive effect of carbon fiber on the tool, while flank wear is caused by both abrasive and adhesive wear. Wang et al. [14] have analyzed the wear effect of different materials on the tool and found that the carbon fiber can reduce the Ti-adhesion on the tool surface, and make the chipping caused by drilling titanium alloy blunt, which increase tool life relative to titanium cutting tools.

At present, the research on tool wear of stacks drilling mainly focuses on the wear rules of CFRP/Ti stacks drilling tool. However, little research has been done on Ti/CFRP stacks, and the effect of different materials on tool wear has not been accurately distinguished. At the same time, different geometrical features of the tool have different effects on material removal in the process of drilling stacks, and the tool wear is also different. However, there is a lack of research on tool wear of different geometric features. In addition, the thrust force will directly affect the delamination size of the CFRP holes. Therefore, in order to prolong the tool life and ensure the quality of the hole, it is still necessary to investigate the relationship between the thrust force and the tool wear.

In this paper, a step drill is applied to investigated the tool wear during drilling CFRP, titanium alloy and Ti/CFRP stacks, and the wear rules and mechanisms of various parts of the tool when drilling different materials are analyzed. It also reveals the carbon fiber/Ti-adhesion interaction when drilling Ti/CFRP stacks, and the influence of tool wear on thrust force.

2 Experiment Method

2.1 Workpiece and Cutting Tool

The Ti/CFRP stacks used in this experiment is composed of titanium alloy and CFRP composites. The titanium alloy is Ti-6Al-4 V, its mechanical properties are shown in Table 1. CFRP is a T800 grade quasi-isotropic laminate in an epoxy matrix, its unidirectional plate mechanical properties are shown in Table 2. The workpiece size is 90 mm × 90 mm × 6 mm. The self-developed step drills are used as the experimental tool. The drill bit substrate is K44UF tungsten carbide, no coating, with submicron grain size. The structure and geometric parameters of experimental tool are shown in Fig. 1.

Table 1. Mechanical properties of the Ti-6Al-4 V

Yield stress Rp0.2%/MPa	Tensile strength Rm/MPa	Elongation A4/%	Area reduction/%	Elastic modulus/GPa
845	915	13	39	114

Table 2. Mechanical properties of the CFRP unidirectional plate

Longitudinal young's modulus/GPa	Longitudinal shear modulus/GPa	Transverse poisson's ratio	Tensile strength/MPa	Compressive strength/MPa
160	6.21	0.36	2843	1553

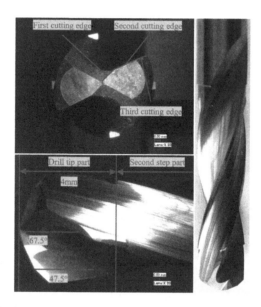

Fig. 1. The structure and geometric parameters of step drill

2.2 Experimental Parameters

The experiments are performed on the VGW210 CNC machining center and the cutting force is recorded by using Kistle 9257B multi-component force sensor. The experimental device is shown in Fig. 2. Three types of hole-making experiments have been performed: drilling titanium alloys, CFRP, and Ti/CFRP stacks. The cutting parameters for single material drilling are shown in Table 3. When drilling Ti/CFRP stacks, the drilling sequence is from Ti to CFRP. Since the machinability of the two materials are different, variable parameters are used to drill different materials. After the second step completely getting out from the Ti plate, change the parameters. When drilling Ti/CFRP stacks, cutting parameters of two materials are the same as those of the single material. 10 holes are drilled for each type of experiment and a total of 30 holes are machined. In order to distinguish the effect of CFRP and titanium alloy on the tool wear, the tool is tested offline once every 2 holes.

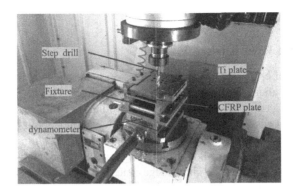

Fig. 2. Experimental setup

Table 3. Experimental process parameters

Material	Cutting parameters				Note
	Spindle speed/(r/min)	Cutting speed/(m/s)	Feed speed/ (mm/min)	Feed rate/ (mm/r)	
CFRP	2000	60	35	0.0175	
Ti	300	9	30	0.1	Peck drill

2.3   Tool Wear Measurement Method

For the twist drill, its flank wear can be divided into three areas as shown in Fig. 3. The chisel edge length of the tool used in this experiment is very short, and peck drill will cause the chisel edge to be under a large intermittent cycle load. And chisel edge is the main factor that causes thrust force and CFRP delamination [1], so the chisel edge wear is analyzed first. On the other hand, the main cutting edge is responsible for the most of material removal, and the wear of second step cutting edge is directly related to the quality of the Ti/CFRP holes. Therefore, the wear of two parts have also been studied. By using the VHX-600E digital microscope from Keyence, microscopic images of different parts of the tool are taken and the 2-D profile of main cutting edge is extracted. Refer to the method in Wang et al. [8] to fit and calculate the CER and flank wear width values.

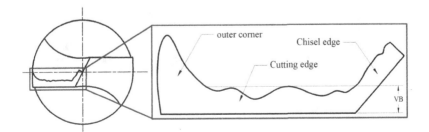

Fig. 3. Twist drill flank wear pattern

3 Step Drill Wear Analysis

3.1 Chisel Edge Wear Analysis

The morphology of chisel edge is shown in Fig. 4(a), and the length of chisel edge of the fresh tool is about 360 μm. As can be seen from Fig. 5, there is a severe Ti-adhesion at the center of chisel edge when drilling Ti/CFRP stacks. While at the corner of the chisel edge, there is a wear band and a chipping about 230 μm in length. The drilling process of Ti/CFRP stacks can be divided into titanium alloy drilling and CFRP drilling. In first titanium alloy drilling stage, it is difficult to discharge chips due to the negative rake angle at the chisel edge, and the Ti-adhesion shown in Fig. 4(b) will be formed on tool surface where severe friction occurs between the chips and the cutting tool. In next CFRP drilling stage, the chisel edge of tool is affected by abrasive carbon fiber, which causes the Ti-adhesion attached to the corner of chisel edge to be removed. Moreover, this interaction can also lead to edge chipping. On the other hand, the cutting speed at the center of chisel edge is lower, and the removal effect of the carbon fiber on Ti-adhesion is more weak. The abrasive carbon fiber will improve the activity of the Ti-adhesion surface, and promote the accumulation of Ti-adhesion at the center of the chisel edge.

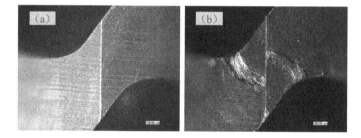

Fig. 4. Morphology of chisel edge (a) fresh tool (b) after drilling titanium

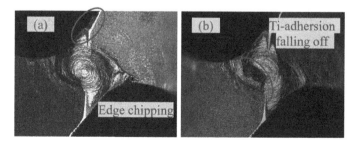

Fig. 5. Morphology of chisel edge after drilling Ti/CFRP stacks (a) after hole 4 (b) after hole 8

Using a digital microscope to extract 2D-profile at the center of the chisel edge as shown in Fig. 6, it is found that Ti-adhesion is always above the plane of the chisel edge during the entire drilling process. This will seriously affect the centering ability of chisel edge and lead to an increase in thrust force. Combined with microscopic images, it is found that after Ti-adhesion reached its maximum at the 6th hole, and then a process of partial fall-off and continued growth appears. Figure 7 shows the size of Ti-adhesion attached to the center of chisel edge during drilling Ti/CFRP stacks, in which Ti-adhesion height and width are measured in the plane of Fig. 6, and the Ti-adhesion length which is the length of chisel edge covered by Ti-adhesion is measured in Fig. 5.

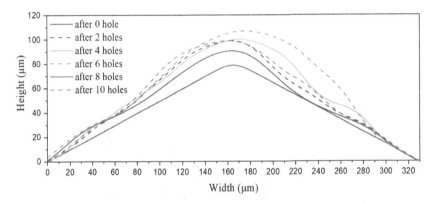

Fig. 6. 2D-profile variation of chisel edge center of step drills during drilling Ti/CFRP stacks

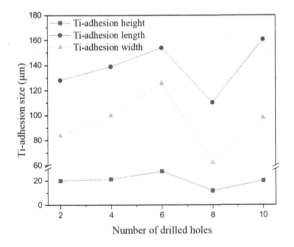

Fig. 7. Size of Ti-adhesion attached to the center of chisel edge

3.2   Cutting Edge Wear Analysis

The tool wear of each cutting edge is shown in Table 4. From the table, we can see that both rake wear and flank wear are sever during drilling Ti/CFRP stacks, and there is a groove wear pattern on the flank face. The 2D-profile of the second cutting edge extracted by the digital microscope is shown in Fig. 8. It can be seen that the rake wear width of the Ti/CFRP stacks cutting tool reaches a maximum length of 97 μm and a depth of 3-4 μm. Combining with the Ti-adhesion attached to surface after drilling titanium alloy in Table 4, It can be determined that the rake wear is caused by Ti-adhesion detachment. The detached Ti-adhesion and a part of the tool material have scratching effect on flank face, which will cause a groove wear pattern.

Table 4. Tool wear of cutting edges in drill tip part (hole 10)

Position	Flank face		Rake face
	Second cutting edge	Third cutting edge	Second cutting edge
Fresh tool			
Tool drilling titanium			Ti-adhesion
Tool drilling Ti/CFRP stacks		Groove wear	Abrasive wear Remaining Ti-adhesion

Using MATLAB to fit 2D-profile of cutting edge, the CER values shown in Fig. 9 are calculated. It can be seen from the figure that the CER of Ti/CFRP stacks cutting tool first increases and then drops, indicating that when the flank wear is within a certain range, the rake face wear has a sharpening effect on the cutting edge, resulting in a decrease of CER. In addition, the second step cutting edge of the Ti/CFRP stacks cutting tool is smaller than the second cutting edge in terms of the maximum value of the CER and its corresponding number of holes. In the view of the wear width of cutting tool, although the rake face adhesion wear on both cutting edge is basically same, the flank wear width of the second cutting edge is smaller. After hole 10, the VB of the second cutting edge is 40 μm or less, and in the same case, the VB of the second

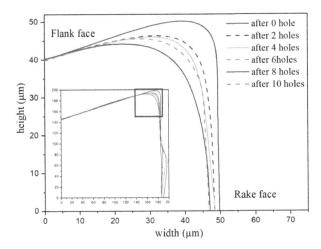

Fig. 8. 2D-profile variation of second cutting edge during drilling Ti/CFRP stacks

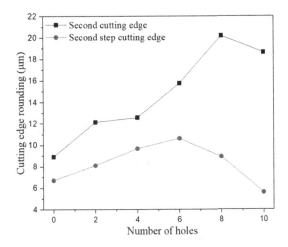

Fig. 9. CER variation during drilling Ti/CFRP stacks with number of holes

step cutting edge is about 80 μm. Therefore, the sharpening effect of the second step cutting edge is stronger. When the number of holes is smaller, the CER shows a decreasing trend.

When drilling single CFRP and Ti/CFRP stacks, the flank face of two cutting tools are severely abraded and a wear band appears. Table 5 shows the measured flank wear width (VB) of the third cutting edge. After hole 4, the flank wear width of the CFRP cutting tool is about 1.5 times that of the Ti/CFRP stacks cutting tool. As the Ti/CFRP stacks cutting tool drills on the titanium alloy, Ti-adhesion will be attached to the flank face of the tool, and its resistance to carbon fiber abrasion is stronger than adhesive

Table 5. Flank wear width(VB) of third cutting edge with number of holes

Number of holes	Flank wear width(VB)/μm	
	CFRP cutting tool	Ti/CFRP stacks cutting tool
2	53.8	41.9
4	101.4	64.1
6	127.4	82.5
8	147.8	98.7
10	182.1	125.7

wear caused by Ti-adhesion falling off. Therefore, the flank wear width of the Ti/CFRP stacks cutting tool is shorter.

3.3   Effect of Tool Wear on Thrust Force

The relationship between the drilling thrust force generated by the drill tip and the number of holes is shown in Fig. 10. There is no significant increase in thrust force when drilling titanium alloys, but it gradually increases when drilling Ti/CFRP stacks and CFRP, which is consistent with the flank wear variation in Sect. 3.2. Figure 11 shows the relationship between the thrust force and the flank wear width. It is found that the thrust force and flank wear are linear when drilling CFRP alone, and the thrust force of stacks drilling is a parabolic curve. Therefore, the difference between thrust force of stacks drilling and single material drilling is analyzed. The CFRP thrust force difference approximately eliminated the effect of flank wear, and the difference curve increases first and then stabilizes, but there is a decrease at hole 7. It can be seen from Fig. 7 that there is a falling off process of Ti-adhesion attached to the chisel edge between the hole 6 and hole 8. Therefore it can be confirmed that the CFRP thrust force difference is caused by Ti-adhesion attached to the chisel edge. The Ti thrust force difference includes the thrust force increment caused by flank wear and Ti-adhesion. And the difference curve also shows a corresponding relationship with Ti-adhesion.

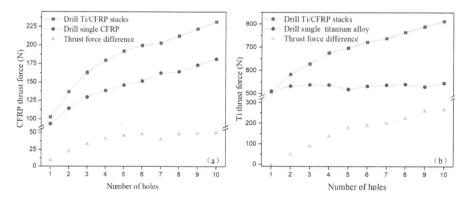

Fig. 10. Thrust force variation with number of holes (a) CFRP (b) Ti

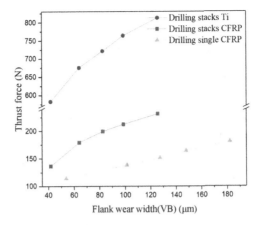

Fig. 11. Thrust force variation with flank wear width(VB)

Therefore, it can be concluded that the thrust force of the drill tip is linearly related to the flank wear, and it is also affected by the Ti-adhesion attached to the chisel edge.

4 Conclusion

In this paper, step drills are used to perform comparative drilling experiments on Ti/CFRP stacks. By analyzing the tool wear of different cutting edges and the effect of tool wear on thrust force, the following conclusions are obtained:

(1) When drilling Ti/CFRP stacks, there is a severe Ti-adhesion attached to the center of chisel edge, and a chipping at the intersection of the corner of chisel edge and the main cutting edge. Carbon fiber can remove Ti-adhesion attached to chisel edge, which is related to cutting speed.

(2) When drilling Ti/CFRP stacks, wear band is found on the flank face. And Ti-adhesion attached to the rake face is removed by fiber which results in adhesive wear. Flank wear and adhesive wear have a sharpening effect on the cutting edge, which causes CER to increase first and then decrease.

(3) The thrust force of Ti/CFRP stacks is related to the flank wear width and Ti-adhesion attached to the chisel edge. The thrust force increase caused by the flank wear is linear with the average width, and the increase caused by the Ti-adhesion is related to the size of the Ti-adhesion. It shows the trend of increasing first and then stabilizing.

Acknowledgments. This work is supported by National Natural Science Foundation of China, No.51575082, National Natural Science Foundation of China-United with Liaoning Province, No. U1508207, National Key Basic Research Program of China (973 Program), No. 2014CB 046503, National Innovative Research Group, No. 51621064.

References

1. Jia, Z., Fu, R., Niu, B., Qian, B., Bai, Y., Wang, F.: Novel drill structure for damage reduction in drilling CFRP composites. Int. J. Mach. Tools Manuf **110**, 55–65 (2016)
2. Rawat, S., Attia, H.: Wear mechanisms and tool life management of WC-Co drills during dry high speed drilling of woven carbon fibre composites. Wear **267**(5-8SI2), 1022–1030 (2009)
3. Wang, F., Qian, B., Jia, Z., De Cheng, Fu, R.: Effects of cooling position on tool wear reduction of secondary cutting edge corner of one-shot drill bit in drilling CFRP. Int. J. Adv. Manuf. Technol. **94**(9), 4277–4287 (2018)
4. Zhang, P.F., Churi, N.J., Pei, Z.J., Treadwell, C.: Mechanical drilling processes for titanium alloys: a literature review. J. Mach. Sci. Technol. **12**(PII 9065730944), 417–444 (2008)
5. Sharif, S., Rahim, E.A.: Performance of coated- and uncoated-carbide tools when drilling titanium alloy. J. Mater. Process. Technol. **185**(1-3SI), 72–76 (2007)
6. Pecat, O., Brinksmeier, E.: Tool wear analyses in low frequency vibration assisted drilling of CFRP/Ti6Al4 V stack material. In: 6th CIRP International Conference on High Performance Cutting (HPC), pp. 142–147 (2014)
7. SenthilKumar, M., Prabukarthi, A., Krishnaraj, V.: Study on tool wear and chip formation during drilling carbon fiber reinforced polymer (CFRP)/titanium alloy (Ti6Al4 V) stacks. In: International Conference On Design and Manufacturing (IConDM), pp. 582–592 (2013)
8. Wang, F., Qian, B., Jia, Z., Fu, R., Cheng, D.: Secondary cutting edge wear of one-shot drill bit in drilling CFRP and its impact on hole quality. J. Compos. Struct. **178**, 341–352 (2017)
9. Wang, X., Kwona, P.Y., Sturtevant, C., Kim, D.D., Lantrip, J.: Tool wear of coated drills in drilling CFRP. J. Manuf. Process. **15**(1), 127–135 (2013)
10. Montoya, M., Calamaz, M., Gehin, D., Girot, F.: Evaluation of the performance of coated and uncoated carbide tools in drilling thick CFRP/aluminum alloy stacks. Int. J. Adv. Manuf. Technol. **68**(9–12), 2111–2120 (2013)
11. Faraz, A., Biermann, D., Weinert, K.: Cutting edge rounding: an innovative tool wear criterion in drilling CFRP composite laminates. Int. J. Mach. Tools Manuf **49**(15), 1185–1196 (2009)
12. Ramulu, M., Branson, T., Kim, D.: A study on the drilling of composite and titanium stacks. J. Compos. Struct. **54**(1), 67–77 (2001)
13. Park, K., Beal, A., Kim, D.D., Kwon, P., Lantrip, J.: A comparative study of carbide tools in drilling of CFRP and CFRP-Ti stacks. J. Manuf. Sci. Eng. Trans. ASME **136**(0145011) (2014)
14. Wang, X., Kwon, P.Y., Sturtevant, C., Kim, D.D., Lantrip, J.: Comparative tool wear study based on drilling experiments on CFRp/Ti stack and its individual layers. Wear **317**(1–2), 265–276 (2014)

The Sigma Level Evaluation Method
of Machine Capability

Sheng-yong Zhang$^{(\boxtimes)}$, Gen-bao Zhang, and Yan Ran

State Key Laboratory of Mechanical Transmission,
Chongqing University, Chongqing, China
rainbowzhang269@163.com, gen.bao.zhang@263.net,
ranyan@cqu.edu.cn

Abstract. Different tolerances causes multiple values of machine capability index(Cmk) in the traditional evaluation method of machine capability. On the basis of normal distribution, a new evaluation method of machine capability, the sigma level evaluation method, is applied to solve the problems above. Combined with the six sigma quality management method, the compensation coefficient Δ_μ and negative stability coefficient Δ_S of the machining process are defined. Multivariate statistical analysis methods are used to analyze the dimensional accuracy dispersion of multi-characteristics parts processing. The subjective and objective combination weighting method is used to evaluate the machine capability of multi-characteristics parts. Taking the transmission housing processing as an example, the feasibility and superiority of the sigma level evaluation method are proved.

Keywords: Machine capability · Sigma level · Compensation coefficient
Multi-characteristics

1 Introduction

Hong [1] standardizes the evaluation method of machine capability of machining center. The concept of Cmk is proposed for acceptance and maintenance of machine, which only considers short-term dispersion and emphasizes the impact of the machine itself on product quality [2].

Product quality data presents various distributions under different conditions, such as the normal distribution, the Weibull distribution [3, 4] and the skew normal distribution [5]. The sample sampling, the sample size [6] and the method of data processing [7, 8] are considered to be the main reason for the non-normal product quality data. Gu et al. [9] analyze the relationship between the process capability index (Cpk) and process yield. Wu et al. [10] improve the evaluation method of the process capability during product acceptance. As for multi-characteristics parts, Shiau et al. [11] extend Castagliola and Castellanos's [12] definitions to MCpk and MCp for multivariate normal processes with flexible specification regions and suggest a method to link the indices to the overall process yield. Pearn [13] proposes the concept of MPCICpk, which is defined for a process with multiple characteristics and two-sided specifications. However, CTpk only provides an approximate rather than an exact

© Springer Nature Singapore Pte Ltd. 2018
S. Wang et al. (Eds.): ICSEE 2018/IMIOT 2018, CCIS 923, pp. 451–462, 2018.
https://doi.org/10.1007/978-981-13-2396-6_42

measure for the overall process yield. Du et al. [14] research the machining accuracy detection of multi-characteristics "S" shaped test piece. Fan et al. [15] study the mathematical modeling and deviation detection about the geometric processing characteristics of multi-characteristics "S" shaped test piece.

With the development of the times, the traditional three sigma standard is transitioning to the six sigma. The finished product rate of 99.73% cannot meet the requirements of improving quality while reducing costs [1]. The evaluation method faces many challenges, while many problems are worth studying.

On the one hand, the traditional Cmk is the ratio of the tolerance to the standard deviation of the data distribution, but the machine capability is an index independent of the tolerance and reflects the machine variability. The premise that controlling the factors other than the machine cannot eliminate the quality fluctuation caused by them, Conversely, the quality fluctuation caused by other factors is constant. Due to the above two points, using Cmk to evaluate machine capability is not accurate enough.

On the other hand, the parts to be machined often have many characteristics, such as porous, multi-surface. The traditional evaluation method of machine capability is only performed for one characteristic, which cannot reflect the real processing and accuracy assurance capability of multi-axis machine tools.

Machine capability is directly and uniquely determined by the quality fluctuations caused by the factor of machine. In view of the above two issues, Multivariate statistical methods are used to analyze the relationship between process and machine quality fluctuation. We apply the sigma level evaluation method to evaluate the machine capability by using quality fluctuations, standard deviation S, to reflect machine capability. And corresponding detection probability of one million chances (DMPO) and machining accuracy are obtained. The sigma level and tolerance correspondence table of the machine is established. For multi-characteristics parts, the subjective and objective combination weighting method is used to determine the overall sigma level.

2 Multivariate Statistical Analysis and Quality Fluctuation

The Basic Theory of Multivariate Statistical Analysis. Suppose one process has m random input variables and r output variables. And n samples are selected randomly from the population to perform independent variable statistical tests. The average value of the test matrix [16] is

$$Y_j = \begin{array}{|cccc|c|}
\overline{X_1} & \overline{X_2} & \cdots & \overline{X_{m-1}} & \overline{X_m} & \text{variables/samples} \\
x_{11} & x_{12} & \cdots & x_{1,m-1} & x_{1,m} & 1 \\
x_{21} & x_{22} & \cdots & x_{2,m-1} & x_{2,m} & 2 \\
\vdots & \vdots & & \vdots & \vdots & \vdots \\
x_{n-1,1} & x_{n-1,2} & \cdots & x_{n-1,m-1} & x_{n-1,m} & n-1 \\
x_{n,1} & x_{n,2} & \cdots & x_{n,m-1} & x_{n,m} & n
\end{array} \quad (j=1,2,\cdots,r). \tag{1}$$

(Where $x_{n,m}$ is the sample mean value of the m-th variable in the n-th sample)

The m variables have a comprehensive effect on the response variable according to statistical method. The sample covariance matrix is

$$D(Y_j) = \begin{bmatrix} \text{cov}(X_1, X_1) & \text{cov}(X_1, X_2) & \cdots & \text{cov}(X_1, X_{m-1}) & \text{cov}(X_1, X_m) \\ \text{cov}(X_2, X_1) & \text{cov}(X_2, X_2) & \cdots & \text{cov}(X_2, X_{m-1}) & \text{cov}(X_2, X_m) \\ \vdots & \vdots & & \vdots & \vdots \\ \text{cov}(X_{m-1}, X_1) & \text{cov}(X_{m-1}, X_2) & \cdots & \text{cov}(X_{m-1}, X_{m-1}) & \text{cov}(X_{m-1}, X_m) \\ \text{cov}(X_m, X_1) & \text{cov}(X_m, X_2) & \cdots & \text{cov}(X_m, X_{m-1}) & \text{cov}(X_m, X_m) \end{bmatrix} \quad (j$$

$$= 1, 2, \cdots, r).$$

$$(2)$$

(Where $\text{cov}(X_i, X_j)$ is the covariance of variable i and j. and $\rho_{ij} = \dfrac{\sigma_{ij}^2}{\sqrt{\sigma_{ii}^2}\sqrt{\sigma_{jj}^2}}$

$\left(\text{cov}(X_i, X_j) = \sigma_{ij}^2\right)$ is the correlation coefficient between the variables i and j)

Multivariate Statistical Analysis and Process Quality Fluctuation. There are six categories of variables influencing the quality of mechanical products: man, machine, material, method, measurement and environment (5M1E). The mathematical model of the quality fluctuations of the workpieces generated by each variable is established as follow:

Set variables of man X_1, machine X_2, material X_3, method X_4, environment X_5, and measurement X_6 to form multiple variables $X = (X_1, X_2, X_3, X_4, X_5, X_6)^T$. Since they are independent variables, then

$$\text{cov}(X_i, X_j)(i \neq j) = 0. \tag{3}$$

$$\rho_{ij} = \frac{\sigma_{ij}^2}{\sqrt{\sigma_{ii}^2}\sqrt{\sigma_{jj}^2}} = 0(i \neq j). \tag{4}$$

Therefore, the impact of total fluctuations is $|D(X)| = \prod\limits_{i=1}^{6} \sigma_{ii}^2$. that is

$$S_{sum} = S_2 \prod_{i=1,3,4,5,6} S_i \tag{5}$$

(Standard deviation $s_i(i = 1, 2, \cdots, 6)$ represents the quality fluctuations caused by variable X_i).

The Cmk evaluation method considers that when the five variables except the machine remain invariable, the value of Cpk equals to Cmk. However, equation above shows that Cpk measured by the traditional method is under a combination impact caused by all variables. At this situation, and Cpk actually is the product of Cmk and the constant k, $\prod\limits_{i=1,3,4,5} s_i$. That is $c_{mk} = kc_{pk}$. As the case stands, the experience in the

United States that 75% of the process variation results from the machine variation [2] indicates machine quality fluctuations account for 75% of process quality fluctuations. That is

$$S_{sum} = \prod_{i=1,3,4,5} S_i \cdot S_2 = \frac{4}{3} S_2 \tag{6}$$

Furthermore, the quality fluctuation is inversely proportional to the quality level, so

$$\sigma_p = \frac{3}{4} \sigma_m \tag{7}$$

(Where σ_p and σ_m represent the sigma level of process and machine capability respectively)

3   Sample Fitting Test and Distribution Standardization

The distributions of random variables and their influences are normally distributed theoretically. However, due to the existence of various artificially irregular operations or processes, the effective measurement data appears a non-normal distribution with multiple peaks and variations, which belongs to system errors rather than accidental errors. The current non-normal data obfuscation can not objectively eliminate the effects of artificially irregular operations or processes. Generally speaking, the sample data normality should be tested firstly.

Sample Fitting Test. We use Skewness and Kurtosis of the sample to test the distribution type [17]. Skewness reflects the degree and direction of deviation of the sample symmetry, and Kurtosis reflects the steepness near the peak and the thickness in the tail of the density function curve of the sample corresponding to the population.

The concepts of Skewness and Kurtosis are defined as follow.

Skewness:

$$G_s = \frac{\frac{1}{n} \sum_{i=1}^{n} (x_i - \bar{x})^3}{(\frac{1}{n} \sum_{i=1}^{n} (x_i - \bar{x})^2)^{\frac{3}{2}}} = \frac{M_3^*}{(M_2^*)^{\frac{3}{2}}} \tag{8}$$

Kurtosis:

$$G_s = \frac{\frac{1}{n} \sum_{i=1}^{n} (x_i - \bar{x})^4}{(\frac{1}{n} \sum_{i=1}^{n} (x_i - \bar{x})^2)^2} - 3 = \frac{M_4^*}{(M_2^*)^2} - 3 \tag{9}$$

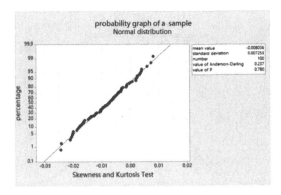

Fig. 1. Anderson-Darling normality skewness and kurtosis test

(Where M_k^* is the value of the k-th center distance of the sample, particularly, the Skewness and Kurtosis of normal distribution in this definition is 0)

In SAS, SPSS, MATBLE and other categories of statistical software, the principle of the Skewness and Kurtosis can be used to test the normality of the data as Fig. 1 shows. If $P > 0.5$, the type of distribution is accepted as normal.

Standardization of Normal Distribution. In order to eliminate the impact of different sizes on the statistical analysis results, the statistical indicators need to be standardized before statistical analysis (Eq. 10).

$$X_j^* = \frac{X_j - E(X_j)}{\sqrt{D(X_j)}} (j = 1, 2, \ldots, n) \tag{10}$$

(Where $E(X_j)$ and $D(X_j)$ represent the expectation and variance of X_j respectively) Therefore, research in this paper is based on the following assumptions:

(1) The process is in a statistically controlled state, which means that the factors influencing the process capability are only random errors.
(2) The quality characteristic of the product follows a normal distribution $N(\mu, \sigma)$.

4   Sigma Level Evaluation Method

Sigma Level. Figure 2 shows an example of a size distribution:

(Where UCL, LCL and CL represent the upper control limit, the lower control limit, and the control center respectively)

If $UCL \leq k_1 S_p$, $LCL \geq -k_2 S_p$, the value of machine capability sigma level σ_m is

$\frac{4}{3} \min\{k_1, k_2\}$, and the corresponding DMPO is $\int_{-\infty}^{k\sigma} \frac{e^{-\frac{x^2}{2\sigma^2}}}{\sigma\sqrt{2\pi}} dx \times 10^6$ *ppm*.

Compensation Coefficient and Sigma Level. For an in-control process with single quality characteristic, the process standard deviation is basically invariable [9].

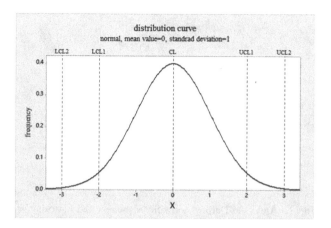

Fig. 2. The distribution of a characteristic size data

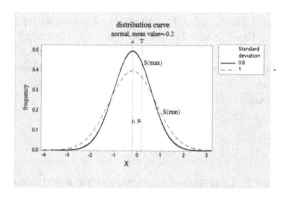

Fig. 3. The distribution of single characteristic size data

Actually, some small beats still exist (Fig. 3), which is defined as negative stability coefficient:

$$\Delta_S = S_{\max} - S_{\min} \tag{11}$$

furthermore, the distribution center and the tolerance center are not coincident. A certain drift exists (Fig. 3), which is defined as the processing compensation coefficient:

$$\Delta_\mu = T_0 - \mu \tag{12}$$

(where the tolerance center $T_0 = \frac{T_l + T_u}{2}$)

When the production process is stable, the center drift caused by various random factors can be kept within $1.5S_p$ [2]. Offset compensation belongs to the core content of process improvement, and the corresponding sigma levels of machine capability before and after compensation are

$$\sigma_m^0 = \frac{4}{3}\min\left\{\frac{T_u - T_0 + \mu}{\sigma_p}, \frac{-T_l + T_0 - \mu}{\sigma_p}\right\} \text{(uncompensated)} \qquad (13)$$

$$\sigma_m^1 = \frac{4}{3}\min\left\{\frac{T_u}{\sigma_p}, \frac{-T_l}{\sigma_p}\right\} \text{(compensated)} \qquad (14)$$

On the basis of the center drift $\Delta_\mu = 1.5S_p$, the sigma level evaluation table of machine capability before and after offset compensation is established to show the importance of offset compensation for improving the quality sigma level.

Table 1 shows that the DMPO of 3 sigma and 4 sigma level after the drift is compensated are respectively located in the 4– 5 sigma and 5–6 sigma level, which indicates the machine capability can be improved by at least one sigma level by offset compensation.

Table 1. Sigma level tolerance and DMPO table before and after offset compensation

Center offset Δ_μ	Process fluctuation	Machine fluctuation	Sigma level	Tolerance table (machine)	Negative stability factor Δ_S	$\Delta_\mu = 1.5S$ DMPO[ppm] (Compensate)	DMPO[ppm] (Uncompensated)
$\mu - T_0$	S_p	$0.75S_p$	3 sigma	$\pm 2.25S_p$	$S_{max} - S_{min}$	2700	66811
			4 sigma	$\pm 3S_p$		63	6210
			5 sigma	$\pm 3.75S_p$		0.57	233
			6 sigma	$\pm 4.5S_p$		0.002	3.4
			k sigma	$\pm 0.75kS_p$		$\int_{-\infty}^{kS_p}\frac{e^{-\frac{x^2}{2\sigma^2}}}{\sigma\sqrt{2\pi}}dx \times 10^6$	$\int_{-\infty}^{kS_p}\frac{e^{-\frac{(x-|\Delta_\mu|)^2}{2\sigma^2}}}{\sigma\sqrt{2\pi}} \times 10^6$

Sigma Level Evaluation of Machine Capability for Multi-characteristics Parts. The overall evaluation of machine capability for multi-characteristics parts is essentially the weighting of each characteristic size. There are mainly three types of weighting methods: subjective, objective and combination of subjective and objective. In consideration of the different application conditions, we adopt the combination weighting method to quantify and differentiate the influence of general, important and key characteristics on the accuracy and performance of the work.

On the basis of the correlation between dimensional tolerances and work performance, the reciprocal of tolerance is used as the weighting cardinal number. The weight of size i is

$$f(i) = \frac{1}{T_i}(i = 1, 2, \cdots, n) \qquad (15)$$

Whether the degree of importance and the reciprocal of the tolerances are directly proportional to each other remains to be questioned. So we superinduce the importance degree coefficient k. And the weight of size i becomes

$$g_k(j) = \frac{[f(j)]^k}{\sum\limits_{i=1}^{n} [f(i)]^k} \quad (j = 1, 2, \cdots, n) \tag{16}$$

Finally, the overall sigma level assessment of machine capability for multi-characteristics parts is obtained as

$$\sigma_m = \sum_{j=1}^{n} g_k(j)\sigma_{mj} \tag{17}$$

The overall sigma level evaluation of multi-characteristics parts is established (Table 2).

Table 2. The overall sigma level evaluation table

σ_m of each size			σ_{m1}	$\cdots$	σ_{mn}
Tolerance of each size			T_1	$\cdots$	T_n
Weight coefficient			$\dfrac{[f(1)]^k}{\sum\limits_{i=1}^{n}[f(i)]^k}$	$\cdots$	$\dfrac{[f(n)]^k}{\sum\limits_{i=1}^{n}[f(i)]^k}$
The overall level	k = 0.5	σ_m	$\sum\limits_{j=1}^{n} g_{0.5}(j)\sigma_{mj}$		
	k = 1	σ_m	$\sum\limits_{j=1}^{n} g_1(j)\sigma_{mj}$		
	k = 1.5	σ_m	$\sum\limits_{j=1}^{n} g_{1.5}(j)\sigma_{mj}$		

5 Applications

Take the transmission housing as an example, the key size tolerances and corresponding measurement data are shown in Fig. 5 below.

Sigma Level Evaluation of Machine Capability for Size 1. According to the calculation formula of the sigma level, the sigma level evaluation chart of size 1 [−0.035, 0.035] is obtained (Fig. 4).
when the machine tolerance range is in [−0.024, 0.008], [−0.029, 0.013], [−0.035, 0.019] and [−0.041, 0.025], the corresponding sigma levels reach 3 sigma, 4 sigma, 5 sigma and 6 sigma level. The sigma level of size 1 is $\frac{4}{3}\min\left\{\frac{|-0.035 + 0.00803|}{0.007253},\right.$ $\left.\frac{0.035 + 0.00803}{0.007253}\right\} = 4.95\,$sigma.

Overall Sigma Level Evaluation of Machine Capability for Multi-characteristics Parts. Taking a domestic transmission housing as an example. After the skewness and kurtosis of characteristic data was tested for normal distribution, the distributions of each size are obtained (Fig. 5).

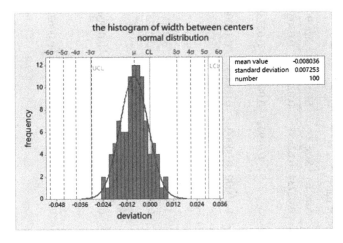

Fig. 4. The machine capability sigma level evaluation chart of size 1

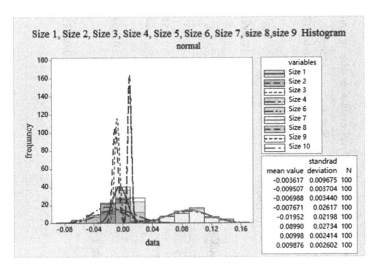

Fig. 5. The fitting distributions of size 1–9

Figure 5 shows that the machine capability sigma levels of size 1, 2, 9 and 10 are higher than size 3, 4, 5, 6, 7 and 8. From (Eqs. 13, 15, 16 and 17) and the sigma level evaluation method of single size, the overall machine capability sigma level of the gearbox housing is evaluated (Table 4).

Table 4 shows that the importance of the each size is (3) > (2) > (1) > (4) = (5) = (6) = (7) = (8) = (9) and the overall sigma level is 4.31, 4.24, 4.22 when k equals to 0.5, 1, 1.5 respectively.

This method takes into account the influence of general and important characteristics on the quality of the part as a whole, and highlights the importance of key characteristics. Moreover, with an increase or decrease in the importance degree

Table 3. Overall sigma level evaluation table of multi-characteristics parts

Each size index			Size 1	Size 2	Size 3	Size 4	Size 5	Size 6	Size 7	Size 8	Size 9
Each size index	Process fluctuations S_p		0.00968	0.00371	0.00344	0.02617	0.02198	0.02734	0.02655	0.02545	0.03061
	Mean μ		−0.00366	−0.00950	−0.00698		−0.00767		−0.01952	0.08990	0.02233
			0.00909	0.08967							
	Tolerance center		0.00000	−0.00850	−0.00700	0.00000	0.00000	0.10000	0.00000	0.00000	0.10000
	Tolerance		[−0.035,0.035] [−0.1,0.1]	[−0.021,0.004] [−0.1,0.1]	[−0.018,0.004] [0,0.2]		[−0.1,0.1]		[−0.1,0.1]	[0,0.2]	
σ_m	4.32		4.13	4.25	4.71		4.88	4.39	3.91	4.76	3.91
The overall level	k = 0.5	Weight	0.12425	0.21305	0.22164	0.07351	0.07351	0.07351	0.07351	0.07351	0.07351
		σ_m	$\sum_{j=1}^{n} g_{0.5}(j)\sigma_j = 4.31152$								
z	k = 1	Weight	0.11011	0.30831	0.35035	0.03854	0.03854	0.03854	0.03854	0.03854	0.03854
		σ_m	$\sum_{j=1}^{n} g_{1}(j)\sigma_j = 4.24469$								
	k = 1.5	Weight	0.05076	0.39800	0.51393	0.00622	0.00622	0.00622	0.00622	0.00622	0.00622
		σ_m	$\sum_{j=1}^{n} g_{1.5}(j)\sigma_j = 4.21539$								

coefficient k, the proximity degree of the overall machine capability sigma level to size 3 increases or decreases. Giving consideration to both the objective law and the specific application situation, we can fractionally adjust the overall sigma level by fine-tuning the value of k.

6 Conclusion

The following results is obtained:

(1) Multivariate statistical analysis methods are applied to establish analysis mathematical model for processing capability. The intrinsic link between process capability and variables such as man, machine, material, method, environment, and measurement method is mathematically analyzed, especially the relationship between process and machine.

(2) The sigma level method is applied to evaluate machine capability, which has solved the problem of multiple exponents resulted by multiple sizes in the traditional Cmk evaluation method.

(3) Grasping the relationship between tolerance levels, machining accuracy and work performance, we propose a combination of subjective and objective weighting method to evaluate the overall machine capability sigma level for multi-characteristics parts.

(4) Problems that need to be further solved: First, how to reduce measurement errors and accomplish offset compensation remains to be resolved. Second, to approach the actual performance of the parts, the importance degree coefficient k still needs to rely on experience and long-term tests.

Acknowledgements. This work is supported by the <National Natural Science Foundation, China> under Grant <No. 51705048; 51575070>; the <National Major Scientific and Technological Special Project for "High-grade CNC and Basic Manufacturing Equipment", China> under Grant <No. 2016ZX04004-005>; and the Fundamental Research Funds for the Central Universities <No. 106112017CDJXY110006>.

References

1. Hong, W.P.: J. Mech. Sci. Technol. **27**(10), 2905 (2013)
2. He, X.Q., Fu, S.J.: Six Sigma Quality Management and Statistical Process Control. Tsinghua University Press, Yangzhou (2016). (In Chinese)
3. Hsu, Y.C., Pearn, W.L., Wu, P.C.: Eur. J. Oper. Res. **191**(2), 517 (2008)
4. Hsu, Y.C., Pearn, W.L., Lu, C.S.: Int. J. Phys. Sci. **6**(19), 4533 (2011)
5. Agudelo, S., Myladis, C., Juan, C.: International Conference on Mechanical, Industrial and Power Engineering (2016)
6. Lepore, A., Palumbo, B., Castagliola, P.: Eur. J. Oper. Res. **267**(1) (2017)
7. Cogollo, M.R., Cogollo-Flórez, J.M., Flórez, A.: Qual. Access Success **18**(158), 50 (2017)
8. Sierra, M.A., Flórez, M.C., Cogollo-Flórez, J.M.: Qual. Access Success **18**(161), 73 (2017)
9. Gu, K., Jia, X., Liu, H., You, H.: Qual. Reliab. Eng. Int. **31**(3), 419 (2013)

10. Wu, C.W., Aslam, M., Jun, C.H.: Eur. J. Oper. Res. **217**(3), 560 (2012)
11. Shiau, J.J.H., Yen, C.L., Pearn, W.L., Lee, W.T.: Qual. Reliab. Eng. Int. **29**(4), 487 (2013)
12. Castagliola, P., Castellanos, J.V.G.: Qual. Technol. Quant. Manage. **2**(2), 201 (2008)
13. Pearn, W.L., Shiau, J.J.H., Tai, Y.T.: Qual. Reliab. Eng. Inter. **29**(2), 159 (2013)
14. Du, L., Zhang, X., Zhang, W., Fu, Z.H., Shi, R.B.: J. Electron. Sci. Technol. Univ. **43**(4), 629 (2017). (In Chinese)
15. Fan, W.J., Lv, W., Tang, Y.H., Liu, K.K.: Manufact. Technol. Mach. Tools **11,** 32 (2017). (In Chinese)
16. Dang, Y.G., Mi, C.M., Qian, W.Y.: Applied Multivariate Statistical Analysis. Tsinghua University Press, Beijing (2012). (In Chinese)
17. Zhong, B., Liu, Q.S., Liu, C.L., Huang, G.H.: Mathematical Statistics (Higher Education Press China 2015). (In Chinese)

Mechanical Transmission System

An Accurate Modeling Method
for the HGM Hypoid Gear

Feiyang Jiang[✉], Tengjiao Lin, Xingxing Lu, Zirui Zhao,
and Shijia Yi

State Key Laboratory of Mechanical Transmission,
Chongqing University, Chongqing, China
963093563@qq.com

Abstract. For hypoid gears manufactured by hypoid generated modified-(HGM), according to gear cutting process and the mutual movement of tools, machine tool and wheel blank, the equations of tooth flank and fillet are derived by the gear meshing theory and gear cutting theory, and the accurate mathematical model for the hypoid gear tooth profile is built. The data of tooth surface are collected and calculated in MATLAB according to the machining parameters of a pair of gears. Imageware software and UG software are used at the same time to establish A hypoid gear solid model with a transition surface. The model with fillet can be used in the digital manufacturing and finite element analysis of hypoid gears.

Keywords: Hypoid gear · Transition surface · Equations of tooth surface
Accurate geometrical modeling

1 Introduction

Hypoid gear is the most complicated type of bevel gear in gear transmission. Its transmission has a series of advantages such as greater coincidence degree, higher bearing capacity, higher transmission efficiency, smoother transmission, less noise, and larger reduction ratio than general cylindrical gear transmission. However, an accurate geometric three-dimensional model cannot be established using the general method.

Tang [1] established a spiral bevel gear tooth surface equation with a tooth root transition arc, and established a three-dimensional model of the spiral bevel gear with Pro/E. Liu [2] developed a set of precise finite element modeling of Spiral bevel gears based on a tooth profile equation of a spiral bevel gear with a transitional arc. Liu [3] utilized MATLAB software to calculate the tooth surface point cloud of HFT hypoid gears, and import it into CATIA software to establish a three-dimensional gear model. Wang [4] took the hypoid gears processed by the HGT method as the object, deduced the theoretical work tooth surface equations and the tooth root transition surface equations. Based on this, a three-dimensional geometric simulation model was established and gear tooth load contact analysis was conducted. Gleason corporation of the United States has its own set of hyperbolic gear CAD/CAE/CAM/CAT closed-loop systems [5], but gleason technology is not open to the outside world. There are few scholars concerned about the modeling method of hypoid gears processed by HGM

© Springer Nature Singapore Pte Ltd. 2018
S. Wang et al. (Eds.): ICSEE 2018/IMIOT 2018, CCIS 923, pp. 465–473, 2018.
https://doi.org/10.1007/978-981-13-2396-6_43

method. This article will use the HGM hypoid gear as research object and propose an modeling method.

According to a set of hypoid gear machining the parameters of the HGM adjustment card [6], MATLAB is applied as a solution tool to calculate the discrete points of the tooth profile surface and transition surface without machining errors. Then, a hypoid gear solid model was established by combination using of Imageware software and UG software.

2 Gear Cutting Principle

The HGM hypoid gear processing is based on a cradle mechanism on the machine tool to simulate an imaginary flat top producing gear [7]. The cutter face mounted on the cradle is a gear tooth of the imaginary gear (see Fig. 1).

Fig. 1. Schematic diagram of hypoid gear cutting

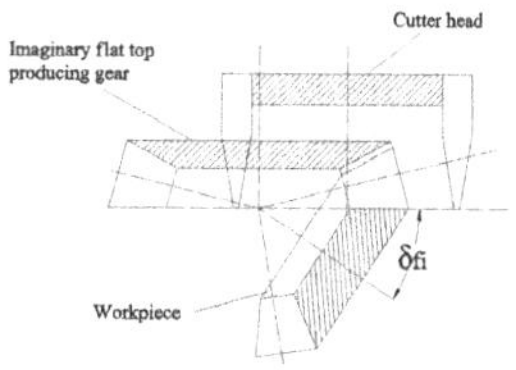

Fig. 2. Principle of flat-top production wheel for processing hypoid gear

The conical cutting surface of the cutter head and the machined tooth surface are a pair of completely conjugate tooth surfaces [6]. The rotation plane of the blade top must be tangent to the root cone of the gear being cut (see Fig. 2).

3 Cutter Equation

The tool geometry of the wheel and the pinion that is processed are shown in Figs. 3 and 4, and the tool tip radius is taken into consideration. The arc between the top edge and the side edge of the cutter tooth is connected by a circular arc. The connection between the arc and the top edge and the side edge is smoothly tangent.

3.1 Cutter Equation for Machining Wheel and Pinion

The machining large wheel adopts single-blade double-side method, namely, a milling cutter simultaneously cuts out the concave surface and convex surface of the gear [8], and the cutter profile is divided into four sections, in the coordinate system $S_t = \{O_t; x_t, y_t, z_t\}$, the equation of the side of the cutter in the four sections is respectively.

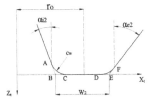

Fig. 3. Tool geometry model for machining wheel

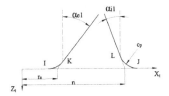

Fig. 4. Tool geometry model for machining pinion

The tool equation of the inner blade

$$r_{21}^t = \begin{bmatrix} (X_A - u_1 \sin(\alpha_{i2})) \cos(\theta) \\ (X_A - u_1 \sin(\alpha_{i2})) \sin(\theta) \\ Y_A - u_1 \cos(\alpha_{i2}) \\ 1 \end{bmatrix} \tag{1}$$

The tool equation of the inner blade tip arc

$$r_{22}^t = \begin{bmatrix} (X_C - c_w \cos(u_2)) \cos(\theta) \\ (X_C - c_w \cos(u_2)) \sin(\theta) \\ -c_w + c_w \sin(u_2) \\ 1 \end{bmatrix} \tag{2}$$

The tool equation of the outer edge of the blade

$$r_{23}^t = \begin{bmatrix} (X_F + u_3 \sin(\alpha_{e2})) \cos(\theta) \\ (X_F + u_3 \sin(\alpha_{e2})) \sin(\theta) \\ Y_F - u_3 \cos(\alpha_{e2}) \\ 1 \end{bmatrix} \tag{3}$$

The tool equation of the outer blade tip arc

$$r_{24}^t = \begin{bmatrix} (X_D + c_w \cos(u_4)) \cos(\theta) \\ (X_D + c_w \cos(u_4)) \sin(\theta) \\ -c_w + c_w \sin(u_4) \\ 1 \end{bmatrix} \tag{4}$$

In the formula: subscript 2 represents wheel; c_w is the arc radius of the blade; α_{i2} is the inner blade angle; α_{e2} is the outer blade profile angle; u_1 is the distance from point A at any point of the inner blade; u_2 is acute angle between the line which connects any point on the inner blade tip arc and tip arc center and X_t axis; u_3 is the distance from the point F at any point on the outer edge of the blade; u_4 is acute angle between the line which connects any point on the outer blade tip arc and tip arc center and X_t axis; θ is the rotational angle of the cutterhead; X_A, X_C, X_F, X_D, Y_A and Y_F can be calculated by the tool geometry model. The calculations are as follows

$$X_A = r_o - 0.5W_2 - c_w \sin(\alpha_{i2})(1 - \sin(\alpha_{i2})) \tag{5}$$

$$X_C = r_o - 0.5W_2 + c_w \cos(\alpha_{i2}) - c_w \sin(\alpha_{i2})(1 - \sin(\alpha_{i2})) \tag{6}$$

$$X_F = r_o - 0.5W_2 - c_w \sin(\alpha_{e2})(1 - \sin(\alpha_{e2})) \tag{7}$$

$$X_D = r_o - 0.5W_2 + c_w \cos(\alpha_{e2}) - c_w \sin(\alpha_{e2})(1 - \sin(\alpha_{e2})) \tag{8}$$

$$Y_A = -c_w(1 - \sin(\alpha_{i2})) \tag{9}$$

$$Y_F = -c_w(1 - \sin(\alpha_{e2})) \tag{10}$$

In the formula: r_o is the nominal cutter radius, W_2 is the top length of the cutter. In the coordinate system $S_t = \{O_t; x_t, y_t, z_t\}$, the normal vector of the four sections is respectively

The normal vector of the inner blade

$$n_{21}^t = \frac{\frac{\partial r_{21}^t}{\partial u_1} \times \frac{\partial r_{21}^t}{\partial \theta}}{\left| \frac{\partial r_{21}^t}{\partial u_1} \times \frac{\partial r_{21}^t}{\partial \theta} \right|} = \begin{bmatrix} \cos(\alpha_{i2})\cos(\theta) \\ \cos(\alpha_{i2})\sin(\theta) \\ -\sin(\alpha_{i2}) \end{bmatrix} \tag{11}$$

The normal vector of the inner blade tip arc

$$n_{22}^t = \frac{\frac{\partial r_{22}^t}{\partial u_2} \times \frac{\partial r_{22}^t}{\partial \theta}}{\left| \frac{\partial r_{22}^t}{\partial u_2} \times \frac{\partial r_{22}^t}{\partial \theta} \right|} = \begin{bmatrix} \cos(u_2)\cos(\theta) \\ \cos(u_2)\sin(\theta) \\ -\sin(u_2) \end{bmatrix} \tag{12}$$

The normal vector of the outer edge of the blade

$$n_{23}^t = \frac{\frac{\partial r_{23}^t}{\partial u_3} \times \frac{\partial r_{23}^t}{\partial \theta}}{\left| \frac{\partial r_{23}^t}{\partial u_3} \times \frac{\partial r_{23}^t}{\partial \theta} \right|} = \begin{bmatrix} \cos(\alpha_{e2})\cos(\theta) \\ \cos(\alpha_{e2})\sin(\theta) \\ \sin(\alpha_{e2}) \end{bmatrix} \tag{13}$$

The normal vector of the outer blade tip arc

$$n_{24}^t = \frac{\frac{\partial r_{24}^t}{\partial u_4} \times \frac{\partial r_{24}^t}{\partial \theta}}{\left| \frac{\partial r_{24}^t}{\partial u_4} \times \frac{\partial r_{24}^t}{\partial \theta} \right|} = \begin{bmatrix} \cos(u_4)\cos(\theta) \\ \cos(u_4)\sin(\theta) \\ \sin(u_4) \end{bmatrix} \tag{14}$$

The pinion's is similar to the wheel, so will not be repeated.

4 Derivation of Tooth Profile Equation

The calculation of the entire cutting process can be transformed into the obtainment of the wheel surface equation and figuring out the relative position and relative motion of the production wheel and the wheel blank. Hypoid gear tooth surface is actually cutter envelope satisfying the meshing equation.

4.1 Coordinate Transformation Matrix

When the production plane along with the cradle rotation develops a tooth surface, both the tool and the tooth blank are in line contact at each position to satisfy the meshing equation. The equation of the production plane is transformed into the gear coordinate system through a series of coordinate transformations, and the radial vector and normal vector equations of the tooth surface are obtained. The coordinate transformation process is: tool-rocker-machine tool-gear. First we need to establish a coordinate system: Let $S_o = \{O_o; x_o, y_o, z_o\}$ be the cradle coordinate system fixed with the machine tool; $S_a = \{O_a; x_a, y_a, z_a\}$ is the wheel blank coordinate system fixed with the machine tool; $S_g = \{O_g; x_g, y_g, z_g\}$ is the moving coordinate system fixed with the cradle; $S_p = \{O_p; x_p, y_p, z_p\}$ is the moving coordinate system fixed with the blank; $S_t = \{O_t; x_t, y_t, z_t\}$ is the coordinate system of the cutterhead fixed with the cradle; $S_f = \{O_f; x_f, y_f, z_f\}$ is the auxiliary coordinate system and fixed with the machine tool (see Fig. 5).

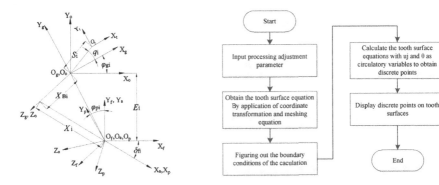

Fig. 5. Coordinate system of hypoid gear processing

Fig. 6. Flowchart of programming for tooth surface equation

The coordinate transformation matrix between coordinates are as follows

$$M_{gt} = \begin{bmatrix} 1 & 0 & 0 & S_i\cos(q_i) \\ 0 & 1 & 0 & \pm S_i\sin(q_i) \\ 0 & 0 & 1 & 0 \\ 0 & 0 & 0 & 1 \end{bmatrix} \tag{15}$$

$$M_{og} = \begin{bmatrix} \cos(\varphi_{gi}) & -\sin(\varphi_{gi}) & 0 & 0 \\ \sin(\varphi_{gi}) & \cos(\varphi_{gi}) & 0 & 0 \\ 0 & 0 & 1 & 0 \\ 0 & 0 & 0 & 1 \end{bmatrix} \tag{16}$$

$$M_{fo} = \begin{bmatrix} 1 & 0 & 0 & -X_i\sin(\delta_{fi}) \\ 0 & 1 & 0 & E_{oi} \\ 0 & 0 & 1 & -X_i\cos(\delta_{fi}) - X_{Bi} \\ 0 & 0 & 0 & 1 \end{bmatrix} \tag{17}$$

$$M_{af} = \begin{bmatrix} \cos(\delta_{fi}) & 0 & \sin(\delta_{fi}) & 0 \\ 0 & 1 & 0 & 0 \\ -\sin(\delta_{fi}) & 0 & \cos(\delta_{fi}) & 0 \\ 0 & 0 & 0 & 1 \end{bmatrix} \tag{18}$$

$$M_{pa} = \begin{bmatrix} 1 & 0 & 0 & 0 \\ 0 & \cos(\varphi_{pi}) & \sin(\varphi_{pi}) & 0 \\ 0 & -\sin(\varphi_{pi}) & \cos(\varphi_{pi}) & 0 \\ 0 & 0 & 0 & 1 \end{bmatrix} \tag{19}$$

In the formula: S_i is the radial tool location; q_i is the angular location of tool; X_{Bi} is the bed location; X_i is the axial wheel position; E_{oi} is the vertical wheel position; δ_{fi} is the root cone angle of the processed gear; φ_{gi} is the rotation angle of the cradle; φ_{pi} is the rotation angle of the workpiece; $i = 1, 2$, 1 represents the pinion, 2 represents the wheel; In composite symbol $\pm$, the positive is for the right-handed gear, and the negative is for the left-handed gear. Calculations of φ_{gi} and φ_{pi} are as follows

$$\varphi_{gi} = \omega_g t \tag{20}$$

$$\varphi_{p2} = i_{pg2}\omega_g t \tag{21}$$

$$\varphi_{p1} = i_{pg1}(c_2\varphi_{g1} - c_2\varphi_{g1}^2) \tag{22}$$

In the formula: ω_g is the cradle rotating speed, assuming $\omega_g = 1$ rad/s; i_{pg1} is roll ratio for machining pinion; i_{pg2} is roll ratio for machining wheel; c_2 is the second-order coefficient of modification; t is the time variable.

4.2   Tooth Profile Equation

The tooth profile machined by the tool is a series of envelope surface formed by tools satisfying the conditions of the meshing equation. That is, any point on the tooth profile should satisfy the following relationship:

$$n \cdot v = 0 \tag{23}$$

In the formula: n is the common normal vector of the meshing point between the production wheel and the workpiece; v is the relative motion speed of the production wheel and the workpiece.

A point is taken on the cutting surface of the cutter, and the radial vector of the point is converted to the workpiece coordinate system by coordinate transformation, and the tooth surface equation is obtained by uniting the meshing equation. The radial vector of any point on the tooth profile in the wheel blank's moving coordinate S_p, and the radial vector and normal vector in the cradle coordinate system fixed with the machine tool S_o are

$$r_{ij}^p = M_{pa}M_{af}M_{fo}M_{og}M_{gt}r_{ij}^t \tag{24}$$

$$r_{ij}^o = M_{og}M_{gt}r_{ij}^t \tag{25}$$

$$n_{ij}^o = L_{og}L_{gt}n_{ij}^t \tag{26}$$

In the formula: L_{og}, L_{gt} are the matrices consisting of the first three rows and the first three columns of M_{og} and M_{gt}, respectively; $i = 1, 2; j = 1, 2, 3, 4$.

The cradle coordinate system fixed with the machine tool S_o, the relative velocity of the contact point between the tool and the blank is

$$v_{ij}^o = (\omega_{gi} - \omega_{pi})r_{ij}^o - \omega_{pi} \times R_i^o \tag{27}$$

In the formula: ω_g and ω_p are the angular velocity vectors of the cradle and wheel blank in the coordinate system of the cutterhead fixed with the cradle S_t; R_i^o is the radial vector of the origin of the cradle coordinate system S_o fixed with the machine tool. The calculations are as follows

$$\omega_{gi} = [0 \quad 0 \quad \omega_g]^T \tag{28}$$

$$\omega_{pi} = [\omega_p \cos(\delta_{fi}) \quad 0 \quad \omega_p \sin(\delta_{fi})]^T \tag{29}$$

$$R_i^o = [-X_i \cos(\delta_{fi}) \quad E_{oi} \quad -X_i \sin(\delta_{fi}) - X_{Bi}]^T \tag{30}$$

According to the meshing principle, the meshing equation of the tooth profile is

$$f_{ij}(u_j, \theta, t) = n_{ij}^o \cdot v_{ij}^o = 0 \tag{31}$$

(31) is a ternary system of nonlinear equations which can be solved to get the corresponding value of t, if u_j and θ are given. The value of t can be brought into (24) to get the tooth profile equation

$$r_{ij} = r_{ij}^p(u_j, \theta) \tag{32}$$

5 The Programming Calculation of Tooth Point Cloud

After deriving the tooth surface equations, a program is designed in MATLAB, and the step length is set to calculate the discrete points of the tooth profile surfaces of the hypoid gears. This article takes the hypoid gear design parameters in Table 1 for example to calculate the discrete points of the tooth profile surfaces (see Fig. 6).

Table 1. Basic parameters of hypoid gear pair

Parameter name	Value	Parameter name	Value
Number of pinion teeth	13	Outer pitch diameter (d_{m2}/mm)	240
Number of wheel teeth	57	Pinion mean spiral angle (β_{m1}/°)	43
Medium normal pressure angle (/°)	20	Addendum working coefficient k_h	4
Shaft angle (Σ/°)	90	Medium Addendum coefficient k_a	0.286
Offset (E/mm)	20	Pinion fillet radius (c_p/mm)	0.2
Wheel width (b_2/mm)	37	Wheel fillet radius (c_w/mm)	0.2
Mean normal module (m_{mn}/mm)	3.036		

6 Geometric Modeling

Constructing a complex surface solid model is difficult for general three-dimensional software, but utilizing Imageware software's powerful surface fitting function and UG software's powerful modeling capabilities can solve this problem.

6.1 Surface Fitting

The point cloud obtained in MATLAB is imported into Imageware software, and the surface function is constructed by interpolation method. After setting the surface fitting order, the tooth surface point cloud is fitted into a smooth tooth surface slice (see Fig. 7).

Fig. 7. Fitting the tooth surface   **Fig. 8.** Hypoid gears model

6.2 The Establishment of Gear Entities

Establish a precise tooth blank model in the UG software and import the tooth surface patches generated in the Imageware software into the model. Utilize The bridging surface function to bridge the two transitional surfaces of the tooth face piece. Since the tooth surfaces are mutually independent, the suture surface function is used to stitch the tooth surfaces into a whole.

The stitched tooth surface piece is used to trim the precise wheel blank model, and then perform corresponding number of arrays of pruning feature according to the actual number of teeth, then an accurate three-dimensional model of the hypoid gear can be obtained (see Fig. 8).

7 Conclusion

The accurate hypoid gear solid model established by the method of this paper can be further used for finite element simulation analysis, such as the analysis of the bending stress of the tooth root and the dynamic meshing stress analysis of the tooth surface contact, so as to better reflect the actual meshing condition of hypoid gear, and a theoretical basis for the CAM/CAE of hypoid gear is provided.

Acknowledgments. The authors are grateful for the financial support provided by the Industrial Common Key Technology Innovation of Chongqing (cstc2015zdcy-ztzx70013) and the Fundamental Research Funds for Central Universities (106112017CDJZRPY0018).

References

1. Tang, J.Y.: Accurate modeling of tooth surface of spiral bevel gear with transitional surface. J. Mach. Sci. Technol. **28**(03), 317–321 (2009)
2. Liu, G.L.: Finite element modeling of spiral bevel gear with tooth root transition surface. Mech. Sci. Technol. **29**(12), 1595–1601 (2010)
3. Liu, C.: A 3D modeling method for hft hypoid gears. J. Sichuan Univ. (Eng. Sci. Ed.) **48**(06), 132–139 (2016)
4. Wang, X.: Accurate modeling and loading analysis of HGT hypoid gears. J. Sichuan Univ. (Eng. Sci. Ed.) **47**(04), 181–185 (2015)
5. Fan, Q.: Developments in Tooth Contact Analysis (TCA) and Loaded TCA for spiral bevel and hypoid gear drives. Gear Technol. **27**(03), 26–35 (2007)
6. Zeng, T.: Design and Processing of Spiral Bevel Gears. Harbin Institute of Technology Press, Harbin (1989)
7. Lin, C.Y.: Computer-aided manufacturing of spiral bevel and hypoid gears with minimum surface-deviation. Mech. Mach. Theory **33**(6), 785–803 (1998)
8. Alfonso, F.A.: Numerical approach for determination of rough-cutting machine-tool settings for fixed-setting face-milled spiral bevel gears. Mech. Mach. Theory **112**, 22–42 (2017)

Analysis of Inherent Characteristics of Torsional Vibration and Its Influence Factors of the Double Planetary Transmission System

Zirui Zhao[1](✉), Tengjiao Lin[1], Jing Wei[1], Feiyang Jiang[1], and Jianbo Liu[2]

[1] State Key Laboratory of Mechanical Transmission, Chongqing University, Chongqing, China
zrzhao@cqu.edu.cn
[2] Chongqing Gearbox Co. Ltd., Chongqing, China

Abstract. This work develops a torsional vibration model with lumped-parameter method and uses it to investigate the torsional vibration characteristics of double planetary transmission system. The natural frequency of torsional vibration and corresponding modes of the transmission system are obtained by solving the vibration differential equation. And then influence of rotational inertia and torsional stiffness on the natural characteristics of torsional vibration of the system is studied. The results show that the natural frequencies of torsional vibration can be improved effectively by increasing the torsional stiffness and reducing the rotational inertia of system under the condition that the total transmission ratio and the dimensional parameters of the gear pairs are constant at all levels.

Keywords: Planetary gear transmission · Torsional vibration
Inherent characteristics

1 Introduction

Torsional vibration is a major form of vibration in power devices and is an important factor influencing their service performance and operation stability. When excitation frequencies of the system are close to the natural frequencies of torsional vibration, the fault of torsional vibration will occur in the power device. Therefore, it is of great engineering significance to analyze the inherent characteristics of torsional vibration of the gear transmission system and its influencing factors.

The inherent characteristics of torsional vibration mainly include natural frequencies of torsional vibration and corresponding vibration modes. Domestic and foreign scholars have done a lot of research work on the analysis of inherent characteristics of torsional vibration of gear transmission system. Lin et al. established lumped parametric models for uniform and uneven distribution of planetary gears respectively, studied the free vibration characteristics of a planetary gear transmission system, and proposed to divide the vibrational modes of the system into the translational mode, the

© Springer Nature Singapore Pte Ltd. 2018
S. Wang et al. (Eds.): ICSEE 2018/IMIOT 2018, CCIS 923, pp. 474–483, 2018.
https://doi.org/10.1007/978-981-13-2396-6_44

torsional mode and planet mode [1, 2]. Song et al. studied the inherent characteristics of the planetary gear system by establishing the pure torsional dynamic model [3, 4]. Taking a vehicle planetary transmission system as the research object, Cai and Yu established the purely torsional vibration model which includes tangential displacements of planet gears and bearing stiffness using the lumped-parameter method. And the amplitude characteristics and inherent characteristics of the transmission system were studied respectively [5, 6]. Synthetically considering the factors of meshing stiffness, backlash and meshing error, Li and Song established the purely inherent vibration model of the planetary gear sets, and then its inherent characteristics are analyzed [7]. Lin et al. established the torsional vibration model of different gear systems respectively and analyzed the natural frequencies of torsional vibration and corresponding vibration modes of the shafting [8, 9].

In this paper, the double planetary transmission system of the vertical mill reducer is taken as the research object. Synthetically considering the joint parameter such as meshing stiffness and torsional stiffness of the shafting, the analysis model of torsional vibration of system is established, and then the natural frequencies of torsional vibration and corresponding modes are obtained. The influence of rotational inertia and torsional stiffness on the natural characteristics of torsional vibration is studied on the basis of all the above.

2   Analysis Model of Torsional Vibration of the Gear System

The schematic diagram of the gear transmission system of the double planetary vertical mill gear reducer is shown as Fig. 1(a). The vibration energy is input by the motor and transmitted in turn to the diaphragm coupling, the small bevel gear, the large bevel gear, the primary planetary gear train, the spline shaft, and the secondary sun gear, and then diverted via five secondary planet gears, finally output by the secondary planet carrier.

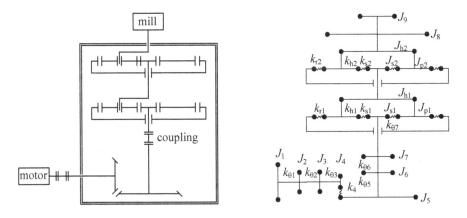

Fig. 1. (a) Analysis model of torsional vibration (b) diagram of the gear transmission system

2.1 Differential Equation of Free Undamped Vibration of the Shafting

To analyze the inherent characteristics of torsional vibration of the transmission system, a torsional vibration model of the shafting is established using lumped-parameter method. In the establishment of the dynamic model, following assumptions shall be made: (1) each part rotating with the shaft is simplified to rigid disc and flexible shaft section in the transmission system; (2) the rotational inertia of shaft is equivalently distributed to the rigid discs at both ends, and masses, rotational inertias of planet gears of the same level are the same; (3) only the torsional vibration of the transmission components are to be considered, regardless of the impact of back-up bearing and the damping; (4) the rings are fixed, with zero displacement; (5) the impact of backlash is ignored. Therefore the analysis model of torsional vibration of the transmission system is obtained as Fig. 1(b).

In Fig. 1(b), k_i denotes the meshing stiffness of the gear pair, $k_{\theta i}$ denotes the torsional stiffness of the shafting, and J_i denotes the rotational inertia of each transmission component plus the partial rotational inertia of the shaft in which it's located.

For a complex mechanical system with multiple degrees of freedom, the Lagrange equation can be expressed as,

$$\frac{d}{dt}\left(\frac{\partial T}{\partial \dot{\theta}}\right) - \frac{\partial T}{\partial \theta} + \frac{\partial V}{\partial \theta} = Q \tag{1}$$

where T and V denote the kinetic and potential energy functions of the transmission system; Q_i denotes the generalized force. And for the undamped free vibration system, $Q_i = 0$.

Considering the influence of the joint between the bevel gear and the primary sun gear, the joint between the primary planet carrier and the secondary sun gear, the differential equations of torsional vibration of the double planetary transmission system can be obtained by applying Lagrange formulation (1) and are given by:

$$\begin{cases} J_1\ddot{\theta}_1 + k_{\theta 1}\theta_1 - k_{\theta 1}\theta_2 = 0 \\ J_2\ddot{\theta}_2 - k_{\theta 1}\theta_1 + (k_{\theta 1} + k_{\theta 2})\theta_2 - k_{\theta 2}\theta_3 = 0 \\ J_3\ddot{\theta}_3 - k_{\theta 2}\theta_2 + (k_{\theta 2} + k_{\theta 3})\theta_3 - k_{\theta 3}\theta_4 = 0 \\ J_4\ddot{\theta}_4 - k_{\theta 3}\theta_3 + (k_{\theta 3} + k_4 r_4^2)\theta_4 - k_4 r_4 r_5 \theta_5 = 0 \\ J_5\ddot{\theta}_5 - k_4 r_5 r_4 \theta_4 + (k_4 r_5^2 + k_{\theta 5})\theta_5 - k_{\theta 5}\theta_6 = 0 \\ J_6\ddot{\theta}_6 - k_{\theta 5}\theta_5 + (k_{\theta 5} + k_{\theta 6})\theta_6 - k_{\theta 6}\theta_7 = 0 \\ J_7\ddot{\theta}_7 - k_{\theta 6}\theta_6 + (k_{\theta 6} + k_{\theta 7})\theta_7 - k_{\theta 7}\theta_{s1} = 0 \\ J_{s1}\ddot{\theta}_{s1} - k_{\theta 7}\theta_7 + (k_{\theta 7} + 3k_{s1}r_{s1}^2)\theta_{s1} - k_{s1}r_{s1}r_{p11}\theta_{p11} - k_{s1}r_{s1}r_{p12}\theta_{p12} \\ \quad - k_{s1}r_{s1}r_{p13}\theta_{p13} - 3k_{s1}r_{s1}r_{h1}\theta_{h1} = 0 \\ J_{p11}\ddot{\theta}_{p11} - k_{s1}r_{p11}r_{s1}\theta_{s1} + (k_{s1} + k_{r1})r_{p11}^2\theta_{p11} + (k_{s1} - k_{r1})r_{p11}r_{h1}\theta_{h1} = 0 \\ J_{p12}\ddot{\theta}_{p12} - k_{s1}r_{p12}r_{s1}\theta_{s1} + (k_{s1} + k_{r1})r_{p12}^2\theta_{p12} + (k_{s1} - k_{r1})r_{p12}r_{h1}\theta_{h1} = 0 \\ J_{p13}\ddot{\theta}_{p13} - k_{s1}r_{p13}r_{s1}\theta_{s1} + (k_{s1} + k_{r1})r_{p13}^2\theta_{p13} + (k_{s1} - k_{r1})r_{p13}r_{h1}\theta_{h1} = 0 \end{cases}$$

$$
\begin{cases}
(J_{h1} + \displaystyle\sum_{i=1}^{3} m_{p1i} r_{h1}^2)\ddot{\theta}_{h1} - 3k_{s1}r_{h1}r_{s1}\theta_{s1} + (k_{s1} - k_{r1})r_{h1}r_{p11}\theta_{p11} + (k_{s1} - k_{r1})r_{h1}r_{p12}\theta_{p12} \\
\quad + (k_{s1} - k_{r1})r_{h1}r_{p13}\theta_{p13} + \left[3(k_{s1} + k_{r1} + k_{h1})r_{h1}^2 + k_{\theta h1}\right]\theta_{h1} - k_{\theta h1}\theta_{s2} = 0 \\
J_{s2}\ddot{\theta}_{s2} - k_{\theta h1}\theta_{h1} + (k_{\theta h1} + 5k_{s2}r_{s2}^2)\theta_{s2} - k_{s2}r_{s2}r_{p21}\theta_{p21} - k_{s2}r_{s2}r_{p22}\theta_{p22} - k_{s2}r_{s2}r_{p23}\theta_{p23} \\
\quad - k_{s2}r_{s2}r_{p24}\theta_{p24} - k_{s2}r_{s2}r_{p25}\theta_{p25} - 5k_{s2}r_{s2}r_{h2}\theta_{h2} = 0 \\
J_{p21}\ddot{\theta}_{p21} - k_{s2}r_{p21}r_{s2}\theta_{s2} + (k_{s2} + k_{r2})r_{p21}^2\theta_{p21} + (k_{s2} - k_{r2})r_{p21}r_{h2}\theta_{h2} = 0 \\
J_{p22}\ddot{\theta}_{p22} - k_{s2}r_{p22}r_{s2}\theta_{s2} + (k_{s2} + k_{r2})r_{p22}^2\theta_{p22} + (k_{s2} - k_{r2})r_{p22}r_{h2}\theta_{h2} = 0 \\
J_{p23}\ddot{\theta}_{p23} - k_{s2}r_{p23}r_{s2}\theta_{s2} + (k_{s2} + k_{r2})r_{p23}^2\theta_{p23} + (k_{s2} - k_{r2})r_{p23}r_{h2}\theta_{h2} = 0 \\
J_{p24}\ddot{\theta}_{p24} - k_{s2}r_{p24}r_{s2}\theta_{s2} + (k_{s2} + k_{r2})r_{p24}^2\theta_{p24} + (k_{s2} - k_{r2})r_{p24}r_{h2}\theta_{h2} = 0 \\
J_{p25}\ddot{\theta}_{p25} - k_{s2}r_{p25}r_{s2}\theta_{s2} + (k_{s2} + k_{r2})r_{p25}^2\theta_{p25} + (k_{s2} - k_{r2})r_{p25}r_{h2}\theta_{h2} = 0 \\
(J_{h2} + J_8 + J_9 + \displaystyle\sum_{i=1}^{5} m_{p2i}r_{h2}^2)\ddot{\theta}_{h2} - 5k_{s2}r_{h2}r_{s2}\theta_{s2} + (k_{s2} - k_{r2})r_{h2}r_{p21}\theta_{p21} \\
\quad + (k_{s2} - k_{r2})r_{h2}r_{p22}\theta_{p22} + (k_{s2} - k_{r2})r_{h2}r_{p23}\theta_{p23} + (k_{s2} - k_{r2})r_{h2}r_{p24}\theta_{p24} \\
\quad + (k_{s2} - k_{r2})r_{h2}r_{p25}\theta_{p25} + 5(k_{s2} + k_{r2} + k_{h2})r_{h2}^2\theta_{h2} = 0
\end{cases}
\tag{2}
$$

where θ_i denotes the angle of each rotational component; m_{p1i} denotes the mass of each planet gear in the primary planetary transmission; r_{h1} denotes the distance from the axis of the primary planet gear to the axis of the primary planet carrier; m_{p2i} denotes the mass of each planet gear in the secondary planetary transmission; r_{h2} denotes the distance from the axis of the secondary planet gear to the axis of the secondary planet carrier; r_4 and r_5 denote the radius of midpoint-based circles of the small bevel gear and the large bevel gear respectively; r_{s1} and r_{p1i} denote the radius of base circles of the primary sun gear and the primary planet gear respectively; r_{s2} and r_{p2i} denote the radius of base circles of the secondary sun gear and the secondary planet gear respectively.

Arrange Eq. (2) into a matrix form in accordance to Eq. (3),

$$
[J][\ddot{\theta}] + [K_\theta][\theta] = 0
\tag{3}
$$

where $[J]$ and $[K_\theta]$ are the inertia matrix and the torsional stiffness matrix of system respectively.

2.2 Equivalent Transformation of the Analysis Model of Torsional Vibration

In order to quickly analyze the inherent characteristics of torsional vibration of the double planetary gear transmission system, the transmission system needs to be converted into a continuous system that rotates at the same rotational speed. Therefore, the displacement variables of each component are converted to the same axis (such as the secondary sun gear shaft). And then the equivalent displacement, equivalent mass and equivalent torsional stiffness of system after equivalent conversion are calculated respectively.

The equivalent displacements of each component of the double planetary gear transmission system to the secondary sun gear are:

$$u_k = \frac{\theta_k}{i_{ks}} r_s \tag{4}$$

where i_{ks} denotes the transmission ratio of the kth component to the sun gear ($k = 1, 2, 3,...,9$, s1, p11, p12, p13, h1, s2, p21, p22, p23, p24, p25, h2).

The transmission ratios of each component of the double planetary gear transmission system to the sun gear are:

$$
\begin{cases}
i_{ks2} = \frac{z_5}{z_4}(1 + z_{r1}/z_{s1}) & (k = 1, 2, 3, 4) \\
i_{ks2} = (1 + z_{r1}/z_{s1}) & (k = 5, 6, 7, s1) \\
i_{ks2} = (1 + z_{r1}/z_{p1}) & (k = p11, p12, p13) \\
i_{ks2} = 1 & (k = h1, s2) \\
i_{ks2} = \frac{1 + z_{r2}/z_{p2}}{1 + z_{r2}/z_{s2}} & (k = p21, p22, p23, p24, p25) \\
i_{ks2} = \frac{1}{1 + z_{r2}/z_{s2}} & (k = h2)
\end{cases}
\tag{5}
$$

where z_4 and z_5 are the teeth number of the small bevel gear and the large bevel gear respectively; z_{s1}, z_{p1} and z_{r1} are the tooth number of the primary sun gear, planet gear and ring respectively; z_{s2}, z_{p2}, z_{r2} are the tooth number of the secondary sun gear, planet gear and ring respectively.

The equivalent masses of each component of the double planetary gear transmission system are:

$$
\begin{cases}
M_k = \frac{J_k i_{ks2}^2}{r_{s2}^2} & (k = 1, 2, 3, \ldots, 9, s1, p11, p12, p13, s2, p21, p22, p23, p24, p25) \\
M_{h1} = \frac{(J_{h1} + \sum\limits_{i=1}^{3} m_{p1i} r_{h1}^2) i_{h1s2}^2}{r_{s1}^2} \\
M_{h2} = \frac{(J_{h2} + J_8 + J_9 + \sum\limits_{i=1}^{5} m_{p2i} r_{h2}^2) i_{h2s2}^2}{r_{s2}^2}
\end{cases}
\tag{6}
$$

And the equivalent stiffness of the kth component of the double planetary gear transmission system is:

$$
\begin{cases}
K_k = k_{\theta k} i_{ks2}^2 / r_{s2}^2 \quad (k = 1,2,3,5,6,7) \\
K_4 = k_4 r_4^2 i_{4s2}^2 / r_{s2}^2 \\
K_{14} = k_{\theta h1} i_{h1s2}^2 / r_{s2}^2 \\
K_8 = k_{s1} r_{s1}^2 i_{s1s2}^2 / r_{s2}^2 \\
K_9 = k_{s1} r_{s1} r_{p1i} i_{p1is2} i_{s1s2} / r_{s2}^2 \ (i = 1,2,3) \\
K_{10} = k_{s1} r_{s1} r_{h1} i_{h1s2} i_{s1s2} / r_{s2}^2 \\
K_{11} = (k_{s1} + k_{r1}) r_{p1i}^2 i_{p1is2}^2 / r_{s2}^2 \\
K_{12} = (k_{r1} - k_{s1}) r_{p1i} r_{h1} i_{h1s2} i_{p1is2} / r_{s2}^2
\end{cases}
$$

$$
\begin{cases}
K_{13} = (k_{s1} + k_{r1} + k_{h1}) r_{h1}^2 i_{h1s2}^2 / r_{s2}^2 \\
K_{15} = k_{s2} r_{s2}^2 i_{s2s2}^2 / r_{s2}^2 \\
K_{16} = k_{s2} r_{s2} r_{p2i} i_{p2is2} i_{s2s2} / r_{s2}^2 \\
K_{17} = k_{s2} r_{s2} r_{h2} i_{h2s2} i_{s2s2} / r_{s2}^2 \quad (i = 1,2,3,4,5) \\
K_{18} = (k_{s2} + k_{r2}) r_{p2i}^2 i_{p2is2}^2 / r_{s2}^2 \\
K_{19} = (k_{r2} - k_{s2}) r_{p2i} r_{h2} i_{h2s2} i_{p2is2} / r_{s2}^2 \\
K_{20} = (k_{s2} + k_{r2} + k_{h2}) r_{h2}^2 i_{h2s2}^2 / r_{s2}^2
\end{cases}
$$

$$(7)$$

Making use of Eqs. (4)–(7) to carry out equivalent transformation for the differential equation of torsional vibration, the equivalent differential equation can be obtained as Eq. (8).

$$
\begin{cases}
M_1 \ddot{u}_1 + K_1 u_1 - K_1 u_2 = 0 \\
M_2 \ddot{u}_2 - K_1 u_1 + (K_1 + K_2) u_2 - K_2 u_3 = 0 \\
M_3 \ddot{u}_3 - K_2 u_2 + (K_2 + K_3) u_3 - K_3 u_4 = 0 \\
M_4 \ddot{u}_4 - K_3 u_3 + (K_3 + K_4) u_4 - K_4 u_5 = 0 \\
M_5 \ddot{u}_5 - K_4 u_4 + (K_4 + K_5) u_5 - K_5 u_6 = 0 \\
M_6 \ddot{u}_6 - K_5 u_5 + (K_5 + K_6) u_6 - K_6 u_7 = 0 \\
M_7 \ddot{u}_7 - K_6 u_6 + (K_6 + K_7) u_7 - K_7 u_{s1} = 0 \\
M_{s1} \ddot{u}_{s1} - K_7 u_7 + (K_7 + 3K_8) u_{s1} - K_9 u_{p11} - K_9 u_{p12} - K_9 u_{p13} - 3K_{10} u_{h1} = 0 \\
M_{p11} \ddot{u}_{p11} - K_9 u_{s1} + K_{11} u_{p11} - K_{12} u_{h1} = 0 \\
M_{p12} \ddot{u}_{p12} - K_9 u_{s1} + K_{11} u_{p12} - K_{12} u_{h1} = 0 \\
M_{p13} \ddot{u}_{p13} - K_9 u_{s1} + K_{11} u_{p13} - K_{12} u_{h1} = 0 \\
M_{h1} \ddot{u}_{h1} - 3K_{10} u_{s1} - K_{12} u_{p11} - K_{12} u_{p12} - K_{12} u_{p13} + (3K_{13} + K_{14}) u_{h1} - K_{14} u_{s2} = 0 \\
M_{s2} \ddot{u}_{s2} - K_{14} u_{h1} + (K_{14} + 5K_{15}) u_{s2} - K_{16} u_{p21} - K_{16} u_{p22} - K_{16} u_{p23} - K_{16} u_{p24} \\
\qquad - K_{16} u_{p25} - 5K_{17} u_{h2} = 0 \\
M_{p21} \ddot{u}_{p21} - K_{16} u_{s2} + K_{18} u_{p21} - K_{19} u_{h2} = 0 \\
M_{p22} \ddot{u}_{p22} - K_{16} u_{s2} + K_{18} u_{p22} - K_{19} u_{h2} = 0 \\
M_{p23} \ddot{u}_{p23} - K_{16} u_{s2} + K_{18} u_{p23} - K_{19} u_{h2} = 0 \\
M_{p24} \ddot{u}_{p24} - K_{16} u_{s2} + K_{18} u_{p24} - K_{19} u_{h2} = 0 \\
M_{p25} \ddot{u}_{p25} - K_{16} u_{s2} + K_{18} u_{p25} - K_{19} u_{h2} = 0 \\
M_{h2} \ddot{u}_h - 5K_{17} u_{s2} - K_{19} u_{p21} - K_{19} u_{p22} - K_{19} u_{p23} - K_{19} u_{p24} - K_{19} u_{p25} + 5K_{20} u_{h2} = 0
\end{cases}
$$

$$(8)$$

The differential equation of free undamped vibration after equivalent transformation of the transmission system is expressed in matrix form in accordance to Eq. (9),

$$[M][\ddot{u}] + [K][u] = 0 \qquad (9)$$

where $[u]$, $[M]$ and $[K]$ are equivalent displacement matrix, equivalent mass matrix, and equivalent stiffness matrix of system respectively.

3 Analysis Model of Torsional Vibration of the Gear System

3.1 Excitation Frequencies of the System

The excitation frequencies of the double planetary transmission system are rotating frequencies f_r of each gear and meshing frequencies f_m of each gear pair, which can be calculated as shown in Table 1.

Table 1. Rotating frequency and meshing frequency at all levels of transmission/Hz

Name		Rotating frequency	Meshing frequency
Input stage	Small bevel gear	16.500	379.500
	Large bevel gear	9.731	
Primary planetary gear train	Primary planet gear	5.414	204.275
	Primary planet carrier	1.559	
Secondary planetary gear train	Secondary planet gear	1.591	44.232
	Secondary planet carrier	0.395	

3.2 Inherent Characteristics of Torsional Vibration

The natural frequencies of torsional vibration and corresponding vibration modes of the double planetary transmission system can be programmed and calculated with Matlab. The torsional vibration natural frequencies are shown in Table 2.

Table 2. Natural frequency of torsional vibration of the transmission system

Frequency	f_1	f_2	f_3	f_4	f_5	f_6	f_7
Value (Hz)	8.15	28.27	53.79	108.41	300.8	483.13	655.29
Frequency	f_8	f_9	f_{10}	f_{11}	f_{12}	f_{13}	f_{14}
Value (Hz)	669.39	732.46	732.46	744.32	854.96	854.96	854.96
Frequency	f_{15}	f_{16}	f_{17}	f_{18}	f_{19}		
Value (Hz)	854.96	1234.03	1539.12	1807.61	4202.02		

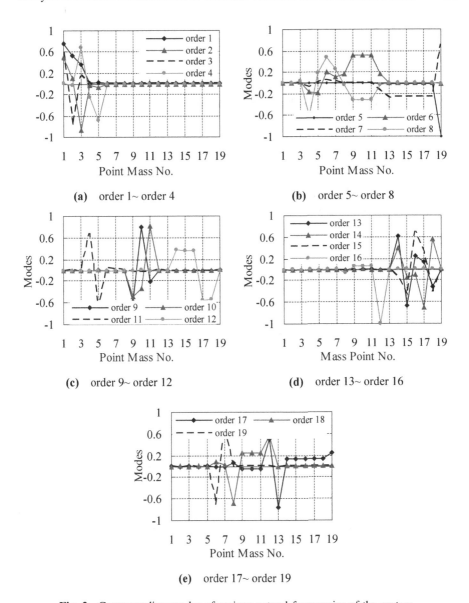

Fig. 2. Corresponding modes of various natural frequencies of the system

The vibration modes corresponding to the first 19 order natural frequencies of torsional vibration of the double planetary transmission system are shown in Fig. 2.

There are two vibration modes in the transmission system: rotational mode and planet mode. f_1–f_8, f_{11}, f_{16}–f_{19} are rotational mode where all components of system are subjected to torsional vibration, and vibrational state of the planets are the same. f_9–f_{10}, f_{12}–f_{15} are planet mode where only the planet gears vibrate, other components except the planet gears do not vibrate, and the algebraic sum of the vibration of each planet is zero. Because the primary planetary gear train has 3 planet gears and the secondary planetary gear train has 5 planet gears, the natural frequencies of the torsional vibration of the transmission system have double roots and quadruple roots respectively.

4   Analysis of Influence Factors of Inherent Characteristics

4.1   Effect of Rotational Inertia on Natural Frequencies

The rotational inertia is a physical quantity that represents the rotational inertia of the rigid body. It is of great significance in the structural design and engineering practice of mechanical parts, and it is also an important factor that describes the inherent characteristics of torsional vibration of the structure. Figure 3 shows that the distribution of the first 10 order natural frequencies of torsional vibration of 4 sets of rotational inertia series (initial rotational inertia J, 0.5 J, 0.75 J, 1.5 J) under the condition that the total gear ratio and dimensional parameters of the gears at all levels are unchanged.

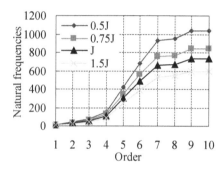 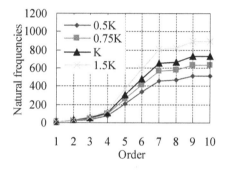

Fig. 3. Natural frequencies of the system under different rotational inertia series

Fig. 4. Natural frequencies of the system under different torsional stiffness series

As shown in Fig. 3, the larger rotational inertia increases the flexibility of the transmission system. Comparing the first 10 natural frequencies of the system, it can be concluded that the natural frequencies of the system significantly decrease with the increase of the rotational inertia. Taking the tenth-order natural frequency as an example, the natural frequencies are 1035.85 Hz, 845.77 Hz, 732.46 Hz and 598.05 Hz respectively.

4.2   Effect of Torsional Stiffness on Natural Frequencies

The torsional stiffness of the shafting not only affects the natural frequencies of the transmission system, but also affects the stability of the entire system. Figure 4 shows that the distribution of the first 10 order natural frequencies of torsional vibration of 4 sets of torsional stiffness series (initial torsional stiffness K, 0.5 K, 0.75 K, 1.5 K) under the condition that the total gear ratio and dimensional parameters of the gears at all levels are unchanged.

As shown in Fig. 4, the smaller torsional stiffness increases the flexibility of the transmission system. Comparing the first 10 natural frequencies of the system, it can be concluded that the natural frequencies significantly decrease with the decrease of the torsional stiffness. Taking the tenth-order natural frequency as an example, the natural frequencies are 897.07 Hz, 732.46 Hz, 634.33 Hz and 517.92 Hz respectively.

5 Conclusion

(1) For the double planetary transmission system the vertical mill reducer ,there are two vibration modes for each mode: rotational mode and planet mode.
(2) For the gear system with N planet gears, the vibration frequencies of planet gears have $N - 1$ multiple roots.
(3) The approximate rates between the natural frequencies and the excitation frequencies are greater than 10%. Thus, it's difficult for the reducer to resonate.
(4) Natural frequencies of torsional vibration can be improved effectively by increasing the torsional stiffness and reducing the rotational inertia of the system under the condition that the total transmission ratio and the dimensional parameters of the gear pairs are constant at all levels.

Acknowledgments. The authors are grateful for the financial support provided by the Industrial Common Key Technology Innovation of Chongqing (cstc2015zdcy-ztzx70013) and the Fundamental Research Funds for Central Universities (106112017CDJZRPY0018).

References

1. Lin, J., Parker, R.G.: Analytical characterization of the unique properties of planetary gear free vibration. J. Vib. Acoust. **121**(3), 316–321 (1999)
2. Lin, J., Parker, R.G.: Structured vibration characteristics of planetary gears with unequally spaced planets. J. Sound Vib. **233**(5), 921–928 (2000)
3. Wang, S., Zhang, C., Song, Y., Yang, T.: Natural mode analysis of planetary gear trains. China Mech. Eng. **16**(16), 1461–1465 (2005)
4. Song, Y., Xu, W., Zhang, C., Wang, S.: Modified torsional model development and natural characteristics analysis of 2 K-H epicyclic gearing. Chin. J. Mech. Eng. **42**(5), 16–21 (2006)
5. Cai, Z., Liu, H., Xiang, C., Zhang, X., Wang, M.: Characteristics of forced torsional vibration and dynamic load for vehicle multistage planetary transmission. J. Jilin Univ. (Eng. Technol. edn.) **42**(1), 19–26 (2012)
6. Yu, H., Zhang, T., Ma, Z., Wang, R.: Torsional vibration analysis of planetary hybrid electric vehicle driveline. Trans. Chin. Soc. Agric. Eng. **29**(15), 57–64 (2013)
7. Li, J., Jin, S., Gong, C., Bierdebieke, W.: Dynamic modeling and eigenvalue evaluation of dual-powerflow transmission. Agric. Equipment Veh. Eng. **53**(8), 17–20 (2015)
8. Li, T., Guo, J., Liu, B., Shen, T.: Junction stiffness analysis and vibration noise prediction of wind power speed-increase gearbox. J. Chongqing Univ. **38**(1), 87–94 (2015)
9. Yang, H., Guo, J., Liu, B., Song, J.: Torsional vibration analysis of transmission system in comprehensive performance testing device for wind-power speed-increasing gearbox. Mech. Res. Appl. **28**(3), 83–90 (2015)

Resonance Reliability and Sensitivity Analysis of Reducer

Yanjun Zhang[1(✉)], Wen Liu[1], Tengjiao Lin[1], Jinhong Zhang[2], Yunlong Cai[3], and Guobing Yu[1]

[1] State Key Laboratory of Mechanical Transmission, Chongqing University, Chongqing 400044, China
1050645940@qq.com
[2] Chongqing BOE Optoelectronics Technology Co., Ltd, Chongqing 400714, China
[3] Jiangsu Tailong Decelerator Machinery Co., Ltd, Taixing 225400, Jiangsu, China

Abstract. Cranes often work under conditions of large power, high torque, and impact loading. Due to the harsh working environment, it is necessary to have reliability analysis for the reducer. Taking the reducer as study object, its parametric model and the reliability analysis model are established by ANSYS software. The constrained modal analysis was done to obtain the natural frequency of gear system. Considering random variation in parameters such as rib thickness, thickness and width of the U-shaped support frame, material elastic modulus and Poisson ratio, the proximity of system natural frequency and excitation frequency will be different. Then, the rules were explored by means of response surface methodology. On this basis, the reliability and sensitivity of the gear system are achieved statistically by Monte Carlo method, which has important engineering significance for improving the reliability of crane.

Keywords: Reducer · Response surface · Monte carlo · Reliability
Sensitivity

1 Introduction

The reliability of mechanical products is determined by various factors such as design, manufacture, use and maintenance, and it will be different in various working conditions. With the increasingly complex structure of gear system, reliability has become an important performance indicator for gear system, and how to improve and maintain its reliability proves to be a crucial issue.

Domestic and overseas scholars have taken up a lot of research on the reliability analysis of gear system. Peng [1] applied the stochastic finite element method to study the fatigue reliability of gear teeth, established a tooth fatigue failure model and compared the calculation results with the Monte-Carlo method. Considering various random factors of reducer work, Sun [2] established a reliability design model for a single-stage assist gear reducer system and the objective function based on the

© Springer Nature Singapore Pte Ltd. 2018
S. Wang et al. (Eds.): ICSEE 2018/IMIOT 2018, CCIS 923, pp. 484–493, 2018.
https://doi.org/10.1007/978-981-13-2396-6_45

independent variable transformation theory. Lou [3] discussed the reliability design method of cylindrical gears, which can quantitatively give the reliability of the gears and reliability design of the gears based on reliability. By the Monte-Carlo method, Guo [4] determined the contact fatigue stress and strength distribution of spiral bevel gears, and studied the reliability to relieve fatigue reliability and the random parameters of the stress. Taking the spindle system of Francis turbine generator unit as the research object, Li [5] proposed a reliability analysis method for nonlinear vibration of hydro generating units with multiple failure modes. Jin [6] proposed an operation reliability evaluation method based on the state information of mechanical equipment, by establishing the mapping model between the information of the equipment running state and the reliability, the calculation of the reliability of the operation is realized. Li [7] presented a non-probabilistic reliability analysis method for active structural vibration control systems. Based on multi-scale method for calculating composite structure, microscopic and macroscopic uncertainty, Zhou [8] proposed a reliability analysis method. Considering the random material strength, the correlation of material properties, and the failure of progressive materials, Dimitrow [9] presented a new structural reliability analysis.

Overall, a great deal of achievements have been made in the reliability analysis of gear system, while the simpler cylindrical gear is generally chosen as the research object, with less research on the reliability of complex gear system. Owing to the effects of manufacturing and assembling, material properties and sizes are usually stochastic. Therefore, parameters such as rib thickness, the width and thickness of the U-shaped support frame, material elastic modulus, and Poisson ratio were comprehensively studied in this paper. The parametric model and the reliability analysis model of the reducer were established by ANSYS software with the comprehensive consideration of random variation in parameters. The closeness of each parameter to the system natural frequency as well as excitation frequency was calculated by means of response surface methodology, and then the reliability and sensitivity of gear system were obtained. The study provides reference for the design of improving operation stability and reliability of the reducer.

2 Modal Analysis of Reducer

2.1 Finite Element Model of the Reducer

The reducer adopts four parallel shaft helical gear transmission. According to the structure and transmission parameters of the gear system, the solid model of the gear system was built which includes the body, gear, transmission shaft, bearing and so on. The meshing relationship of the helical gear pair and the supporting relationship between the inner and outer rings of the bearing were simulated by spring element. The reducer's finite element model is shown in Fig. 1, from which we can see how the boundary conditions and the engaging force of gear pair were applied.

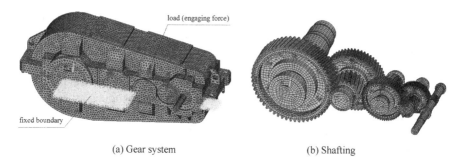

(a) Gear system   (b) Shafting

Fig. 1. Finite element model of reducer

2.2   Constraint Modal Analysis

Based on the finite element model of the reducer, the Block Lanczo method was used to carry out the restrained modal analysis of the gear system. Table 1 shows the first 20 natural frequencies of the gear system.

Table 1. The first 20 natural frequencies of the reducer

Modal modular	1	2	3	4	5	6	7	8	9	10
Natural frequency (Hz)	69.00	99.08	131.36	152.41	224.31	231.91	265.04	308.58	331.49	347.82
Modal modular	11	12	13	14	15	16	17	18	19	20
Natural frequency (Hz)	367.24	391.11	427.34	430.24	471.52	516.28	556.28	568.73	578.55	568.73

Table 2. The rotational frequency of transmission shaft and meshing frequency of reducer

Items	Input shaft	Intermediate shaft I	Input stage
Rotating frequency (Hz)	25	6.52	450
Items	Output shaft	Intermediate shaft II	Intermediate stage I
Rotating frequency/Hz	0.20	1.99	117.39
Items	Output stage	Intermediate shaft III	Intermediate stage II
Rotating frequency/Hz	11.69	0.61	33.83

According to the input speed and gear parameters, the frequency of each drive shaft and the gear meshing of each gear pair can be obtained, as shown in Table 2. It can be seen that the maximum incentive is 450 Hz. When the high-order natural frequency of the system is far greater than 450 Hz, the modal energy is relatively lower, and the system vibration will be less affected. At the same time, the rotating frequency or meshing frequency in each level is far from the low order natural frequency of the gear system, so it is unlikely to arouse the resonance of the crane.

3   Resonance Reliability Analysis of Reducer

When the excitation frequency is close to a certain natural frequency of the system, resonance occurs with the significantly increasing amplitude of the system. When the mechanical system resonates, it will produce some dynamic response that exceeds the limit value, causing the destruction of the structure and failure of the transmission. Therefore, in order to prevent resonance with an appropriate probability during the designing process, reliability analysis and sensitivity research on the resonance problem are essential to guide the selection of the design parameters.

3.1   System Resonance Failure Range

In the analysis of the resonance problem, resonance failure is considered to occur when the excitation frequency p_j is sufficiently close to the natural frequency ω_i. In order to measure the closeness of the excitation frequency to the natural frequency, the ratio of the absolute value of the difference between p_j and ω_i to ω_i is chosen as the output variable Z.

$$Z = \frac{|p_j - \omega_i|}{\omega_i} \tag{1}$$

When it comes to the analysis of resonance reliability, using Z as the output variable to determine the failure range, the reliability to avoid resonance can be obtained. In engineering, 10% is generally taken as the cut-off point of Z. If Z < 10%, it is considered that the system will produce resonance failure, in other words, the probability of Z > 10% is the reliability of the system without resonance failure.

3.2   Gear System Resonance Reliability Analysis Model

The explicit function relationship between the state function and the random variable is difficult to be directly derived, and the Monte Carlo method requires extensive sampling of parameters and excitation frequencies, which will consume a lot of computing resources and time, however, the response surface methodology uses polynomial to fit and approximate the test sample points with higher computational efficiency. Therefore, the response surface methodology was selected to analyze the resonance reliability of the reducer. Taking the reducer as the research object, on the basis of modal calculation, the resonance reliability analysis file was compiled with APDL, and the resonance reliability of the gear system was analyzed. The response surface function used can be expressed as:

$$g(x) = \beta_0 + \sum_{i=1}^{n} \beta_i x_i + \sum_{i} \sum_{j} \beta_{ij} x_i x_j + \sum_{i=1}^{n} \beta_{ii} x_i^2 \tag{2}$$

In the formula, x, y are random basic variables, and β_0, β_i, β_{ij}, β_{ii} are undetermined parameters. By viewing the modal analysis of the crane gear reducer carried out in

Sect. 1.1, it was found that the meshing frequency of the intermediate stage I gear pair was 117.39 Hz, which was close to the 2nd and 3rd order modal frequencies of the system. Therefore, the ratio of the absolute value of the difference between the excitation frequency F_1 (117.39 Hz) and the second and third-order modes ω_i of the system to the corresponding ω_i was selected as the output variable.

$$Z_j = \frac{|F_1 - \omega_i|}{\omega_i} \tag{3}$$

In the formula, i represents the order of the natural frequency. By ordering it as 2 and 3 respectively, Z_j is correspondingly to be Z_1 and Z_2. When Z_1 and Z_2 are greater than 10%, the resonance does not occur in the gear system, and the resonance reliability is

$$R = R(Z_1 \geq 0.1) \cdot R(Z_2 \geq 0.1) \tag{4}$$

The random variables selected and their distribution type and distribution parameters are shown in Table 3. In the table, $JBBH$ means the rib thickness, UBH means the U-shaped support frame thickness, $UBK1$ means the U-shaped support frame width at the output shaft, $UBK2$ means the U-shaped support frame width at the intermediate shaft III, $UBK3$ means the U-shaped support frame width at the intermediate shaft II, EE means the elasticity modulus, PP means the density, F_1 means excitation frequency.

Table 3. The random variable parameters of reducer

Random variable	Mean value	Standard deviation	Coefficient of variation	Distribution type
$JBBH/$(mm)	10	0.05	0.005	Gauss
$UBH/$(mm)	6	0.03	0.005	Gauss
$UBK1/$(mm)	130	0.65	0.005	Gauss
$UBK2/$(mm)	120	0.6	0.005	Gauss
$UBK3/$(mm)	100	0.5	0.005	Gauss
$EE/$(Pa)	2.06×10^{11}	7.245×10^9	0.0345	Gauss
$PP/$(kg·m^{-3})	7850	157	0.02	Gauss
$F_1/$(Hz)	117.39	0.11739	0.001	Gauss

3.3   Reliability Analysis of Gear System Resonance

The experiment was designed on the basis of the number of random input variables, and then the value and quantity of sample point are determined. The numerical values of the input variables and output variables were obtained by finite element numerical calculation. The approximate relationship between input and output was constructed, and the approximate expression was used to replace the finite element model. Then Monte Carlo simulation technology was used to call this function and thousands of simulations were performed on the output variables. After statistical processing, statistical characteristics and probability cumulative distribution function of the output variables were achieved, and reliability analysis was performed according to the performance function.

The response surfaces of the gear system variables to the state function are compared and some surfaces with an obvious effect on the state function are shown in Fig. 2. As can be seen from the figure, with the decrease of EE (F_1 and PP), Z_1 (Z_2) will increase evidently, while the influence of PP and $UBK3$ ($JBBH$ and UBH) is smaller.

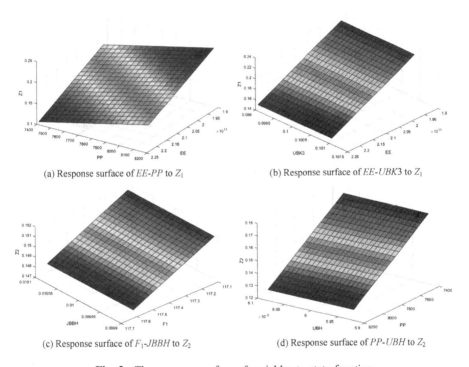

(a) Response surface of EE-PP to Z_1 (b) Response surface of EE-$UBK3$ to Z_1

(c) Response surface of F_1-$JBBH$ to Z_2 (d) Response surface of PP-UBH to Z_2

Fig. 2. The response surface of variables to state function

On the basis of determining the response surface, Monte Carlo method was used to randomly sample 100,000 times, and the sampling process curve of each random variable was obtained. Figure 3 shows the sampling curve of random basic variables such as $JBBH$, UBH, $UBK1$, EE, PP, and F_1. From the sampling curve of each random variable, it can be seen that each random variable fluctuates around its mean value.

The calculation accuracy of Monte Carlo depends on the number of random sampling. To verify the accuracy of the method, the probability density histogram of each random variable was viewed which should be the most effective way to determine the number of random sampling. When the probability density histogram is close to the normal distribution curve, it indicates that the sampling times are sufficient. Figure 4 shows the probability density histogram of each random variable of the reducer.

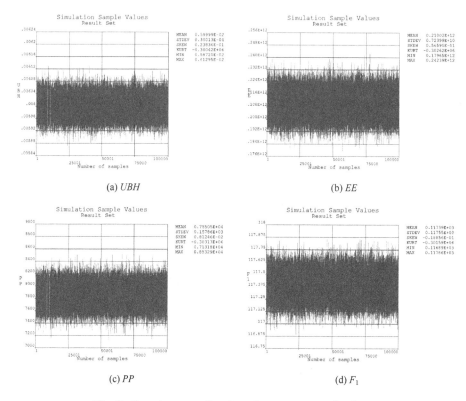

Fig. 3. Sample curve of each random parameter of reducer

Figure 5 is the cumulative distribution function curve of the state functions Z_1, Z_2, and the probability that the state function is greater than 10% can be obtained from it. It can be seen that $R_1 = 1, R_2 = 0.998936(R_1, R_2$ are the probability of Z_1, Z_2 greater than 0.1), then the reliability of the gear system resonance of the reducer is $R = R_1 \cdot R_2 = 0.998936$.

3.4   Sensitivity Analysis of Gear System Resonance

In order to adjust the natural frequency close to the excitation frequency easily, it is necessary to calculate the sensitivity of the resonance reliability and analyze the influence of each random input parameter on the reliability. Taking the output variable Z_2 as an example, a resonance sensitivity analysis is performed on a random input variable. Figure 6 shows the sensitivity of the output variable Z_2 to the basic variable. A positive value represents a positive correlation between the random variable and the reliability. On the contrary, there is a negative correlation.

As shown in Fig. 6, Z_2 is positively correlated with *EE*, *JBBH*, *UBH*, *UBK*1, *UBK*2, and *UBK*3. When these parameters increase, Z_2 also increases correspondingly, and the reliability increases. Z_2 is negatively correlated with *PP* and F_1. When these parameters increase, Z_2 will decrease accordingly, and the reliability will decrease,

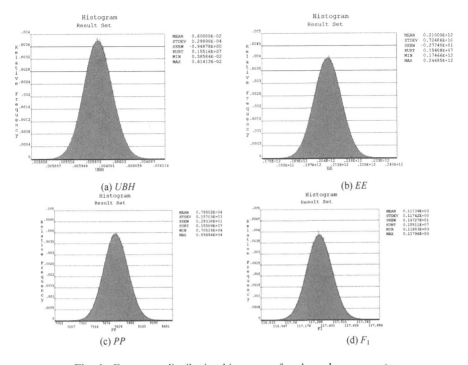

Fig. 4. Frequency distribution histogram of each random parameter

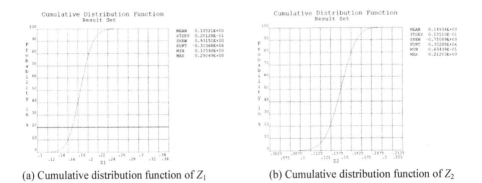

(a) Cumulative distribution function of Z_1

(b) Cumulative distribution function of Z_2

Fig. 5. The cumulative distribution function curve of state function Z

which is consistent with the previous response surface analysis. The elastic modulus EE and density PP of the material have a great influence on the Z_2. In the dimension parameters, the $UBK3$ has a relatively large influence on the reliability of the gear system. In the resonant reliability design, it should be considered seriously.

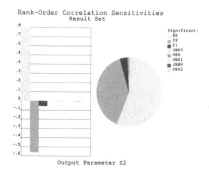

Fig. 6. The sensitivity distribution of the random parameter of state function Z_2

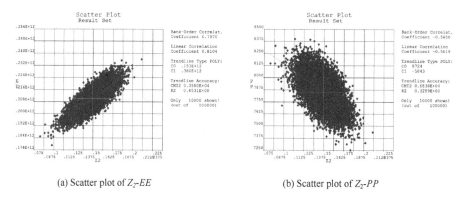

(a) Scatter plot of Z_2-EE   (b) Scatter plot of Z_2-PP

Fig. 7. Scatter diagram between Z_2 and each random parameter

Through the above analysis, we are clear about which variables can be adjusted to improve reliability, but can't determine how to adjust the variables and the adjustment scope. Therefore, it is necessary to analyze the scatter plot of the state function Z_2 on the basic variables. The straight lines that are orthogonal to each other in the scatter plot are their average values, and the straight line that intersects the mean line is the trend line. The slope of trend line represents the degree of correlation, and the correlation between Z_2 and variable is positive if the line has a positive slope, otherwise the correlation is negative. Figure 7 shows the scatter plot of the state function Z_2 on the basic variables. In the scatter plot, the slope of the Z_2-EE trend line is positive, and the slope of the Z_2-PP trend line is negative, which is consistent with the previous sensitivity analysis.

4   Conclusion

Taking the reducer as the research object, its parametric model and the reliability analysis model were established by ANSYS software in the paper. We have the following tentative conclusions:

(1) The material parameters and structural system dimension parameters were selected as the random input variables, while the proximity of the natural frequency and the excitation frequency were selected as the output random variables. Then, the response surface methodology was used to construct an approximate relationship between the input and output. The Monte Carlo simulation technique was adopted to carry out multiple sampling. The results have shown that the resonance reliability of the reducer was 99.89%.

(2) With the analysis of resonance reliability sensitivity, it is found that the elastic modulus, density, excitation frequency and the U-shaped support frame width at the output shaft have a greater influence on the reliability of the 3rd order resonance. The 3rd order resonance reliability is positively correlated with ribs thickness, elastic modulus, the thickness and width of the U-shaped support frame, and negatively correlated to density and excitation frequency.

Acknowledgments. The work described in this article was supported by the Major Industry Common Key Technology Innovation of Chongqing (cstc2015zdcy-ztzx70013) and the Fundamental Research Funds for Central Universities (106112017CDJZRPY0018).

References

1. Peng, X.Q.F.: A stochastic finite element method for fatigue reliability analysis of gear teeth subjected to bending. Comput. Mech. **21**(3), 253–261 (1998)
2. Zhili Sun, F.: Mechanical transmission system reliability design model-A case study of single-stage cylindrical gear reducer. Shenyang J. Northeast. Univ. **24**(9), 854–857 (2003)
3. Yun Lou, F.: Gear reliability design method based on tooth surface contact strength and tooth root bending strength. Mech. Des. **23**(9), 31–32 (2006)
4. Yaobin Guo, F.: Reliability analysis of contact fatigue of spiral bevel gear based on monte carlo method. Chin. J. Agric. Mach. **39**(4), 157–159 (2008)
5. Li Zhaojun, F.: Multi failure mode nonlinear reliability model for hydro generating units. J. Mech. Eng. **49**(16), 170–176 (2013)
6. Jin Yibo, F.: Development and consideration of reliability evaluation of mechanical equipment. Chin. J. Mech. Eng. **50**(2), 171–186 (2014)
7. Li, Y.F.: Non-probabilistic stability reliability measure for active vibration control system with interval parameters. J. Sound Vib. **387**, 1–15 (2017)
8. Zhou, X.Y.F.: Stochastic multi-scale finite element based reliability analysis for laminated composite structures. Appl. Math. Modell. **45**, 457–473 (2017)
9. Dimitrov, N.F.: Spatial reliability analysis of a wind turbine blade cross section subjected to multi-axial extreme loading. Struct. Saf. **66**, 27–37 (2017)

Effect of Gear Profile Modification on Vibration and Howling Noise of Gearbox

Guobing Yu[1(✉)], Wen Liu[1], Tengjiao Lin[1], Jun Liu[2],
Hesheng Lv[3], and Yanjun Zhang[1]

[1] State Key Laboratory of Mechanical Transmission,
Chongqing University, Chongqing, China
1914540456@qq.com
[2] Chery Automobile Co., Ltd., Anhui 241009, China
[3] CN GPower Gearbox Co., Ltd., Chongqing 400714, China

Abstract. Aiming at the one planetary stage and two parallel-axes wind power gear transmission system, the dynamic equation of the gearbox transmission system was established by lumping parameters method, the variable-length Runge-Kutta method was used to solve the system dynamic differential equations, the dynamic transmission errors of gear pair was obtained before and after gear profile modification. The dynamics model of the rigid-flexible coupling of the gearbox was established in LMS software, the transmission errors was imported into it. The modal superposition method was used to obtain the bearing reaction force of the gearbox, then it was used as the boundary condition of the acoustic-vibration coupling model. Acoustic finite element method was adopted to estimate vibration and noise of gearbox and research the influence of gear profile modification on the vibration and howling noise of gearbox. The research results show that there have some improvements on vibration and howling noise of gearbox with gear profile modification.

Keywords: Dynamic equations · Gear profile modification · Howling noise

1 Introduction

In 2009, Peng Guomin [1, 2] studied that the howling noise of the transmission was decreased by reducing the internal excitation. According to the tooth surface load distribution and the contact spot test, the micro-morphological modification of the tooth surface was carried out. Then the static transmission errors of the gear pair was reduced, the howling noise of the transmission was decreased. In 2010, Shi Quan [3] verified that the noise source came from meshing gear pair according to the transmission vibration howling noise test, the gear pair was optimized by reducing the backlash, gear profile modification etc., the meshing impact and howling noise were reduced. In 2013, Oh [4] established a static model of gearbox transmission in ROMAX software, the static transmission errors of the helical gear pair was predicted after applying the torque. The tooth surface is optimized and the gear noise was reduced. In 2015, Zheng Taishan [5] analyzed the crusher gear transmission system base on the high-frequency howling noise in ROMAX software and tested the

© Springer Nature Singapore Pte Ltd. 2018
S. Wang et al. (Eds.): ICSEE 2018/IMIOT 2018, CCIS 923, pp. 494–505, 2018.
https://doi.org/10.1007/978-981-13-2396-6_46

high-frequency howling component of the gear transmission system by the ODS test method. In 2016, Carbonelli [6] studied transmission radiated noise from gear static transmission errors and meshing stiffness fluctuation, the meshing stiffness wave equation was deduced with different loads. The robustness optimization methods was applied to correct the tooth profile modification. Fang Yuan [7] analyzed the vibration performance of reducer through experiments, then the source of howling noise was determined. In order to reduce noise, multi-objective and multi-parameter optimization was carried out base on genetic algorithm, the optimal gear modification profile program was obtained. In 2017, Liu Wen [8] established a bending-torsion-axial coupled lumped parameter dynamic model of one planetary stage and two parallel-axes transmission system with considering the factors of time-varying mesh stiffness, mesh damping, gear modification and transmission errors, gearbox noise and vibration were predicted by using acoustic finite element method.

To sum up, there has been lots of research on the howling noise and production mechanism of the gearbox, many results have been obtained that mainly focused on the influence of the tooth profile on the static transmission errors, thus the vibration and howling noise was reduced. This article will mainly calculate the dynamic transmission errors of the gear meshing base on the gear profile modification and consider it as the main excitation. the acoustic-vibration coupling model of the gearbox was established to estimate the vibration and howling noise.

2   The Dynamic Model Analysis of Gear Transmission System

The basic parameters of multi-stage gear transmission system in this article are shown in Table 1.

Table 1. Parameters of multi-stage gear transmission system

	Rotating speed r/min Input/Output	Modulus/mm	Number of teeth	Pressure angle/(°)	Helix angle/(°)
First stage	16.756/95.966	14	22/41/104	20	–
Second stage	95.968/444.943	10	102/22	20	7
Third stage	444.943/1800	7	89/22	20	16

For the multi-stage gear transmission system consisting of the one planetary stage and two parallel-axes helical gears as shown in Table 1, the lumped parameter method was adopted to establish the analysis model of the bending-torsion-axis coupling vibration as shown in Fig. 1. In order to simplify the calculation, friction between tooth flank was not taken into consideration. For planetary spur gear transmission, there was no axial force, only the torsion and radial deformation of the planet gear, sun gear and planet carrier were taken into consideration.

In the gear transmission system, the ring gear was fixed and the others are moving parts. In order to set up independent coordinate systems for the planet carrier and each gear, the coordinate origins of the sun gear, planet carrier and helical gear 1 to 4 are the

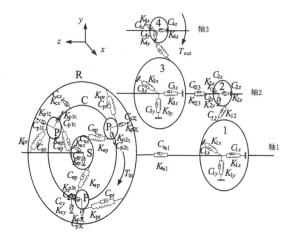

Fig. 1. The dynamic model of multi-stage gear transmission system

own centers. the coordinate directions were as shown in Fig. 1. The planet's rotation coordinate system is fixed on the planet carrier with the planet center as its coordinate origin. When defining the angular displacement need to take the tangential and radial displacements into account, the rotation direction of each gear according to the input torque is positive, the relative displacement direction of each meshing line according to the direction of pressure on the tooth surface is positive.

2.1   The Dynamic Model of Gear Transmission System

For the first planet gear transmission, the ring gear was fixed, the planet carrier was input, and the sun gear was output.

The relative displacements of the sun gear-planet gears and the planet gears-ring gear along the normal line of the meshing point are x_{pis}, x_{pir} (i = 1, 2, 3):

$$\begin{cases} x_{pis} = r_{bpi}\theta_{pi} - r_{bs}\theta_s + r_c\theta_c \cos\alpha + (x_c - x_s)\cos(\varphi_i + \alpha) - (y_c - y_s)\sin(\varphi_i + \alpha) + \\ \qquad \eta_{pi}\cos\alpha - \xi_{pi}\sin\alpha - e_{pis}(t) \\ x_{pir} = r_{bpi}\theta_{pi} - r_c\theta_c \cos\alpha - x_c\cos(\alpha + \varphi_i) + y_c\sin(\alpha + \varphi_i) - \\ \qquad \eta_{pi}\cos\alpha + \xi_{pi}\sin\alpha - e_{pir}(t) \end{cases}$$

$$(1)$$

In the formula: $e_{pis}(t)$, $e_{pir}(t)$ are normal static transmission error. x_c, y_c, θ_c are the lateral displacement, longitudinal displacement and twist angle of the planet carrier. x_s, y_s, θ_s are the lateral displacement, longitudinal displacement and twist angle of the sun gear. η_{pi}, ζ_{pi}, θ_{pi} are tangential displacement, radial displacement and torsion angle of the planet gears. r_{bs}, r_{bpi} are the base circle radius of the sun gear and planet gears, r_c is the radius of the planet carrier (the distribution radius of the planets). α is the pressure angle of planet gears, φ_i is the position angle of the planet gears ($\varphi_i = 2\pi(i-1)/3$, $i = 1, 2, 3$).

The relative displacement along the normal direction of the meshing point due to vibration and error between the meshing points of the second stage driving and driven helical gears is x_{12n}:

$$
\begin{aligned}
x_{12n} = {}& (r_{b1}\theta_1 - r_{b2}\theta_2)\cos\beta_{12b} + (z_1 - z_2)\sin\beta_{12b} + (y_1 - y_2)\sin\alpha_{12n} + \\
& (x_1 - x_2)\cos\alpha_{12t}\cos\beta_{12b} - e_{12}(t)
\end{aligned}
\tag{2}
$$

In the formula: β_{12b} is the base circle helix angle of helical gear 1 and 2, α_{12n} is the normal pressure angle of helical gear 1 and 2, α_{12t} is the face pressure angle of helical gear 1 and 2. r_{b1}, r_{b2} are the base circle radius of the helical gear 1 and 2. x_1, y_1, z_1, θ_1 is the lateral displacement, longitudinal displacement, axial displacement and twist angle of the helical gear 1. x_2, y_2, z_2, θ_2 is the lateral displacement, longitudinal displacement, axial displacement and twist angle of the helical gear 2. $e_{12}(t)$ is the normal static transmission errors of the gear pair.

The relative displacement along the normal direction of the meshing point due to the vibration and error between the meshing points of the third stage driving and driven helical gears is x_{34n}:

$$
\begin{aligned}
x_{34n} = {}& (r_{b3}\theta_3 - r_{b4}\theta_4)\cos\beta_{34b} + (z_3 - z_4)\sin\beta_{34b} + (y_3 - y_4)\sin\alpha_{34n} - \\
& (x_3 - x_4)\cos\alpha_{34t}\cos\beta_{34b} - e_{34}(t)
\end{aligned}
\tag{3}
$$

In the formula: β_{34b} is the base circle helix angles of helical gear 3 and 4, α_{34n} is the normal pressure angle of helical gear 3 and 4, α_{34t} is the face pressure angle of helical gear 3 and 4. r_{b3}, r_{b4} are the base circle radius of the helical gear 3 and 4. x_3, y_3, z_3, θ_3 is the lateral displacement, longitudinal displacement, axial displacement and twist angle of the helical gear 3. x_4, y_4, z_4, θ_4 is the lateral displacement, longitudinal displacement, axial displacement and twist angle of the helical gear 4. $e_{34}(t)$ is the normal static transmission errors of the gear pair.

A 31-degree-of-freedom bending-torsional-axis coupled lumped parameter vibration differential equation was established for the gearbox transmission system by Lagrangian energy method. The first stage planetary transmission were expressed as the formula (4)–(6), the second-stage helical gear transmission was expressed as the formula (7), the third stage of helical gear transmission was expressed as the formula (8). The planetary carrier dynamics equation is:

$$
\left\{
\begin{aligned}
& I_{cp}\ddot{\theta}_c + K_{c\theta}\theta_c + \sum K_{sp}(t)x_{pis}r_c\cos\alpha - \sum K_{pr}(t)x_{pir}r_c\cos\alpha + C_{c\theta}\dot{\theta}_c + \\
& \sum C_{sp}\dot{x}_{pis}r_c\cos\alpha - \sum C_{pr}\dot{x}_{pir}r_c\cos\alpha = T_{in} \\
& m_{cp}\ddot{x}_c + K_{cx}x_c + \sum K_{sp}(t)x_{pis}\cos(\varphi_i+\alpha) - \sum K_{pr}(t)x_{pir}\cos(\varphi_i+\alpha) + C_{cx}\dot{x}_c + \\
& \sum C_{sp}\dot{x}_{pis}\cos(\varphi_i+\alpha) - \sum C_{pr}\dot{x}_{pir}\cos(\varphi_i+\alpha) = 0 \\
& m_{cp}\ddot{y}_c + K_{cx}y_c - \sum K_{sp}(t)x_{pis}\sin(\varphi_i+\alpha) + \sum K_{pr}(t)x_{pir}\sin(\varphi_i+\alpha) + C_{cy}\dot{y}_c - \\
& \sum C_{sp}\dot{x}_{pis}\sin(\varphi_i+\alpha) + \sum C_{pr}\dot{x}_{pir}\sin(\varphi_i+\alpha) = 0
\end{aligned}
\right.
\tag{4}
$$

In the formula: I_{cp} is the equivalent moment of inertia of the planet carrier and the planet gears, m_{cp} is the equivalent mass of the planet carrier and the planet gears, K_{cj}, $C_{cj}(j = x, y)$ are the support stiffness and support damping of the planet carrier. $K_{c\theta}$, $C_{c\theta}$ are the torsional stiffness and torsional damping of the planet carrier. $K_{sp}(t)$, $K_{pr}(t)$ are the time-varying meshing stiffness of the sun gear-planet gears and planet gears-ring gear pair. C_{sp}, C_{pr} are gear pair meshing damping of the sun gear-planet gear and planet gear-ring gear. T_{in} is the input torque of the planet carrier.

The sun gear dynamics equations is:

$$\begin{cases} I_s\ddot{\theta}_s + K_{\theta s1}(\theta_s - \theta_1) - \sum K_{sp}(t)x_{pis}r_{bs} + C_{\theta s1}(\dot{\theta}_s - \dot{\theta}_1) - \sum C_{sp}\dot{x}_{pis}r_{bs} = 0 \\ m_s\ddot{x}_s + K_{sx}x_s - \sum K_{sp}(t)x_{pis}\cos(\varphi_i + \alpha) + C_{sx}\dot{x}_s - \sum C_{sp}\dot{x}_{pis}\cos(\varphi_i + \alpha) = 0 \quad (5) \\ m_s\ddot{y}_s + K_{sy}y_s + \sum K_{sp}(t)x_{pis}\sin(\varphi_i + \alpha) + C_{sy}\dot{y}_s + \sum C_{sp}\dot{x}_{pis}\sin(\varphi_i + \alpha) = 0 \end{cases}$$

In the formula: I_s is the moment of inertia of the sun gear, m_s is the mass of the sun gear, $K_{\theta s1}$, $C_{\theta s1}$ are the torsional stiffness and torsional damping of shaft 1. K_{sj}, $C_{sj}(j = x, y)$ are the lateral support stiffness, longitudinal support stiffness and support damping of the sun gear.

The planet gears dynamics equations is:

$$\begin{cases} I_{pi}\ddot{\theta}_{pi} + K_{sp}(t)x_{pis}(r_{bpi}) + K_{pr}(t)x_{pir}(r_{bpi}) + C_{sp}\dot{x}_{pis}(r_{bpi}) + C_{pr}\dot{x}_{pir}(r_{bpi}) = 0 \\ m_{pi}\ddot{\xi}_{pi} - K_{sp}(t)x_{pis}\sin\alpha + K_{pr}(t)x_{pir}\sin\alpha + K_{pi\xi}\xi_i - C_{sp}\dot{x}_{pis}\sin\alpha + \\ C_{pr}\dot{x}_{pir}\sin\alpha + C_{pi\xi}\dot{\xi}_i = 0 \quad (6) \\ m_{pi}\ddot{\eta}_{pi} + K_{sp}(t)x_{pis}\cos\alpha - K_{pr}(t)x_{pir}\cos\alpha + K_{pi\eta}\eta_i + C_{sp}\dot{x}_{pis}\cos\alpha - \\ C_{pr}\dot{x}_{pir}\cos\alpha + C_{pi\eta}\dot{\eta}_i = 0 \end{cases}$$

In the formula: $I_{pi}(i = 1, 2, 3)$ are the moment of inertia of the planet gears, $m_{pi}(i = 1, 2, 3)$ are the mass of the planet gears, K_{pij}, $C_{pij}(i = 1, 2, 3, j = \eta, \xi)$ are support stiffness and support damping of the planet gears.

The second stage helical gear dynamics equations is:

$$\begin{cases} I_1\ddot{\theta}_1 - K_{\theta s1}(\theta_s - \theta_1) + K_{12}(t)x_{12n}r_{b1}\cos\beta_{12b} - C_{\theta s1}(\dot{\theta}_s - \dot{\theta}_1) + C_{12}\dot{x}_{12n}r_{b1}\cos\beta_{12b} = 0 \\ m_1\ddot{x}_1 + K_{1x}x_1 + K_{12}(t)x_{12n}\cos\alpha_{12t}\cos\beta_{12b} + C_{1x}\dot{x}_1 + C_{12}\dot{x}_{12n}\cos\alpha_{12t}\cos\beta_{12b} = 0 \\ m_1\ddot{y}_1 + K_{1y}y_1 + K_{12}(t)x_{12n}\sin\alpha_{12n} + C_{1y}\dot{y}_1 + C_{12}\dot{x}_{12n}\sin\alpha_{12n} = 0 \\ m_1\ddot{z}_1 + K_{1z}z_1 + K_{12}(t)x_{12n}\sin\beta_{12b} + C_{1z}\dot{z}_1 + C_{12}\dot{x}_{12n}\sin\beta_{12b} = 0 \\ I_2\ddot{\theta}_2 - K_{12}x_{12n}r_{b2}\cos\beta_{12b} + K_{\theta 23}(\theta_2 - \theta_3) - C_{12}\dot{x}_{12n}r_{b2}\cos\beta_{12b} + C_{\theta 23}(\dot{\theta}_2 - \dot{\theta}_3) = 0 \\ m_2\ddot{x}_2 + K_{2x}x_2 - K_{12}(t)x_{12n}\cos\alpha_{12t}\cos\beta_{12b} + C_{2x}\dot{x}_2 - C_{12}\dot{x}_{12n}\cos\alpha_{12t}\cos\beta_{12b} = 0 \\ m_2\ddot{y}_2 + K_{2y}y_2 - K_{12}(t)x_{12n}\sin\alpha_{12n} + C_{2y}\dot{y}_2 - C_{12}\dot{x}_{12n}\sin\alpha_{12n} = 0 \\ m_2\ddot{z}_2 + K_{2z}z_2 - K_{12}(t)x_{12n}\sin\beta_{12b} + C_{2z}\dot{z}_2 - C_{12}\dot{x}_{12n}\sin\beta_{12b} = 0 \end{cases}$$

$$(7)$$

In the formula: $I_i(i = 1, 2)$ $I_i(i = 1, 2)$ are the moment of inertia of the helical gear 1 and 2, $m_i(i = 1, 2)$ are the mass of the helical gear 1 and 2, K_{ij}, $C_{ij}(i = 1, 2.j = x, y, z)$ are the gear support stiffness and support damping of the helical gear 1 and 2, $K_{\theta23}$, $C_{\theta23}$ are the torsional stiffness and torsional damping of shaft 2. $K_{12}(t)$, C_{12} are time-varying meshing stiffness and meshing damping of the gear pair.

The third stage helical gear dynamics equations is:

$$
\begin{cases}
I_3\ddot{\theta}_3 - K_{\theta23}(\theta_2 - \theta_3) + K_{34}(t)x_{34n}r_{b3}\cos\beta_{34b} - C_{\theta23}(\dot{\theta}_2 - \dot{\theta}_3) + C_{34}\dot{x}_{34n}r_{b3}\cos\beta_{34b} = 0 \\
m_3\ddot{x}_3 + K_{3x}x_3 - K_{34}(t)x_{34n}\cos\alpha_{34t}\cos\beta_{34b} + C_{3x}\dot{x}_3 - C_{34}\dot{x}_{34n}\cos\alpha_{34t}\cos\beta_{34b} = 0 \\
m_3\ddot{y}_3 + K_{3y}y_3 + K_{34}(t)x_{34n}\sin\alpha_{34n} + C_{3y}\dot{y}_3 + C_{34}\dot{x}_{34n}\sin\alpha_{34n} = 0 \\
m_3\ddot{z}_3 + K_{3z}z_3 + K_{34}(t)x_{34n}\sin\beta_{34b} + C_{3z}\dot{z}_3 + C_{34}\dot{x}_{34n}\sin\beta_{34b} = 0 \\
I_4\ddot{\theta}_4 - K_{34}x_{34n}r_{b4}\cos\beta_{34b} - C_{34}\dot{x}_{34n}r_{b4}\cos\beta_{34b} = -T_{out} \\
m_4\ddot{x}_4 + K_{4x}x_4 + K_{34}(t)x_{34n}\cos\alpha_{34t}\cos\beta_{34b} + C_{4x}\dot{x}_4 + C_{34}\dot{x}_{34n}\cos\alpha_{34t}\cos\beta_{34b} = 0 \\
m_4\ddot{y}_4 + K_{4y}y_4 - K_{34}(t)x_{34n}\sin\alpha_{34n} + C_{4y}\dot{y}_4 - C_{34}\dot{x}_{34n}\sin\alpha_{34n} = 0 \\
m_4\ddot{z}_4 + K_{4z}z_4 - K_{34}(t)x_{34n}\sin\beta_{34b} + C_{4z}\dot{z}_4 - C_{34}\dot{x}_{34n}\sin\beta_{34b} = 0
\end{cases}
$$

$$(8)$$

In the formula: $I_i(i = 3, 4)$ are the moment of inertia of the helical gear 3 and 4, $m_i(i = 3, 4)$ are the mass of the helical gear 3 and 4, K_{ij}, $C_{ij}(i = 3, 4.j = x, y, z)$ are the support stiffness and support damping of the helical gear 3 and 4, $K_{34}(t)$, C_{34} are time-varying meshing stiffness and meshing damping of the helical gear pair. T_{ou} is the output torque.

The required parameters such as time-varying meshing stiffness and static transmission error are substituted into the formula (1)–(8). The Runge-Kutta method with 4–5 order variable step lengths was used to solve the vibration differential equations of the gearbox transmission system. The calculation time is 4 s, the vibration displacement, vibration speed and vibration acceleration of each transmission component can be obtained. The gear twist angle displacement that obtained by solving the dynamic differential equations of the gearbox transmission system was substituted into transmission error formula, the dynamic transmission error of each gear pair can be calculated.

3   Vibration and Noise Analysis of Gearbox

3.1   Dynamic Response Analysis of Gearbox

First, the gearbox was made to be flexible in the ANSYS software and the constraint mode was calculated. Then, the flexible model and modal results were imported into the LMS Virtual. Lab software. Combining with the gearbox transmission system, a rigid-flexible coupling calculation model was constructed for the gearbox.

In the motion module of LMS Virtual. Lab software, the modal superposition method was adopted to analyze the dynamic response of the gearbox with the modal analysis results of the gearbox, the time and frequency domain data of reaction forces

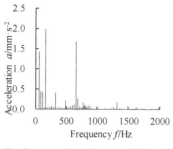

(a) The frequency domain curve of Y direction
acceleration at point 1

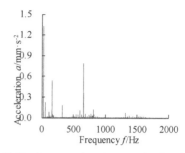

(b) The frequency domain curve of Y direction
acceleration at point 2

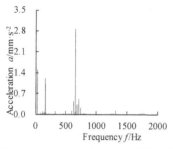

(c) The frequency domain curve of Y direction
acceleration at point 3

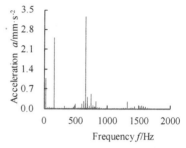

(d) The frequency domain curve of Y direction
acceleration at point 4

Fig. 2. The frequency domain curve of Y direction acceleration at each evaluation point

were gotten at each bearing of the gearbox. it prepared for the subsequent analysis of howling noise of gearbox. The set time step is $\Delta t = 5 \times 10^{-5}$s, the solve total time is $t = 4$ s.

The frequency domain curves of the vertical(Y direction) vibration acceleration of the node on the surface of the gearbox as shown in Fig. 2.

From Fig. 2, it can be seen that the vibration response exhibit a certain periodicity, the response spectrum maps of each point reflect the spectral components of the gear transmission errors. The frequency domain response peaks of all points mostly occur at the planetary stage (input stage) and the third-stage helical gear pair (output stage) with the meshing frequency of 29 Hz, 660 Hz and double frequency. The acceleration frequency domain response of evaluation points 1 and 2 was also occur at the second-stage gear with the meshing frequency of 163 Hz, which reflected the coupling effect of transmission errors excitation at all stages.

3.2   Establishment of Acoustic Coupling Model and Noise Prediction of Gearbox

For the acoustic-vibration coupling calculation method, the structural vibration and sound field distribution were calculated at the same time in a coupled environment. At the coupling boundary, the vibration velocity in the structural normal direction was the same as the vibration velocity in the fluid direction. In this case, the sound would produce sound pressure that load on the structure in normal direction, the structural vibration velocity would produce speed input on the sound, the sound field and structure field were coupled to each other.

The structure grid, acoustic grid and field grid of the gearbox were imported into the acoustic module Acoustics of the LMS software, a acoustic-vibration coupling calculation model was established as shown in Fig. 3.

Fig. 3. The acoustics finite element model of the gearbox

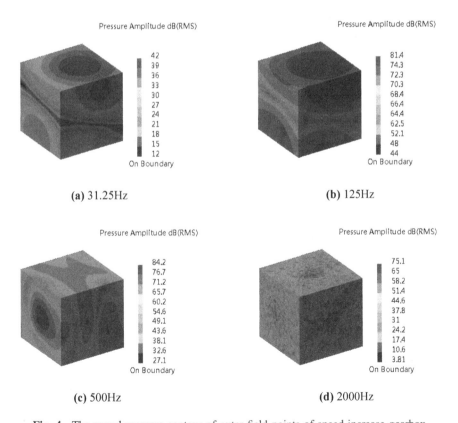

(a) 31.25Hz

(b) 125Hz

(c) 500Hz

(d) 2000Hz

Fig. 4. The sound pressure contour of outer field points of speed-increase gearbox

The frequency domain process data of the bearing support reaction force was used as the boundary conditions for acoustic-vibration coupling. The frequency domain loads were added at the rigid coupling points of the nine bearing bores. The acoustic-vibration coupling finite element method was used to calculate the radiation noise of the gearbox. The data exchange between the structural grid and acoustic grid need to be calculated by interpolation. The acoustic grid need to envelope the structural grid completely and the envelope element was established at the interface. Meanwhile, the field grid was established at 1 m from the gearbox outer surface.

The air properties that the gearbox's working environment was set in LMS Virtual. Lab software: the air density is 1.225 kg/m^3, the speed of sound in the air is 340 m/s, the reference sound pressure is 2×10^{-5}Pa. Then the calculation parameters such as solving scope, solving space, solving accuracy etc. was set. Combining the results of the constraint modal of the gearbox, the acoustic-vibration coupling finite element method was adopted to solve the howling noise of the gearbox. Figure 4 shows the sound pressure cloud diagram of howling noise at the external field of the gearbox. It can be seen from the figure that the maximum sound pressure at the field point is 84.2 dB, which occurs at a frequency of 500 Hz.

4 Effect of Gear Profile Modification on Vibration and Noise of Gearbox

4.1 Analysis of Gear Profile Modification

In this section, the addendum modification was adopted on gears, the influence of it on the gear vibration and howling noise was researched. Based on the modification formula [9] that H. Sigg's studied to calculate the theoretical modification of spur and helical gear, the addendum modification of each gear in the gearbox transmission system is obtained. As shown in Table 2.

Table 2. The value of each gear tooth modification

Gear	First stage			Second stage		Third stage	
	Sun gear	Planet gear	Inner ring gear	Driving gear	Driven gear	Driving gear	Driven gear
Gear tooth modification $\Delta/\mu m$	62.57	55.07	62.57	46.86	51.86	27.77	32.77

4.2 Dynamic Response Analysis of Gearbox After Modification

The dynamic transmission error of gears at all stages is reduced after gear profile modification. The changed gear dynamic transmission error was substituted into the rigid-flexible coupling model of the gearbox, then the box surface vibration response

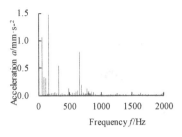

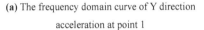

(a) The frequency domain curve of Y direction
acceleration at point 1

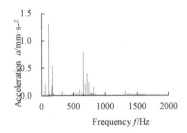

(b) The frequency domain curve of Y direction
acceleration at point 2

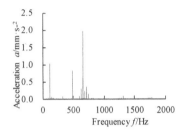

(c) The frequency domain curve of Y direction
acceleration at point 3

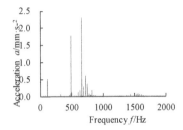

(d) The frequency domain curve of Y direction
acceleration at point 4

Fig. 5. The frequency domain curve of Y direction acceleration at each evaluation point after addendum modification

was solved and the frequency domain curve of Y direction acceleration at each evaluation point was extract. As shown in Fig. 5.

As can be seen from the Fig. 5, the vibration acceleration of the gearbox is reduced by approximately 0.2 to 0.3 times of each gears after addendum modification, the root mean square acceleration of nodes 1 to 4 is 2.37 m/s^2, 2.08 m/s^2, and 2.83 m/s^2 respectively. It can be seen from the time-domain curve that the change rule of acceleration of each node before and after the gear profile modification is same basically, the peak-to-peak acceleration is reduced after the modification. Comparing with the frequency domain curve, the vibration acceleration peak still occur at the meshing frequency and double frequency, the amplitude is greatly reduced after the addendum modification.

4.3 Prediction of Noise of Gearbox After Modification

The dynamic transmission errors of the gear pair after addendum modification was substituted into the rigid-flexible coupling model of the gearbox. The reaction force of the bearing was calculated and it used as the load excitation of the acoustic-vibration coupling model of the gearbox. The acoustic-vibration coupling model was calculated to get the gearbox howling noise cloud diagram as shown in Fig. 6. Comparing with the howling noise of the gearbox before modification, the value of howling noise of the

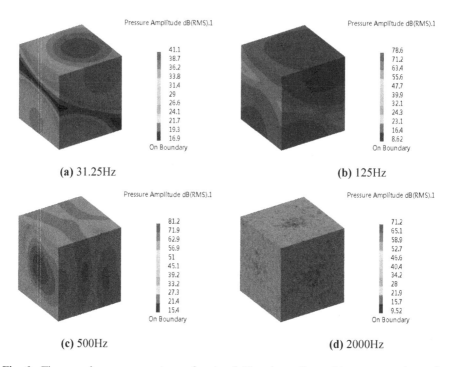

Fig. 6. The sound pressure contour of outer field points of speed-increase gearbox after addendum modification

gearbox in each frequency band is reduced by about 2 to 3 dB after modification, the maximum value of howling noise is 81.2 dB, which occurs at 500 Hz. frequency band.

5 Conclusion

(1) Considering the addendum modification of different gear to estimate the vibration of the gearbox and analyze the influence of modification on the vibration of the gearbox surface. The results show that the vibration of the gearbox surface is reduced by about 0.2–0.3 times after the addendum modification.

(2) Considering the addendum modification of different gear to estimate the howling noise of the gearbox and analyze the influence of modification on the surface noise of the gearbox. The results show that the value of howling noise of the gearbox in each frequency band is reduced by about 2 to 3 dB after the addendum modification.

Acknowledgments. The work described in this article was supported by the Major Industry Common Key Technology Innovation of Chongqing (cstc2015zdcy-ztzx70013) and the Fundamental Research Funds for Central Universities (106112017CDJZRPY0018).

References

1. Guomin, P., Liyun, K., Haijun, R.: Transmission errors analysis and optimization of transmission gear. Automot. Technol. **12**, 95–99 (2009)
2. Ruhai, G., Xuyi, J., Wentao, Y.: Application of tooth surface micro modification in noise reduction of automotive transmission. Automot. Eng. **31**(6), 27–33 (2009)
3. Quan, S., Yuequan, L., Xiaohui, S., et al.: Research on transmission gear parameters optimization and howling noise control. Noise Vibr. Control **21**(3), 43–50 (2010)
4. Oh, S., Kang, J., Lee, I., et al.: A study on modeling and optimization of tooth microgeometry for a helical gear pair. Int. J. Precis. Eng. Manuf. **14**(3), 423–427 (2013)
5. Taishan, Z., Yuewei, W.: Noise analysis of cone crusher gear drive system based on Romax. Electr. Mech. Eng. Technol. **44**(2), 38–42 (2015)
6. Carbonelli, A., Rigaud, E., Perret-Liaudet, J.: Vibro-acoustic analysis of geared systems— predicting and controlling the whining noise. In: Fuchs, A., Nijman, E., Priebsch, H.-H. (eds.) Automotive NVH Technology. SAST, pp. 63–79. Springer, Cham (2016). https://doi.org/10. 1007/978-3-319-24055-8_5
7. Yuan, F., Tong, Z., Yi, L., et al.: Research on the howling noise quality of electric vehicle gear based on gear profile modification. J. Vibr. Shock **35**(9), 123–128 (2016)
8. Wen, L., Jun, L., Tengjiao, L., Hesheng, L.: Transmission errors analysis and vibration noise prediction of gearbox. J. Chongqing Univ. **40**(03), 12–23 (2017)
9. Shaojun, L.: Research Gear Profile Modification of Involute Cylindrical and its Influence on Transmission Performance. Nanjing University of Aeronautics and Astronautics, Nanjing (2010)

Calculation of Mesh Stiffness of Gear Pair with Profile Deviation Based on Realistic Tooth Flank Equation

Quancheng Peng[1](✉), Tengjiao Lin[1], Zeyin He[2], Jing Wei[1], and Hesheng Lv[3]

[1] State Key Laboratory of Mechanical Transmissions, Chongqing University, Chongqing 400044, China
20150701014@cqu.edu.cn
[2] School of Mechatronics and Vehicle Engineering, Chongqing Jiaotong University, Chongqing 400074, China
[3] Chongqing Gearbox Company Limited, Chongqing 402263, China

Abstract. Due to the compatibility with accurate geometry of contact surface, finite element analysis (FEA) is an efficient method for tooth contact analysis of gear pair with profile deviation. However, it usually requires a dense grid along the height of the tooth in order to simulate the elliptically distributed contact pressure. In consideration of reducing the node number, the grid model of spur gear pair with profile deviation is firstly established based on the realistic tooth flank equation and then locally refined at the vicinity of theoretic contact point. With the refined grid model, global linear deformation and local nonlinear contact deformation of tooth can be accurately calculated, and mesh stiffness of gear pair with different profile deviation and load are obtained correspondingly. According to the results, the influence of each profile deviation on mesh stiffness, the coupling effect of different profile deviation, and the nonlinear relevance between load and mesh stiffness are analyzed and can be used to provide reference for further dynamic analysis of gear pair.

Keywords: Profile deviation · Local refinement · Contact FEA
Mesh stiffness

1 Introduction

During the running process of gear pair, the simultaneously meshing teeth number are changing alternatively, and the mesh stiffness and profile deviation of a meshing tooth are also changing continuously. Stiffness excitation and error excitation will be aroused then and lead to vibration of gear pair [1, 2]. As the stiffness excitation and error excitation are both relevant to composite meshing errors [3, 4] which is greatly influenced by profile deviation, the analysis of influence of profile deviation on mesh stiffness is of importance to the prediction of internal excitation of gear pair.

Common calculation method for mesh stiffness includes material mechanics method [5], elastic mechanics method [6], finite element method [7], etc. With suitable disposal of gear profile deviation, these methods can also be applied to calculate mesh

© Springer Nature Singapore Pte Ltd. 2018
S. Wang et al. (Eds.): ICSEE 2018/IMIOT 2018, CCIS 923, pp. 506–517, 2018.
https://doi.org/10.1007/978-981-13-2396-6_47

stiffness of gear pair with profile deviation. And due to the profile modification can be measured in the same way as profile deviation, it is helpful to refer to the calculation method of mesh stiffness of gear pair with profile modification.

For material mechanics method, the total tooth deformation is separated into bending deformation, compressive deformation, shear deformation, fillet-foundation deformation and Hertz contact deformation [8], however, the cantilever beam assumption does not coincide precisely with gear tooth and the tooth fillet curve is usually ignored. For finite element method, the total tooth deformation is often separated into a global and a local term [9], however, the boundary conditions of the partial FE model for correction of the global term have not been well studied. As a result, the local refinement of tooth grid model is adopted [10], however, the existing literatures are based on gear grid model without consideration of profile deviation or modification, which is not totally consistent with gear pair under realistic condition.

Through adjusting position of gird nodes of gear tooth without profile deviation, the contact grid model of gear pair with profile deviation is established. The contact FEA of a spur gear pair is then carried out to calculate the mesh stiffness. According to calculation results, influence of profile deviation on mesh stiffness are analyzed.

2 Locally Refined Grid of Gear Pair with Profile Deviation

To build the grid model of gear pair with profile deviation, the idealistic profile is firstly discretized and locally refined. Through adjusting the obtained discretization points according to profile deviation, profile grid nodes of gear pair with profile deviation are obtained and used by block mapping method to generate end face grid.

2.1 Discretization and Local Refinement of Idealistic Profile

In order to obtain the locally refined discretization points of idealistic profile, two coordinate systems are firstly established. A global coordinate system O-xy shown in Fig. 1 is built where the origin is at gear center and the y axis coincides with tooth symmetric line. Assuming the intersection point of tooth profile and contact path is i as is shown in Fig. 1, a local coordinate system O_i-x_iy_i is built with the intersection O_i of contact path and base circle as origin and x axis along the radial direction.

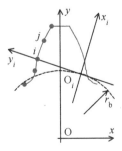

Fig. 1. Coordinate system of tooth profile.

Local coordinate of tooth profile is shown in Eqs. (1) and (2). And for the mating tooth, similar local coordinate system O_{mi}-$x_{mi}y_{mi}$ and profile equation can be obtained.

$$x_{i,j} = r_b \cos \theta_{i,j} + r_b \tan \alpha_j \sin \theta_{i,j} - r_b \tag{1}$$

$$y_{i,j} = -r_b \sin \theta_{i,j} + r_b \tan \alpha_j \cos \theta_{i,j} \tag{2}$$

where, r_b is base circle radius, α_j is pressure angle of point j, and $\theta_{i,j} = \tan\alpha_j - \tan\alpha_i$.

Coordinate transformation from local coordinate system O_i-x_iy_i to global coordinate system O-xy can be expressed as Eqs. (3) and (4).

$$x_j = (x_{i,j} + r_b) \cos \eta_i + y_{i,j} \sin \eta_i \tag{3}$$

$$y_j = -(x_{i,j} + r_b) \sin \eta_i + y_{i,j} \cos \eta_i \tag{4}$$

where, η_i can be calculated as Eq. (5).

$$\eta_i = \alpha_i - \frac{s}{r} + 2(\text{inv } \alpha_i - \text{inv } \alpha) \tag{5}$$

Before local refinement of profile, half contact band width is estimated as follows.

$$b_H = \sqrt{\frac{4}{\pi}(\frac{1 - v_1^2}{E_1} + \frac{1 - v_2^2}{E_2})\frac{F_n}{b_w}\frac{\rho_1\rho_2}{\rho_1 + \rho_2}} \tag{6}$$

where, v_1, v_2, E_1 and E_2 are respectively the material Poison ratio and elastic modulus of relevant gear, F_n is the normal meshing force, b_w is the effective gear width, ρ_1 and ρ_2 are respectively the curvature radius of relevant gear at contact point i.

With load applied, contact point i will be expanded to a contact band with width $2b_H$. In order to reflect the local contact deformation, it is necessary to generate a dense grid in the vicinity of point i. Firstly, the addendum pressure angle α_a is taken into Eq. (1) to calculate the local coordinate $x_{i,a}$, and for the mating tooth, the coordinate $x_{mi,a}$ is calculated. Then, according to $x_{i,a}$ and $x_{mi,a}$, at most N + 1 and at least N/2 + 1 (N is an even integer) local refinement profile points are generated as follows:

Case 1. $x_{i,a} \leq 2b_H$

Calculate local coordinates $x_{i,j}$ ($0 \leq j \leq$ N) of N + 1 points as Eq. (7) where $\Delta l_H = 4b_H/N$. Choose the point c which is closest to point i as the contact center point.

$$x_{i,j} = x_{i,a} - j\Delta l_H \tag{7}$$

Case 2. $x_{mi,a} \leq 2b_H$

Calculate local coordinate $x_{i,j}$($0 \leq j \leq N/2 + \lfloor x_{mi,a}/b_H \rfloor$) of N/2 + $\lfloor x_{mi,a}/b_H \rfloor$ + 1 points with Eq. (8). Choose the point c which is closest to point i as the contact center point.

$$x_{i,j} = -x_{mi,a} + j\Delta l_H \tag{8}$$

Case 3. $x_{i,a} \geq 2b_H$ and $x_{mi,a} \geq 2b_H$

Calculate local coordinate $x_{i,j}$ ($0 \leq j \leq N$) of N + 1 points with Eq. (9). Choose the first N/2 point c as the contact center point and $x_{i,c}$ is always equal to 0.

$$x_{i,j} = (j - \frac{N}{2})\Delta l_H \tag{9}$$

Here, the local coordinate $x_{i,c}$ of contact center point might be unequal to 0 for case 1 and 2. And with the local coordinate $x_{i,j}$ of local refinement point j, the corresponding pressure angle α_j can be obtained with bisection method based on Eq. (1). With α_j, corresponding local coordinate $y_{i,j}$ can be calculated with Eq. (2), which is finally taken into Eqs. (3) and (4) to calculate the global coordinate of point j.

For unrefined involute part, discretization points can be calculated as usual and equidistantly distributed according to the involute arc length.

2.2 Discretization of Realistic Tooth Profile with Flank Deviation

If a measured or assumed profile deviation e_j is existing for idealistic profile point j, then a corresponding point j' on realistic profile can be obtained as Eqs. (10) and (11). From the equation, for each point j' on realistic profile, there is a corresponding point j on idealistic profile, and profile composed of all these corresponding points j are called the hypothetical idealistic profile of realistic profile.

$$x_{i,j'} = r_b \cos \theta_{i,j} + (r_b \tan \alpha_j - e_j) \sin \theta_{i,j} - r_b \tag{10}$$

$$y_{i,j'} = -r_b \sin \theta_{i,j} + (r_b \tan \alpha_j - e_j) \cos \theta_{i,j} \tag{11}$$

For each locally refined point j on idealistic profile, through letting $x_{i,j'}$ in Eq. (10) equals to $x_{i,j}$, a new pressure angle α_j can be calculated through bisection method and then taken into Eq. (11) to calculate $y_{i,j'}$.

For each unrefined point j on idealistic profile, its new pressure angle α_j can be calculated with bisection method through taking its global coordinate x_j and y_j into Eq. (12) due to that $x_{i,j'}$ and $y_{i,j'}$ are both relied on α_j according to Eqs. (10) and (11). And along with α_j, local coordinates $x_{i,j'}$ and $y_{i,j'}$ of point j are obtained.

$$x_j^2 + y_j^2 = (x_{i,j'} + r_b)^2 + y_{i,j'}^2 \tag{12}$$

Transformation from local coordinate $x_{i,j'}$ and $y_{i,j'}$ to global coordinate $x_{j'}$ and $y_{j'}$ is the same as Eqs. (3) and (4), and then locally refined discretization point of realistic profile with flank deviation is obtained.

2.3   Locally Refined Grid Model of Gear Pair

Through taking the above profile discretization point as the profile grid node, the block mapping method is used to generate quadrilateral grid on end face as Fig. 2. As is shown, a special block partition scheme is adopted to divide denser grid for meshing tooth, and the tooth thickness direction is also refined beneath the tooth flank. Figure 3 shows example grid of the 3 cases in 2.1, where case 1 and 2 always appear at the same time (when one tooth is in case 1, its mating tooth will be in case 2).

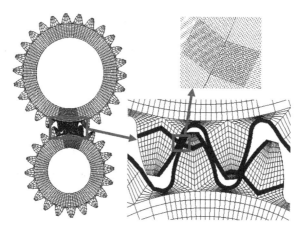

Fig. 2. Locally refined grid model of gear pair

With the gear pair grid model, contact center point chosen in 2.1 is taken as a pair of possible contact nodes, and through traversing nodes on profile along the positive and negative directions of $x_{i,j}$ respectively from contact center point, nodes met successively on driving and driven gear are chosen as a new pair of possible contact nodes. The initial contact gap ε of the contact node pair can be determined through calculation of distance between the two nodes along contact path direction.

3   Contact Finite Element Equation of Gear Pair

At a given meshing position, the system stiffness matrix $[K]$ of the above grid model is firstly calculated and then adjusted according to the relevant constraints as shown in the following four steps. The adjustment of displacement and load vector is similar to stiffness matrix and is skipped over for conciseness considerations.

(1) For each node i on inner ring of driving gear, its displacement and force in global coordinate system O-xy is transformed to local coordinate system O_i-x_iy_i as shown in Fig. 4, and resultant stiffness matrix is expressed as $[K_i]$.

(2) In consideration of zero displacement constraint in radial and longitudinal directions of inner ring nodes of driving gear, and zero displacement constraint for

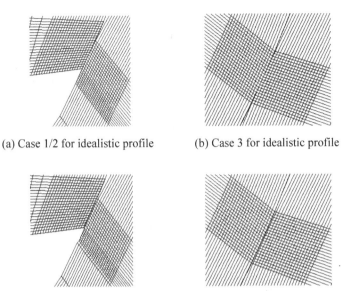

(a) Case 1/2 for idealistic profile   (b) Case 3 for idealistic profile

(c) Case 1/2 for profile with deviation (d) Case 3 for profile with deviation

Fig. 3. Grid refinement of different cases

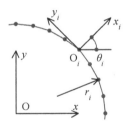

Fig. 4. Local coordinate system of inner ring nodes of driving gear

all inner ring nodes of driven gear, the corresponding rows and columns of $[K_i]$ are crossed out and the resultant stiffness matrix is expressed as $[K_c]$.

(3) Choosing the tangent displacement of all inner ring nodes of driving gear and the displacement of all contact nodes as master freedom, and condensing all other node displacements in $[K_c]$, a resultant stiffness matrix $[K_m]$ is obtained.

(4) The contact displacement constraint and the constraint that all inner ring nodes of driving gear have the same tangential displacement are imported into $[K_m]$ through Lagrange method, and resultant system equation is shown in Eq. (13).

$$\begin{bmatrix} K_m & N^{AB,T} & N^{t,T} \\ N^{AB} & 0 & 0 \\ N^t & 0 & 0 \end{bmatrix} \begin{Bmatrix} u_m \\ \lambda^{AB} \\ \lambda^t \end{Bmatrix} = \begin{Bmatrix} F_m \\ -\varepsilon^{AB} \\ 0 \end{Bmatrix} \quad (13)$$

where, $[N^{AB}]$ and $[N^t]$ are respectively the transformation matrix of contact constraint and inner ring nodes displacement constraint, $\{\varepsilon^{AB}\}$ is initial normal contact gap vector, $\{\lambda^{AB}\}$ and $\{\lambda^t\}$ are the corresponding Lagrange multiplier vector.

Procedure for establishing and solving Eq. (13) is shown in Fig. 5. And in order to calculate the mesh stiffness, the tangential displacement u_t of inner ring nodes of driving gear is transferred to an arc length of base circle as shown in Eq. (14).

$$k = \frac{F_n/b_w}{r_{b1}u_t/r_{i1}} \tag{14}$$

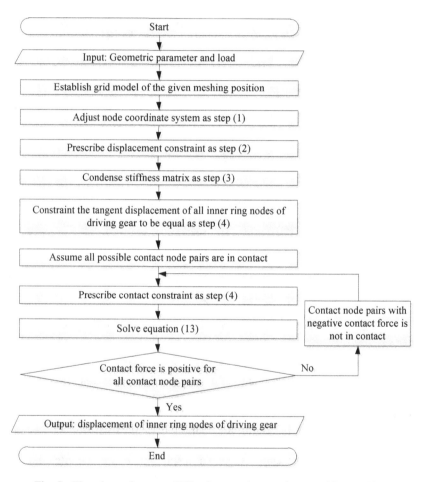

Fig. 5. Flowchart of contact FEA of gear pair at a given meshing position

4 Influence of Profile Deviation on Mesh Stiffness

Choosing a tooth on driving gear as the reference tooth, the influence of profile deviation only located at this reference tooth on mesh stiffness is analyzed. For gear with idealistic profile, the curvature radius of reference tooth profile at contact point is used to represent different meshing positions. And for gear with realistic profile, the curvature radius of its hypothetical idealistic profile mentioned in 2.2 is used to represent different meshing positions. For the following stiffness curves, the abscissa called meshing positions means this curvature radius.

For profile slope deviation $f_{H\alpha,j}$ of profile point j on reference tooth, linear distribution rule shown in Eq. (15) is adopted, and for profile form deviation $f_{f\alpha,j}$ of profile point j on reference tooth, sinusoidal distribution rule shown in Eq. (16) is adopted. The adoption of these distribution rules is acceptable according to the tooth flank topography separation [11].

$$f_{H\alpha,j} = f_{H\alpha T} \frac{\rho_j - \rho_s}{\rho_e - \rho_s} \tag{15}$$

$$f_{f\alpha,j} = f_{f\alpha T} \sin(\frac{\rho_j - \rho_s}{\rho_e - \rho_s} \pi) \tag{16}$$

where, $f_{H\alpha T}$ is the profile slope tolerance, $f_{f\alpha T}$ is the profile form tolerance, s and e respectively mean the starting and ending point of the involute. The value of profile deviation is assumed to be positive when material is taken away from tooth flank.

For gear pair shown in Table 1 with idealistic profile, the procedure shown in Fig. 5 is adopted to carry out the contact FEA with load $T = 12$ N·m. The resultant half contact band width b_H and load sharing ratio (LSR) of the reference tooth of driving gear at different mesh positions are shown in Fig. 6. The half contact band width b_H calculated by Eq. (6) is also shown in Fig. 6(a). From the figure, the b_H calculated by FEA method and analytical method are close to each other, and then the effectiveness of the above FEA procedure is verified. At mesh position $\rho = 6$ mm, the contact force distribution of contact nodes in contact band of the reference tooth is shown in Fig. 6 (c). From the figure, contact force distribution along contact band width direction is elliptic and is consistent with the Hertz contact pressure distribution.

For gear pair shown in Table 1 with different profile deviation ($e_j = f_{H\alpha,j}$ or $e_j = f_{f\alpha,j}$) of class 2 and 3, mesh stiffness k_H and K_α are calculated and compared to mesh stiffness k with idealistic profile as is shown in Fig. 7. From the figure, mesh stiffness decreases when profile deviation is considered and this conclusion is consistent with reference [8]. Reason for the decrease of mesh stiffness is that contact force undertaken by points with positive deviation will decrease under the same meshing deformation, compared to deviation ignoring cases.

Figure 8 shows the calculated mesh stiffness $k_{H+\alpha}$ of gear pair with composition of profile slope and form deviation ($e_j = f_{H\alpha,j} + f_{f\alpha,j}$) of class 3, and the mesh stiffness k_s obtained through subtracting the sum of mesh stiffness decrease ($\Delta k_H + \Delta K_\alpha$) caused by single profile deviation from mesh stiffness k is also shown. From the figure, with composition of profile slope and form deviation, decrease amount of mesh stiffness is

Table 1. Geometric parameters of gear pair.

Parameter	Driving gear	Driven gear
Number of teeth	20	26
Modulus/mm	1.5	
Pressure angle/°	25	
Addendum coefficient	1.0	
Bottom clearance coefficient	0.2	
Shifting coefficient	0.0	0.0
Face width/mm	4.0	
Working center distance/mm	34.5	
Hub inner ring radius/mm	8.0	12.5

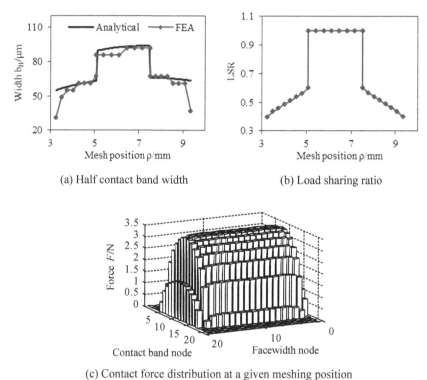

(a) Half contact band width   (b) Load sharing ratio

(c) Contact force distribution at a given meshing position

Fig. 6. Contact band width, LSR and force distribution of contact FEA

less than the sum of mesh stiffness decrease caused by single profile deviation respectively. This indicates the influence of different profile deviation on mesh stiffness is coupled and it is consistent with reference [12].

Due to the nonlinear local contact deformation, it is necessary to analyze the influence of load on mesh stiffness. Figure 9(a) shows mesh stiffness k_T of gear pair

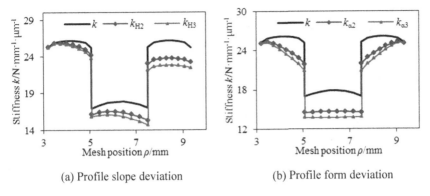

(a) Profile slope deviation   (b) Profile form deviation

Fig. 7. Mesh stiffness of gear pair with different profile deviation

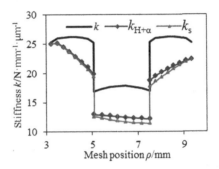

Fig. 8. Mesh stiffness of gear pair under composition of profile slope and form deviation

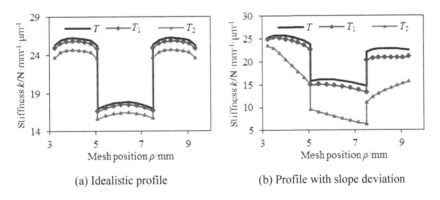

(a) Idealistic profile   (b) Profile with slope deviation

Fig. 9. Mesh stiffness of gear pair under different load

with idealistic profile under three different loads T_1 = 12kN·m, T_2 = 7.5kN·m and T_3 = 1.2kN·m, and Fig. 9(b) shows mesh stiffness $k_{H,T}$ of gear pair with profile slope deviation of classification 3 under the same three loads. From the figure, mesh stiffness of gear pair with idealistic profile and realistic profile will both increase along with increase of load. This conclusion is consistent with reference [13], and the reason for increase of stiffness is that along with the increase of applied load, the contact band width will also increase. And due to the wider contact band, there will be more points to undertake the contact force which can finally result in the increase of mesh stiffness for gear pair with or without profile deviation.

5   Conclusions

According to realistic flank equation with consideration of profile deviation, the contact finite element model of gear pair with local refinement is established to calculate the mesh stiffness of gear pair with profile deviation:

(1) Due to the decrease of load undertaken by contact points with profile deviation, the gear mesh stiffness will decrease under consideration of profile deviation, and as the deviation become larger, the mesh stiffness decrease will also be larger;

(2) With composition of profile slope and form deviation, decrease amount of mesh stiffness is not equal to sum of mesh stiffness decrease with single profile deviation, which indicates a coupling influence of different profile deviation;

(3) Due to the increase of the number of contact points caused by increase of contact band width, the mesh stiffness will also increase for gear pair with idealistic profile or realistic profile along with the increase of applied load.

Acknowledgments. This project is supported by the Industrial Common Key Technology Innovation of Chongqing (cstc2015zdcy-ztzx70013) and the Fundamental Research Funds for Central Universities (106112017CDJZRPY0018).

References

1. Velex, P., Maatar, M.: A mathematical model for analyzing the influence of shape deviations and mounting errors on gear dynamic behaviour. J. Sound Vib. **191**(5), 629–660 (1996)
2. Li, R., Wang, J.: Gear System Dynamics: Vibration, Shock, Noise. Science Press, Beijing (1996)
3. Yang, Y., Lin, T., Liu, W., Zhang J.: Multi-body dynamic simulation and vibro-acoustic coupling analysis of bridge crane gearbox. In: 2016 International Conference on Advanced Manufacture Technology and Industrial Application, pp. 307–311, Shanghai (2016)
4. Chang, L., Liu, G., Wu, L.: Determination of composite meshing errors and its influence on the vibration of gear system. Chin. J. Mech. Eng. **51**(1), 123–130 (2015)
5. Weber, C.: The deformations of loaded gears and the effect on their load-carrying capacity, in: sponsored research. In: British Department of Scientific and Industrial Research, Report No 3, (1949)
6. Terauchi, Y., Nagamura, K.: Study on deflection of spur gear teeth (1st report). Bull. of JSME **23**(184), 1682–1688 (1980)
7. Wallace, D., Seireg, A.: Computer simulation of dynamic stress, deformation, and fracture of gear teeth. J. Eng. Ind. **95**(4), 1108–1114 (1973)

8. Chen, Z., Shao, Y.: Mesh stiffness calculation of a spur gear pair with tooth profile modification and tooth root crack. Mech. Mach. Theory **62**, 63–74 (2013)

9. Andersson, A., Vedmar, L.: A dynamic model to determine vibrations in involute helical gears. J. Sound Vib. **260**(2), 195–212 (2003)

10. Li, S.: Effects of misalignment error, tooth modifications and transmitted torque on tooth engagements of a pair of spur gears. Mech. Mach. Theory **83**, 125–136 (2015)

11. Shi, Z., Lin, H.: Multi-degrees of freedom theory for gear deviation. Chin. J. Mech. Eng. **50** (1), 55–60 (2014)

12. Lin, T., He, Z.: Analytical method for coupled transmission error of helical gear system with machining errors, assembly errors and tooth modifications. Mech. Syst. Signal Pr. **91**, 167–182 (2017)

13. Liu, B., Du, Q., Wen, Q.: Calculation and analysis of meshing stiffness of helical gear considering installation error. J. Mech. Transm. **41**(3), 33–37 (2017)

Nonlinear Dynamics of Hypoid Gears in Automobile

Xingxing Lu[(⊠)], Tengjiao Lin, Feiyang Jiang, and Zirui Zhao

State Key Laboratory of Mechanical Transmission,
Chongqing University, Chongqing, China
1612703716@qq.com

Abstract. In this paper, the dynamic model of an 8-degree-of-freedom hypoid gear pair model with time-varying stiffness, comprehensive gear error and the nonlinearity backlash is established. The numerical integration method is applied to solve the dynamic responses. With help of bifurcation diagrams, time history, phase plane, frequency spectrum and Poincaré maps, the effects exaction frequency, load coefficient and support damping are investigated by using the numerical integration method. The results reveal that system exhibits a diverse range of one-period responses, multi-periodic responses, bifurcation and chaotic responses when the parameters are changed. Some results presented in this study provide some useful reference to dynamic design and vibration control of the gear transmission system.

Keywords: Hypoid gears · Nonlinear · Bifurcation · Chaos

1 Introduction

Hypoid gear systems are widely used in automotive rear axle applications due to their ability to transmit large torque between two perpendicular, non-intersecting shafts. Specifically, its applications can be found in automotive systems, off-highway vehicles, wind turbines or other industrial machineries with speed reducing mechanisms. How the system parameters affect the form of the gear transmission and the bifurcation and chaos characteristics of the system is an important part of studying the form of gear transmission.

From the available published works in gear dynamics. Kahraman et al. [1] studied the nonlinear frequency response characteristic of a spur gear pair with external and internal excitations. Tang et al. [2] established the torsional vibration equations of spiral bevel gear system, which included time-varying stiffness and gear backlash. Wang et al. [3] built a generalized nonlinear time-varying dynamic model of a hypoid gear pair with backlash nonlinearity. Kiyono et al. [4] established a 2-DOF dynamic model of a pair of bevel gears, and analyzed the stability of the vibration model. Mohammadpour et al. [5] set up an 8-DOF tribo-dynamic model of hypoid gear system, and analyzed the dominant frequency from the transmission system onto the differential casing. Peng et al. [6] established a 14-DOF hypoid geared rotor dynamic model, and

© Springer Nature Singapore Pte Ltd. 2018
S. Wang et al. (Eds.): ICSEE 2018/IMIOT 2018, CCIS 923, pp. 518–528, 2018.
https://doi.org/10.1007/978-981-13-2396-6_48

comparatively analyzed of the rotor gyroscopic effect on dynamic response. Yang et al. [7] established a 7-DOF dynamic model of the spiral bevel gear system, and investigated the system parameters influence bifurcation and chaotic behavior of the gear system. Yang et al. [8] performed dynamic analysis of hypoid gear system by means of nonlinear vibration models relate time-varying stiffness, static transmission error, and the nonlinearity backlash. However, most of the dynamic characteristics researches are the analysis of spur or helical gear. The dynamics analysis of hypoid gear system relate the coupled bending-torsional vibration is also rarely reported.

In this paper, a nonlinear vibration equations of the hypoid gear pair relate time-varying meshing stiffness, comprehensive gear error and the backlash is formulated. The Runge-Kutta numerical method is applied to solve differential equations of hypoid gear system, and interpreted the nonlinear characteristics of the hypoid gear system by construction of the time history, phase plane, frequency spectrum, Poincaré map, and bifurcation diagram. The influence of internal and external periodic excitation on the coupled vibration of the system is investigated systematically.

2 Dynamic Model

According to the meshing characteristics of the hypoid gear pair, a dynamic model to stimulate hypoid gear system is shown in Fig. 1. A dynamic model for hypoid gear Pair based on lumped parameter method. The following assumptions are following: (1) the mass and inertia of the rotating shaft are concentrated onto the gear, and the rotating shaft is modeled as massless rigid body; (2) Ignoring the twist vibration of hypoid gears, only axial vibration, torsional vibration and transverse bending vibration are considered Coupling between motions. O_g and O_p are the centroid of the gear and pinion. The coordinates of pinion (x_p, y_p, z_p, θ_p) and gear (x_g, y_g, z_g, θ_g) are defined relative to their local inertial reference frames illustrated in Fig. 1 with the origin of the local coordinate systems at the centroid of pinion and gear bodies respectively.

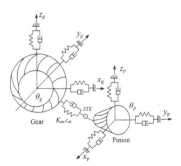

Fig. 1. Bending-torsional dynamic model of a hypoid gear system

The generalized coordinate vector of the nonlinear dynamic model can be described as

$$q = \{x_p, y_p, z_p, \theta_p, x_g, y_g, z_g, \theta_g\}^T \tag{1}$$

Where x_p and x_g are the x direction displacements of pinion and gear; y_p and y_g are the y direction displacements of pinion and gear; z_p and z_g are the y direction displacements of pinion and gear; θ_{ly} are the y direction torsional displacements of the pinion and gear, respectively.

The internal vibratory excitations originate from kinematic transmission error which is a displacement type excitation. The coordinate transformation vectors h_p and h_g in internal excitation component can be defined as:

$$h_l = \{n_{lx}, n_{ly}, n_{lz}, \lambda_{ly}\} \qquad l = p, g \tag{2}$$

$$\lambda_{ly} = z_l n_{lx} - x_l n_{lz} \qquad l = p, g \tag{3}$$

Where vector $\{n_{lx}, n_{ly}, n_{lz}\}$ stands for the unit normal vector of line of action and $\{x_l, z_l\}$ is mesh point vector.

The dynamic transmission error indicates the displacement difference between pinion and gear along the line of action during operation which can be written as:

$$\lambda = h_p^T \{x_p, y_p, z_p, \theta_{py}\} - h_g^T \{x_g, y_g, z_g, \theta_{gy}\} - e_n(t) \tag{4}$$

Here $e_n(t)$ indicates comprehensive gear error, $e_n(t)$ can be expressed in the form

$$e_n(t) = \sum_{l=1}^{N_e} A_{ei} \cos(i\Omega_h t + \phi_{ei}) \tag{5}$$

Where A_{ei} is the ith amplitude of comprehensive gear error, Ω_h is meshing frequency, and Φ_{ei} is the ith phase angle.

Since the periodicity of the motion of the system, $k_h(t)$ can be obtained by means of a Fourier expansion:

$$k_h(t) = k_m + \sum_{i=1}^{N_k} A_{ki} \cos(i\Omega_h t + \phi_{ki}) \tag{6}$$

Here, k_m is the average mesh stiffness value, A_{ki} is the ith stiffness fluctuation amplitude, and Φ_{ki} is the ith phase angle.

The backlash function $f(\lambda)$ is nonlinear displacement function, which can be expressed as

$$f(\lambda) = \begin{cases} \lambda - b & \lambda > b \\ 0 & -b < \lambda < b \\ \lambda + b & \lambda < b \end{cases} \tag{7}$$

Where b represents half of normal backlash.

The normal meshing force F_m of gear pair meshing point can be calculated as

$$F_m = k_h(t)f(\lambda) + c_m f'(\lambda) \tag{8}$$

The differential equations of coupled bending-torsional vibration model of the nonlinear dynamics system with comprehensive gear error, gear backlash and time-varying stiffness, as shown in Fig. 1, can be written as:

$$\begin{cases} m_p \ddot{x}_p + c_{px} \dot{x}_p + k_{px} x_p = -n_{px} F_m \\ m_p \ddot{y}_p + c_{py} \dot{y}_p + k_{py} y_p = -n_{py} F_m \\ m_p \ddot{z}_p + c_{pz} \dot{z}_p + k_{pz} z_p = -n_{pz} F_m \\ J_{py} \ddot{\theta}_{py} = T_L - \lambda_{py} F_m \\ m_g \ddot{x}_g + c_{gx} \dot{x}_g + k_{gx} x_g = n_{gx} F_m \\ m_g \ddot{y}_g + c_{gy} \dot{y}_g + k_{gy} y_g = n_{gy} F_m \\ m_g \ddot{z}_g + c_{gz} \dot{z}_g + k_{gz} z_g = n_{gz} F_m \\ J_{gy} \ddot{\theta}_{gy} = -T_D + \lambda_{gy} F_m \end{cases} \tag{9}$$

Where m_l $(l = p, g)$ are the mass; I_l $(l = p, g)$ are the mass moments of inertias; T_p and T_g are mean load torques on pinion and gear. c_{lj} $(l = p, g; j = x, y, z)$ are support damping coefficients; k_{lj} $(l = p, g; j = x, y, z)$ are the support stiffness coefficients of the roller bearings; F_j $(j = x, y, z)$ are the direction x, y, and z dynamic meshing force for the pinion and gear, respectively; r_p is the base radius of the pinion; r_g is base radius of the gear.

The dynamic transmission error λ between the meshing points of tooth surfaces is taken as a new degree of freedom, the Eq. (9) can be nondimensionalized as Eq. (10)

$$
\begin{bmatrix} 1 & 0 & 0 & 0 & 0 & 0 & 0 \\ 0 & 1 & 0 & 0 & 0 & 0 & 0 \\ 0 & 0 & 1 & 0 & 0 & 0 & 0 \\ 0 & 0 & 0 & 1 & 0 & 0 & 0 \\ 0 & 0 & 0 & 0 & 1 & 0 & 0 \\ 0 & 0 & 0 & 0 & 0 & 1 & 0 \\ -n_{px} & -n_{py} & -n_{pz} & n_{gx} & n_{gy} & n_{gz} & 1 \end{bmatrix}
\begin{bmatrix} \ddot{X}_p \\ \ddot{Y}_p \\ \ddot{Z}_p \\ \ddot{X}_g \\ \ddot{Y}_g \\ \ddot{Z}_g \\ \ddot{\lambda} \end{bmatrix}
+
\begin{bmatrix} \zeta_{px} & 0 & 0 & 0 & 0 & 0 & n_{px}\zeta_{mpx} \\ 0 & \zeta_{py} & 0 & 0 & 0 & 0 & n_{py}\zeta_{mpy} \\ 0 & 0 & \zeta_{pz} & 0 & 0 & 0 & n_{pz}\zeta_{mpz} \\ 0 & 0 & 0 & \zeta_{gx} & 0 & 0 & -n_{gx}\zeta_{mgx} \\ 0 & 0 & 0 & 0 & \zeta_{gy} & 0 & -n_{gy}\zeta_{mgy} \\ 0 & 0 & 0 & 0 & 0 & \zeta_{gz} & -n_{gz}\zeta_{mgz} \\ 0 & 0 & 0 & 0 & 0 & 0 & C\zeta_m \end{bmatrix}
\begin{bmatrix} \dot{X}_p \\ \dot{Y}_p \\ \dot{Z}_p \\ \dot{X}_g \\ \dot{Y}_g \\ \dot{Z}_g \\ \dot{\lambda} \end{bmatrix}
$$

$$
+
\begin{bmatrix} \bar{k}_{px} & 0 & 0 & 0 & 0 & 0 & n_{px}\bar{k}_{mpx} \\ 0 & \bar{k}_{py} & 0 & 0 & 0 & 0 & n_{py}\bar{k}_{mpy} \\ 0 & 0 & \bar{k}_{pz} & 0 & 0 & 0 & n_{pz}\bar{k}_{mpz} \\ 0 & 0 & 0 & \bar{k}_{gx} & 0 & 0 & -n_{gx}\bar{k}_{mgx} \\ 0 & 0 & 0 & 0 & \bar{k}_{gy} & 0 & -n_{gy}\bar{k}_{mgy} \\ 0 & 0 & 0 & 0 & 0 & \bar{k}_{gz} & -n_{gz}\bar{k}_{mgz} \\ 0 & 0 & 0 & 0 & 0 & 0 & C\bar{k}_h \end{bmatrix}
\begin{bmatrix} f(\bar{X}_p) \\ f(\bar{Y}_p) \\ f(\bar{Z}_p) \\ f(\bar{X}_g) \\ f(\bar{Y}_g) \\ f(\bar{Z}_g) \\ f(\bar{\lambda}) \end{bmatrix}
=
\begin{bmatrix} 0 \\ 0 \\ 0 \\ 0 \\ 0 \\ 0 \\ \bar{F}_{pm} + \bar{F}_{pv} + \bar{F}_e \end{bmatrix}
\tag{10}
$$

Introducing Eq. (10) non-dimensional parameters, which are calculated as following:

$$\bar{X}_l = x_l/b, \ \bar{Y}_l = y_l/b, \ \bar{Z}_l = z_l/b, \ m_e = J_p J_g/(J_g r_{bp}^2 + J_p r_{bg}^2), \ \omega_n = k_m/m_e,$$

$$\zeta_{lj} = c_{lj}/(2m_l\omega_n), \ \zeta_m = c_m/2m_e\omega_n, \ \bar{k}_{lj} = k_{lj}/(m_l\omega_n^2), \ \bar{k}_h = 1 + \sum_{i=1}^{N_k} \frac{A_{ki}}{k_m}\cos(i\Omega_h t + \phi_{ki}),$$

$$\bar{F}_{pm} = F_m/m_e b\omega_n^2, \ \bar{F}_e = 1 + \sum_{i=1}^{N_e} \frac{A_{ei}}{b_m}(i\omega_h)^2 \cos(i\Omega_h t + \phi_{ei}), f(\lambda)$$

$$= \begin{cases} \lambda - 1 & \lambda > 1 \\ 0 & |\lambda| \leq 1 \\ \lambda + 1 & \lambda < -1 \end{cases}$$

3   Numerical Result and Discussion

The main parameters of the hypoid gear system are given in Table 1, an 8-DOF nonlinear dynamic system with time-varying meshing stiffness, comprehensive gear error and gear backlash shown in Fig. 1. The Runge-Kutta numerical integration method is applied to solve the dimensionless equations expressed in Eq. (10). The time history data corresponding to the first 2000 revolution of the system are excluded from the dynamic response to ensure that the data related to steady state condition. Bifurcation diagram, Time series, Fourier spectra, phase diagrams and Poincare map are used to identify the occurrence of chaotic motion to understand the dynamic response of nonlinear model.

Table 1. The parameters of the hypoid gear system.

Parameters	Pinion	Gear
Teeth numbers/z_1, z_2	10	43
Offset/mm	31.8	
Pitch angle/°	16.9	72.71
Spiral angle/°	46	33.86
Tooth width/mm	47.8	

3.1   Excitation Frequency

As show in Fig. 2, the nonlinear dynamic behavior of the steady condition of the hypoid gear system with the dimensionless excitation frequency changes. The dimensionless excitation frequency is regarded as a control variable parameter in range of $0.1 \leq \Omega \leq 1.5$. For our subsequent numerical analysis, set the damping ratio $\zeta = 0.02$, the backlash $b = 150 \ \mu m$, amplitude of comprehensive gear error as $e_n = 0.5$. When the dimensionless excitation frequency $\Omega = 0.1 \sim 0.72$, the nonlinear system performs periodic motion, then enters into chaos. At $\Omega = 0.35$, the system occurs

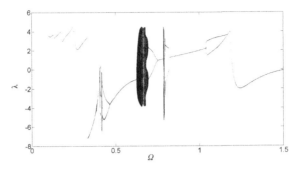

Fig. 2. Bifurcation diagram with dimensionless excitation frequency Ω as control parameter

frequency hopping. When the dimensionless excitation frequency $\Omega = 0.8$, the system degenerates from chaos to periodic motion. At $\Omega = 0.84$, the system enters into a transient chaotic motion. When the dimensionless excitation frequency increases to $\Omega = 1.5$, the nonlinear system performs periodic motion.

Comparing time history, phase plane, frequency spectrum and Poincaré map presented in Figs. 2, 3, 4 and 5, with different the dimensionless excitation frequency, we can find that the system experiences different types motions and complex and irregular bifurcation, when the system control variable parameters change slightly. Therefore, we need to avoid the system enter into the chaos.

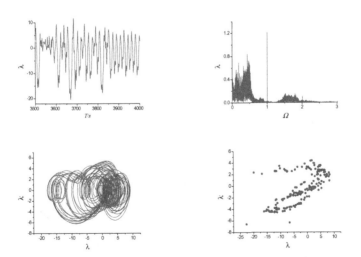

Fig. 3. Time history, phase plane, frequency spectrum and Poincaré map at $\Omega = 0.7$

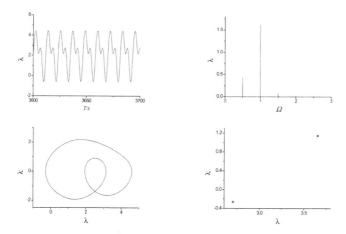

Fig. 4. Time history, phase plane, frequency spectrum and Poincaré map at $\Omega = 1.08$

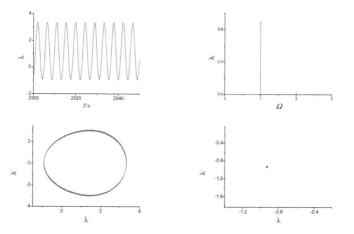

Fig. 5. Time history, phase plane, frequency spectrum and Poincaré map at $\Omega = 1.3$

3.2   Load Coefficient

Figure 6 presents the bifurcation diagram with dimensionless load coefficient f as control parameter. For Eq. (10), set the dimensionless excitation frequency $\Omega = 1$, the backlash $b = 150$ μm and amplitude of comprehensive gear error as $e_n = 0.5$. As the load coefficient increasing, we can find that the dynamic behavior of the system from the chaotic motion into periodic motion. Different vibration characteristics will be shown under different loads. Time series, Fourier spectra, phase diagram and Poincare maps are shown in Figs. 7 and 8. Figures 7 and 8 show dynamic responses for light loaded condition and heavy loaded condition at the dimensionless mesh frequency $\Omega = 1$, As illustrated in Fig. 8, the motion state is periodic harmonic motion under heavy loaded condition. It can be seen that the hypoid gear system is in chaotic motion

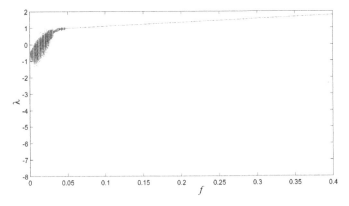

Fig. 6. Bifurcation diagram with dimensionless load coefficient f as control parameter

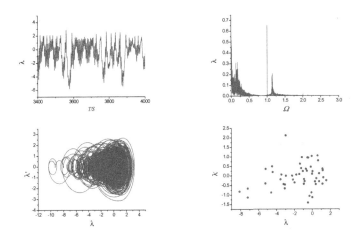

Fig. 7. Time history, phase plane, frequency spectrum and Poincaré map at $f = 0.05$

under light loaded condition and the response of the system is irregular in the chaotic state from Fig. 7. Furthermore, chaotic phenomenon is more likely to occur in light loaded condition compared with heavy loaded condition without changing other conditions.

3.3 Supporting Damping

Figure 9 presents the bifurcation diagram with dimensionless support damping ζ as control parameter. For Eq. (10), set the dimensionless excitation frequency $\Omega = 1$, the backlash $b = 150$ μm and amplitude of comprehensive gear error as $e_n = 0.5$. As the dimensionless Support damping growing, we can observe that the dynamic behavior of the system from the chaotic motion into periodic motion. Figures 10 and 11 are the different types of dynamic behaviors of the system, which presents the system abundant dynamic motions. At $\zeta = 0.02$, the dynamic behavior behaves as chaotic motion, as

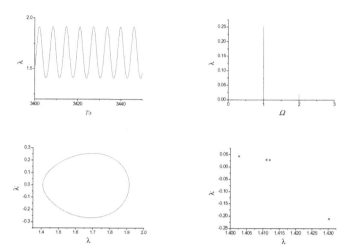

Fig. 8. Time history, phase plane, frequency spectrum and Poincaré map at $f = 0.3$

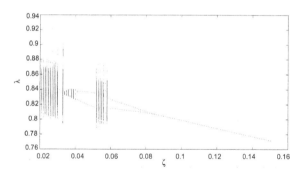

Fig. 9. Bifurcation diagram with dimensionless Support damping ζ as control parameter

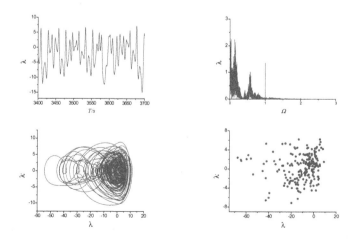

Fig. 10. Time history, phase plane, frequency spectrum and Poincaré map at $\zeta = 0.02$

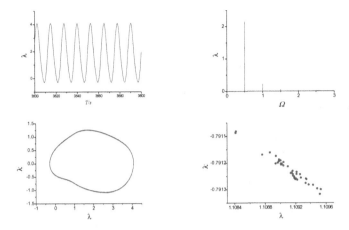

Fig. 11. Time history, phase plane, frequency spectrum and Poincaré map at $\zeta = 0.1$

shown in Fig. 10. When $\zeta = 0.1$, the dynamic behavior behaves as periodic motion, as shown in Fig. 11. According to the comparison of Time series, Fourier spectra, phase plane and Poincare maps with different damping ratio values, it can be observed that the increase in ζ tends to decrease the nonlinearity dynamic responses.

4   Conclusion

The effects of the parameters of system excitation frequency, support damping and load coefficient on the bifurcation and chaos characteristics and stability of the system are studied by qualitative methods. The conclusions are as follows:

(1) The system performs different motion states with the change of the excitation frequency under the fixed gear backlash and supporting condition. With the increase of the excitation frequency, the system changes from period state of motion to chaos, then from chaotic to dual-period. Subsequently, from the double-cycle movement to the four-cycle movement through the period of bifurcation, after the inverse cycle of bifurcation to dual-period movement, and finally into a single-period movement.

(2) Within a certain range, the load coefficient and support damping changes the system dynamic characteristics. And the increase of supporting damping and load coefficient will reduce the effect of nonlinearity effect and decrease the chaotic region of the gear system.

Acknowledgments. The authors are grateful for the financial support provided by the Industrial Common Key Technology Innovation of Chongqing (cstc2015zdcy-ztzx70013) and the Fundamental Research Funds for Central Universities (106112017CDJZRPY0018).

References

1. Kahraman, A.: Non-linear dynamics of a spur gear pair. J. Sound Vib. **142**(1), 49–75 (1990)
2. Tang, J.Y.: Effect of static transmission error on dynamic responses of spiral bevel gears. J. Central South Univ. **20**(3), 640–647 (2013)
3. Wang, J.: Dynamics of a hypoid gear pair considering the effects of time-varying mesh parameters and backlash nonlinearity. J. Sound Vib. **308**(1), 302–309 (2007)
4. Kiyono, S.: Analysis of vibration of Bevel gear. JSME Int. J. **24**(188), 441–446 (1981)
5. Mohammadpour, M.: Effect of tapered roller bearing supports on the dynamic behavior of hypoid gear pair differentials. Proc. Inst. Mech. Eng. Part D J. Automobile Eng. **230**(8) (2016)
6. Peng, T.: Influence of gyroscopic effect on hypoid and bevel geared system dynamics. SAE Int. J. Passeng. Cars Mech. Syst. **2**(1), 1377–1386 (2009)
7. Yang, X.Y.: Bifurcation and chaos of nonlinear systems with spiral bevel gears. J. Vib. Shock **27**(11), 115–125 (2008)
8. Yang, H.B.: Non-linear dynamics of hypoid gears. Autom. Eng. **22**(1), 51–54 (2000)

Rotordynamics of a High Speed
Quill Shaft Coupling

Sheng Feng, Baisong Yang, Haipeng Geng$^{(\boxtimes)}$, and Lie Yu

State Key Laboratory for Strength and Vibration of Mechanical Structures,
Xi'an Jiaotong University, Xi'an 710049, Shaanxi, China
`feng-7531@163.com, 309586755@qq.com, 371868218@qq.com,`
`245135984@qq.com`

Abstract. In this paper, a quill shaft coupling is built and analyzed. The quill shaft coupling is a solid and thin shaft with two flexural elements on the both ends of the shaft. The flexural element is represented by an angular stiffness and a radial stiffness. The equation of motion of the quill shaft coupling is derived by the finite element method. Three groups of the quill shaft coupling are analyzed. They are a stiff coupling, a radial stiff but an angular flexible coupling, and a coupling flexibly in both the radial and angular directions. The effects of the stiffness of the flexural element and the length of the quill shaft on the first bending critical speed are studied. The results show that these two parameters could be used to raise the first bending critical speed of the quill shaft coupling above the operating speed of the system.

Keywords: Rotordynamics · A quill shaft coupling · Critical speed
Stiffness

1 Introduction

A quill shaft coupling, with a solid and thin shaft, transfer the torque moment from a primer machine to a driven shaft to realize the high speed rotation demand. The quill shaft coupling has many advantages when comparing with the other plain couplings, which can great reducing the overhung weight, torsional vibrations and pulsations; using much smaller seal as a result of the small diameter of the quill shaft.

The quill shaft coupling, which can be used together with one or two flexural elements attached to the two ends of the quill-shaft. Figure 1 shows a quill shaft coupling with two thin diaphragms on the ends of the shaft. A quill shaft coupling with two splines is sketched in Fig. 2, while Fig. 3 shows a quill shaft with a flange on each end of the quill shaft coupling. There are also many forms of a quill shaft coupling, here only name a few of them.

In the past, the rotordynamics of the quill shaft coupling rotor systems have been investigated. Anderson [1] sketched two types of quill shaft couplings applied in turbo compressor. They listed the advantages of using these quill-shaft couplings. Heinrich et al. [2] studied a high speed turbo-compressor system connected by flexible intermediate shafts. They classified the intermediate shafts as solid couplings and developed the design and usage of the solid couplings. The critical speeds of their high speed

© Springer Nature Singapore Pte Ltd. 2018
S. Wang et al. (Eds.): ICSEE 2018/IMIOT 2018, CCIS 923, pp. 529–539, 2018.
https://doi.org/10.1007/978-981-13-2396-6_49

Fig. 1. A quill shaft coupling with a circular plate on the each end

Fig. 2. Schematic of a quill shaft coupling with a spline on each end

Fig. 3. A quill shaft coupling with a flanges on each end

system connected with different couplings were analyzed. These couplings contain a flexible-disc or gear coupling, solid couplings. They found that the solid couplings enable compressors to rotate at higher speeds. Kelm and Leader [3] modeled a flexible coupling by a long quill shaft with one flexural element on its one end. The flexural element of the quill shaft was represented by a lateral and torsional stiffnesses in the finite element models. A quill shaft with a length of 285 mm and a diameter 30 mm was used to connect a motor and a compressor together in Schmied and Pradetto's paper [4]. They concluded that using such quill shaft coupling enables the rotor has higher natural frequencies than with the result of a diaphragm coupling and the maximum speed gained sufficient margin to the second bending mode of the compressor. In Vanniniet's et al. [5] test rig, a quill shaft coupling was also used. Of which the quill shaft coupling is used to connected the gearbox and bolts are used to connect the intermediate shaft. Walton II et al. [6] explained a quill-shaft coupling with two attached flanges used to connect the shafts. Heshmat, Walton II and Hunsberger [7] studied a high-speed power turbogenerator connected by a quill shaft. McLuckie did a high speed seal experiment on a rotor system with a solid quill shaft coupling [8]. Feng, Geng and Yu analyzed the dynamics of a generator and a turbine rotor connected by a quill shaft coupling. The quill shaft coupling has an angular flexible but rigid in radial direction [9]. The literature shows that a solid quill shaft coupling is usually used to maintain the bending critical speed of the system below the maximum operating speed. However, there are three parameters of a quill shaft as known. They are the length of the quill shaft, the radial stiffness and the angular stiffness. However, how these parameters affect the bending critical speed of the system was not studied.

This paper provides an extensive study on the effects of parameters of the quill shaft coupling. The finite element method is used to model the quill shaft coupling. Variable stiffness is used to model the flexural element. Then the first bending critical speed of the quill shaft coupling is analyzed.

2 Model Development

2.1 Structure

Figure 4 shows a quill shaft coupling used to connect two shafts together. The quill shaft coupling contains a quill shaft and two flexural elements attached to two ends of the quill shaft. A radial stiffness and angular stiffness shown in Fig. 5 is used to the model the flexural element of the quill shaft coupling.

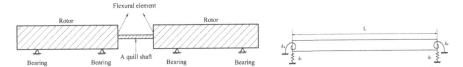

Fig. 4. A quill shaft coupling used to connect two rotors

Fig. 5. A quill shaft coupling

2.2 Modeling

Seen from Fig. 5, the quill shaft coupling is splitted into the flexural element and the shaft, and the corresponding finite element models can be explained as follows.

Shaft. A Timoshenko beam finite element is used to model the shaft and the effects of rotary inertia and transverse shear deformation are taken into account [10–12]. Each node of the Timoshenko beam element has two translational and two rotational motions and the nodal displacement vector can be illustrated in Fig. 6.

$$\{ \mathbf{q}_1 \quad \mathbf{q}_2 \}^T = [u_1 \quad v_1 \quad \beta_1 \quad \alpha_1 \quad u_2 \quad v_2 \quad \beta_2 \quad \alpha_2]^\mathrm{T} \tag{1}$$

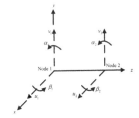

Fig. 6. Timoshenko beam model

Then equation of motion (EOM) of the above model can be expressed by the Lagrangian form:

$$[\mathbf{M}_\mathrm{e}]\left\{\begin{matrix}\ddot{\mathbf{q}}_1\\\ddot{\mathbf{q}}_2\end{matrix}\right\} + \Omega[\mathbf{G}_\mathrm{e}]\left\{\begin{matrix}\dot{\mathbf{q}}_1\\\dot{\mathbf{q}}_2\end{matrix}\right\} + [\mathbf{K}_\mathrm{e}]\left\{\begin{matrix}\mathbf{q}_1\\\mathbf{q}_2\end{matrix}\right\} = \{\mathbf{F}_\mathrm{con}\} \tag{2}$$

where $[\mathbf{K_e}]$, $[\mathbf{G_e}]$ and $[\mathbf{M_e}]$ are the stiffness matrix for a beam element, the gyro-scopic matrix and the mass matrix, respectively; $\{\mathbf{F_{con}}\}$ is interconnecting force on the beam element. Their expressions can be found in the book written by Friswell et al. [10].

The Flexural Element. The flexural element follows the governing equation

$$[\mathbf{K_c}]\{\mathbf{q_c}\} = \{\mathbf{F_c}\} \tag{3}$$

where $[\mathbf{K_c}]$ is the stiffness matrix of the flexural element, $\{\mathbf{F_c}\}$ is the external force and the displacement vector $\{\mathbf{q_c}\}$ of the flexural element can be represented by

$$\{\mathbf{q_c}\} = \{\, u_c \quad v_c \quad \beta_c \quad \alpha_c \,\}^T \tag{4}$$

2.3   Equation of Motion

After combining the matrices of the shafts and the flexural element, we can drive the EOM of the system as follows

$$[\mathbf{M}]\{\ddot{\mathbf{q}}\} + \Omega[\mathbf{G}]\{\dot{\mathbf{q}}\} + [\mathbf{K}]\{\mathbf{q}\} = \{\mathbf{0}\} \tag{5}$$

where adding the mass matrices of the shaft $[\mathbf{M_e}]$ to get the mass matrix. The matrix $[\mathbf{G}]$ includes the gyroscopic moment shaft $[\mathbf{G_e}]$. The stiffness matrix $[\mathbf{K}]$ contains the stiffness matrix of the shaft elements $[\mathbf{K_e}]$ and the flexural element $[\mathbf{K_c}]$. The vector $\{\mathbf{q}\}$ consists of the displacement vector at the nodes.

3   Dynamics of the Quill-Shaft Coupling

In order to get the parameter of the quill shaft effects on the dynamics of the system, the natural frequencies and mode shapes needs to find. They can be derived by solving the eigenvalues of Eq. (5). To get the eigenvalues, we need convert the EOM into a state space

$$\begin{bmatrix} \Omega[\mathbf{G}] & [\mathbf{M}] \\ [\mathbf{M}] & \mathbf{0} \end{bmatrix} \frac{d}{dt} \left\{ \begin{array}{c} \{\mathbf{q}\} \\ \{\dot{\mathbf{q}}\} \end{array} \right\} + \begin{bmatrix} [\mathbf{K}] & [\mathbf{0}] \\ [\mathbf{0}] & -[\mathbf{M}] \end{bmatrix} \left\{ \begin{array}{c} \{\mathbf{q}\} \\ \{\dot{\mathbf{q}}\} \end{array} \right\} = \{\mathbf{0}\} \tag{6}$$

Using the state vector $\{\mathbf{x}\} = \{\, \{\mathbf{q}\} \quad \{\dot{\mathbf{q}}\} \,\}^T$, the first-order differential equation takes the form

$$[\mathbf{A}]\{\dot{\mathbf{x}}\} + [\mathbf{B}]\{\mathbf{x}\} = \{\mathbf{0}\} \tag{7}$$

where

$$[\mathbf{A}] = \begin{bmatrix} \Omega[\mathbf{G}] & [\mathbf{M}] \\ [\mathbf{M}] & [\mathbf{0}] \end{bmatrix}, [\mathbf{B}] = \begin{bmatrix} [\mathbf{K}] & [\mathbf{0}] \\ [\mathbf{0}] & -[\mathbf{M}] \end{bmatrix} \tag{8}$$

Assuming the solutions of the Eq. (8) take the form

$$\{\mathbf{q}(t)\} = \{\mathbf{\Psi}\}e^{\lambda t} \tag{9}$$

then $\{\mathbf{x}(t)\} = \{\mathbf{X}\}e^{\lambda t} = \{\{\mathbf{\Psi}\} \quad \lambda\{\mathbf{\Psi}\}\}^{\mathrm{T}}e^{\lambda t}$ can be derived. Substituting the expression of $\{\mathbf{x}\}$ into Eq. (7) yields

$$\lambda[\mathbf{A}]\{\mathbf{X}\} + [\mathbf{B}]\{\mathbf{X}\} = \mathbf{0} \tag{10}$$

Equation (10) can be rewritten as

$$[\mathbf{H}]\{\mathbf{X}\} = \lambda\{\mathbf{X}\} \tag{11}$$

where

$$[\mathbf{H}] = -[\mathbf{A}]^{-1}[\mathbf{B}] = \begin{bmatrix} [\mathbf{0}] & [\mathbf{I}] \\ -[\mathbf{M}]^{-1}[\mathbf{K}] & -\Omega[\mathbf{M}^{-1}][\mathbf{G}] \end{bmatrix} \tag{12}$$

Matrix [**H**] is asymmetrical and Eq. (11) becomes a real asymmetrical eigenvalue problem, and the eigenvalues λ of this equation consist of pure imaginary conjugate pairs. The magnitude of the pure imaginary conjugate pairs corresponds to the natural frequencies of the system [10]. In the same way, the corresponding eigenvectors $\{\mathbf{x}\}$ also have a form of complex conjugate pairs. Using the knowledge of rotordynamics, we can obtain the whirl direction and the mode shape of the rotor. The details of decision of the whirl direction of mode can be found in the book written by Friswell et al. [10].

4 Numerical Analysis

These values are used in the simulation:$E = 2.1 \times 10^{11}$ Pa, $\mu = 0.3$, $D_q = 10$ mm. Three groups of the quill shaft coupling are given, which are a stiff case when $k_r \to \infty$ and $k_a \to \infty$, an angular flexibility case when $k_r \to \infty$, and an angular and radial flexibility case when both k_r and k_a have a finite value. The units of k_r and k_a are N/m and Nm/rad, respectively.

4.1 A Stiff Case

In this case, both of k_r and k_a have an infinite value. Table 1 shows the first four bending critical speeds of the system. It should be noted that the differences between ω_1, ω_2 and ω_3, ω_4 are small. This is due to the thin and long of the quill shaft, thus the gyroscopic moment has a minimal impact on the natural frequency of the system. This can be easily found in the natural frequency map of the quill shaft coupling in Fig. 7. The differences between the two groups of lines in Fig. 7 are still marginally small although they are enlarged in the boxed areas.

Table 1. The first four bending critical speeds of the stiff case (rev/min)

L	$\omega 1$	$\omega 2$	$\omega 3$	$\omega 4$
100	261450	264500	665000	691400
120	184700	186700	481200	496000
140	137500	138500	362600	371500
160	105900	106500	282480	287960
180	84100	84400	225850	229420
200	68350	68620	184500	186920
220	56650	56820	153400	155140
240	47700	47820	129500	130700

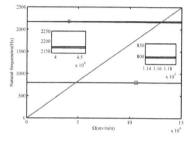

Fig. 7. The natural frequency map of the quill shaft coupling for L = 240 mm

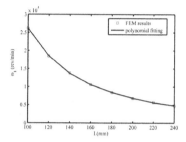

Fig. 8. The first bending critical speed of the quill shaft coupling

From Table 1 it is seen that the length of the quill shaft affects the first bending critical speed of the system significantly. The first bending critical speed ω_1 increases 450% when the length of the quill shaft decreases from 240 mm to 100 mm. If the maximum operating speed of the system is 60,000 rev/min, then the first bending critical speed for L = 200 mm has an additional margin of 13.9%.

To further understand the effect of the length on the first bending critical speed of the quill shaft coupling. The relationship between ω_1 and L was approximated by means of polynomial functions. The line in Fig. 8, fitted by a second-order polynomial approximations, can be written as

$$\omega_1 = 159240 - 26300L + 180L^2 \tag{13}$$

Figure 9 shows the first four bending modes for $\Omega = 40000$ rev/min and L = 240 mm. Figure 9(a) and (b) are a pair of the first bending modes and Fig. 9(c) and (d) are a pair of the second bending modes.

4.2   An Angular Flexibility Case

This case corresponds to $k_r \rightarrow \infty$ and a finite value of k_a. The first bending critical speed is plotted against L for several values of the angular stiffness k_a in Fig. 10, and their values are listed in Table 2.

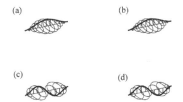

Fig. 9. Modes from 1 to 4 when $\Omega = 40000$ rev/min (a) mode 1 (795 Hz) (b) mode 2 (796 Hz) (c) mode 3 (2166 Hz) (d) mode 4 (2172 Hz)

The first bending critical speed of the quill shaft coupling increases with an increase of k_a and decreases with an increase of the length of the quill shaft coupling. If the maximum operating speed of the system is 60,000 rev/min, the ranges of length L and k_a on the upper right corner of the lines in Table 2 are available for the system. Combining Table 2 with Table 1, when L = 220 mm or 240 mm, changing the value of k_a can not increase the first bending critical speed above 60,000 rev/min. It can be realized by reducing the length of the quill shaft coupling. However, when the length of the quill shaft is smaller than 200 mm, it would be possible to increase the first bending critical speed above 60000 rev/min either by increasing the angular stiffness k_a or decreasing the length of the quill shaft coupling.

Table 2. The first bending critical speed of the quill shaft coupling for $k_r \to \infty$ (rev/min)

L	k_a =100	k_a =1000	k_a=10000	k_a =100000	k_a =1000000
100	122300	139500	204500	252150	260400
120	85800	99700	148100	179250	184200
140	63500	75200	112500	133700	136900
160	48910	58900	88050	103400	105600
180	38850	47500	70950	82320	83920
200	31610	39200	58420	67050	68240
220	26240	32970	48930	55650	56550
240	22140	28140	41580	47050	47600

4.3   An Angular and Radial Flexibility Case

For $k_r = 10^6, 10^7, 10^8$, the first bending critical speed of the system is plotted against L for several values of the radial stiffness k_a in Figs. 11, 12 and 13, respectively. More specially, the values of the first bending critical speed are listed in Tables 3, 4 and 5, respectively.

It can be seen that the gaps between the lines in Fig. 11 becomes larger with an increase of L. However, these gaps keep almost constant for Fig. 12 and become smaller with increase of L for Fig. 13.

From Table 3, if the maximum operating speed is 60,000 rpm, neither reducing the length of the quill shaft nor increasing the angular stiffness k_a can not increase the first bending critical speed above 60,000 rev/min.

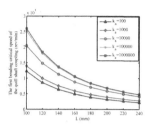

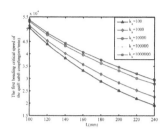

Fig. 10. The first bending critical speed of a stiff quill shaft coupling for different radial stiffness constants k_a

Fig. 11. The first bending critical speed of a flexible quill shaft coupling for $k_r = 10^6$ N/m

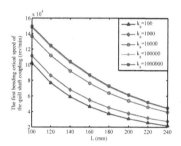

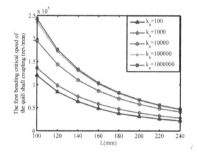

Fig. 12. The first bending critical speed of a flexible quill shaft coupling for $k_r = 10^7$ N/m

Fig. 13. The first bending critical speed of a flexible quill shaft coupling for $k_r = 10^8$ N/m

Table 3. The first bending critical of the quill shaft when $k_r = 10^6$ N/m

L	$k_a = 100$	$k_a = 1000$	$k_a = 10000$	$k_a = 100000$	$k_a = 1000000$
100	50556	51440	53122	53652	53717
120	43936	45340	47762	48464	48547
140	38211	40175	43354	44227	44330
160	33201	35690	39567	40602	40723
180	28837	31750	36212	37390	37528
200	25075	28285	33182	34475	34626
220	21865	25247	30142	31786	31945
240	19141	22590	27868	29284	29450

Similarly, the lines in Tables 4 and 5 are separate lines of the operating speed 60,000 rev/min. It is found that the available ranges of the L and k_a in Table 4 are wider than that of Table 5.

It is found that increasing the radial stiffness k_r can widen the available range of the first bending critical speed above the operating speed from Tables 3, 4 and 5.

Table 4. The first bending critical speed of the quill shaft coupling for $k_r = 10^7 \text{N/m}$

L	k_a=100	k_a=1000	k_a=10000	k_a =100000	k_a =1000000
100	102390	111610	136670	147870	149390
120	76831	86325	111930	123540	125140
140	59066	68130	92068	102940	104420
160	46530	54890	76275	85805	87116
180	37485	45088	63776	71840	72930
200	30790	37675	53860	60570	61460
220	25720	31958	45950	51480	52220
240	21795	27460	39575	44160	44765

Table 5. The first bending critical speed of the quill shaft when $k_r = 10^8$ N/m

L	k_a=100	k_a=1000	k_a=10000	k_a =100000	k_a =1000000
100	120170	136300	195240	235810	242570
120	84893	98380	143820	172090	176580
140	63701	74502	110070	130200	133250
160	48685	58512	86850	101560	103710
180	37820	47271	70250	81264	82824
200	31540	39055	57960	66416	67580
220	26190	32870	48650	55250	56140
240	22110	28083	41401	46660	47350

5 Conclusions

Based on the model of the quill shaft coupling and finite element method, the EOM of the system has been obtained and analyzed. Of which the shaft was represented by Timoshenko beam element and the quill shaft coupling was modeled by a radial stiffness and an angular stiffness. The available ranges of the first bending critical speed above the operating speed were analyzed.

From discussions above, we can draw some conclusions as follows:

1. For L = 220 and L = 240 mm, changing the radial stiffness and angular stiffness would not make the first bending critical speed above the maximum operating speed 60,000 rev/min. It can be realized by reducing the length of quill shaft.
2. When the length of the quill shaft ranges from 100 mm to 240 mm, and ka ranges from 100 Nm/rad to 1000000 Nm/rad, all the values of the first bending critical speed are below the maximum operating speed 60,000 rev/min.
3. Increasing the radial stiffness kr can widen the available range of the first bending critical speed above the operating speed.

Acknowledgments. The authors are pleased to acknowledge the support of the 973 project of China (Grant No. 2013CB035704), and the NSFC Grants No. 51375366, 51139005.

Appendix

Notation

A_e	the cross-sectional area of the quill shaft
D_q, E	diameter of the quill shaft and elastic modulus
FEM	Finite Element Method
$\{\mathbf{F}_c\}$, $\{\mathbf{F}_{con}\}$	external force vector and connecting forces on the quill shaft coupling
$[\mathbf{G}]$, $[\mathbf{G}_e]$	gyroscopic matrix of the system and a beam element
I_e	the second moment of area of a beam element's cross-section
$[\mathbf{K}]$, $[\mathbf{K}_c]$, $[\mathbf{K}_e]$	stiffness matrix of the system, the quill shaft coupling and beam
l_e, L	the beam element's length and the quill shaft coupling's length
$[\mathbf{M}]$, $[\mathbf{M}_e]$	mass matrix of the system and beam element
k_r, k_a	radial stiffness and angular stiffness of the quill shaft coupling
u, v	lateral (x- and y-direction) displacements, respectively.
α, β	rotation around x- and y-direction, respectively.
ρ, v	density and Poisson ratio
ω_i	the ith bending critical speed of the quill shaft coupling, i=1,2,3,4
Ω	spinning speed of the system
T	transpose of the matrix
c, e	the quill shaft coupling element and beam element

References

1. Anderson, J.H.: Turbocompressor drive couplings. ASME J. Eng. Power **84**, 115–121 (1962)
2. Heinrich, L., Niedermann, E.A., Wattinger, W.: Solid couplings with flexible intermediate shafts for high speed turbocompressor trains. In: Proceedings of the Eighteenth Turbomechinery Symposium, Texas (1989)
3. Kelm, R.D., Leader, M.E.: Improving the reliability of a high speed refrigeration compressor. In: Proceedings of the 36th Turbomachinery Symposium, Texas (2007)
4. Schmied, J., Pradetto, J.C.: Rotor dynamic behavior of a high-speed oil-free motor compressor with a rigid coupling supported on four radial magnetic bearings. NASA, USA (1994). N94-35911
5. Vannini, G., Cioncolini, S., Calicchio, V., et al.: Development of a high pressure rotordynamic test rig for centrifugal compressors internal seals characterization. In: Proceedings of the Fortieth Turbomachinery Symposium, Houston (2011)
6. Walton II, J.F., Heshmat, H., Tomaszewski, M.: Power loss in high-speed turbomachinery - an experimental study. In: Proceedings of ASME Turbo Expo 2012, Copenhagen (2012)
7. Heshmat, H., Walton II, J.F., Hunsberger, A.: Oil-free 8 KW high-speed and high specific power turbogenerator. In: Proceedings of ASME Turbo Expo 2014: Turbine Technical Conference and Exposition, GT 2014, Dusseldorf (2014)
8. McLuckie, I.R.W.: Instability studies of an 'O'-ring flexibly supported, gas bearing, mounted, cool air unit. Cranfield Institute of Technology, UK (1990). Doctor of Philosophy

9. Feng, S., Geng, H.P., Yu, L.: Rotordynamics analysis of a quill-shaft coupling-rotor-bearing system. Proc. IMechE Part C J. Mech. Eng. Sci. (2014). https://doi.org/10.1177/0954406214543673
10. Friswell, M.I., Penny, J.E.T., Garvey, S.D., et al.: Dynamics of Rotating Machines. Cambridge University Press, New York (2010)
11. To, C.W.S.: A linearly tapered beam finite element incorporating shear deformation and rotary inertia for vibration analysis. J. Sound Vib. **78**, 475–484 (1981)
12. Thomas, D.L., Wilson, J.M., Wilson, R.R.: Timoshenko beam finite elements. J. Sound Vib. **31**, 315–330 (1973)

Kinematics Based Sliding-Mode Control for Trajectory Tracking of a Spherical Mobile Robot

Wei Li[1,2] and Qiang Zhan[2(✉)]

[1] Ecole Centrale de Pékin, Beihang University,
37 Xueyuan Road, Beijing 100191, China
[2] Robotics Institute, Beihang University,
37 Xueyuan Road, Beijing 100191, China
qzhan@buaa.edu.cn

Abstract. Spherical mobile robot (spherical robot in short) has remarkable stability, flexible motion as well as significant advantages in the exploration of unmanned environments when compared with traditional mobile robots. However, as a special under-actuated nonholonomic system spherical robot cannot be transformed to the classic chained form and is difficult to control. At present, there has not been a kinematics based trajectory tracking controller which could track both the position states and the attitude states of spherical robot simultaneously. This paper deduced a three states (two position states and one attitude state) trajectory tracking controller using sliding-mode control method and based on the kinematic model of a spherical mobile robot BHQ-1. The jittering on the sliding surface was reduced under the effect of a saturation function in the controller. The effectiveness of the proposed trajectory tracking controller were verified through MATLAB simulations for both a linear trajectory and a circular trajectory.

Keywords: Spherical mobile robot · Nonholonomic kinematics
Trajectory tracking · Sliding-mode control

1 Introduction

Spherical mobile robot is a fully enclosed robot which envelopes all its mechanisms and devices in a ball-shaped outer shell. Spherical robot has very compact structure, flexible motion and remarkable stability as a roly-poly that can make it regain balance when it collides with obstacles or even falls down from a high place. Hence, spherical robot is very suitable to work in unmanned environments like outer planets. However, spherical mobile robot is a special highly underactuated nonholonomic system which cannot be transformed to the classic chained form, so new control methods should be researched.

Open loop control is developed in Refs. [1–5] to validate the mathematical models of spherical robots and test those robot's motions. But the control accuracy is not high enough for practical applications. Hence, the closed loop control of spherical robot is required. Trajectory tracking control plays an important role among the closed loop

© Springer Nature Singapore Pte Ltd. 2018
S. Wang et al. (Eds.): ICSEE 2018/IMIOT 2018, CCIS 923, pp. 540–547, 2018.
https://doi.org/10.1007/978-981-13-2396-6_50

control, because it is the basis to independently implement tasks in unmanned environments. The trajectory tracking controllers proposed in Refs. [6–9] can track the position states, but the pose of spherical robot is not controlled. When the robot moves along a desired path, it swings with large amplitude. This is not acceptable to the practical applications, because the inside equipment of the robot needs a stable working platform. References [10, 11] take the control of pose into account, but the controllers are based on the dynamic model which depends on the structure of robot. Thus it is difficult to apply them to other spherical robots with different models or different structures.

However, a kinematics based controller has generality and can be applied by other spherical robots. To the best of our knowledge, there has not been a trajectory tracking controller based on the kinematic model of spherical robot which can track both the position states and the attitude states. This paper proposed a three-state trajectory tracking controller for a spherical robot BHQ-1 (Fig. 1) based on its kinematic model, which can track two position states and one attitude state simultaneously.

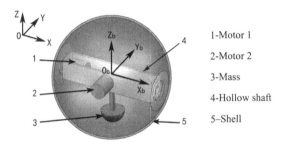

Fig. 1. Mechanical structure of BHQ-1

The structure of the paper is organized as follows: In Sect. 2, the mechanical structure and the kinematic model of BHQ-1 are presented. In Sect. 3, a sliding-mode trajectory tracking controller is proposed. In Sect. 4, the simulation results for the linear trajectory tracking and the circular trajectory tracking are provided. The conclusions of the paper are given in Sect. 5.

2 Mechanical Structure and Kinematic Model of Spherical Robot BHQ-1

2.1 Mechanical Structure

The spherical robot BHQ-1 (Fig. 1) is a pendulum-driven spherical robot which can move by changing the center of its gravity. It is composed of a shell, a mass, two motors and a hollow shaft. Two motors can control the forward and veer motion through the following principles. When only motor 1 rotates around axis X_b, the rotation of the pendulum makes the robot moves forward or backward under the action of the gravity torque. When the two motors rotate simultaneously, the mass and the hollow shaft will tilt to make the robot veer.

2.2   Kinematic Model

As illustrated in Fig. 2, we use ZYX Euler angle which is denoted by (ψ, β, φ) to describe the pose of BHQ-1. $OXYZ$, $O_bX_bY_bZ_b$ and $O'X'Y'Z'$ are three right-hand coordinate frames that respectively correspond to the world frame, the frame fixed on the outer shell, and the frame which is fixed on the geometrical center of the spherical robot and parallel to the reference frame.

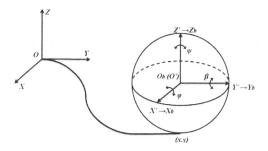

Fig. 2.   Euler angles and coordinate frames of BHQ-1

The spherical robot's configuration can be described by $p = [x \quad y \quad \psi \quad \beta \quad \varphi]^T$, where (x, y) denotes the position of the geometric center of the robot. Then, the kinematic model is expressed as following:

$$\dot{p}(t) = J(p) \cdot u(t) \tag{1}$$

In Eq. (1), $u = \begin{bmatrix} \dot{\varphi} & \dot{\beta} \end{bmatrix}^T$ is the angular velocity of the spherical robot, J is the Jacobian matrix that can be expressed as

$$J(p) = \begin{bmatrix} R \sin\psi \cos\beta & R \cos\psi \\ -R \cos\psi \cos\beta & R \sin\psi \\ \sin\beta & 0 \\ 0 & 1 \\ 1 & 0 \end{bmatrix}$$

where R is the radius of the spherical robot.

3 Trajectory Tracking Controller

3.1 Sliding-Mode Control

Sliding Mode Control (SMC in short) is a variable structure control method that uses discontinuous control signal to force the system to slide along the boundaries of the system's normal states. [12] The geometrical locus including the boundaries is called "sliding surface" and this kind of motion along the sliding surface is called "sliding mode". The major advantage of sliding mode is high robustness to system's parameters and external disturbances.

The design of a sliding-mode controller could be divided to two steps:

(1) Design the switching function $s(x)$ to ensure the asymptotical stable of the sliding mode;
(2) Design the sliding-mode control law $u(x)$ to make the sliding-mode achievable.

3.2 Trajectory Tracking Controller Design

In this section, we propose a three-state trajectory tracking controller for BHQ-1 using sliding-mode control. The three states of the spherical robot to be controlled are denoted by $X = [x \quad y \quad \psi]^T$ and the desired trajectory of the three states is denoted by $X_d = [x_d \quad y_d \quad \psi_d]^T$. Then the three states trajectory tracking problem based on the kinematic equation Eq. (1) can be described by

$$\dot{X} = G \cdot u \tag{2}$$

Where

$$G = \begin{bmatrix} R \sin \psi \cos \beta & R \cos \psi \\ -R \cos \psi \cos \beta & R \sin \psi \\ \sin \beta & 1 \end{bmatrix},$$

$$u = \begin{bmatrix} \dot{\varphi} & \dot{\beta} \end{bmatrix}^T$$

Therefore, the tracking error is got as following:

$$e = X_d - X = \begin{bmatrix} e_x & e_y & e_\psi \end{bmatrix}^T = \begin{bmatrix} x_d - x \\ y_d - y \\ \psi_d - \psi \end{bmatrix} \tag{3}$$

We define the switching function of the sliding-mode controller as following:

$$s = \begin{bmatrix} s_1 & s_2 & s_3 \end{bmatrix}^T = C \cdot e \tag{4}$$

where C is a constant matrix defined as

$$C = \begin{bmatrix} c_x & 0 & 0 \\ 0 & c_y & 0 \\ 0 & 0 & c_\psi \end{bmatrix}, c_x > 0, c_y > 0, c_\psi > 0$$

And we use the exponential reaching law to force the system to attain the sliding surface $s = 0$

$$\dot{s} = -\varepsilon \cdot SGN(s) - ks \tag{5}$$

where ε and k are two positive constants that represent the reaching speed and SGN is the sign function from a 3×1 vector to a 3×1 vector.

In order to reduce the chattering along the sliding surface, we replaced the sign function with a saturation function defined as

$$SAT(s) = \begin{bmatrix} sat(s_1) \\ sat(s_2) \\ sat(s_3) \end{bmatrix}, \delta = \begin{bmatrix} \delta_1 \\ \delta_2 \\ \delta_3 \end{bmatrix}, sat(s_i) = \begin{cases} 1, & s_i > \delta_i \\ \frac{s_i}{\delta_i}, & |s_i| \le \delta_i \\ -1, & s_i < -\delta_i \end{cases} (i = 1, 2, 3)$$

where δ is a vector of three small positive constants. The improved reaching law becomes

$$\dot{s} = -\varepsilon \cdot SAT(s) - ks \tag{6}$$

Then we define $V = \frac{1}{2} s^T s$ as a Lyapunov function candidate, therefore its time derivative is

$$\dot{V} = \dot{s}s = -\varepsilon \cdot SAT(s) \cdot s - ks \cdot s \le 0 \tag{7}$$

and

$$\dot{V} = 0 \leftrightarrow s = 0 \leftrightarrow e = 0 \tag{8}$$

Hence, $\dot{V}$ is negative definite and s is asymptotical stable.

We can get the time derivate of s from Eqs. (2)–(4) as

$$\dot{s} = C \cdot \dot{e} = C \cdot (\dot{X}_d - \dot{X}) = C \cdot (\dot{X}_d - Gu) \tag{9}$$

Then we can calculate the control law u from Eqs. (6) and (9).

$$C \cdot (\dot{X}_d - Gu) = -\varepsilon \cdot SAT(s) - ks \tag{10}$$

$$\rightarrow u = G^+ \cdot \left[\dot{X}_d + C^{-1}(\varepsilon \cdot SAT(s) + ks) \right] \tag{11}$$

where G^+ denotes the generalized inverse of matrix G.

4   Simulations for Trajectory Tracking

In order to verify the effectiveness of the controller, we take two typical trajectories into account for the simulations in MATLAB: the linear trajectory and the circular trajectory. We first define the desired trajectory of the three states to track along a straight line and the initial configuration of all the five states as follows:

$$X_d(t) = \begin{bmatrix} x_d(t) \\ y_d(t) \\ \psi_d(t) \end{bmatrix} = \begin{bmatrix} \frac{\sqrt{2}}{2}t \\ \frac{\sqrt{2}}{2}t \\ -\frac{\pi}{4} \end{bmatrix} \tag{12}$$

$$p_0 = \begin{bmatrix} x_0 & y_0 & \psi_0 & \beta_0 & \varphi_0 \end{bmatrix}^T = \begin{bmatrix} 0 & 1 & 0 & 0 & 0 \end{bmatrix}^T$$

All the eight parameters in the sliding-mode control law are defined as follows:

$$\varepsilon = 0.2, k = 1, c_x = 10, c_y = 0.05, c_\psi = 1, \delta_1 = \delta_2 = 0.01, \delta_3 = 0.05$$

Figures 3 and 4 show the simulation results of linear trajectory tracking. Figure 3 shows the relationship between the desired trajectory and the actual trajectory of the robot's position. Figure 4 shows the tracking errors of the three states. We can observe from Fig. 4 that the robot achieves stability in 5 s. The tracking error of two position states and the attitude state ψ can be limited respectively within $0.01\,\text{m}$ $(1\,\text{cm})$ and $0.05\,\text{rad}$ $(2.9°)$, which are consistent with the parameters δ_1, δ_2 and δ_3.

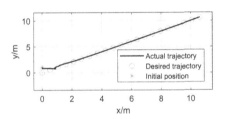

Fig. 3. Linear trajectory tracking simulation

Similarly, we simulate the circular trajectory tracking with the desired trajectory, and the initial configuration and the parameters are defined as follows:

$$X_d(t) = \begin{bmatrix} x_d(t) \\ y_d(t) \\ \psi_d(t) \end{bmatrix} = \begin{bmatrix} cos(t) \\ sin(t) \\ t \end{bmatrix} \tag{13}$$

$$p_0 = \begin{bmatrix} x_0 & y_0 & \psi_0 & \beta_0 & \varphi_0 \end{bmatrix}^T = \begin{bmatrix} 1.5 & 0 & 0 & 0 & 0 \end{bmatrix}^T$$

$$\varepsilon = 0.2, k = 5, c_x = 0.2, c_y = 2, c_\psi = 10, \delta_1 = \delta_2 = 0.01, \delta_3 = 0.05$$

Figures 5 and 6 show the simulation results of circular trajectory tracking. Figure 5 shows the desired trajectory and the actual trajectory of the robot's position. Figure 6 shows the tracking errors of the three states. From Fig. 6 we can observe that the robot reaches stability in 8 s. The tracking error of two position states and the attitude state ψ can be limited respectively within 0.01 m (1 cm) and 0.02 rad (1°).

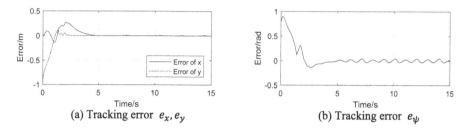

(a) Tracking error e_x, e_y (b) Tracking error e_ψ

Fig. 4. Tracking errors of three states

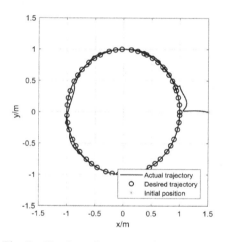

Fig. 5. Circular trajectory tracking simulation

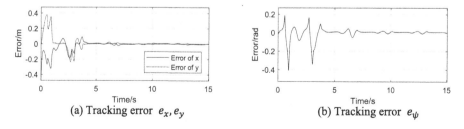

(a) Tracking error e_x, e_y (b) Tracking error e_ψ

Fig. 6. Tracking errors of three states

5 Conclusions

This paper proposed a three states trajectory tracking controller using sliding-mode control based on the kinematic model of a spherical robot. In order to reduce the jittering on the sliding surface, we defined a saturation function to improve the exponential reaching law. The asymptotical stability of the sliding mode was demonstrated through Lyapunov's method. The simulations for the linear trajectory tracking and the circular trajectory tracking were used to verify the effectiveness of the proposed controller. The simulation results showed that the tracking errors could be limited within desired values when the system converged to stability.

References

1. Zhan, Q., Jia, C., Ma, X., Zhai, Y.: Mechanism design and motion analysis of a sphericle mobile robot. Chin. J. Mech. Eng. **18**(4), 542–545 (2005)
2. Tomik, F., Nudehi, S., Flynn, L.L., Mukherjee, R.: Design, fabrication and control of spherobot: a spherical mobile robot. J. Intell. Robot. Syst. **67**(2), 117–131 (2012)
3. Mahboubi, S., Fakhrabadi, M.M.S., Ghanbari, A.: Design and implementation of a novel spherical mobile robot. J. Intell. Robot. Syst. **71**(1), 43–64 (2013)
4. Chen, W.H., Chen, C.P., Tsai, J.S., Yang, J., Lin, P.C.: Design and implementation of a ball-driven omnidirectional spherical robot. Mech. Mach. Theory **68**(68), 35–48 (2013)
5. Dejong, B.P., Karadogan, E., Yelamarthi, K., Hasbany, J.: Design and analysis of a four-pendulum omnidirectional spherical robot. J. Intell. Robot. Syst. **86**(1), 1–13 (2017)
6. Muralidharan, V., Mahindrakar, A.D.: Geometric controllability and stabilization of spherical robot dynamics. IEEE Trans. Automat. Control **60**(10), 2762–2767 (2015)
7. Kayacan, E., Bayraktaroglu, Z.Y., Saeys, W.: Modeling and control of a spherical rolling robot: a decoupled dynamics approach. Robotica **30**(4), 671–680 (2012)
8. Cai, Y., Zhan, Q., Yan, C.: Two-state trajectory tracking control of a spherical robot using neurodynamics. Robotica **30**(2), 195–203 (2012)
9. Yu, T., Sun, H., Jia, Q., Zhang, Y.: Stabilization and control of a spherical robot on an inclined plane. Res. J. Appl. Sci. Eng. Technol. **5**(6), 2289–2296 (2013)
10. Zhan, Q., Liu, Z., Cai, Y.: A back-stepping based trajectory tracking controller for a non-chained nonholonomic spherical robot. Chin. J. Aeronaut. **21**(5), 472–480 (2008)
11. Urakubo, T., Monno, M., Maekawa, S., Tamaki, H.: Dynamic modeling and controller design for a spherical rolling robot equipped with a gyro. IEEE Trans. Control Syst. Technol. **24**(5), 1669–1679 (2016)
12. Sliding mode control. https://en.wikipedia.org/wiki/Sliding_mode_control

Design and Control of Two Degree of Freedom Powered Caster Wheels Based Omni-Directional Robot

Tianjiang Zheng[1], Jie Zhang[1], Weijun Wang[1], Sunhao song[1],
Junjie Li[1], Qiang Liu[1], Guodong Chen[2], Guilin Yang[1(✉)],
Chin-Yin Chen[1], and Chi Zhang[1]

[1] Zhejiang Key Laboratory of Robotics and Intelligent Manufacturing
Equipment Technology, Ningbo Institute of Materials Technology
and Engineering, CAS, Ningbo 315201, China
{zhengtianjiang, zhangjie, wangweijun, songsunhao,
lijunjie, liuqiang, glyang, chenchinyin,
zhangchi}@nimte.ac.cn

[2] Innovation Center of Suzhou Nano Science and Technology,
Soochow & University of Suzhou, Suzhou, China
guodongxyz@gmail.com

Abstract. Omni-directional robot has the ability of 0–360° motions are received much attention in recent years. They have locomotive advantages and are widely deployed in larger range of application fields especially in constrained narrow space. This paper introduce a novel omni-directional robot with four powered caster wheels, each caster wheel has two degree of freedom (DOF) and made by two outer rotor motors connected mechanically. The kinematics of the system are analyzed, the prototype has been developed. The developed omni-directional robot is able to realize the moving motions along x and y axis and rotate about z-axis. All of the software are implemented on Robot Operation Systems (ROS) and the velocity trajectory planner is employed and embedded in the software. The squared position curve is given and tested by using lase tracker, the result is analyzed, and it shown that the following error of the system is about 2.5 cm while the width of the square is 70 cm.

Keywords: Omni-directional robot · Powered caster wheels
Direct motor · Kinematics · Control

1 Introduction

The intelligent manufacturing and E-commerce logistics producing a huge demands on the Automated Guided Vehicle (AGV) which motivated the development of mobile robot technology [1]. The mobile robot have to fulfill various movement and tasks, especially, they should have a strong pass through ability to fit for narrow and crowd environment. Also they need to adaptive, safe, and flexible for intelligent factory applications [2]. These properties are hard to achieve by traditional differential mobile robot due to they need a big turning radius while moving.

© Springer Nature Singapore Pte Ltd. 2018
S. Wang et al. (Eds.): ICSEE 2018/IMIOT 2018, CCIS 923, pp. 548–560, 2018.
https://doi.org/10.1007/978-981-13-2396-6_51

There are many omni-directional mobile has been developed, the platforms are employed ball wheels [3], Mecanum wheels [4] and Caster wheels [5, 6] in normally. But the ball wheel is usually have the problems that it is hard to control, moreover, it is easy to get dirty that slow down their motion accuracy. They are seldom been built for industrial applications but only in laboratory. The mecanum wheels has been already used for some omni-directional roots [7, 8], but the problem is that the sliding friction exists between the wheels and the ground while the robot moving, this will restrict their application area. The robot with powered caster wheels is designed by Holmberg and Slater in 2002, their caster wheels has one problem that the steering motion of the caster wheels will generate a parasite rolling motion inevitably which make it hard to design the system controller [9]. Wada et al. developed the powered active caster wheel by using dual-ball transmission, but they are taking two balls as the transmission mechanisms [10]. Professor Yang [11] et al. have been developed the decoupled active caster wheels are applied in their mobile robot system, which showing a high performance on the robot behaving. But the designed robot need the gear system to decouple the roll motion and steer motion where the gear system will slow down the system positioning accuracy due to the backlash.

To avoid the above problems, this paper developed a novel decoupled caster wheels which is able to do the rolling motion and steering motion independently and simultaneously. The steering motion and rolling motion are decoupled. The caster is made of two outer rotor motors, the rolling motor is hang under the steering motor, these motors are designed as direct drive motor which doesn't have the reduction box and don't need the decouple mechanisms so that the motions of the caster wheels can be accurately.

In this paper we developed a two DOF wheeled power casters and built the entire omni-directional robot prototype based on it. The following Sects. 2 and 3 will introducing the mechanical design of the robot, the kinematics, and the control system will introduced at Sect. 4, final section is the experiment results and discuss about this omni-directional robot system.

2 Robot Mechanical Design

2.1 The Mobile Prototype Design

The intelligent manufacturing have the strong demands that the factory should have the flexible ability, where mobile robot will be an important execution unit of the system. The developed omni-direction mobile robot is aim to serve the major link of the intelligent manufacturing and act as a transport tool for the factory such as the cargo transfer and storage. The application environments are commonly favorable indoor sites crowded with equipment and materials, the omni-direction mobile robot is required to move flexibly and have the ability of moving towards to any direction or it can be say that have 3 DOF, that is moving along x and y axis and rotate about z axis. Our mobile robot prototype is shown in Fig. 1. Which are included four developed powered caster wheels. Figure 1(a) is the 3D model and Fig. 1(b) is the prototype.

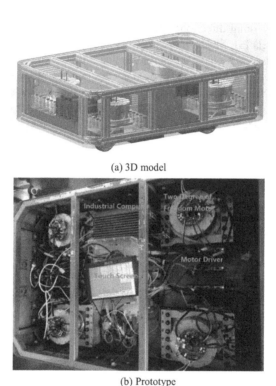

(a) 3D model

(b) Prototype

Fig. 1. Omni-directional mobile robot 3D model and the prototype machine (a) 3D model (b) prototype

2.2   The Two Degree of Freedom Caster Design

As mentioned before, our two DOF caster wheel is made of two outer rotor motor, as shown in Fig. 2(a) and (b). In Fig. 2(a) motor 1 is used to produce the steering motion and motor 2 is used to produce rolling motion. Motor 1 has been designed as center hollow structure so that the drive cable and encode cable of the motor 2 can be pass through of it. The motor 2 is hang under the motor 1 which is actually been designed as a hub motor. A modular structure with spring buffer connector mechanism has been considered in the wheel system as shown in Fig. 2(c). The spring buffer connector has been arranged in two rows (six of each) and mounted in parallel at both sides of the wheels which can absorb the shock energy and some damping energy. The stiffness of the spring was calculated according to the typical loads of the design requirements. Normally the roll motor is contact to the ground directly, it may producing the vibrations in the platform. To solve this problem we use polyurethane adhesive process to deal with the out layer of the motor.

The parameters of the omni-directional mobile system are shown in Table 1, this prototype is designed for the application of car engine transportation workshop.

(a) The 3D model of the two DOF caster   (b) the prototype of the two DOF caster

(c) The modular of the wheels with suspension system

Fig. 2. The active two DOF caster wheel and its suspension system.

Table 1. Parameters of the omni-directional mobile robot platform

Description	Quantity
Body length	1.2 m
Body width	0.8 m
High from the ground	0.38 m
Wheel diameter	0.128 m
Wheel bias	0.05 m
Mass of the body	150 kg
Maximum Load	200 kg
Max velocity of the body	1 m/s^2
Max rotational velocity of the body	2.5 rad/s

The weight of the car engine is 180 kg which is offered by the car producer company. So the typical load for the mobile robot is designed as 200 kg. Here the steering motor and the rolling motor should have a bias which will allowing the robot produce pure rolling motion without slip [12].

3 Kinematics

The developed omni-directional robot prototype employed four powered active caster wheel. The wheels mounted in symmetrically at the four corner of the robot. The simplified schematic of the robot is shown in Fig. 3.

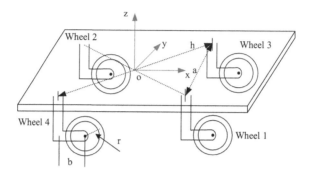

Fig. 3. The simplified robot schematic

In Fig. 3 the coordinates system has been attached on the robot, where h is the length of the diagonal line, a is the length between wheel 1 and wheel 2, b is the bias of the steering motor and rolling motor, r is the radius of the rolling wheel. Since the four wheels are arranged symmetrically, one of the two DOF caster wheels can be treated as a modular, then the kinematics of the system can be calculated first by only take one modular. Figure 4 shown the kinematics geometric relationship for one modular in 2D plane.

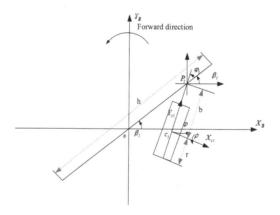

Fig. 4. Kinematics geometric relationship for one modular in 2D plane

In Fig. 4, the x-axis and y-axis of the coordinate system XYZ in Fig. 3 has been renamed as X_B and Y_B. Here we attached a new coordinate system on the rolling motor and X_{ci}, Y_{ci} is the name of x-axis and y-axis. φ_i is the angle between the rolling motor y-axis and the prototype body diagonal line. β_i is the angle between the prototype body x-axis and the body diagonal line. Then the velocity of the wheel center shown in frame $X_{BO}Y_B$ is given by:

$$^B v_{ci} = {}^B v + {}^B \omega \times {}^B P_{ci} \tag{1}$$

The velocity of $^B v_{Ci}$ can be also expressed as alongside the wheels and perpendicular to the wheels due to the no slip condition:

$$^B v_{ci} = {}^B v_{cix} + {}^B v_{ciy} \tag{2}$$

Combine Eqs. (1) and (2) gives:

$$^B v + {}^B \omega \times {}^B P_{ci} = b\dot{\phi}_i {}^B x_{ci} + r\dot{\rho}_i {}^B y_{ci} \tag{3}$$

where

$$^B x_{ci} = \begin{bmatrix} \sin(\beta_i + \varphi_i) \\ -\cos(\beta_i + \varphi_i) \end{bmatrix} {}^B Y_{ci} = \begin{bmatrix} -\cos(\beta_i + \varphi_i) \\ -\sin(\beta_i + \varphi_i) \end{bmatrix} \tag{4}$$

Equation (1) can be also written as:

$$^B \omega \times {}^B P_{ci} = \omega e_z \times {}^B P_{ci} = \omega {}^B t_{ci} \tag{5}$$

Notice that ω is a scalar, then the Eq. (3) is given by:

$$\begin{bmatrix} I_{2\times2} & {}^B t_{ci} \end{bmatrix} \begin{bmatrix} {}^B v \\ \omega \end{bmatrix} = \begin{bmatrix} b^B X_{ci} & r^B Y_{ci} \end{bmatrix} \begin{bmatrix} \dot{\phi}_i \\ \dot{\rho}_i \end{bmatrix} \tag{6}$$

where

$$^B t_{ci} = e_z \times {}^B P_{ci}, \quad e_z = \begin{bmatrix} 0 & 0 & 1 \end{bmatrix}^T,$$

$$^B P_{ci} = \overrightarrow{BP_i} + \overrightarrow{P_i\,C_i} = \overrightarrow{BP_i} + \left(b^B Y_{Ci}\right)$$

Then the inverse kinematics can be rewritten as matrix style:

$$\mathbf{AX} = \mathbf{B\dot{q}} \Rightarrow \dot{\mathbf{q}} = B^{-1} A \dot{\mathbf{X}} \tag{7}$$

where

$$\dot{\mathbf{q}} = [b\dot{\varphi}_i \quad r\dot{\rho}_i]^T, \ \mathbf{A} = \begin{bmatrix} 1 & 0 & -h\sin\beta_i + b\sin(\beta_i + \varphi_i) \\ 0 & 1 & h\cos\beta_i - b\cos(\beta_i + \varphi_i) \end{bmatrix},$$

$$\mathbf{B} = \begin{bmatrix} \sin(\beta_i + \varphi_i) & -\cos(\beta_i + \varphi_i) \\ -\cos(\beta_i + \varphi_i) & -sin(\beta_i + \varphi_i) \end{bmatrix}$$

Then, the inverse kinematics of four wheels is given by:

$$\dot{\mathbf{q}} = \begin{bmatrix} \sin(\beta_1 + \varphi_1) & -\cos(\beta_1 + \varphi_1) & -h\cos(\varphi_1) + b \\ -\cos(\beta_1 + \varphi_1) & -sin(\beta_1 + \varphi_1) & -h\sin(\varphi_1) \\ \sin(\beta_2 + \varphi_2) & -\cos(\beta_2 + \varphi_2) & -h\cos(\varphi_2) + b \\ -\cos(\beta_2 + \varphi_2) & -sin(\beta_2 + \varphi_2) & -h\sin(\varphi_2) \\ \sin(\beta_3 + \varphi_3) & -\cos(\beta_3 + \varphi_4) & -h\cos(\varphi_3) + b \\ -\cos(\beta_3 + \varphi_3) & -sin(\beta_3 + \varphi_4) & -h\cos(\varphi_3) + b \\ \sin(\beta_4 + \varphi_4) & -\cos(\beta_3 + \varphi_4) & -h\cos(\varphi_4) + b \\ -\cos(\beta_4 + \varphi_4) & -sin(\beta_3 + \varphi_4) & -h\cos(\varphi_4) + b \end{bmatrix} \dot{\mathbf{X}}$$

where $\beta_2 = \pi + \beta_1$ $\beta_4 = \pi + \beta_3$ and $\beta_1 = a\cos(a/h)$.

The forward kinematics can be written as: $\dot{\mathbf{X}} = \mathbf{A}^{-1}\mathbf{B}\dot{\mathbf{q}}$ or by solving the equation $\mathbf{A}\dot{\mathbf{X}} = \mathbf{B}\dot{\mathbf{q}}$

4 Robot Control System and Software System

4.1 The Robot Control System

The robot chassis layer have the mechanical body and powered caster wheels modular mounted on it, also with the motor driver and battery. The parameters of our motors are shown in Table 2, and the incremental magnetic grating encoder has embedded into the

Table 2. The parameters of the motors

Steering motor	Power	48 V, 200 W
	Diameter	0.145 m
	Continuous current	6.8A
	Maximum current	12A
	Continuous torque	6 N
	Maximum toque	15 N
Rolling motor	Power	48 V, 100 W
	Diameter	0.128 m
	Continuous current	3.5A
	Maximum current	8.3A
	Continuous torque	3 N.m
	Maximum toque	9 N

motors with 2048 pulse/circle, the capacity of the battery is 48 V 40 Ah. The motor driver is Copley and the maximum continuous current of the driver is 20 A.

The control layer is equipped with an industrial computer and a motion control card form Galil which is mounted into the PCI slot of Industrial PC. The motor encoder message has already separate into two copy's, one is send to the motor driver for local velocity and current control and the other copy is send to motion control card used for the velocity close-loop control. The motion control card send the analog signal to the driver according to the calculated kinematic results. Different with the traditional mobile platform, the caster wheel based mobile robot need to know the precision position of each steering wheel so that we need to initialize each steering wheel at the initial start time. To help the steering motor find the initial position, some infrared switches are mounted at the mechanical initial position of the body. The bumpers and ultrasonic sensors also mounted and used for obstacle avoidance. The Bluetooth joystick from Sony are used for the wireless velocity control of the robot, Wi-Fi module allowing for robot remote control via socket protocol, a touch screen is used for robot local operation. The block diagram of the omni-directional robot hardware is shown in Fig. 5.

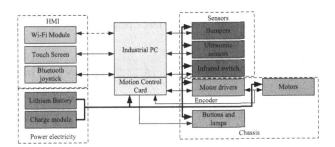

Fig. 5. The block diagram of the omni-directional robot

4.2 The Robot Software System

The software is based on the ROS system, ROS is the robot operational system which are widely used for robot program, it available for c++ code and python code, by using this software platform, the code for each function can be built as a node, you don't need care about how the software deal with the data and exchanged between different node by using ROS operation system.

The omni-directional robot software has been designed as three mainly part, part I is the chassi controller for solving the kinematics and inverse kinematics, part II is the lowlevel controller used for accedence avoidance and joystick control, part III is the trajectory planner and highlevel control. The chassi movement node accept the external velocity information from the robot operational space and deal with the kinematics module and inverse kinematic node, the S-curve producer is used to generate the continuous taskspace velocity for the robot. The inverse kinematic module used to calculate the position of each joint. The motion controller card will accept the joint space velocity command and send to the driver, the odometry information was calculated by forward kinematics and encoder then sent it to high-level controller, the high-level controller is designed for mapping, localization and navigation, especially, the path planning node will find the optimized the robot path point according to the mapping information, the trajectory planner module will deal with the path points and generate a interpolated trajectory points for the real robot mobile moving (for example generate the square curve), the joystick control node will used to send manually control command for the low-level controller, the bumper and ultrasonic sensors are programed for the obstacle avoidance function. The program block diagram is shown in Fig. 6.

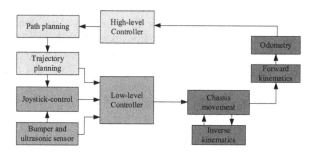

Fig. 6. Software block diagram

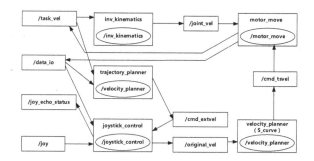

Fig. 7. The block diagram of the software node in ROS

The node information schematics of the programed ROS shown in Fig. 7 (where in this paper, we are not address the localization and navigation function of the omni-directional robot system).

5   Experiment Results

Based on the hardware and software configuration, we developed the prototype of the omni-directional mobile robot, and the robot can achieved motions towards x and y direction and rotate about z axis, that is, the system has three DOF.

When a velocity command has been send from the task space, the joint space velocity will get by using the inverse kinematics. In Fig. 8 we are take two of the caster

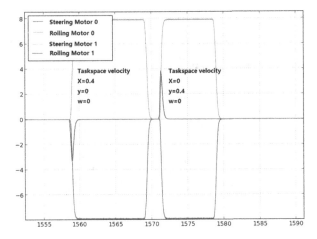

Fig. 8. The robot velocity curve

Taskspace Velocity x=0.4 y=0 w=0

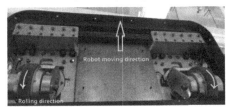

Taskspace Velocity x=0 y=0.4 w=0

Fig. 9. The robot wheels motion while task space velocity are given

wheels as the example, the velocity are recoded at Steering motor and Rolling motor, it can be see that the Steering velocity only have the value when the robot change their taskspace velocity, and the velocity of the steering motor will be goes to zero after a while. From the robot side we can see that the wheels are goes to the opposite side of the robot velocity direction, which are shown in Fig. 9.

In addition, we are carry out the trajectory following test to analysis the system accuracy, the laser tracker is used to record the actual value of the robot position. The test rig is shown in Fig. 10. The square trajectory are planned for test and the sampling time is set as 0.01 s, the test result is shown in Fig. 11, it can be seen that the maximum of the robot error is about 2.5 cm while width of the square is 70 cm (3.5%). But the

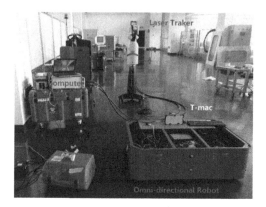

Fig. 10. The robot test rig

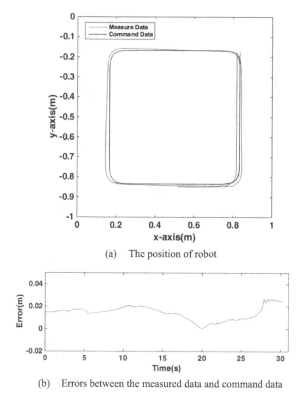

(a)   The position of robot

(b)   Errors between the measured data and command data

Fig. 11. The tested results (a) the position of the robot, (b) the errors between the measured and commanded data.

test result might different when the robot running at different type of the ground due to the different friction force. In this system, we got the accuracy on each motor is about 0.3 mm (the encoder can produce 1024 pulse for each circle).

6 Conclusions

This paper introduced a new mobile robot with two degree of freedom powered caster wheels, and each powered caster wheel is designed with two directly derived motor there are no gear system existed in the wheels so that the system doesn't have errors from the gear system. which will make the system accurate than normal mobile robot system, the prototype of the robot is built, the hardware and software are also developed and the ROS system is used for software building, the experiment is carried out at the developed prototype which is shown that the maximum error of the robot about 2.5 cm at 70 cm squared trajectory following, the error percentage is 3.5%. The designed prototype robot have one problem is that the power cables and the encoder cables of rolling motor have to go through the steering motor, this need to be solve in the future and the localization and navigation system will be also considered in the future.

Acknowledgements. Zhejiang Key Laboratory of Robotics and Intelligent Manufacturing Equipment Technology as well as NSFC-Zhejiang Joint Found For the Integration and information (U1509202), Ningbo International Cooperation Project (2017D10023), Ningbo IndustrialMajor Project (2017B10012) and Major Project and Key S&T Program of Ningbo (2016B10019).

References

1. Stampa, M., Rohrig, C., Kunemund, F., et al.: Estimation of energy consumption on arbitrary trajectories of an omnidirectional automated guided vehicle. In: IEEE International Workshop on Intelligent Data Acquisition and Advanced Computing Systems-Technology and Applications-IDAACS, New York, pp. 873–878 (2015)
2. Qian, J., Zi, B., Wang, D., et al.: The design and development of an omni-directional mobile robot oriented to an intelligent manufacturing system. Sensors, **17**(12) (2017)
3. Ghariblu, H.: Design and modeling of a ball wheel omni-directional mobile robot. In: Second International Conference on Computer Engineering and Applications, Changsha, China (2010)
4. Chu, B., Nat, K., Gumi, et al.: Mechanical and electrical design about a mecanum wheeled omni-directional mobile robot. In: 10th International Conference on Ubiquitous Robots and Ambient Intelligence, Jeju, Korea (2013)
5. Afaghani, A.Y., Yuta, S., Lee, J.H.: Jacobian-matrix-based motion control of an omnidirectional mobile robot with three active caster. In: 2011 IEEE/SICE International Symposium on System Integration (SII) (2011)
6. Yang, G., Lim, Y., Lim, T.M., et al.: Decoupled powered caster wheel for omnidirectional mobile platforms. In: IEEE Conference on Industrial Electronics and Applications, Melbourne, Australia (2014)

7. KUKA. KUKA omniMove[EB/OL] (2018). https://www.kuka.com/en-us/products/mobility/mobile-platforms/kuka-omnimove

8. Indiveri, G.: Swedish wheeled omnidirectional mobile robots: kinematics analysis and control. IEEE Trans. Rob. **25**(1), 164–171 (2009)

9. Holmberg, R., Slater, J.C.: Powered caster wheel module for use on omni-directional drive systems (2002)

10. Wada, M., Hirama, T., Inoue, Y.: Traction analysis for Active-caster Omnidirectional Robotic Drive with a Ball Transmission (ACROBAT). In: IEEE ASME International Conference on Advanced Intelligent Mechatronics, pp. 274–279. IEEE, New York (2013)

11. Yang, G.L., Li, Y.P., Lim, T.M., et al.: Decoupled powered caster wheel for omnidirectional mobile platforms. In: IEEE Conference on Industrial Electronics and Applications. IEEE, New York (2014)

12. Oetomo, D., Li, Y.P., Ang, M.H., et al.: Omnidirectional mobile robots with powered caster wheels. In: Design Guidelines from Kinematic Isotropy Analysis, pp. 2708–2713. IEEE, New York (2005)

A Dual-Loop Dual-Frequency Torque Control Method for Flexible Robotic Joint

Chongchong Wang[1], Guilin Yang[1(✉)], Chin-Yin Chen[1], and Qiang Xin[1,2]

[1] Zhejiang Key Laboratory of Robotics and Intelligent Manufacturing Equipment Technology, Zhejiang, China
glyang@nimte.ac.cn
[2] University of Chinese Academy of Sciences, 19 A Yuquan Road, Shijingshan District, Beijing 100049, People's Republic of China

Abstract. The impedance control of most flexible joints generally has a cascaded structure with both inner torque feedback and outer position feedback loops. The torque control accuracy and bandwidth have great effects on their impedance control performance. But in practical applications, the improvement of the torque control performance are limited by many factors, such as the high noise level of torque sensor and the model uncertainty and nonlinearity. This paper proposes a dual-loop torque control structure with a dual-frequency control in the inner loop and a disturbance observer in the outer loop. The dual-frequency control uses a frequency-separated controller design method that employs two controllers in low and high frequency, respectively. The high frequency controller with relatively conservative gains is designed to ensure the system stability. Thus, the low frequency controller can focus on improving the torque control accuracy, without experiencing the limitations of system stability and torque sensor noise. Moreover, the disturbance observer is introduced to compensate the model uncertainty and nonlinearity. Simulations are conducted to verify the effectiveness of the proposed dual-loop dual-frequency torque controller.

1 Introduction

In recent years, collaborative robots have been developed for human environments, allowing physical interaction and cooperation with human operators [1]. For robots to achieve compliant interaction, the impedance control scheme has been established, which aims at achieving a mass-damping-spring relationship between the external forces and the robot position [2,3].

Impedance control is a conventional topic in robot control and has been widely employed for rigid-body robot systems [4,5]. For a collaborative robot, its joints inherently have high flexibility as a result of light-weight design. A straightforward application of the conventional impedance control method to a light-weight robot with flexible joints usually will not lead to a satisfactory performance [6]. As such, a number of modified control methods have been proposed

© Springer Nature Singapore Pte Ltd. 2018
S. Wang et al. (Eds.): ICSEE 2018/IMIOT 2018, CCIS 923, pp. 561–570, 2018.
https://doi.org/10.1007/978-981-13-2396-6_52

by taking the joint flexibility into consideration. These methods include singular perturbation and integral manifold [7], feedback linearization [8], and dynamic feedback linearization along with adaptive control techniques [9,10]. Singular perturbation based controllers are easy to implement, but their performance is limited to the case of a weak elasticity of the joints. Feedback linearization based control method are theoretically well constructed, but when it comes to the multiple joints system, the implementation is difficult because of the involved computations, the lack of robustness on parameters and model uncertainties even if the adaptive control technique is applied [6].

An efficient method for the flexible joint robot control is the passivity based approach that can provide a high degree of robustness to un-modeled robot dynamics and in the contact with unknown environments [11,12]. This method is easy to be implemented because it is based only on the available motor position and joint torque signals, as well as their first-order derivatives. Therefore, the passivity based control method is widely applied to the flexible joint robots impedance control. The passivity-based flexible joint impedance control system generally has a cascaded structure with both inner torque feedback and outer position feedback loops. The position feedback loop is used to define the flexible joint impedance behaviors. The torque feedback loop is designed to make the motor more like an ideal torque source, which has a critical influence on the impedance control performance and system stability.

However, in practical applications, many factors influence the torque control performance [12,13]. On the one hand, considering the high noise level of the torque sensor and system stability, the torque feedback gains cannot be set to be too large. This limits the improvement of both torque control accuracy and bandwidth. On the other hand, the torque control accuracy will be greatly degraded by the nonlinearity that is mainly caused by frictions in the driven motor. In addition, due to load inertia variations during manipulation applications, the model uncertainty is large, which further makes it difficult for torque control.

This paper proposes a frequency-separated (FS) torque feedback control structure, which conducts the torque controller design separately in different frequencies. In high frequency, with the system stability in mind during the torque control design, relatively conservative controller gains are chosen. Then the gain of low frequency controller can be tuned without experiencing the limitations of sensor noise and stability considerations. Thus, larger controller gains can be applied to increase the torque control bandwidth, and achieving better ability to attenuate the model uncertainty and nonlinearity. Meanwhile, the FS control method makes it easier for torque controller gains tuning. Furthermore, a disturbance observer (DOB) is introduced to the closed torque control loop to further compensate the model uncertainty and nonlinearity. The effectiveness of the proposed torque controller is validated by simulations on a single flexible joint.

Section 2 is devoted to establish the dynamic model of the flexible joint as well as analyzes the system nonlinearity and model uncertainty. Section 3 describes the controller design idea. Simulations are then presented in Sect. 4. Conclusions are addressed in Sect. 5.

2 Dynamic Modeling of the Flexible Joint

2.1 Flexible Joint Dynamics Modeling

Modular designed robot joint which integrated electronics and other mechanical components into a single joint is a well-established technique. And it is widely used in most light-weight robots as the core module. The mechanical structure of the modular joint is shown in Fig. 1.

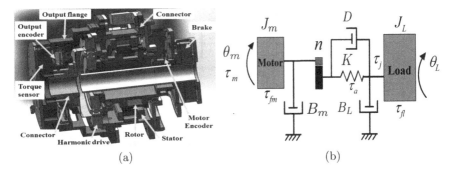

(a)   (b)

Fig. 1. Flexible joint:(a) Mechanical structure Modular designed joint; (b) Schematic diagram

Since an electric motor in a direct drive fashion was not sufficient to fulfill the torque requirement for locomotion, gear reduction is necessary to amplify the motor torque. Harmonic drives are commonly used due to their desirable characteristics of light weight, compactness, high torque capacity, high gear ratio and near-zero backlash. In particularly, strain-gauge-based torque-sensors are often integrated in the joint. Besides harmonic drives and torque sensors, also couplings, shafts, bearings and many other components used in the assembly of the modular joint.

The analysis of integrated modular joint dynamic can be divided into three parts, which consists of motor side mass-damping part with inertia and damping denoted as J_M and B_M respectively, joint output side (load side) mass-damping part with inertia and damping of J_L and B_L, and flexible transmission part modeled as a linear spring-damping system with stiffness of K and damping of D. Schematic diagram of the flexible joint can be expressed as shown in Fig. 1(b). Thus, the dynamic equation of the flexible joint is

$$\tau_m - \tau_{fm} - \frac{\tau_a + K^{-1}D\dot{\tau}_a}{n} = J_M\ddot{\theta}_M + B_M\dot{\theta}_M$$

$$\tau_a + K^{-1}D\dot{\tau}_a + \tau_{ext} - \tau_{fl} = J_L\ddot{\theta}_L + B_L\dot{\theta}_L + \tau_g \quad (1)$$

$$\tau_a = K\left(\frac{\theta_M}{n} - \theta_L\right)$$

Herein, τ_m represents the motor torque. τ_a is the spring torque, which can be measured by the joint torque sensor. θ_M and θ_L are the motor and load side positions, obtained by position encoders mounted at the motor and link side respectively. τ_{fm} and τ_{fl} are the frictions on motor and link side respectively. n is the reduction gear ratio of harmonic drive. τ_{ext} represents the external force acting on the load side. τ_g is the load gravity.

Then the equivalent two inertia system block diagram shown in Fig. 2 can be used for the flexible joint system dynamic analysis and controller design. Herein, τ_j is the torque from spring-damping part with $\tau_j = \tau_a + K^{-1}D\dot{\tau}_a$. The load gravity τ_g is eliminated for elaboration simplification.

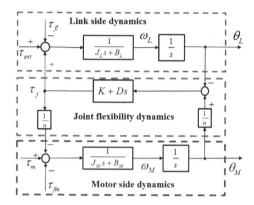

Fig. 2. The equivalent two-inertia system block diagram.

To identify the flexible joint model, firstly the frequency response from the motor driven current to motor position θ_M and spring torque τ_a are measured respectively. The motor driven current signals are given sine by sine ranging from 1 Hz to 60 Hz with an amplitude of 2 A (The motor rated current is 6 A). The joint is located on horizontal plane to eliminate the effect of gravity. The frequency responses are given as in Fig. 3 with the blue solid lines marked by asterisks. Notice that, due to the sampling delay, the phase lag in high frequency is continuously decreasing.

The anti-resonance frequency and resonance frequency are located at 16 Hz and 19 Hz, respectively. Since motor-side inertia is obtained from a CAD model and the load-side inertia is 1.2 kg·m² in the experiment, based on the measured resonance frequency, the joint stiffness can be calculated using Eq. 1. Then the motor and load side damping, together with the D can be calculated to fit the measured frequency response.

Furthermore, the system identification accuracy is validated. The red solid lines is Fig. 3 are the frequency response of the plant models. For all frequencies, the magnitude fitting errors of the position response are all within 3 dB. The magnitude fitting errors of the torque response are a little larger, but the maximum error is still within 5 dB. However, as for the phase response fitting,

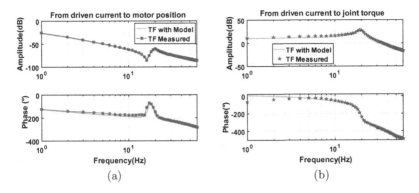

Fig. 3. Comparison between the measured and the modeling frequency responses:(a) From i to θ_M; (b) From i to τ_a. (Color figure online)

the fitting errors is relatively large, with position phase errors of $10°$, and torque phase errors of about $30°$ in low frequencies.

2.2   Model Uncertainty and Nonlinearity Analysis

Notice that the integrated flexible joint electromechanical system is subjected to various nonlinear varying factors, such as the friction and the efficiency of harmonic driver. These nonlinear varying factors result in large model variations of the flexible joint system. To analyze these nonlinearities, the flexible joint torque frequency response are measured with amplitude of sinusoidal excitation current varying from $1\,\mathrm{A}$ to $6\,\mathrm{A}$ (see Fig. 4(a)).

It can be observed that the joint torque response shows large differences according to the magnitude of input driven currents, especially in low frequencies below $10\,\mathrm{Hz}$. Commonly, a nominal model is used in the flexible joint system

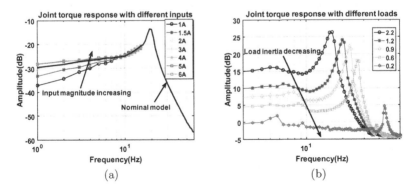

Fig. 4. Frequency response:(a)From i to τ_a with varying input amplitude;(b)From τ_m to τ_a with varying load

analysis and controller design. The thick continuous line shown in Fig. 4(a) represents the nominal model $P_{\tau n}(s)$, which is obtained by averaging the magnitudes of the frequency responses. The flexible joint torque control accuracy will be greatly degraded by these nonlinearities. In addition, since the load-side inertia often changes for manipulator applications, the joint torque responses from τ_m to τ_a with different loads are measured and shown in Fig. 4(b).

Obviously, the flexible joint system is subject to large model variations due to the load inertia varying. On the one hand, reducing load inertia is shown to increase resonant frequency. On the other hand, the amplitude of joint torque is significantly reduced as the load inertia decreasing, because the load inertia carries less energy for smaller values of J_L.

3   Controller Design

The passivity based impedance control generally has a cascaded structure with both inner torque feedback and outer position feedback loops [11,13]. The position loop controller behaves as an impedance controller which defines the flexible joint impedance behavior between the joint output position and the external torque. The inner torque control is used to improve the torque response performance from the applied torque on motor side to the joint torque that actuates its load. Then, the joint can be considered as a torque source which tracks the reference torque command obtained from the impedance controller. Therefore, the flexible joint impedance performance will be largely influenced by the accuracy and bandwidth of the torque control loop.

However, as the flexible joint system has large model uncertainty and nonlinearity especially in low frequency, the torque control accuracy will be greatly reduced. Considering that the disturbance observer control structure is generally used to (1) estimate and cancel disturbances; (2) compensate for the variation of plant dynamics by treating the variation as an equivalent disturbance, DOB control algorithm would be a good choice for flexible joint torque control to compensate the model variation and nonlinearity.

But, since the flexible joint system is subjected to such large model variations for manipulator applications, many problems will raise if the DOB is directly applied for the joint torque control. Firstly, to guarantee the system stability, the magnitude of the low pass Q-filter in DOB is limited by the boundary of the modal uncertainty. As the magnitude of flexible joint system model uncertainty boundary function is obviously greater than one in low frequency, the magnitude of the low pass Q-filter should be less than one, which cannot ensure a good system performance at low frequencies. Secondly, due to large model variations, the nominal model in DOB would unavoidably have large differences from actual system model, which would reduce or even make the system performance worse. In this paper, a torque feedback controller is used to attenuate the joint model variation firstly, and then DOB is applied to the closed-loop torque control system.

Traditionally, a proportional-derivative (PD) torque feedback controller is used in the passivity-based impedance control structure for flexible joint.

A physical interpretation of the joint torque feedback is given as the shaping of the motor inertia [13]. For a torque control with feedback gain of K_p, both the motor-side moment inertia J_M and the friction τ_{fm} are scaled down by the ratio $K_p + 1$. Hence, the system resonance frequency is pushed to a higher frequency by the torque feedback control. From the point of view of system control, a higher system resonance frequency will lead to a higher control bandwidth and a more effective ability for vibration suppression. In addition, since the friction is scaled down, the torque control accuracy can be improved.

However, during the implementation of the torque feedback controller, many limitations also exist. On the one hand, commonly the controller parameters tuning is done based on a nominal model which capture the behavior of the physical plant well at low frequencies, but are unable to capture the higher frequency dynamics. Therefore, the typical feedback controller gains are chosen to be relatively conservative to guarantee an enough stability margin. On the other hand, the torque feedback gain is also limited by the high noise level of the torque sensor. Thus, both the achievable torque accuracy and the bandwidth of torque loop cannot be improved in practical applications.

As such, the FS control scheme is introduced which is a combination of two separated controllers and each of them takes part in lower and higher frequencies separately. The overall joint torque control structure is given in Fig. 5.

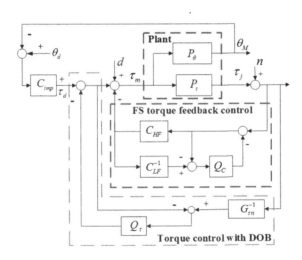

Fig. 5. Flexible joint impedance control system structure.

Here, τ_d is the command torque obtained from the impedance controller C_{imp}. P_θ is the open loop transfer function from τ_m to the motor position θ_m. P_τ is the open loop transfer function from τ_m to the joint torque τ_j. d is the disturbance existing in the torque control loop and n is the torque sensor noise. C_{LF} and C_{HF} is the controller used in the FS torque feedback framework. Q_C is a low pass filter whose bandwidth is designed to be the desired torque feedback closed-loop bandwidth.

The transfer function of FS feedback torque controller $C_\tau(s)$ can be expressed as follows:

$$C_\tau = \frac{C_{HF}(s)\,C_{LF}(s)}{C_{LF}(s) + Q_C(s)\,(C_{HF}(s) - C_{LF}(s))} \tag{2}$$

Roughly speaking, $C(s)$ behaves like $C_{LF}(s)$ in the pass-band of $Q_C(s)$ and behaves like $C_{HF}(s)$ otherwise. By using this FS feedback framework, the system stability can be guaranteed by the design of $C_{HF}(s)$ with relatively conservative gains. While, because tuning the feedback controller $C_{LF}(s)$ would just affect the system performance within the desired torque feedback closed-loop bandwidth, the controller gains in $C_{LF}(s)$ can be tuned without experiencing the limitations such as the system stability and torque sensor noise considerations. $G_{\tau n}$ is the nominal transfer function of the torque feedback closed-loop. $G_{\tau n}^{-1}(s)$ is the inverse transfer function of the FS torque feedback close-loop. In this paper, Q_τ is a second order Butterworth filter with cutoff frequency of ω_τ. This ensures proper causality of the inverse plant model $G_{\tau n}^{-1}$ and also defines the bandwidth under which the torque DOB is effective.

4   Joint Impedance Control Performance Simulation

The flexible joint torque control performance with the proposed FS torque feedback scheme and DOB control structure is simulated based on the two inertia system model. The simulation is performed in the cases as listed in Table 1.

Table 1. Controller parameters used in simulation.

Controller schemes	Controller parameters
PD	$K_p = 4; K_d = 0.117$
FS-PD	$C_{LF} : K_p = 8; K_d = 0.214$
	$C_{HF} : K_p = 4; K_d = 0.117$
	$\omega_C = 126$
PD with DOB	$K_p = 4; K_d = 0.117$
	$\omega_\tau = 94$
FS-PD with DOB	$C_{LF} : K_p = 8; K_d = 0.214$
	$C_{HF} : K_p = 4; K_d = 0.117$
	$\omega_C = 126; \omega_\tau = 94$

The command torque is a step signal with an amplitude of $10\,Nm$. The joint torque step response is shown in Fig. 6(a) with the static friction of $0.15Nm$ in the motor side, as well as the white torque sensor noise with an amplitude of $1Nm$. Then the impedance controller $C_{imp}(s)$ is applied which is a simple PD controller with $K_p = 3000$ and $K_d = 320$. The impedance control performance

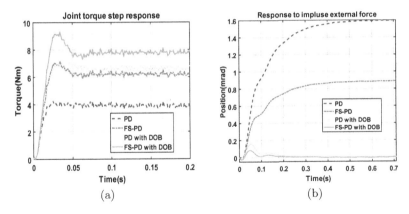

Fig. 6. The simulated flexible joint system frequency response with different controllers.

can be validated by observing the flexible joint position response to an impulse external force signal, on condition that the reference position is zero. The amplitude of the external force is $10Nm$. The joint position response with different torque controllers are shown in Fig. 6(b).

Comparing the performances of PD torque controller with the FS-PD controller in Fig. 6, not only the torque tracking response is improved, but also the ability to attenuate the motor-side disturbances in low frequency is strengthen. This is benefit from the larger torque feedback gains in FS-PD control schemes. The joint torque step responses in Fig. 6(a) illustrate that the torque control errors decrease by 36.7% from $6Nm$ to $3.8Nm$ by using the FS-PD controller. Furthermore, the torque control accuracy will be improved further by adding the DOB scheme not matter for PD controller or FS-PD controller. By using the DOB control method, the motor-side disturbance in lower frequency are greatly attenuated(see Fig. 6(b)), which means a better robust to the model uncertainties and disturbance.

Obviously, the impedance response is accelerated by using FS-PD torque control scheme, as the rise time decreasing from $0.7\,s$ to $0.5\,s$ compared with the PD torque controller. Because of the static friction is compensated by the DOB, the joint position can be back to zero. This illustrates the effectiveness of the DOB control scheme in torque control loop. Thus, all the simulation results have demonstrated that the flexible joint torque control performance as well as the impedance control performance can be improved by introducing the FS and DOB control schemes in the torque control loop.

5   Conclusion

In this paper, the dynamic model and the model uncertainty of the flexible joint is analyzed. And the FS and DOB torque control method are introduced to improve torque response of the flexible joint. The FS torque control scheme is based on the concept of different torque controller design in different frequency domains, which not only improves the performance of torque control but also simplifies the torque controller parameters tuning to guarantee the flexible joint system stability. The injection of DOB structure into the torque control loop is an effective to improve the torque control accuracy by compensating the disturbance and model uncertainty of the flexible joint system. The simulation results demonstrated the effectiveness of the proposed FS and DOB control schemes.

Acknowledgement. The work was supported by NSFC-Zhejiang Joint Found For the Integration and Information (U1509202) and Chinese Postdoctoral Science Foundation (2016M601987).

References

1. Albu-Schaffer, A., et al.: Soft robotics. IEEE Robot. Autom. Mag. **15**(3) (2008)
2. Hogan, N.: Impedance control - an approach to manipulation. i - theory. ii - implementation. iii - applications. Gerontologist **107**(1), 304–313 (1985)
3. Haddadin, S., Albuschaffer, A., Hirzinger, G.: Safe physical human-robot interaction: measurements, analysis and new insights. In: International Symposium on Robotics Research, pp. 439–450 (2010)
4. Caccavale, F., Natale, C., Siciliano, B., Villani, L.: Six-DOX impedance control based on angle/axis representations. IEEE Trans. Robot. Autom. **15**(2), 289–300 (1999)
5. Oliveira, M.D., Mo, J.: Modeling and control of robot manipulators : lorenzo sciavicco and bruno siciliano. Automatica **37**(10), 1681–1682 (2001). ISBN 0-07-114726-8
6. Albu-Schäffer, A., et al.: The DLR lightweight robot: design and control concepts for robots in human environments. Ind. Robot Int. J. **34**(5), 376–385 (2007)
7. Spong, M.W.: Modeling and control of elastic joint robots. Asme J. Dyn. Sys. Meas. **109**(4), 310–319 (1987)
8. Readman, M.C.: Flexible Joint Robots (1994)
9. De Luca, A., Lucibello, P.: A general algorithm for dynamic feedback linearization of robots with elastic joints. In: Proceedings of IEEE International Conference on Robotics and Automation, vol. 1, pp. 504–510 (1998)
10. Ott, C., Albu-Schaffer, A., Hirzinger, G.: Comparison of adaptive and nonadaptive tracking control laws for a flexible joint manipulator. In: IEEE/RSJ International Conference on Intelligent Robots and Systems, vol. 2, pp. 2018–2024 (2002)
11. Ott, C., Albu-Schaffer, A., Kugi, A., Stamigioli, S., Hirzinger, G.: A passivity based cartesian impedance controller for flexible joint robots-part i: Torque feedback and gravity compensation. In: 2004 IEEE International Conference on Robotics and Automation, Proceedings. ICRA 2004, vol. 3. IEEE, pp. 2659–2665 (2004)
12. Albu-Schaffer, A., Ott, C., Hirzinger, G.: A passivity based cartesian impedance controller for flexible joint robots-part ii: Full state feedback, impedance design and experiments. In: Proceedings of 2004 IEEE International Conference on Robotics and Automation, ICRA 2004, vol. 3, pp. 2666–2672. IEEE (2004)
13. Atzei, N., Bartoletti, M., Cimoli, T.: A survey of attacks on ethereum smart contracts (SoK). In: Maffei, M., Ryan, M. (eds.) POST 2017. LNCS, vol. 10204, pp. 164–186. Springer, Heidelberg (2017). https://doi.org/10.1007/978-3-662-54455-6_8

A Gecko Inspired Wall-Climbing Robot Based on Vibration Suction Mechanism

Rui Chen[✉], Yilin Qiu, Li Wu, Jinquan Chen,
Long Bai, and Qian Tang

The State Key Laboratory of Mechanical Transmissions,
Chongqing University, Chongqing 400044, China
cr@cqu.edu.cn

Abstract. This paper presents the design, analysis and fabrication of a quadruped wallclimbing robot. The robot can stick on the wall surface based on a novel negative pressure adsorption technology named as vibration suction mechanism. By combining the unique properties of vibration suction mechanism and the bionic gait design of the gecko, the robot has advantages of light weight, low energy consumption, flexible movement and high adaptability to different wall surfaces. Climbing experiments on the surface of a high-rise glass window are demonstrated, and the robot can climb vertically at the highest speed of 13.75 mm/s.

Keywords: Vibration suction · Wall-climbing robot · Gecko-inspired robot

1 Introduction

Climbing robots are widely used in exterior wall cleaning [1], military reconnaissance [2], bridge crack detection [3] and so on. Mankind can be saved from carrying out tasks in a harsh working environment because of the creative combination of suction technology and mobile mechanism possessed by the climbing robots. Considering the precondition of walking on vertical wall, a stable and considerable suction force is one of the most important aspects for climbing robots. The second is to choose a reasonable mobile mechanism and a flexible walking gait for the robot to deal with the complex working environment.

As for the suction technology, they can mainly be divided into three categories which are respectively based on negative pressure, magnetic force and van der Waals force, and the most widely-used and mature is based on negative pressure [4, 5]. However, most of the climbing robots using negative pressure need to carry an onboard pump and fan, which will lead to a complex structure and low speed and load capacity [6, 7]. It's reasonable to believe that some extraordinary impacts will happen in related field if a simple-driving, low mass and fast-shifting climbing robot could be invented. Unlike some common wall-climbing robots based on negative pressure, the robot herein was designed to generate vacuum in suckers by a creative mechanism—vibration suction.

In essence, vibration suction is also a strategy to produce negative pressure, while its negative pressure is created through the vibration of suction cups [8]. It doesn't have

© Springer Nature Singapore Pte Ltd. 2018
S. Wang et al. (Eds.): ICSEE 2018/IMIOT 2018, CCIS 923, pp. 571–580, 2018.
https://doi.org/10.1007/978-981-13-2396-6_53

any strict requirements for climbing with a large adsorption force on a rough wall. Therefore, it has lots of advantages including its low energy consumption, low noise, low mass, and reliable suction [9]. The specific design details and adsorption principles will be described furtherly in the second part of this paper.

The selection of locomotive mechanism is another important aspect for designing a climbing robot, and the common options include wheel type [10], leg type [11], track type [12] and the mixture of these three types [13]. In this paper, a novel wall-climbing robot using a four-legged locomotive mechanism is also developed. As for the gait planning, a tripod gait inspired by geckos was studied [14]. The specific kinematic and dynamic analysis and calculation will be discussed in the next part. Different from a real gecko sticking its body on wall by Van der Waals force, the wall-climbing robot herein is based on Vibration adsorption. After experimental verification, it is found that the robot can move with load on the vertical rough wall with certain obstacle crossing and turning ability.

2   Design of the Robot

The structure of the robot can be classified into two parts: foot module and main body. In this part, the design details of the foot module is introduced and the experiment is conducted to verify its function. A locomotive mechanism of the robot was designed according to a series of researches about the gecko's gait in order to prove the reliability of the adsorption module and the rationality of motor selection, a simulation analysis of the model was carried out.

2.1   Configuration Design of Foot Module

Vibration adsorption is driven by a vibration mechanism instead of fan, air pump or other airflow sources, so it belongs to passive negative pressure adsorption. It is found that there is a long negative pressure process in the inner environment of a single sucker during a vibration period. However, there will also be a short period of positive pressure inside the sucker during the final stage of the compression process, which will result in a failure of the adsorption state. In other words, during every vibration cycle of the suckers, there will be a periodic change of "adsorption-desorption" so that the foot module cannot work properly. The pressure change inside of the suction cup is shown in Fig. 1.

The average pressure during the vibration adsorption process of a single sucker is similar to that of a sinusoidal curve. According to the superposition principle, the influence of positive pressure process can be offset if two sinusoidal waves whose phase difference is π, while the amplitude and the period are the same. The principle can be depicted as

$$A\sin(2\pi t) + A\sin(2\pi t + \pi) = 0 \tag{1}$$

After the analysis above, we need to design a mechanism to drive the two suction cup groups vibrating alternately to produce a sustained average negative pressure so

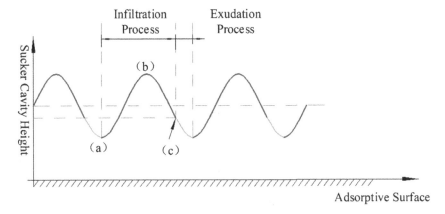

Fig. 1. Pressure change inside of the suction cup. (a)-(b)-(c) negative pressure inside of the suction cup; (c)-(a) positive pressure inside of the suction cup.

that the foot module can adhered on the wall stably. The foot module is designed as follow.

Mechanical Structure of Vibration and Guiding. The core part of the mechanical structure of vibration is a crank block mechanism. The alternating vibration with the phase difference of π in two groups of suckers is realized by controlling the relative position of the eccenter and the output shaft of the motor. The motor rotates the eccenter and causes the relative motion of the upper and lower mounting plates, which leads to the vibration of the two sets of suckers. The mechanical structure of vibration is shown in Fig. 2.

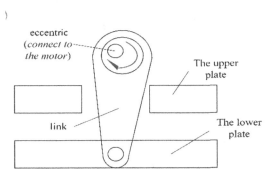

Fig. 2. Mechanical structure of vibration.

It is necessary to design a guiding mechanism between the upper and lower plates since it is easy to oscillate during the vibration process, even lead to the mechanism jam which seriously affects the stable operation of the device without the guiding mechanism. The guide of linear bearing and guide column are selected, as shown in Fig. 3.

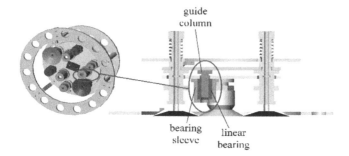

Fig. 3. Guiding mechanism.

Arrangement of the Suction Cups. The suction force is brought by the pressure difference between the inside and outside of the suction cups. Therefore, the suction cups are the key components of the whole foot module, and their performance will directly affect the magnitude and reliability of the suction force. We also found that the arrangement of the suction cups can be linear, annular, and rectangular and so on, and we finally select the annular arrangement since it has the characteristics of compact structure and suction stability. In addition, the vibration adsorption module needs two sets of suction cups, and the number and layout of the two sets of suction cups should be the same. The number of the suction cups in each group should be no less than three. Therefore, we choose six suction cups to distribute evenly. The arrangement of the suction cups is shown in Fig. 4.

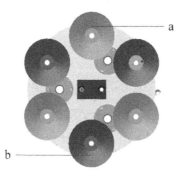

Fig. 4. Annular arrangement of suckers. (a) green suckers are connecting to the lower plate; (b) blue suckers are connecting to the upper plate. (Color figure online)

Design of the Separation Mechanism. In order to make the suction cups switch between the adsorption state and the desorption state, a separation mechanism is designed. A two-position and seven-way valve is used to control the relative pressure inside of the suction cups. Two-position is "on" and "off" which is corresponding to "desorption" and "adsorption" respectively, and seven-way means that six interfaces of the valve body are connected with six suction cups, while the last one interface is connected with the external atmosphere. The separation mechanism is shown in Fig. 5.

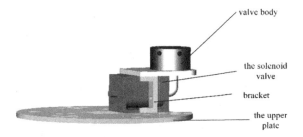

Fig. 5. Separation mechanism.

Design of the Stabilization Mechanism. In order to reduce the harmful vibration of the foot module to the robot body, a stabilizing mechanism is designed. The stabilizing mechanism is composed of stabilizing ring, damping spring, spring column and adjusting nut, which are shown in Fig. 6. With the stabilization mechanism, the damping spring will always be in the state of compression so that the stabilizing ring can be fastened onto the wall in every vibration cycle. The legs of the robot are fixed directly on the stabilizing ring, which ensures the stability of the robot body.

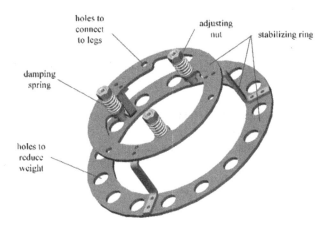

Fig. 6. Stabilization mechanism.

Since the robot designed in this paper is used to climb on vertical walls, the main indicator for evaluating the adsorption effect of the foot module is its lateral load capacity. We tested the static suction force and dynamic suction force of the foot module respectively on different walls, the experiments are shown in Fig. 7 and the results are shown in Table 1. The results show that the vibration suction theory is feasible.

dynamometer

Fig. 7. Experiments of the foot module.

Table 1. Results of the foot module experiments

Material	Glass		Ceramics		Wood	
State	Static	Dynamic	static	Dynamic	Static	Dynamic
Force(N)	43	39	40	29	36	34

2.2 Gait Analysis

Geckos usually take different walking modes when they climb on flat ground, vertical wall and ceiling. Geckos mainly take diagonal gait on flat ground and walls to achieve a larger speed which means diagonal legs are lifted up or laid down at the same time. They often climb on ceilings in tripod gait which means three legs always adhere to the wall for stability [15, 16].

In order to achieve the highest stability of the robot crawling on the wall, the gecko's tripod gait is studied in this paper.

The gecko-inspired robot gets the max stability margin using 1-3-2-4 order in tripod gait as shown in Fig. 8. However, when the first foot and the third foot move, a parallel mechanism is formed by the other three legs adsorbed on the wall, which

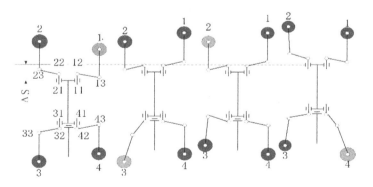

Fig. 8. Tripod gait: The robot moves the single leg in order of 1-3-2-4. The absorbed legs are blue, and non-contact legs are green (Color figure online)

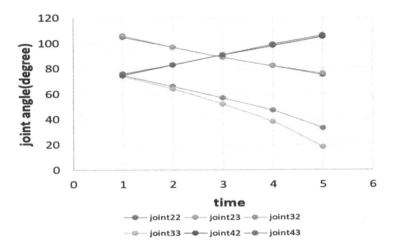

Fig. 9. Joint angles of three legs absorbed in the first step of straight tripod climbing gait.

makes the rotation angles of the joints not independent. The movement process needs to be analyzed. The first step can be planned using interpolation method to make rotations of the joint angles in each movement roughly equal to reduce impacts. The result is shown in Fig. 9.

2.3 Design of the Main Body Structure

According to observations of gecko's structure and gait, dynamics analysis of the robot were carried out in this character. In this paper, a simplified kinematic model of a real gecko was proposed. As show in Fig. 10(b), the gecko's limb was simplified as a series of links, where ankle joint was simplified as a one-freedom low pair, hip joint was simplified as a two-vertical-freedom low pair and the tail was simplified as a one-freedom low pair. As shown in Fig. 10(c), Each joint is driven by a servomotor.

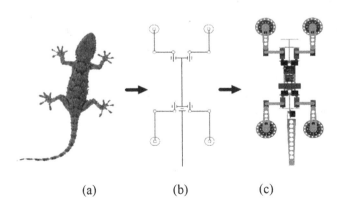

(a)   (b)   (c)

Fig. 10. A schematic of gecko-inspired motion model. (a) real gecko; (b) simplified kinematic model; (c) CAD model of the robot.

The control board and battery is placed in the middle and the sensors are located on the head. The tail equipped with a universal wheel keeps close contact with the wall can not only produce an anti-overturning moment but also reduce the friction force.

The dynamics of the robot is studied using the simulation software ADAMS. The robot model is 414 mm long, 125 mm wide. Its material is aluminum alloy and weighs 3.2 kg. According to the above experiment of the vibration suction module, the preload force of each single foot is set as 30 N. The motion cycle of the robot walking straightly with three feet is set as 12 s. The rotation of the servo motors studied above is the input for the dynamic simulation.

The driving torque of the joint between the thigh and shank during the forward gait is studied and the results are shown in Fig. 11. The maximum value of the joint torque is 57 N·mm, which happens in the leg 2 during the preparing state.

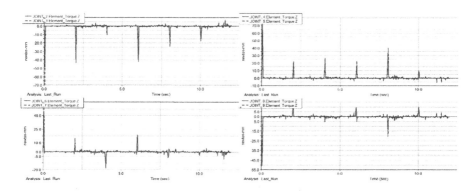

Fig. 11. Torques needed by joints between thigh and shank in the order of 1-2-3-4

3 Experiments and Discussions

The overall weight of the robot is 1.6 kg including the electronic board and the battery. The total length is 1000 mm including the tail and width is 408 mm. The robot is equipped with 9 servo motors, 4 gear motors and 4 solenoid valves. Servo motors provide high torques to lift the legs and tail of the robot. Gear motors is used for driving the vibration mechanism. Solenoid valves are used for controlling the separation mechanism. When the robot is climbing on the wall, it always moves with a single leg in the order of "1-3-2-4" while the other three legs stably stick on the wall surface by vibration suction. As shown in Fig. 12, the robot is climbing on a vertical glass surface and the highest speed is about 13.75 mm/s.

The experimental results show that the feasibility and robustness of the robot are acceptable. However, there are still some improvements need to be made in future. Compared with the test of a single foot, the vibration suction module is applied in a more complicated stress state during the movement of the robot and a slight unintended left-right vibration happens, which will affect the overall robustness of the robot.

Fig. 12. Photo snapshots of the robot climbing on the surface of a glass

A possible solution to this problem is to optimize the guiding mechanism of the foot module, reduce the assembly clearance or add some lubricating fluid.

4 Conclusions

Compared with other wall-climbing robots, the gecko-inspired robot based on vibration suction mechanism proposed in this paper has the advantages of no need of gas source, large suction force and strong environmental adaptability. In this paper, a compact vibration suction module was designed and manufactured. The tripod gait of the robot is simulated and achieved in the robot prototype. The experiment proves that it can climb on the vertical surface of glass at the highest speed of 13.75 mm/s. The unsolved problems of the current prototype include obstacle avoidance and autonomous navigation, which will be solved in the next generation of prototype by equipping with cameras and other peripheral devices.

References

1. Zhan, H., et al.: A series of pneumatic glass-wall cleaning robots for high-rise. J. Buildings Ind. Robot **2**(34), 150–160 (2007)
2. Jizhong, X,. et al.: Design of mobile robots with wall climbing capability. In: Proceedings of IEEE AIM, Monterey, pp. 438–443(2005)
3. Liu, Y., Dai, Q., Liu, L.: Adhesion-adaptive control of a novel bridge-climbing robot. In: 3rd Annual International Conference on IEEE, pp. 102–107 (2013)
4. Nishi, A.: A wall climbing robot using propulsive force of propeller. In: Fifth International Conference on IEEE, pp. 320–325 (1991)
5. Miyake, T., Ishihara, H.: Basic studies on wet adhesion system for wall climbing robots. In: IEEE/RSJ International Conference on IROS 2007, pp. 1920–1925. IEEE (2007)
6. Zhang, Y., Nishi, A.: Low-pressure air motor for wall-climbing robot actuation. Mechatronics **13**, 377–392 (2003)

7. La Rosa, G., et al.: A low-cost lightweight climbing robot for the inspection of vertical surfaces. Mechatronics **12**(1), 71–96 (2002)
8. Yang, H., Liu, R., Hong, Q., He, N.: A miniature multi-joint wall climbing robot based on new vibration suction robotic foot. In: Proceedings of IEEE International Conference on Automation and Logistics, pp. 1160–1165, September 2008
9. Zhu, T., et al.: Principle and application of vibrating suction method. In: Proceedings of the IEEE Robotics and Biomimetics Conference, pp. 491–495 (2006)
10. Fischer, W., Tche, F., Siegwart, R.: Inspection system for very thin and fragile surfaces, based on a pair of wall climbing robots with magnetic wheels. In: International Conference on Intelligent Robots and Systems, San Diego (2007)
11. Zhu, J., Sun, D., Tso, S.K.: Development of a tracked climbing robot. J. Intell. Robot. Syst. **35**(4), 427–444 (2002)
12. Menon, C., Li, Y., Sameoto, D., Martens, C.: Abigaille-I: towards the development of a spider-inspired climbing robot for space use. In: 2nd IEEE RAS & EMBS International Conference on Biomedical Robotics and Biomechatronics, BioRob, pp. 384–389 (2008)
13. Yin, H., et al.: Motion control of a wheel-leg-track compound mobile robot. In: Information and Automation, Piscataway, pp. 770–775 (2008)
14. Son, D., et al.: Gait-planning based on kinematics for quadruped gecko model with redundancy. Robot. Autonomous Syst. **53**(5), 648–656 (2010)
15. Li, H., et al.: Angular observation of joints of Geckos moving on horizontal and vertical surfaces. Chin. Sci. Bull. **54**, 592–598 (2009)
16. Zaaf, A., et al.: Spatio-temporal gait characteristics of level and vertical locomotion in a ground-dwelling and a climbing gecko. J. Exp. Biol. **204**, 1233–1246 (2001)

Author Index

Printed in the United States
By Bookmasters